Rick Steves'
BEST OF
EUROPE
1998

Europe

500 KM
300 MI

John Muir Publications
Santa Fe, New Mexico

Other JMP travel guidebooks by Rick Steves
Asia Through the Back Door
Europe Through the Back Door
Europe 101: History and Art for the Traveler (with Gene Openshaw)
Mona Winks: Self-Guided Tours of Europe's Top Museums
    (with Gene Openshaw)
Rick Steves' France, Belgium & the Netherlands (with Steve Smith)
Rick Steves' Germany, Austria & Switzerland
Rick Steves' Great Britain & Ireland
Rick Steves' Italy
Rick Steves' Russia & the Baltics (with Ian Watson)
Rick Steves' Scandinavia
Rick Steves' Spain & Portugal
Rick Steves' Phrase Books: German, French, Italian, Spanish/
    Portuguese, and French/German/Italian

John Muir Publications, P.O. Box 613, Santa Fe, NM 87504
Copyright © 1998, 1997, 1996 by Rick Steves
Cover copyright © 1998 by John Muir Publications
All rights reserved.

Printed in the United States of America
Second printing May 1998

For the latest on Rick's lectures, guidebooks, tours, and public television
series, contact Europe Through the Back Door, Box 2009, Edmonds, WA
98020, tel. 425/771-8303, fax 425/771-0833, e-mail rick@ricksteves.com,
or on the Web at www.ricksteves.com.

ISSN: 1096-7702
ISBN: 1-56261-384-7

Europe Through the Back Door Editor Risa Laib
John Muir Publications Editors Krista Lyons-Gould, Chris Hayhurst
Production Janine Lehmann, Nikki Rooker
Design Linda Braun
Cover Design Janine Lehmann
Typesetting Dave Cox
Maps David C. Hoerlein
Research Assistance Steve Smith
Printer Banta Company
Cover Photo Il Duomo (cathedral and temple); Siena, Italy: Leo de Wys
Inc./Jacobs

Distributed to the book trade by
Publishers Group West
Berkeley, California

Europe's Best Destinations

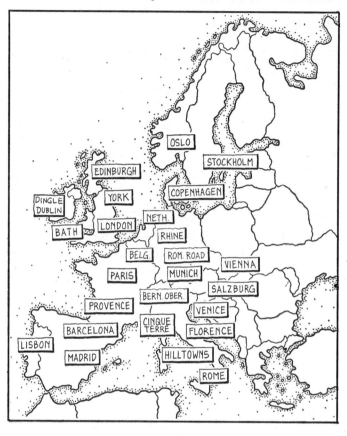

CONTENTS

ITALY
From *Rick Steves' Italy*

THE NETHERLANDS
From *Rick Steves' France, Belgium & the Netherlands*

PORTUGAL
From *Rick Steves' Spain & Portugal*

SCANDINAVIA
From *Rick Steves' Scandinavia*

SPAIN
From *Rick Steves' Spain & Portugal*

SWITZERLAND
From *Rick Steves' Germany, Austria & Switzerland*

INTRODUCTION

This book breaks Europe into its top big-city, small-town, and rural destinations. It then gives you all the information and opinions necessary to wring the maximum value out of your limited time and money in each of them. If you plan two months or less in Europe, this lean and mean book is all you need.

Experiencing Europe's culture, people, and natural wonders economically and hassle-free has been my goal during more than 20 years of traveling, tour guiding, and travel writing. With this book, I pass on to you the lessons I've learned, updated for 1998.

Rick Steves' Best of Europe is the crème de la crème of places featured in six of my Country Guides. This book is balanced to include a comfortable mix of exciting big cities and cozy small towns: from Paris, London, and Rome to traffic-free Riviera ports, avalanche-zone Alpine villages, and mom-and-pop châteaus. It covers the predictable biggies and mixes in a healthy dose of Back Door intimacy. Along with Leonardo in the Louvre, you'll enjoy Caterina in her Cantina. I've been very selective. For example, rather than listing the countless castles, hill towns, and Riviera resorts, I recommend the best three or four of each.

The best is, of course, only my opinion. But after two busy decades of travel writing, lecturing, and tour guiding, I've developed a sixth sense for what tickles the traveler's fancy.

This Information Is Accurate and Up-to-Date

This book is updated every year. Most publishers of guidebooks that cover Europe from top to bottom can afford an update only every two or three years (and even then, it's often by letter). Since this book covers only my favorite places, we are able to personally update it each year. Even with an annual update, things change. But if you're traveling with the current edition of this book, I guarantee you're using the most up-to-date information available. If you're packing an old book, you'll learn the seriousness of your mistake . . . in Europe. Your trip costs at least $10 per waking hour. Your time is valuable. This guidebook saves lots of time.

Planning Your Trip

This book is organized by destinations. Each destination is covered as a mini-vacation on its own, filled with exciting sights and homey, affordable places to stay. In each chapter, you'll find these sections:

Planning Your Time, a suggested schedule with thoughts on how to best use your limited time.

Orientation, including tourist information, transportation within a destination, and an easy-to-read map designed to make the text clear and your arrival smooth.

Sights with ratings: ▲▲▲—Don't miss; ▲▲—Try hard to see; ▲—Worthwhile if you can make it; No rating—Worth knowing about.

Sleeping and Eating, with addresses and phone numbers of my favorite budget hotels and restaurants.

Transportation Connections to nearby destinations by train, bus, or car.

The Appendix is a traveler's tool kit, with telephone tips, a climate chart, and a list of national tourist offices.

Browse through this book, choose your favorite destinations, and link them up. Then have a great trip! You'll travel like a temporary local, getting the absolute most out of every mile, minute, and dollar. You won't waste time on mediocre sights because, unlike other guidebooks, I cover only the best. Since your major financial pitfall is lousy, expensive hotels, I've worked hard to assemble the best accommodations values for each stop. And, as you travel the route I know and love, you'll be meeting some of my favorite Europeans.

Trip Costs

Five components make up your trip cost: airfare, surface transportation, room and board, sightseeing, and shopping/entertainment/miscellany.

Airfare: Don't try to sort through the mess yourself. Get and use a good travel agent. A basic round-trip flight between the United States and Europe should cost $600 to $1,000, depending on where you fly from and when. Always consider saving time and money in Europe by flying "open-jaws" (flying into one city and out of another, such as flying into London and out of Rome).

Surface Transportation: Your best mode of transportation depends upon the time you have and the scope of your trip. For many it's a Eurailpass: three weeks-$698; one month-$864; two months-$1,224; 15 days in two months-$836. You can save money if you're traveling with one or more companions (get Eurail Saverpasses); if you're under 26 (get a second-class Eurailpass); or if you're focusing your trip within Europe's core countries–France, Germany, Switzerland, Italy, and Spain (get a Europass). Train passes are normally available only outside of Europe. You might find it cheapest to simply buy tickets as you go (see Transportation, below).

Drivers can figure $200 per person per week (based on two people splitting the cost of the car, tolls, gas, and insurance). Car rental is cheapest to arrange from the U.S.A. Leasing, for trips over three weeks, is even cheaper.

Room and Board: You can thrive in Europe on an overall average of $60 a day per person for room and board. A $60-a-day budget allows $10 for lunch, $15 for dinner, and $35 for lodging (based on two people splitting the cost of a $70 double room that includes breakfast). That's doable. Students and tightwads will do it on $40 ($15–20 per bed, $20 for meals and snacks). But budget sleeping and eating require the skills and information covered below (and much more extensively in *Rick Steves' Europe Through the Back Door*).

Sightseeing: In big cities, figure $5 to $10 per major sight, $2 for minor ones, and $25 for splurge experiences (e.g., tours, lifts, gelato binges). An overall average of $15 a day works for most. Don't skimp here. After all, this category directly powers most of the experiences all the other expenses are designed to make possible.

Shopping/Entertainment/Miscellany: This can vary from nearly nothing to a small fortune. Figure $1 per postcard, $2 per coffee, beer, or ice-cream cone, and $10 to $20 for evening entertainment. Good budget travelers find that this category has little to do with assembling a trip full of life-long and wonderful memories.

Exchange Rates
I've priced things in local currencies throughout this book.

Country	$1 equals roughly . . .
Austria	12 Austrian schillings (AS)
Belgium	35 Belgian francs (BF)
Denmark	7 kroner (kr)
France	5.5 francs (F)
Germany	1.7 Deutsche marks (DM)
Great Britain	.60 pound (£)
Ireland	.60 punt (£)
Italy	1,600 lire (L)
Netherlands	1.9 guilders (f)
Norway	7 kroner (kr)
Portugal	170 escudos ($)
Spain	140 pesetas (ptas)
Sweden	7 kroner (kr)
Switzerland	1.5 Swiss francs (SF)

Prices, Times, and Discounts
The prices in this book, as well as the hours and telephone numbers, are accurate as of late 1997. But Europe is always changing. I know you'll understand that this, like any other guidebook, starts to yellow even before it's printed.

In Europe—and in this book—you'll be using the 24-hour clock. After 12:00 noon, keep going—13:00, 14:00, and so on. For anything over 12, subtract 12 and add p.m. (14:00 is 2 p.m.).

This book lists peak-season hours for sightseeing attractions (July–August). Off-season, roughly October through April, expect generally shorter hours, more lunchtime breaks, fewer activities, and fewer guided tours in English. If traveling off-season, be careful to confirm opening times.

Europe's Best 70 Days

While discounts for sights and transportation are not listed in this book, seniors (60 and over), students (with International Student Identity Cards), and youths (under 18) can sometimes get discounts—but only by asking.

When to Go

May, June, September, and October are the best travel months. Generally, peak season offers the sunniest weather and the most exciting slate of activities—but the worst crowds. During this crowded time, it's best to arrive early in the day or to call your next hotel in advance. (The hotel receptionist can help you.) As a very general rule of thumb any time of year, the climate north of the Alps is mild (like Seattle), while south of the Alps it's like southern California. For information on weather, check the climate chart in the Appendix. If you wilt in the heat, avoid the Mediterranean in the summer. If you want blue skies in the Alps, Britain, and Scandinavia, travel in the height of summer. Plan your itinerary to beat the heat (spring trip, start in the south and work north) but also to moderate culture shock (start in mild Britain and work south and east) and minimize crowds. Touristy places in the core of Europe (Germany, the Alps, France, Italy, and Greece) suffer most from crowds.

Sightseeing Priorities

Depending on the length of your trip, here are my recommended priorities. Assuming you're traveling by train, I've taken geographical proximity into account.

5 days:	London, Paris
7 days, add:	Amsterdam, Haarlem
10 days, add:	Rhine, Rothenburg, Munich
14 days, add:	Salzburg, Swiss Alps
17 days, add:	Venice, Florence
21 days, add:	Rome, Cinque Terre
24 days, add:	Siena, Bavaria
30 days, add:	Arles, Barcelona, Madrid, Toledo
36 days, add:	Vienna, Berlin, Bath/Cotswolds
40 days, add:	Copenhagen, Edinburgh
70 days:	See Europe's Best 70 Days map on page 4

Red Tape, News, and Banking

Red Tape: You currently need a passport but no visa and no shots to travel in Europe. Crossing borders is easy. Sometimes you won't even realize it's happened. When you do change countries, however, you change money, postage stamps, phone cards, gas prices, ways to flush a toilet, words for "hello," figurehead monarchs, and breakfast breads. Plan ahead for these changes. Coins and stamps are worthless outside their home countries. Just before crossing a border, I use up my coins on gas, candy, souvenirs, or a telephone call home.

News: Americans keep in touch with the *International Herald Tribune* (published almost daily via satellite throughout Europe). Every Tuesday, the European editions of *Time* and *Newsweek* hit the stands with articles of particular interest to European travelers. Sports addicts can get their fix from *USA Today*. News in English will be sold only where there's enough demand: in big cities and tourist centers. If you're concerned about how some event might affect your safety as an American traveling abroad, call the U.S. consulate or embassy in the nearest big city for advice.

Banking: Bring traveler's checks in dollars along with some plastic (ATM, credit, or debit cards). Regular banks have the best rates for cashing traveler's checks. For a large exchange, it pays to compare rates and fees. Post offices and train stations usually change money if you can't get to a bank.

To get a cash advance from a bank machine, you'll need a four-digit PIN (numbers only, no letters) with your bank card. Before you go, verify with your bank that your card will work, then use it whenever possible. Beware that the distances between these machines can be great, and bring enough traveler's checks as backup.

Visa and MasterCard are more commonly accepted than American Express. Just like at home, credit or debit cards work

Europe's Best Three Weeks

easily at larger hotels, restaurants, and shops, but smaller businesses prefer payment in local currency.

You should use a money belt. Thieves target tourists. A money belt (call 425/771-8303 for our free newsletter/catalog) provides peace of mind. You can carry lots of cash safely in a money belt.

Don't be petty about changing money. The greatest avoidable money-changing expense is wasting time every few days to return to a bank. Change a week's worth of money, get big bills, stuff it in your money belt, and travel!

Travel Smart

Upon arrival in a new town, lay the groundwork for a smooth departure. Reread this book as you travel, and visit local tourist information offices. Buy a phone card and use it for reservations, reconfirmations, and double-checking hours. Enjoy the friendliness of the local people. Ask questions. Most locals are eager to point you in their idea of the right direction. Wear your money belt, learn the local currency, and develop a simple formula to quickly estimate rough prices in dollars. Keep a notepad in your

Europe's Best Three-Week Trip by Car

Day	Plan	Sleep in
1	Arrive in Amsterdam	Haarlem
2	Amsterdam	Haarlem
3	Haarlem, drive to Rhine	Bacharach
4	Cruise Rhine, Rheinfels Castle	Rothenburg
5	Rothenburg	Munich
6	Munich	Munich
7	Castle day in Bavaria and Tirol	Reutte
8	Drive to Venice	Venice
9	Venice	Venice
10	Drive to Siena	Siena
11	Florence	Siena
12	Rome	Rome
13	Rome	Rome
14	Civita di Bagnoregio	Vernazza
15	Italian Riviera, Cinque Terre	Vernazza
16	Drive into the Alps, Interlaken	Gimmelwald
17	Alps hike, Jungfrau/Schilthorn	Gimmelwald
18	Bern, Beaune in Burgundy	Beaune
19	Versailles, drop car	Paris
20	Paris	Paris
21	Paris	Paris

While this 21-day itinerary is designed to be done by car, with a few small modifications it works great by train. The gas and tolls for this trip, if you take all the autobahns, will cost around $600 ($75 for tolls in Italy, $25 in France; $30 for your Swiss autobahn sticker; $15 for the Brenner Pass in Austria; 3,000 miles at 28 mpg = 107 gallons of gas at $4 a gallon = $430, plus parking—grand total = $600).

By train, this route would cost about $585 (sample 1998 prices for second-class train tickets: Amsterdam–Frankfurt $90, Frankfurt–Munich $90, Munich–Venice $65, Venice–Rome $50, Rome–Interlaken $90, Interlaken–Paris $110, and Paris–Amsterdam $100). First class is 50 percent more. A ten-days-in-two-months Eurail Flexipass ($634), giving you first-class comfort, convenience, and the freedom to change your plans, costs only a little more than second-class point-to-point tickets.

pocket for organizing your thoughts and practice the virtue of simplicity. Those who expect to travel smart, do.

As you read this book, note the days of markets, festivals, and when sights are closed. Anticipate problem days: Mondays are bad in Munich, Dachau, Florence, and Rome; Tuesdays are bad in

Paris. Museums and sights, especially large ones, usually stop admitting people 30 to 60 minutes before closing time.

Sundays have the same pros and cons as they do for travelers in the United States. Sightseeing attractions are generally open, shops and banks are closed, and city traffic is light. Rowdy evenings are rare on Sundays. Saturdays in Europe are virtually weekdays with earlier closing hours. Hotels in tourist areas are most crowded on Fridays and Saturdays.

Plan ahead for banking, laundry, post office chores, and picnics. Mix intense and relaxed periods. Every trip (and every traveler) needs at least a few slack days. Pace yourself. Assume you will return.

Tourist Information

The tourist information office is your best first stop in any new city. Try to arrive, or at least telephone, before it closes. In this book, I'll refer to a tourist information office as a TI. Throughout Europe, you'll find TIs are usually well organized, with English-speaking staff.

As national budgets tighten, many TIs have been privatized. This means they become sales agents for big tours and hotels, and their "information" becomes unavoidably colored. While the TI has listings of all the rooms and is eager to book one for you, use their room-finding service only as a last resort. Across Europe, room-finding services are charging commissions from hotels, taking fees from travelers, blacklisting establishments that buck their materialistic rules, and are unable to give hard opinions on the relative value of one place over another. The accommodations stakes are too high to go potluck through the TI. By using the listings in this book, you can avoid that kind of "help."

Tourist Offices, U.S.A. Addresses: Each country has a national tourist office in the U.S.A. (see the Appendix for addresses). Before your trip, you can ask for the free general information packet and any specific information you may want (such as city maps and schedules of upcoming festivals).

Recommended Guidebooks

You may want some supplemental information, especially if you'll be traveling beyond my recommended destinations. When you consider the improvements they'll make in your $3,000 vacation, $25 or $35 for extra maps and books is money well spent. Especially for several people traveling by car, the weight and expense are negligible.

The **Lonely Planet** guides to various European countries are thorough, well researched, and packed with good maps and hotel recommendations for low- to moderate-budget travelers. The hip **Rough Guide** series (British researchers, more insightful) and the highly opinionated **Let's Go** series (by Harvard students) are great for students and vagabonds. If you're a backpacker with a train pass, and interested in the youth and night scene, get Let's Go. The popular, skinny green **Michelin** guides to most southern countries and French regions are excellent, especially if you're driving. They're known for their city and sightseeing maps, dry but concise and helpful information on all major sights, and good cultural and historical background. English editions are sold locally at tourist shops and gas stations.

Rick Steves' Books and Videos

Rick Steves' Europe Through the Back Door (Santa Fe, N.M.: John Muir Publications, 1998) gives you budget travel tips on minimizing jet lag, packing light, planning your itinerary, traveling by car or train, finding budget beds without reservations, changing money, avoiding rip-offs, outsmarting thieves, hurdling the language barrier, staying healthy, taking great photographs, using your bidet, and much more. The book also includes chapters on my 37 favorite "Back Doors."

Rick Steves' Country Guides are a series of seven guidebooks with extensive coverage of Britain/Ireland, France/Belgium/ Netherlands, Italy, Spain/Portugal, Scandinavia, Germany/Austria/ Switzerland, and Russia/Baltics. If you wish this book covered more of any particular country, my Country Guides are for you. They are updated annually and come out each January.

Europe 101: History and Art for the Traveler (co-written with Gene Openshaw, John Muir Publications, 1996) gives you the story of Europe's people, history, and art. Written for smart people who were sleeping in their history and art classes before they knew they were going to Europe, *101* really brings Europe's sights to life.

Mona Winks (co-written with Gene Openshaw, John Muir Publications, 1996) gives you 400 pages of fun, easy-to-follow, self-guided tours of major museums and historic highlights featured in this book, including Amsterdam's Rijksmuseum and Van Gogh Museum; Venice's St. Mark's, Doge's Palace, and Accademia Gallery; Florence's Uffizi Gallery, Bargello, Michelangelo's *David*, and a Renaissance walk; Rome's Colosseum, Forum, Pantheon, Vatican Museum, and St. Peter's Basilica; and Paris' Louvre, the exciting Orsay Museum, the Pompidou Modern Art Museum, and a tour of Europe's greatest palace, Versailles. If you plan to tour these sights, *Mona* will be a valued friend.

Rick Steves' Phrase Books: After 20 years as an English-only traveler struggling with other phrase books, I've designed a series of practical, fun, and budget-oriented phrase books to help you ask the gelato man for a free little taste and the hotel receptionist for a room with no street noise. If you want to chat with your cabbie and make hotel reservations over the phone, the new pocket-sized Rick Steves' Phrase Books for French; German; Italian; Spanish and Portuguese; and French, Italian, and German together will come in very handy (John Muir Publications, 1996).

My television series, *Travels in Europe with Rick Steves*, includes 52 half-hour shows on Europe, with 13 brand-new shows for 1998. Call your local public TV station or the Travel Channel to find out when to tune in. These shows are also available as home videos (2–3 shows per tape), along with my two-hour slideshow lectures (call us at 425/771-8303 for our free newsletter/catalog.

Maps

The maps in this book, drawn by Dave Hoerlein, are concise and simple. Dave, who is well-traveled in Europe, has designed the maps to help you locate recommended places and get to the tourist offices, where you can pick up a more indepth map (usually free) of the city or region.

European bookstores, especially in tourist areas, have good selections of maps. For drivers, I'd recommend a 1:200,000 or 1:300,000 scale map for each country. Train travelers can usually manage with the freebies they get with their train pass and at the local tourist offices.

Transportation in Europe

By Car or Train?

Each has pros and cons. Cars are an expensive headache in big cities but give you more control for delving deep into the countryside. Groups of three or more go cheaper by car. If you're packing heavy (with kids), go by car. Trains are best for city-to-city travel and give you the convenience of doing long stretches overnight. By train, I arrive relaxed and well-rested—not so by car. The latest permutation of the train pass is a popular rail 'n' drive version, which lets you mix train and car travel. When thoughtfully used, this economic pass gives you the best of both transportation worlds.

Traveling by Train

A major mistake Americans make is relating public transportation in Europe to the pathetic public transportation they're used to at home. By rail you'll have the Continent by the tail. And every year the trains of Europe are getting speedier and more comfortable. While many simply buy tickets as they go ("point to point"), the various train passes give you the simplicity of ticket-free unlimited travel, and depending on how much travel you do, often offer a tremendous savings over regular point-to-point tickets. The Eurailpass gives you several options (explained in the box on page 11). For a free 40-page booklet analyzing the railpass and point-to-point ticket deals available both in the U.S.A. and in Europe, call my office at 425/771-8303. The booklet is updated each January. Regardless of where you get your train pass, this information will help you get the right one for your trip.

1998 Eurail Passes

1998 EURAILPASSES, SAVERPASSES, AND YOUTHPASSES

These passes cover all 17 Eurail countries: Austria, Belgium, Denmark, Finland, France, Germany, Greece, Hungary, Ireland, Italy, Luxembourg, Netherlands, Norway, Portugal, Spain, Sweden, and Switzerland.

	First Class Eurailpass	First Class Saverpass	Second Class Youthpass
10 days in 2 months flexi	$634	$540	$444
15 days in 2 months flexi	836	710	585
15 consecutive days	538	458	376
21 consecutive days	698	594	489
1 month consec. days	864	734	605
2 months consec. days	1224	1040	857
3 months consec. days	1512	1286	1059

Saverpass prices are per person for 2 or more traveling together. Youthpasses are for travelers under age 26 only, no discounts for companions. Children 4-11 pay half, under 4 travel free.

1998 EUROPASSES

All Europasses include France, Germany, Switzerland, Italy and Spain.

	1st class	"Partner"	Youth 2nd
5 days in 2 months	$326	$196	$216
With 1 add-on zone	386	232	261
With 2 add-on zones	416	250	286
With 3 add-on zones	436	262	301
With 4 add-on zones	446	268	309

Europass add-on days: Add up to 10 extra days.
Price per day: .... 42 .... 25 29

Europass add-on zones
Choose from:
▼ Austria/Hungary
▼ Belgium/Netherlands/ Luxembourg
▼ Portugal
▼ Greece

Europasses are good for use only in the countries shown above. Kids 4-11 half price. Adding days does not increase your 2 month validity period. The Greece add-on zone includes the Brindisi, Italy to Patras, Greece boat. There are nasty penalties for sneaking through countries not on your pass.

✔ *40% OFF EUROPASS "PARTNER" DEAL:*
When a traveler buys any first class Europass at full fare, one companion can buy an identical pass for 40% off. Partners must travel together at all times. No "partner" discounts for additional traveling companions, or for 2nd class Youthpasses.

Eurailpass and the Europass

The granddaddy of European railpasses, Eurail gives you unlimited rail travel on the national trains of 17 European countries. That's 100,000 miles of track through all of western Europe including Ireland, Greece, and Hungary (but excluding Great Britain and eastern Europe). The pass includes many bonuses such as boat rides on the Rhine, Mosel, Danube, and lakes of Switzerland; several international ferries (Ireland–France,

EurailDrive Pass

1998 FIRST CLASS EURAILDRIVE PASSES

4 first class rail days and 3 car days in a 2 month period.

Car categories	2 adults	1 adult	Extra car day	Extra rail day
A-Economy	$350	$435	$58	$55
B-Compact	380	495	78	55
C-Intermediate	395	525	88	55

Prices are approximate per person. Third and fourth persons sharing car get a 4-day out of 2-month railpass for approx. $268 (kids 4-11 $134). You can add up to 5 extra rail and car days.

1998 FIRST CLASS EUROPASS DRIVE

3 first class rail days and 2 car days in a 2 month period.

Car categories	2 adults	1 adult	Extra car day
A-Economy	$265	$315	$55
B-Compact	280	355	75
C-Intermediate	290	370	85
D-Compact Automatic	310	415	105
Each add'l rail day	42	42	

Prices are approximate per person. You can add rail days (max. 12) and car days (no limit).

Sweden–Finland, Italy–Greece); and many buses, including the Romantic Road bus tour through Germany. The new scaled-down five- to 12-country Europass offers a cheaper, more focused version of the Eurailpass. (Prices listed on page 11 are good through 1998, kids 4 to 11 pay half fare, those under 4 ride free.)

Eurail Analysis

Break-even point? For an at-a-glance break-even point, remember that a one-month Eurailpass pays for itself if your route is Amsterdam–Rome–Madrid–Paris on first class or Copenhagen–Rome–Madrid–Copenhagen on second class. A one-month Eurail Youthpass saves you money if you're traveling from Amsterdam to Rome to Madrid and back to Amsterdam. Passes pay for themselves more quickly in the north, where the cost per kilometer is higher. Check the map on page 13, Europe by Rail: Time and Cost, to see if your planned travels merit the purchase of a train pass. If it's about even, go with the pass for the convenience of not having to wait in line to buy tickets, and for the fun and freedom to travel "free."

   Using one Eurailpass versus a series of country passes: While nearly every country has its own mini-version of the Eurail-pass, trips covering several countries are usually cheapest with the budget whirlwind traveler's old standby, the Eurailpass (or its budget cousin, the Europass). This is because the more days that are included in a pass, the cheaper your per-day cost is. A group of short country passes will each be high on that curve of diminishing per-day costs, while a Eurailpass with a longer life span offers a better deal overall. While a patchwork of individual country passes

Europe by Rail: Time and Cost

This map can help you determine quickly and painlessly whether a railpass is right for your trip. Add up the ticket prices for your route. If your total is about the same or more than the cost of a pass, buy the pass.

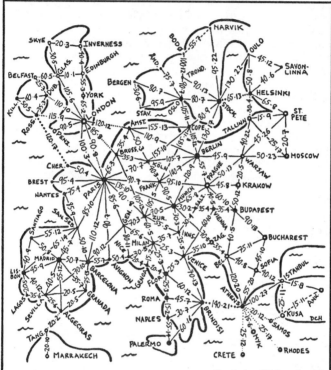

Map designed by Dave Hoerlein

The **first number** between cities = cost in $US for a 1-way, 2nd class ticket.
The **second number** = number of hours the trip takes.
● = Cities served by Eurailpass.
○ = Cities **not** served by Eurailpass (for example, if you want to go from Munich to Prague, you'll need to pay extra for the portion through the Czech Republic).
••• = Boat crossings covered by Eurailpass.
•••• = Boat crossings **not** covered by Eurailpass.
Important: These fares and times are based on the Eurail Tariff Guide. Actual prices may vary due to currency fluctuations and local promotions. Local competition can cut the actual price of some boat crossings (from Italy to Greece, for example) by 50% or more. For approx. 1st class rail prices, multiply the prices shown by 1.5. In some cases faster trains (like the TGV in France) are available, cutting the hours indicated on the map. Travelers under age 26 can receive up to 1/3 off the 2nd class fares shown. Eurailpasses are **not** honored in the U.K., Turkey or Eastern Europe (except for Hungary).

is usually more expensive and restrictive than the basic Eurailpass, if you're traveling in a single country an individual country railpass (such as Francerail or Germanrail) is a better value.

EurailDrive Pass analysis: The EurailDrive Pass is a great deal compared to the Eurail Flexipass if two are traveling together and would like three days of car rental. When you subtract the cost of a four-day Flexipass (based on 80 percent of the cost of a five-day pass), the drive option gives you three driving days at about $14 a day ($7 per person, not including gas or CDW insurance). That's better than the best weekly car rental rate, with the flexibility of a day here and a day there. Great areas for a day of joyriding include: the Dutch countryside; the Rhine, Mosel, or Bavaria in Germany; the Loire, Burgundy, Alsace, Provence, and the Pyrenees in France; Tuscany, Umbria, and the Dolomites in Italy; the hill towns of Andalusia in Spain; Norway's fjord country; or "car hiking" in the Alps. When considering prices, remember that each day of car rental comes with about $30 of extra expenses (CDW insurance, gas, parking) which you'll divide by the number in your party.

Car Rental

It's cheaper to arrange European car rentals in the United States, so check rates with your travel agent. Rent by the week, with unlimited mileage. If you'll be renting for three weeks or more, ask your agent about leasing, a scheme to save on insurance and taxes. I normally rent the smallest, least expensive model. Explore your drop-off options (and costs).

For peace of mind, I spring for CDW insurance (Collision Damage Waiver, about $14 per day), which gives a zero-deductible rather than the standard value-of-the-car "deductible." Ask your travel agent about money-saving alternatives to CDW (such as Travel-Guard's insurance package). A few "gold" credit cards cover CDW; quiz your credit card company on the worst-case senario.

Driving

For most of Europe, all you need is your valid U.S. driver's license and a car. Ask your rental company whether an international license is required. While gas is expensive, if you keep an eye on the big picture, paying $4 per gallon is more of a psychological trauma than a financial one. I use the freeways whenever possible. They are free in the Netherlands and Germany; you'll pay $6 as you enter Austria for a week's use of the roads ($12 for two months) and a one-time road fee of about $30 as you enter Switzerland; and the Italian autostradas and French autoroutes are punctuated by toll booths (charging about $1 for every ten minutes). The alternative to these super-freeways often is being marooned in rural traffic. The autobahn/autostrada route usually saves enough time, gas, and nausea to justify its expense. Mix scenic country-road rambling with high-speed autobahning, but don't forget that in Europe, the shortest distance between two points is the autobahn.

Metric: Outside of Britain, get used to metric. A liter is about a quart, four to a gallon. A kilometer is six-tenths of a mile. I figure kilometers to miles by cutting them in half then adding back 10 percent of the original (120 km: 60 + 12 = 72 miles, 300 km: 150 + 30 = 180 miles).

Parking: Parking is a costly headache in big cities. You'll pay about $20 a day to park safely. Ask at your hotel for advice. I keep a pile of coins in my ashtray for parking meters, public phones, laundromats, and wishing wells.

Telephones and Mail

Smart travelers learn the phone system and use it daily to reserve or reconfirm rooms, find tourist information, or phone home. Many European phone booths take phone cards rather than coins. Each country sells phone cards good for use in that country's phones. (For example, you can use a Swiss phone card to make local and international calls from Switzerland, but it won't do a thing for you in France.) Buy a phone card from post offices, newsstands, or tobacco shops. Insert the card into the phone, make your call, and the value is automatically deducted from your card. If you use coins instead, have a bunch handy.

Dialing Direct: You'll usually save money by dialing direct. You just need to learn to break the codes. When calling long distance within a country, first dial the area code (which usually starts with zero), then dial the local number.

For example, Munich's area code is 089 and the number of my favorite Munich hotel is 264-349. To call it from Frankfurt, dial 089/264-349. When dialing internationally, dial the international access code (of the country you're calling from), the country code (of the country you're calling to), the area code (without the initial zero), and the local number. To call the Munich hotel from the U.S.A., dial 011 (U.S.A.'s international access code), 49 (Germany's country code), 89 (Munich's area code without the zero), then 264-349. To call my office from Munich, I dial 00 (Germany's international access code), 1 (U.S.A.'s country code), 425 (Edmond's area code), and 771-8303. For a listing of international access codes, country codes, and exceptions, see the Appendix.

USA Direct Services: Calling home from Europe is easy from any kind of phone if you have an AT&T, MCI, or Sprint calling card. Each card company has a toll-free number in each European country that puts you in touch with an English-speaking operator who takes your card number and the number you want to call, puts you through, and bills your home phone number for the call (at the cheaper U.S.A. rate of about a dollar a minute, after $3 for the first minute, plus a $2.50 service charge). You'll save money on calls of three minutes or more. Hanging up when you hear an

answering machine will cost you around $5.50. Avoid this by mak-
ing a five-second call using a small-value coin or European phone
card. For about 25 cents you can get through long enough to say
"call me," or to make sure an answering machine is off so you can
call back using your USA Direct number. European time is six/nine
hours ahead of the east/west coast of the U.S.A. For a list of
AT&T, MCI, and Sprint calling card operators, see the Appendix.
Avoid using USA Direct for calls between European countries; it's
much cheaper to call direct using coins or a phone card.

Mail: To arrange for mail delivery (allow ten days for a letter
to arrive), reserve a few hotels along your route in advance and give
their addresses to friends, or use American Express Company's mail
services (available to anyone who has at least one Amex traveler's
check). Federal Express makes two-day deliveries—for a price.
Phoning is so easy that I've dispensed with mail stops all together.

Sleeping
In the interest of smart use of your time, I favor hotels and restaurants handy to your sightseeing activities. Rather than list hotels
scattered throughout a city, I describe my favorite two or three
neighborhoods and recommend the best accommodations values
in each, from $10 bunks to $150 doubles.

Now that hotels are so expensive and tourist information
offices' room-finding services are so greedy, it's more important
than ever for budget travelers to have a good list of rooms and call
directly to make reservations. This book gives you a wide range of
budget accommodations to choose from: hostels, bed and breakfasts, guest houses, pensions, small hotels, and splurges. I like
places with firm beds that are clean, small, central, traditional,
friendly, and not in other guidebooks. Most places listed are a
good value, having at least five of these seven virtues.

Rooms with private bathrooms are often bigger and renovated, while the cheaper rooms without bathrooms often will be
on the top floor or not yet refurbished. Any room without a bathroom has access to a bathroom in the corridor (free unless otherwise noted). Rooms with tubs often cost more than rooms with
showers. All rooms have a sink. Unless I note a difference, the cost
of a room includes a continental breakfast. When breakfast is not
included, the price is usually posted in your hotel room.
Before accepting, confirm your understanding of the complete
price. The only tip the hotels I've listed would like is a friendly,
easygoing guest. The accommodations prices listed in this book
should be good through 1998. I appreciate feedback on your hotel
experiences.

Sleep Code
To give maximum information in a minimum of space, I use the
code below to describe accommodations listed in this book. Prices

are per room, not per person. When there is a range of prices in one category, the price will fluctuate with the season, size of room, or length of stay.

S = Single room or price for one person using a double.
D = Double or twin room. Double beds are usually two twins pushed together—comfortable for non-romantic couples.
T = Three-person room (often a double bed with a single bed moved in).
Q = Four-adult room (an extra child's bed is usually cheaper).
b = Private bathroom with toilet and shower or tub.
t = Private toilet only (the shower is down the hall).
s = Private shower or tub only (the toilet is down the hall).
CC = Accepts credit cards (V = Visa, M = MasterCard, A = American Express). If CC is not mentioned, assume they accept only cash.
SE = Speaks English. This code is used only when it seems predictable you'll encounter English-speaking staff.
NSE = Does not speak English. Used only when it's unlikely you'll encounter English-speaking staff.

According to this code, a couple staying in Madrid at a "Db-6,000 ptas, CC:V, SE" hotel would pay a total of 6,000 pesetas (about $43) for a double room with a private bathroom. The hotel accepts Visa or Spanish cash in payment, and the staff speaks English.

Hotels

While most hotels listed in this book cluster around $60 to $80 per double, listings range from about $25 (very simple, toilet and shower down the hall) to $150 (maximum plumbing and more) per double. The cost is higher in big cities and heavily touristed cities and lower when off the beaten track. Three or four people can nearly always save lots of money by requesting one big room. Traveling alone can get expensive: A single room is often only 20 percent cheaper than a double. If you'll accept a room with twin beds and you ask for a double, you may needlessly be turned away. Get in the habit of asking for "a room for two people" if you'll take a twin or a double.

Rooms are generally very safe, but don't leave valuables lying around. More (or different) pillows and blankets are usually in the closet or available on request. Remember, in Europe towels and linen aren't always replaced every day. Drip-dry and conserve.

A very simple continental breakfast is almost always included. (Breakfasts in Europe, like towels and people, get smaller as you go south.) If you like juice and protein for breakfast, supply it yourself. I enjoy a box of juice in my hotel room and often supplement the skimpy breakfast with a piece of fruit and cheese. (A ziplock baggie is handy for light eaters to grab an extra breakfast roll and slice of cheese, when provided, for a fast and free lunch.)

Making Reservations

It's possible to travel at any time of year without reservations, but given the high stakes, erratic accommodations values, and the quality of the gems I've found for this book, I'd highly recommend calling ahead for rooms a day or two in advance as you travel. Even if a hotel clerk says the hotel is full, you can try calling between 9:00 and 10:00 on the day you plan to arrive. That's when the hotel clerk knows who'll be checking out and just which rooms will be available. I've taken great pains to list telephone numbers with long-distance instructions (see the Appendix). Use the telephone and the convenient phone cards. Most hotels listed are accustomed to English-only speakers. A hotel receptionist will trust you and hold a room until 17:00 without a deposit, though some will ask for a credit card number. Honor (or cancel by phone) your reservations. Long distance is cheap and easy from public phone booths. Don't let these people down—I promised you'd call and cancel if for some reason you won't show up. Don't needlessly confirm rooms through the tourist office; they'll take a commission.

If you know exactly which dates you need and really want a particular place, reserve a room well in advance before you leave home. To reserve from home, call, fax, or write the hotel. Phone and fax costs are reasonable, and simple English is usually fine. To fax, use the form in the Appendix. If you're writing, add the zip code and confirm the need and method for a deposit. A two-night stay in August would be "two nights, 16/8/98 to 18/8/98"—European dates are written day/month/year, and hotel jargon counts your stay from your day of arrival through your day of departure. You'll often receive a letter or fax requesting one night's deposit. A credit card and expiration date will usually be accepted as a deposit, though you may need to send a signed traveler's check or a bank draft in the local currency. If your credit card is the deposit, you can pay with your card or cash when you arrive; if you don't show up, you'll be billed for one night. Reconfirm your reservations a day in advance for safety.

Bed and Breakfasts

You can stay in private homes throughout Europe and enjoy double the cultural intimacy for about half the cost of hotels. You'll find them mainly in smaller towns and in the countryside (so they are most handy for those with a car). In Germany, look for *Zimmer* signs. For Italian *affitta camere* and French *chambre d'hôte* (CH), ask at local tourist offices. Doubles cost about $50, and you'll often share a bathroom with the family. While your European hosts will rarely speak English (except in Switzerland, the Netherlands, Belgium, and Scandinavia), they will almost always be enthusiastic and a delight to share a home with.

Youth Hostels

For $10 to $20 a night, you can stay at one of Europe's 2,000 youth hostels. While most hostels admit non-members for an extra fee, it's best to join the club and buy a hostel card before you go. Except in Bavaria (where you must be under 27 to stay in a hostel), travelers of any age are welcome as long as they don't mind dorm-style accommodations and making lots of traveling friends. Cheap meals are sometimes available, and kitchen facilities are usually provided for do-it-yourselfers. Expect crowds in the summer, snoring, and lots of youth groups giggling and making rude noises while you try to sleep. Family rooms and doubles are often available on request, but it's basically boys' dorms and girls' dorms. Many hostels are locked up from about 10:00 until 17:00, and a 23:00 curfew is often enforced. Hosteling is ideal for those traveling single: Prices are by the bed, and you'll have an instant circle of friends. More and more hostels are getting their business acts together, taking credit card reservations over the phone and leaving sign-in forms on the door for each available room. In the north, many hostels have a telex reservation system that allows you to reserve and pay for your next hostel. If you're serious about traveling cheaply, have a card, carry your own sheet, and cook in the members' kitchens.

Camping

For $4 to $10 per person per night, you can camp your way through Europe. "Camping" is an international word—you'll see signs everywhere. All you need is a tent and a sleeping bag. Good campground guides are published, and camping information is also readily available at local tourist information offices. Europeans love to holiday camp. It's a social rather than a nature experience, and a great way for traveling Americans to make local friends. Many campgrounds will have a small grocery and washing machines, and some even come with discos and mini-golf. Camping is ideal for families traveling by car on a tight budget.

Eating European

Europeans are masters at the art of fine living. That means eating long and eating well. Two-hour lunches, three-hour dinners, and endless hours sitting in outdoor cafés are the norm. Americans eat on their way to an evening event and complain if the check is slow in coming. For Europeans, the meal is an end in itself, and only rude waiters rush you.

Even those of us who liked dorm food will find that the local cafés, cuisine, and wines become a highlight of our European adventure. This is sightseeing for your palate, and even if the rest of you is sleeping in cheap hotels, your taste buds will want an occasional first-class splurge. You can eat well without going broke. But be careful: You're just as likely to blow a small fortune on a mediocre meal as you are to dine wonderfully for $12.

Restaurants
When restaurant hunting, choose a place filled with locals, not the place with the big neon signs boasting "We Speak English and Accept Credit Cards." Look for menus posted outside; if you don't see one, move along. Also look for set-price menus (called the tourist menu, *menù del giorno*, *prix-fixe*, or simply *le menu*) that give you several choices among several courses. Combination plates (*le plat* in France, *plato combinado* in Spain) provide daily specials at reasonable prices. Galloping gourmets should bring a menu translator. (*The Marling Menu Master*, available in French, Italian, and German editions, is excellent.) These days, tipping is included in the bill in most cafés and restaurants. If it's not, the menu will tell you. Still, it's polite to leave the change (under 5 percent) if the service was good.

When you're in the mood for something halfway between a restaurant and a picnic meal, look for food stands selling take-out sandwiches and drinks, delis with stools or a table, a department store cafeteria, or simple little eateries for fast and easy, sit-down restaurant food. Many restaurants offer a good value, three- to five-course "menu" at lunch only. The same menu often costs much more at dinner.

Picnics
So that I can afford the occasional splurge in a nice restaurant, I like to picnic. Besides the savings, picnicking is a great way to sample local specialties. And, in the process of assembling your meal, you get to plunge into local markets like a European.

Gather supplies early. Some small shops close for a lunch break. While it's fun to visit the specialty shops, *supermarchés* give you the same quality with less color, less cost, and more efficiency.

When driving I organize a backseat pantry in a cardboard box with plastic cups, paper towels, a water bottle (the standard, disposable, European half-liter plastic mineral water bottle works fine), a damp cloth in a ziplock baggie, a Swiss army knife, and a petite tablecloth. To take care of juice once and for all, stow a rack of liter boxes of orange juice in the trunk. (Look for "100%" on the label or you'll get a sickly sweet orange drink.)

Picnics (especially French ones) can be an adventure in high cuisine. Be daring: Try the smelly cheeses, midget pickles, ugly pâtés, sissy quiches, and minuscule yogurts. Local shopkeepers are happy to sell small quantities of produce and even slice and stuff a sandwich for you. A typical picnic for two might be fresh bread (half loaves on request), two tomatoes, three carrots, 100 grams of cheese (about a quarter-pound, called an *etto* in Italy), 100 grams of meat, two apples, a liter box of orange juice, and yogurt. Total cost for two: about $8.

Stranger in a Strange Land

We travel all the way to Europe to enjoy differences—to become temporary locals. You'll experience frustrations. Certain truths that we find "God-given" or "self-evident," like cold beer, ice in drinks, bottomless cups of coffee, hot showers, body odor smelling bad, and bigger being better, are suddenly not so true. One of the benefits of travel is the eye-opening realization that there are logical, civil, and even better alternatives. A willingness to go local ensures that you'll enjoy a full dose of local hospitality.

If there is a negative aspect to the European image of Americans, we are big, loud, aggressive, impolite, rich, and a bit naive. While Europeans look bemusedly at some of our Yankee excesses—and worriedly at others—they nearly always afford us individual travelers all the warmth we deserve.

Back Door Manners

While updating this book, I heard over and over again that my readers are considerate and fun to have as guests. Thank you for traveling as temporary locals who are sensitive to the culture. It's fun to follow you in my travels.

Send Me a Postcard, Drop Me a Line

If you enjoy a successful trip with the help of this book and would like to share your discoveries, fill out and send the survey at the end of this book to me at Europe Through the Back Door, Box 2009, Edmonds, WA 98020. I personally read and value all feedback. Thanks in advance—it helps a lot.

For our latest travel information, tap into our Web site at www.ricksteves.com. My e-mail address is rick@ricksteves.com. Anyone is welcome to request a free issue of our Back Door quarterly newsletter (it's free anyway).

Judging from all the positive feedback and happy postcards I receive from travelers who have used this book, it's safe to assume you're on your way to a great vacation—independently, inexpensively, and with the finesse of an experienced traveler. Thanks, and happy travels!

BACK DOOR TRAVEL PHILOSOPHY

As Taught in *Rick Steves' Europe Through the Back Door*

Travel is intensified living—maximum thrills per minute and one of the last great sources of legal adventure. Travel is freedom. It's recess, and we need it.

Experiencing the real Europe requires catching it by surprise, going casual . . . "Through the Back Door."

Affording travel is a matter of priorities. (Make do with the old car.) You can travel—simply, safely, and comfortably—anywhere in Europe for $60 a day plus transportation costs. In many ways, spending more money only builds a thicker wall between you and what you came to see. Europe is a cultural carnival, and time after time, you'll find that its best acts are free and the best seats are the cheap ones.

A tight budget forces you to travel close to the ground, meeting and communicating with the people, not relying on service with a purchased smile. Never sacrifice sleep, nutrition, safety, or cleanliness in the name of budget. Simply enjoy the local-style alternatives to expensive hotels and restaurants.

Extroverts have more fun. If your trip is low on magic moments, kick yourself and make things happen. If you don't enjoy a place, maybe you don't know enough about it. Seek the truth. Recognize tourist traps. Give a culture the benefit of your open mind. See things as different but not better or worse. Any culture has much to share.

Of course, travel, like the world, is a series of hills and valleys. Be fanatically positive and militantly optimistic. If something's not to your liking, change your liking. Travel is addicting. It can make you a happier American, as well as a citizen of the world. Our Earth is home to nearly 6 billion equally important people. It's humbling to travel and find that people don't envy Americans. They like us, but with all due respect, they wouldn't trade passports.

Globetrotting destroys ethnocentricity. It helps you understand and appreciate different cultures. Travel changes people. It broadens perspectives and teaches new ways to measure quality of life. Many travelers toss aside their hometown blinders. Their prized souvenirs are the strands of different cultures they decide to knit into their own character. The world is a cultural yarn shop. And Back Door travelers are weaving the ultimate tapestry. Come on, join in!

VIENNA
(WIEN)

Vienna is a head without a body. For 600 years the capital of the once-grand Habsburg Empire, she started and lost World War I and, with it, her far-flung holdings. Today you'll find an elegant capital of 1.6 million people (20 percent of Austria's population) ruling a small, relatively insignificant country. Culturally, historically, and from a sightseeing point of view, this city is the sum of its illustrious past. The city of Freud, Kafka, Brahms, a gaggle of Strausses, Maria Theresa's many children, and a dynasty of Holy Roman emperors is right up there with Paris, London, and Rome.

Vienna has always been the easternmost city of the West. In Roman times it was Vindobona, on the Danube facing the Germanic barbarians. In medieval times Vienna was Europe's bastion against the Ottoman Turks (a "horde" of 300,000 was repelled in 1683). While the ancient walls held out the Turks, World War II bombs destroyed 22 percent of the city's buildings. In modern times Vienna took a big bite out of the USSR's Warsaw Pact buffer zone. Read a coin—it says "Österreich." That's "Kingdom of the East."

The truly Viennese person is not Austrian but a second-generation Habsburg cocktail, with grandparents from the distant corners of the old empire—Polish, Serbian, Hungarian, Romanian, Czech, or Italian. Vienna is the melting-pot capital of an empire of 60 million—of which only 8 million are Austrian.

In 1900, Vienna's 2.2 million inhabitants made it the world's fifth-largest city (after New York, London, Paris, and Berlin). But the average Viennese mother has 1.3 children and the population is down to 1.6 million. (Dogs are the preferred "child.")

Of the Habsburgs who ruled Austria from 1273 to 1918, Maria Theresa (ruled 1740–1765) and Franz Josef (ruled 1848–1916) are the most famous. People are quick to remember Maria Theresa as the mother of 16 children (12 survived). This was actually no big deal back then (one of her daughters had 18 kids and a son fathered 16). Maria Theresa's reign followed the Austrian defeat of the Turks, when Europe recognized Austria as a great power. She was a strong and effective queen. (Her rival, the Prussian emperor, said, "When at last the Habsburgs get a great man, it's a woman.") She was a great social reformer. During her reign she avoided wars and expanded her empire by skillfully marrying her children into the right families. With daughter Marie Antoinette's marriage into the French Bourbon family (to Louis XVI), for instance, a country that had been an enemy became an ally. (Unfortunately for Marie, she arrived in time for the Revolution and lost her head.) In tune with her age and a great reformer, Maria Theresa's "Robin Hood" policies helped Austria slip through the "age of revolution" without turmoil. She taxed the church and the nobility and provided six years of obligatory education to all children and free health care to all in her realm. She also welcomed the boy genius Mozart into her court.

As far back as the 12th century, Vienna was a mecca for musicians—both secular (troubadours) and sacred. The Habsburg emperors of the 17th and 18th centuries were not only generous supporters of music but fine musicians and composers themselves. (Maria Theresa played a mean double bass.) Composers like Haydn, Mozart, Beethoven, Schubert, Brahms, and Mahler gravitated to this music-friendly environment. They taught each other, jammed together, and spent a lot of time in Habsburg palaces. Beethoven was a famous figure, walking—lost in musical thought—through Vienna's still-inspirational parks and woods.

After the defeat of Napoleon and the Congress of Vienna (in 1815, which shaped 19th-century Europe), Vienna enjoyed its violin-filled belle époque, which shaped our romantic image of the city (fine wine, chocolates, cafés, and waltzes). The waltz was the rage, and "Waltz King" Johann Strauss and his brothers kept Vienna's 300 ballrooms spinning.

This musical tradition (that continues in our century) leaves some prestigious Viennese institutions for today's tourists to enjoy: the opera, the boys' choir, and the great Baroque halls and churches, all busy with classical and waltz concerts.

Planning Your Time

As far as big cities go, Vienna has to be one of Europe's most pleasant and laid-back. Vienna is worth two days and two nights. Not only is it packed with great sights, but it's also a joy to spend time in. It seems like Vienna was designed to help people simply meander through a day.

Day 1:
    9:00 Circle the Ring by tram, following the tour explained below (or take this tour the night before with a stop at

the Kursalon for Strauss).

10:00 Stroll Kärntner Strasse (take care of TI and ticket needs, possibly tour Kaisergruft tombs).

11:00 Tour the Opera (lunch at Rosenberger).

13:00 Tour Hofburg (visiting Augustinian church, royal apartments, treasury, Neue Burg).

16:00 Walk Kohlmarkt, take Graben to the cathedral, then tour cathedral.

19:00 Choose classical music, Heuriger wine garden, Prater amusement park, or an Opera performance. Spend some time wandering the old center.

Day 2:

9:00 Schönbrunn Palace

13:00 Kunsthistorisches Museum after lunch.

16:00 Strauss waltz coffee concert at Kursalon?

Orientation
(tel. code within Austria: 0222; from outside: 1)

Vienna, or Wien (VEEN) in German, is bordered on three sides by the Vienna Woods (Wienerwald) and the Danube (Donau). To the southeast is industrial sprawl. The Alps, which arc across Europe from Marseilles, end at Vienna's wooded hills. These provide a popular playground for walking and new-wine drinking. This greenery's momentum carries on into the city. You'll notice more than half of Vienna is park land, filled with ponds, gardens, trees, and statue memories of Austria's glory days.

Think of the city map as a target. The bull's-eye is the cathedral, the first circle is the Ring, and the second is the Gürtel. The old town snuggles around towering St. Stephan's Cathedral south of the Donau, bound tightly by the Ringstrasse. The Ring, marking what was the city wall, circles the first district (or *Bezirk*). The Gürtel, a broader ring road, contains the rest of downtown (Bezirkes 2–9).

Addresses start with the Bezirk, followed by street and building number. Any address higher than the ninth Bezirk is beyond the Gürtel, far from the center. The middle two digits of Vienna's postal codes show the district, or Bezirk. The address "7, Lindengasse 4" is in the seventh district, #4 on Linden Street. Its postal code would be 1070. Nearly all your sightseeing will be done in the core first district or along the Ringstrassse. As a tourist, concern yourself only with this small old center, and sprawling Vienna suddenly becomes manageable.

Tourist Information

The "tourist offices" at the train stations and airport are hotel agencies in disguise. Vienna's real tourist office, near the Opera House at Kärntner Strasse 38, is excellent (daily 9:00–19:00, tel. 0222/211-140 or 0222/513-8892). Stop here first with a list of needs and questions, to confirm your sightseeing plans, and to pick up the free and essential city map (best of its kind in Europe—use the town center inset), the museum brochure (listing hours, phone numbers), the monthly program of concerts, and the fact-filled *Young Vienna Scene* magazine. Consider investing in the handy 50-AS *Vienna from A to Z* booklet. Every important building has a numbered flag banner that keys into this guidebook. *A to Z* numbers are keyed into the TI's city map. When lost, find one of the "famous-building flags" and match its number to your map. If you're at a "famous building," check the map to see what other key numbers are nearby, then check the *A to Z* book to see if you want to drop in. Many of my recommended accommodations keep enough tourist maps and brochures on hand to make a TI trip unnecessary. The much-promoted 180-AS "Vienna Card" gives you a three-day transit pass (worth 130 AS) and tiny discounts at museums on the push list (which you probably won't visit). Skip it.

Arrival in Vienna

By Train at the West Station: Most train travelers arrive at the Westbahnhof. Pick up a free city map at the "Reisebüro am Bahnhof" at the station. To get to the city center (and most likely, your hotel), catch the U-3 subway. Buy a 24-hour pass from the *Tabak* (tobacco) shop in the station or from a machine in the underground (50 AS, good on trams and buses, too). The subway has an entrance within the station. Follow the U-3 signs down the long escalator. If you still need a ticket or pass, stop at a VOR-Fahrkarten machine, push the yellow "24-Stunden" button, and the window display will read "50 AS." Insert 50 AS in coins (or a 100–AS bill and get change) and get your 24-hour ticket (individual tickets cost 17 AS). On the same level as the ticket machines, you'll see an "Information/Vorverkauf" office, where you can get transit advice, tickets and passes, and a tiny, free metro map. One more level down takes you to the U-3 tracks. Catch a train in the direction of U-3-Erdberg. Ride five stops to Stephansplatz, escalate in the exit direction "Stephansplatz," and you hit the cathedral. The TI is a five-minute stroll down the busy Kärntner Strasse pedestrian street.

The Westbahnhof station has a grocery store (daily 6:00–22:50), change offices, storage facilities, and rental bikes (see Getting Around, below).

By Plane: The airport (16 km from town) is connected by 70-AS shuttle buses (3/hr) to either the Westbahnhof (35 min) or the City Air Terminal (20 min) near the river in the old center. Taxis into town cost about 400 AS.

Getting Around Vienna

By Bus, Tram, and Subway: To take simple and economical advantage of Vienna's fine transit system of buses, trams, and

Vienna

HOTELS:
- ❶ Nossek
- ❷ Aclon
- ❸ Pertsky
- ❹ Neuer Markt
- ❺ Suzanne
- ❻ Wiener Staats
- ❼ Dr. Geissler
- ❽ Schweizer Solderer

HOFBURG DETAILS:
- Ⓐ Neue Burg
- Ⓑ In der Burg Square
- Ⓒ Albertina

Ⓤ U-bahn Station

sleek, easy subways, buy the 24-hour (50-AS) or 72-hour (130-AS) subway/bus/tram pass at a station machine or at Tabak shops near any station. Take a moment to study the eye-friendly city center map on metro station walls to internalize how the metro and tram system can help you. I use it mostly to zip along the Ring (tram #1 or #2) and subway to more outlying sights or hotels. The 15-AS transit map is overkill. The necessary routes are listed on the free tourist city map. Without a pass, either buy individual tickets (17 AS, good for one journey with necessary changes) from metro ticket windows or buy blocks of five tickets for 85 AS (17 AS apiece). If you buy from the bus driver, you'll pay 20 AS per ticket. Eight-strip, eight-day, 265-AS transit passes, called "8 Tage Umwelt Streifennetzkarte," can be shared (for instance, four people for two days each, a 33 percent savings over the cheap 24-hour pass).

Stamp your pass as you enter the system or tram (which puts a time on it). Rookies often miss stops because they fail to open the door. Push buttons, pull latches, do whatever it takes to get on or off. Study your street map before you exit the subway; by choosing the right exit, you'll save yourself lots of walking.

By Taxi: Vienna's comfortable, honest, and easy-to-flag-down taxis start at 26 AS and mount quickly; you'll pay about 60 AS for a five-minute ride (tel. 0222/40106).

By Bike: Good as the city's transit system is, you may want to rent a bike at any train station (daily 4:00–midnight, 90 AS/day with railpass or train ticket, 150 AS without; rent early in morning before supply runs out). Pedal Power offers rental bikes (350 AS/day for "trekking" bike, 395 AS includes delivery and pick-up from your hotel) and four-hour city tours (daily at 10:00, 280 AS includes bike and guide, Austellungsstrasse 3, U-1 to Praterstern, tel. 0222/729-7234, run by American Rick Watts and others).

By Buggy: Rich romantics get around by traditional horse and buggy. You'll see the *Fiakers* clip-clopping tourists on 20-minute (500 AS) or 40-minute (800–1,000 AS) tours.

Helpful Hints

Bank Alert: There is a mix of decent and rip-off banks in the city and at the airport. Save 5 percent by checking the rates at three before changing. Avoid the rip-off Rieger "Bank." Bank hours are roughly Monday through Friday from 8:00 to 15:00 and until 17:30 on Thursday. After hours, you can change money at train stations, the airport, the main post office on Postgasse in the city center (open 24 hours daily, also has handy metered phones), or the Verkehrsbüro at Stephansplatz 10 (daily 9:00–18:30). Commissions of 80 AS are sadly normal. A happy exception is the American Express office, which charges no commissions to change Amex checks (Monday–Friday 9:00–17:30, Saturday 9:00–12:00, Kärntner Strasse 21-23, tel. 0222/51540).

English Bookstores: The British Bookshop is at the corner of Weihburggasse and Seilerstätte (Monday–Friday 9:00–18:30, Saturday 10:00–17:00), and Shakespeare & Co. is at Sterngasse 2, north of the Höher Markt square (Monday–Friday 9:00–19:00, Saturday 9:00–17:00, tel 535-50-5354; as a bonus for coming here at noon, the clock in Höher Markt does a musical act with moving figures).

Do-It-Yourself Bus Orientation Tour

▲▲**Ringstrasse Tour**—In the 1860s, Emperor Franz Josef had the city's ingrown medieval wall torn down and replaced with a grand boulevard 190 feet wide, arcing nearly 3 miles around the city's core. The road predates all the buildings that line it. So what you'll see is neo-Gothic, neoclassical, and neo-Renaissance. One of Europe's great streets, it's lined with many of the city's top sights.

Trams #1 and #2 circle the whole route and so should you.

In fact, start your Vienna visit with this do-it-yourself, 20-AS, 30-minute, circular tour. "Tours" leave every five minutes. Tram #1 goes clockwise; tram #2, counterclockwise. Since most of the sights are on the outside of the Ring, tram #2 is best (sit on the right in the front of the front car). Ideally, catch it at the Opera House at Opernring and Kärntner Strasse (but anywhere will do). With a 24-hour ticket, you can jump on and off as you go. This is great, since trams come every few minutes. (Otherwise, buy your 20-AS ticket, good for only one ride, as you board.) All described sights on this tour are on the right unless I say "on left." Let's go:

• Just past the Opera (on left): The city's main pedestrian drag, Kärntner Strasse, leads to the zigzag roof of St. Stephan's Cathedral. This tour makes a 360-degree circle, staying about this far from that spire.

• At the first bend: Look towards the tall fountain. Schwartzenberg Platz—with its equestrian statue of Prince Charles Schwartzenberg, who battled Napoleon—leads to the Russian monument (behind the fountain). This monument was built in 1945 as a forced thanks to the Soviets for liberating Austria from the Nazis. Formerly a sore point, now it's just ignored.

• Going down Schubertring: The white and yellow concert hall behind the trees is the Kursalon, opened in 1867 by the Strauss brothers, who directed many waltzes here. (See below for concert times.) The huge Stadtpark (city park) honors 20 great Viennese musicians and composers with statues.

• Immediately after next stop: In the park, the gilded statue of Waltz King Johann Strauss holds his violin as he did when he conducted his orchestra.

• While at next stop at end of park: On the left, a green and white statue of Dr. Karl Lueger honors the popular man who was mayor of Vienna until 1910.

• At next bend in road: The quaint building with military helmets decorating the windows was the Austrian ministry of war, back when that was a serious operation. Field Marshal Radetzky, a military big-shot in the 19th century under Franz Josef, still sits on his high horse.

• At next corner: The white-domed building is the Urania, Franz Josef's 1910 observatory. Lean forward and look behind it for a peek at the huge red cars of the giant 100-year-old Ferris wheel in Vienna's Prater Park.

• Now you're rolling along the Danube Canal. This "Baby Danube" is one of the many small arms of the river that once made up the Danube at this point. The rest have been gathered together in a mightier modern-day Danube, farther to the right. This was the site of the original Roman town, Vindobona. In 3 long blocks, on the left (opposite the BP station), you'll see the ivy-covered walls and round Romanesque arches of St. Ruprechts, the oldest church in Vienna (built in the 11th century on a bit of Roman ruins). By about 1200, Vienna had grown to fill the area within this ring road.

• Leaving the canal, turning up Schottenring, at first stop: On the left, the pink and white neo-Renaissance temple of money, the Börse, is Vienna's stock exchange.

• Next stop, at corner: The huge frilly neo-Gothic church is a "votive church," built in 1853 as a thanks to God when an assassination attempt on Emperor Franz Josef failed. Ahead on the right is the Vienna University building, which faces (on the left, behind the gilded angel) a chunk of the old city wall.

• At next stop: The neo-Gothic city hall, flying the flag of Europe, towers over Rathaus Platz, a festive site of outdoor movies and concerts. Immediately across the street (on left) is the Hofburg Theater.

• At next stop: The neo-Greek temple of democracy houses the Austrian Parliament. The lady with the golden helmet is Athena, goddess of wisdom. Across the street (on left) is the royal park called the Volksgarten.

• At next stop: Ahead on the right is the Natural History Museum, the first of Vienna's huge twin museums. Next door is the Kunsthistorisches Museum, containing the city's greatest collection of paintings. A statue of Empress Maria Theresa sits between the museums, facing the grand gate to the Hofburg, the emperor's palace (on your left). Of the five arches, only the emperor used the center. The gate, a modern addition, is located where Vienna's medieval city wall once stood.

• Fifty yards after the next stop, through a gate in the black iron fence: On the left is the statue of Mozart in the Burggarten, which until 1880 was the private garden of the emperor. A hundred yards later (on your left), Goethe sits in a big thought-provoking chair playing Trivia with Schiller (on your right). Behind the statue of Schiller is the Academy of Fine Arts. Vienna had its share of intellectual and creative geniuses.

• Hey, there's the Opera again. Jump out and see the rest of the city. (In front of the Opera there's a person who'd love to take you on a bus tour of what you just did . . . for 220 AS.)

Sights—Vienna's Old Center
(These sights are in walking order.)

▲▲▲**Opera**—The Staatsoper, facing the Ring, just up from Stephansdom and next to the TI, is a central point for any visitor. While the critical reception of the building 130 years ago led the architect to commit suicide, and it's been rebuilt since the World War II bombings, it's a dazzling place (60 AS, by guided 35-minute tour only, offered daily in English, July and August at 11:00, 13:00, 14:00, 15:00, and often at 10:00 and 16:00; other months, afternoons only). Tours are often canceled for rehearsals and shows, so check the posted schedule or call 0222/51444.

The Vienna State Opera, with the Vienna Philharmonic Orchestra in the pit, is one of the world's top opera houses. There are performances almost nightly, except in July and August (when the singers are on vacation, but music still trills in Vienna—see Summer Music Scene, below). Expensive seats and shows are normally sold out. Unless Pavarotti is in town, it's easy to get one of 500 *Stehplatz* (standing-room spots, which are 20–30 AS; the downstairs spots are best). Join the Stehplatz lineup at the Abendkasse side door, where the number of available places is posted. The ticket window opens an hour before each performance. Buy your place at the padded leaning rail. Since the spots aren't numbered, tie your belt or scarf to the rail and you can slip out for a snack and return to enjoy the performance. If less than 500 people are in line, there's no need to line up early.

Between the Opera and the TI is Philharmoniker Strasse; take a left to the Sacher Café, home of every chocoholic's fantasy, the Sachertorte (100 AS for cake and coffee). Continue past café to the . . .

Monument against War and Fascism—Behind the Opera House, on Albertinaplatz, a modern white split statue is Vienna's monument remembering the victims of the 1938–1945 Nazi rule of Austria. In 1938, Germany annexed Austria, saying Austrians were wanna-be-Germans anyway. Austrians are *not* Germans— never were, never will be. They're quick to tell you that while Austria was founded in 976, Germany wasn't born until 1870. For seven years (1938–1945) there was no Austria. In 1955, after ten years of joint occupation by the victorious Allies, Austria regained her independence.

Across the street, the **Albertina Museum**, with its great collection of sketches and graphic art, sits atop the Augustiner Beerhall (colorful lunch place; see Eating, below). This building is the beginning of the huge Hofburg Palace complex.

To get to the pedestrian street, Kärntner Strasse, either retrace your steps or take Maysedergasse, off Albertinaplatz, passing the recommended Rosenberger Markt (see Eating, below).

▲**Kärntner Strasse**—This grand but hamburgerized mall (traffic-free since 1974) is the people-watching delight of this in-love-with-life city. It points south in the direction of the southern Austrian state of Kärnten (for which it's named). Starting from the Opera, you'll find the TI, city Casino (at #41, the former Esterhazy palace), many fine stores, pastry shops, the American Express office (#21–23), and the cathedral.

▲▲**St. Stephan's Cathedral**—Stephansdom is the Gothic needle around which Vienna spins. It's survived all of Vienna's many wars and symbolizes the city's freedom. Locals call it "Steve" (*Steffl*). Hundreds of years of history are carved in its walls and buried in its crypt (40 AS, open at odd times, tel. 0222/515-52-526). Tours are usually in German, but English tours are offered in July and August. The information board near the entry has tour schedules and the time of the impressive 50-minute daily Mass. You can ascend both towers, the north (via crowded elevator) and the south (by spiral staircase). The north shows you a big bell (the 21-ton Pummerin, cast from the cannon captured from the Turks in 1683) but a mediocre view (40 AS, daily 9:00–18:00, enter inside). The 450-foot-high south tower, also called St. Stephan's Tower, offers a great view—343 tightly wound steps away, up the spiral staircase at the watchman's lookout, 246 feet above the postcard stand (25 AS, daily 9:00–17:00, enter outside and burn about one Sachertorte of calories). From the top, use your *Vienna from A to Z* to locate the famous sights. The church is open daily from 6:00 to 22:00.

Outside, the last bit of the 11th-century Romanesque church can be seen in the west end (above the entry): the portal and the round windows of the towers. The church survived the bombs of WWII but, in the last days of the war, fires from the street-fighting between Russian and Nazi troops leapt to the rooftop; the original timbered Gothic rooftop burnt, and the cathedral's huge bell crashed to the ground. With a financial outpouring of civic pride, the roof of this symbol of Austria was rebuilt in its original splendor by 1952. The ceramic tiles are purely decorative (and each has the name of a local who contributed money to the rebuilding). Photos of the war damage can be seen inside.

The interior is grand in general, but it's hard to get thrilled about any particular bit. An exception is the Gothic sandstone pulpit in the middle of the nave (on left or north). A spiral stairway winds up to the lectern surrounded and supported by the four Latin Church Fathers: St. Ambrose, St. Gerome, St. Gregory, and St. Augustine. The work of Anton Pilgram, this has all the elements of Flamboyant Gothic in miniature. But this was 1515. The Italian Renaissance was going strong in Italy and, while Gothic persisted in the north, the Renaissance spirit had already arrived. Pilgram included a rare self-portrait bust in his work (the guy with sculptor's tools, looking out a window under the stairs). Gothic art was to the glory of God. Artists were anonymous. In the more humanist Renaissance, man was allowed to shine—and artists became famous.

The peaceful **Cathedral Museum** (Dom und Diözesan Museum) gives a close-up look at piles of religious paintings, statues, and a treasury (40 AS, Tuesday–Saturday 10:00–16:00, behind the church and past the buggy stand, Stephansplatz 6). Near the church entrance, descend into the Stephansplatz subway stop for a peek into the 13th-century Virgilkapelle.

▲▲**Stephansplatz, Graben, and Kohlmarkt**—The atmosphere of the church square, Stephanplatz, is colorful and lively. At the nearby Graben Street (which was once a *Graben* or "ditch"), topnotch street entertainment dances around an exotic plague monument. In medieval times, people did not understand the causes of plagues and figured they were a punishment from God. It was common for survivors to thank God with a monument like this one from the 1600s. Just beyond the monument is a fine set of Jugendstil public toilets (5.50 AS). St. Peter's Church faces the toilets. Step into this festival of Baroque (from 1708) and check out the jeweled skeletons—anonymous martyrs donated by the pope. Kohlmarkt (at the end of Graben), Vienna's most elegant shopping street, leads left to the palace. Wander down here, checking out the edible window displays at Demel (Kohlmarkt 14). Then drool through the interior (coffee and cake for 100 AS). Shops like this one and the one across the street boast "K. u. K." This means a shop considered good enough for the *Köenig und Kaiser* (king and emperor—same guy). Kohlmarkt leads to Michaelerplatz. The stables of the Spanish Riding School face this square. Notice the Roman excavation in the center. Enter the Hofburg Palace by walking through the gate and into the first square (In der Burg).

Sights—Vienna's Hofburg Palace

▲▲Hofburg—The complex, confusing, imposing Imperial Palace, with 640 years of architecture, demands your attention (and with so many turnstiles, a lot of your money). This first Habsburg residence (13th century) grew in an ad-lib manner until 1913, when the new wing (Neue Burg) was opened. The winter residence of the Habsburg rulers until 1918, it's still the home of the Spanish Riding School, the Vienna Boys' Choir, the Austrian President's office, and several important museums.

While you could lose yourself in its myriad halls and courtyards, I'd focus on three things: the apartments, treasury, and new palace. Orient yourself to the complex from the In der Burg square. The statue is of Emperor Franz II (grandson of Maria Theresa and grandfather of Franz Josef). Behind him is a tower with three kinds of clocks (the yellow disc shows the stage of the moon tonight). On the right, a door leads to the imperial apartments and Hofburg model. Franz II is facing the oldest part of the palace. The gate (which used to have a drawbridge) leads to the 13th-century Swiss Court (named for the Swiss mercenary guards who used to be stationed here) with the Schatzkammer (treasury) and the palace chapel (Hofburgkapelle), where the boys' choir sings the Mass. Continuing out opposite the way you entered In der Burg, you'll find the Hero's Square and the Neue Burg. The *A to Z* book sorts out this time-blackened, jewel-stained mess. Or, if overwhelmed, tour the Imperial Apartments first; here you can buy a big, glossy, detailed Hofburg guidebook in English with great photos and special emphasis on apartments (95 AS). Leave In der Burg for the Imperial Apartments, where you'll find a marvelous model of the whole darn place under a glass pyramid. Study that.

▲▲Imperial Apartments (Kaiserappartements)—These lavish, Versailles-type "wish-I-were-God" royal rooms are a small, downtown version of the grander Schönbrunn Palace. If rushed, see one palace or the other. These suffice. The Apartments are next to the Silver and Porcelain Collection (Silberkammer). You can tour either for 80 AS or get a Kombi-Ticket for 95 AS and see them both (daily 9:00–17:00, from courtyard through St. Michael's Gate, just off Michaelerplatz, tel. 0222/533-7570). An optional guided tour, in German only, costs 20 AS extra.

▲▲Treasury—The Weltliche and Geistliche Schatzkammer (secular and religious treasure room) is expensive, but if you want historic and lavish jewels, these are by far the best on the Continent. Reflect on the glitter of 21 rooms filled with scepters, swords, crowns, orbs, weighty robes, a 96-inch-tall and 500-year-old unicorn horn (or maybe the horn of a narwhal), double-headed eagles, gowns, dangles, and gem-studded bangles. Remember that these were the Holy Roman Emperor's—the divine monarch's. The highlight is Room 11, with the Reich-skrone—the tenth-century crown of the Holy Roman Emperor—and two cases of Karls des Grossen (Charlemagne's) riches (80 AS, Wednesday–Monday 10:00–18:00, closed Tuesday, follow Schatzkammer signs through the red/gold/black arch leading from the main courtyard into the Schweizerhof, tel. 0222/533-7931). Included with your admission is an Art-guide; strap this infrared computer around your neck and point it at display cases to get information (deposit: passport or 500 AS).

▲Neue Burg (New Palace)—This is the last and most impressive addition to the palace. Dating from this century, it was built for Franz Ferdinand but never used. Its grand facade arches around Heldenplatz, or Hero's Square. The featured heroes are Prince Eugene of Savoy (who saved the city from the Turks) and Archduke Charles Schwartzenberg (first to beat Napoleon in a battle, breaking Nappy's image of invincibility and heralding the end of the Napoleonic age). The palace houses three museums: an armory, historical musical instruments, and classical statuary from ancient Ephesus. The musical instruments are particularly entertaining, and free radio headsets (when they work) play appropriate music in each room. Wait at the orange dots for the German description to finish, and you might hear the instruments you're seeing. Stay tuned in, as graceful period music accompanies your wander through the neighboring halls of medieval weaponry—a killer collection of crossbows, swords, and armor. An added bonus is the chance to wander all alone among those royal Habsburg halls, stairways, and painted ceilings (30 AS for all three collections, Wednesday–Monday 10:00–18:00, closed Tuesday, almost no tourists).

More Sights—Vienna

▲▲▲Kunsthistorisches Museum—This exciting museum near the Hofburg Palace showcases the great Habsburg collection of work by Dürer, Rubens, Titian, Raphael, and especially Brueghel. There's also a fine display of Egyptian, classical, and applied arts, including a divine golden saltshaker by Cellini. The museum sells a pamphlet on the top 21 paintings (20 AS) and offers English tours (usually at 11:00 and 15:00 Tuesday–Sunday April–October). The paintings are hung on one floor, and clear charts guide you (95 AS, higher depending on special exhibitions, Tuesday–Sunday 10:00–18:00, Thursday until 21:00, closed Monday, tel. 0222/525-240).

Natural History Museum—In the twin building facing the art museum, you'll find moon rocks, dinosaur stuff, and the *Venus of Willendorf*—at 30,000 years old, the world's oldest sex symbol, found near Vienna in the Danube Valley (Wednesday–Monday 9:00–18:00, closed Tuesday; off-season 9:00–15:00).

▲**Academy of Fine Arts**—This small but exciting collection includes works by Bosch, Botticelli, and Rubens; a Venice series by Guardi; and a self-portrait by 15-year-old Van Dyck (30 AS, Tuesday, Thursday, and Friday 10:00–14:00, Wednesday 10:00–13:00 and 15:00–18:00, Saturday and Sunday 9:00–13:00, three minutes from the Opera at Schillerplatz 3, tel. 0222/588-16-225).

▲**Kaisergruft, the Remains of the Habsburgs**—Visiting the imperial remains is not as easy as you might imagine. These original organ donors left their bodies—147 in all—in the Kaisergruft (Capuchin Crypt, 40 AS, daily 9:30–16:00, a block behind the Opera on Neuer Markt, 5-AS map with a Habsburg family tree and a chart locating each coffin), their hearts in St. George Chapel in the Augustinian Church (church open daily, but to see the goods you'll have to talk to a priest; near the Hofburg, Augustinerstrasse 3), and their entrails in the crypt below St. Stephan's Cathedral. Don't tripe. Rather than chasing down all these body parts, remember that the magnificence of this city is the real remains of the Habsburgs. Pan up. Watch the clouds glide by the ornate gables of Vienna.

Nearby, step into the Augustinian Church, where the Habsburg weddings took place. Don't miss the exquisite Canova tomb (neoclassical, 1805) of Maria Theresa's favorite daughter, Maria Christina, with its incredibly sad white-marble procession. The church has the burial vault for the hearts of the Habsburgs (by appointment only).

▲**Belvedere Palace**—The elegant palace of Prince Eugene of Savoy (the still-much-appreciated conqueror of the Turks), and later home of Franz Ferdinand, houses the Austrian Gallery of 19th- and 20th-century art. Skip the lower palace and focus on the garden and the top floor of the upper palace (Oberes Belvedere) for a winning view of the city and a fine collection of Jugendstil art, Klimt, and Kokoschka (60 AS, Tuesday–Sunday 10:00–17:00, closed Monday, entrance at Prince Eugen Strasse 27, tel. 0222/795-570). Your ticket includes the Austrian Baroque and Gothic art in the Lower Palace.

▲▲▲**Schönbrunn Palace**—Schloss Schönbrunn is second only

to Versailles among Europe's palaces. Located 7 kilometers from the center, it was the Habsburgs' summer residence. It is big—1,441 rooms—but don't worry, only 40 rooms are shown to the public. (The families of 260 civil servants actually rent simple apartments in the rest of the palace.)

While the exterior is Baroque, the interior was finished under Maria Theresa in the Rococo style. The chandeliers are either of hand-carved wood with gold-leaf gilding or of Bohemian crystal. Thick walls hid the servants as they ran around stoking the ceramic stoves from the back, and so on. Most of the public rooms are decorated in neo-Baroque as they were under Franz Josef (1890). While WWII bombs rained on the city and the palace grounds, the palace itself took only one direct hit; that bomb, which crashed through three floors, including the sumptuous central ballroom, was a dud.

There are two different tours you can take. Both come with free headphones that describe the sights in English as you walk through the rooms on your own. The Imperial Tour covers 22 rooms (90 AS) and the Grand Tour covers those 22 rooms plus 18 others (120 AS). Both include the special Empress Elizabeth exhibit. Optional guided tours in English are scheduled roughly every two hours (25 AS extra); you can call in advance for tour times or you can just show up and kill waiting time in the gardens or coach museum (palace open 8:30–17:00, until 16:30 off-season; from the Westbahnhof, either take bus #58 or take subway U-6 to Längenfeldstrasse, then transfer to U-4 and get off at Schönbrunn stop—take exit "Schönbrunn Palace" at train level, tel. 0222/8111-3239). The palace is the most crowded right at opening time and on weekends; it's least crowded from 12:00 to 14:00 and after 16:00.

Wagenburg, the adjacent coach museum, is impressive, with more than 50 royal carriages and sleighs, including a death-black hearse carriage and an extravagantly gilded job, pulled by a dozen horses, that seems pumpkin-bound (30 AS, daily 9:00–18:00; off-season 10:00–16:00 and closes on Monday). The sculpted gardens (with a palm house) lead up to the Gloriette, a purely decorative monument celebrating an obscure Austrian military victory and offering a fine city view (and an expensive cup of coffee). The park is free and open until dusk.

▲City Park—Vienna's Stadtpark is a waltzing world of gardens, memorials to local musicians, ponds, peacocks, music in bandstands, and local people escaping the city. Notice the Jugendstil entry at the Stadtpark subway station. The Kursalon Orchestra plays Strauss waltzes daily in summer: 16:00 to 18:00, 20:00 to 21:00, and 21:30 to 22:30 (tel. 0222/713-2181). You can buy a front-row seat or join the local seniors and ants on the grass for free.

▲Prater—Vienna's sprawling amusement park tempts any visitor with its huge 220-foot-high, famous, and lazy Ferris wheel (Riesenrad), roller coaster, bumper cars, Lilliputian railroad, and endless eateries. This is a fun, goofy place to share the evening with thousands of Viennese (daily 9:00–24:00 in summer; subway: Praterstern). For a local-style family dinner, eat at Schweizerhaus (great beer) or Wieselburger Bierinsel.

Sunbathing—Like most Europeans, the Austrians worship the sun. Their lavish swimming centers are as much for tanning as for swimming. For the best man-made island beach scene, head for the "Danube Sea," Vienna's 20 miles of beach along Danube Island (subway: Donauinsel).

▲**Naschmarkt**—Vienna's ye olde produce market bustles daily, near the Opera along Wienzeile Street. It's likeably seedy and surrounded by sausage stands, Turkish döner kebab stalls, cafés, and theaters. Each Saturday it is infested by a huge flea market where, in olden days, locals would come to hire a monkey to pick little critters out of their hair (Monday–Friday 6:00–18:30, Saturday 6:00–17:00). For a park to picnic in, walk 1 block down Schleifmuhlgasse.

City Tours—Get the *Walks in Vienna* brochure at the TI. Of Vienna's many guided walks, only a few are in English (126 AS, not including admissions, 90 min, tel. 0222/51450, ext. 257). The 75-minute "Getting Acquainted" German/English bus tour is essentially what I covered above in the Ring Tour, with a detour to the Upper Belvedere Palace (220 AS, daily from the Opera at 10:30, 11:45, 15:00, and, in summer, 16:30; no reservations necessary; tel. 0222/712-4683). While pricey, it's intensely informative and a good introduction if you're lazy. Cut out at the palace (which is near the end) if you'd like to see its collection of Klimt and Art Nouveau. The TI has a booklet listing all city tours. Eva Prochaska can book you an excellent private guide who charges 1,180 AS for a half-day (1, Weihburggasse 13-15, tel. 0222/513-5294).

KunstHausWien—This "make yourself at home" modern-art museum, opened in 1990, is a real hit with modern art lovers. It features the work of local painter/environmentalist Hundertwasser (90 AS, daily 10:00–19:00; 3, Weissgerberstrasse 13, nearest metro: U-3 Landstrasse, tel. 0222/712-0491). Nearby, the one-with-nature Hundertwasserhaus (at Löwengasse and Kegelgasse) is a complex of 50 lived-in apartments. This was built in the 1980s as a breath of architectural fresh air in a city of blocky, suicidally predictable apartment complexes. It's not open to visitors but worth visiting for its fun-loving exterior, the Hundertwasser festival of shops across the street, and for the pleasure of annoying its residents.

▲**Jugendstil**—Vienna gave birth to its own curvaceous brand of Art Nouveau around the turn of the century. Jugendstil art and architecture are popular around Europe these days, and many come to Vienna solely in search of it. The TI has a brochure laying out Vienna's 20th-century architecture. The best of Vienna's scattered Jugendstil sights include the Belvedere Palace collection, the clock on Höher Markt (which does a musical act at noon), that WC on the Graben, and the Karlsplatz subway stop, where you'll find the gilded-cabbage-domed gallery with the movement's slogan: "To each century its art and to art its liberty." Klimt, Wagner, and friends (who called themselves the Vienna Succession) first exhibited their "liberty style" art here in 1897.

Spanish Riding School—Performances are usually sold out in advance (tickets 250–900 AS, standing room 200 AS), but training sessions in a chandeliered Baroque hall are open to the public (100 AS at the door, Tuesday–Saturday 10:00–12:00 roughly February–June, September, and mid-October–December; long line; Innerer Burghof in the Hofburg).

Honorable Mention—There's much, much more. The city museum brochure lists everything. If you're into butterflies, Esperanto, undertakers, tobacco, clowns, fire fighting, or the homes of dead composers, you'll find them all in Vienna. Several good museums that try very hard but are submerged in the greatness of Vienna include: **Historical Museum of the City of Vienna** (Tuesday–Sunday 9:00–16:30, Karlsplatz), **Folkloric Museum of Austria** (8, Laudongasse 15, tel. 0222/438-905), and **Museum of Military History**, one of Europe's best if you like swords and shields (Heeregeschichtliches Museum, Saturday–Thursday 10:00–16:00, closed Friday; 3, Arsenal, Objekt 18). The best-value shopping street, with more than 2,000 shops, is Mariahilfer Strasse. For a walk in the Vienna Woods, catch the U-4 subway to Heiligenstadt then bus #38A to Kahlenberg, where there are great city views and a café terrace overlooking the city. From there it's a peaceful 45-minute downhill hike to the Heurigen of Nussdorf or Grinzing to enjoy some wine.

Vienna's Cafés and Wine Gardens

▲**Viennese Coffeehouse**—In Vienna the living room is the coffeehouse down the street. This tradition is just another example of the Viennese expertise in good living. Each of Vienna's many long-established (and sometimes even legendary) coffeehouses has its individual character (and characters). They offer newspapers, pastries, sofas, elegance, a smoky ambience, and a "take all the time you want" charm for the price of a cup of coffee. You may want to order *Malange* (with a little milk) rather than *Schwarzer* (black).

Some of my favorites are: **Café Hawelka**, with a rumpled, "brooding Trotsky" atmosphere, paintings on the walls by struggling artists who couldn't pay, a saloon-wood flavor, chalkboard menu, smoked velvet couches, an international selection of newspapers, and a phone that rings for regulars (8:00–2:00, Sunday from 16:00, closed Tuesday, Dorotheergasse 6, just off the Graben); the **Café Central**, with Jugendstil decor and great *Apfelstrudel* (8:00–20:00, closed Sunday, Herrengasse 14); the Jugendstil

Café Sperl, dating from 1880 (7:00–23:00, closed Sunday in summer, Gumpendorfer 11, just off Naschmarkt); and the basic, untouristy **Café Ritter** (daily 8:00–20:00, Mariahilfer Strasse 73, at the Neubaugasse subway stop near several of my recommended hotels).

▲**Wine Gardens**—The Heurige is a uniquely Viennese institution celebrating the *Heuriger*, or new wine. It all started when the Habsburgs let Vienna's vintners sell their own wine tax-free for 300 days a year. Several hundred families opened Heurigen wine-garden restaurants clustered around the edge of Vienna, and a tradition was born. Today they do their best to maintain their old-village atmosphere, serving the homemade new wine (the last vintage, until November 11th) with light meals and strolling musicians.

Of the many Heurigen suburbs, **Grinzing** (tram #38 or #38A) is the most famous and lively—but it comes with tour buses. **Nussdorf** is less touristy but still characteristic and popular with locals (two fine places are right at the end of tram D). For more crowds and music with your meal, visit **Beethoven's home** (on Heiligenstadt (on Pfarrplatz, tram #38A or #37 and a ten-minute walk, tel. 0222/371-287). While Beethoven lived here in 1817 (to be near a spa he hoped would cure his worsening deafness), he composed his Sixth Symphony ("Pastoral"). These suburbs are all within a 15-minute stroll of each other.

At any Heurige you'll fill your plate at a self-serve cold-cut buffet (75–125 AS for dinner). Waitresses will then take your wine order (30 AS per quarter-liter). Many locals claim it takes several years of practice to distinguish between Heuriger and vinegar. For a near-Heurigen experience right downtown, drop by Gigerl Stadtheuriger (see Eating, below).

Summer Music Scene

Vienna is Europe's music capital. It's music *con brio* from October through June, with things reaching a symphonic climax during the Vienna Festival each May and June. Sadly, in July and August, the Boys' Choir, the Opera, and many more music companies are—like you—on vacation. But Vienna hums year-round with live classical music. In the summer, you have these basic choices:
Touristy Mozart and Strauss concerts—Quality but touristy powdered-wig orchestra performances are given almost nightly in grand traditional settings (400–600 AS). Music is becoming a tourist trap in Vienna. Pesky wigged and powdered Mozarts peddle tickets in the streets. At the touristy Wiener Mozart Konzerte, the orchestra, clad in historic costumes and looking better than it sounds, performs Mozart's greatest hits, including his famous opera arias. The Strauss concerts feature formal waltzers and the Salon Orchestra of the "Wiener Volksoper" inside the Kursalon, where the Waltz King himself directed wildly popular concerts 100 years ago.
▲▲**"Programm"**—Serious concerts, including the Opera, are

listed in the "Programm," a free monthly brochure available at the TI. Events cost between 150 and 700 AS. Tickets booked in advance or through a box office come with a stiff 25 percent booking fee (one's next to the TI behind the Opera). If you call a concert hall directly, they can advise you on the availability of (cheaper) tickets at the door. Vienna takes care of its starving artists (and tourists) by offering cheap standing-room tickets to top-notch music and opera. (The Philharmonic plays at each opera; see Opera, above.)

▲**Free music**—For a festive and free slice of the local music scene, ask about free concerts at the Rathaus (city hall) and on the big screen in front of the Opera. You can also freeload on the Kursalon outdoor Strauss concerts by sitting in the fringes.

▲**Strauss in the Kursalon**—This is your easiest, most affordable option, with daily concerts (April–mid-October) and all your three-quarter favorites in a romantic outdoor setting (weather permitting). Check schedule by calling 0222/713-2181. Pay at the door. Seats are always available (40 AS for orchestra only from 16:00–18:00, or 195 AS for orchestra, dancers, and champagne: 20:00–21:00 or 21:30–22:30).

▲**"Summer of Music" Festival**—This assures that from June through September you'll find lots of top-notch concerts, choirs, and symphonies (special "Klang Bogen" brochure at TI; tickets at the Wien Ticket pavilion on Kärntner Strasse next to the Opera House, or go direct to the location of the particular event; tel. 0222/4000-8410 for information).

▲▲**Vienna Boys' Choir**—The boys sing (heard but not seen, from a high balcony) at Mass in the Imperial Chapel of the Hofburg (entrance at Schweizerhof) at 9:15 on Sundays, except from July through mid-September. Seats must be reserved at least two months in advance (60–280 AS), but standing room is free and open to the first 60 or 70 who line up. Concerts (on stage in the Konzerthaus, or Concert Hall) are also given Fridays at 15:30 in May, June, September, and October (390–430 AS, fax 011-431-587-1268 from U.S.A. or write Reisebüro Mondial, Faulmanngasse 4, 1040 Wien). They're nice kids but, for my taste, not worth all the commotion.

Sleeping in Vienna
(12 AS = about $1, tel. code within Austria: 0222; from outside: 1)
Sleep Code: **S**=Single, **D**=Double/Twin, **T**=Triple, **Q**=Quad, **b**=bathroom, **t**=toilet only, **s**=shower only, **CC**=Credit Card (Visa, MasterCard, Amex). English is spoken at each place.

Call accommodations a few days in advance. If you're calling from outside Austria, replace the "0222" area code with "1." Most places will hold a room without a deposit if you promise to arrive before 17:00. My recommendations stretch along the likeable

Mariahilfer Strasse from the Westbahnhof (West Station) to the town center. Unless otherwise noted, prices include a sparse continental breakfast.

Street addresses start with the district. Postal code is 1XX0, with XX being the district.

Sleeping outside the Ring, along Mariahilferstrasse

Lively Mariahilfer Strasse connects the West Station with the center. The U-3 subway line, starting at the Westbahnhof, goes down Mariahilfer Strasse to the cathedral. While most places are on stern and quiet no-nonsense side roads, the nearby and very Viennese Mariahilfer Strasse is a comfortable and vibrant area filled with local shops and cafés.

Privatzimmer F. Kaled is bright, airy, homey, quiet, and has TVs (with CNN) in each of the four rooms. Hardworking Tina is a mini tourist information service. Being Hungarian, she has good contacts for people visiting Budapest (S-400 AS, Sb-450 AS, D-550 AS, Db-650 AS, T-800 AS, 150 AS for extra bed, skip the 75-AS breakfast in bed, prices through 1998, secure reservation with CC, but room bills must be paid in cash, tell Tina or Fred when you'll arrive; 7, Lindengasse 42, 1070 Wien, near intersection with Neubaugasse, tel. & fax 0222/523-9013). Across the street, Zur Lindenwirtin is a hole-in-the-wall serving big salads and reasonable meals. The Zimmer is a 15-minute walk from the station or a quick two-stop metro ride on U-3 to Neubaugasse (exit to Neubaugasse at train level).

Pension Lindenhof is worn but clean, filled with plants, and run with a unique combination of Bulgarian and Armenian warmth (S-360 AS, Sb-460 AS, D-600 AS, Db-820 AS, cheaper in winter, hall showers-20 AS, most rooms are spacious; 7, Lindengasse 4, 1070 Wien, metro: U-3 Neubaugasse—take "Stiftgasse" exit, tel. 0222/523-0498, fax 0222/523-7362).

Pension Hargita, with 19 generally small, bright, and tidy rooms (mostly twins), is handy—right at the U-3 Zieglergasse stop—and next to a sex shop (S-400 AS, Ss-450 AS, D-550 AS, Ds-650 AS, Db-800 AS, Ts-800 AS, Tb-1,000 AS, Qb-1,100 AS, breakfast-40 AS extra, cheaper for longer stays off-season, corner of Mariahilfer Strasse and Andreasgasse at 7, Andreasgasse 1, 1070 Wien, tel. 0222/526-1928, fax 0222/526-0492).

Budai Ildiko, in a Jugendstil building with a vintage elevator, has high-ceilinged rooms and classy furnishings (small S-350 AS, D-560 AS, T-820 AS, Q-1,050 AS, laundry-20 AS; 7, Lindengasse 39/5, 1070 Wien, tel. 0222/523-1058, tel. & fax 0222/526-2595, run by a charming Hungarian woman).

Hotel Kummer is a 100-room turn-of-the-century hotel with all the comforts (Sb-990–1,490 AS, Db-1,250–2,400 AS, the upper price range applies in May, September, and October, show book to get lower price outside those months, elevator, some no-smoking rooms, CC:VMA, right at the U-3 Neubaugasse stop, 6, Mariahilfer Strasse 71A, 1060 Wien, tel. 0222/58895, fax 0222/587-8133, e-mail: kummer@austria-hotels.co.at).

Privatzimmer Hilde Wolf, 3 blocks off Naschmarkt near U-2 Karlsplatz, is a homey place one floor above an ugly entry, with four huge rooms like old libraries. Hilde loves her work, will do your laundry if you stay two nights, and even offers to baby-sit if traveling parents need a break. Her helpful husband, Otto, speaks English. From West Station, take tram #6 or #18 five stops to Eichenstrasse, then tram #62 six stops to Paulanergasse (two stops from Opera). For a real home in Vienna, unpack here (S-450 AS, D-650 AS, T-955 AS, Q-1,225 AS, with a big, friendly, family-style breakfast, prices through 1998; 4, Schleifmühlgasse 7, 1040 Vienna, tel. 0222/586-5103, reserve by telephone and CC; if you can't make it, call to cancel).

Pension Quisisana is tired and ramshackle, but is a fine value for bohemians in search of the old days and a clean dive (S-330 AS, Ss-380 AS, D-520 AS, Ds-600–640 AS, Db-700–740 AS, 640 AS for a big corner room, third person-260 AS, prices good through 1998 with this book, Db rooms are a better value than the D rooms with head-to-toe twin beds; a block south of Mariahilfer Strasse at 6, Windmuhlgasse 6, 1060 Wien, tel. 0222/587-7155, fax 0222/587-715-633).

West of the Westbahnhof, **Pension Funfhaus** is big, clean, stark, and quiet, with 97 beds split between the main building and an annex. Although the neighborhood is rundown, this place is a great value, especially the spacious and bright doubles with bathrooms (S-390 AS, Sb-470 AS, D-560 AS, Db-640 AS, T-840 AS, Tb-910 AS, two-bedroom apartments for four-1,120 AS, free and easy street parking, closed mid-November–February; 15, Sperrgasse 12, 1150 Wien, tel. 0222/892-3545 or 0222/892-0286, Frau Susi Tersch SE, her mama doesn't). From the station, either ride tram #52 or #58 two stops or walk 7 blocks away from downtown on Mariahilfer Strasse, to Sperrgasse.

Sleeping North of Mariahilfer Strasse

These listings are 4 to 8 blocks north of Mariahilfer Strasse.

Jugendherbergen Myrthengasse/Neustiftgasse is actually two hostels near each other. Both are cheery and well-run, will hold rooms until 16:00, have a lock-out period from 9:00 to 16:00 and a 1:00 curfew, and offer 60-AS meals. The **IYHF** hostel charges 165 AS per person plus 40 AS for non-members (includes sheets and breakfast, three- to six-bed rooms; 7, Myrthengasse 7, 1070 Wien, tel. 0222/523-6316, fax 0222/523-5849). Across the street is **Believe It Or Not**, a friendly and basic place with two big coed rooms for up to ten travelers under age 30. It's locked up from 10:30 to 12:30, has kitchen facilities, and has no curfew (160 AS per bed, 110 AS November–Easter; 7, Myrthengasse 10, no

Vienna: Hotels Outside the Ring

❶ FUNFHAUS
❷ F. KALED
❸ LINDENHOF
❹ HARGITA
❺ KUMMER
❻ QUISIANA
❼ HILDE WOLF

❽ HOSTELS
❾ BELIEVE IT OR...
❿ WILD
⓫ ANDREAS

Ⓤ U-BAHN

sign, ring apt. #14, tel. 0222/526-4658, run by Gosha).

Pension Wild has 14 fine rooms (though a few have a stale smell) and a good, "keep-it-simple-and-affordable" attitude. There are handy extras, like an elevator, full kitchen facilities on each floor, and cheap passes to the health club downstairs (S-450 AS, Ss-550 AS, D-590 AS, Ds-690 AS, Db-790 AS, T-860 AS, Ts-960 AS, reserve with CC:VMA but pay cash, near U-2 Rathaus; 8, Langegasse 10, 1080 Vienna, tel. 0222/406-5174, fax 0222/402-2168).

Pension Andreas is past-its-prime classy and quiet, but a bit smoky (St-580–690 AS, Ds-780–850 AS, Db-890–930 AS, big Db-990 AS, elevator, CC:VMA, near U-2 Rathaus at 8, Schlösselgasse 11, 1080 Wien, tel. 0222/405-3488, fax 0222/405-348-850).

Sleeping within the Ring, in the Old City Center

These places offer less room per schilling but are comfortable, right in the town center, and elevatored, with easy subway connections from West Station. The first four are nearly in the shadow of St. Stephan's Cathedral, on or near the Graben, where the elegance of Old Vienna strums happily over the cobbles. The next two listings are near the Opera (subway: Karlsplatz) just off the famous Kärntner Strasse, near the tourist office and five minutes from the cathedral.

At **Pension Nossek** an elevator takes you above any street noise into Frau Bernad's and Frau Gundolf's world, where the children seem to be placed among the lace and flowers by an interior designer. Street musicians, a pedestrian mall filled with cafés, and the plague monument are outside your door. This is the best value of these first three (Ss-650 AS, Sb-800–900 AS, small Db-1,050 AS, big Db-1,100 AS, apartment-1,500 AS; 1, Graben 17, tel. 0222/5337-0410, fax 0222/535-3646). This pension borders on the square with the Jugendstil WCs.

Pension Aclon is quiet, elegant, sternly run, a block off the Graben, and above a classic Vienna café. The owner, Frau Michlmayer, is curt (S-500 AS, Sb-730 AS, D-860 AS, Db-1,200 AS, T-1,230 AS, Tb-1,620, Q-1,600, Qb-2,000; 1, Dorotheergasse 6-8, tel. 0222/512-79-400, fax 0222/513-8751).

Pension Pertschy is more hotelesque than the others. Its big rooms are huge (ask to see a couple), and those on the courtyard are quietest (Sb-800 AS, Db-1,180–1,440 AS depending on size, apartments with kitchenette for the same price—just ask, cheaper off-season, extra person-300 AS, CC:VM; 1, Habsburgergasse 5, tel. 0222/53449, fax 0222/534-4949).

Pension Neuer Markt, also just off Graben, has cheap-looking doors but the rooms are comfy and pleasant and the location is great (Ss-900 AS, St-800 AS, Sb-1,100 AS, Ds-1,050 AS, Dt-980 AS, Db-1,380 AS, prices soft if business is slow, TVs and phones, CC:VMA; 1, Seilergasse 9, 1010 Wien, tel. 0222/512-2316, fax 0222/513-9105). Ask for a view of Naschmarkt.

Pension Suzanne, as Baroque and doily as you'll find in this price range, is wonderfully located a few yards from the Opera. Suzanne is professional and quiet, with pink elegance bouncing on every bed (Sb-850–880 AS, Db-1,050–1,300 AS, third person-500 AS, TV and phones, reserve with CC but cash preferred as payment; 1, Walfischgasse 4, 1010 Wien, tel. 0222/513-2507, fax 0222/513-2500). From the Westbahnhof, take U-3 to Volkstheater, then transfer to U-2 and get off at Karlsplatz (Opera exit).

Hotel zur Wiener Staatsoper is quiet, rich, and hotelesque. Its rooms come with high ceilings, chandeliers, and fancy carpets on parquet floors—a great value for this locale and ideal for people whose hotel taste is a cut above mine (Sb-1,100 AS, Db-1,600 AS, Tb-1,850 AS, CC:VMA; 1, Krugerstrasse 11, 1010 Wien, tel. 0222/513-1274, fax 0222/513-127-415). Take subway to Karlsplatz, or walk five minutes from U-3: Stephansplatz.

Schweizer Pension Solderer, in the family for three generations, is warmly run by two friendly sisters, Monica and Anita. Enjoy the homey feel, comfortable rooms, parquet floors, and lots of tourist info (S-430 AS, Ss-650 AS, Sb-700 AS, D-700 AS, Ds-860 AS, Db-980 AS, quirky elevator costs 1 AS, laundry-150 AS, non-smoking, Heinrichsgasse 2, 1010 Wien; from West station, take U-3 to Volkstheater, then U-2 to Schottenring; tel. 0222/533-8156, fax 0222/535-6469).

Eating in Vienna

The Viennese appreciate the fine points of life, and right up there with the waltz is eating. The city has many atmospheric restaurants. As you ponder the menus, remember that Vienna's diverse empire may be gone, but its flavor lingers. You'll find Slavic and Eastern European specialties here, along with wonderful desserts and local wine.

On nearly every corner you can find a colorful *Beisl* (Viennese tavern) filled with poetry teachers and their students, couples loving without touching, housewives on their way home from cello lessons, and waiters who thoroughly enjoy serving hearty food and good drink at an affordable price. Ask at your hotel for a good *Beisl*.

All my recommended eateries are within a five-minute walk of the cathedral.

These **wine cellars** are fun and touristic but typical, in the old center of town, with painless prices and lots of smoke. **Zu den Drei Hacken** is famous for its local specialties (Monday–Friday 9:00–24:00, Saturday 10:00–24:00, closed Sunday, indoor/outdoor seating, CC:VA, Singerstrasse 28). The less touristy **Pürstner** restaurant is pleasantly drenched in Old World atmosphere but doesn't encourage lingering (daily 11:00–24:00, indoor/outdoor seating, 150-AS meals, a block away at Riemergasse 10, tel. 0222/512-6357). **Melker Stiftskeller**, the least touristy, is a *Stadtheuriger* in a deep and rustic cellar with hearty, inexpensive meals and new wine (Monday–Saturday 17:00–24:00, closed Sunday, halfway between Am Hof and the Schottentor subway stop at Schottengasse 3, tel. 0222/533-5530).

For a near-Heuriger experience (a la Grinzing, see above) without leaving the center, eat at **Gigerl Stadtheuriger**. Just point to what looks good. Food is sold by the weight (cheese and cold meats cost about 35 AS/100 grams, salads are about 15 AS/100 grams). They also have menu entrees, along with spinach strudel, quiche, *Apfelstrudel*, and, of course, the new and local wines. Meals run 100 to 150 AS (daily 11:00–24:00, indoor/outdoor seating, near the cathedral, a block off Kärntner Strasse, a few cobbles off Rauhensteingasse on Blumenstock, tel. 0222/513-4431).

Brezel-Gwölb, a wonderfully atmospheric wine cellar with outdoor dining on a quiet square, serves delicious, moderately priced light meals, fine *Krautsuppe*, and local dishes. It's ideal for a romantic late-night glass of wine (daily 11:30–1:00, Ledererhof 9, take Drahtgasse off Am Hof). Around the corner, **Zum Scherer Sitz u. Stehbeisl** is just as untouristy, with indoor or outdoor seating, a soothing woody atmosphere, intriguing decor, and local specialties (Monday–Saturday 11:00–1:00, Sunday 17:00–24:00, Judenplatz 7, near Am Hof).

Augustinerkeller is fun, inexpensive, and touristy (daily 10:00–24:00, next to the Opera under the Albertina Museum on Augustinerstrasse). **Figlmüller** is a popular *Beisl* famous for its giant schnitzels (one can easily feed two) near St. Stephan's Cathedral (daily 11:00–22:30, just down the Stephansplatz 6 alley at Wollzeile 5, watch for thieves and rip-off waiters).

For a fast, light, and central lunch, **Rosenberger Markt Restaurant**, a popular highway chain, has an elegant super-branch a block toward the cathedral from the Opera. This place, while not cheap, is brilliant: friendly and efficient, with special theme rooms to dine in, offering a fresh and healthy cornucopia of food and drink and a cheery break from the heavy, smoky, traditional eateries (daily 11:00–23:00, lots of fruits and vegetables, just off Kärntner Strasse at Maysedergasse 2, head downstairs). You can stack a small salad or veggie plate into the tower of gobble for 30 AS.

Buffet Trzesniewski is justly famous for its elegant and cheap finger sandwiches (9 AS) and small beers (9 AS). Three sandwiches and a *Kleines Bier* (Pfiff) make a fun, light lunch (Monday–Friday 8:30–19:30, Saturday 9:00–17:00, just off the Graben, nearly across from the brooding Café Hawelka, on Dorotheergasse).

Naschmarkt, five minutes beyond the Opera, is Vienna's best Old World market, with plenty of fresh produce, cheap eateries, cafés, and döner kebab and sausage stands (Monday–Friday 6:00–18:30, Saturday until 17:00, closed Sunday). For about the cheapest hot meal in town, lunch at the nearby Technical University's **mensa** (cafeteria) in the huge, modern, light-green building just past Karlsplatz (Monday–Friday 11:00–14:30, Wiedner Hauptstrasse 8-10, second floor). Anyone is welcome to eat here with a world of students. The snack bar is less crowded, but the bigger mensa on the same floor has a more interesting selection. The popular **Italian Eis** at Schwedenplatz has great gelato; survey the evening scene from their sidewalk benches.

Wherever you're eating, some vocabulary will help. Three interesting drinks to try are *Grüner Veltliner* (dry white wine, any time), *Traubenmost* (a heavenly grape juice on the verge of wine, autumn only, sometimes just called *Most*), and *Sturm* (barely fermented *Most*, autumn only). The local red wine (called *Portuguese*) is pretty good. Since the Austrian wine is often very sweet, remember the word *Trocken* (German for "dry"). You can order your wine by the *Viertel* (quarter-liter) or *Achtel* (eighth-liter). Beer comes in a *Krugel* (half-liter) or *Seidel* (third liter).

Transportation Connections—Vienna

Vienna has two main train stations: the Westbahnhof, serving Munich, Salzburg, Switzerland, and Budapest; and the Südbahnhof, serving Italy, Budapest, and Prague. The third station, Franz Josefs, serves Krems and the Danube Valley. Subway line U-3 connects the Westbahnhof with the center, tram D takes you from the Südbahnhof and from the Franz Josefs to downtown, and tram #18 connects West and South Stations. Train info: tel. 0222/1717.

By train to: **Melk** (hrly, 75 min), **Krems** (10/day, 1 hr), **Salzburg** (hrly, 3 hrs), **Innsbruck** (3/day, 5.5 hrs), **Budapest** (3/day, 4 hrs), **Prague** (4/day, 5.5 hrs), **Munich** (10/day, 4.5 hrs), **Berlin** (2/day, 14 hrs), **Zurich** (4/day, 9 hrs), **Rome** (3/day, 14 hrs), **Venice** (6/day, 9 hrs), **Frankfurt** (7/day, 7.5 hrs), **Amsterdam** (2/day, 14 hrs).

To Eastern Europe: Vienna is the natural springboard for a quick trip to Prague and Budapest. Vienna is four hours by train from Budapest (360 AS, 580 AS round-trip, free with Eurail) and 5.5 hours from Prague (488 AS one-way, 976 AS round-trip, 652 AS with Eurail). Visas are not required. Train tickets are purchased easily at most travel agencies (such as Intropa, next to the TI on Kärntner Strasse).

SALZBURG, SALZKAMMERGUT, AND HALLSTATT

Enjoy the sights and sounds of Salzburg, Mozart's hometown, then commune with nature in the Salzkammergut, Austria's *Sound of Music* country. Amid hills alive with the S.O.M., you'll find the tiny town of Hallstatt, as pretty as a postcard (and about the same size).

SALZBURG

With a well-preserved old town, gardens, churches, and lush surroundings, set under Europe's biggest intact medieval castle, its river adding an almost seaside ambience, Salzburg is forever smiling to the tunes of Mozart and *The Sound of Music*.

This town knows how to be popular. Eight million tourists crawl its cobbles each year. That's a lot of Mozart balls. But all that popularity has led to a glut of businesses hoping to catch the tourist dollar, and an almost desperate greediness. The town's creative energy is invested in ways to soak the tourist rather than share its rich cultural heritage. Salzburg makes for a pleasant visit, but for most, a day is plenty. With a few exceptions, it's hard to get English information, and music costs about 350 AS per event.

Planning Your Time

While Vienna measures much higher on the Richter scale of sightseeing thrills, Salzburg is simply a joy. A touristy and expensive joy, but a joy nevertheless. If you're going into the nearby Salzkammergut lake country anyway, you don't need to take the *Sound of Music* tour. But this tour kills a nest of sightseeing birds with one ticket (city overview, S.O.M. sights, a luge ride, and a fine drive through the lakes). If you're not planning a detour through the lakes, allow half a day for this tour. That means a minimum of two nights for Salzburg. Of course, the nights are important for concerts and swilling beer in atmospheric local gardens. The actual town sights are mediocre. It's the town itself—a Baroque treat—that you should enjoy. If you like things slow, bike down the river or hike across the Mönchsberg.

Orientation (tel. code: 0662)

Salzburg, a city of 150,000 (Austria's fourth-largest) is divided into old and new. The old town, sitting between the Salzach River and the 1,600-foot-high hill called Mönchsberg, is a bundle of Baroque holding all the charm and most of the tourists.

Tourist Information: Salzburg's three tourist offices (at the train station; on Mozartplatz in the old center—daily 8:00–20:00; and on the freeway entrance to the city, tel. 0662/88987) are helpful. Ask for a city map, the "hotel plan" map, a list of sights with current hours, and a schedule of events. Book a concert upon arrival. The TIs also book rooms (30-AS fee, or 60 AS for three people or more).

Arrival in Salzburg: The Salzburg station makes getting set up easy. The TI is at track 2A. Downstairs is the place to leave bags, rent bikes, buy tickets, and get train information (at "Reisebüro am Bahnhof"). This lower street level faces the bus station (where buses 1, 5, 6, and 51 go to the old center; get off at the first stop after you cross the river). To walk downtown (15 minutes), leave the station ticket hall near window #8 through the door marked "Zentrum" and walk absolutely straight down Rainerstrasse, which leads you under the tracks past Mirabellplatz, changes its name to Dreitaltigkeits-gasse, and takes you to the *Staatsbrucke* (bridge) which deposits you in the old town. For a more dramatic approach, leave the same way but follow the tracks to the river, turn left, and walk the riverside path toward the castle.

American Express: The Amex office holds mail for their check- or credit card–users, and doesn't charge a commission for cashing Amex checks (Monday–Friday 9:00–17:30, Saturday 9:00–12:00, Mozartplatz 5, A-5010 Salzburg, tel. 0662/8080).

Getting Around Salzburg

By Bus: Single-ride tickets are sold on the bus for 19 AS. Daily passes, called Tageskarte, cost 38 AS (good for one calendar day only). The "Salzburg Card" is not worth it for most (24-hour bus pass and 24 hours free entrance to all the city sights for 180 AS). Bus information: tel. 0662/872-145.

By Bike: Salzburg is bike-friendly. From 7:00 until midnight, the train station rents good road bikes for 50 AS and mountain bikes for 150 AS; without a railpass or train ticket, you'll pay 50 AS more (no deposit required, pay at counter #3, pick it up at "left luggage"). Georg, who runs Velo-Active, rents bikes on Residenz-platz under the glockenspiel in the old town. He offers carriers of this book a one-day rental for 100 AS (daily 9:00–18:00, passport number for security, extra charge for mountain bikes, tel. 0663/435-595).

By Funicular and Elevator: The old town is connected to Mönchsberg (and great views) via road, funicular, and elevator. The funicular whisks you up to the imposing Hohensalzburg fortress (32 AS round-trip, 67 AS includes fortress admission). The elevator on the east side of the old town propels you to Café Winkler, the recommended Naturfreundehaus (see Sleeping, below), and lots of wooded paths (27 AS round-trip).

Sights—Salzburg's Old Town

▲▲**Old Town Walking Tour**—The two-language, one-hour guided walks of the old town are informative and worthwhile if you don't mind listening to a half-hour of German (80 AS, start at TI on Mozartplatz at 12:15, Monday–Saturday, May–October, tel. 0662/847-568), but you can easily do it on your own. Here's a basic old-town orientation walk (start on Mozartplatz in the old town):

Mozartplatz features a statue of Mozart erected in 1842. Mozart spent most of his first 20 years (1756–1777) in Salzburg. The tourist information office and American Express Company face this square. Salzburg was the greatest Baroque city north of the Alps. Walk to the next square with the huge fountain.

Residenz Platz: Salzburg's energetic Prince-Archbishop Wolf Dietrich (who ruled from 1587–1612) was raised in Rome, counted the Medicis as his buddies, and had grand Renaissance ambitions for Salzburg. After a convenient fire destroyed much of the old town, he set about building "the Rome of the North." This square with his new cathedral and palace was the centerpiece of his new, Italian-designed Baroque city. A series of interconnecting squares lead from here through the old town.

For centuries, Salzburg's leaders were both important church leaders and princes of the Holy Roman Empire, hence their title mixing sacred and secular authority. Wolf Dietrich abused his power and spent his last five years imprisoned in the Salzburg castle.

The fountain is as Italian as can be, with a Triton matching Bernini's famous *Triton Fountain* in Rome. As the north became aware of the exciting things going on in Italy, things Italian were respected. Local architects even Italianized their names in order to raise their rates.

Dietrich's palace, the **Residenz**, is connected to the cathedral by a skyway. A series of fancy rooms are open to visitors but only with a German-language tour (not worth the boredom or the 50-AS price, English fact sheet available, tel. 0662/8042-2690). The Residenz also has an art gallery.

Opposite the Residenz is the new Residenz, which has long been a government administration building (and post office with a handy bank of pay phones). Atop the new Residenz is the famous **Glockenspiel**, or bell tower. Its carillon of 35 17th-century bells (cast in Antwerp) chimes throughout the day and plays a tune (that changes each month) at 7:00, 11:00, and 18:00. There was a time when Salzburg could afford to take tourists to the top of the tower to actually see the big adjustable barrel turn . . . pulling the right bells in the right rhythm—a fascinating show.

Look back past Mozart's statue to the 4,220-foot-tall Gais-berg (the forested hill with the television tower). A road leads to the top for a commanding view. It's a favorite destination for local bikers. Opposite the church is a picnic-friendly grocery store with an orange awning (Monday–Friday 8:30–18:00, Saturday 8:00–16:00). Walking under the Prince-Archbishop's skyway, step into Domplatz, the cathedral square.

Salzburg Cathedral, built in the 17th century, claims to be the first Baroque building north of the Alps (free, daily 6:00–20:00). The dates on the iron gates refer to milestones in the church's history: In 774 the previous church (long since destroyed) was founded by St. Virgil, to be replaced in 1628 by the church you see today. In 1959, the reconstruction was completed after a bomb blew through the dome in WWII.

Check out the organ draped over the entrance; it was played only when the archbishop walked in and out of the cathedral. Gape up. The interior is marvelous. Concert and Mass schedules are posted at the entrance; Sunday Mass (10:00) is famous for its music.

Under the skyway, a stairway leads down to the excavation site under the church with a few second-century Christian Roman mosaics and the foundation stones of the previous Romanesque and Gothic churches (20 AS, Wednesday–Sunday 9:00–17:00). The Cathedral (or *Dom*) Museum has a rich collection of church art (entry at portico).

The cathedral square is surrounded by "ecclesiastical palaces." The statue of Mary (1771) is looking away from the church, but if you stand in the rear of the square immediately under the middle arch, you'll see how she's positioned to be crowned by the two angels on the church facade.

From the arch, walk back across the square to the front of the cathedral and turn right (going past the underground public toilets) to the next square where you'll see locals playing chess on the giant board. Past the chessboard, a small road leads up to the castle (and castle lift). On the right, a gate reading "St. Peter's" leads past a traditional old bakery (near the waterfall) and into a cemetery.

St. Peter's Cemetery is a collection of lovingly tended mini-gardens (butted up against the Mönchberg's rock wall). The graves are cared for by relatives; anyone residing in the cemetery for over 30 years without living kin gets booted out. Early Christ-ian catacombs are carved into the rock wall above the graveyard (12 AS, 10:00–17:00). This was where the Trapp family hid out in the *Sound of Music*. Walk through the cemetery and out the oppo-site end. Drop into St. Peter's Church, a Romanesque basilica done up beautifully Baroque. Continue through another square and past another church to Universitätsplatz, with its busy open-air produce market. This is Salzburg at its liveliest and most real (mornings, daily except Sunday). Take one of several covered arcades from here to Getreidegasse.

Salzburg

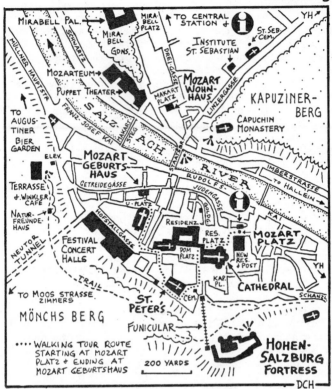

WALKING TOUR ROUTE STARTING AT MOZART PLATZ & ENDING AT MOZART GEBURTSHAUS

200 YARDS

Getreidegasse was old Salzburg's lively and colorful main drag. Famous for its old wrought-iron signs, it still looks much as it did in Mozart's day. *Schmuck* means jewelry. Wolfgang was born on this street. Find his very gold house.

▲**Mozart's Birthplace (Geburtshaus)**—Mozart was born here in 1756. It was in this building that he composed most of his boy-genius works. This most popular Mozart sight in town, filled with scores of scores, portraits, and old keyboard instruments and violins, is worthy of a pilgrimage. If you're a fan, you'll have to check it out. It's right in the old town on colorful Getreidegasse #9 (65 AS, or 100 AS for combined ticket to Mozart's Wohnhaus—see below, daily 9:00–19:00, shorter hours off-season).

▲**Hohensalzburg Fortress**—Built on a rock 400 feet above the Salzach River, this castle, one of Europe's mightiest, dominates Salzburg's skyline and offers great views of the city and surrounding hills. The castle interior is so-so unless you catch a tour (35 AS admission plus 30 AS for a tour; confirm that it will be in English as well as German). Check out the sound-and-vision show. The museum has the noisiest floorboards in Europe, but even so, the princess had a chastity belt. You can see it next to other gruesome torture devices that need no explanation. Upstairs, the mediocre military museum on WWI honors the nice-looking young men who fought in the war Austria started. You can walk up to the fortress, but the funicular is effortless (32 AS round-trip, every ten minutes, 69 AS includes fortress admission). The castle is open daily from 8:00 to 19:00, until 18:00 in the off-season (tel. 0662/842-430).

▲**The Hills are Alive Walk**—For a most enjoyable approach to the castle, consider riding the elevator to the Café Winkler and walking 20 minutes through the woods high above the city to Festung Hohensalzburg (stay on the high paved paths to avoid a needless climb back up to the castle).

Sights—Across the River

▲**Mozart's Wohnhaus (a.k.a. Mozarts Ton- und Filmmuseum)**—Even better than the birthplace is this newly renovated museum, previously Mozart's second home (his family moved here when he was 17). A headphone, free with admission, lets you hear English throughout. Along with the usual scores and old pianos, the highlight is an intriguing film which leaves you wanting to know more about Mozart and his remarkable family (65 AS, or 100 AS for combined ticket to birthplace, guidebook-58 AS, daily 10:00–18:00, just over the river at Marktplatz 8, tel. 0662/8834-5440).

▲**Mirabell Gardens and Palace (Schloss)**—The bubbly gardens are always open and free. You may recognize the statues featured in the *Sound of Music*. To properly enjoy the lavish Mirabell Palace, get a ticket to a *Schlosskonzerte*. Baroque music flying around a Baroque hall is a happy bird in the right cage. Tickets are around 360 AS and are rarely sold out (tel. 0662/848-586).

More Sights—Salzburg

▲▲**Riverside Bike Ride**—The Salzach River has smooth, flat, and scenic bike paths along each side. On a sunny day, I can think of no more shout-worthy escape from the city. Hallein is a pleasant destination (with a salt-mine tour, about 12 kilometers away, north or new-town side of river is most scenic). Even a quickie ride from one end of town to the other gives you the best possible views of Salzburg. In the evening, it's a hand-in-hand, floodlit-spires world.

▲▲*Sound of Music* **Tour**—I took this tour skeptically (as part of my research chores) and liked it. It includes a quick but good general city tour, stops for a luge ride (in season, fair weather, 30 AS extra), hits all the S.O.M. spots (including the stately home, gazebo, and wedding church), and shows you a lovely stretch of the Salzkammergut. The Salzburg Panorama Tours Company charges 350 AS for the four-hour, English-only tour (from Mirabellplatz daily at 9:30 and 14:00, tel. 0662/874-029, e-mail: Panorama@alpin.or.at; ask for a reservation and a free hotel pickup if you like; travelers with this book who buy their ticket at the Mirabellplatz ticket booth get a 10-percent discount on this and any other tour they do). This is worthwhile for S.O.M. fans without a car, or those who won't otherwise be going into the Salzkammergut. Warning: Many think rolling through the Austrian countryside with 30 Americans singing "Doe, a deer" is pretty schmaltzy. And local Austrians don't understand all the commotion.

There are several similar and very competitive tour companies which offer every conceivable tour of and from Salzburg (Mozart sights, Berchtesgaden, salt mines, Salzkammergut lakes and mountains). Some hotels have their brochures and get a healthy commission. The only minibus tours going are Bob's Tours (two different tours: S.O.M. or Berchtesgaden and Bavarian Alps, Kaigasse 19, tel. 0662/849-511).

▲**Hellbrunn Castle**—The attractions here are a garden full of clever trick fountains and the sadistic joy the tour guide gets from soaking tourists. The archbishop's mediocre 17th-century palace is open by tour only (30 AS, hrly, 20 minutes). His Baroque garden, one of the oldest in Europe, is pretty enough, and now features the "I am 16, going on 17" gazebo (70 AS for the 40-minute tour and admission, daily 9:00–17:00, until 22:00 in July and August, until 16:30 in April and October, closed November–March, tel. 0662/820-372). The castle is 3 miles south of Salzburg (bus #55 from the station or downtown, twice hourly, 20-minute ride). It's most fun on a sunny day or with kids, but it's a lot of trouble for a few water tricks.

Music Scene

▲▲**Salzburg Festival**—Each summer from late July to the end of August, Salzburg hosts its famous Salzburger Festspiele, founded in 1920 to employ Vienna's musicians in the summer. This fun and festive time is crowded, but there are plenty of beds (except for a few August weekends). Except for the big shows, tickets are normally available the day of the concert (ticket office on Mozartplatz). You can contact the Austrian National Tourist Office in the U.S.A. for specifics on this year's festival schedule and tickets (Box 1142 Times Square, New York, NY 10108-1142, tel. 212/944-6880, fax 212/730-4568, Web site: www.anto.com, e-mail: antonyc@ix.netcom.com), but I've never planned in advance and have enjoyed great concerts with every visit.

▲▲**Musical events outside of Festival time**—Salzburg is busy throughout the year with 2,000 classical performances in its palaces and churches annually. (While you may find folk evenings twice a week in the summer, Innsbruck is better for these.) Pick up the events calendar at the TI (free, comes out monthly). Whenever you visit, you'll have a number of concerts to choose from. There are nearly nightly concerts at the Mirabell Palace and up in the fortress (both with open seating and 360-AS tickets, concerts at 20:30, doors open at 20:00). The Schlosskonzerte at the Mirabell Palace offers a fine Baroque setting for your Mozart (tel. 0662/848-586). The fortress concerts, called *Festungskonzerte*, are held in the "prince's chamber" (usually chamber music—a string quartet, tel. 0662/825-858 to reserve, you can pick up tickets at the door). This medieval-feeling room atop the castle has windows overlooking the city. The extra 32-AS round-trip lift gives you a chance to enjoy a stroll through the castle courtyard and enjoy the grand city view.

The almost daily "5:00 Concert" next to St. Peter's is cheaper, since it features young artists (120 AS, daily except Wednesday, 45 minutes, tel. 0662/844-57-619). While the series is named after the brother of Joseph Haydn, it features music from various masters.

The Marionette Theater performs operas with fine marionettes and recorded music (250–400 AS, nearly nightly May–September, tel. 0662/872-406).

Sights—Near Salzburg

▲**Bad Dürnberg Salzbergwerke**—Like its salty neighbors, this salt-mine tour and cable-car ride above the town of Hallein (12 kilometers from Salzburg) respects only the German speakers. You'll get information sheets or headphones but none of the jokes. Still, it's a fun experience wearing white overalls, sliding down the sleek wooden chutes, and crossing underground from Austria into Germany (daily 9:00–17:00, easy bus and train connections from Salzburg, tel. 06245/82121 or 06245/852-8515).

▲**Berchtesgaden**—This Alpine resort just across the German border (20 km from Salzburg) flaunts its attractions effectively, and you may find yourself in a traffic jam of desperate tourists looking for ways to turn their money into fun. From the station and the TI (tel. 08652/9670), buses go to the salt mines (a 30-minute walk otherwise) and the idyllic Königsee (21.50 DM, two-hour scenic cruises, 2/hr, stopovers anywhere, tel. 08652/963-618).

At the salt mines, you put on the traditional miners' outfits, get on funny little trains, and zip deep into the mountain. For one hour you'll cruise subterranean lakes; slide speedily down two long, slick, wooden banisters; and learn how they mined salt so long ago. Call for crowd-avoidance advice. You can buy a ticket early and browse through the town until your appointed tour time (19.50 DM, daily 9:00–17:00; winter Monday–Saturday, 12:30–15:30, tel. 08652/60020).

Hitler's famous (but overrated) "Eagle's Nest" towered high

above Obersalzberg near Berchtesgaden. The site is open to visitors, but little remains of the Alpine retreat Hitler visited only five times. The bus ride up the private road and the lift to the top (a 2,000-foot altitude gain) cost 26 DM from the station, 20 DM from the parking lot. If the weather's cloudy, as it often is, you'll Nazi a thing.

Berchtesgaden is a train ride from Munich (hrly, 2.5 hrs, with one change). From Salzburg, ride the scenic and more-direct-than-train bus (2/hr, 60 min). Berchtesgaden caters to long-term German guests. During peak season, it's not worth the headaches for the speedy tourist.

Sleeping in Salzburg
(12 AS = about $1, tel. code: 0662, zip code: 5020)
Sleep Code: **S**=Single, **D**=Double/Twin, **T**=Triple, **Q**=Quad, **b**=bathroom, **t**=toilet only, **s**=shower only, **CC**=Credit Card (Visa, MasterCard, Amex).

Finding a room in Salzburg, even during the music festival, is usually easy. Unless otherwise noted, all my listings come with breakfast and at least some English is spoken. The more expensive places charge more during the music festival (late July and August).

Sleeping in or above the Old Town
Gasthaus Zur Goldenen Ente, run by the Family Steinwender, is a great splurge if you'd like to sleep in a 600-year-old building above a fine restaurant as central as you can be on a pedestrian street in old Salzburg. Somehow the 15 modern and comfortable doubles fit into this building's medieval-style stone arches and narrow stairs (Sb-680 AS and Db-980 AS with this book, higher prices in high season, extra person-450 AS, parking deals, CC:VMA, Goldgasse 10, tel. 0662/845-622, fax 0662/845-6229). The breakfast is buffet-big and their restaurant is a treat (see Eating, below).

Hotel Restaurant Weisses Krentz is a classy, comfy, family-run place on a cobbled back street near the castle (Sb-600 AS, Db-1,000 AS, Tb-1,400, reserve ahead, Bierjodlgasse 6, tel. 0662/845-641, fax 0662/845-6419).

Gasthof Hinterbrühl is a smoky, ramshackle old place with a handy location, minimal plumbing, and not a tourist in sight (S-420 AS, D-520 AS, T-600 AS, plus optional 50-AS breakfast, above a bar that can be noisy, workable parking, CC:V, on a village-like square just under the castle at Schanzlgasse 12, tel. 0662/846-798).

Naturfreundehaus, also called Gasthaus Bürgerwehr, is a local version of a mountaineer's hut. It's a great budget alternative in a forest guarded by singing birds and snuggled in the remains of a 15th-century castle wall overlooking Salzburg, with magnificent old-town and mountain views (D-280 AS, 120 AS per person in four- to six-bed dorms, breakfast-30 AS, dinner-68–108 AS, curfew-1:00, open May–September, Mönchsberg 19, two minutes from the top of the 27-AS round-trip Mönchsberg elevator, tel. 0662/841-729). High above the old town, it's the stone house to the left of the glass Café Winkler.

Sleeping on Linzergasse and near Kapuzinerberg

All of these listings are a 15-minute walk from the train station in the "new" section of town, across the river from the old town. The first three are on lower Linzergasse, directly across the bridge from Mozartville. Its bustling crowds of shoppers overwhelm the few shy cars that venture onto it. The last two listings are farther from the city center (a ten-minute walk).

Institute St. Sebastian is close to the old town and newly renovated, offering the town's best doubles and dorm beds for the money (Sb-300 AS, Db-600 AS, Tb-870 AS, elevator, Linzergasse 41, enter through arch at #37, tel. 0662/871-386, fax 0662/8713-8685). They usually have rooms available, as well as 200-AS spots in ten-bed dorms (30 AS less if you have sheets, no lock-out time, lockers, free showers). Anyone is welcome to use the self-service kitchen on each floor. Fridge space is free; just ask for a key. This friendly, clean, historic building has lots of spacious public areas and a roof garden. The doubles come with modern baths and head-to-toe twin beds. Some Mozarts are buried in the courtyard.

Hotel Pension Goldene Krone is big, quiet, and creaky-traditional but modern, with comforts rare in this price range (Sb-500–570 AS, D-700–800 AS, Db-800–970 AS, Tb-1,100–1,300 AS, elevator, Linzergasse 48, tel. 0662/872-300).

Troglodytes love **Hotel zum Jungen Fuchs**. It's very plain but clean and wonderfully located in a funky, dumpy old building (S-280 AS, D-400 AS, T-500 AS, no breakfast, across from Institute St. Sebastian at Linzergasse 54, tel. 0662/875-496).

Pension Bergland is a classy oasis of calm, with rustic rooms and musical evenings (S-460 AS, Sb-530 AS, two dim D-620 AS, Db-820–880 AS depending on size, Tb-1,010 AS, music room open 17:00–21:30, bike rental, English library, laundromat nearby, Rupertgasse 15, southeast of the station, tel. 0662/872-318, fax 0662/872-3188, e-mail: pknhn@sol.at, run by Peter Kuhn).

Gasthaus Ganslhof, 3 blocks away from the Bergland, is clean, comfortable, and back in the real world with Motel 6 ambience and a parking lot (Sb-480 AS, Db-800 AS, 150 AS more per person in the summer, elevator, TV, and phone, CC:VMA, Vogel-weiderstrasse 6, tel. 0662/873-853, fax 0662/873-85-323).

Bed and Breakfasts

These are generally roomy, modern, comfortable, and come with a good breakfast. Off-season, competition softens prices. They are a bus ride from town, but with a day pass and the frequent service, this shouldn't keep you away. Unsavory Zimmer skimmers lurk at the station. If you have a reservation, ignore them. If you need a place . . . they need a customer.

Brigitte Lenglachner fills her big, traditional home with a warm welcome and lots of tourist information (S-270 AS, D-480 AS, bunk bed D-390 AS, Db-550 AS, T-690 AS, apartment available, two nights preferred, one night costs 10 percent more, breakfast served in room, tel. & fax 0662/438-044). It's in a chirpy neighborhood a ten-minute walk northwest of the station: From the station, cross the pedestrian Pioneer bridge, turn right, pass the park, and take the third left to Scheibenweg 8.

Trude Poppenberger, near Brigitte's place, also offers lots of tourist info. It's three pleasant rooms share the same long balcony and a mountain view (S-280 AS, D-460 AS, T-690 AS; if you stay two nights she'll do your laundry for 80 AS; Wachtelgasse 9, tel. & fax 0662/430-094). It's a 20-minute walk northwest of the station (she will pick you up for free) and a short bus ride (on #49 or #95) into the old town.

Zimmers on Moosstrasse: The street called Moosstrasse, southwest of Mönchsberg, is lined with Zimmer. Those farther out are farmhouses. From the station, catch bus #1 and change to bus #60 immediately after crossing the river. From the old town, ride bus #60 (get off at "Marienbad," the stop after the American High School). If you're driving from the center, go through the tunnel, straight on Neutorstrasse, and take the fourth left onto Moosstrasse. **Maria Gassner** rents ten sparkling clean, comfortable rooms in her modern house (St-250 AS, Sb-400 AS, D-440 AS, Db-500 AS, big Db-600 AS, 10 percent more for one-night stays, family deals, CC:VM, 60-AS coin-op laundry, Moosstrasse 126-B, tel. 0662/824-990, fax 0662/822-075).

Frau Ballwein offers cozy, charming rooms in an old farmhouse (S-200 AS, Ss-240 AS, D-400 AS, Db-480 AS, farm-fresh breakfasts, Moosstrasse 69A, tel. 0662/824-029).

The **Ziller Family Farm** rents three huge rooms with kitchenettes in a kid-friendly, horse-filled environment (Db-600 AS, minimum two nights, Moosstrasse 76, tel. 0662/824-940, Gabi speaks English).

Gästehaus Blobergerhof is rural and comfortable (Sb-350 AS, Db-550 AS, 10 percent more for one-night stays, CC:VM; breakfast buffet, bike rental, will pick up at station, Hammerauerstrasse 4, Querstrasse zur Moosstrasse, tel. 0662/830-227, fax 0662/827-061).

Helga Bankhammer rents recently renovated, pleasant rooms in a farmhouse with farm animals nearby (DB-440–500 AS, most with private bath, Moosstrasse 77, tel. 0662/830-067).

Eating in Salzburg

Salzburg boasts many inexpensive, fun, and atmospheric places to eat. I'm a sucker for big cellars with their smoky Old World atmosphere, heavy medieval arches, time-darkened paintings, antlers, and hearty meals to match. These places are famous with visitors but also enjoyed by the locals.

Gasthaus "Zum Wilder Mann" is the place if the weather's bad and you're in the mood for Hofbräu atmosphere and a hearty, cheap meal at a shared table in one small, well-antlered room (Monday–Saturday 11:00–21:00, closed Sunday, two minutes from Mozart's place—enter from Getreidegasse 20 or Griesgasse 17, tel. 0662/841-787). For a quick 100-AS lunch, get the *Bauernschmaus*, a mountain of dumpling, kraut, and peasant's meats.

Krimplestätter employs 500 years of experience serving authentic old-Austrian food in its authentic old-Austrian interior or its cheery garden (10:00–24:00, closed Monday all year, closed Sunday September–April, Müllner Hauptstrasse 31, ten minutes north of the old town near the river). For fine food with a wild finale, eat here and drink at the nearby Augustiner Bräustübl.

Augustiner Bräustübl, a monk-run brewery, is so rustic and crude that I hesitate to show my true colors by recommending it. On busy nights it's like a Munich beer hall with no music but the volume turned up. When it's cool, you'll enjoy a historic setting with beer-sloshed and smoke-stained halls. On balmy evenings you'll eat under trees in a pleasant outdoor beer garden. Local students mix with tourists eating hearty slabs of schnitzel with their fingers or cold meals from the self-serve picnic counter. It'll bring out the barbarian in you (Augustinergasse 4, head up Müllner Hauptstrasse northwest along the river, and ask for "Müllner-bräu," its local nickname). Don't be fooled by second-rate gardens serving the same beer nearby—this huge, 1,000-seat place is in the Augustiner brewery (daily 15:00–23:30). Order carefully, prices can sting. Pick up a half-liter (28–32 AS) or full-liter mug (56–64 AS) of the great beer, pay the lady, and give Mr. Keg your empty mug. For dessert, after a visit to the strudel kiosk, enjoy the incomparable floodlit view of old Salzburg from the nearby pedestrian bridge and then stroll home along the river. Delicious memories.

Stiftskeller St. Peter has been in business for more than 1,000 years. It's classier (with strolling musicians), more central, and a good splurge for traditional Austrian cuisine in medieval sauce (daily 11:00–24:00, outdoor and indoor seating, meals 100–200 AS, CC:VMA, next to St. Peter's Church at the foot of Mönchsberg, tel. 0662/841-268).

Gasthaus Zur Goldenen Ente (see Sleeping, above) serves great food. The chef, Robert, specializes in roast duck (*Ente*) and seafood, along with "Salzberger Nockerl," the mountainous sweet soufflé served all over town. It's big enough for four (Monday–Friday 11:00–21:00, closed Saturday and Sunday, Goldgasse 10, tel. 0662/845-622).

Stieglkeller is a huge, atmospheric institution which has several rustic rooms and outdoor garden seating with a great rooftop view of the old town (daily 10:00–22:00, 50 yards uphill from the lift to the castle, Festungsgasse 10, tel. 0662/842-681). They offer the latest S.O.M. spin-off, a *Sound of Music* Dinner Show, featuring songs from the movie and local dances (520 AS includes dinner, 360 AS for show only, daily May–September, tel. 0662/832- 029). Since the Stieglkeller has lots of rooms, you can skip the show and still enjoy the restaurant.

Picnics: The University Square, just behind Mozart's house, hosts a bustling morning **produce market** daily except Sunday.

Lunch: Classy Salzburg delis serve good, cheap, sit-down lunches on weekdays. Have them make you a sandwich or something hot, toss in a carrot, a piece of fruit, yogurt, and a box of milk, and sit at a small table with the local lunch crowd.

Café Glockenspiel, on Mozartplatz 2, does a good, if pricey, lunch (80–160 AS). The following cheaper places are all just across the river from the old town: **Frauenberger** is friendly, picnic-ready, and inexpensive, with indoor or outdoor seating (Monday 8:00–14:00, Tuesday–Friday 8:00–14:00 and 15:00–18:00, Saturday 8:00–12:30, closed Sunday, across from Linzergasse 16); their take-out window is open until midnight. **Café Haydn Stube**, run by the local music school, is cheap and popular with students (Monday–Friday 9:00–18:00, later in summer, Mirabellplatz 1, at the entry to the Aicherpassage). **Mensa Aicherpassage** serves even cheaper meals in the basement (Monday–Friday 11:30–14:30, go under arch, enter metal door to "Mozarteum," and go down one floor).

Transportation Connections—Salzburg
By train to: Innsbruck (every 2 hrs, 2 hrs), **Vienna** (2/hr, 3.5 hrs), **Hallstatt** (hrly, 50 min to Attnang Puchheim, 20-minute wait, 1.5 hrs to Hallstatt), **Reutte** (every 2 hrs, 4 hrs, transfer in Innsbruck), **Munich** (hrly, 2 hrs).

SALZKAMMERGUT LAKE DISTRICT AND HALLSTATT
Commune with nature in Austria's Lake District. "The hills are alive," and you're surrounded by the loveliness that has turned on everyone from Emperor Franz Josef to Julie Andrews. This is *The Sound of Music* country. Idyllic, majestic, but not rugged, it's a gentle land of lakes, forested mountains, and storybook villages rich in hiking opportunities and inexpensive lodging. Settle down in the postcard-pretty, fjord-cuddling town of Hallstatt.

Planning Your Time
While there are plenty of lakes, Hallstatt is really the only one that matters. One night and two hours to browse is all you'll need to fall in love. To relax or take a hike in the surroundings, give it two nights and a day. It's a good stop between Salzburg and Vienna. A

visit here (with a bike ride along the Danube) balances out your
Austrian itinerary.

Orientation (tel. code: 06134)

Lovable Hallstatt is a tiny town bullied onto a ledge between a
selfish mountain and a swan-ruled lake, with a waterfall ripping
furiously through its middle. It can be toured on foot in about ten
minutes. The town is one of Europe's oldest, going back centuries
before Christ. The charm of Hallstatt is the village and its lakeside
setting. Go there to relax, nibble, wander, and paddle. (In August,
tourist crowds trample much of Hallstatt's charm.) The lake is
famous for its good fishing and pure water (8 km by 2 km, 125
meters deep at 508 meters altitude).

Tourist Information: The TI can always find you a room.
Its hotel "guest card" gives you free parking and sightseeing discounts (Monday–Friday 9:00–18:00, weekends 10:00–14:00, less
off-season, tel. 06134/8208).

Arrival in Hallstatt: Hallstatt's train station is a wide spot on
the tracks across the lake. *Stefanie* (a boat) meets you at the station
and glides across the lake into town (20 AS, with each train until
18:35—don't arrive after that). The boat ride is gorgeous.

Sights—Hallstatt

Prehistory Museum—The humble Prehistory Museum adjacent
to the TI is interesting because little Hallstatt was the important
salt-mining hub of a culture which spread from France to the
Balkans during what archaeologists call the Hallstatt Period
(800–400 B.C.). Back then Celtic tribes dug for precious salt and
Hallstatt was, as its name means, the "salt mine." Your 40-AS Prehistory Museum ticket also gets you into the cute Heimat Museum
of folk culture (daily 10:00–18:00 in summer). Historians like the
English booklet that covers both museums (25 AS). The Janu
sport shop across from the TI recently dug into a prehistoric site,
and now its basement is another small museum.

▲▲Hallstatt Church and Cemetery—Hallstatt has two
churches. The Protestant church is at lake level. The more interesting Catholic church, with a giant St. Christopher (protector of
us travelers) on its outside wall, overlooks the town from above.
From near the boat dock, hike up the covered wooden stairway to
the church. The lovely church has 500-year-old altars and frescoes
dedicated to the saints of mining and salt. Space is so limited in
Hallstatt that bones have only 12 peaceful buried years in the
church cemetery before making way for the freshly dead. The
result is a fascinating chapel of bones in the cemetery (Beinhaus,
10 AS, daily 10:00–18:00). Each skull is lovingly named, dated, and
decorated, with the men getting ivy, and the women, roses. They
stopped this practice in the 1960s, about the same time the
Catholic Church began permitting cremation.

Salzkammergut and Hallstatt

▲▲Salt Mine Tour—If you have yet to do a salt mine, Hallstatt's is as good as any. You'll ride a frighteningly steep funicular high above the town (97 AS round-trip, 85 AS with guest card), take a ten-minute hike, put on old miners' clothes, take an underground train, slide down the banisters, and listen to an English tape-recorded tour while your guide speaks German (135 AS, 120 AS with guest card, daily 9:30–16:30, closes early off-season, no children under age 4, tel. 06134/8251). The well-publicized ancient Celtic graveyard excavation sites nearby are really dead. The scenic 50-minute hike back into town is (with strong knees) a joy.

▲Boating, Hiking, and Spelunking—Those into relaxation can rent a sleepy motorboat to enjoy town views from the water (75 AS/30 minutes, 120 AS/one hour, one or two people, two speeds:

slow and stop, from Das Boot in the center or from the bus terminal just south of town). Mountain lovers, hikers, and spelunkers keep busy for days using Hallstatt as their home base. Get information from the TI on the various caves with their ice formations, the thunderous rivers, mountain lifts, nearby walks, and harder hikes. The best short and easy walk is the two-hour round-trip up the Echerhal Valley to a waterfall and back. With a car, consider hiking around nearby Altaussee (flat, three-hour hike) or along Grundlsee to Tolpitzsee. Regular buses connect Hallstatt with Gosausee for a pleasant walk around that lake. The TI can recommend a great two-day hike with an overnight in a nearby mountain hut.

Sleeping in Hallstatt
(12 AS = about $1, tel. code: 06134, zip code: 4830)
Hallstatt's TI can almost always find you a room. July and August can be tight, and early August is worst. A bed in a private home costs about 200 AS with breakfast. It's hard to get a one-night advance reservation. But if you drop in and they have a spot, they're happy to have you. Prices include breakfast, lots of stairs, and a silent night. *"Zimmer mit Aussicht?"* means "Room with view?"—worth asking for.

Gasthof Simony is my stocking-feet-tidy, 500-year-old favorite, right on the square with a lake view, balconies, creaky wood floors, slip-slidey rag rugs, antique furniture, a lakefront garden, and a huge breakfast. Call friendly Susan Scheutz for a reservation. For safety, reconfirm a day or two before you arrive (Sb-500 AS, Db-850 AS, price can vary according to the plumbing, view, season, and length of stay, 250 AS for third person, cheaper for families, Markt 105, tel. 06134/8231, SE). Downstairs Frau Zopf runs a traditional Austrian restaurant; try her delicious homemade desserts.

Pension Seethaler is a homey old lodge with 45 beds and a breakfast room mossy with antlers, perched a little above the lake on the parking-lot side of town (215 AS per person in S, D, T, or Q, 280 AS per person in rooms with private bath, cheaper if you stay more than one night, no extra for great views, Dr. Morton Weg 22, tel. 06134/8421, fax 06134/84214; Frau Seethaler).

Pension Sarstein has 25 beds, mostly in rooms with flower-bedecked lake-view balconies. The charming building, a few minutes' walk along the lake from the center, is run by friendly Frau Fisher. You can swim from her lakeside garden (D-420 AS, Ds-550 AS, Db-600 AS with this book; one-night stays cost 20 AS per person extra; Gosaumühlstrasse 83, tel. 06134/8217). Her sister, friendly **Frau Zimmermann**, runs a small Zimmer (as her name implies) in a 500-year-old ramshackle house with low beams, time-polished wood, and fine lake views just down the street (200-AS-per-person bed and breakfast in a double or triple, can be musty, Gosaumühlstrasse 69, tel. 06134/8309). These elderly ladies speak almost no English, but you'll find yourself caught up in their charm and laughing together like old friends.

Helga Lenz has a big, sprawling, woodsy house on top of the town with great lake and town views and a garden perch. It's ideal for those who sleep well in tree houses (180 AS per person in two-, three-, or four-bed rooms, 20 AS more for one-night stays, high above the paddleboat dock at Hallberg 17, tel. 06134/8508, SE).

Gasthof Zauner is a business machine offering modern pine-flavored rooms with all the comforts on the main square, and a restaurant specializing in grilled meat and fish (Db-1,190 AS, CC:VM, Marktplatz 51, tel. 06134/8246, fax 06134/82468).

Gasthaus Mühle Naturfreunde-Herberge has the best cheap beds in town and is clearly the place to eat well on a bud-get—great pizzas (145 AS per bed with sheets in two- to 20-bed coed dorms, 110 AS if you BYO hostel sheet, 40-AS breakfast, closed in November, the restaurant is closed on Wednesday, Kirchenweg 36, just below the tunnel car park, tel. & fax 06134/8318, run by Ferdinand Törö). "Nature's friends' houses" are found throughout the Alps. Like mountaineers' huts, they're a good, basic, fun bargain.

The nearby village of Obertraun is a peaceful alternative to Hallstatt in August. Check out the ice caves on a hot day. You'll find plenty of Zimmer and a luxurious hostel (135-AS beds with breakfast, tel. 06131/1360).

Transportation Connections—Hallstatt
By train to: Salzburg (hrly, 90 min to Attnang Puchheim, 10-to 30-min wait, 50 min to Salzburg), **Vienna** (hrly, 90 min to Attnang Puchheim, 10-to 30-min wait, 2.5 hrs to Vienna). Daytrippers to Hallstatt can either check their bags or use the lockers at Attnang Puchheim station.

BRUGES (BRUGGE)

With Renoir canals, pointy gilded architecture, time tunnel art, and stay-awhile cafés, Bruges is a heavyweight sightseeing destination, as well as a joy. Where else can you ride a bike along a canal, munch mussels, wash them down with the world's best beer, savor heavenly chocolate, and see Flemish Primitives and a Michelangelo, all within 300 yards of a bell tower that rings out "Don't worry, be happy" jingles every 15 minutes? And there's no language barrier.

The town is Brugge (broo-gha) in Flemish. It's Bruges (broozh) in French and English. Before it was Flemish or French, the name was a Viking word for "wharf" or "embarkment." Right from the start, Bruges was a trading center. By the 14th century, Bruges' population was 35,000, in a league with London, and the city was the most important cloth market in northern Europe. By the 16th century, the harbor had silted up and the economy had collapsed. In the 19th century, a new port, Zeebrugge, brought renewed vitality to the area. But today, Bruges prospers mainly because of tourism: It's a uniquely well-preserved Gothic city and a handy gateway to Europe. It's no secret, but even with the crowds, it's the kind of city where you don't mind being a tourist.

The tourists' Bruges (you'll be sharing it) is contained within a 1-kilometer-square canal, or moat. Nearly everything of interest and importance is within a cobbled and convenient swath between the train station and the Market Square (a 15-minute walk).

Planning Your Time
Bruges needs at least two nights and a full, well-organized day. Even non-shoppers enjoy browsing here, and the Belgian love of life makes a hectic itinerary seem a little senseless. With one day, the speedy visitor could do this:

9:30, climb the belfry. 10:00, catch the minibus orientation town tour. 11:00, tour the Burg sights (visit the TI if necessary). 12:15, walk to the brewery, have lunch, and catch the 13:00 tour. 14:30, walk through the Beguinage. 15:00, tour the Memling Museum (six paintings). 15:45, see the Michelangelo in the church. 16:00, tour the Groeninge Museum (closes at 17:00).

Rent a bike for an evening ride through the quiet back streets (or take a 900BF half-hour horse-and-buggy tour or catch a canal-boat tour). Lose the tourists and find a dinner. (If this schedule seems insane, skip the belfry and the brewery.)

Orientation (tel. code: 050)

Tourist Information: The main office is on Burg Square (Monday–Friday 9:30–18:30, Saturday and Sunday 10:00–12:00 and 14:00–18:30; off-season closes at 17:00, tel. 050/448-686, public WC in courtyard). The other TI is at the train station office (daily 10:30–18:30; off-season closes at 17:00 and on Sunday). Both TIs sell a great 25BF all-inclusive Bruges visitors' guide with a map and listings of all of the sights and services. The free *Exit* includes a monthly calendar of the many events the town puts on to keep its hordes of tourists entertained. It's entirely in Dutch but almost readable (i.e., *Harmonieconcert*). Skip the TI's "combo" museum ticket. They also have train schedule information and specifics on the various kinds of tours available. Bikers will want the "5X On The Bike Around Bruges" map/guide for 20BF, showing five routes through the countryside.

Arrival in Bruges

By Train: From the train, you'll see the square belfry tower on the main square. Upon arrival, stop by the station TI to pick up the Bruges visitors' guide (map in centerfold). Most buses (#1, #3, #4, #6, #8, #11, #13, #16) go right to the Market Square (40BF ticket, buy from driver, good for an hour). Taxi fare to most hotels is 250BF. It's a 20-minute walk from the station to the center: cross the busy street and canal in front of the station, head up Oostmeers, and turn right on Steenstraat to reach Market Square. You could rent a bike at the station for the duration of your stay (325BF/day with a 500BF deposit), but other bike rental shops are closer to the center (see below).

By Car: Park at the train station for just 100BF a day and pretend you arrived by train; show your parking receipt on the bus to get a free ride into town. The pricier underground parking garage at t'Zand costs 350BF/day.

Helpful Hints

Change traveler's checks at Brussels Lambert Bank (Monday–Friday 9:00–12:30 and 13:30–16:30, Saturday 9:00–12:00, on the Market Square). The post office is on Market Square near the belfry

(Monday–Friday 9:00–19:00, Saturday 9:00–12:00). Shops are open from 9:00 to 18:00; a little later on Friday. Grocery stores are usually closed on Sunday. Market day is Wednesday morning (Market Square) and Saturday morning (t'Zand). On Saturday and Sunday afternoons there is a flea market along Dijver (in front of Groeninge Museum). October through March is off-season (when some museums close on Tuesday). A botanical garden blooms in the center of Astrid Park.

Sights—Bruges

Bruges' sights are listed here in walking order: from the Market Square, to the Burg, to the cluster of museums around the Church of Our Lady, to the Beguinage (a ten-minute walk from beginning to end). Like Venice, the ultimate sight is the town itself, and the best way to enjoy that is to get lost on the back streets away from the lace shops and ice-cream stands.

Market Square (Markt)—Ringed by banks, the post office, lots of restaurant terraces, great old gabled buildings, and the belfry, this is the modern heart of the city. Most city buses go from here to the station. Under the belfry are two great Belgian French-fry stands and a quadralingual braille description and model of the tower. In its day, a canal went right up to the central square of this formerly great trading center.

▲▲**Belfry (Belfort)**—This bell tower has towered over Market Square since 1300. In 1486, the octagonal lantern was added, making it 83 meters high—that's 366 steps (daily 9:30–17:00, October–March closed 12:30–13:30, WC in courtyard). The view is worth the climb and the 100BF. Survey the town. On the horizon you can see the towns along the coast. Just before you reach the top, peek into the carillon room. The 47 bells can be played mechanically with the giant barrel and movable tabs (as they do on each quarter-hour) or with a manual keyboard (as it does for regular concerts) with fists and feet rather than fingers. Be there on the quarter-hour when things ring. It's *bellissimo* at the top of the hour. Carillon concert times are listed at the base of the belfry (usually Wednesday, Saturday, and Sunday 14:15–15:00). With your back to the belfry, turn right on Breidelstraat to get to Burg Square.

▲▲**Burg Square**—The opulent square called Burg is Bruges' civic center, historically the birthplace of Bruges and the site of the ninth-century castle of the first Count of Flanders. Today it's the scene of outdoor concerts, a parking place for horse buggies, and home of the TI (with a public WC). It's surrounded by six centuries of architecture. Sweeping counterclockwise 360 degrees, you'll go from Romanesque (the round arches and thick walls of the brick basilica in the corner, best seen inside the lower chapel), to the pointed Gothic arches of the Town Hall (with its "Gothic Room"), to the well-proportioned Renaissance windows of the Old Recorder's House (next door, under the gilded statues), past the TI

Bruges

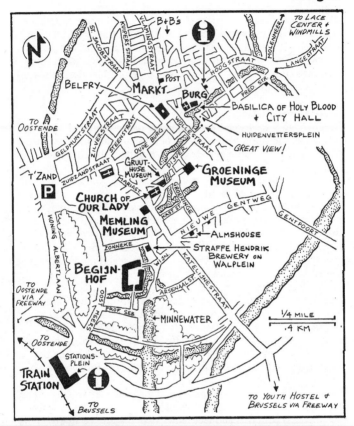

and the park to the elaborate 17th-century Baroque of the
Provost's House.

▲**Basilica of the Holy Blood**—Originally the Chapel of Saint
Basil, it is famous for its relic of the blood of Christ, which,
according to tradition, was brought to Bruges in 1150 after the
Second Crusade. The lower chapel (through door labeled
"Basiliek") is dark and solid—a fine example of Romanesque (with
some beautiful statues). The upper chapel (separate entrance,
climb the stairs) is decorated Gothic and is often filled with
appropriately contemplative music. An English flier tells about
the relic, art, and history. The Basilica Museum is small but
sumptuous and contains the gem-studded hexagonal reliquary
that carries the relic on its yearly Ascension Day trip through the
streets of Bruges (museum is next to the upper chapel, 40BF,

daily 9:30–12:00 and 14:00–18:00; shorter hours and closed Wednesday afternoon off-season).

▲**City Hall's Gothic Room**—Built around 1400, this is the oldest in the Low Countries. Your ticket gives you a room full of old town maps and paintings, and a grand "Gothic Hall" beautifully restored. Its painted and carved wooden ceiling features "hanging arches" (explained by an English flier). The free ground-level lobby is a picture gallery of Belgium's colonial history, from the Spanish Bourbon king to Napoleon (100BF, includes admission to Renaissance Hall, daily 9:30–17:00, off-season closed 12:30–14:00, Burg 12).

Renaissance Hall (Brugse Vrije)—This is just one ornate room with an impressive Renaissance chimney. If you're into heraldry, the symbolism, explained in the free English flier, makes this worth a five-minute stop. If you're not, you'll wonder where the rest of the museum is (100BF, includes admission to City Hall, Tuesday–Sunday 9:30–12:30 and 13:15–17:00, closed Monday, entry in corner of square).

From Burg to Fish Market to View—From Burg, walk under the Goldfinger family down Blinde Ezelstraat. Just after you cross the bridge, the persistent little fish market (*Vismarkt*) is on your left. Take an immediate right to Huidevettersplein, a tiny, picturesque, and restaurant-filled square. Continue a few steps to the street Rozenhoedkaai, where you can get a great photo of the belfry reflected in the canal. Can you see its tilt? It leans about 4 feet. Down the canal (past a flea market on weekends) looms the huge brick spire of the Church of Our Lady (tallest spire in the Low Countries). Between you and the church are the next three museums.

▲▲▲**Groeninge Museum**—This diverse and classy collection shows off mostly Flemish art from Memling to Magritte. While it has plenty of worthwhile modern art, the highlights are its vivid and pristine Flemish Primitives. ("Primitive" here means before the Renaissance.) Flemish art is shaped by its love of detail, its merchant patrons' egos, and the power of the Church. Lose yourself in the halls of Groeninge: Gaze across 15th-century canals, into the eyes of reassuring Marys, and through town squares littered with leotards, lace, and lopped-off heads (200BF, daily 9:30–17:00; October–March closed 12:30–14:00 and Tuesday, Dijver 12). The Brangwyn Museum (Arentshuis), next door, is only interesting if you are into lace or the early-20th-century art of Brangwyn (80BF, daily 9:30–17:00; off-season closed 12:30–14:00 and Tuesday, Dijver 16).

▲**Gruuthuse Museum**—A wealthy brewer's home, this is a sprawling smattering of everything from medieval bedpans to a guillotine. There's no information inside, so to understand the crossbows, dark old paintings, and what a beer merchant's doing with box seats peeking down on the altar of the Church of Our Lady next door, you'll have to buy or browse through the 600BF guidebook (130BF, daily 9:30–17:00, shorter hours off-season, Dijver 17).

▲▲**Church of Our Lady**—The church stands as a memorial to the power and wealth of Bruges in its heyday. A delicate *Madonna and Child* by Michelangelo is near the apse (to the right, if you're facing the altar). It's said to be the only Michelangelo statue to leave Italy in his lifetime (cloth money). If you like tombs and church art, pay to wander through the apse (60BF, Michelangelo free, art-filled apse Monday–Friday 10:00–11:30 and 14:30–16:30, closes at 16:00 on Saturday; Sunday open 14:30–16:30; on Mariastraat).

▲▲**St. Jans Hospital/Memling Museum**—Just beyond the Church of Our Lady is a medieval hospital with six much-loved paintings by the greatest of the Flemish Primitives, Hans Memling. The fascinating medieval hospital is due to reopen in August 1998, but the Memling art is wide open year round. His *Mystical Wedding of St. Catherine* triptych deserves a close look. Catherine and her "mystical groom," the baby Jesus, are flanked by a headless John the Baptist and a pensive John the Evangelist. The chairs are there so you can study it. If you understand the Book of Revelations, you'll understand St. John's wild and intricate vision. The Reliquary of St. Ursula, an ornate little mini-church in the same room, is filled with impressive detail (100BF, open daily 9:30–17:00; off-season closed 12:30–14:00 and Wednesday, Mariastraat 38).

▲▲**Straffe Hendrik Brewery Tour**—Belgians are Europe's beer connoisseurs. This fun and handy tour is a great way to pay your respects. The happy gang at this working family brewery gives entertaining and informative 45-minute/four-language tours (usually by friendly Inge, 140BF including a beer, piles of very steep steps, a great rooftop panorama, daily on the hour 11:00–17:00, occasionally skipping 14:00, October–March 11:00 and 15:00 only, 1 block past church and canal, take right down skinny Stoofstraat to #26 on Walplein square, tel. 050/332-697). Originally "Henri Maes," this delicious brew is now known as Straffe Hendrik (strong Henry). They remind their drinkers: "The components of the beer are vitally necessary and contribute to a well-balanced life-pattern. Nerves, muscles, visual sentience, and a healthy skin are stimulated by these in a positive manner. For longevity and life-long equilibrium, drink Straffe Hendrik in moderation!"

Their bistro, where you'll be given your included-with-the-tour beer, serves a quick and hearty lunch plate (the 150BF "bread with paste and vegetables" is the best value, although the 250BF "meat selection and vegetables" is a beer-drinker's picnic for two). You can eat indoors with the smell of hops or outdoors with the smell of hops. This is a great place to wait for your tour or to linger afterwards—just watch out for the medieval whoopee cushions on the tables.

▲▲**Beguinage**—For military (and various other) reasons, there were more women than men in the medieval Low Countries.

Towns provided Beguinages, a dignified place in which these "Beguines" could live a life of piety and service (without having to take the same vows a nun would). You'll find Beguinages all over Belgium and Holland. Bruges' Beguinage almost makes you want to don a habit and fold your hands as you walk under its wispy trees and whisper past its frugal little homes. For a thin slice of Beguinage life, walk through the simple museum (Beguine's House, 60BF with English flier, daily 10:00–12:00 and 13:45–18:00, shorter hours off-season).

Minnewater—Beyond the Beguinage is Minnewater, an idyllic, clip-clop world of flower boxes, canals, swans, and tour boats packed like happy egg cartons. Beyond that is the train station.

Almshouses—Walking from the Beguinage back to the center, you might detour along Nieuwe Gentweg to visit one of about 20 almshouses in the city. At #8, go through the door (free) into the peaceful courtyard. This was a medieval form of housing the poor. The rich would pay for someone's tiny room here in return for lots of prayers.

More Bruges' Sights and Experiences

Chocolate—Bruggians are connoisseurs of fine chocolate. You'll be tempted by chocolate-filled display windows all over town. Godiva is the best big-factory/high-price/high-quality local brand, but for the finest small-family operation, drop by Maitre Chocolatier Verbeke. While Mr. Verbeke is busy downstairs making chocolates, Mrs. Verbeke makes sure customers in the shop get the chocolate of their dreams. Ask her to assemble a bag of your favorites. (The smallest amount sold is 100 grams, about seven pieces, for 82BF). Most are "pralines," which means they're filled. While the "hedgehogs" are popular, be sure to get a "pharaoh's head." Pray for cool weather, since it's closed when it's very hot. (Open at least in the mornings on Tuesday, Wednesday, Friday, and Saturday, and on cooler afternoons, a block off Market Square at Geldmuntstraat 25, tel. 050/334-198.)

Lace and Windmills by the Moat—A ten-minute walk from the center to the northeast end of town brings you to four windmills strung out along a pleasant grassy setting on the "big moat" canal (between Kruispoort and Dampoort, on the Bruges side of the moat). One of the windmills (St. Janshuismolen) is open for visitors (40BF, 9:30–12:30 and 13:15–17:00, closed October–March, at the end of Carmersstraat).

To actually see lace being made, drop by the nearby Lace Centre, where ladies toss bobbins madly while their eyes go bad (60BF includes demonstration and a small lace museum called Kantcentrum, next to the Jerusalem church, Monday–Friday 10:00–12:00 and 14:00–18:00, until 17:00 Saturday, closed Sunday, Peperstraat 3). The Folklore Museum, in the same neighborhood, is cute but forgettable (80BF, daily 9:30–17:00, less off-season, Rolweg 40). To find either place, ask for the Jerusalem church.

▲▲Biking—While the sights are close enough for easy walking, the town is a treat to bike through, and you'll be able to get away from the tourist center. Consider a peaceful evening ride through the back streets and around the outer canal. Rental shops have maps and ideas. The TI sells a handy "5X On The Bike Around Bruges" map/guide for 20BF, narrating five differ- ent bike routes (ranging from 18–30 kilometers) through the idyllic nearby countryside. The best basic trip is 30 minutes along the canal out to Damme and back. The Netherlands/Bel- gium border is a 40-minute pedal beyond Damme. Two shops rent bikes under the belfry on Hallestraat for the same rates: 70BF/one hour, 150BF/four hours, 250BF/day. Both offer free city maps and child seats. **Popelier Eric's** doesn't require any kind of deposit and sells a good-quality map of the countryside for 80BF (daily 9:00–21:00 in summer, 10:00–19:00 in winter, Hallestraat 14, a few steps farther from the belfry, tel. 050/343- 262). **'T Koffie Boont Je** asks for a deposit of 1,000BF, your passport, or a credit-card imprint. They sell an annoying double- sided photocopy of the TI's biking brochure for 20BF; the map is on one side and the directions—inconveniently—are on the other (Hallestraat 4, closer to the belfry, tel. 050/338-027). The less central **De Ketting** rents bikes for less (150BF/day, Gentpoortstraat 23, tel. 050/344-196).

Bryggia, my Love **Multivision Show**—Shown in a former neo- Gothic church, this multi-screen film tells of Bruges' Golden Age under the Dukes of Burgundy (mid-1300s–mid-1400s). Dial your audiophone to English and sit near the back to see all of the screens. The 30-minute show, which is informative yet uneven, beats standing in the rain. Parents might find a medieval grope or two objectionable (190BF, daily April–October 10:00–17:00, show every hour on the hour, Vlamingstraat 8, tel. 050/347-572). The same company offers a medieval dinner show—skip it.

Dolfinarium—At Boudewijnpark, just outside of town, dolphins make a splash at 10:00, 11:00, and 14:00 (275BF, Debaeckestraat 12, call to confirm show times, tel. 050/383-838). The theme park's roller-skating rink is open in the afternoon (and turns into an ice- skating rink off-season). From Bruges, catch the "Sint Michiels" bus #7 or #17 from Kuipersstraat.

Tours of Bruges

Bruges by Bike—The Backroad Bike Company leads daily bike tours through the nearby countryside (450–500BF, 30 km, 3 hrs, tel. 050/343-045, fax 050/841-709). Shorter, longer, and evening tours are available.

Bruges by Boat—The most relaxing and scenic (if not informa- tive) way to see this city of canals is by boat, with the captain narrating. Boats leave from all over town (copycat 35-minute rides, 170BF, 10:00–18:00).

City Minibus Tours—"City Tour Bruges" gives 50-minute/380BF rolling overviews of the town in a 13-seat, three-skylight minibus, with dial-a-language headsets and earphones. The tour leaves hourly (on the hour, 10:00–19:00 in summer, until 18:00 in spring and fall) from the Market Square. The audio is clean, and the narration gives a good history as you tour the town the lazy way.

Bus Tours of Countryside—Quasimodo Tours is a hip outfit offering those with extra time two all-day tours through the rarely visited Flemish countryside. You can do "Flanders Fields" on Sunday, Tuesday, and Thursday from 9:00 to 16:30 and see WWI battlefields, trenches, memorials, and poppy-splattered fields. On Monday, Wednesday, and Friday from 9:00 to 16:00, it's "Triple Treat": the port of Damme, a castle, monastery, brewery, and chocolate factory, and sampling the treats—a waffle, chocolate, and beer. Tours are in English only (1,400BF, CC:VM, 29-seat bus, canceled if eight don't sign up, lots of walking, pick-up at your hotel or the train station, non-smoking, tel. 050/370-470 to book, fax 050/374-960). **Sightseeing Line** offers a bus trip to Damme and a boat ride back (660BF, daily April–June at 14:00, July–September at 16:00, 2 hours, leaves from Market Square).

Walking Tours—Local guides walk small groups through the core of town daily in July and August (120BF, depart from TI at 15:00, 1,200BF for a private guide). The tours, while earnest, are heavy on history and in two languages, so they may be less than peppy. Still, to propel you beyond the pretty gables and canal swans of Bruges, they are good medicine.

Sleeping in Bruges
(35BF = about $1, tel. code 050, zip code: 8000)
Sleep Code: **S**=Single, **D**=Double/Twin, **T**=Triple, **Q**=Quad, **b**=bathroom, **t**=toilet only, **s**=shower only, **CC**=Credit Card (**V**isa, **M**asterCard, **A**mex). Everyone speaks English.

Most places are located between the train station and the old center, with the most distant (and best) being a few blocks beyond the market to the north and east. All include breakfast, are on quiet streets, and (with two exceptions) keep the same prices throughout the year. Assuming you'll arrive at the Market Square by foot or bus, I'll give hotel directions using a 12-hour clock, as if you were standing with your back to the belfry.

Hotels
Hansa Hotel offers 20 rooms in a completely modernized old building. It's bright and tastefully decorated in elegant pastels, and has all the amenities. This is a great splurge, with best prices Sunday through Thursday nights (Sb-2,700–3,650BF, Db-3,000–3,950BF, extra bed-1,250BF, CC:VMA, elevator, Niklaas Desparsstraat 11, a

block north of Market Square, tel. 050/338-444, fax 050/334-205, e-mail: information@hansa.be, run by Johan and Isabelle). Head for Vlamingstraat at 1:00 and take the first left.

Hans Memling gets more interesting as its owner, Gilbert, does. The parrot speaks Flemish, while the first king and queen of an independent Belgium (Leopold I and Louise Marie, 1835) peer down on you through the chandeliers as you breakfast. There's Mozart in the morning and Beethoven in the afternoon. The giant living/breakfast room is palatial, while the 17 huge upstairs bedrooms are decorated with a man's touch (Sb-1,750BF, Db-2,300BF, Tb-2,800BF, Qb-3,400BF, CC:VM, cheaper in winter, skimpy continental breakfast, elevator, Kuipersstraat 18, 2 blocks north of Market, easy phone reservations if arriving before 18:00, tel. 050/332-096). At 11:00, take Sint Jakobsstraat for 1 block, then angle right through Eiermarkt Square to Kuipersstraat.

Hotel Cavalier, across the street from Hans Memling, is tall and skinny with less character, but serves a hearty buffet breakfast in a royal setting (Sb-1,800BF, Db-2,300BF, Tb-2,800BF, Qb-3,200BF, two lofty "backpackers doubles" on the fourth floor for 1,600BF, CC:VM, Kuipersstraat 25, tel. 050/330-207, fax 050/347-199, run by friendly Viviane De Clerck).

Hotel Karel de Stoute has pleasant rooms in a 15th-century house with carved railings and a huge chandelier (Sb-2,400BF, Db-2,900BF, Tb-3,600BF, CC:VMA, Moerstraat 23, tel. 050/343-317, fax 050/344-472). Take Sint Jakobsstraat at 11:00, first left on Geldmuntstraat, first right on Geerwiynstraat, then left on Moerstraat.

Hotel Botaniek has three stars, nine fine rooms, and a quiet location a block from Astrid Park. Rooms have TVs and phones, and some have a fridge at no extra cost—ask (Sb-2,300BF, Db-2,700BF, Tb-3,000BF, CC:VMA, Waalsestraat 23, tel. 050/341-424, fax 050/345-939). Immediately to your right at 4:00, take Briedelstraat to Burg, then Blinde Ezelstraat (under Goldfinger family); continue straight (with fish market on your left) for 2 blocks to Waalsestraat.

Hotel Rembrandt-Rubens has 18 rooms in a creaky 500-year-old building, with tipsy floors, a mysterious floor plan, tacky rooms, elephant tusks, a gallery of creepy old paintings, and probably the holy grail in a drawer somewhere (S-1,000BF, Ss-1,400BF, one D-1,500BF, Ds-2,000BF, Db-2,300BF, Tb-2,900BF, Qb-3,800BF, locked up at 24:00, on a quiet square between the Memlings and the brewery at Walplein 38, tel. 050/336-439). The breakfast room (which must have been the knights' hall) overlooks a canal (while Rembrandt and Rubens overlook you from an ornately carved and tiled 1648 chimney). There's a little warmth behind Mrs. DeBuyser's crankiness. The hotel has been in her family for 50 years. At 8:00, take Steenstraat 2 blocks to the square, turn left on Mariastraat, then right on Walstraat.

Hotel **De Pauw** is family-run with straightforward rooms on a quiet street across from a church (two D-1,750BF, Db-2,100–2,350BF, CC:VMA, cable TV and phones, Sint Gilliskerkhof 8, tel. 050/337-118, fax 050/345-140).

Hotel **t'Keizershof** is a dollhouse of a hotel that lives by its motto, "Spend a night, not a fortune." It's simple and tidy, with eight small, cheery rooms split between two floors, a shower and toilet on each (S-925BF, D-1,350BF, T-1,980BF, free and easy parking, laundry service, Oostmeers 126, a block in front of the train station, tel. 050/338-728, run by Stefaan and Hilde).

Hotel **Maison Printaniere**, outside of Bruges, has seven doubles (D-from 1,300BF, Db-from 1,800BF, CC:VM, Kapelleweg 7, 8200 Brugge Sint Andries, 20-minute walk from station or take bus #25 "Olympia" to the stop "Vogelzang," tel. 050/385-067, fax 050/380-081).

Bed and Breakfasts

These places offer the best value. Each is central, run by people who enjoy their work, and offers lots of stairs and three or four doubles you'd pay 2,000 to 2,200BF for in a hotel.

Koen and Annemie Dieltiens are a youngish couple who enjoy translating for the guests who eat a hearty breakfast around a big table in their bright, homey, comfortable house. They are a friendly wealth of information on Bruges (S-1,200BF, Sb-1,500BF, D-1,500BF, Db-1,800BF, T-2,000BF, Tb-2,300BF, Qb-2,800BF, no smoking, free street parking, Sint-Walburgastraat 14, 3 blocks east of Market Square, reserve in advance for this popular place, tel. 050/334-294, fax 050/335-230, e-mail: koen.dieltiens@skynet.be). At 1:00, take Philipstockstraat, turn left on Wapenmakersstraat, then take first right. The Dieltiens also rent a cozy studio and apartment for two to six people in a nearby 17th-century house (two pay 10,500BF per week for studio; 12,000BF per week for apartment; prices higher for shorter stays and more people; cheaper off-season).

Paul and Roos Gheeraert, around the corner from the Dieltiens, live on the first floor while their guests take the second. With big, bright, comfy rooms, this is a fine value (Sb-1,400BF, larger Sb-1,600BF, Db-1,600BF, larger Db-1,800BF, Tb-2,300BF; rooms have coffee makers, some have fridge; Ridderstraat 9, 4 blocks east of Market, tel. 050/335-627, fax 050/345-201, e-mail: paul.gheeraert@skynet.be).

Chris Deloof's rooms are a good bet in the old center. The ones with showers are more elegant, but the upstairs A-frame loft room is fun (Ss-1,100BF, D-1,500BF, Ds-1,900BF, pleasant breakfast room, Geerwiynstraat 14, tel. 050/340-544, fax 050/340-544). The upstairs rooms are great for a family or group, with a shared kitchenette/microwave. At 11:00, take Sint Jakobsstraat to the first left on Geldmuntstraat, then first right on Geerwiynstraat.

Yvonne De Vriese rents three basic B&B rooms on a corner overlooking two canals (S-1,000BF, D-1,500BF, Db-1,800BF, plus 500BF for third or fourth person, breakfast served in your room; double rooms have fridge, TV, stereos, and books; CC:VMA, free parking, Predikherenstraat 40, 4 blocks east of Burg Square, bus #6 or #16 from station, tel. 050/334-224). The Db-room is smaller, on the ground floor, and closer to traffic. D-rooms are large and bright: One overlooks both canals, and the other is on the quiet back side. At 4:00, take Breidelstraat to the Burg Square, go through archway, pass fish market, turn left on Braambergstraat, which becomes Predikherenstraat.

Jan Degeyter, a block away, rents two airy, spacious, wood-floored rooms on a quiet street (Db-1,800BF, Tb-2,300BF, Qb-2,800BF, CC:VMA, Waalsestraat 40, tel. 050/331-199, fax 050/347-857).

The **Van Nevel family** rents two attractive top-floor rooms with built-in beds in a 16th-century house (S-1,300–1,400BF, D-1,400–1,700BF, Carmersstraat 13, 10-minute walk from Market Square, tel. & fax 050/346-860). Robert speaks much better English than his wife Lievetje. Take Vlamingstraat at 1:00, turn right on Academiestraat, continue on Spinolarei (runs along right side of canal) and turn right on Carmersstraat.

Arnold Dewolf's B&B is in a stately, quiet neighborhood on a dead-end street. To keep the peace, the rooms lack TVs and radios (S-900BF, D-1,300BF, one big family room-1,400–2,200BF depending on the number of people, free parking, Oostproostse 9, 20-minute walk from center, near the windmills, tel. 050/338-366). Follow directions to Van Nevel's (above), continue on Carmersstraat, turn left on Peterseliestraat, then right on Leestenburg to Oostprootse.

Gastenhuis Het Wit Beertje has three fine rooms a 20-minute walk from Market Square (Db-1,500BF, rooms with phones and TV, Witte Beerstraat 4, 8200 Brugge, over freeway past 't Zand, bus #5 or #15 from the station, tel. 050/318-762, run by Jean Pierre Defour).

Hostels

Bruges has several good hostels offering beds for around 350BF in two- to eight-bed rooms (singles go for around 550BF). Pick up the hostel info sheet at the station TI. Smallest, loosest, and closest to the center are: **Snuffel Travelers Inn** (Ezelstraat 47, tel. 050/333-133), **Bauhaus International Youth Hotel** (Langestraat 135, tel. 050/341-093), and **Passage** (Dweerstraat 26, tel. 050/340-232, its hotel next door has 1,200BF doubles). Bigger, more modern, and less central are: **International Youth Hostel Europa** (Baron Ruzettelaan 143, tel. 050/352-679), **IYH Herdersbrug** (Louis Coiseaukaai 46, tel. 050/599-321), and the **Merkenveld Scout Center** (Merkenveldweg 15, tel. 050/277-698).

Eating in Bruges

Specialties include mussels cooked a variety of ways (one order can feed two people), fish dishes, grilled meats, and French fries. Touristy places on the square are affordable, while candle-cool bistros flicker on back streets.

Wittekop is very Flemish, specializing in the beer-soaked equivalent of *beef bourgignon* (18:00–24:00, closed Sunday and Monday, terrace in the back, Sint Jakobsstraat 14). **De Kluiver** offers great "seasnails in spiced bouillon" simmered in a whispering jazz ambience (19:00–1:00, closed Wednesday and Thursday, Hoogstraat 12). For jazz and hearty budget spaghetti (210BF), head for **Estaminet**, on the northern border of peaceful Astrid Park (open from 11:30 on, closed Monday afternoon and all day Thursday, Park 5). Another jazzy place to join locals for dinner is **De Versteende Nacht Jazzcafe** on Langestraat 11 (19:00–2:00, closed Sunday and Monday).

Locals like **La Dentelliere** for its good food, service, and prices (CC:VMA, Wijngaardstraat 33, tel. 050/331-898) and **Vlissinghe 1515**, a pub at Blekersstraat 2, for its friendly atmosphere (open from 11:30 on, closed Tuesday). Two restaurants popular for their high-quality lunch specials (345BF) are the classy **'t Heerenhuys** (12:00–14:30, closed Thursday and Sunday, Vlamingstraat 53, tel. 050/346-178) and the **Brasserie Georges** (12:00–14:30, closed Sunday, Vlamingstraat 58, tel. 050/343-565).

Bistro 't Gezelleke (next door to the Van Nevel B&B and near the Bauhaus hostel) offers fine fresh food at bring-'em-in prices (weekdays 12:00–24:00, Saturday from 18:00, closed Sunday, Carmersstraat 15, tel. 050/338-102). **Restaurant 't Gulden Plies**, just off Burg, is also good (from 19:00 on, closed Monday and Tuesday, Mallebergplaats 17).

Picnics: Geldmuntstraat is a handy street when you're hungry. A block off the Market Square at Geldmuntstraat 1, the **Spegelaere** deli serves sandwiches and salads by weight—100g is a tiny tub (8:00–18:30, closed Sunday, counter seating). Across the street, **Pickles Frituur** serves the best sit-down fries in town. A block farther, past the Verbeke chocolate shop, the **Nopri Supermarket** is great for picnics (push-button produce pricer lets you buy as little as one mushroom, open 9:00–18:00, closed Sunday). The small **Delhaize** grocery store is on Market Square opposite the belfry (8:00–12:00 and 13:30–18:00, closed Sunday). **Selfi** has cheap sandwiches to go (Breidelstraat 16, between Burg and Market Square). For midnight munchies, head to the tiny **Nightshop** grocery just off Market Square (daily 14:00–2:00, Philipstockstraat 14).

Frietjes: These local French fries are a treat. Proud and traditional *frituurs* serve tubs of fries and various local-style shish kebabs. Belgians dip their *frietjes* in mayonnaise, but ketchup is there for the Yankees (along with spicier sauces). For a quick, cheap, and scenic meal, hit a *frituur* and sit on the steps or benches overlooking the Market Square, about 50 yards past the post office.

Beer: Belgium boasts more than 350 types of beer. Straffe Hendrik (strong Henry), a potent local brew, is, even to a Bud Lite kind of guy, obviously great beer. Among the more unusual of the others to try: Kriek (a cherry-flavored beer), Dentergems (with coriander and orange peel), and Trappist (a dark, monk-made beer). Non-beer drinkers enjoy Kriek and Frambozen (the cherry and raspberry-flavored beers). Each beer is served in its own unique glass. Any pub carries the basic beers, but for a selection of more than 300 types, drink at **t'Brugs Beertje** (Kemelstraat 5, open 16:00–1:00, closed Wednesday). When you've finished those, step next door, where **Dreupel Huisje "1919"** serves more than 100 Belgian gins and liqueurs (closed Tuesday). Another good place to gain an appreciation of the Belgian beer culture is **de Garre**, off Breidelstraat (between Burg and Markt) on the tiny Garre alley (daily 12:00–24:00).

Transportation Connections—Bruges
From Brussels, all of Europe is at your fingertips. Train information tel. 050/382-382.

By train to: Brussels (2/hr, 1 hr), **Ghent** (3/hr, 20 min), **Oostende** (3/hr, 15 min), **Köln** (6/day, 4 hrs), **Paris** (6/day, 4 hrs, via Brussels), **Amsterdam** (hrly, 3.5 hrs).

Trains from England: Bruges is an ideal "welcome to Europe" stop after crossing the English Channel. From England, catch the London/Victoria–Ramsgate train (2 hrs), then the Ramsgate–Oostende catamaran (2 hrs), then the Oostende–Bruges train (15 min). Five boats run daily (cost of ferry crossing: 800BF one way, same price for the cheap five-day return ticket; call at least three days in advance to book with credit card, otherwise just call to reserve a seat and pay at the dock; CC:VMA, tel. 059/559-955). Or you can take the Eurostar train from London to Brussels under the English Channel (5–8/day, 3 hrs), then transfer to Bruges (hrly, 1 hour). Call 1-800-EUROSTAR in the U.S.A. for the latest fares.

PARIS

Paris offers sweeping boulevards, sleepy parks, world-class art galleries, chatty crêpe stands, Napoleon's body, sleek shopping malls, the Eiffel Tower, and people-watching from outdoor cafés. Climb the Notre-Dame and the Eiffel Tower, cruise the Seine and the Champs-Élysées, and master the Louvre and Orsay museums. Save some after-dark energy for one of the world's most romantic cities. Many people fall in love with Paris. Some see the essentials and flee, overwhelmed by the huge city. With the proper approach and a good orientation, you'll fall head over heels for Europe's capital city.

Planning Your Time
Best of Paris in Two Days

Day 1
Morning: Historic walk (described later) featuring Île de la Cité, Notre-Dame, Latin Quarter, and Sainte-Chapelle.
Afternoon: Métro to Arc de Triomphe and walk down the Champs-Élysées and through the Tuilleries. Tour the Louvre late, when it's less crowded and half-price.
Twilight: Métro to Trocadero for a closer look at the Eiffel Tower.
Touristy night options: Trip up Eiffel Tower, Seine cruise, Montmartre, Latin Quarter. The Pompidou Modern Art Gallery is the only museum open late.

Day 2
Morning: Consider these options: Métro to Bastille to do the Marais walk (described later). Visit the Rodin Museum and enjoy a

picnic lunch in its garden. Historians may prefer paying homage to Napoleon and his military museum at Les Invalides across the street. Poets shop on rue Cler to assemble a moveable feast for lunch.

Midday: Pick up your art history where the Louvre left off by touring the Orsay Gallery.

Afternoon: At 15:00, take an efficient RER trip from Orsay to Versailles. To avoid crowds, see the park first and the palace late.

Day 3
Do our two-day plan—only enjoy yourself.

Orientation

Paris is split in half by the Seine River, divided into 20 *arrondissements* (proud and independent governmental jurisdictions), and circled by a ring-road freeway (the *périphérique*). You'll find Paris easier to negotiate if you know which side of the river you're on, which *arrondissement* you're in, and which subway (Métro) stop you're closest to. Remember, if you're north of the river (above on any city map) you're on the Right Bank (*rive droite*), and if you're south of it you're on the Left Bank (*rive gauche*).

Arrondissements are numbered, starting at Notre-Dame (ground zero) and moving in a clockwise spiral out to the ring road. The last two digits in a Parisian zip code are the *arrondissement* number, and the notation for the Métro stop is "Mo." In Parisian jargon, Napoleon's tomb is on *la rive gauche* (the Left Bank) in the 7ème (*arrondissement*), zip code 75007, Mo: Invalides. Paris Métro stops are a standard aid in giving directions.

Tourist Information

Avoid the Paris TIs—long lines, short information, and a 5F charge for maps. This book, the *Pariscope* magazine (described below), and one of the freebie maps available at any hotel are all you need for a short visit. The main TI is at 127 avenue des Champs-Élysées (open 9:00–20:00), but the TIs at the Louvre, Eiffel Tower, and train stations are handier. You'll find TIs at these train stations: Gares de Lyon, Montparnasse, Austerlitz, Nord, and Est. Hours: daily 8:00 to 20:00, except at Austerlitz, which closes at 15:00 during off-season. *(Note: Austerlitz and Montparnasse TIs might close permanently in 1998).*

The *Pariscope* weekly magazine (or one of its clones, 3F at any newsstand, explained below) lists museum hours, concerts and music festivals, plays, movies, nightclubs, and special art exhibits. For a complete list of museum hours and scheduled English museum tours, pick up the free *Musées, Monuments Historiques, et Expositions* booklet from any museum.

While it's easy to pick up free maps of Paris once you've arrived (your hotel has them), they don't show all the streets, and

Paris Overview

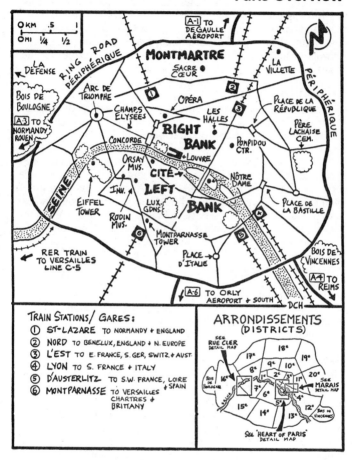

TRAIN STATIONS/ GARES:
① ST-LAZARE TO NORMANDY & ENGLAND
② NORD TO BENELUX, ENGLAND & N. EUROPE
③ L'EST TO E. FRANCE, S. GER, SWITZ, & AUST.
④ LYON TO S. FRANCE & ITALY
⑤ D'AUSTERLITZ TO S.W. FRANCE, LOIRE & SPAIN
⑥ MONTPARNASSE TO VERSAILLES, CHARTRES & BRITTANY

ARRONDISSEMENTS (DISTRICTS)

you may want the huge Michelin #10 map of Paris. For an
extended stay, consider the pocket-size and street-indexed *Paris
Practique*, or *Paris par Arrondissement* map books, as well as two
fine guidebooks: *Michelin Green Guide* (somewhat scholarly) and
the more readable *Paris Access Guide*.

There are many English-language bookstores in Paris where
you can pick up guidebooks (for nearly double their American
price). A few are: Shakespeare and Company (12:00–24:00, lots of
used travel books, 37 rue de la Boucherie, across the river from
Notre-Dame), W. H. Smith (248 rue de Rivoli), and Brentanos
(37 avenue de L'Opéra).

The American Church is a nerve center for the American èmigrè community and distributes the *Free Voice*, a handy monthly English-language newspaper, with useful reviews of concerts, plays, and current events in Paris, and *France—U.S.A. Contacts*, an advertisement paper, full of useful information for those looking for work or long-term housing (facing the river between Eiffel and Orsay at 65 quai d'Orsay, Métro: Invalides).

Arrival in Paris

By Train: Paris has six train stations, all connected by Métro and bus, most with banks and TIs and none that will check bags (blame terrorism). Hop the Métro to your hotel (see Getting Around Paris, below).

Paris' train stations serve different destinations. The Gare de l'Est handles the east; the Gare du Nord and Gare St. Lazare serve northern and central Europe; the Gare d'Austerlitz and Gare du Lyon cover southern Europe, and the Gare Montparnasse handles western France and TGV service to France's southwest. (Any train station can give you schedule information, make reservations, and sell tickets for any destination.) Buying tickets is handier from an SNCF neighborhood office (eg: Louvre, Orsay, Versailles, airports) or at your neighborhood travel agency—worth their small fee (SNCF signs in their window indicate they sell train tickets). For schedule information, call 08 36 35 35 35 (3F/minute).

By Plane: For detailed information on getting from Paris' airports to downtown Paris (and vice versa), see Transportation Connections at the end of this chapter.

Helpful Hints

Theft Alert: Use your money belt, and never carry a wallet in your back pocket or a purse over your shoulder. Thieves target tourists at tourist areas, in subway stations, and on the Métro.

Museums: The Louvre and many other museums are closed on Tuesday. Versailles and the Orsay and Rodin museums are closed Monday. Most offer reduced prices and shorter hours on Sunday. Many begin closing rooms 45 minutes before the actual closing time. For the fewest crowds, visit very early, at lunch, or very late. The best Impressionist art museums are the Orsay, Marmottan, and L'Orangerie (all described below). Most museums have slightly shorter hours October through March. French holidays can really mess up your sightseeing plans (Jan. 1, May 1, May 8, July 14, Nov. 1, Nov. 11, and Dec. 25).

Mona Winks: This guidebook (by Rick Steves and Gene Openshaw) is particularly heavy on Paris, with extensive self-guided walking tours of the Louvre, the Orsay, the Pompidou Gallery, Versailles, and the Historic Core of Paris.

The Paris Museum Pass: In Paris there are two classes of sightseers: those with this pass and those without. Serious sightseers save time (less time in lines) and money by getting this pass. Sold at museums, main Métro stations, and tourist offices, it pays for itself in two admissions and gets you into sights with no lining up (one day-80F, three consecutive days-160F, five consecutive days-240F). Included sights (and admission prices without the pass) you're likely to visit: Louvre (45F), Orsay (39F), Sainte-Chapelle (32F), Arc de Triomphe (35F), Army Museum and Napoleon's Tomb (37F), Pompidou Gallery (35F), Carnavalet Museum (35F), Conciergerie (32F), Sewer Tour (25F), Cluny Museum (30F), Notre-Dame towers (30F) and crypt (32F), L'Orangerie (30F), Picasso Museum (30F), Rodin Museum (28F), and the elevator to the top of the Grand Arche de La Defense (40F). Outside Paris, the pass covers the Palace of Versailles (45F) and its Grand Trianon (25F) and Château Chantilly (35F). Notable sights not covered: Marmottan Museum, Eiffel Tower, Montparnasse Tower, the ladies of Pigalle, and Disneyland Paris. Tally it up. But remember, an advantage of the pass is that you skip to the front of all lines—saving hours of waiting in the summer (though everyone must pass through the slow-moving metal detector lines). With the pass you'll pop painlessly into sights that you're walking by (even for a few minutes) that you'd otherwise probably skip (e.g., Notre-Dame crypt, Cluny Museum, Conciergerie, Victor Hugo's House). The free museum and monuments directory that comes with your pass is handy, with the latest hours, phone numbers, and specifics on which kids pay. The cut-off age for free entry varies from 5 to 18. Most major art museums let young people up to age 18 in for free. For some reason, anyone over age 5 has to pay to tour the sewers.

Toilets: Carry small change for pay toilets, or walk into any outdoor café like you own the place and find the toilet in the back. Remember, the toilets in museums are free and generally the best you'll find. Modern super-sanitary street booths provide both relief and a memory.

Telephone Cards: Pick up the essential France *tèlécarte* at any *tabac* (tobacco shop), post office, or tourist office (*une petite carte* is 42F; *une grande* is 98F). Smart travelers check things by telephone. Most public phones use these cards.

Useful Telephone Numbers: American Hospital, 01 46 41 25 25; American pharmacy, 01 47 42 49 40 (Opéra); Police, 17; U.S. Embassy, 01 43 12 22 22; Paris and France directory assistance, 12; AT&T operator, 0800 99 00 11; MCI, 0800 99 00 19; Sprint, 0800 99 00 87.

Getting Around Paris

By Métro: Europe's best subway is divided into two systems—the Métro (puddle-jumping everywhere in the city) and the RER (which makes giant speedy leaps around town and connects suburban destinations). You'll be using the Métro for almost all your trips. In Paris you're never more than a ten-minute walk from a Métro station. One ticket takes you anywhere in the system with unlimited transfers. Save 40 percent by buying a *carnet* (car-nay) of ten tickets for 47F at any Métro station (a single ticket is 8F). Métro tickets work on city buses, though one ticket cannot be used as a transfer between subway and bus.

The Formule 1 pass (30F) allows unlimited travel for a single day on all bus and Métro lines. If you're staying longer, the Carte d'Orange pass gives you free run of the bus and Métro system for one week (72F and a photo, ask for the Carte d'Orange Coupon Vert) or a month (243F, ask for the Carte d'Orange Coupon Orange). These pass prices cover only central Paris; you can pay more for passes covering regional destinations (e.g., Versailles). The weekly pass begins Monday and ends Sunday, and the monthly pass begins the first day of the month and ends the last day of that month, so mid-week or mid-month purchases are generally not worthwhile. All passes can be purchased at any Métro station (most have photo booths).

To get to your destination, determine which "Mo." stop is closest to your destination and which line or lines will get you there. The lines have numbers, but they're best known by their *direction* or end-of-the-line stop. (For example, the Saint Denis/ Châtillon line runs between Saint-Denis in the north and Châtillon in the south.)

Once in the Métro station, you'll see blue and white signs directing you to the train going in your direction (e.g., *direction: Saint-Denis*). Insert your ticket in the automatic turnstile, pass through, reclaim and *keep your ticket until you exit the system* (fare inspectors accept no excuses from anyone). Transfers are free and can be made wherever lines cross. When you transfer, look for the orange *correspondence* (connections) signs when you exit your first train, then follow the proper *direction* sign.

Before you *sortie* (exit), check the helpful *plan du quartier* (map of the neighborhood) to get your bearings, locate your destination, and decide which *sortie* you want. At stops with several *sorties*, you can save lots of walking by choosing the best exit. Remember your essential Métro words: *direction, correspondance, sortie, carnet* (cheap set of ten tickets), and *Donnez-moi mon porte-monnaie!* (Give me back my wallet!) Thieves thrive in the Métro.

By RER: The RER (Réseau Express Régionale, ehr-uh-ehr) suburban train system (thick lines on your subway map identified by letters A, B, C, etc.) works like the Métro but is much speedier because it makes only a few stops within the city. One Métro ticket is all you need for RER rides within Paris. You can transfer between the Métro and RER systems with the same ticket, and unlike the Métro, you need to insert your ticket in a turnstile to exit the RER system. To travel outside the city (to Versailles or the airport, for example) you'll need to buy another ticket at the

Paris

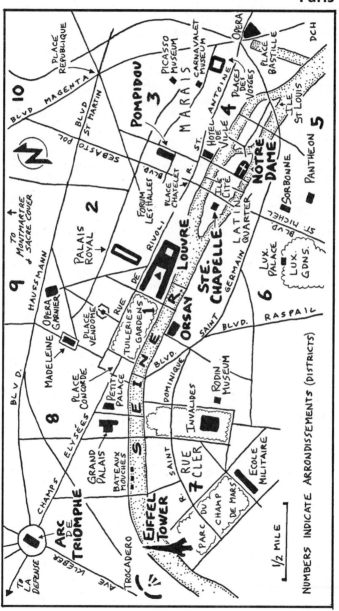

NUMBERS INDICATE ARRONDISSEMENTS (DISTRICTS)

station window before boarding, and make sure your stop is served by checking the signs over the train platform (not all trains serve all stops).

By City Bus: The trickier bus system is worth figuring out. Métro tickets are good on both bus and Métro, though you can't use the same ticket to transfer between the two systems. One ticket gets you anywhere in central Paris, but if you leave the city center (shown as section 1 on the diagram onboard the bus) you must validate a second ticket. While the Métro shuts down about 00:45, some buses continue much later. Schedules are posted at bus stops.

Big system maps, posted at each bus and Métro stop, display the routes. Individual route diagrams show the exact route of the lines serving that stop. Major stops are painted on the side of each bus. Enter through the front doors. Punch your Métro ticket in the machine behind the driver, or pay the higher cash fare. Get off the bus using the rear door. Even if you're not certain you've figured it out, do some joyriding (outside of rush hour). Lines #24, #63, and #69 are Paris' most scenic routes and make a great introduction to the city. Bus #69 is particularly handy, running between the Eiffel Tower, the recommended hotels around rue Cler, the Orsay Gallery, the Louvre, the Marais/Bastille area (more recommended hotels), and the Père Lachaise Cemetery.

By Taxi: Parisian taxis are almost reasonable. A ten-minute ride costs about 50F (versus about 5F to get anywhere in town on the Métro). You can try waving one down, but it's easier to ask for the nearest taxi stand ("oo-ay la tet de stah-see-oh taxi") or ask your hotel to call for you. Sunday and night rates are higher, and if you call from your hotel the meter starts as soon as the call is received. Taxis are tough to find on Friday and Saturday night, especially after the Métro closes.

Sights—The "Historic Core of Paris" Walk

These sights are best done as described in this self-guided tour. (This information is distilled from the Historic Paris Walk chapter in *Mona Winks*, by Gene Openshaw and Rick Steves.) Allow four hours, including sightseeing. Start your visit where the city did—on the Île de la Cité—facing the Notre-Dame and following the dotted line on the "Heart of Paris" map. To get to the Notre-Dame, ride the Métro to Cité, Hotel de Ville, or St-Michel and walk to the big square facing the . . .

▲▲**Notre-Dame Cathedral**—The 700-year-old cathedral is packed with history and tourists. Study its sculpture (Notre-Dame's forte) and windows, take in a Mass, eavesdrop on guides, and walk all around the outside. (Open daily 8:00–18:45; treasury 15F, 9:30–17:30. Ask about the free English tours, normally Wednesday and Thursday at noon and Saturdays at 14:30. Clean 2.70F toilets in front of the church near Charlemagne's statue.) Sun-

day Masses are at 8:00, 8:45, 10:00, 11:30, 12:30, and 18:30. Climb
to the top for a great gargoyle's-eye view of the city (entrance on
outside, north tower open 9:30–17:30, closed at lunch and earlier
off-season, Métro: Cité). You get more than 400 stairs for only 30F.

The Cathedral facade is worth a close look. The church is
dedicated to "Our Lady" (Notre-Dame). Mary is center stage—
cradling Jesus, surrounded by the halo of the rose window. Adam
is on the left and Eve is on the right.

Below Mary and above the arches is a row of 28 statues
known as the Kings of Judah. During the French Revolution,
these Biblical kings were mistaken for the hated French kings. The
citizens stormed the church, crying, "Off with their heads." All
were decapitated but have since been recapitated.

Speaking of decapitation, look at the carving above the doorway on the left. The man with his head in his hands is St. Denis.
Back when there was a Roman temple on this spot, Christianity
began making converts. The fourth-century bishop of Roman
Paris, Denis, was beheaded. But these early Christians were hard
to keep down. The man who would become St. Denis got up,
tucked his head under his arm, and headed north until he found
just the right place to meet his maker: Montmartre, which means
"mountain of the martyr." The Parisians were convinced of this
miracle, Christianity gained ground, and a church soon replaced
the pagan temple.

Medieval art was OK if it embellished the house of God and
told Bible stories. For a fine example, move to the base of the
central column (at the foot of Mary, about where the head of St.
Denis could spit if he was real good). Working around from the
left, find God telling a barely created Eve, "Have fun but no
apples." Next, the sexiest serpent I've ever seen makes apples à la
mode. Finally, Adam and Eve, now ashamed of their nakedness,
are expelled by an angel. This is a tiny example (featuring a story
most of us know) in a church covered with meaning.

Now move to the right and study the carving above the central portal. It's the end of the world, and Christ sits on the throne
of Judgment (just under the arches, holding his hands up). Below
him, an angel and a demon weigh souls in the balance. The
"good" stand to the left, looking up to heaven. The "bad" ones to
the right are chained up and led off to . . . Versailles on a Tuesday.
The "ugly" ones must be the crazy sculpted demons to the right,
at the base of the arch.

Wander through the interior. You'll be routed around the
ambulatory, much as medieval pilgrims would have been. Don't
miss the rose windows filling each of the transepts. Back outside,
walk around the church through the park on the riverside for a
close look at the flying buttresses.

The neo-Gothic 90-meter spire is a product of the 1860
reconstruction. Around its base are apostles and evangelists (the

Heart of Paris

green men) as well as Viollet-le-Duc, the architect in charge of the
work. Notice how the apostles look outward, blessing the city,
while the architect (at top, seen from behind the church) looks up,
admiring his spire.

The archaeological crypt is a worthwhile 15-minute stop
with your museum pass (enter 100 yards in front of church; 32F,
50F with Notre Dame's tower; daily 10:00–18:00, closes at 17:00
October–April). You'll see Roman ruins, trace the street plan of
the medieval village, and see diagrams of how the earliest Paris
grew and grew, all thoughtfully explained in English.

If you're hungry near Notre-Dame, the only grocery store
on the Île de la Cité is tucked away at #16 rue Chanoinesse, 1
block north of the church (9:00–13:30, 16:00–20:30, closed Sunday). Nearby Île St. Louis has inexpensive creperies and grocery
stores open daily on its main drag. Plan a picnic for the quiet
bench-filled park immediately behind the church (public WC).

Behind the Notre-Dame, squeeze through the tourist buses,
cross the street, and enter the iron gate into the park at the tip of
the island.

▲▲Deportation Memorial (Mémorial de la Déportation)—
This memorial to the 200,000 French victims of the Nazi concentration camps draws you into their experience. As you descend the steps, the city around you disappears. Surrounded by walls, you have become a prisoner. Your only freedom is your view of the sky and the tantalizing glimpse of the river below.

Enter the dark, single-file chamber ahead. Inside, the circular plaque in the floor reads, "They descended into the mouth of the earth and they did not return."

A hallway stretches in front of you, lined with 200,000 lighted crystals, one for each French citizen that died. Flickering at the far end is the eternal flame of hope. The tomb of the unknown deportee lies at your feet. Above, the inscription reads, "Dedicated to the living memory of the 200,000 French deportees sleeping in the night and the fog, exterminated in the Nazi concentration camps."

Above the exit as you leave is the message you'll find at all Nazi sights: "Forgive but never forget." (Free, open daily 8:30–21:45, weekends and holidays from 9:00, less off-season, east tip of the island near Île St. Louis, behind Notre-Dame, Métro: Cité.)
Île St-Louis—Back on street level, look across the river to the Île St-Louis. If the Île de la Cité is a tugboat laden with the history of Paris, it's towing this classy little residential dinghy laden only with boutiques, characteristic restaurants, and famous sorbet shops (see recommended restaurants under Eating in Paris, below). This island wasn't developed until much later (18th century). What was a swampy mess is now harmonious Parisian architecture. The pedestrian bridge (Pont Saint Louis) connects the two islands leading right to rue Saint Louis en l'Île. This spine of the island is lined with interesting shops. A short stroll takes you to the famous Bertillon ice-cream parlour (#31). Loop back to the pedestrian bridge along the park-like quays (walk north to the river and turn left). This riverside walk is about as peaceful and romantic as Paris gets.

Before walking to the opposite end of the Île de la Cité, loop through the Latin Quarter (as indicated on the map). From the Deportation Memorial, cross the bridge onto the Left Bank and enjoy the riverside view of the Notre-Dame and window-shop among the characteristic green book stalls that sell used books, vintage posters, and souvenirs. At the little park and church (over the bridge from the front of Notre-Dame), venture inland a few blocks, basically arcing through the Latin Quarter and returning to the island two bridges down at place St-Michel.
▲The Latin Quarter—This area, which gets its name from the language used here when it was an exclusive medieval university district, lies between the Luxembourg Gardens and the Seine, centering around the Sorbonne University and boulevards St-Germain and St-Michel. This is the core of the Left Bank—it's crowded with international eateries, far-out bookshops, street singers, and

jazz clubs. For colorful wandering and café-sitting, afternoons and evenings are best. (Métro: St-Michel.)

Along rue Saint-Severin you can still see the shadow of the medieval sewer system. (The street slopes into a central channel of bricks.) In the days before plumbing and toilets, when people still went to the river or neighborhood wells for their water, "flushing" meant throwing it out the window. Certain times of day were flushing times. Maids on the fourth floor would holler "*Garde de l'eau!*" (Look out for the water!) and heave it into the streets where it would eventually be washed down into the Seine.

The **Cluny Museum**, a treasure trove of medieval art, fills the old Roman baths, offering close-up looks at stained glass, Notre-Dame carvings, fine goldsmithing and jewelry, and rooms of tapestries—the best of which is the exquisite Lady with the Unicorn. In five panels, a delicate-as-medieval-can-be noble lady introduces a delighted unicorn to the senses of taste, hearing, sight, smell, and touch (30F, daily 9:15–17:45, closed Tuesday, near the corner of boulevards St-Michel and St-Germain, tel. 01 53 73 78 00, Métro: Cluny).

Place St. Michel (facing the St-Michel bridge) is the traditional core of the Left Bank's artsy, liberal, hippie, Bohemian district of poets, philosophers, winos, and tourists. In less commercial times, place St-Michel was a gathering point for the city's malcontents and misfits. Here, in 1871, the citizens took the streets from the government troops, set up barricades *Les Miz*–style, and established the Paris Commune. In World War II, the locals rose up against their Nazi oppressors (read the plaques by the St. Michael fountain). And in the spring of 1968, a time of social upheaval all over the world, young students, battling riot batons and tear gas, took over the square and demanded change.

From place St-Michel, look across the river and find the spire of Sainte-Chapelle Church and its weathervane angel (below). Cross the river on the Pont St-Michel and continue along boulevard du Palais. On your left you'll see the high-security doorway to Sainte-Chapelle. But first, carry on another 30 meters and turn right at a wide pedestrian street, the rue de Lutece.

Cité "Métropolitain" Stop—Of the 141 original turn-of-the-century subway entrances, this is one of 17 survivors now preserved as a national art treasure. The curvy, plantlike ironwork is a textbook example of Art Nouveau, the style that rebelled against the erector-set squareness of the Industrial Age (e.g., Mr. Eiffel's tower).

The flower market on place Louis Lepine is a pleasant detour. On Sunday this square chirps with a busy bird market. And across the way is the Prefecture de Police, where Inspector Clouseau of *Pink Panther* fame used to work, and where in August 1944 the local resistance fighters took the first building from the Nazis, leading to the allied liberation of Paris a week later.

Pause here to admire the view. Sainte-Chapelle is a pearl in an ugly architectural oyster, part of a complex of buildings that includes the Palace of Justice (to the right of Sainte-Chapelle, behind the fancy gates). Return to the entrance of Sainte-Chapelle. You'll need to pass through a metal detector to get in. Toilets are ahead, on the left. The line into the church may be long. (Museum card holders can go directly in; pick up the excellent English info sheet.) Enter the humble ground floor. . . .

▲▲▲Sainte-Chapelle—The triumph of Gothic church architecture is a cathedral of glass like no other. It was speedily built from 1242 to 1248 for St. Louis IX (France's only canonized king) to house the supposed Crown of Thorns. Its architectural harmony is due to the fact that it was completed under the direction of one architect in only six years—unheard of in Gothic times. (Notre-Dame took more than 200 years to build.)

The design clearly shows an Old Regime approach to worship. The basement was for staff and other common folk. Royal Christians worshiped upstairs. The ground-floor paint job, a 19th-century restoration, is a reasonably accurate copy of the original.

Climb the spiral staircase to the *Chapelle Haute*. Fill the place with choral music, crank up the sunshine, face the top of the altar, really believe that the Crown of Thorns was there, and this becomes one awesome space.

"Let there be light." In the Bible, it's clear: Light is divine. Light shining through stained glass was a symbol of God's grace shining down to earth. Gothic architects used their new technology to turn dark stone buildings into lanterns of light. The glory of Gothic shines brighter here than in any other church.

There are 15 separate panels of stained glass (6,500 square feet—two-thirds of it 13th-century original), with more than 1,100 different scenes, mostly from the Bible. In medieval times, scenes like these helped teach Bible stories to the illiterate.

The altar was raised up high to better display the relic around which this chapel was built—the Crown of Thorns. The supposed Crown cost King Louis three times as much as this church. Today it is kept in the Notre-Dame Treasury and shown only on Good Friday.

Louis' little private viewing window is in the wall to the right of the altar. Louis, both saintly and shy, liked to go to church without dealing with the rigors of public royal life. Here he could worship still dressed in his jammies.

Lay your camera on the ground and shoot the ceiling. Those pure and simple ribs growing out of the slender columns are the essence of Gothic.

Books in the gift shop explain the stained glass in English. There are concerts (120F) almost every summer evening. (32F, daily 9:30–18:30, even Tuesday, off-season 10:00–16:30, tel. 48 01 91 35 for concert information, handy free public toilets just outside, Métro: Cité.)

Palais du Cité—Back outside, as you walk around the church exterior, look down and notice how much Paris has risen in the 800 years since Sainte-Chapelle was built. You're in a huge complex of buildings that has housed the local government since ancient Roman times. It was the site of the original Gothic palace of the early kings of France. The only surviving medieval parts are the Sainte-Chapelle church and the Conciergerie prison.

Most of the site is now covered by the giant Palais de Justice, home of France's supreme court (built in 1776). "*Liberté, Egalité, Fraternité*" over the doors is a reminder that this was also the headquarters of the revolutionary government.

Now pass through the big iron gate to the noisy boulevard du Palais and turn left (toward the Right Bank). On the corner is the site of the oldest public clock (built in 1334) in the city. While the present clock is said to be Baroque, it somehow still manages to keep accurate time.

Turn left onto Quai de l'Horologe and walk along the river. The round medieval tower just ahead marks the entrance to the Conciergerie. Pop in to visit the courtyard and lobby (free). Step past the serious-looking guard into the courtyard.

Conciergerie—The Conciergerie, a former prison, is a gloomy place. Kings used it to torture and execute failed assassins. The leaders of the Revolution put it to similar good use. The tower next to the entrance, called "the babbler," was named for the painful sounds that leaked from it.

Look at the stark lettering above the doorways. This was a no-nonsense revolutionary time. Everything, even lettering, was subjected to the test of reason. No frills or we chop 'em off.

Step inside; the lobby, with an English-language history display, is free. Marie-Antoinette was imprisoned here. During a busy eight-month period in the Revolution, she was one of 2,600 prisoners kept here on their way to the guillotine. The interior (28F, daily 9:30–18:30, 10:00–17:00 in winter, good English), with its huge vaulted and pillared rooms, echoes with history but is pretty barren. You can see Marie-Antoinette's cell, housing a collection of her mementos. In another room, a list of those made "a foot shorter at the top" by the "national razor" includes ex-King Louis XVI, Charlotte Corday (who murdered Marat in his bathtub), and the chief revolutionary who got a taste of his own medicine, Maximilien Robespierre.

Back outside, wink at the flak-vested guard, fake right, and turn left. Listen for babbles and continue your walk along the river. Across the river you can see the rooftop observatory—flags flapping—of the Samaritaine Department Store, where this walk will end. At the first corner, veer left past France's supreme court building and into a sleepy triangular square called place

Dauphine. Marvel at how such quaintness could be lodged in the
midst of such greatness as you walk through the park to the end
of the island. At the equestrian statue of Henry IV, turn right
onto the bridge and take refuge in one of the nooks on the Eiffel
Tower side.

Pont Neuf—This "new bridge" is now Paris' oldest. Built during
Henry IV's reign (around 1600), its 12 arches span the widest part
of the river. The fine view includes the park on the tip of the
island (note Seine tour boats), the Orsay Gallery, and the Louvre.
These turrets were originally for vendors and street entertainers.
In the days of Henry IV, who originated the promise of "a chicken
in every pot," this would have been a lively scene.

Directly over the river, the first building you'll hit on the
Right Bank is the venerable old department store, Samaritaine.

▲**Samaritaine Department Store Viewpoint**—Enter the store
and go to the rooftop. Ride the glass elevator from near the Pont
Neuf entrance to the ninth floor (you'll be greeted by a WC, check
out the sink). Pass the tenth-floor terrace for the 11th-floor
panorama (tight spiral staircase; watch your head). Quiz yourself.
Working counterclockwise, find: the Eiffel Tower, Invalides/
Napoleon's Tomb, Montparnasse Tower, Henry IV statue on the
tip of the island, Sorbonne University, the dome of the Panthéon,
Sainte-Chapelle, Notre-Dame, Hôtel de Ville (city hall), Pompidou
Center, Sacré-Coeur, Opéra, and Louvre. The Champs-Élysées
leads to the Arc de Triomphe. Shadowing that—even bigger, while
twice as distant—is the Grand Arche la Defense. You'll find light,
reasonably priced, and incredibly scenic meals on the breezy terrace, and a supermarket in the basement. (Rooftop view is free,
daily 9:30–19:00, tel. 01 40 41 20 20, Métro: Pont Neuf.)

Sights—Paris' Museums near the Tuileries Gardens

The newly renovated Tuileries gardens was once private property
of kings and queens. It's Paris' grandest public park and links these
four museums:

▲▲▲**The Louvre**—This is Europe's oldest, biggest, greatest,
and possibly most crowded museum. Metal detectors create a line
in front of the pyramid; with a museum pass you can avoid the
line by entering under the Richelieu wing, though there is no
grander entry than through the pyramid. Pick up the free *Louvre
Handbook in English* at the information desk under the pyramid as
you enter. Don't try to cover the museum thoroughly. The 90-
minute English-language tours, which leave six times daily except
Sunday, boil this overwhelming museum down to size (33F, tour
tel. 01 40 20 52 09). Clever new 30F digital audio tours (after
ticket booths, at top of stairs) give you a receiver and a directory
of about 130 masterpieces, allowing you to dial a rather dull commentary on included works as you stumble upon them. Rick's

museum guidebook, *Mona Winks* (buy in U.S.A.), includes a self-guided tour of the Louvre.

If you can't get a guide, start in the Denon wing and visit the following highlights in this order: Michelangelo's *Slaves*, Ancient Greek and Roman (Parthenon frieze, *Venus de Milo*, Pompeii mosaics, Etruscan sarcophagi, Roman portrait busts, Nike of Samothrace); Apollo Gallery (jewels); French and Italian paintings in the Grande Galerie (¼-mile long and worth the hike); the *Mona Lisa* and her Italian Renaissance roommates; the nearby neoclassical collection (*Coronation of Napoleon*); and the Romantic collection, with works by Delacroix (*Liberty at the Barricades*—see your 100F note) and Géricault (*Raft of the Medusa*).

Admission is 45F until 15:00, 26F after 15:00 and all day Sunday, free on the first Sunday of the month and if you're under age 18. Open daily from 9:00 to 18:00; key wings open Monday until 21:45, all wings open Wednesday until 21:45, closed Tuesday. You can enter the pyramid for free until 21:30. Go in at night and see it glow. Tel. 01 40 20 53 17 or 01 40 20 51 51 for recorded information. Métro: Palais-Royal/Musée du Louvre. Note: The old "Louvre" Métro stop called "Louvre Rivoli" no longer goes to the Louvre.

The newly-renovated Richelieu wing and the underground shopping mall extension add the finishing touches to Le Grand Louvre Project (that started in 1989 with the pyramid entrance). To explore this most recent extension of the Louvre, enter through the pyramid then walk toward the inverted pyramid and uncover a post office, a handy TI and SNCF office, glittering boutiques and a dizzying assortment of good-value eateries (up the escalator), and the Palais-Royal Métro entrance. Stairs at the far end take you right into the Tuileries Gardens, a perfect antidote to the stuffy, crowded rooms of the Louvre. My First Evening Orientation Walk (see More Paris Walks, below) also leaves from the Louvre.

▲L'Orangerie—This small, quiet, and often-overlooked museum houses Monet's water lilies, many famous Renoirs, and a scattering of other great Impressionist works. The breezy round rooms of water lilies are two of the most enjoyable rooms in Paris (30F, 9:45–17:15, closed Tuesday, located in the Tuileries Gardens near the place de la Concorde, Métro: Concorde tel. 01 42 97 4816).

Jeu de Paume—This one-time home to the Impressionist art collection (now located in the Musée d'Orsay) hosts rotating exhibits of top contemporary artists (38F, 12:00–19:00, until 21:30 on Tuesdays, weekends 10:00–19:00, closed Monday; on place de la Concorde, just inside the Tuileries gardens on the rue de Rivoli side; Métro: Concorde).

▲▲▲Orsay Museum—This is Paris' 19th-century art museum (actually, art from 1848–1914), including Europe's greatest collection of Impressionist works (call for 38F English tour schedule, usually daily at 11:30, not Sunday). Start on the ground floor. The "pretty" conservative establishment art is on the right. Then cross left into the brutally truthful and, at that time, very shocking art of the realist rebels and Manet. Then ride the escalators at the far end (detouring at the top for a grand museum view) to the series of Impressionist rooms (Monet, Renoir, Dégas, et al). Don't miss the Grand Ballroom (room 52, Arts et Decors de la IIIème Republique) and Art Nouveau on the mezzanine level. The museum is housed in a former train station (Gare d'Orsay) across the river and ten minutes downstream from the Louvre (39F, 27F for the young and old, under 18 free, late June–late September and all Sundays 9:00–18:00, other days 10:00–18:00, Thursday until 21:45, closed Monday, most crowded around 11:00 and 14:00; 1 rue Bellechasse, tel. 01 40 49 48 14, reception tel. 01 40 49 48 48; Métro: Solferino or, better, the RER: Musée d'Orsay). City museum passes are sold in the basement; if there's a long line you can skip it by buying one there, but you can't skip the metal detector line into the museum. Note: From the Orsay Museum, it's a convenient straight shot to Versailles on the RER, and a 20-minute walk to the Rodin Museum (turn left out of the museum and walk down rue Bellechasse, then right on rue de Varenne).

Sights—Southwest Paris

▲▲▲**Eiffel Tower**—Crowded and expensive but worth the trouble. Go early (arrive by 9:30) or late in the day (after 18:00) to avoid most crowds; weekends are worst. The higher you go, the more you pay. The view from the 400-foot-high second level is plenty. *Pilier Nord* (the north pillar) has the biggest elevator and the fastest moving line. Begin at the first floor, read the informative signs (in English) describing the major monuments, see the entertaining free movie on the history of the tower, and consider a drink overlooking all of Paris at the café or at the reasonable restaurant Altitude 95 (decent 100F meals until 20:00, and Paris' best view bar). Take the elevator to the second floor for even greater views. It costs 20F to go to the first level, 40F to the second, and 57F to go all the way for the 1,000-foot view (not included with museum pass). On a budget? You can climb the stairs to the second level for only 12F (summers daily 9:00–24:00, off-season 9:30–23:00, tel. 01 44 11 23 23, Métro: Trocadero, RER: Champs de Mars). For another great view, especially at night, enjoy the tower (and the wild roller-blading scene) by approaching via the Trocadero Métro stop. Have a picnic dinner in front of the tower in the Champs de Mars park after the grass guards have left (about 20:00).

The Paris Sewer Tour (Egouts)—This quick and easy visit takes you along a few hundred yards of underground water tunnel lined with interesting displays, well-described in English, explaining the evolution of the world's longest sewer system (if you lined up Paris' sewers they would reach beyond Istanbul). Don't miss the slide show, fine WCs just beyond the gift shop, and the occasional tours in English (32F, 11:00–17:00, closed Thursday and Friday, where the Pont de l'Alma hits the Left Bank, tel. 01 47 05 10 29).

▲▲**Napoleon's Tomb and the Army Museum**—The emperor lies majestically dead inside several coffins under a grand dome—a goose-bumping pilgrimage for historians. Napoleon is surrounded by the tombs of other French war heroes and Europe's greatest military museum in the Hôtel des Invalides. Follow signs to the "crypt," where you'll find Roman Empire–style reliefs listing the accomplishments of Napoleon's administration. The restored dome glitters with 26 pounds of gold (37F, daily 10:00–18:00, off-season 17:00, tel. 01 44 42 37 67, Métros: La Tour Maubourg or Varennes).

▲▲**Rodin Museum**—This user-friendly museum is filled with passionate works by the greatest sculptor since Michelangelo. See *The Kiss, The Thinker, The Gates of Hell,* and many more. Don't miss the room full of work by Rodin's student and mistress, Camille Claudel. (28F, 18F on Sunday, 5F for gardens only, which may be Paris' best deal as many works are well-displayed in the beautiful gardens; 9:30–17:45, closed Monday and at 17:00 off-season, 77 rue de Varennes, tel. 01 44 18 61 10, Métro: Varennes, near Napoleon's Tomb.) Good self-serve cafeteria and idyllic picnic spots in family-friendly back garden.

▲▲**The Marmottan**—In this private, intimate, less-visited museum you'll find more than 100 paintings by Claude Monet (thanks to his son Michel), including the *Impressions of a Sunrise* painting that gave the movement its start—and name (40F, 10:00–17:30, closed Monday, no museum pass, 2 rue Louis Boilly, Métro: La Muette, follow the museum signs 6 blocks through a park to the museum, tel. 01 42 24 07 02).

Sights—Southeast Paris

▲**Latin Quarter**—See the "Historic Core of Paris" walk above.

St-Germain des Prés—A church was first built on this site in A.D. 452. The church you see today was constructed in 1163. The area around the church hops at night with fire-eaters, mimes, and scads of artists (Métro: St-Germain-des-Prés).

▲**St. Sulpice Organ Concert**—For pipe-organ enthusiasts, this is a delight. The Grand-Orgue at St. Sulpice has a rich history, with a line of 12 world-class organists (including Widor and Dupre) going back 300 years. Marcel Dupre started the tradition of opening the loft to visitors after the 10:30 service on Sundays. The friendly-in-three-languages Daniel Roth continues to welcome guests as he plays five keyboards at once. The 10:30 Sunday Mass is followed by a 20-minute recital at 11:40. At 12:00 the small unmarked door opens (left of entry as you face the rear) and visitors scamper like 16th notes up spiral stairs to a world of 6,000 pipes, where they can watch the master perform, friends warming his bench, and a committee scrambling to pull and push the 110 stops (Métro: St. Sulpice or Mabillon).

▲Luxembourg Gardens—Paris' most beautiful, interesting, and enjoyable garden/park/recreational area is a great place to watch Parisians at rest and play. Challenge the card and chess players to a game (near the tennis courts) or find a free chair near the main pond and take a breather. Notice any pigeons? A poor Ernest Hemingway used to hand-hunt (read: strangle) them here. The grand neoclassical-domed **Panthéon** (now a mausoleum housing the tombs of several great Frenchmen) is a block away and is only worth entering if you have a museum pass. The park is open until dusk (Métro: Odéon). If you enjoy the Luxembourg Gardens and want to see more, visit **Parc Monceau** (Métro: Monceau) and the **Jardin des Plantes** (Métro: Jussieu).

▲Montparnasse Tower—This 59-floor superscraper—it's cheaper and easier to get to the top than it is to that of the Eiffel Tower—offers one of Paris' best views, since the Eiffel Tower is in it and the Montparnasse Tower isn't. Buy the photo guide to the city, then go to the rooftop and orient yourself (42F, daily in summer 9:30–23:00, off-season 10:00–22:00, disappointing after dark, entrance on rue l'Arrivé, Métro: Montparnasse). This is efficient when combined with a day trip to Chartres, which begins at the Montparnasse train station.

Sights—Northwest Paris

▲▲Place de la Concorde and the Champs-Élysées—This famous boulevard is Paris' backbone and greatest concentration of traffic. All of France seems to converge on the place de la Concorde, the city's largest square. It was here that the guillotine took the lives of thousands—including King Louis XVI. Back then it was called the place de la Revolution.

Catherine de Medici wanted a place to drive her carriage, so she started draining the swamp that would become the Champs-Élysées. Napoleon put on the final touches, and it's been the place to be seen ever since. The Tour de France bicycle race ends here, as do all parades (French or foe) of any significance. While the boulevard has become a bit hamburgerized, a walk here is a must. Take the Métro to the Arc de Triomphe (Métro: Étoile) and saunter down the Champs-Élysées (Métro stops every few blocks: FDR, George V, and Étoile).

▲▲▲Arc de Triomphe—Napoleon had the magnificent Arc de Triomphe constructed to commemorate his victory at the Battle of Austerlitz. It was finished in 1836, just in time to be a part of the emperor's funeral parade. Today it commemorates heroes of past wars. There's no triumphal arch bigger (50 meters high, 40 meters wide). And, with 12 converging boulevards, there's no traffic circle more thrilling to experience—either behind the wheel or on foot (take the underpass). Eleven major boulevards feed into the place Charles de Gaulle (Étoile) that surrounds the arch. Study the traffic "system." Underneath the arch is the eternal flame and tomb of the unknown soldier. An elevator or a spiral staircase leads to a cute museum about the arch and a grand view from the top, even after dark (35F, Tuesday–Saturday 9:00–23:00, Sunday and Monday 9:30–18:00, tel. 01 43 80 31 31, Métro: Étoile).

▲Grande Arche, La Defense—The centerpiece of Paris' ambitious skyscraper complex (La Defense) is the Grande Arche. Built to celebrate the 200th anniversary of the 1789 French Revolution, the place is big—38 floors on more than 200 acres. It holds offices for 30,000 people. Notre-Dame Cathedral could fit under its arch. The La Defense complex is an interesting study in 1960s land-use planning. Over 100,000 workers commute here daily, directing lots of business and development away from downtown and allowing central Paris to retain its more elegant feel. This aspect makes sense to most Parisians, regardless of whatever else they feel about this controversial complex. You'll enjoy city views from the Arche elevator (40F includes a film on its construction and art exhibits, daily 9:00–20:00, 9:00–19:00 off-season, tel. 01 49 07 27 57, Métro or RER: La Defense, follow signs to Grande Arche).

Sights—North and Northeast Paris

Note: For more information on this neighborhood (Pompidou and Beaubourg), see the Bastille/Marais/Beaubourg walk, below.

▲▲Pompidou Center—Europe's greatest collection of far-out modern art, the **Musée National d'Art Moderne** is housed in this colorfully exoskeletal building. After so many Madonnas and Children, a piano smashed to bits and glued to the wall is refreshing. It's a social center with lots of people, street theater, and activity inside and out—a perpetual street fair. Ride the escalator for a free city view from the café terrace on top and don't miss the free exhibits on the ground floor (35F, 24F for the young and old, Monday–Friday 12:00–22:00, weekends and most holidays 10:00–22:00, closed Tuesday, tel. 01 44 78 12 33, Métro: Rambuteau).

▲Picasso Museum (Hôtel Salé)—This is the world's largest collection of Pablo Picasso's paintings, sculpture, sketches, and ceramics, and includes his personal collection of Impressionist art. It's well-explained in English and worth ▲▲▲ if you're a fan (30F, 9:30–18:00, closed Tuesday, 5 rue Thorigny, tel. 01 42 71 25 21, Métro: St. Paul or Chemin Vert).

▲Père Lachaise Cemetery—Littered with the tombstones of many of the city's most illustrious dead, this is your best one-stop look at the fascinating and romantic world of the "permanent Parisians." The place is confusing, but maps will direct you to the graves of Chopin, Molière, and even the American rock star Jim Morrison (who died in Paris). In section 92, a series of statues memorializing the war makes the French war experience a bit more real (10F maps at flower store near entry, closes at dusk, Métro: Père Lachaise or bus #69).

▲▲**Sacré-Coeur and Montmartre**—This Byzantine-looking church, while only 100 years old, is impressive. It was built as a "praise the Lord anyway" gesture, after the French were humiliated by the Germans in a brief war in 1871. The church is open daily until 23:00. One block from the church, the place du Tertre was the haunt of Toulouse-Lautrec and the original Bohemians. Today it's mobbed by tourists and unoriginal Bohemians, but still fun. Watch the artists, tip the street singers, have a dessert crêpe, and wander down the rue Lepic to the two remaining windmills (there were once 30). Rue des Saules leads to Paris' only vineyard. Plaster of Paris comes from the gypsum found on this *mont*. Place Blanche is the white place near where they used to load it, sloppily. Métros: Anvers (one Métro ticket, use the funicular to avoid stairs) or the closer but less scenic Abbesses. A taxi may be worth the splurge.

Pigalle—Paris' red-light district, the infamous "Pig Alley," is at the foot of Butte Montmartre. Ooh la la. More shocking than dangerous. Stick to the bigger streets, hang on to your wallet, and exercise good judgment. Cancan can cost a fortune, as can con artists in topless bars. After dark, countless tour buses line the streets, reminding us that tour guides make big bucks by bringing their groups to touristic nightclubs like the famous Moulin Rouge (Métro: Pigalle and Abbesses).

Promenade Plantée Park—This 3-mile narrow garden walk, elevated above the city, was once a train track and is now a joy. It runs from the opéra de la Bastille (Métro: Bastille) along Avenue Daumesnil to Saint-Mandé (Métro: Michel Bizot).

Disappointments *de* Paris

While Paris can drive you in Seine with superlatives, here are a few negatives to help you manage with limited time:

La Madeleine is a big stark neoclassical church with a postcard facade and a postbox interior. The famous aristocratic deli behind the church, Fauchon, is elegant, but so are many others handier to your hotel.

The old Opéra Garnier has a great Chagall-painted ceiling but is in a pedestrian-mean area. Don't go to American Express (behind the Opéra) just to change money. You'll get a better rate at many other banks.

Paris' Panthéon (nothing like Rome's) is another stark neoclassical edifice filled with mortal remains of great Frenchmen who mean little to the average American tourist.

The Bastille is Paris' most famous nonsight. The square is there, but confused tourists look everywhere and can't find the famous prison of Revolution fame. The building's gone and the square is good only as a jumping-off point for the Marais walk (see below).

Montmartre, the once-artsy now-touristy original haunt of the Bohemians, is overrun with big-bus tourists and those who live off of them. The view—from the steps of Sacré-Coeur—is marred by hustlers.

And the Latin Quarter is a frail shadow of its characteristic self. It's more Tunisian, Greek, and Woolworth's than old-time Paris. The café life that turned on Hemingway and endeared Boul Miche and Boulevard St-Germain to so many poets is also trampled by modern commercialism.

Best Shopping

Forum des Halles is a huge subterranean shopping center. It's fun, mod, and colorful, but lacks a soul (Métro: Halles). The Galleries Lafayette behind the opera house is your best elegant, Old World, one-stop, Parisian department store and shopping center. Also, visit the Printemps store and the historic (as well as handy) Samaritaine department store near Pont Neuf. Ritzy shops surround the Ritz Hotel at place Vendôme (Métro: Tuileries).

More Paris Walks

Before setting out on each of these walks, mark your route on the free tourist map at your hotel. (Your receptionist can help.) Be certain you splice in visits to the recommended sights you'll pass along the way.

▲First Evening Orientation Walk—If you just landed in Europe, an evening walk will show you some of Paris' delights and keep your jet-laggy body moving until a reasonable European bedtime. Bring a map and, when you run out of steam, hop the nearest Métro and head home.

Start with a Métro ride to the "Louvre Rivoli" stop (not the "Palais-Royal/Musée du Louvre" stop). This art-filled subway station offers a tiny sneak preview of the culture Paris offers. Exiting the station you get more art: The Métro entrance itself is Art Nouveau. Walk along the imposing facade of the Louvre palace (on your right), with a spindly Gothic church on your left to the river. Fake left to the Île de la Cité, then jog right and cross the pedestrian-only bridge (Pont des Arts). Grab a bench. Savor this spot. If facing the history-laden Île de la Cité, turn around and you'll see the Eiffel Tower. Just to its right, the Orsay Museum still looks like a train station. Further right, the Louvre seems to go on forever.

Cross to the dome which welcomes you to the Left Bank. This is the Palais de l'Institut de France, part of which is the

Académie Française. Circle the building on the right, past the statue of the all-knowing Voltaire. Then angle up the modern art gallery–lined rue de Seine. Consider a stop at the very Parisian La Palette café—if you've yet to encounter a Turkish-type toilet. . . . A block beyond La Palette, turn right on rue Jacob. After about 3 blocks, turn left to follow rue Bonaparte to the church of Germain-des-Pres, with the oldest bell tower in Paris. Explore this Romanesque landmark (from 1163, English info sheet inside). One of Paris' most expensive and famous cafés, Les Deux Magots, faces the church. (Ernest Hemingway hung out here while writing *The Sun Also Rises*, back when they didn't charge $12 for a glass of champagne.)

Follow the famous boulevard St-Germain (with the church on your left and the Montparnasse skyscraper towering in the distance on your right) for about 4 blocks. This lively café and shopping scene is typical of the Left Bank. At the five-screen cinema and Métro stop, turn right on Carrefour de l'Odéon, which leads straight to the templelike Theatre de l'Odéon. Behind that is Paris' most beautiful park, the Luxembourg Gardens. Grab a chair by the center fountain and contemplate where you are—Paris. (The recommended Polidor Restaurant is nearby. The handiest Métro stop from here is Luxembourg or Odéon, back where you left boulevard St-Germain.)

▲**Eiffel Tower/Rue Cler/Rodin Museum/Orsay Museum**

Walk—Take the Métro to Trocadero. Exit the subway and follow the *Sortie Tour Eiffel* signs to one of Europe's great views (gloriously floodlit at night). From here the tower seems to straddle the military school (École Militaire). Napoleon lies, hand tucked under a rib, beneath the golden dome of Les Invalides to the left. From the Trocadero terrace balcony, enjoy the lively people scene with tourists, hustlers, and daredevil roller bladers. The Naval Museum (one of Europe's best, with lots of ship models) and the National Museum of French Monuments (closed in 1998) are both here in the Chaillot Palace (free with museum pass). Le Totem Café (open noon–2:00, entrance next to the Naval Museum) offers the best-kept secret café view of the Eiffel Tower.

Hike across the river to the Eiffel Tower. Ride the elevator up to the second level. Then walk away from the river through the park. Follow the third cross street (rue de Grenelle) left and turn right on rue Cler for a rare bit of village Paris (shops closed 13:00–16:00 and on Monday; for recommended hotels and restaurants, see Sleeping and Eating, below).

Assemble a picnic on the rue Cler, then turn left on the avenue de la Motte Piquet to the grand esplanade des Invalides, a fine picnic spot. The Hôtel des Invalides, with Napoleon's Tomb and the Army Museum, is on your right. Cross the esplanade, turn right on boulevard des Invalides, and look for the Rodin Museum (Hôtel Biron) on the left. Tour the great sculpture museum. You can picnic or eat in the pricey cafeteria surrounded by Rodin's works in the elegant backyard.

Now it's on to the crowd-pleaser of Paris' museums, the Orsay. Turn right out of the Rodin Museum onto the rue Varenne, then take a left on the rue Bellechasse (allow 20 minutes to the Orsay). If you still have energy after touring the Musée d'Orsay, walk away from the river and hook up with one of Paris' best people-watching, shopping, and café streets, the boulevard St-Germain.

▲▲Bastille/Marais/Beaubourg Walk—This walk takes you through one of Paris' most characteristic quarters. When in Paris, the natural inclination is to concentrate only on the big sights. But to experience Paris you need to experience a vital neighborhood. This is a good one, containing more pre-Revolutionary buildings than anywhere else in town. It's Paris at its best, with the body of yesterday and the pulse of today. Ride the Métro to Bastille and follow the dotted path outlined on the Marais map. (As a recommended hotel neighborhood, you'll find the map and lots of good hotels and eateries listed later in this chapter.)

At **Place de la Bastille**, there are more revolutionary images in the Métro station murals than on the square. Exit the Metro following signs to rue Saint Antoine. Ascend onto a noisy square dominated by the bronze *Colonne de Juillet* (July Column). Victims of the revolutions of 1830 and 1848 are buried in a vault 55 meters below this guilded statue of liberty. The actual Bastille, a royal fortress-then-prison that once symbolized old regime tyranny and now symbolizes the Parisian emancipation, is long gone. While only a brick outline of the fortress' round turrets survives (under the traffic where rue Saint Antoine hits the square), the story of the Bastille is indelibly etched on the city's psyche.

For centuries the Bastille was used to defend the city (mostly from its own people). On July 14, 1789, the people of Paris stormed the prison, releasing its seven prisoners and hoping to find arms. They demolished the brick fortress and decorated their pikes with the heads of a few big wigs. Shedding blood, the leaders of the gang made sure it would be tough to turn back the tides of revolution. Ever since, the French have celebrated July 14th as their independence day—Bastille Day.

The flashy, glassy-grey, and controversial **Opéra-Bastille** dominates (some say overwhelms) the square. Designed by the Canadian architect Carlos Ott, this latest Parisian grand project was opened with great fanfare by François Mitterrand on the 200th Bastille Day, July 14, 1989.

Turn your back to the statue and, passing the Banque de France on your right (good rates, long lines, opposite a fine map of the area on your left), head straight down the busy rue Saint Antoine about 4 blocks into the Marais.

The **Marais**, still filled with pre-Revolutionary lanes and buildings, is more characteristic than touristy (unlike the Latin Quarter). It's medieval Paris. This is how much of the city looked until, in the mid-1800s, Napoleon III had Baron Haussmann blast through the boulevards (open and wide enough for the guns and marching ranks of the army, too wide for revolutionary barricades), creating modern Paris.

Leave rue Saint Antoine at #62, turn right through two elegant courtyards of Hotel de Sully (62 rue Saint Antoine, open until 19:00, good Marais map on corridor wall). Originally a swamp (*marais*), during the reign of Henry IV it became the hometown of the French aristocracy. In the 17th century, big shots built their private mansions (*hôtels*) like this one—close to Henry's place des Vosges. *Hôtels* that survived the revolution now house museums, libraries, and national institutions. The aristocrats may be gone, but the Marais—which, until recently, was a dumpy Bohemian quarter—is today a thriving, trendy but real-feeling community and a joy to explore.

To get to the **place des Vosges**, continue through the Hotel de Sully. The small door on the far right corner of the second courtyard pops you out into one of Paris' finest squares (closes at dusk). Walk to the center, where Louis XIII sits on a horse surrounded by locals enjoying their community park. Children frolic in the sandbox, lovers warm benches, and pigeons guard their fountains, while trees shade this retreat from the glare of the big city. Henry IV built this centerpiece of the Marais in 1605. As hoped, this turned the Marais into Paris' most exclusive neighborhood. Victor Hugo lived at #6 (18F, corner closest the Bastille, open to the public).

To leave the square, walk behind Louis' horse to the arcade. Follow it left past art galleries and antique shops onto the boutique-filled rue des Francs Bourgeois (the store at #17 sells used silver, often from famous restaurants, by weight). Browse 2 blocks off the place des Vosges to corner of rue de Sévigné, where you'll see the Musée Carnavalet (on right).

The **Carnavalet (History of Paris) Museum**, housed inside a fine Marais mansion with classy courtyards and statues, features paintings of Parisian scenes, French Revolution paraphernalia, old Parisian store signs, a guillotine, a model of 16th-century Île de la Cité (notice the bridge houses), and rooms full of 15th-century Parisian furniture. Unfortunately, explanations are in French only (30F, 10:00–17:30, closed Monday, 23 rue de Sévigné, tel. 01 42 72 21 13, Métro: St. Paul).

To continue the Marais walk, go another block along rue des Francs Bourgeois (peeking through the gate on the right) and turn left at the post office (Picasso Museum, described above, is up 1 block to the right). From rue Pavée, bend right onto rue Rosiers, which runs straight for 3 blocks through Paris' lively (except on Saturday) Jewish Quarter.

The **Jewish Quarter** is lined with colorful shops and kosher eateries. Jo Goldenberg's delicatessen/restaurant (first corner on left, at #7—scene of a terrorist bombing in darker times) is worth poking into. You'll be tempted by kosher pizza and plenty of 20F falafel-to-go (*emporter*) joints. Rue Rosiers deadends into rue du Vieille du Temple. Turn right.

Frank Bourgeois is waiting at the corner postcard/print shop. Turn left. He leads past the national archives (peek inside the courtyard) and turns into rue Rambuteau.

The pipes and glass of the **Pompidou Center** reintroduce you to our century. Pass that huge building on your left to join the fray in front of the center (also called the Centre Beaubourg). Survey this popular spot from the top of the sloping square. A tubular series of escalators leads up the building (free, entry inside, fine view terrace with café on top, modern Pompidou art gallery on fourth floor—described above).

The Centre Georges Pompidou follows with gusto the 20th-century architectural axiom "form follows function." To get a more spacious and functional interior, the guts of this exoskeletal building are draped on the outside and color coded: vibrant red for people lifts, cool blue for air conditioning, eco-green for plumbing, don't-touch-it yellow for electrical stuff, and white for bones. Explore the always-titillating interior. The ground floor and three-floor library (second-floor entrance) are free. The Centre's many contemporary exhibits make it the most visited sight in Paris. Back outside, wander left to the *Homage to Stravinsky* fountain. Jean Tingley designed this new-wave fountain as a tribute to Stravinsky . . . every fountain represents one of his hard-to-hum scores.

With your back to Centre Pompidou's escalators, walk the cobbled pedestrian mall, crossing the busy boulevard Sebastopol to the ivy-covered pavilions of Les Halles. After 800 years as Paris' down-and-dirty central produce market, this was replaced by a glitzy but soulless modern shopping center in the late 1970s. The most endearing layer of the mall is its grassy rooftop park. The fine Gothic Saint Eustache church overlooking this contemporary scene has a famous 8,000-pipe organ. The Louvre and Notre-Dame are just a short walk away. The mall is served by Paris' busiest Métro hub (the Chatelet-Les Halles station).

Near Paris: Versailles

▲▲▲**The Palace of Versailles**—Every king's dream, Versailles was the residence of the French king and the cultural heartbeat of Europe for about 100 years—until the Revolution of 1789 ended the notion that God deputized some people to rule for Him on Earth. Louis XIV spent half a year's income of Europe's richest country turning his dad's hunting lodge into a palace fit for a divine monarch. Louis XV and Louis XVI spent much of the 18th century gilding Louis XIV's lily. About 50 years after the royal family was evicted, King Louis Philippe opened the palace as a museum in 1837. Europe's next-best palaces are Versailles wannabes.

Information: There's a helpful tourist information office across the street from Versailles' R.G. station (tel. 01 39 50 36 22), two information desks on the approach to the palace, and a very helpful TI at entrance C. The useful brochure, "Versailles Orientation Guide," explains your sightseeing options.

Tickets: Your choices are the main palace with a basic self-guided walk, several main-palace sections tourable only with guided walks, and two smaller palaces in the backyard. Thus, admissions are complicated. In the main palace, the self-guided one-way palace romp, including the Hall of Mirrors, costs 45F (35F after 15:30, on Sunday, or for those under 26). To take a private tour through the other sections, you'll need to pay the 45F base price then add 25F for a one-hour guided tour, 37F for a 90-minute guided tour, or 25F for a self-guided Walkman-cassette tour.

Hours: Tuesday through Sunday 9:00 to 18:30, October through April 9:00 to 17:30, last entry 30 minutes before closing, closed Monday, information tel. 01 30 84 76 18 or 01 30 84 74 00. Crowds are a problem from 10:00 to 15:00. Tuesday and Sunday are most crowded. If you dislike crowds, arrive after 15:30, pay a reduced admission charge, then tour the main palace, and tour the gardens after the palace closes. The palace is great late. On my last visit, at 18:00, I was the only tourist in the Hall of Mirrors, even on a Tuesday.

For the basic self-guided tour, join the line at entrance A. Enter the palace and take a one-way walk through the state apartments from the "King's Wing," through the magnificent Hall of Mirrors, and out via the "Queen's Wing."

The Hall of Mirrors was the ultimate hall of the day—250 feet long, 17 arched mirrors matching 17 windows with royal garden views, 24 gilded candelabra, eight busts of Roman emperors, and eight classical-style statues (seven of them actually ancient originals). The ceiling is decorated with stories of Louis' triumphs. Imagine this place filled with silk gowns and powdered wigs, lit by thousands of candles. The mirrors—a luxurious rarity at the time—were a reflection of a time when aristocrats felt good about their looks and their fortunes. In another age altogether, this was the room in which the Treaty of Versailles was signed, ending World War I.

Before going downstairs at the end, take a historic stroll clockwise around the long room filled with the great battles of France murals. If you don't have *Mona Winks*, the guidebook called *The Châteaux, The Gardens, and Trianon* gives a room-by-room rundown.

Versailles

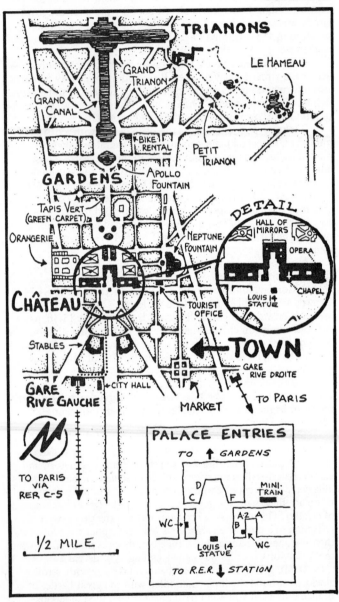

TRIANONS

LE HAMEAU

GRAND
TRIANON

GRAND
CANAL

BIKE
RENTAL

PETIT
TRIANON

GARDENS

APOLLO
FOUNTAIN

TAPIS VERT
(GREEN CARPET)

ORANGERIE

NEPTUNE
FOUNTAIN

DETAIL

HALL OF
MIRRORS

OPERA

CHAPEL

LOUIS 14
STATUE

CHÂTEAU

TOURIST
OFFICE

STABLES

TOWN

GARE
RIVE DROITE

GARE
RIVE GAUCHE

CITY HALL

TO PARIS

MARKET

TO PARIS
VIA
RER C-5

½ MILE

PALACE ENTRIES

TO ↑ GARDENS

D
C   F

MINI-
TRAIN

WC

A2   A
B
WC

LOUIS 14
STATUE

TO R.E.R. ↓ STATION

For a private tour, pay the base-price admission at the same time you pay for your tour (entrance D). The 60- or 90-minute tours, led by an English-speaking art historian, take you through sections of Versailles not included in the base-price visit. Groups are limited to 30. Of the several tours offered, the 90-minute version covering Louis XV and Louis XVI's apartments and the opera is best. Pay and get your tour appointment at entrance D. Tour times are normally all allotted for the day by 13:00. Tours leave from entrance F. If the line's long and you're in a hurry, the self-guided Walkman-cassette tour of the King's Chamber (25F, entrance C, last entry at 15:00) covers Louis XIV's rooms and is a good option. If you're waiting for your tour, have finished a tour, or have a Paris Museum pass, you can go directly into the main palace with no line at the A2 gate.

The Palace Gardens: The gardens offer a world of royal amusements. Outside the palace is the L'Orangerie. Louis, the only one who could grow oranges in Paris, had an orange grove on wheels that could be wheeled in and out of his greenhouses according to the weather. A promenade leads from the palace to the Grand Canal, an artificial lake that, in Louis' day, was a mini-sea with nine ships, including a 32-cannon warship. France's royalty used to float up and down the canal in Venetian gondolas.

While Louis cleverly used palace life at Versailles to "domesticate" his nobility, turning otherwise meddlesome nobles into groveling socialites, all this pomp and ceremony hampered the royal family as well. For an escape from the public life at Versailles, they built more intimate palaces as retreats in their garden. Before the Revolution there was plenty of space to retreat—the grounds were enclosed by a 25-mile-long fence.

The beautifully restored **Grand Trianon Palace** is as sumptuous as the main palace but much smaller. With its pastel pink colonnade and more human scale, this is the place where you may experience a little palace envy.

The nearby Petit Trianon, which has a fine neoclassical exterior with a skippable interior, was Marie Antoinette's favorite residence.

You can almost see princesses bobbing gaily in the branches as you walk through the enchanting forest, past the white marble temple of love (1778) to the queen's fake-peasant hamlet. Palace life really got to Marie Antoinette. Sort of a back-to-basics queen, she retreated further and further from her blue-blooded reality. Her happiest days were at the hamlet, under a bonnet, tending her perfumed sheep and her manicured gardens in a thatch-happy wonderland.

Getting around the gardens: It's a 30-minute hike from the palace, down the canal, past the two mini-palaces to the hamlet. You can rent bikes (30F/hr). The pokey tourist train (30F, five/hr, four stops, you can hop on and off as you like, nearly worthless commentary) is handy for the very slow or very tired; it's only 10F from the canal back to the chateau.

Garden admissions: Except for fountain-filled Sundays, the gardens are free and open from 7:00 to sunset (as late as 21:30). Grand and Petit Trianon are open May through September 10:00 to 18:00 (Grand Trianon, 25F; Petit Trianon, 15F; 30F for both; off-season 10:00–17:00, closed Monday). The park is picnic-perfect. Food is not allowed into the palace, but those with a picnic can check bags (and picnics) at doors A or C. There's a kiosk selling good sandwiches and a decent restaurant on the canal in the gardens.

Fountain Spectacles: Every Sunday, May through October, music fills the king's backyard and the garden's fountains are in full squirt (25F garden admission on these days only, 11:15–11:35 and 15:30–17:00). Louis had his engineers literally reroute a river to fuel these fountains. Even by today's standards they are impressive.

Getting to Versailles: Versailles, 12 miles from downtown Paris, is an easy direct 30-minute ride on the RER train. While two other trains go to Versailles, RER is the most efficient for the tourist. Métro to any RER-C station (Austerlitz, St-Michel, Orsay, Invalides, Pont de l'Alma, or Champs de Mars/Tour Eiffel) and follow the RER signs to trains (usually named VICK) bound for Versailles R.G. (Rive Gauche station). Do not ride Versailles C.H. trains; they stop at a different Versailles station, farther from the palace. (26F round-trip, covered by railpasses, 30 minutes each way; trains run every 15 minutes; most but not all trains go to Versailles R.G. Check the stops listed on signs over the platform and confirm with a local. Turn right out of the Versailles R.G. station, then left on the major boulevard to reach the palace, ten minutes.) The Paris–Versailles taxi fare is about 100F—a money saver for groups of four. To save a long walk (but do things in a less logical order), consider having the taxi drop you at the Little Hamlet (Petit Hameau).

The Town of Versailles (zip code: 78000): After the palace closes and the tourists go, the prosperous and pleasant little town of Versailles feels wholesome and a long way from Paris. The central market thrives on Tuesday, Friday, and Saturday (on place du Marche; leaving the RER station, turn right and walk ten minutes). Consider the wisdom of picking up or dropping your rental car here rather than in Paris. The Hertz and Avis offices are at the Gare des Chantiers (train station served by Paris' Montparnasse station), a six-minute walk from the RER station.

For a laid-back alternative to Paris within easy reach of the big city (30 minutes by RER, five/hour), with free and safe parking, Versailles can be a good overnight stop. **Hôtel Le Cheval Rouge****, built in 1676 as Louis XIV's stables, now houses tourists comfortably. It's a block behind the place du Marche in a quaint corner of town on a large quiet courtyard (Ds-265F, Db-

325–400F, extra bed-90F, CC:VM, 18 rue Andre Chenier, 78000 Versailles, tel. 01 39 50 03 03, fax 01 39 50 61 27). **Ibis Versailles****, a slick business-class place, offers all the comfort with none of the character (Db-390–490F, CC:VMA, across from the RER station, 4 ave du Gen de Gaulle, tel. 01 39 53 03 03, fax 01 39 50 06 31, SE). **Hotel du Palais**, facing the RER station, has cheap and handy beds; get one off the street. It's a pink and funky place, dumpy enough to lack stars but proud enough to put candy on the beds (D-170F, Ds-220F, Db-250F, 30F per additional person, miles of stairs, 6 place Lyautey, tel. 01 39 50 39 29, fax 01 39 50 80 44, NSE). **Hotel d'Angleterre**** is a peaceful, well-worn old place near the palace (Db-300–350F, extra bed-60F, CC:VM, first-floor rooms are best, 2 rue de Fontenay, tel. 01 39 51 43 50, fax 01 39 51 45 63).

More Side Trips from Paris

▲▲▲**Chartres**—In 1194 a terrible fire destroyed the church at Chartres with the much-venerated veil of Mary. With almost unbelievably good fortune, the monks found the veil miraculously preserved in the ashes. Money poured in for the building of a bigger and better cathedral. Bigger and better it was, as the grand new church was decorated with 2,000 carved figures and some of France's best stained glass. The cathedral feels too large for the city because it was designed to accommodate huge crowds of pilgrims. One of those pilgrims, an impressed Napoleon, declared after a visit in 1811: "Chartres is no place for an atheist." Rodin called it "the Acropolis of France." British Francophile Malcolm Miller or his impressive assistant give great "Appreciation of Gothic" tours daily (except Sunday and off-season, usually at noon and 14:45, verify in advance, call the TI at tel. 02 37 21 50 00). Each 30F tour is different; many stay for both tours. Just show up at the church (7:00–19:00).

Find time to explore Chartres' pleasant city center and discover the picnic-friendly park behind the cathedral. The helpful TI, next to the cathedral, has a map with a self-guided tour of Chartres (9:30–18:45). Chartres is a one-hour train trip from Paris (hourly departures from the Gare Montparnasse, about 140F round-trip) and is a delightful overnight stop.

For acceptable rooms and a well-respected restaurant, find the **Hôtel le Boeuf Couronne****, a few blocks up from the train station (D-160F, Db-285F, Tb-300F, CC:VM, 15 place Chatelet, tel. 02 37 18 06 06, fax 02 37 21 72 13).

▲▲**Château of Chantilly** (shan-tee-yee)—One of France's best château experiences is 30 minutes and 40F by RER train from Paris's Gare du Nord station, and then a 20-minute walk. This château has it all: moat, drawbridge, sculpted gardens, little hamlet (the prototype for the more famous *hameau* at Versailles), a lavish interior that rivals Versailles', a world-class art collection (including two Raphaels), and manageable crowds. (35F includes required French-language tour, 15F for gardens only, open daily except Tuesday 10:00–18:00, off-season 10:30–12:45 and 14:00–17:00, tel. 01 44 57 08 00.) Horse lovers will enjoy the nearby stables (expensive), built for a prince who believed he'd be reincarnated as a horse. The quaint and impressively preserved medieval town of Senlis is a 30-minute bus ride from the Chantilly station.

▲**Giverny**—Monet spent 43 of his most creative years (1883–1926) here at the Camp David of Impressionism. Monet's gardens and home are split by a busy road. Buy your ticket, walk through the gardens, and take the underpass into the artist's famous lilypad land. The path leads you over the Japanese Bridge, under weeping willows, and past countless scenes that leave artists aching for an easel. For Monet fans, it's strangely nostalgic. Back on the other side, continue your visit with a wander through his more robust and structured garden and his mildly interesting home. The jammed gift shop at the exit is the actual skylit studio Monet used to paint his waterlily masterpieces.

While lines may be long and tour groups may trample the flowers, true fans still find magic in those lilypads. Arrive after 16:00 for fewest crowds. (35F, 25F for gardens only, open April 1– October 31 10:00–18:00, closed Monday and off-season, tel. 02 32 51 28 21.) Take the Rouen train from Paris' Gare St. Lazare station to Vernon (about 140F round-trip). To get from the Vernon train station to Monet's garden (4 km away), take the Vernon–Giverny bus (five/day, scheduled to meet most trains), hitch, taxi (60F), or rent a bike at the station (55F, busy road). Ask at the ticket office in Giverny for return bus times or to call a taxi. Big tour companies do a Giverny day trip from Paris for around $60.

The new **American Impressionist Art Museum** (100 yards down the lane from Monet's place) is devoted to American artists who followed Claude to Giverny. Giverny had a great influence on American artists of Monet's day. This bright, modern gallery is well-explained in English, has a good little Mary Cassatt section, and gives Americans a rare chance to see French people appreciating our artists (same price and hours as Monet's home, pleasant café).

▲▲**Vaux-le-Vicomte**—This château is considered the prototype for Versailles. In fact, when its owner, Nicolas Fouquet, gave a grand party, Louis XIV was so jealous that he arrested the host and proceeded with the construction of the bigger and costlier (but not necessarily more splendid) palace of Versailles. Vaux-le-Vicomte is a joy to tour, elegantly furnished, surrounded by royal gardens, and not crowded. It's difficult to get to without a car. Take the train from Paris' Gare de Lyon (*Départs Banlieues*) to Melun. Rent a bike (crummy ride on a busy road) or taxi (about 70F) the 6 kilometers to the château. (Steep 56F admission, gardens only 30F, open daily 10:00–13:00 and 14:00–18:00. Special

candlelit visits cost 75F and are on Saturday May–October
20:30–23:00, and Friday and Saturday in July and August. The
fountains run April–October on the second and last Saturday of
each month 15:00–18:00, tel. 01 64 14 41 90.)

▲▲**Disneyland Paris**—Europe's Disneyland is basically a modern
remake of the one in California, with most of the same rides and
smiles. The main difference is that Mickey Mouse speaks French
(and you can buy wine with your lunch). My kids went ducky.
Locals love it. It's worth a day if Paris is handier than Florida or
California. Crowds are a problem. Avoid Saturday, Sunday,
Wednesday, school holidays, and July and August, if you can. The
park is occasionally so crowded that they close the gates at 60,000
people (tel. 01 64 74 30 00 for the latest). After dinner the crowds
are gone, and you'll walk right on to rides that had a 45-minute
wait three hours earlier. Food service is fun but expensive. Save
money with a picnic. Disney brochures are in every Paris hotel.
The RER (37F each way, direct from downtown Paris–Station
Marne-la-Vallee in 30 minutes) drops you right into the park. The
last train to Paris leaves shortly after midnight. (195F for adults,
150F for kids ages 3–11, 25F less in spring and fall. Open daily
9:00–23:00 late June–early September and Saturday and Sunday
off-season, shoulder-season weekdays 9:00–19:00, off-season
10:00–18:00, tel. 01 60 30 60 30 for park and hotel reservations.)
To sleep reasonably at the huge Disney complex, try **Hotel Sante
Fe** (550F family rooms for two to four people, 450F off-season;
ask for their hotel and park package deal). If all this ain't enough, a
new Planet Hollywood restaurant opened just outside the park a
five-minute walk from the RER stop.

Sleeping in Paris
(5.5F = about $1)
Sleep Code: **S**=Single, **D**=Double/Twin, **T**=Triple, **Q**=Quad,
b=bathroom, **t**=toilet only, **s**=shower only, **CC**=Credit Card
(Visa, MasterCard, Amex), **SE**=Speaks English, **NSE**=No English,
* =French hotel rating system (0–4 stars).

Remember, French hotels are rated by stars. One star is simple, two has most of the comforts, and three is, for this book,
plush (stars are indicated here by an *). Old, characteristic, budget
Parisian hotels have always been cramped. Retrofitted with elevators, toilets, and private showers (as most are today), they are even
more cramped. Even three-star hotel rooms are small. Some hotels
include the hotel tax (*taxe de sejour*, about 5F per person per day),
though most will add this to your bill. Almost every hotel accepts
Visa and MasterCard. Few take American Express.

Quad rooms usually have two double beds. Recommended
hotels have an elevator unless otherwise noted. Because double
beds and showers are cheaper than twin beds and baths, room
prices vary within each hotel. To keep things manageable, I've

focused on three safe, handy, and colorful neighborhoods (listing good hotels, restaurants, and helpful hints for each).

You can save about 100F by finding the increasingly rare room without a private shower, though some hotels charge for down-the-hall showers. Breakfasts cost 20F to 50F extra. Café or picnic breakfasts are cheaper. Singles (except for the rare closet-type rooms that fit only one twin bed) are simply doubles inhabited by one person, renting for only a little less than a double.

Conventions clog Paris in September (worst), October, May, and June. Reserve in advance during these months. July and August are no problem. Most hotels accept telephone reservations and require prepayment with a credit-card number and prefer a faxed follow-up to be sure everything is in order. Get advice for safe parking. Meters are free in August. Garages are plentiful (about 140F per day, with special rates through some hotels). Self-serve Laundromats (*laverie automatique*) are common; ask your hotelier for the nearest one.

Sleeping in the Rue Cler Neighborhood
(7th district, Métro: École Militaire, zip code: 75007)

Rue Cler, a villagelike pedestrian street, is safe, tidy, and makes me feel like I must have been a poodle in a previous life. How such coziness lodged itself between the high-powered government/business district and the expensive Eiffel Tower and Invalides areas, I'll never know. Living here ranks with the top museums as one of the city's great experiences. (But if you're into nightlife, consider one of the other two neighborhoods I list.)

On rue Cler you can eat and browse your way through a street full of tart shops, colorful outdoor produce stalls, cheeseries, and fish vendors. From rue Cler it's a short stroll to the Eiffel Tower, Les Invalides, the Seine, and the Orsay and Rodin museums. **Warning:** The first two hotels are popular with my readers.

Hôtel Leveque* has been entirely renovated and the new owner has made all the right moves. Rather than three stars, it's "one star deluxe," with a helpful staff and a singing maid. It's a fine value with the best location on the block, comfortable rooms, cable TV, hair dryers, safes, an ice-machine, and tasteful decor throughout (Sb-250F, Db-350–420F, Tb-515F, breakfast-30F, CC:VM, 29 rue Cler, tel. 01 47 05 49 15, fax 01 45 50 49 36, Web site: http://interresa.ca/hotel/leveque). The friendly staff speaks English, except for cheery Michele, who is very creative at communicating.

Hôtel du Champs de Mars**, with its cozy, pastel rooms and helpful English-speaking owners, Françoise and Stephane, is a good rue Cler option. The hotel has a Provence-style small-town feel from top to bottom—rooms are comfortable but tight. Single rooms can work as tiny doubles (Db-390–420F, Tb-505F, CC:VM, cable TV, 30 yards off rue Cler at 7 rue du Champs de Mars, tel. 01 45 51 52 30, fax 01 45 51 64 36, e-mail: stg@club-internet.fir).

Paris, Rue Cler Neighborhood

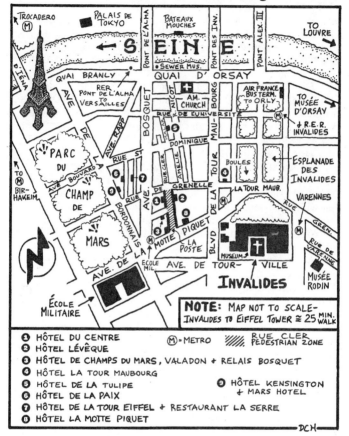

NOTE: MAP NOT TO SCALE—
INVALIDES TO EIFFEL TOWER ≅ 25 MIN. WALK

❶ HÔTEL DU CENTRE   Ⓜ = METRO   ▨ RUE CLER PEDESTRIAN ZONE
❷ HÔTEL LÉVÊQUE
❸ HÔTEL DE CHAMPS DU MARS, VALADON + RELAIS BOSQUET
❹ HÔTEL LA TOUR MAUBOURG
❺ HÔTEL DE LA TULIPE   ❾ HÔTEL KENSINGTON
❻ HÔTEL DE LA PAIX   + MARS HOTEL
❼ HÔTEL DE LA TOUR EIFFEL + RESTAURANT LA SERRE
❽ HÔTEL LA MOTTE PIQUET

—DCH—

Hôtel la Serre*, across the street from Leveque, is a
simple hotel with shabby hallways, big ambitions, a charming location, and new, friendly owners (D-260F, Db-370–400F, Tb-475F,
cable TV, CC:VM, 24 rue Cler, tel. 01 47 05 52 33, fax 01 40 62
95 66, SE).

Hôtel Relais Bosquet***, bright, spacious, and newly renovated, is upscale and comfortable (Db-575–810F, CC:VMA, 19
rue du Champs de Mars, tel. 01 47 05 25 45, fax 01 45 55 08 24,
SE). The similar Hotel Beaugency*** is also very comfortable,
but quieter, more friendly, and popular with Germans (Db-680F,
includes a buffet breakfast, 21 rue Duvivier, tel. 01 47 05 01 63,
fax 01 45 51 04 96).

Hôtel Le Valadon**, on a quiet street with a plain lobby

and spacious, comfy rooms, has a shy Parisian cuteness (Db-400–520F, Tb-550F, 16 rue Valadon, tel. 01 47 53 89 85, fax 01 44 18 90 56, friendly Tatiana SE).

Hôtel de la Tour Eiffel**, with petite, wicker-pleasant rooms, is like a small wilting salad with lots of dressing (Sb-320F, Db-370F, Tb-470F, CC:VMA, 17 rue de l'Exposition, tel. 01 47 05 14 75, fax 01 47 53 99 46, Muriel SE).

Hôtel de l'Alma*** is a tight and tidy place with 32 delightful look-alike rooms all with TV and minibar (Sb-400F, Db-450F, breakfast included, no triples but a kid's bed can be moved in for free, popular with Mexican and Russian groups, CC:VMA, 32 rue de l'Exposition, tel. 01 47 05 45 70, fax 01 45 51 84 47, SE).

Hôtel La Tour Maubourg*** feels like a slightly faded, elegant manor house with spacious old world rooms. It overlooks a cheery green within sight of Napoleon's tomb (Sb-550–650F, Db-690–850F, suites for up to four 900–1,400F, prices include breakfast with fresh-squeezed juice, prices reduced from mid-July–mid-August, CC:VM, immediately at the La Tour Maubourg Métro stop, 150 rue de Grenelle, tel. 01 47 05 16 16, fax 01 47 05 16 14, e-mail: victor@worldnet.fr, SE).

Mars Hôtel** has a richly decorated lobby, spacious—if well-worn—rooms, and a beam-me-up-Maurice coffin-sized elevator. The front rooms look out on the Eiffel Tower (large Sb-305F, Db-355F, Twin/b-400F, CC:VM, 117 avenue de la Bourdonnais, tel. 01 47 05 42 30, fax 01 47 05 45 91).

Hôtel Kensington**, near the Mars Hotel, is bigger, more professional, and well-worn, but a fair value (Sb-315F, Db-400–500F, extra bed 80F, CC:VMA, 79 avenue de La Bourdonnais, tel. 01 47 05 74 00, fax 01 47 05 25 81).

Hotel Prince** is a fair value on a busy street with pleasant owners (Db-400–450F, 66 avenue Bosquet, tel. 01 47 05 40 90, fax 01 47 53 06 62).

These places are lesser values but, in this fine area, acceptable last choices: **Hôtel Eiffel Rive Gauche**** (Ds-260F, Db-370–475F, 6 rue du Gros-Caillou, tel. 01 45 51 24 56, fax 01 45 51 11 77), **Hôtel de la Tulipe**** (Db-510–560F, wood-beamed with a leafy courtyard, no elevator, 33 rue Malar, tel. 01 45 51 67 21, fax 01 47 53 96 37), **Hôtel Royal Phare**** (Db-310–410F, facing the École Militaire Métro stop, 40 avenue de la Motte Piquet, tel. 01 47 05 57 30, fax 01 45 51 64 41), **Hôtel la Motte Piquet**** (Db-350–440F, duplex suites-730F, CC:VM, 30 avenue de la Motte Piquet, tel. 01 47 05 09 57, fax 01 47 05 74 36), and **Hôtel de la Paix** (S-165F, Ds-305F, Db-335F, Tb-460F, well-worn, quiet, run agreeably by English-speaking Noél, no elevator, 19 rue du Gros-Caillou, tel. 01 45 51 86 17).

Rue Cler Helpful Hints: Become a local at a rue Cler café for breakfast, or join the afternoon crowd for *une bière pression* (a draft beer). Cute shops and bakeries line rue Cler. Ask your hotelier for the nearest laundromat. The Métro station (École Militaire) and a post office with phone booths are at the end of rue Cler, on avenue de la Motte Piquet. Taxi stands are on avenue de Tourville at avenue la Motte Piquet (near the metro stop), and on avenue Bosquet at rue St-Dominique. Your neighborhood TI is at the Eiffel Tower (open May–September 11:00–18:00, tel. 01 45 51 22 15). There's a small late-night grocery on rue de Grenelle at rue des Expositions. The Bank Populaire (across from the Hôtel Leveque) changes money.

At 65 quai d'Orsay you'll find the American Church and College, the community center for Americans living in Paris. The interdenominational service at 11:00 on Sunday, the coffee hour after church, and the free Sunday concerts (18:00) are a great way to make some friends and get a taste of émigré life in Paris. Stop by and pick up copies of the *Free Voice* and *France–U.S.A. Contacts* newspapers (tel. 01 47 05 07 99) for information on housing and employment through the community of 30,000 Americans living in Paris.

Afternoon *boules* (lawn bowling) on the esplanade des Invalides is a relaxing spectator sport. Look for the dirt area to the upper right as you face the Invalides.

Rue Cler is a moveable feast. The entire street is clogged with connoisseurs of good eating. Only the health-food store is not busy. For a magical picnic dinner, assemble it in no fewer than six shops on rue Cler and lounge on the best grass in Paris (the police don't mind after dark) with the dogs, Frisbees, a floodlit Eiffel Tower, and a cool breeze in the Parc du Champs de Mars. (More eating specifics below.)

For an after-dinner cruise on the Seine, it's just a short walk to the river to the Bâteaux Mouches.

Sleeping in the Marais Neighborhood
(4th district, Métro: St. Paul or Bastille, zip code: 75004)

Those interested in a more Soho/Greenwich, gentrified, urban-jungle locale would enjoy making the Marais their Parisian home. The Marais is a cheaper and more happening locale than rue Cler. It's narrow medieval Paris at its finest. Only 15 years ago it was a forgotten Parisian backwater, but now the Marais is one of Paris' most popular residential areas. It's a short walk to Notre-Dame, Île St. Louis, and the Latin Quarter. The St-Paul Métro stop puts you right in the heart of the Marais.

Castex Hôtel** is pleasant, clean, cheery, and run by the very friendly Bouchand family (son Blaise, pronounced "blaze," speaks English) who, unfortunately, are selling it. As the new owners will not assume control until early 1998, assume these prices are correct. This place is a great value, with comfortable rooms, many stairs, and a great location on a relatively quiet street (Ss-230F, Sb-250–280F, Ds-310–330F, Db-330–350F, Tb-450F, CC:VM, no elevator, 5 rue Castex, just off place de la Bastille and rue Saint Antoine, Métro: Bastille, tel. 01 42 72 31 52, fax 01 42 72 57 91). Reserve by phone and leave your credit-card number.

The security code marked on your key opens the front door after hours.

Grand Hôtel Jeanne d'Arc**, a cozy and welcoming place with thoughtfully appointed rooms on a quiet street, is a haven for connoisseurs of the Marais and a fine value (small Db-310F, Db-400–490F, Tb-530F, Qb-590F, extra bed 75F, CC:VM, 3 rue Jarente, tel. 01 48 87 62 11, fax 01 48 87 37 31, SE). Sixth-floor rooms have a view. Corner rooms are wonderfully bright in the city of light.

Hotel Bastille Speria*** feels warm and family-run while offering a serious business-type service. Perfectly located, its spacious lobby and 45 rooms are mod, cheery, and pastel. It's English language–friendly, from the *Herald Tribunes* in the lobby to the history of the Bastille in the elevator (Sb-525– 550F, Db-570–635F, Tb-770F, fold-out sofas let two kids stow away for free in larger doubles, CC:VMA, 1 rue de la Bastille, tel. 01 42 72 04 01, fax 01 42 72 56 38, e-mail: speria@micronet.fr, SE).

Hôtel de la Place des Vosges**, quasi-classy with a linoleum antique feel, charges the limit for its 16 rooms but is ideally located on a quiet street (Db-475–490F, CC:VMA, 12 rue de Biraque, just off the elegant place des Vosges and just as snooty, tel. 01 42 72 60 46, fax 01 42 72 02 64).

Hotel des Chevaliers***, 1 block northwest of the place des Vosges, has renovated its pleasant and comfortable rooms, adding all the comforts from hair dryers to cable TV (Db-610–660F, CC:VMA, skip the over-priced breakfasts, tel. 01 42 72 73 47, fax 01 42 72 54 10).

Hotel de la Herse D'Or is industrial-strength, three-coats-of-paint simple, with a good location, tortured floor plan, and hard-to-beat prices (S-160F, D-200F, Db-280F, showers 10F, no elevator, 20 rue St. Antoine, tel. 01 48 87 84 09, fax 01 48 87 94 01).

Hôtel Pratic* has a slightly Arabic feel in its cramped lobby. The tidy rooms are simple but not confined, stairs are many, and it's right on a great people-friendly square. Single rooms are disappointing (S-180F, D-245F, Ds-290F, Db-340F, no elevator, 9 rue d'Ormesson, tel. 01 48 87 80 47, fax 01 48 87 40 04).

The bare-bones and dumpy **Hôtel Moderne**, next to the Hôtel Pratic, might be better than a youth hostel if you need privacy. The only thing "moderne" about it is the name—which is illegible on the broken sign (D-160F, Ds-190F, Db-220F, 3 rue Caron, tel. 01 48 87 97 05).

Hôtel de 7ème Art** is a Hollywood-nostalgia place (run by young, hip Marais types) with dull rooms, a full service café/bar, and Charlie Chaplin murals (Sb-300F, Db-420–490F, CC:VMA, 20 rue St. Paul, tel. 01 44 54 85 00, fax 01 42 77 69 10).

Hôtel de Nice** is a cozy "Marie Antoinette does tie-dye" place with lots of thoughtful touches on the Marais' busy main drag (Sb-380F, Db-450F, Tb-550F, CC:VM, 42 bis rue de Rivoli,

Paris, Marais Neighborhood

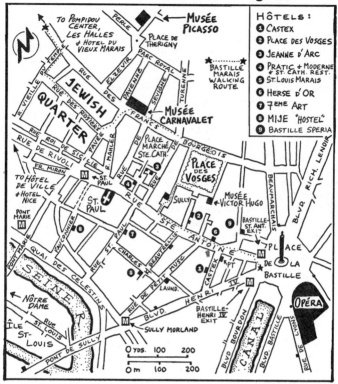

HÔTELS:
❶ CASTEX
❷ PLACE DES VOSGES
❸ JEANNE D'ARC
❹ PRATIC + MODERNE + ST. CATH. REST.
❺ ST. LOUIS MARAIS
❻ HERSE D'OR
❼ 7ᵉᵐᵉ ART
❽ MIJE "HOSTEL"
❾ BASTILLE SPERIA

tel. 01 42 78 55 29, fax 01 42 78 36 07). Twin rooms, which cost the same as doubles, are roomier but on the street side (effective double-pane windows).

Hotel de Vieux Marais*** offers just-renovated and quite comfortable rooms with air-conditioning; tucked away on a quiet street near the Pompidou Center (Sb-450F, Db-575–650F, Tb-725F, CC:VM, just off rue des Archives at 8 rue du Platre, tel. 01 42 78 47 22, fax 01 42 78 34 32).

MIJE "Youth Hostels": The Maison Internationale de la Jeunesse des Étudiants (MIJE) runs three classy old residences in the Marais for travelers under age 30. Each offers simple, clean, single-sex, mostly four-bed rooms for 126F per bed, including shower and breakfast. Singles cost 200F. Rooms are locked from 12:00 to 16:00 and at 1:00. MIJE Fourcy (6 rue de Fourcy, just south of the rue Rivoli), MIJE Fauconnier (11 rue Fauconnier), and the best, MIJE Maubisson (12 rue des Barres), share one telephone number (01 42 74 23 45) and Métro stop (St. Paul).

Reservations are taken only one week ahead. MIJE Fourcy offers very cheap dinners.

Marais Helpful Hints: Place des Vosges, Paris' oldest square, the new Bastille opera house, and the Jewish Quarter (rue des Rosiers) are all nearby. The Marais' main drag, rue St. Antoine, starts at the Bastille and leads west towards the hopping Beaubourg/Les Halles area. Paris' biggest and best budget department store is BHV, next to the Hôtel de Ville. Marais post offices are on rue Castex and on the corner of rues Pavée and Francs Bourgeois. (See the Marais walk, above, for neighborhood details.) You'll find a cyber-café at Café Hamman (4 rue des Rosiers, tel. 42 78 04 45).

The nearest TIs are in the Louvre and Gare de Lyon (arrival level open 8:00–20:00, tel. 01 43 43 33 24). The Bank of France changes money, offering good rates and long lines (where rue St-Antoine hits the place de la Bastille, 9:00–11:45 and 13:30–15:30 Monday–Friday). Most banks, shops, and other services are on rue St-Antoine between Métro stops St-Paul and Bastille. You'll find one taxi stand on the north side of St-Antoine where it meets rue Castex, and another on the south side of St-Antoine in front of the St. Paul church.

Bus 69 rolls you scenically from the Marais (rue St. Antoine) to the recommended rue Cler neighborhood via the Louvre and Orsay museums.

Sleeping in the Contrescarpe Neighborhood
(5th district, Métro: Place Monge, zip code: 75005)
This lively, colorful neighborhood—just over the hill from the Latin Quarter and behind the Panthéon, is walking distance from Notre-Dame, Île de la Cité, Île St. Louis, Luxembourg Gardens, and the grand boulevards St-Germain and St-Michel. The rue Mouffetard and delightfully Parisian place Contrescarpe are the heart and soul of this area. Rue Mouffetard is a market street by day and restaurant row by night. Fewer tourists sleep here and I find the hotel values consistently better than most other neighborhoods.

Hôtel des Grandes Écoles** offers an idyllic, very peaceful oasis with three buildings protecting a flowering garden courtyard. This romantic place is deservedly popular, so call well in advance (Db-490–570F, Tb-620–670F, Qb-670–750F, 75 rue de Cardinal Lemoine, tel. 01 43 26 79 23, fax 01 43 25 28 15, mellow Marie SE).

Hôtel Central* has a charming location, a steep and slippery castlelike stairway, simple rooms (all with shower, though toilets are down the hall), so-so beds, and plenty of smiles (Ss-155–180F, Ds-220–250F, no elevator, 6 rue Descartes, tel. 01 46 33 57 93, NSE). It's nothing fancy but a good budget option.

The low-energy, bare-bones **Hôtel du Commerce** is run by Monsieur Mattuzzi, who must be a pirate gone good (S-140F, D-150F, Ds-160F, Ts-220F, Qs-270F, showers-15F, no elevator, takes no reservations, call at 10:00 and he'll say *"oui"* or *"non,"* 14 rue de La Montagne Sainte-Geneviève, Métro: Place Maubert, tel. 01 43 54 89 69, NSE). This 300-year-old place (with vinyl that looks it) is a great rock-bottom deal and as safe as any dive next to a police station can be. In the morning, the landlady will knock and chirp, *"Restez-vous?"* (Are you staying tonight?)

Hotel de l'Esperance** gives you nearly three stars for the price of two. It's quiet, fluffy, and very comfortable, with thoughtfully appointed rooms complete with canopy beds, hair dryers, and cable TV (Sb-370–400F, Db-400–450F, Tb-510F, Qb-560F, CC:VM, rue Pascal 15, Métro: Censier-Daubenton, tel. 01 47 07 10 99, fax 01 43 37 56 19, SE).

Hotel Pascal* is a good value with spotless, simple rooms, tiny bathrooms, and some particularly French (small) double beds (S-155F, Db-250F, Tb-300F, Qb-450F, 20 rue Pascal, Métro: Censier-Daubenton, tel. 01 47 07 41 92, fax 01 47 07 43 80).

The **Hotel de France****, on a busy street, has good modern rooms and hard-working, helpful owners (Sb-360F, Db-410–430F, CC:VM, 108 rue Monge, Métro: DaubentonCensier, tel. 01 47 07 19 04, fax 01 43 36 62 34). Its best and quietest rooms are *sur le cour* (on the courtyard).

Y&H Hostel offers a great location, easygoing English-speaking management, and basic but acceptable hostel-like conditions (100F-beds in rooms of four, 120F-beds in double rooms, 15F for sheets, rooms closed 11:00–17:00 though reception stays open, no reservations, 80 rue Mouffetard, tel. 01 45 35 09 53, fax 01 47 07 22 24).

Contrescarpe Helpful Hints: The nearest TI is in the Gare d'Austerlitz (Monday–Saturday 8:00–15:00, it may be closed in 1998). The post office (PTT) is between rue Mouffetard and rue Monge at 10 rue de l'Épée du Bois. Place Monge hosts a colorful outdoor market (Wednesday, Friday, and Sunday until 13:00). The street market at the bottom of rue Mouffetard (bustles daily 8:00–12:00 and 15:30–19:00, 5 blocks down past the place Contrescarpe) and the always lively place Contrescarpe hops in the afternoon and well after dark. Best midday café sitting is at the Café Le Mouffetard (corner of rue Mouffetard and rue de l'Arbalete).

The flowery Jardin des Plantes park is close by and great for afternoon walks, as are Luxembourg Gardens, which justify the 15-minute walk. The doorway at 49 rue Monge leads to a hidden Roman arena (**Arènes de Lutèce**). Today, *boules* players occupy the stage, while couples cuddle on the seats. Walk to the Panthéon, admire it from the outside, and go into the wildly beautiful St. Étienne-du-Mont church.

Eating in Paris

Paris is France's wine and cuisine melting pot. While it lacks a style of its own, it draws from the best of France. Paris could hold a gourmet's Olympics—and import nothing.

Picnic or go to bakeries for quick take-out lunches, or

stop at a café for a lunch salad or *plat du jour*, but linger longer
over dinner. You can eat very well, restaurant-style, for 100F to
140F. Ask your hotel to recommend a small nearby restaurant in the
60F to 100F range. Remember, cafés and simple small restaurants
are happy to serve a *plat du jour* (garnished plate of the day, about
60F) or a chef-like salad (35–50F) day or night. Famous places are
often overpriced, overcrowded, and overrated. Find a quiet neighborhood and wander, or follow a local recommendation. Don't
arrive before 19:00. Small local favorites get crowded after 21:00.

Cafeterias and Picnics

Many Parisian department stores have huge supermarkets hiding
in the basement and top-floor cafeterias offering not really cheap
but low-risk, low-stress, what-you-see-is-what-you-get meals. For
picnics, you'll find handy little groceries (*épiceries*) and delis (*char-
cuteries*) all over town but rarely near famous sights. Good picnic
fixings include roasted chicken, drinkable yogurt, fresh bakery
goods, melons, and exotic pâtés and cheeses. Great take-out deli-
type foods like gourmet salads and quiches abound. *Boulangeries*
make good cheap miniquiches and sandwiches. While wine is
taboo in public places in the U.S.A., it's *pas de problème* in France.
The general budget eating tips in this book's introduction will
save piles of francs in Paris.

Good Picnic Spots: The pedestrian bridge, Pont des Arts,
with unmatched views and plentiful benches, and the park under
the Eiffel Tower are my favorite dinner-picnic places. Bring your
own dinner feast and watch the riverboats or the Eiffel Tower
light up the city for you. The Palais Royal (across the street from
the Louvre) is a good spot for a peaceful and royal picnic. Also try
the little triangular Henry IV Park on the west tip of the Île de la
Cité, people-watching at the Pompidou Center, the elegant place
des Vosges (closes at dusk), the Rodin Museum gardens, and the
Luxembourg Gardens.

Restaurants

The Parisian eating scene is kept at a rolling boil. Entire books
(and lives) are dedicated to the subject. If you are traveling outside
Paris, save your splurges for the countryside, where you'll enjoy
better cooking for less money. I've listed places that conveniently
fit a busy sightseeing schedule and places near recommended
hotels. If you'd like to visit a district specifically to eat, consider
the many romantic restaurants that line the cozy Île St. Louis'
main street, and the colorful, touristic but fun string of eateries
along rue Mouffetard behind the Panthéon.

Restaurants in the Rue Cler Neighborhood

The rue Cler neighborhood isn't famous for its restaurants.
That's why I eat here. Several small family-run places serve great
dinner menus for 100F and *plats du jour* for 60 to 80F.

Café du Marche (corner rue Cler and rue Champs du Mars), with the best seats and prices on rue Cler, serves hearty salads and great 60F lunch and dinner *plats du jour*. Grab a table and shuffle yourself in with the neighborhood gang. A chalkboard listing the plates of the day—each a meal—will momentarily be hung in front of you. The less hip **Café La Roussillon** also offers a quintessential café experience: peopled and decorated *belle epoche*. Sip a 7F wine at the bar and grab a light lunch at a table (hearty 50F *plats du jour* and salads, corner of Grenelle and Cler, closes at 19:00). The tiny rue Grenelle grocery store next door is open nightly until midnight.

For a special dinner, survey the handful of fine places that line the rue de l'Exposition, between rue St. Dominique and rue de Grenelle: **Restaurant La Serre**, at #29, has ambience and food worth the splurge (*plats* 50–70F, open daily from 19:00, often a wait after 21:00, great onion soup and duck specialties, tel. 01 45 55 20 96, Marie-Alice and Philippe SE). The quieter **La Maison de Cosima** at # 20 offers a more refined, creative French cuisine (excellent 94F and 140F menu with several choices including a vegetarian option, dinners only, closed Sunday, 20 rue de l'Exposition, tel. 01 45 51 37 71, friendly Helene SE). The softly-lit tables of **Auberge du Champs de Mars** at #18 draw a romantic crowd in search of fine cuisine (100F menu, closed Sunday, tel. 01 45 51 78 08). Around the corner, just off rue de Grenelle, friendly **La Varanque** is unpretentious and is a good budget bet with 60F *plats* and a 80F menu (27 rue Augereau, tel. 01 47 05 51 22).

One block east of rue Cler, **Leo le Lion** has been run by Mimi for 18 years. A charming souvenir of old Paris, it's popular with locals (105F menu, 23 rue Duvivier, closed Sunday, tel. 01 45 51 41 77). **L'Ami de Jean** is a lively place to sample Basque cuisine (27 rue Malar, closed Sunday, tel. 01 47 05 86 89). The dressy **Thoumieux** is a bustling and very traditional *brasserie* (79 rue St. Dominique, tel. 01 47 05 49 75). The **Ambassade du Sud-Ouest**, a wine and food boutique/restaurant, specializes in French Southwest cuisine such as *daubes de canard* (46 avenue de la Bourdonnais, tel. 01 45 55 59 59).

Rue Cler gives fast-food a good name. A festival of food, the street is lined with people whose lives seem to be devoted to their specialty: stacking polished produce, rotisserie chicken, crêpes, or cheese squares. The crêpe stand next to the Café du Marche does a wonderful top-end dinner crêpe for 25F. An Asian deli, **Traiteur Asie** (across from Hôtel Leveque, another across from the Hotel de Champs de Mars), has tasty low-stress, low-price take-out treats. Its two tables offer the cheapest place to sit, eat, and enjoy the rue Cler ambiance. For quiche, cheese pie, or a pear/chocolate tart, try **Tarte Julie's** (take-out or stools, 28 rue Cler). The elegant **Flo Prestige** charcuterie (at École Militaire Metro) is open until 23:00 and offers mouthwatering meals to go. The *boulangerie* on the corner of rue de

Champs de Mars is the place for a fresh baguette, sandwich, tiny quiche, or *pain au chocolat*, but the almond croissants at the *boulangerie* on rue de Grenelle at rue Cler make my day.
The **Real McCoy** is a little shop selling American food and sandwiches (194 rue de Grenelle).

The almost no-name **Maison Altmayer** is a hole-in-the-wall place for a drink quietly festooned with reality (next to Hôtel Eiffel Rive Gauche at 6 rue du Gros Caillou, open 9:00–19:30). Cafés like this originated (and this one still functions) as a place where locals enjoyed a drink while their heating wood, coal, or gas was prepared for delivery.

Restaurants in the Marais Neighborhood

The windows of the Marais are filled with munching sophisticates. The epicenter is the tiny square where rue Caron and rue d'Ormesson intersect, midway between the St. Paul Métro stop and the place des Vosges. **Le Marais Ste. Catherine** is a good value at 5 rue Caron (100F menu, daily from 19:00, extra seating in their candlelit cellar, tel. 01 42 72 39 94). **Auberge de Jarente** (117F menu, closed Sunday and Monday, just off the square at 7 rue Jarente, tel. 01 42 77 49 35) offers a more elaborate and traditional cuisine. Across the street, **La Soupe aux Cahards** serves good *plats du jour* (70F) in a fun, relaxed atmosphere (closed Sunday and Monday).

Dinners under the candle-lit arches of the place des Vosges are *très* romantic: **Nectarine** at #16 serves fine salads, quiches, and *plats du jour* day and night, while **Ma Bourgogne** is where locals go for a splurge (at the northwest corner, daily, tel. 01 42 78 44 64). Hobos picnic on the place des Vosges itself, trying not to make the local mothers with children nervous (closes at dusk). Gourmet take-out places do a brisk business all along rue St. Antoine (**Flo Prestige**, on the tiny square where rue Tournelle and rue St. Antoine meet, is open until 23:00). Those same hobos stretch their francs at the supermarket in the basement of the Monoprix department store (closest to place des Vosges on rue St. Antoine). A few small grocery shops are open until 23:00 on the rue St. Antoine.

For a fast, cheap change of pace, eat at (or take-out from) the Chinese/Japanese **Delice House**. Two can split 200 grams of chicken curry (or whatever, 26F) and a heaping helping of rice (20F). Lots of seating, with pitchers of water at the ground-floor tables and a roomier upstairs (81 rue St. Antoine, open until 21:00).

Near the Hôtel Castex, the restaurant **La Poste** and the **Crêperie** across the street (13 rue Castex) offer inexpensive, light meals (both closed on Sunday). I like **La Bastoche's** cozy ambience and good 100F menu (7 rue St. Antoine, tel. 01 48 04 74 34). Across the street, **Le Paradis de Fruit** serves salads and organic foods to a young local crowd (on the small square at rues Tournelle and St. Antoine). The couscous restaurant next door, **La Perle** (open till wee hours), is good and very cheap. Several cafés on the Boulevard Henri IV (like **Brasserie Le Reveil** at #29, near the rue Castex), offer very reasonable and good *plats du jour* and salads.

For a worthwhile splurge, try the romantic and traditional **L'Excuse** (185F menu, 14 rue Charles V, closed Sunday, tel. 01 42 77 98 97, call ahead). Across the street, **L'Énoteca** has lively and reasonable Italian cuisine in a relaxed, open setting (across from Hôtel du 7ème Art at 20 rue St. Paul, closed Sunday, tel. 01 42 78 91 44).

For a cheap breakfast, warm a stool at the tiny *boulangerie/ pâtisserie* where the hotels buy their croissants (coffee machine, 3F; 10F baby quiches, 5F *pain au chocolat*, 1 block off place Bastille, corner of rue St. Antoine and rue de Lesdiguieres).

Restaurants in the Contrescarpe Neighborhood
The rue Mouffetard and the rue du Pot-de-Fer are lined with inexpensive, lively, and forgettable restaurants. Study the many menus, compare crowds, then dive in. A fine neighborhood restaurant with excellent value menus at 68F and 118F is the **Restaurant l'Epoque** (1 block off place Contrascarpe at 81 rue Cardinal Lemoine, tel. 01 46 34 15 84). The **Restaurant Le Vigneron** (20 rue du Pot-de-Fer) is well respected and serves traditional French cuisine, and the **Savannah Cafe**'s creative Mediterranean cuisine attracts a loyal, artsy crowd (27 rue Descartes, tel. 01 43 29 45 77). **Café Tournebride** serves delicious salads (104 rue Mouffetard).

Restaurants in the Latin Quarter
La Petite Bouclerie is a cozy place with classy family cooking (70F menu, closed Monday, 33 rue de la Harpe, center of touristy Latin Quarter, tel. 01 43 54 18 03). The popular **Restaurant Polidor** is an old turn-of-the-century-style place, with great *cuisine bourgeois*, a vigorous local crowd, and a historic toilet. Arrive at 19:00 to get a seat in the restaurant (65F *plat du jour*, 100F menus, 41 rue Monsieur le Prince, midway between Odéon and Luxembourg Métro stops, tel. 01 43 26 95 34).

Restaurants on the Île St. Louis
Cruise the island's main street for a variety of good options from simple crêperies to romantic restaurants. Don't leave the island without tasting some of the best sorbet and ice cream in Paris at any place advertising *les glaces Berthillon* (31 rue St. Louis en l'Île is the original Berthillon shop).

All listings below are on the rue St. Louis en l'Île. I like the pleasant **Relais de L'Isle** (120F menu, #37, tel. 01 46 34 72 34). My romantic splurge is **Le Tastevin** (135F and 200F menus, #46, tel. 01 43 54 17 31). **La Castafiore** at #51–53 serves fine Italian dishes in a cozy setting (100F menu, arrive by 20:00), and for crazy, touristy cellar atmosphere and hearty fun food, feast at

La Taverne du Sergeant Recruiter. The "Sergeant Recruiter" used to get young Parisians drunk and stuffed here, then sign them into the army. It's all-you-can-eat, including wine and service, for 190F (daily from 19:00, #41, tel. 01 43 54 75 42). There's a near-food-fight clone next door at **Nos Ancêtres Les Gaulois** ("Our Ancestors the Gauls," 190F, daily at 19:00, tel. 01 46 33 66 07).

Restaurants near the Pompidou Center
The **Mélodine** self-service is right at the Rambuteau Métro stop. **Dame Tartine** overlooks the *Homage to Stravinsky* fountain, serves a young clientele, and offers excellent, cheap, lively meals. The popular **Café de la Cité** fills one long line of tables with locals enjoying their 44F lunches and 65F dinner specials (22 rue Rambuteau, tel. 01 48 04 30 74).

Elegant Dining on the Seine
La Plage Parisienne is a nearly dress-up riverfront place popular with locals, serving elegant, healthy meals at good prices (Metro: Javel, Port de Javel-Haut, tel. 01 40 59 41 00).

Parisian Entertainment
A Tour of Pariscope
Newsstands sell weekly magazines listing all the events and happenings in Paris. *Pariscope* (3F) or *L'Officiel des Spectacles* (2F) are cheap and essential if you want to know what's happening. Pick one up and page through it. For a headstart, *Pariscope* has a Web site: www.pariscope.fr.

Each begins with culture news. Skip the bulky *"Theatres"* and *"Diners/Spectacles"* sections and anything listed as *"des environs"* (outside of Paris). *"Musique"* or *"Concerts Classiques"* follow, listing each day's events (program, location, time, and price). Venues with phone numbers and addresses are listed in an *"Adresses des Salles de Concerts"* sidebar. Touristic venues (such as Sainte-Chapelle and Église de la Madeleine) are often featured in display ads. Operas, Traditional Music, Ballet/Dance, and Jazz/Pop/Folk/Rock listings follow.

Half of these magazines are devoted to Cinema—a Paris forte. After the *"Films Nouveaux"* section trumpets new releases, the *"Films en Exclusivite"* pages list all the films playing in town. While a code marks films as *"Historique,"* *"Karate,"* *"Erotisme,"* and so on, the key mark for tourists is "vo," which means *version original* (American films have their English soundtracks and French subtitles). Films are listed alphabetically, with theaters and their *arrondissements* at the end of each entry. Later films are listed by neighborhood (*Salles Paris*) and by genre. To find a showing near your hotel, simply match the *arrondissement*. (But don't hesitate to hop on the Métro for the film you want.) *Salles Peripherie* is out in the suburbs Film festivals are also listed.

Pariscope has a small English "Time Out" section listing the week's events. The *"Musées"* sections (*Monuments, Jardins, Autres Curiosites, Promenades, Activites Sportives, Piscines*) give the latest hours of the sights, gardens,curiosities, boat tours, sports, swimming pools, and so on. *Clubs de Loisirs* are various athletic and social clubs. *Pour les Jeunes* is for young people (kids' films, animations/cartoons, marionettes, circuses, and amusement parks such as Asterix and Disney). *Conferences* are mostly lectures. For cancan mischief, look under *"Paris la nuit,"* cabarets, or the busty *"spectacles erotiques."*

Finally, you'll find a TV listing. Paris has four country-wide stations: TF1, France 2, France 3, and the new *Arte* station (a German/French cultural channel). M6 is filled with American series. Canal Plus (channel 4) is a cable channel that airs an American news show at 7:00 and an American sports event on Sunday evening.

Jazz Clubs

Caveau de la Huchette is the handiest characteristic old jazz club for visitors, filling an ancient Latin Quarter cellar with live jazz and frenzied dancing every night (60F weekday, 70F weekend admission, 30F drinks, open 21:30–2:30 or later, closed Monday, 5 rue de la Huchette, tel. 01 43 26 65 05). You'll also find several well-reputed clubs bordering the Forum shopping center in Les Halles area on the rue Berger.

Transportation Connections—Paris

Paris is Europe's transportation hub. You'll find trains and buses (day and night) to any French or European destination. Paris has six central stations, each serving different regions.

Gare St. Lazare: Serves Upper Normandy. To **Rouen** (15/day, 75 min), **Honfleur** (6/day, 3 hrs, via Lisieux then bus), **Bayeux** (9/day, 2.5 hrs), **Caen** (12/day, 2 hrs).

Gare Montparnasse: Serves Lower Normandy and Brittany and offers TGV service to the Loire Valley and southwestern France. To **Chartres** (10/day, 1 hr), **Mont St. Michel** (2/day, 4.5 hrs, via Rennes), **Dinan** (7/day, 3 hrs, via Rennes and Dol), **Bordeaux** (14/day, 3.5 hrs), **Toulouse** (7/day, 5 hrs, possible transfer in Bordeaux), **Albi** (6.5 hrs, via Toulouse), **Carcassonne** (6.5 hrs, via Toulouse), **Tours** (14/day, 1 hr).

Gare d'Austerlitz: Provides non-TGV service to the Loire Valley, southwestern France, Spain, and Portugal. To **Amboise** (8/day, 2.5 hrs), **Sarlat** (5/day, 5.5 hrs), **Cahors** (5/day, 7 hrs), **Barcelona** (3/day, 13 hrs), **Madrid** (5/day, 16 hrs), **Lisbon** (1/day, 24 hrs).

Gare du Nord: Serves northern France and international destinations. To **Brussels** (10/day, 3.5 hrs), **Amsterdam** (10/day, 5.5 hrs), **Copenhagen** (3/day, 16 hrs), **Koblenz** (3/day, 7 hrs), **London** via Eurostar Chunnel (5/day, 3 hrs).

Gare de l'Est: Serves eastern France and points east. To **Colmar** (6/day, 5.5 hrs, transfer in Strasbourg or Mulhouse), **Strasbourg** (10/day, 4.5 hours), **Reims** (8/day, 2 hrs), **Verdun** (5/day, 3 hrs), **Munich** (4/day, 8.5 hrs), **Vienna** (3/day, 13 hrs), **Zurich** (4/day, 6 hrs).

Gare du Lyon: Offers TGV and regular service to southeastern France, Italy, and other international destinations. To **Beaune** (8/day, 2–3 hrs), **Dijon** (13/day, 1.5 hrs), **Chamonix** (3/day, 9 hrs, transfer in Lyon and St. Gervais, one direct and very handy night train), **Annecy** (8/day, 4–7 hrs), **Lyon** (12/day, 2.5 hrs), **Avignon** (10/day, 4 hrs), **Arles** (10/day, 5 hrs), **Nice** (8/day, 7 hrs), **Venice** (5/day, 11 hrs), **Rome** (3/day, 15 hrs), **Bern** (5/day, 5 hrs).

Buses: Buses provide cheaper, if less comfortable and less flexible, transportation to major European cities. The main bus station is Gare Routière du Paris-Gallieni at Métro Gallieni, on avenue du General de Gaulle, in the suburb of Bagnolet (tel. 01 49 72 51 51). Eurolines buses depart from here.

Charles de Gaulle Airport

There are three main terminals: T-1, T-2, and T-9. Air France uses T-2, charters dominate T-9, and most airlines serving the U.S.A. use T-1. The terminals are connected every few minutes by a free shuttle bus called a *navette*.

At T-1 you'll find an American Express cash machine, an automatic bill changer (at baggage claim 30), and a bank exchange window (at baggage claim 18). The TI (open until 23:00) at the "Meeting Point" has free Paris city maps and sightseeing information. You can buy a *télécarte* (phone card) at the Relais H at the Meeting Point and pick up French currency at the bank or ATM machine near gate 16 (barely acceptable rates). Car rental offices are found on the arrival level from gates 10 to 22, and a handy SNCF (train) office is at gate 22. For flight information, call 01 48 62 22 80.

Transportation between Paris and Charles de Gaulle Airport: Three efficient public-transportation routes link the airport's T-1 terminal and central Paris. The free shuttle bus (*navette*) runs between gate 28 and the **RER Roissy Rail** station, where a train zips you into Paris' subway system in 30 minutes (45F, stops at Gare du Nord, Chatelet, St-Michel, and Luxembourg Gardens). The **Roissy Bus** runs every 15 minutes between gate 30 and the old Paris Opéra (stop is on the rue Scribe, in front of the American Express), costs 40F (use the automatic ticket machine), and takes 40 minutes but can be jammed. The **Air France Bus** leaves every 15 minutes from gate 34 and serves the Arc de Triomphe and the Porte Maillot in about 40 minutes for 55F, and the Montparnasse Tower in 60 minutes for 65F. For most people the RER Roissy Rail works best. **A taxi ride** with luggage costs about 230F; there is a taxi stand, often with long waits, at gate 16. The Disneyland express bus departs from gate 32.

The Roissy bus, Air France buses, and RER trains described above also connect T-2 and Paris with the same frequency and for the same prices as from T-1.

Transportation between Charles de Gaulle Airport and Other Destinations in France: A new TGV rail station (located at T-2, take Navette bus from T-1, gate 26) links this airport at blistering speeds with Lille to the north and Lyon, Avignon, Nîmes, Marseille, and Montpellier to the south, without passing through Paris. You can transfer easily from these cities to many other French and European destinations.

Sleeping at or near Charles de Gaulle Airport: Those with early flights may want to sleep in T-1 at **Cocoon** (60 "cabins," Sb-250F, Db-300F, CC:VM, tel. 01 48 62 06 16, fax 01 48 62 56 97). Take the elevator down to "boutique level" or walk down from the departure level; it's near the Burger King. You get 16 hours of silence buried under the check-in level with TV and toilet. The **Hôtel IBIS** (at the Roissy Rail station; free shuttle bus to either terminal takes two minutes) offers more normal accommodations (Db-400F, CC:VMA, tel. 01 49 19 19 19, fax 01 49 19 19 21).

Drivers who want to stay near the airport should consider the pleasant city of Senlis, a 15-minute drive. **Hostellerie de la Porte Bellon** is comfortable (Sb-215F, Db-365–420F, CC:VM, 51 rue Bellon, tel. 03 44 53 03 05, fax 03 44 53 29 94).

Orly Airport

This airport feels small. Orly has only two terminals: Sud and Ouest. Most flights arrive at Sud (where this book assumes you will arrive). After customs and baggage claim (near gate H) you'll see ADP, a quasi–tourist office that offers free city maps and information. Near ADP is a CFF exchange desk (decent rates), a Métro info/ticket desk, and a SNCF French rail desk (sells train tickets and even Eurailpasses). Downstairs, you'll find a sandwich bar, bank (lousy rates), newsstand (buy *télécarte* phone card), and post office (great rates for cash or American Express traveler's checks). For flight info, call 01 49 75 15 15.

Transportation between Paris and Orly Airport: The Air France Bus, which runs between gate F and Paris' Invalides Métro stop (40F, 4 hour 30 min), is best for those staying in the rue Cler neighborhood. For the Marais area and other destinations, take the **Jetbus** (22F, bus #285, every 15 min) from near gate F to the Villejuif Métro stop, buy a *carnet* of Métro tickets, and take the Métro. Get off at Sully Morland for the Marais area. For the RER (line C-2) into Paris, take the shuttle bus from gate H to the Rungis—Aéroport d'Orly stop. Shuttle buses and trains run every 15 minutes (35F) to several central Paris Metro stations from which you can connect to the Paris Métro. Allow 150F for a taxi into central Paris.

Sleeping near Orly Airport: The only reasonable hotel is the **IBIS** (Db-400F, CC:VMA, tel. 01 46 87 33 50, fax 01 46 87 29 92), with free shuttle service to the terminal. Chartres and Versailles are convenient to Orly by car—beware of rush hour on the freeways. Check hotels under Versailles, above.

PROVENCE

This magnificent region is shaped like a wedge of quiche. From its sunburnt crust fanning out along the Mediterranean coast from Nîmes to Nice, it stretches north along the Rhône Valley to Orange. The Romans were here in force and left many ruins—some of the best anywhere. Seven popes, great artists like van Gogh, Cézanne, and Picasso, and author Peter Mayle all enjoyed their years in Provence. Provence offers a splendid recipe of arid climate (but brutal winds known as the mistral), captivating cities, exciting hill towns, and remarkably varied landscapes.

Wander through the ghost town of ancient Les Baux and under France's greatest Roman ruin, the Pont du Gard. Spend your starry, starry nights where van Gogh did, in Arles. Explore its Roman past, then find the linger-longer squares and café corners that inspired Vincent. Some may prefer Avignon's more elegant feel and softer edge as a home base. Youthful but classy Avignon bustles in the shadow of its brooding popes' palace.

Planning Your Time

Make Arles or Avignon your base (Italophiles prefer Arles, while poodles pick Avignon). Avignon (well-connected to Arles by train) is the regional transportation hub for destinations north of Arles (Pont du Gard, Uzès, and Orange). You'll want a full day for sightseeing in Arles (ideally on a Wednesday or Saturday, when the morning market rages), a half day for Avignon, and a day or two for the villages and sights in the countryside.

Getting Around Provence

The yellow Michelin map to this region is essential for drivers. Public transit is fairly good: Frequent trains link Avignon, Arles,

Provence

and Nîmes; Les Baux is accessible by bus from Arles; and the Pont du Gard and Uzès are accessible by bus from Avignon.

ARLES

By helping Julius Caesar defeat Marseille, Arles earned the imperial nod and was made an important port city. With the first bridge over the Rhône, Arles was a key stop on the Roman road from Italy to Spain, the Via Domitia. After reigning as a political center of the early Christian church (the seat of an archbishop for centuries) and thriving as a trading city on and off until the 18th century, Arles all but disappeared from the map. Van Gogh settled here a hundred years ago but left only memories. American bombers destroyed much of Arles in WWII, but today Arles thrives again. This compact city is alive with great Roman ruins, some fine early Christian art, an eclectic assortment of museums, made-for-ice-cream pedestrian zones, squares that play hide-and-seek with visitors, and too many cars. Arles is a fine springboard for Provence explorations.

Tourist Information: Arles has two TIs. The one at the train station is relaxed and easy by car (open 9:00–13:00 and 14:00–18:00, Sunday 10:00–14:00; closed Sunday off-season). The main TI on esplanade Charles de Gaulle is a high-powered mega-information site (open 9:00–19:00, Sunday 9:00–13:00, off-season closing at 18:00, tel. 04 90 18 41 20). Pick up the free and handy *Guide Touristique 1998* and ask about bullfights.

Laundry: You'll find two Laundromats near the place Voltaire—one at 12 rue Portagnel (closed 12:00–14:00). Another, on 6 rue Cavalarie near place Voltaire, has a confusing central command panel: 20F for wash—push machine number on top row; 10F for 25 minutes of dryer—push dryer number on third row five times slowly; 2F for flakes—button #11 (daily 7:00–21:00, later once you're in; recommended Saveurs Provençales restaurant is 1 block away for dining while you clean).

Supermarket: Place Lamartine has a big, handy Monoprix supermarket/department store (8:30–19:25, closed Sunday).

Banks: Several banks change money on the place de la République, across from the St. Trophime church.

Arrival in Arles

By Train and Bus: Both stations sit side by side on the river, a ten-minute walk from the city center. To reach the old town, walk to the river and turn left.

By Car: Follow signs to *centre-ville*, then be on the lookout for signs to the *gare* SNCF (the train station; go there for the TI). You'll come to a huge roundabout (place Lamartine), with a Monoprix store to the right. There is parking on the left along the base of the wall. Pay attention to no-parking signs on Wednesday and Saturday until 13:00—they mean it. Theft is a problem; park at your hotel if possible. Take everything out of your car for safety. From place Lamartine, walk into the city through the two stumpy towers.

Getting Around Arles

Arles faces the Mediterranean more than Paris. Its spaghetti streetplan disorients the first-time visitor. Landmarks hide in the medieval tangle of narrow, winding streets. Everything is deceptively close. While Arles sits on the Rhône, it completely ignores the river. The elevated riverside walk does provide a direct—if lonesome—return to the station. Hotels have free city maps, but Arles works best if you simply follow the numerous street-corner signs pointing you toward the sights and hotels of the town center. Racing cars seem to enjoy Arles' medieval lanes, turning sidewalks into tightropes and pedestrians into leaping targets.

By Minibus: The free "Starlette" shuttle minibus, which circles the town's major sights twice an hour, is worthwhile only to get to or from the distant ancient history museum (just wave at the driver and hop in, 7:30–19:30, never on Sunday).

By Bike and Car: The Peugeot store rents bikes (15 rue du Pont, tel. 04 90 96 03 77) as does the newsstand next to the main

TI. You can rent cars at Avis (at the train station, tel. 04 90 96 82 42) and Europcar (downtown at 15 boulevard Victor Hugo, tel. 04 90 93 23 24).

By Taxi: Arles' taxis charge a minimum flat fee of 50F. Nothing in town is worth a taxi ride (figure 100F to Les Baux).

Sights—Arles

Arles' *global billet* covers all the sights (55F, sold at each sight). Otherwise, it's 15F per sight and museum (35F for the ancient history museum). While any sight is worth a few minutes of your time, many aren't worth the individual admission. For the small price of a *global billet*, the city is yours. All sights are open June 1 through September 15, 9:00 to 19:00; April, May, and September 16 to 30, 9:00 to 12:30 and 14:00 to 19:00; otherwise, 10:00 to 12:30 and 14:00 to 17:30; sights close one hour earlier in winter.

▲▲**Place du Forum**—This café-crammed square, while always lively, is best at night. Named for the Roman Forum that stood here, only two columns from a second-century temple survive. They are incorporated into the wall of the Hotel Nord Pinus. (After a few drinks at the Café van Gogh, the corner of that hotel actually starts to look phallic.) Van Gogh hung out here under these same plane trees. In fact, his *Starry Starry Night* was painted from this square. The bistros on the square, while no place for a fine dinner, put together a good salad, and when you sprinkle in the ambience that's 45F well spent. The guy on the pedestal is Frederic Mistral who, in 1904, received the Nobel Prize for literature. He used his prize money to preserve and display the folk identity of Provence at a time when France was rapidly centralizing. (He founded the Arlaten museum—see below.)

▲▲**Wednesday and Saturday Market**—On these days until around noon, Arles' ring road (boulevard Emile Combes on Wednesday, boulevard Lices on Saturday) erupts into an outdoor market of fish, flowers, produce, and you-name-it. Join in, buy flowers, try the olives, sample some wine, and slap a pickpocket. On the first Wednesday of the month it's a grand flea market.

▲▲▲**Ancient History Museum (Musée de L'Arles Antique)**— The sights of Roman Arles make maximum sense if you start your visit in this well-organized museum. Models and original sculpture (with the help of the free English handout) re-create the Roman city of Arles, making workaday life and culture easier to imagine. Models of Arles' arena even illustrate the moveable stadium cover, good for shade and rain. While virtually nothing is left of Arles' chariot racecourse, the model shows how it must have rivaled Rome's Circus Maximus. Jewelry, fine metal and glass artifacts, and fine mosaic floors make it clear—Roman Arles was a city of art and culture. The finale is an impressive row of pagan and early Christian sarcophagi (second to fifth centuries). In the early days of the

Arles

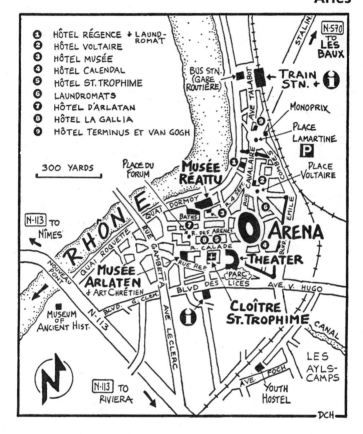

- **①** HÔTEL RÉGENCE ↓ LAUNDROMAT
- **②** HÔTEL VOLTAIRE
- **③** HÔTEL MUSÉE
- **④** HÔTEL CALENDAL
- **⑤** HÔTEL ST. TROPHIME
- **⑥** LAUNDROMATS
- **⑦** HÔTEL D'ARLATAN
- **⑧** HÔTEL LA GALLIA
- **⑨** HÔTEL TERMINUS ET VAN GOGH

Church, Jesus was often portrayed beardless and as the good shepherd—with a lamb over his shoulder.

Built at the site of the chariot racecourse, this museum is a 15-minute walk from Arles along the river. Turn left at the river and follow it to the big, modern building past the new bridge—or ride the free Starlette shuttle bus. (35F, April–September 9:00–19:00, 10:00–18:00 off-season, tel. 04 90 18 88 88.)

▲▲**Roman Arena (Amphithéàtre)**—Nearly 2,000 years ago, gladiators fought wild animals here to the delight of 20,000 screaming fans—cruel. Today matadors fight wild bulls to the delight of local fans—still cruel. While the ancient third row of arches is long gone, three towers survive from medieval times when the arena was used as a fortress. In the 1800s it corralled 200 humble homes and functioned as a town within the town. Today modern gladiators fight bulls, and if you don't mind the gore, it's an exciting show. Climb the tower. Walk through the inner corridors of this 440- by 350-foot oval and notice the similarity to 20th-century stadium floor plans.

▲▲Bullfights (Courses Camarguaise)—Occupy the same seats fans have been sitting in for 1,900 years and take in one of Arles' most memorable treats—a bullfight *à la* Provençale. Three classes of bullfights take place here. The *course protection* is for aspiring matadors; it's a daring dodge-bull game of scraping hair off the angry bull's nose for prize money offered by local businesses (no blood). The *trophée de l'avenir* is the next class, with amateur matadors. The *trophée des as excellence* is the real thing *à la* Spain: outfits, swords, spikes, and the whole gory shebang. (In Arles, Saturday, Sunday, and holidays from April–early October. Skip their "rodeo" spectacle. Tickets 30–50F, tel. 04 90 96 03 70 or TI.) There are nearby village bullfights in small wooden bullrings nearly every weekend (TI has schedule).

Classical Theater (Théâtre Antique)—Precious little survives from this Roman theater, which served as a handy town quarry throughout the Middle Ages. Two lonely Corinthian columns look from the stage out over the audience. The 10,000 mostly modern seats are still used for local concerts and festivals. Take a stroll backstage through broken bits of Rome. Sit in a seat and contemplate a society that enjoyed Greek dramas one night and gladiator battles the next.

▲▲St. Trophime Cloisters and Church—This church, named after a third-century bishop of Arles, sports the finest Romanesque west portal (main doorway) I've seen anywhere.

But first enjoy the place de la République. Sit on the steps opposite the church. The Egyptian obelisk used to be the centerpiece of Arles' Roman Circus. Watch the peasants—pilgrims, locals, buskers—nothing new about this scene. Like a Roman triumphal arch, the church trumpets the promise of Judgment Day. The tympanum is filled with Christian symbolism. Christ sits in majesty surrounded by symbols of the four evangelists (Matthew—the winged man, Mark—the winged lion, Luke—the ox, and John—the eagle). The 12 apostles are lined up below Jesus. Move up closer. This is it. Some are saved and others aren't. Notice the condemned—a chain gang on the right bunny-hopping over the fires of hell. For them the tune trumpeted by the three angels on the very top isn't a happy one. Ride the exquisite detail back to a simpler age. In an illiterate medieval world long before the vivid images of our technicolor age, this message was a neon billboard over this town's everything square. A chart just inside the church helps explain the carvings. On the right side of the nave, a fourth-century early Christian sarcophagus is used as an altar.

The adjacent cloisters are the best in Provence (15F, enter from the square 20 meters to the right of the church). Enjoy the sculpted capitals of the rounded 12th-century Romanesque columns and the pointed 14th-century Gothic columns. The second floor offers only a view of the cloisters from above.

Musée Réattu—Highlights of this museum are a fun collection of 70 Picasso drawings (some two-sided, and all done in a flurry of creativity) andHenri Rousseau's Camargue watercolors.

▲**Musée Arlaten**—This cluttered folklore museum, given to Arles by Monsieur Mistral, is filled with interesting odds and ends of Provence life. The employees wear the native costumes. Like a failed turn-of-the-century garage sale, you'll find shoes, hats, wigs, old photos, bread cupboards, and the beetle-dragon monster. If you're into folklore, this museum is for you.

Sleeping in Arles
(5.5F = about $1, zip code: 13200)
Sleep Code: **S**=Single, **D**=Double/Twin, **T**=Triple, **Q**=Quad, **b**=bathroom, **t**=toilet only, **s**=shower only, **CC**=Credit Card (Visa, MasterCard, Amex), **SE**=Speaks English, **NSE**=No English, ***** =French hotel rating system (0–4 stars).

Hôtel Régence** has an unappealing exterior but is immaculate and comfortable within, with good beds, easy train station access, and safe parking. Helpful and gentle Sylvie speaks English (one Ds-150–180F, Db-200–280F, Tb-250–335F, Qb-330F, choose river view or quiet courtyard rooms, CC:VM, 5 rue Marius Jouveau, from place Lamartine turn right immediately after passing through the towers, tel. 04 90 96 39 85, fax 04 90 96 67 64).

Hôtel du Musée** is a quiet, delightful manor house hide-away with spacious rooms and a terrific courtyard terrace. Its friendly owners, M. and Mme. Dubreuil, speak some English (Sb-185F, Db-225–310F, Tb-340–400F, Qb-430F, parking-40F, mostly air-conditioned rooms, CC:VMA, 11 rue de la Grande Prieure, follow signs to Musée Réattu, tel. 04 90 93 88 88, fax 04 90 49 98 15).

Hôtel Calendal** is *trés* Provençal, with a peaceful outdoor garden, thoughtfully decorated rooms, and three-star ambience for the price of two (Db-250–380F, Tb-350–450F, Qb-420F, garage-50F, air-conditioned rooms with strong beds and modern bathrooms, CC:VMA, located above the arena at 22 place Pomme, tel. 04 90 96 11 89, fax 04 90 96 05 84, Cecile and Catherine SE).

Hôtel d'Arlatan***, one of France's more affordable classy hotels, comes with a beautiful lobby, courtyard terrace, and air-conditioned, antiques-filled rooms. In the lobby of this 15th-century building, a glass floor looks down into Roman ruins (Db-460–720F, Db/suites-820–1,400F, garage-60F, elevator, very central, CC:VMA, 1 block off the place du Forum at 26 rue du Sauvage, tel. 04 90 93 56 66, fax 04 90 49 68 45, SE).

Hotel Terminus et Van Gogh*, 1 block from the train station facing a busy square at the gate of the old town, has spacious, bright rooms. Joelle proudly posts photos and pictures showing that her building is in the painting of van Gogh's house, which was bombed in WWII (D-145 with no shower available, Ds-180F, Db-200F, CC:VM, 5 place Lamartine, tel. & fax 04 90 96 12 32, SE).

Hotel St. Trophime** is very central with a grand entry, spacious rooms, and helpful owners (Sb-210F, Db-290–320F, CC:VM, 16 rue de la Calade, near the place de la Republique, tel. 04 90 96 88 38, fax 04 90 96 92 19).

Starving artists can afford these three clean but spartan places. **Hôtel Voltaire*** rents 12 dumpy rooms with great balconies overlooking a caffeine-stained square a block below the arena (D-120–130F, Ds-140F, add 40F per person for three or four, CC:VM, 1 place Voltaire, tel. 04 90 96 13 58). **Hotel Lamartine*** is a pay-in-advance kind of place featuring industrial simplicity. It's well-located and handier than a youth hostel (D-130F, Ds-170F, Db-200F, Ts-220F, beds of variable quality—worth checking, just inside the place Lamartine gate at 2 rue Cavalerie, tel. 04 90 96 13 83, fax 04 90 96 08 84). **Hôtel La Gallia** is another sleepable cheapie (D-125F, Dt-145F, above a friendly café, 22 rue de l'Hôtel de Ville, tel. 04 90 96 00 63).

Eating in Arles

The restaurants and cafés, such as **Le Bistro Arlesien** and **Le Pub** (good 45F *salade niçoise*) and **L'Estaminet**, on place du Forum, serve basic food with great atmosphere. The well-respected **l'Olivier** offers fine provençale cuisine (145F menu, near the Hotel du Musée, 1 bis rue Reattu, tel. 04 90 49 64 88). **Les Saveurs Provençales** serves regional specialties (115F menu, closed Monday, 1 block below the arena at 65 rue Amédée Pichot, tel. 04 90 96 13 32). To dine under Gothic arches at bargain prices, try **Le Medieval** (78F menu, 9 rue Truchet, 1 block toward the river from the place du Forum). **La Vitamine** offers great salads and pastas (closed weekends, just below place du Forum on 16 rue Dr. Fanton, tel. 04 90 93 77 36). **Le Constantin** is almost elegant, quite friendly, and cheap (70F menu, near the recommended hotels du Musée and d'Arlatan on place du Sauvage, tel. 04 90 93 48 64). The riverfront walk is a good spot for a picnic dinner.

Transportation Connections—Arles

By bus to: Les Baux (4/day, 30 min; departs Arles' bus station and #16 boulevard Clemenceau in downtown Arles, tel. 04 90 49 38 01). Service is reduced November through March and on Sunday and holidays.

By train to: Paris (2 direct TGV, 4.5 hrs; otherwise, transfer in Avignon, 8/day, 5.5 hrs), **Avignon** (8/day, 20 min, check for afternoon gaps), **Carcassonne** (8/day, 3 hrs, usually with painless transfer in Narbonne), **Beaune** (3/day, 5 hrs, transfer in Lyon), **Nice** (8/day, 3 hrs, likely transfer in Marseille), **Barcelona** (3/day,

7 hrs, at least one transfer), **Italy** (3/day, via Marseille and Nice; from Arles, it's 5 hrs to Ventimiglia on the border, 9 hrs to the Cinque Terre, 9 hrs to Milan, 11 hrs to Florence, 13 hrs to Venice or Rome). Train information tel. 04 90 96 43 94.

AVIGNON

Famous for its nursery rhyme, medieval bridge, and brooding Palace of the Popes, contemporary Avignon bustles and prospers behind its walls. During the 68 years (1309–1377) that Avignon played Franco Vaticano, it grew from an irrelevant speck on the map to the thriving city it is today. This city combines a young, hip student population with a white-collar, sophisticated city feel. Street mimes play to crowds enjoying Avignon's slick cafés and chic boutiques. If you're here in July, save evening time for Avignon's rollicking theater festival and reserve your hotel early. The streets throng with jugglers, skits, and singing, as visitors from around the world converge on Avignon.

The cours Jean Jaurés (which turns into the rue de la République) leads from the train station to place de l'Horloge and the Palace of the Popes, forming Avignon's spine. Climb to the parc de Rochers des Doms for a fine view, enjoy the people scene on place de l'Horloge, and meander the back streets. Avignon's shopping district fills the pedestrian streets where the rue de la République meets the place de l'Horloge. Walk across the Pont Daladier for a great view back on Avignon and the Rhône River.

Tourist Information: The main TI is between the train station and the old town at 41 cours Jean Juarés (open Monday–Friday 9:00–18:00, Saturday 9:00–12:00 and 14:00–17:00, tel. 04 90 82 65 11), while a smaller branch is on the Rhône River at the Pont St. Bénezet. They have regional bus and train schedules and information on Isle sur la Sorgue and the wine villages north of Avignon and the Luberon.

Arrival in Avignon

By Train: In front of the bus or train station, the cours Jean Juarés—that becomes rue de la République—leads into the old city center (20-minute walk, TI on right in a few blocks).

By Car: Drivers enter Avignon following *centre-ville* signs. Park along the wall close to the Pont St. Bénezet (ruined old bridge) and use that TI. Hotels have advice for smart overnight parking.

Sights—Avignon

▲**Palace of the Popes (Palais des Papes)**—In 1309, a French pope was elected (Pope Clement V). At the urging of the French king, His Holiness decided he'd had enough of unholy Italy. So he loaded up his carts and moved out of the chaos north to Avignon for a steady rule under a friendly, supportive king. The Catholic

Church literally bought Avignon, then a two-bit town, and popes resided here until 1403. From 1378 on, there were twin popes, one in Rome and one in Avignon, causing a split in the Catholic Church that wasn't fully resolved until 1417.

The pope's palace is two distinct buildings, one old and one older. Along with lots of big, barren rooms, you'll see brilliant frescoes, enormous tapestries, and remarkable floor tiles. While scheduling your day around the English tour times can be a hassle, guided tours can be worthwhile. (35F, 8F more for the guided tour, occasional supplements for special exhibits, open April–November 1, daily 9:00–19:00, until 20:00 in summer, 9:00–12:45 and 14:00–18:00 in off-season, ticket office closes one hour earlier, tours in English twice daily March–October, tel. 04 90 27 50 74 to confirm.)

▲**Musée du Petit Palais**—This palace superbly displays collections of 14th- and 15th-century Italian painting and sculpture. Since the Catholic Church was the patron of the arts in those days, all 350 paintings deal with Christian themes. Visiting this museum before going to the Palace of the Popes gives you a sense of art and life during the Avignon papacy. Notice the improvement in perspective in the later paintings (20F, open 9:30–12:00 and 14:00–18:00, closed Tuesday).

▲**Parc de Rochers des Doms and Pont St. Bénezet**—Hike above the Pope's Palace for a panoramic view over Avignon and the Rhône valley. At the far end drop down a few steps for a good view of the Pont St. Bénezet. This is the famous "sur le Pont d'Avignon," whose construction and location were inspired by a shepherd's religious vision. Imagine a 22-arch, 3,000-foot-long bridge extending across two rivers to that lonely Tower of Philippe the Fair (the bridge's former tollgate on the distant side). The island the bridge spanned is now filled with campgrounds. You can pay 10F to walk along a section of the ramparts and do your own jig on the bridge, but it's best appreciated from where you are. The castle on the right, the St. André Fortress, was once another island in the Rhône. Cross Daladier Bridge for the best view of the old bridge and Avignon's skyline.

Sleeping in Avignon
(5.5F = about $1, zip code: 84000)
The cozy, pleasant **Hôtel Blauvac**** is in the pedestrian zone 1 block off the rue de la République on 11 rue de La Bancasse (Db-310–410F, Tb-390–475F, Qb-500F, CC:VMA, tel. 04 90 86 34 11, fax 04 90 86 27 41). Right on the rue de la République at #17, the bright and cheery **Hotel Danelli**** offers modern and comfortable rooms in shiny surroundings (Db-400F, Tb-450F, CC:VM, tel. 04 90 86 46 82, fax 04 90 27 09 24). The clean, compact, and friendly **Hôtel Mignon*** is simpler, but a good value (Sb-150F, Db-185–250F, 12 rue Joseph Vernet, tel. 04 90 82 17 30, fax 04 90 85 78

46). **Hôtel Splendid*** rents firm beds in pleasant rooms near the station, on the small park near the TI (Ss-140–170F, Ds-170–220F, 17 rue Agricol Perdiguier, tel. 04 90 86 14 46). Across the street at #17, **Hotel du Parc*** is another good value (Ds-140–170F, Db-180F, tel. 04 90 82 71 55, fax 04 90 85 64 86).

Transportation Connections—Avignon

By train to: Arles (8/day, 20 min), **Orange** (hrly, 15 min), **Nîmes** (hrly, 21 min), **Nice** (10/day, 4 hrs, a few direct, but most require transfer in Marseille), **Carcassonne** (10/day, 3 hrs, possible transfer in Narbonne), **Paris'** Gare de Lyon (10 TGVs/day, 4 hrs), **Barcelona** (2/day, 5 hrs, possible transfer in Narbonne; direct night train is convenient).

Bus service to Pont du Gard and **Uzès** (3/day, 1 hr) can leave you stranded for hours. Consider visiting the Pont du Gard, then continuing on to Uzès or Nîmes (both merit exploration) and returning to Avignon from there (trains run hourly from Nîmes to Avignon). Make sure you're waiting for the bus on the right side of the road at the Pont du Gard (ask at the small inn: "Nîmes? Uzès? Avignon? *Par ici?*"). The Avignon TI has all schedules. Note reduced or no service on Sunday and holidays. The bus station (tel. 04 90 82 07 35) is adjacent to the train station.

Sights—Provence

▲▲▲**Les Baux**—This rock-top ghost town is worth visiting for the lunar landscape alone. Arrive by 9:00 or after 17:00 to avoid the crowds. A 12th-century regional powerhouse with 6,000 fierce residents, Les Baux was razed in 1632 by a paranoid Louis XIII, afraid of these trouble-making upstarts. What remains are a reconstructed "live city" of tourist shops and snack stands, and the "dead city" ruins carved into, out of, and on top of a 600-foot-high rock. Spend most of your time in the dead city—it's most dramatic and enjoyable in the morning or early evening light. Don't miss the slide show on van Gogh, Gauguin, and Cézanne in the small chapel near the entry. Spend some time in the small museum as you enter (good exhibits) and pick up the English explanations before exploring the dead city. In the tourist-trampled live city you'll find artsy shops, several interesting Renaissance homes, and a fine exhibit of paintings by Yves Brayer (20F), who spent his final years here. The dead city is open Easter through October, 9:00 to dusk, otherwise 19:00 to 20:00 and 9:30 to 17:30 (35F, tickets include entry to all the town's sights, TI tel. 04 90 54 34 39).

If tempted to sleep and eat here, try the **Hotel Reine Jeanne****, 50 yards on your right after the main entry (Db-270–330F, menus from 110F, CC:VM, 13520 Les Baux, tel. 04 90 54 32 06, fax 04 90 54 32 33). Four daily buses serve Les Baux from Arles' train station, and two daily buses (summers only) leave from Avignon. Les Baux is 15 kilometers northeast of Arles, just past Fontvielle.

St. Rémy—This *trés* Provençale town with a pleasant center is a scenic ride just over the hill from Les Baux. Here you'll find the crumbled ruins of **Glanum**, a once-thriving Roman city located at the crossroads of two ancient trade routes between Italy and Spain, and the mental ward where Vincent van Gogh was sent after cutting off his ear. Glanum is just outside St. Rémy, on the road to Les Baux (D-5). Walk to the gate and peek in to get a feel for its scale. The ruins are worth the effort if you have the time and haven't been to Pompeii or Ephesus (32F, open April–September, daily 9:00–12:00 and 14:00–19:00, otherwise, 9:30–12:00 and 14:00–17:00). Across the street and opposite the entry is a free Roman arch and tower. The arch marked the entry into Glanum. The tower is a memorial to the grandsons of Emperor Augustus, located there as a reminder to folks entering or leaving Glanum.

Across the street from Glanum is the still-functioning mental hospital that housed van Gogh, Clinique St. Paul. Wander into the small chapel and peaceful cloisters. Vincent's favorite walks outside the hospital are clearly signposted. If St. Rémy charms you into a longer visit, sleep at **Canto Cigalo** (Db-300–340F, chemin Canto Cigalo, tel. 04 90 92 14 28, fax 04 90 92 24 48). Wednesday is market day in St. Rémy.

▲▲▲**Pont du Gard**—One of Europe's great treats, this remarkably well-preserved Roman aqueduct was built before the time of Christ. It was the missing link of a 35-mile canal that, by dropping 1 foot for every 300, supplied 44 million gallons of water to Nîmes daily. While the top is now closed to daredevils, just walking under it is a marvel. Study it up close—no mortar, just expertly cut stones. Signs direct you to "panoramas" above the bridge on either side. The best view of the aqueduct is from the cool of the river below, floating flat on your back—bring a swimsuit. Buses run from Nîmes, Uzès, or Avignon. Combine Uzès and the Pont du Gard for an ideal day excursion from Avignon. By car, the Pont du Gard is an easy 30-minute drive due west of Avignon (follow Nîmes) and 45 minutes northwest of Arles (via Tarascon). Park on the *rive droite* side (you'll see signs).

Uzès—A pleasant, less-trampled town near the Pont du Gard, Uzès is best seen slowly on foot, with a long coffee break in its mellow main square, the place aux Herbes (not so mellow during the colorful Sunday morning market). Check out the Tour Fenestrelle and the Duché de Uzès. Uzès is a short hop west of the Pont du Gard and is well-served by bus from Nîmes (9/day) and Avignon (3/day).

The Camargue—This is one of the few truly "wild areas" of France, where pink flamingos, wild bulls, and the famous white horses wander freely amid rice fields and lagoons. Even so, skip it.

The Camargue's biggest town is Aigue Mortes. That means "dead town," and it should stay that way.

▲▲Orange—This most northern town in Provence is notable for its Roman arch and theater. Its 60-foot-tall Roman Arch (from 25 B.C.) shows off Julius Caesar's defeat of the Gauls in 49 B.C. Its Roman theater, the best-preserved in existence, still seats 10,000. Of particular interest is its 120-foot-high stage wall, the likes of which you'll see nowhere else (30F, open April–early October, daily 9:00–18:30, winter 9:00–12:00, 13:30–17:00, ticket includes entrance to the city museum across the street with more Roman art, orange TI tel. 04 90 34 70 88). Trains run hourly between Avignon and Orange (15 min ride, bus #2 takes you the mile from the Orange station to the old town center). From Orange, drivers can tour the adjacent wine region, described below.

Loop Trip for Wine Lovers—If you have a car (or a bike, best rented in Vaison la Romaine—ideal riding from here) and a fondness for fine wine, take a loop trip of Provence's wine country. From Avignon, head to Carpentras (a great city itself), then connect the Côte du Rhône wine villages of Vaqueryas, Gigondas, Rasteau, Sablet, and adorable, if over-restored, Seguret (100-km round-trip from Avignon). This is a hospitable and relaxed wine-tasting region, with generous samples and little pressure to buy. Near Rasteau village, at Le Domaine des Girasols, friendly Francoise will take your palate on a tour of some of the area's best wine. It's well-marked and worth a stop, and while you aren't pressured to buy, their wine is a good value. Ideally, have lunch in Gigondas at the remarkable outdoor restaurant on the small town square and consider sleeping and eating at the very comfortable **Hostellerie les Florets***** (Db-400F, exquisite 200F menu, 84190 Gigondas, tel. 04 90 65 85 01, fax 04 90 65 83 80). The nearby wine village of Sablet, which makes a good base for budget travelers, is chock-full of *Chambres d'Hôte*. Try **Madame Fert's Chambres** (Db-300F, breakfast included, follow the signs, tel. 04 90 46 94 77).

THE RHINE AND MOSEL VALLEYS

These valleys are storybook Germany, a fairy-tale world of Rhine legends and robber-baron castles. Cruise the most castle-studded stretch of the romantic Rhine as you listen for the song of the treacherous Loreley. For hands-on castle thrills, climb through the Rhineland's greatest castle, Rheinfels, above the town of St. Goar. Then, for a sleepy and laid-back alternative, mosey through the neighboring Mosel Valley. On the Rhine, stay in St. Goar or Bacharach. On the Mosel, choose Zell.

Planning Your Time

The Rhineland does not take much time. The blitziest tour is one hour on the train. For a better look, cruise in, tour a castle, sleep in a medieval town, and train out. With limited time, cruise less and be sure to get into a castle. Ideally, spend two nights here, sleep in Bacharach, cruise the best hour of the river (from Bacharach to St. Goar), and tour the Rheinfels Castle. Those with more time could bike the riverside bike path. With two days, split your time between the Rhine and Mosel, seeing Burg Eltz and Cochem.

THE RHINE

Ever since Roman times, when this was the Empire's northern boundary, the Rhine has been one of the world's busiest shipping rivers. You'll see a steady flow of barges with 1,000- to 2,000-ton loads. Tourist-packed buses, hot train tracks, and highways line both banks.

Many of the castles were "robber baron" castles, put there by petty rulers (there were 300 independent little countries in medieval Germany) to levy tolls on passing river traffic. A robber baron would put his castle on, or even in, the river. Then, often with the help of chains and a tower on the opposite bank, he'd stop each ship and get his toll. There were ten customs stops between Mainz and Koblenz alone (no wonder merchants were early proponents of the creation of larger nation-states).

Rhine and Mosel Valleys

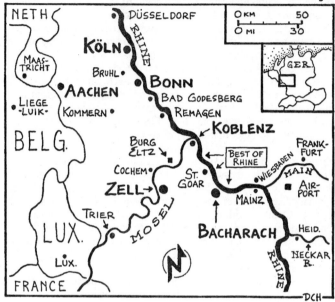

Some castles were built to control and protect settlements, and others were the residences of kings. As times changed, so did the lifestyles of the rich and feudal. Many castles were abandoned for more comfortable mansions in the towns.

Most of the Rhine castles date from the 11th, 12th, and 13th centuries. When the pope successfully asserted his power over the German emperor in 1076, local princes ran wild over the rule of their emperor. The castles saw military action in the 1300s and 1400s, as emperors began reasserting their control over Germany's many silly kingdoms.

The castles were also involved in the Reformation wars in which Europe's Catholic and "protesting" dynasties fought it out using a fragmented Germany as their battleground. The Thirty Years' War (1618–1648) devastated Germany. The outcome: Each ruler got the freedom to decide if his people would be Catholic or Protestant, and one-third of Germany was dead. Production of Gummi Bears ceased entirely.

The French destroyed most of the castles prophylactically (Louis XIV in the 1680s, the revolutionary army in the 1790s, and Napoleon in 1806). They were often rebuilt in neo-Gothic style in the Romantic Age—the late 1800s—and today are enjoyed as restaurants, hotels, hostels, and museums. Check out the Rhine Web site at www.loreleytal.com.

Getting Around the Rhine

While the Rhine flows from Switzerland to Holland, the stretch
from Mainz to Koblenz hoards all the touristic charm. Studded
with the crenelated cream of Germany's castles, it bustles with
boats, trains, and highway traffic. Have fun exploring with a mix of
big steamers, tiny ferries, bikes, and trains.

By Boat: While many travelers do the whole trip by boat, the
most scenic hour is from St. Goar to Bacharach. Sit on the top deck
with your handy Rhine map-guide (or the kilometer-keyed tour in
this chapter) and enjoy the parade of castles, towns, boats, and vineyards. Rhine boats cruise only from Easter through October.
Off-season is so quiet that many hotels close down.

There are several boat companies, but most travelers sail on the
bigger, more expensive, and romantic Köln–Düsseldorf (K-D) line
(free with Eurail, otherwise about 15 DM for the first hour, then
progressively cheaper per hour, tel. 06741/ 1634 in St. Goar). Boats
run daily in both directions (no express boat on Monday) from April
through October, with fewer boats off-season. Complete, up-to-
date, and more complicated schedules are posted in any station,
Rhineland hotel, TI, or current Thomas Cook Timetable. Purchase
tickets at the dock five minutes before departure. The boat is never
full. (Confirm times at your hotel the night before.)

The smaller Bingen–Rüdesheimer line is 25 percent cheaper
than K-D (Eurail not valid, buy tickets on the boat, tel. 06721/
14140), with three two-hour round-trip St. Goar–Bacharach trips
daily in summer (12 DM one way, 16 DM round-trip; departing St.
Goar at 11:00, 14:10, and 16:10; departing Bacharach at 10:10,
12:30, 15:00).

Drivers have these options: (1) skip the boat; (2) take a
round-trip cruise from St. Goar or Bacharach on the Bingen–
Rüdesheimer line; (3) draw pretzels and let the loser drive, prepare
the picnic, and meet the boat; (4) rent a bike, bring it on the boat for
free, and bike back; or (5) take the boat one way and return by train.

By Train: Hourly milk-run trains down the Rhine hit every
town: St. Goar–Bacharach, 12 min; Bacharach–Mainz, 60 min;
Mainz–Frankfurt, 45 min. (Some train schedules list St. Goar but
not Bacharach as a stop, but any schedule listing St. Goar also
stops at Bacharach.)

By Bike: In St. Goar you can rent bikes at the Golf Pavilion
along the Rhine (13 DM/day, 10 DM/4 hrs, 50 DM or passport as
deposit, open April–October 10:00–21:00, tel. 06741/1360). In
Bacharach try Pension Lettie (15 DM/day, 10 DM/4 hrs, no
deposit for guests, otherwise passport or credit-card imprint, tel.
06743/2115), Hotel Gelberhof (20 DM/day for ten-speeds, 25
DM for "trekking" bikes, 5 DM for child's seat, tel. 06743/1017,
ring bell when closed), Hotel Hillen (15 DM/day, 10 DM/half-
day, cheaper for guests, lots of bikes), or Frau Feldhege (free if
you rent a room from her, see Sleeping, below). The best riverside

Best of the Rhine

TO KÖLN — EHRENBREITSTEIN
KOBLENZ
BURG ELTZ
LAHNECK
MARKSBURG
MOSEL R.
COCHEM STOLZENFELS
STERRENBURG
LIEBENSTEIN
BOPPARD 'MAUS'
←TO TRIER 'KATZ'
LORELEI
RHEINFELS GUTENFELS
ST. GOAR
SCHOENBURG NOLLICH
OBERWESEL PFALZ
STAHLECK EHRENFELS
BACHARACH NIEDERWALD MONUMENT
HEIMBURG
SOONECK BROEMERSBURG
REICHENSTEIN ←MOUSE TOWER
RHEINSTEIN →TO FRANKFURT
KLOPP
✳NOT TO SCALE·BINGEN
TO KOBLENZ = 50 MILES
BINGEN
DCH

bike path is from Bacharach to Bingen. The path is also good from St. Goar to Bacharach, but it's closer to the highway. Consider sailing to Bingen and biking back, visiting Rheinstein Castle (you're on your own to wander the well-furnished castle) and Reichenstein Castle (admittance with groups), and maybe even taking a ferry across the river to Kaub (where a tiny boat shuttles sightseers to the better-from-a-distance castle on the island). While there are no bridges between Koblenz and Mainz, several small ferries do their job constantly and cheaply.

Sights—The Romantic Rhine
(These sights are south to north, from Bingen to Koblenz.)
▲▲▲**Der Romantische Rhine Blitz Zug Fahrt**—One of Europe's great train thrills is zipping along the Rhine in this fast train tour. Here's a quick and easy, from-the-train-window tour (also works for car, boat, or bike) that skips the syrupy myths and the life story of Dieter von Katzenelnbogen that fill normal Rhine guides.

For more information than necessary, buy the handy *Rhine Guide from Mainz to Cologne* (7-DM book with foldout map, at

1998 Rhine Cruise Schedule

Koblenz	Boppard	St. Goar	Bacharach ⟶
—	9:00	10:15	11:20
9:00	10:50	12:05	13:05
11:00	12:50	14:05	15:05
14:00	15:50	17:05	18:05
11:05	11:30	11:50	12:10*
⟵			
13:00	11:45	10:50	9:05
14:15	13:10	12:15	11:30
—	14:00	13:15	12:30
17:55	16:45	15:50	15:05
20:00	18:50	18:00	17:20

* Hydrofoil, Koblenz-Bacharach, 8 DM with Eurail, 22.40 DM without.
Note: Schedule applies to summer; fewer boats run in spring and fall.

most shops). Sit on the right (river) side of the train going north from Bingen. While nearly all the castles listed are viewed from this side, clear a path to the left window for the times I yell, "Crossover."

You'll notice large black-and-white kilometer markers along the riverbank. I put those up years ago to make this tour easier to follow. They tell the distance from the Rhinefalls where the Rhine leaves Switzerland and becomes navigable. Now the river-barge pilots have accepted these as navigational aids as well. We're tackling just 36 miles of the 820-mile-long Rhine. Your Blitz Rhine Tour starts near Mainz, Rüdesheim, and Bingen. If you're going the other direction, it still works. Just follow the kilometer markings.

Km 528: Niederwald Monument—Across from the Bingen station on a hilltop is the 120-foot-high Niederwald monument, a memorial built with 32 tons of bronze in 1877 to commemorate "the re-establishment of the German Empire." A lift takes tourists to this statue from the famous and extremely touristy wine town of Rüdesheim.

Km 530: Ehrenfels Castle—Opposite Bingerbrück and the Bingen station, you'll see the ghostly Ehrenfels Castle (clobbered by the Swedes in 1636 and by the French in 1689). Since it had no view of the river traffic to the north, it built the cute little *Mäuseturm* (Mouse Tower) on an island (the yellow tower you'll see near the train station today). Rebuilt in the 1800s in neo-Gothic style, today it's used as a Rhine navigation signal station.

Km 533: Burg Rheinstein, and Km 534: Burg Reichen-stein—Cross to the other side of the train to see some of the first castles to be rebuilt in the Romantic era (both are privately owned, tourable, and connected by a pleasant trail; info at TI).

Km 538: Castle Sooneck—Cross to the other side of the train. Built in the 11th century, this castle was twice destroyed by people sick and tired of robber barons.

Km 540: Lorch—This pathetic stub of a castle is barely visible from the road. Notice the small car ferry, one of several between Mainz and Koblenz, where there are no bridges.

Km 543: Bacharach and Burg Stahleck—Cross to the other side of the train. Bacharach is a great stop (see details and accommodations below). Some of the Rhine's best wine is from this town, whose name means "altar to Bacchus." (The local vintners brag that the medieval Pope Pius II ordered it by the cartload.) Perched above the town, the 13th-century Burg Stahleck is now a hostel.

Km 546: Burg Gutenfels and Pfalz Castle—Burg Gutenfels (see the white painted "Hotel" sign) and the ship-shape Pfalz Castle (built in the river in the 1300s, notice the overhanging his-and-hers "outhouses") worked very effectively to tax medieval river traffic. The town of Kaub grew rich as Pfalz raised its chains when boats came and lowered them only when the merchants had paid their duty. Those who didn't pay spent time touring its fascinating prison, on a raft at the bottom of its well. In 1504, a pope called for the destruction of Pfalz, but a six-week siege failed. Pfalz is tourable but bare and dull (3-DM ferry from Kaub, 4 DM, Tuesday–Sunday 9:00–13:00 and 14:00–18:00, closed Monday, tel. 06774/570).

Km 550: Oberwesel—Cross to the other side of the train. Oberwesel was a Celtic town in 400 B.C., then a Roman military station. It now boasts some of the best Roman wall-and-tower remains on the Rhine. Notice how many of the train tunnels have entrances designed like medieval turrets built in the Romantic 19th century. OK, back to the riverside.

Km 554: The Loreley—Steep a big slate rock in centuries of legend and it becomes a tourist attraction, the ultimate Rhine-stone. The Loreley (two flags on top, name painted near shore-line) rises 450 feet over the narrowest and deepest point of the Rhine. (In the old days, the fine echoes here were thought to be ghostly voices, fertilizing the legendary soil.)

Because of the killer reefs just upstream (at km 552, called the "Seven Maidens"), many ships never made it to St. Goar. Sailors (after days on the river) blamed their misfortune on a *wunderbar Fräulein* whose long blond hair almost covered her body. (You can see her statue at about km 555.) Heinrich Heine's *Song of Loreley* (the *Cliffs Notes* version is on local postcards) tells the story of a count who sent his men to kill or capture this siren after his son was killed because of her. When the soldiers cornered the nymph in her cave, she called her father (Father Rhine) for help. Huge waves, the likes of which you'll never see today, rose from the river and carried her to safety. And she has never been seen since.

But alas, when the moon shines brightly and the tour buses are parked, a soft, playful Rhine whine can still be heard from the Loreley. As you pass, listen carefully ("Sailors . . . sailors . . . over my bounding mane").

Km 556: Burg Katz—From the town of St. Goar, you'll see Burg Katz (Katzenelnbogen) across the river. Look back on your side of the river to see the mighty Rheinfels Castle over St. Goar.

Together, Burg Katz (b. 1371) and Rheinfels had a clear view up and down the river and effectively controlled traffic. There was absolutely no duty-free shopping on the medieval Rhine. Katz got Napoleoned in 1806 and rebuilt around 1900; today it's a convalescent home.

Km 557: St. Goar and Rheinfels Castle—The pleasant town of St. Goar (gwahr) was named for a sixth-century home-town monk. It originated in Celtic times (really old) as a place where sailors would stop, catch their breath, send home a post-card, and give thanks after surviving the seductive and treacherous Loreley crossing. St. Goar is worth a stop (see Sleeping below) to explore its Rheinfels Castle. Sitting like a dead pit bull above St. Goar, this mightiest of Rhine castles rumbles with ghosts from its hard-fought past. Burg Rheinfels (built in 1245) withstood a siege of 28,000 French troops in 1692, but was creamed by the same team in 1797. It was huge, the biggest on the Rhine, then used as a quarry. Today this hollow but interesting shell offers your best single hands-on castle experience on the river. Follow the castle map with English instructions (.30 DM from the ticket window, English brochure-3.5 DM, tiny flashlight-5 DM). Follow the castle's perimeter, circling counterclockwise and downward, to find an easy-to-explore chunk of the several miles of spooky tunnels. Bring your flashlight (and bayonet). These tunnels were used to lure and entomb enemy troops. You'll be walking over the remains (from 1626) of 300 unfortunate Spanish soldiers. The reconstruction of the castle in the museum shows how much bigger it was before Louis XIV destroyed it. The museum's fine exhibits are well-explained in English. Climb to the top for the Rhine view (5 DM, daily 9:00–18:00, last entry at 17:00; Saturday and Sunday only in winter; gather ten English-speaking tourists to get a cheaper ticket and a free English tour, tel. 06741/383). It's a 15-minute steep hike up from St. Goar or you can call a taxi (7-DM lift from the boat dock to the castle, 11 DM for a mini-bus, tel. 06741/93100).

The St. Goar TI offers free left-luggage service (Monday–Friday 8:00–12:30 and 14:00–17:00, Saturday 9:30–12:00

May–October; closed Sunday and earlier in winter, tel. 06741/
383). You can rent a bike at the Golf Pavilion near the river (13
DM/day).

St. Goar's waterfront park is hungry for a picnic. The small
EDEKA supermarket on main street is fine for picnic fixings
(Monday–Friday 8:30–19:00, Saturday 8:00–16:00, closed Sunday).

The friendly and helpful Montag family in the shop under
Hotel Montag has Rhine guidebooks (Koblenz–Mainz), fine steins,
and copies of this guidebook.

For a good two-hour hike from St. Goar, catch the ferry
across to St. Goarshausen, hike to the Katz castle, and traverse
along the hillside from there to the top of the Loreley. From the
Loreley, the trail winds down to the river and then takes you back
to the St. Goarshausen to St. Goar ferry (4/hr, 3-DM round-trip).

Km 559: Burg Maus—The Maus got its name because the
next castle was owned by the Katzenelnbogen family. In the 1300s, it
was considered a state-of-the-art fortification . . . until Napoleon had
it blown up in 1806 with state-of-the-art explosives. It was rebuilt
true to its original plans around 1900.

Km 567: Burg Sterrenberg and Burg Liebenstein—These
are the "Hostile Brothers" castles (with the white square tower).
Take the wall between the castles (actually designed to improve
the defenses of both castles), add two greedy and jealous brothers
and a fair maiden, and create your own legend. The castles are
restaurants today.

Km 570: Boppard—Once a Roman town, Boppard has some
impressive remains of fourth-century walls. Notice the Roman
tower just after the Boppard train station and the substantial chunk
of Roman wall just before. Boppard is worth a stop. Just above the
market square are the remains of the Roman wall. Below the square
is a fascinating church. Notice the carved Romanesque crazies at
the doorway. Inside, to the right of the entrance, you'll see Christian symbols from Roman times. Also notice the painted arches and
vaults. Originally most Romanesque churches were painted this
way. Down by the river, look for the high water (*Hochwasser*) marks
on the arches from various flood years. (Throughout the Rhine and
Mosel Valleys you'll see these flood marks.)

Km 580: Marksburg—This castle (with the three modern
chimneys behind it) is the best-looking of all the Rhine castles and
the only surviving medieval castle on the Rhine. Because of its
commanding position, it was never attacked. It's now open as a
museum with a medieval interior second only to the Mosel's Burg
Eltz (7 DM, daily 10:00–17:00, tour required—in German, worth
a visit only if you can tag along with a rare English tour, call
ahead, tel. 02627/206).

Km 585: Burg Lahneck—Above the modern autobahn
bridge over the Lahn River, this castle was built in 1240 to defend
local silver mines, ruined by the French in 1688, and rebuilt in the

St. Goar

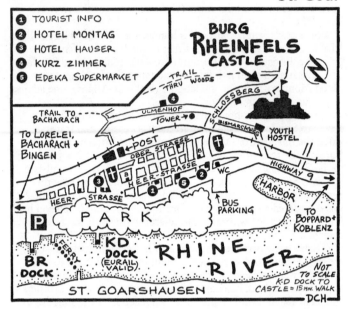

❶	TOURIST INFO
❷	HOTEL MONTAG
❸	HOTEL HAUSER
❹	KURZ ZIMMER
❺	EDEKA SUPERMARKET

BURG **RHEINFELS** CASTLE

TRAIL THRU WOODS

SCHLOSSBERG

TRAIL TO BACHARACH

ULMENHOF TOWER

TO LORELEI, BACHARACH + BINGEN

BISMARCKWEG

YOUTH HOSTEL

POST STRASSE

OBER STRASSE

HEER-STRASSE

WC

HIGHWAY 9

HEER-STRASSE

BUS PARKING

HARBOR

P   PARK

TO BOPPARD + KOBLENZ

KD DOCK (EURAIL VALID)

RHINE RIVER

BR DOCK

FERRY

NOT TO SCALE
KD DOCK TO CASTLE ≈ 15 MIN. WALK

ST. GOARSHAUSEN

—DCH—

1850s in neo-Gothic style. Burg Lahneck faces the yellow Schloss Stolzenfels (out of view above the train, a ten-minute climb from the tiny car park, open for touring, closed Monday).

Km 590: Koblenz—The Romantic Rhine thrills and the Blitz Rhine Tour ends at Koblenz. It's not a nice city (it was really hit hard in World War II), but its place as the historic *Deutsches-Eck* (German corner)—the tip of land where the Mosel joins the Rhine—gives it a certain magnetism. Koblenz, Latin for "confluence," has Roman origins. Walk through the park, noticing the reconstructed memorial to the Kaiser. Across the river, the yellow Ehrenbreitstein Castle now houses a hostel. It's a 30-minute hike from the station to the Koblenz boat dock.

BACHARACH

Bacharach, once prosperous from the wine and wood trade, is now just a pleasant medieval village that misses most of the tourist glitz. Among its 14th-century fortifications is a tower that holds my favorite Rhine hotel—the Hotel Kranenturm—5 screaming yards from the train tracks.

The TI is on the main street a block from the train station; you'll get a town history and blurry photocopied map. Look for the "i" sign (Monday–Friday 9:00–12:30 and 13:30–17:00, Saturday 10:00–12:00, tel. 06743/1297; the TI might move closer "downtown" on Oberstrasse to the Posthof, just before the church and the intersection with Blücherstrasse).

The huge Jost beer stein "factory outlet" carries everything a shopper could want. It has one shop across from the church in the main square and a slightly cheaper shop a block away on Rosen-strasse 16 (Monday–Friday 8:30–18:00, Saturday 8:30–17:00, Sunday 10:00–17:00, ships overseas, 10 percent discount with this book on non-sale items, CC:VM, tel. 06743/1224).

Get acquainted with Bacharach by taking a walking tour. Herr Rolf Jung, retired headmaster of the Bacharach school, gives excellent guided tours in English with plenty of history and photos (50 DM, 1.5 hrs, tel. 06743/1519). Or try this self-guided walk:

Introductory Tour of Bacharach

Start at the Köln–Dusseldorf ferry dock (next to a fine picnic park). View the town from the parking lot—a modern landfill. The Rhine used to lap against Bacharach's town wall. Two of its original 16 towers are visible from here (up to five if you look real hard). The huge roadside wine keg declares this town was built on the wine trade. Reefs up the river forced boats to unload upriver and reload here. As a result, Bacharach became the biggest wine trader on the Rhine. A riverfront crane hoisted huge kegs of prestigious "Bacharach" wine (which in practice was from anywhere in the region). The tour buses next to the dock remind you today's economy is basically tourism.

At the big town map and public WC, take the underpass, ascend on the right, and walk under the train tracks through the medieval gate (one out of an original six 14th-century gates) and to the two-tone Protestant church which marks the town center. From this intersection, Bacharach's main street (Oberstrasse) goes right to the half-timbered Altes Haus (from 1368, the oldest house in town) and left to the TI and train station. To the left (or south) of the church, duck into old Posthof. Notice the fascist eagle—on the left doorstep as you enter—and the fine view of a chapel and church. This post station dates from 1724, when stagecoaches ran from Köln to Frankfurt.

Two hundred years ago this was the only road along the Rhine. Napolean widened it to fit his cannon wagons. The steps alongside the church lead to the castle.

Inside the church you'll find grotesque and brightly painted capitals and a mix of round Romanesque and pointed Gothic arches. In the upper left corner some medieval frescos survive where an older Romanesque arch was cut by a pointed Gothic one.

Walk past Bacharach's main intersection and past the Altes Haus to the old mint (Münze) marked by a crude coin in its sign. Across from the mint, the wine garden of Fritz Bastian is the liveliest place in town after dark. Above you in the vineyards stands a ghostly black and gray tower—your destination. Wander

Bacharach

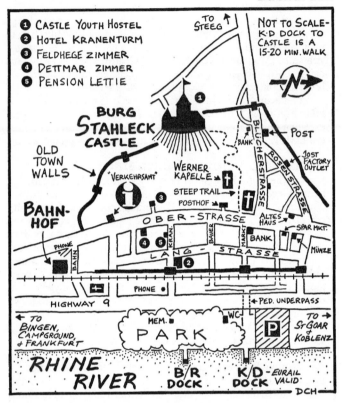

30 meters up Rosenstrasse to the well. Notice the sundial and the wall painting of 1632 Bacharach with its walls intact. Climb the tiny stepped lane behind the well up into the vineyard and to the tower. The slate steps deposit you at a viewpoint atop the stubby remains of the old town wall just above the tower's base.

A grand medieval town spreads before you. When Frankfurt had 15,000 residents, medieval Bacharach had 6,000. For 300 years (1300–1600) Bacharach was big, rich, and politically powerful.

From this perch you can see the chapel ruins and six of the nine surviving city towers. Visually trace the wall to the castle, home of one of seven electors who voted in the Holy Roman Emperor in 1275. To protect their own power, these elector princes did their best to choose the weakest guy on the ballot. The elector from Bacharach helped select a two-bit prince named Rudolf von Habsburg (from a two-bit castle in Switzerland). The underestimated Rudolf brutally silenced the robber barons along the Rhine and established the mightiest dynasty in European history. His family line, the Habsburgs, ruled the Austro-Hungarian empire until 1918.

Plagues, fires, and the Thirty Years War (1618–1648) finally did Bacharach in. The town has slumbered for several centuries, with a population of about a thousand.

In the mid-19th century, artists and writers such as Victor Hugo were charmed by the Rhineland's romantic mix of past glory, present poverty, and rich legend. They put this part of the Rhine on the old "grand tour" map as the "Romantic Rhine." Victor Hugo pondered the ruined 15th-century chapel which you can see under the castle. In his 1842 travel book, *Rhein Reise*, (Rhine Travels) he wrote, "No doors, no roof or windows, a magnificent skeleton puts its sillouette against the sky. Above it, the ivy-covered castle ruins provide a fitting crown. This is Bacharach, land of fairy tales, covered with legends and sagas."

A path leads along the wall up the valley to the next tower and down onto the street. The road leads under the gate and back into the center. If you're enjoying the Romantic Rhine, thank Victor Hugo and company.

Sleeping on the Rhine
(1.7 DM = about $1)
Sleep Code: **S**=Single, **D**=Double/Twin, **T**=Triple, **Q**=Quad, **b**=bathroom, **t**=toilet only, **s**=shower only, **CC**=Credit Card (**V**isa, **M**asterCard, **A**mex), **SE**=Speaks English, **NSE**=No English. All hotels speak some English. Most Zimmer do not. Breakfast is included unless otherwise noted.

The Rhine is an easy place for cheap sleeps. Zimmer and Gasthäuser with 35-DM beds abound (and Zimmer normally discount their prices for longer stays). Several exceptional Rhine-area hostels offer even cheaper beds (for travelers of any age). Each town's helpful TI is eager to set you up, and finding a room should be easy any time of year (except for wine-festy weekends in September and October). Bacharach and St. Goar, the best towns for an overnight stop, are about 10 miles apart, connected by milk-run trains, river boats, and a riverside bike path. Bacharach is less touristy, St. Goar has the famous castle.

Sleeping in Bacharach
(tel. code: 06743, zip code: 55422)

Hotels
Hotel Kranenturm gives you the feeling of a castle without the climb. This is my choice for the best combination of comfort and hotel privacy with Zimmer warmth, central location, and medieval atmosphere. Owned and run by hardworking Kurt Engel and his intense but friendly wife, Fatima, this hotel is actually part of the

medieval fortification. Its former *Kranen* (crane) towers are now round rooms. When the riverbank was higher, cranes on this tower loaded barrels of wine onto Rhine boats. Hotel Kranenturm is 5 yards from the train tracks (just under the medieval gate at the Frankfurt end of town), but a combination of medieval sturdiness, triple-paned windows, and included ear plugs makes the riverside rooms sleepable (Sb-60–65 DM, Db-90–95 DM, Tb-125–130 DM, Qb-160–165 DM with this book, cheaper price is for stays of at least two days, kid-friendly, Rhine views come with train noise, the back rooms—some with castle views—are quieter, laundry service, CC:VMA but prefer cash, reservations easiest by phone with CC, Langstrasse 30, tel. 06743/1308, fax 06743/1021, Fatima SE). Kurt, a great cook, serves fine 15 to 20 DM dinners. His big-enough-for-three Kranenturm ice-cream special may ruin you (10.20 DM). For a quick trip to Fiji in a medieval German cellar, check out his tropical bar. From the train station, take the main street (Oberstrasse), then turn right on Kranenstrasse.

Hotel Altkölnischer Hof, on the main square, rents attractive rooms, some with balconies overlooking the quaint square (Sb-90–95 DM, Db-110–130 DM, Db with terrace-140 DM, with balcony-150–160 DM, TV and phones in rooms, elevator, attached restaurant, CC:VA, tel. 06743/1339 or 06743/2186, fax 06743/2793, some English spoken).

Hotel Gelberhof has bright, comfortable rooms worthy of a splurge (S-55 DM, Sb-75–85 DM, one small Db-110 DM, Db-120–140 DM, popular with groups, attached restaurant, elevator, bike rental, CC:M, Blucherstrasse 26, tel. 06743/910-100, fax 06743/910-1050, e-mail: gelberhof@fh-bingen.de). Coming from the train station, turn left at the main square on Blucherstrasse.

Hotel Hillen, a block south of the Hotel Kranenturm, has less charm and as much train noise, with friendly owners and lots of rental bikes (S-45 DM, Sb-60 DM, D-80 DM, Db-90 DM, Tb-126 DM, CC:VMA, Langstrasse 18, tel. 06743/1287, fax 06743/1037, some English spoken).

Pensions and Private Rooms

Friendly **Pension Lettie** offers four cheery, newly remodeled rooms (Sb-55–60 DM, Db-80–90 DM, Tb-115–120 DM with this book, cheaper price is for longer stays, non-smoking, CC:VMA but prefers cash, a few doors down from Hotel Kranenturm, Kranenstrasse 6, tel. & fax 06743/2115, SE). Lettie also does laundry (16 DM per load, guests only) and rents bikes (15 DM/day, no deposit for guests, non-guests need to leave a passport or credit-card imprint).

Frau Feldhege rents two rooms in her quiet, homey, traditional place (Db-55 DM, no breakfast, Oberstrasse 13, in the old center on a small lane a few yards off the main street, tel. 06743/1271). Guests get a cushy living room, a self-serve kitchen, and free use of bikes.

Entreprenurial **Annelie und Hans Dettmar** rent four smoke-free rooms in a modern house on the main drag in the center (Db-50–70 DM, Tb-75 DM, Qb-100 DM, free use of bikes for guests, laundry-17 DM, Oberstrasse 8, tel. 06743/2661, fax 06743/2979, SE). One room is huge, easily fits a family of four, and has a kitchenette that costs 20 DM if you use it. Skip their other building up the hill; it's a long, steep walk away. Readers give this couple mixed reviews, but their place is handy for those who need a smoke-free option.

Ursula Orth offers four small, bright rooms in her home around the corner from the Dettmars' in the town center (Sb-30 DM, Db-55–60 DM, Tb-75 DM for one night and less for two, Spurgasse 3, tel. 06743/1557, some English spoken). Coming from the station, her place is about a block past the TI; turn right on alley.

The home of **Herr und Frau Theilacker** is a German-feeling Zimmer with comfortable rooms and no outside sign, and is likely to have a room when others don't (S-30 DM, D-60 DM, in the town center behind the Altes Haus at Oberstrasse 57, tel. 06743/1248, NSE).

Hostel

Bacharach's hostel, **Jugendherberge Stahleck**, is a 12th-century castle on the hilltop, 500 steps above Bacharach, with a royal Rhine view. Open to travelers of any age, this is a newly redone gem with eight beds and a private modern shower and WC in each room. A 15-minute climb on the trail from the town church, the hostel is warmly and energetically run by Evelyn and Bernhard Falke (FALL-kay), who serve hearty, 9-DM buffet all-you-can-eat dinners. The hostel pub serves cheap local wine until midnight (23.50-DM dorm beds with breakfast; 6 DM extra if over 26, without a card, or in a double; groups are welcome for 32 DM per bed with breakfast and dinner; accepts traveler's checks, no smoking in rooms, easy parking, beds normally available but call and leave your name, they'll hold a bed until 18:00, can help you find a place if full, tel. 06743/1266, SE).

Sleeping in St. Goar
(tel. code 06741, zip code: 56329)

Hotel Montag is just across the street from the world's largest free-hanging cuckoo clock. Manfred Montag, his wife, Maria, and son Mike speak New Yorkish. Even though Montag gets a lot of bus tours, it's friendly, laid-back, and comfortable (Sb-70 DM, Db-130 DM, price can drop if you arrive late or it's a slow time, CC:VMA, Heerstrasse 128, tel. 06741/1629, fax 06741/2086). Check out their adjacent crafts shop (heavy on beer steins).

Hotel Hauser, very central and newly redone, is warmly run by Frau Velich (S-42 DM, D-88 DM, Db-98 DM, Db with Rhine-view balconies-110 DM, show this book to get these prices, cheaper in off-season, CC:VMA, Heerstrasse 77, telephone reservations easy, tel. 06741/333, fax 06741/1464, SE).

Hotel am Markt, well-run by Herr and Frau Velich, is rustic with all the modern comforts, featuring a hint of antler with a pastel flair and bright rooms in the center of town (18 rooms, Ss-65 DM, Sb-80 DM, Db-100 DM, Tb-140 DM, Qb-160 DM, cheaper off-season, open March–November, CC:VMA, Am Markt 1, tel. 06741/1689, fax 06741/1721, SE).

Hotel Silberne Rose has comfortable rooms with older decor, some with Rhine views (Sb-65 DM, Db-100 DM, Tb-120–140 DM, cheaper price for longer stays, across street from dock, Heerstrasse 63, tel. 06741/7040, fax 06741/2865).

St. Goar's best Zimmer deal is the home of **Frau Kurz**, with a breakfast terrace, fine view, easy parking, and all the comforts of a hotel (S-34 DM, D-60 DM, Db-70 DM, showers-5 DM, one-night stays cost extra, confirm prices, Ulmenhof 11, tel. & fax 06741/459, some English spoken). From the train station, it's a steep three-minute hike (memorable with luggage). Exit left from the station, take an immediate left at the post office and go under the tracks to the paved path. Take a right part way up the stairs, then climb just a few more stairs to a road where you'll find the Zimmer.

The Germanly run **St. Goar Hostel**, the big beige building under the castle, is a good value, with two to 12 beds per room, a 22:00 curfew, and hearty 9-DM dinners (19.50-DM beds with breakfast, 5-DM sleep sacks, open all day, Bismarckweg 17, tel. 06741/388, SE).

Eating in Bacharach

For inexpensive and atmospheric dining in Bacharach, try **Hotel Kranenturm** (see above) or **Altes Haus** (the oldest building in town, on main square, 20-DM dinners, closed Wednesday). **Bastian Weingut** offers delicious cold lunches and the **Posthof** beer garden has good, cheap pub grub, served outside in the courtyard.

Wine Tasting: Drop in on entertaining Fritz Bastian's **Weingut zum Gruner Baum** wine bar (just past the Altes Haus, tel. 06743/1208, evenings only, closed Thursday). He's the president of the local vintner's club and his calling is giving travelers an understanding of the subtle differences among the Rhine wines. Groups of two to ten people pay 26 DM for a "carousel" of 15 glasses of 14 different white wines and one lonely red. Spin the lazy Susan, share a common cup, and discuss the taste.

Transportation Connections—Rhine

Milk-run trains stop at all Rhine towns each hour starting around 6:00. Koblenz, Boppard, St. Goar, Bacharach, Bingen, and Mainz are each about 15 minutes apart. From Koblenz to Mainz takes 75 minutes. To get a faster big train, go to Mainz or Koblenz.

From Mainz by train to: Bacharach/St. Goar (hrly, 1 hr),

Cochem (hrly, 2.5 hrs, changing in Koblenz), **Köln** (3/hr, 90 min), **Baden-Baden** (hrly, 2.5 hrs), **Munich** (hrly, 4 hrs), **Frankfurt** (3/hr, 45 min), **Frankfurt airport** (3/hr, 25 min).

From Frankfurt by train to: Koblenz (hrly, 90 min), **Rothenburg** (hrly, 3 hrs, transfers in Würzburg and Steinach), **Würzburg** (hrly, 90 min), **Munich** (hrly, 3.5 hrs), **Amsterdam** (8/day, 5 hrs), **Paris** (4/day, 6.5 hrs).

MOSEL VALLEY

The misty Mosel is what many visitors hoped the Rhine would be—peaceful, sleepy, romantic villages slipped between the steep vineyards and the river, fine wine, a sprinkling of castles, and lots of friendly Zimmer. Boat, train, and car traffic here is a trickle compared to the roaring Rhine. While the swan-speckled Mosel moseys 300 miles from France's Vosges Mountains to Koblenz, where it dumps into the Rhine, the most scenic piece of the valley lies between the towns of Bernkastel-Kues and Cochem. I'd savor only this section.

Throughout the region on summer weekends and during the fall harvest time, wine festivals with oompah bands, dancing, and colorful costumes are powered by good food and wine.

Getting Around the Mosel Valley

The train gets you to Cochem or Trier in a snap. Regular buses connect the smallest train stations with Mosel villages. The Beilstein–Cochem bus takes 15 minutes (7/day, fewer on weekends, 4 DM). Consider a boat ride from Cochem to Zell (2/day, 3 hrs, 23 DM one-way, 33 DM round-trip) or Beilstein (5/day, 60 min, 12 DM one-way, 17 DM round-trip, tel. 02673/1515). The K-D (Köln–Düsseldorf) line sails once a day in each direction (May–mid-October, Koblenz to Cochem 10:00–14:30, or Cochem to Koblenz 15:50–20:10, free with Eurail). You can also rent bikes at some stations and leave them at others, or rent a bike in Cochem from the K-D line kiosk at the dock (summers only) or year-round from Kreutz at the Shell station on Ravenestrasse 7 (7 DM/4 hrs, 14 DM/day, no deposit required, just your passport number). If you find yourself stranded, hitching isn't bad.

Sights—Mosel Valley

Cochem—With a majestic castle and picturesque medieval streets, Cochem is the very touristic hub of this part of the river. The Cochem TI has a free town history and a walking tour brochure. The pointy Cochem Castle is the work of overly imaginative 19th-century restorers (6 DM, daily mid-March–October 9:00–17:00, 15-minute walk from Cochem, tel. 02761/255). German-language tours, with written English explanation, are given frequently. Try to gather a group of ten to 12 English

Mosel Valley

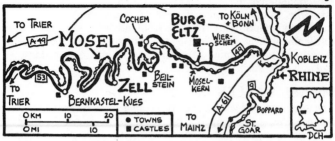

speakers to get part of the tour in English.

The Cochem TI books rooms (same day only), keeps a thorough 24-hour listing in its window, and offers lots of brochures and concert info (Monday–Friday 10:00–13:00 and 14:00–17:00, summer Saturday 10:00–15:00 and Sunday 10:00–12:00, off-season closed weekends, tel. 02671/3971). The "Moselle Wine Road" flyer is perfect for wine-lovers. Day-trippers can check luggage at the station. Many train travelers end up sleeping in Cochem (see Sleeping, below). Stroll along the pleasant paths that line the river. Cochem is right on the train line (to Koblenz, hrly, 60 min; to Trier, hrly, 60 min).

▲▲▲**Burg Eltz**—My favorite castle in all of Europe lurks in a mysterious forest, has been left intact for 700 years, and is furnished throughout as it was 500 years ago. Thanks to smart diplomacy and clever marriages, Burg Eltz was never destroyed. (It survived one five-year siege.) It's been in the Eltz family for 820 years. The countess arranges for new flowers in each room weekly. The only way to see the castle is with a one-hour tour (included in admission ticket). German tours (with pathetic English fact sheets) go constantly. Organize an English tour. (Corral 20 English-speakers in the inner courtyard—they'll thank you for it. Push the red button on the white porch and politely beg for an English guide. This is well worth a short wait. You can also telephone ahead to see if there's an English-language group scheduled that you could tag along with.)

Reaching Burg Eltz by train, walk one steep hour from Moselkern station (midway between Cochem and Koblenz; trail is slippery when wet) through a pine forest where sparrows carry crossbows, and maidens, disguised as falling leaves, whisper "watch out." Driving to Burg Eltz, leave the river at Moselkern (shortest drive) or Hatzenport (but not Muden), following the white "Burg Eltz P&R" signs to the castle car park, a ten-minute walk from the castle. There are three "Burg Eltz" parking lots; only this one is close enough for an easy walk (8 DM, daily April–October 9:30–17:30, constant 1.50-DM shuttle bus service from car park, tel. 02672/1300).

▲**Beilstein**—Farther upstream is the quaintest of all Mosel towns (see Sleeping, below). Beilstein is Cinderella land. Check out the narrow lanes, ancient wine cellar, resident (and very territorial) swans, and ruined castle. The small 1.50-DM ferry goes constantly back and forth. Two shops rent bikes for the pleasant riverside roll (toward Zell is best). The TI is in a café (summer Tuesday–Sunday 9:00–18:00, closed Monday, tel. 02673/1417).

▲**Zell**—This is the best Mosel town for an overnight stop (see Sleeping, below). It's peaceful, with a fine riverside promenade, a pedestrian bridge over the water, plenty of Zimmer, and a long pedestrian zone filled with colorful shops, restaurants, *Weinstubes*, and a fun oompah folk band on weekend evenings on the main square. Walk up to the medieval wall's gatehouse and through the cemetery to the old munitions tower for a village view. The fine little Wein und Heimat Museum features Mosel history (Wednesday and Saturday 15:00–17:00). Locals know the town for its Schwarze Katz (Black Cat) wine. (TI open Monday–Friday 8:00–12:30 and 13:30–17:00, Saturday 9:00–14:00, off-season closed on Saturday, tel. 06542/4031.)

Sleeping on the Mosel
(1.7 DM = about $1)

Sleeping in Cochem
(tel. code: 02671, zip code: 56812)
All places include breakfast. The little town is strung along the river. Exit right from the station onto Ravenestrasse. A seven-minute walk brings you to the TI (on your left, past the bus lanes). To get to the main square (Markt), continue under the bridge, then angle right and follow Bernstrasse.

Gästezimmer Hüsgen is a good and handy value that welcomes one-night stays (Ss-40–45 DM, D-64 DM, Ds-68 DM, Db-82 DM, family deals, ground-floor rooms, small view terrace, Ravenestrasse 34, near the station, tel. 02671/5817, Andrea SE). Across the street, the **Ravene** offers six rooms varying in size and quality from odd to comfortable (Sb-60 DM, Db-80–100 DM, Tb-132 DM, add 5 DM per person for one-night stay, Ravenestrasse 43, tel. 02671/980-177, fax 02671/91119, some English spoken).

The rustic **Hotel Lohspeicher**, just off the main square, is for those who want a real hotel (and much higher prices). The best values are the bigger #4 and small view room #8 (Sb-75–95 DM, Db-170 DM, elevator, CC:VMA, Obergasse 1, on tiny-stepped street off main square, tel. 02671/3976, fax 02671/1772, Ingo SE). Farther up the quiet street, you'll find the **Stolz Zimmer** at 20 Obergasse, with big rooms that look like they were decorated by an elderly aunt (Ss-30 DM, Sb-30 DM, Ds-60 DM, Db-60 DM, less for stays of two nights or more, tel. 02671/1509, friendly Mrs. Stolz NSE).

Haus Andreas has small but modern rooms (S-25 DM, Sb-40 DM, Db-60 DM, Schlosstrasse 16, tel. 02671/1370 or 02671/5155, fax 02671/1370). From the main square, take Herren-strasse; after 1 block, angle right uphill on Schlosstrasse.

Sleeping in Zell
(tel. code: 06542, zip code: 56856)

If the Mosel charms you into spending the night, do it in Zell. By car, this is a natural. By train, you'll need to go to Bullay (from Cochem or Trier), where the bus takes you to little Zell (2.60 DM, 2/hr, 10 min; bus stop is across street from Bullay train station; check yellow MB schedule for times). Its hotels are a disappointment, but its private homes are great. The owners speak almost no English and discount their rates if you stay more than one night. They can't take reservations long in advance for one-night stays; just call a day ahead. They ask that you honor your reservations. My favorites are on the south end of town, a two-minute walk from the town hall square and the bus stop. Breakfast is included.

Gästhaus Gertrud Thiesen is classy, with a TV-living-breakfast room and a river view. The Thiesen house has big, bright rooms and is on the town's first corner overlooking the Mosel from a great terrace (S or D-70 DM, Balduinstrasse 1, tel. 06542/4453, SE).

Friendly **Natalie Huhn**, your German grandmother, has the cheapest beds in town in her simple but comfortable house (S-30 DM, D-60 DM, cheaper for two-night stays, near the pedestrian bridge behind the church at Jakobstrasse 32, tel. 06542/41048).

Weinhaus Zum Fröhlichen Weinberg offers cheap, basic rooms (D-60 DM, family Zimmer, Mittelstrasse 6, tel. 06542/4308) above a *Weinstube* disco (noisy on Friday and Saturday nights). **Gästehaus Am Römerbad** is also central and a decent value (Db-80 DM, Am Römerbad, tel. 06542/41602, Elizabeth Münster).

The comfortable and modern home of **Fritz Mesenich** is quiet, friendly, clean, central, and across from a good wine bar (D-60 DM, 50 DM if you stay two nights, Oberstrasse 3, tel. 06542/4753, NSE). Herr Mesenich can take you into his cellar for a look at the *Haus* wine. Notice the flood (*Hochwasser*) marks on the wall across the street.

If you're looking for room service, a sauna, pool, and elevator, sleep at **Hotel Grüner Kranz** (Db-160 DM with Mosel views, 140 DM without, CC:VMA, tel. 06542/98610, fax 06542/986-180). **Weinhaus Mayer**, a classy—if stressed out—old pension next door, is perfectly central with Mosel-view rooms (13 rooms, Db-120 DM, Balduinstrasse 15, tel. 06542/4530, fax 06542/61160).

Sleeping in Beilstein
(tel. code: 02673, zip code: 56814)

Cozier and farther north, Beilstein (BILE-shtine) is very small and quiet (no train; 7 buses/day to nearby Cochem, fewer buses on weekends; 15-minute trip). Breakfast is included.

Hotel Haus Lipmann is your chance to live in a medieval mansion with hot showers and TVs. A prize-winner for atmosphere, it's been in the Lipmann family for 200 years. The creaky wooden staircase and the elegant dining hall, with long wooden tables surrounded by antlers, chandeliers, and feudal weapons will get you in the mood for your castle sightseeing, but the riverside terrace may mace your momentum (five rooms, Db-120–150 DM, tel. 02673/1573, fax 02673/1521).

Gasthaus Winzerschenke an der Klostertreppe is comfortable and a great value, right in the tiny heart of town (Db-75 DM, bigger Db-95 DM, discount for two-night stays, tel. 02673/1354, Frau Sausen).

The half-timbered, riverfront **Altes Zollhaus Gästzimmer** has crammed all the comforts into tight, bright (if a bit musty), and modern rooms (Db-95 DM, deluxe Db-135 DM, 15 DM more on Friday and Saturday, open March–October, tel. 02673/1574 or 02673/1850, fax 02673/1287).

ROTHENBURG

Dive into the Middle Ages via Rothenburg (ROE-ten-burg), Germany's best-preserved walled town. Countless renowned travelers have searched for the elusive "untouristy Rothenburg." There are many contenders (such as Michelstadt, Miltenberg, Bamberg, Bad Windsheim, and Dinkelsbühl), but none holds a candle to the king of medieval German cuteness. Even with crowds, overpriced souvenirs, Japanese-speaking night watchmen, and yes, even with *Schneeballs*, Rothenburg is best. Save time and mileage, and be satisfied with the winner.

Planning Your Time
The best one-day look at the heartland of Germany is the Romantic Road bus tour. Eurail travelers pay only a 10-DM registration fee for a ride (daily, Frankfurt to Munich or Füssen, and vice versa). Drivers can follow the route laid out in the tourist brochures (available at any TI). The only stop worth more than a few minutes is Rothenburg. Twenty-four hours is ideal for this town. Two nights and a day is a bit much, unless you're actually relaxing on this trip.

Rothenburg in a day is easy, with four essential experiences: the Medieval Crime and Punishment Museum, the Riemenschneider wood carving in St. Jacob's Church, the city walking tour, and a walk along the wall. With more time there are several mediocre but entertaining museums, walking and biking in the nearby countryside, and lots of cafés and shops. Make a point to spend at least one night. The town is yours after dark, when the groups vacate, and the town's floodlit cobbles wring some romance out of any travel partner.

ROTHENBURG
In the Middle Ages, when Frankfurt and Munich were just wide spots on the road, Rothenburg was Germany's second-largest

Rothenburg

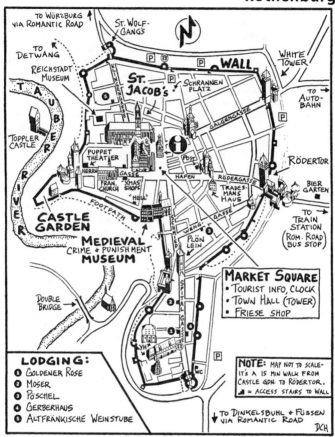

free imperial city, with a whopping population of 6,000. Today it's her best-preserved medieval walled town, enjoying tremendous tourist popularity without losing its charm. Get medievaled in Rothenburg.

Orientation (tel. code: 09861)

To orient yourself in Rothenburg, think of the town map as a human head. Its nose—the castle garden—sticks out to the left, and the neck is the skinny lower part, with the hostel and my favorite hotels in the Adam's apple. The town is a joy on foot. No sight or hotel is more than a 15-minute walk from the train station or each other.

During Rothenburg's heyday, from 1150 to 1400, it was the

crossing point of two major trade routes: Tashkent–Paris and Hamburg–Venice. Most of the buildings you'll see were built by 1400. The city was born around its long-gone castle, which was built in 1142, destroyed in 1356, and is now the site of the castle garden. You can see the shadow of the first town wall, which defines the oldest part of Rothenburg, in its contemporary street plan. A few gates from this wall survive. The richest and therefore biggest houses were in this central part. The commoners built higgledy-piggledy (read: picturesquely) farther from the center near the present walls. Today the great trade is tourism; two-thirds of the townspeople are employed to serve you. Too often Rothenburg brings out the shopper in visitors before they've had a chance to appreciate the historic city. True, this is a great place to do your German shopping, but first see the town. While 2.5 million people visit each year, a mere 500,000 spend the night. Rothenburg is most enjoyable early and late, when the tour groups are gone.

Tourist Information: The TI is on the market square (Monday–Friday 9:00–12:30 and 14:00–18:00, Saturday 9:00–12:00 and 14:00–16:00, closed Sunday; off-season closed Saturday afternoon, tel. 09861/40492, after-hours board lists rooms still available). Pick up a map and the "Sights Worth Seeing and Knowing" brochure (a virtual walking guide to the town; read it all). The TI's free "Hotels and Pensions of Rothenburg" map has the greatest detail and names all streets. Confirm sightseeing plans and ask about the daily 14:00 walking tour (April–December) and evening entertainment. The best town map is available free at the Friese shop, two doors toward Rothenburg's "nose."

Arrival in Rothenburg: Exit left from the train station, and turn right on the first busy street (Ansbacher Strasse). It'll take you to Rothenburg's market square within ten minutes. Day-trippers can leave luggage in lockers at the station (2 DM). The travel agency in the station is the place to arrange train and *couchette* (sleeper) reservations.

Tours of Rothenburg

The TI on the market square offers 90-minute guided **walking tours** in English (6 DM, daily April–October at 14:00 from the market square). The equally informative but more dramatic **Night Watchman's Tour** leaves each evening at 20:00 (6 DM, April–December, in English). Or you can hire a private guide. For 85 DM, a local historian—who's usually an intriguing character as well—will bring the ramparts alive. Eight hundred years of history are packed between Rothenburg's cobbles. (Manfred Baumann, tel. 09861/4146, and Anita Weinzierl, tel. 09868/7993, are good guides.) If you prefer riding to walking, **horse-and-buggy rides** last 30 minutes and cost 10 DM per person for a minimum of three people.

Sights—Rothenburg

▲▲**Walk the Wall**—Just over a mile around, providing great views and a good orientation, this walk can be done by those under 6 feet tall without a camera in less than an hour, and requires no special sense of balance. Photographers go through lots of film, especially before breakfast or at sunset, when the lighting is best and the crowds are fewest. The best fortifications are in the Spitaltor (south end). Walk from there counterclockwise to the "forehead." Climb the Rödertor en route. The names you see along the way are people who donated money to repair the wall after WWII.

▲**Rödertor**—The wall tower nearest the train station is the only one you can climb. It's worth the hike up for the view and a fascinating rundown on the bombing of Rothenburg in the last weeks of World War II—the northeast corner of the city was destroyed (2 DM, daily 9:00–17:00, closed off-season, photos, English translation).

▲▲**Town Hall Tower**—The best view of Rothenburg and the surrounding countryside, and a close-up look at an old tiled roof from the inside are yours for 1 DM and a rigorous (214 steps, 180 feet) but interesting climb (daily 9:30–12:30 and 13:00–17:00; off-season Saturday and Sunday 12:00–15:00 only). Entrance is on the market square. Women, beware: Some men find the view best from the bottom of the ladder just before the top.

▲▲**Medieval Crime and Punishment Museum**—It's the best of its kind, full of fascinating old legal bits and *Kriminal* pieces, instruments of punishment and torture, even a special cage—complete with a metal gag—for nags. Exhibits are in English (5 DM, daily 9:30–17:30, shorter hours in winter, fun cards, and posters).

▲▲**St. Jacob's Church**—Here you'll find a glorious 500-year-old wooden altarpiece by Tilman Riemenschneider, located up the stairs and behind the organ. Riemenschneider was the Michelangelo of German woodcarvers. This is the one required art treasure in town (2.50 DM, Monday–Saturday 9:00–17:30, Sunday 10:45–17:30, off-season 10:00–12:00 and 14:00–16:00, free helpful English info sheet).

Meistertrunk Show—Be on the market square at 11:00, 12:00, 13:00, 14:00, 15:00, 20:00, 21:00, or 22:00 for the ritual gathering of the tourists to see the less-than-breathtaking reenactment of the Meistertrunk story. In 1631, the Catholic army took the Protestant town and was about to do its rape, pillage, and plunder thing when, as the story goes, the mayor said, "Hey, if I can drink this entire 3-liter tankard of wine in one gulp, will you leave us alone?" The invading commander, sensing he was dealing with an unbalanced people, said, "Sure." Mayor Nusch drank the whole thing, the town was saved, and the mayor slept for three days. Hint: For the best show, don't watch the clock; watch the open-mouthed tourists gasp as the old windows flip open. At the late shows, the square flickers with flash attachments.

▲**Toy Museum**—Two floors of historic *Kinder* cuteness is a hit with many (5 DM, 12 DM per family, daily 9:30–18:00, just off the market square, downhill from the fountain, Hofbronneng 13).

▲**Historical Vaults**—Under the town hall tower is a city history museum that gives a waxy but good look at medieval Rothenburg and a good-enough replica of the famous Meistertrunk tankard (3 DM, 9:00–18:00, closed in winter, well-described in English).

Museum of the Imperial City (Reichsstadt Museum)—This stuffier, less sensational museum, housed in the former Dominican Convent, gives a more scholarly look at old Rothenburg, with some fine art and the supposed Meistertrunk tankard, labeled "Kürfurstenhumpen" (4 DM, daily 9:30–17:30, in winter 13:00–16:00).

St. Wolfgang's Church—This fortified Gothic church is built into the medieval wall at Klingentor (near the "forehead"). Explore its dungeon-like passages below and check out the shepherd's dance exhibit to see where they hot-oiled the enemy back in the good old days (2 DM, daily 10:00–13:00 and 14:00–17:00, closed in winter).

Alt Rothenburger Handwerkerhaus—This tradesman's house, 700 years old, shows the typical living situation of Rothenburg in its heyday (3 DM, daily 9:00–18:00, closed in winter, Alter Stadtgraben 26, near the Markus Tower).

▲▲**Herrngasse and the Castle Garden**—Any town's *Herrngasse*, where the richest patricians and merchants (the *Herren*) lived, is your chance to see its finest old mansions. Wander from the market square down Herrngasse (past the old Rothenburg official measurement rods on the City Hall wall) and drop into the lavish front rooms of a ritzy hotel or two. Pop into the Franciscan Church (free, daily 10:00–12:00 and 14:00–16:00, built in 1285—the oldest in town, with a Riemenschneider altarpiece), continue on down past the old-fashioned puppet theater, through the old gate (notice the tiny after-curfew door in the big door and the frightening mask mouth from which hot Nutella was poured onto attackers) and into the garden that used to be the castle (great picnic spots and Tauber Riviera views at sunset).

▲**Walk in the Countryside**—Just below the *Burggarten* (castle garden) in the Tauber Valley is the cute, skinny, 600-year-old castle/summer home of Mayor Toppler (2 DM, 13:00–16:00 on Friday, Saturday, and Sunday). On the top floor, notice the photo of bombed-out 1945 Rothenburg. Then walk on past the covered bridge and huge trout to the peaceful village of Detwang. Detwang (from 968, the second-oldest village in Franconia) is actually older than Rothenburg, and also has a Riemen- schneider altarpiece in its church. For a scenic return, loop back to Rothenburg through the valley along the river, past a café with outdoor tables, great desserts, and a town view to match.

Festivals—Rothenburgers dress up in medieval costumes and beer gardens spill out into the street to celebrate Mayor Nusch's Meistertrunk victory (Whitsun, six weeks after Easter) and 700 years of history in the Imperial City Festival (second weekend in September, with fireworks).

Swimming—Rothenburg has a fine modern recreation center, with an indoor/outdoor pool and sauna. It's just a few minutes' walk down Dinkelsbühl Road (Friday–Wednesday 8:00–20:00, opens at 10:00 on Thursday, tel. 09861/4565).

Sights—Near Rothenburg

A Franconian Bike Ride—For a fun, breezy look at the country-side around Rothenburg, rent a bike from Rad & Tat (25 DM/day, Monday–Friday 9:00–18:00, Saturday 9:00–14:00, closed Sunday, Bensenstrasse 17, outside of town behind the "neck," near corner of Bensenstrasse and Erlbacherstrasse, no deposit except passport number, tel. 09861/87984). Return the bike the next morning before 10:00. For a pleasant half-day pedal, bike south down to Detwang via Topplerschlosschen. Go north along the level bike path to Tauberscheckenbach, then huff and puff uphill about 20 minutes to Adelshofen and south back to Rothenburg.

Franconian Open-Air Museum—A 20-minute drive from Rothenburg in the undiscovered "Rothenburgy" town of Bad Windsheim is a small, open-air folk museum that, compared with others in Europe, isn't much. But it's trying very hard and gives you the best look around at traditional rural Franconia (6 DM, Tuesday–Sunday 9:00–18:00, closed Monday, shorter hours off-season).

Shopping

Be careful . . . Rothenburg is one of Germany's best shopping towns. Do it here, mail it home, and be done with it. Lovely prints, carvings, wineglasses, Christmas-tree ornaments, and beer steins are popular.

The Kathe Wohlfahrt Christmas trinkets phenomenon is spreading across the half-timbered reaches of Europe. In Rothenburg tourists flock to two Kathe Wohlfahrt Christmas Villages (on either side of Herrngasse, just off the market square). This Christmas wonderland is filled with enough twinkling lights to require a special electric hookup, instant Christmas spirit mood music (best appreciated on a hot day in July), and American and Japanese tourists hungrily filling little woven shopping baskets with 5-DM to 10-DM goodies to hang on their trees. (OK, I admit it, my Christmas tree sports a few KW ornaments.) Note: Prices have hefty tour-guide kickbacks built into them.

The Friese shop (just off the market square, west of the tourist office on the corner across from the public WC) offers a charming contrast. Cuckoo with friendliness, it gives shoppers with this book tremendous service: a 10 percent discount,

14 percent tax deducted if you have it mailed, and a free Rothenburg map. Anneliese, who runs the place with her sons, Frankie and Berni, charges only her cost for shipping, changes money at the best rates in town with no extra charge, and lets tired travelers leave their bags in her back room for free. Her pricing is good, but to comparison shop, go here last.

For prints, etchings, and paintings 10 percent off marked prices with this book and a free shot of German brandy, visit the Ernst Geissendörfer print shop, where the market square hits Schmiedgasse. For characteristic wineglasses and oinkology gear, drop by the Weinladen am Plonlein (Plonlein 27).

Shoppers who mail their goodies home can get handy boxes at the post office (Monday–Friday 9:00–12:30 and 14:00–17:00, Saturday 9:00–12:00, Milchmarkt 5).

Those who prefer to eat their souvenirs shop the *Bäckerei* (bakeries). Their succulent pastries, pies, and cakes are pleasantly distracting. Skip the good-looking but bad-tasting Rothenburger Schneeballs.

Sleeping in Rothenburg
(1.7 DM = about $1, tel. code: 09861, zip code: 91541)
Sleep Code: **S**=Single, **D**=Double/Twin, **T**=Triple, **Q**=Quad, **b**=bathroom, **t**=toilet only, **s**=shower only, **CC**=Credit Card (Visa, MasterCard, Amex), **SE**=Speaks English, **NSE**=No English. Unless otherwise indicated, room prices include breakfast.

Rothenburg is crowded with visitors, including probably Europe's greatest single concentration of Japanese tourists. But when the sun sets, most retreat to the predictable plumbing of their big-city high-rise hotels. Except for the rare Saturday night, room-finding is easy throughout the year.

Many hotels and guest houses will pick up desperate heavy packers at the station. You may be greeted at the station by the Zimmer skimmer trying to waylay those on their way to a reserved room. If you arrive without a reservation, try talking yourself into one of these more desperate bed-and-breakfast rooms for a youth-hostel price. Be warned: Some take you to distant hotels and then charge you for a ride back if you decline a room.

Hotels
I stay in **Hotel Goldene Rose**, where scurrying Karin serves breakfast and stately Henni keeps everything in good order. The hotel has only one shower for two floors of rooms, and the street-side rooms can be noisy, but the rooms are clean and airy and you're surrounded by cobbles, flowers, and red-tiled roofs (one small S-25 DM, S-35 DM, D-65 DM, Ds-82 DM, Db-87 DM in classy annex behind the garden, some triples, and a spacious family apartment: for four-190 DM, for five-225 DM; closed in January and February, kid-friendly, ground-floor rooms in annex,

CC:VMA, Spitalgasse 28, tel. 09861/4638, fax 09861/86417, Henni SE). The Favetta family also serves good, reasonably priced meals. Remember to keep your key to get in after they close (at the side gate in the alley). The hotel is a 15-minute walk from the station or a seven-minute (without shopping) walk downhill from the market square (walk downhill on Schmiedgasse, which becomes Plonlein, which becomes Spitalgasse).

Gasthof Greifen is a big, traditional 600-year-old place with all the comforts. It's family-run and creaks just the way you want it to (Sb-64–80 DM, one D-74 DM, Db-115–135 DM, Tb-180 DM, CC:VMA; half a block downhill from the market square at Obere Schmiedgasse 5, tel. 09861/2281, fax 09861/86374, SE).

Right on the market square, Herr Rosner's **Gasthof Marktplatz** has simple rooms and a cozy atmosphere (S-40 DM, D-69 DM, Ds-80 DM, Db-87 DM, T-89 DM, Ts-102 DM, Tb-115 DM, Grüner Markt 10, tel. & fax 09861/6722, some English spoken).

Gastehaus Raidel, a 500-year-old house packed with antiques, offers large rooms with cramped facilities down the hall. Run by grim people who make me want to sing the *Addams Family* theme song, it works in a pinch (S-35 DM, D-69 DM, Db-89 DM, Wenggasse 3, tel. 09861/3115, some English spoken).

In the modern world, a block from the train station, you'll find just-the-basics rooms at **Pension Willi und Helen Then**, run by a cool guy who played the sax in a jazz band for seven years after the war and is a regular at the English Conversation Club (D-70 DM, Db-80 DM, on a quiet street across from a handy Laundromat, Johannitergasse 8, tel. 09861/5177, fax 09861/86014).

Splurges

Hotel Gerberhaus, a classy new hotel in a 500-year-old building, is warmly run by Inge and Kurt, who mix modern comforts into bright and airy rooms while maintaining the half-timbered elegance. Great buffet breakfasts, a guests' washer and dryer, and pleasant garden in back (Sb-80 DM, Db-100–140 DM, Tb-165 DM, family room for five-185 DM, all with TV and telephones; CC:VM but prefer cash, Spitalgasse 25, tel. 09861/ 94900, fax 09861/86555, e-mail: Gerberhaus@t-online.de, SE). Claudia's café, downstairs, serves huge sandwiches.

Even classier than the Gerberhaus and my best Rothenburg splurge, **Hotel Klosterstuble** is deep in the old town near the castle garden. Jutta greets her guests while husband Rudolf does the cooking (Sb-90 DM, Db-120–150 DM, some luxurious family rooms, discounts for families, buffet breakfast, 10-DM parking garage, CC:V, Heringsbronnengasse 5, tel. 09861/6774, fax 09861/6474, some English spoken).

Bohemians with bucks enjoy the **Hotel Altfränkische Weinstube am Klosterhof**. Mario and Hanne run this dark and smoky

pub in a 600-year-old building. Upstairs they rent *Gemütliche*
rooms with upscale Monty Python atmosphere, TVs, modern
showers, open-beam ceilings, and *"Himmel"* beds—canopied four-
poster "heaven" beds (Sb-79 DM, Db-89 DM, Tb-109–119 DM,
kid-friendly, CC:VM, walk under St. Jacob's church, take second
left off Klingengasse at Klosterhof 7, tel. 09861/6404, fax 09861/
6410, SE). Their pub is a candlelit classic, serving hot food until
22:30, closing at 1:00. You're welcome to drop by on Wednesday
evening (18:30–24:00) for the English Conversation Club.

Pensions

Pension Pöschel is friendly with seven cozy rooms (S-35 DM,
D-60 DM, T-90 DM, small kids free, Wenggasse 22, tel. 09861/
3430, NSE).

Pension Kittlitz has six pleasant, ground-floor rooms with
views of parked cars on a quiet street (Sb-40 DM, Db-80 DM, will
pick up at the station, Millergasse 6, tel. 09861/1880; at tel. & fax
09861/3424, Christiana SE).

Erich Endress offers five airy, comfy rooms with woody
decor above his grocery store (S-45 DM, D-70–90 DM, cheaper
for three-night stays, non-smoking, Rodergasse 6, tel. 09861/2331,
some English spoken). Coming from the station, look for the
Endress grocery on your left, a few blocks within the town walls.

The recommended **Zum Schmolzer** restaurant (see Eating,
below) rents 14 well-maintained but drab-colored rooms, ideal if
you like olive green (Sb-55 DM, Db-90 DM, Stollengasse 29, tel.
09861/3371, fax 09861/7204, SE).

Cafe Uhl offers several fine, slightly frayed rooms over a bakery (Sb-55–65 DM, Db-95–100 DM, CC:VA, Plonlein 8, tel.
09861/4895, fax 09861/92820, some English spoken).

Private Rooms

For the best real, with-a-local-family, comfortable, and homey
experience, stay with **Herr und Frau Moser** (D-65 DM, T-95
DM, back room has view—ask for *mit Ausblick*, Spitalgasse 12, tel.
09861/5971). This charming retired couple speak little English but
try very hard. Speak slowly, in clear, simple English. They ask that
readers honor their reservations.

Frau Guldemeister rents two simple ground-floor rooms
(Ss-40 DM, Ds-60 DM, Db-70 DM, breakfast in room, minimum
two-night stay, off the market square behind the Christmas shop,
Pfaffleinsgasschen 10, tel. 09861/8988, NSE).

Hostel

The fine **Rossmühle Youth Hostel** has two buildings. The
droopy-eyed building (the old town horse-mill, used when the
town was under siege and the river-powered mill was inaccessi-
ble) houses groups and the hostel office. The adjacent and newly

renovated hostel is for families and individuals (22-DM bed and breakfast, Db-54 DM, 5.50-DM sheets, 9-DM dinners, Muhlacker 1, tel. 09861/ 94160, fax 09861/941-620, e-mail: JHRothen@aol.com, SE). The reception is open from 7:00 to 19:00 and 20:30 to 22:00, and will hold rooms until 18:00 if you call. This popular place takes reservations (even more than a year in advance). Here in Bavaria, hosteling is limited to those under 27, except for families traveling with children under 18.

Sleeping in nearby Detwang and Bettwar

The town of Detwang, a 15-minute walk below Rothenburg, is loaded with quiet Zimmer. The clean, quiet, and comfortable old **Gasthof zum Schwarzen Lamm** in Detwang (D-85 DM, Db-110 DM, tel. 09861/6727, fax 09861/86899) serves good food, as does the popular and very local-style Eulenstube next door. **Gastehaus Alte Schreinerei** offers good food and quiet, comfy, reasonable rooms a little farther down the road in Bettwar (Db-70 DM, 8801 Bettwar, tel. 09861/1541)

Eating in Rothenburg

Most places serve meals only from 11:30 to 13:30 and 18:00 to 20:00. At **Goldene Rose** (see Sleeping, above), Reno cooks up traditional German fare at good prices (11:30–14:00, 17:30–21:00, closed Tuesday evening and all day Wednesday, in sunny weather the garden terrace is open in the back, Spitalgasse 28).

Galgengasse (Gallows Lane) has two cheap and popular standbys: **Pizzeria Roma** (11:30–24:00, 10-DM pizzas and normal schnitzel fare, Galgengasse 19) and **Gasthof zum Ochsen** (Friday–Wednesday 11:30–13:30 and 18:00–20:00, closed Thursday, uneven service but decent 10-DM meals, Galgengasse 26). **Landsknechtstuben**, at Galgengasse 21, is pricey but friendly, with some cheaper schnitzel choices. The smoky **Zum Schmolzer** is a local favorite for its cheap beer and good food (Rosengasse 21, at intersection with Stollengasse, a block south of Galgengasse, closed Wednesday).

Gasthaus Siebersturm serves up tasty, reasonable meals in a bright, airy dining room (Spitalgasse). For a break from schnitzel, the **Lotus China** serves good Chinese food daily (2 blocks behind TI near the church, Eckele 2, tel. 09861/86886).

There are two **supermarkets** near the wall at Rödertor (the one outside the wall to the left is cheaper).

Evening Fun and Beer Drinking

The best beer garden for balmy summer evenings is at Gasthof Rödertor, just outside the wall at the Rödertor (red gate). Two popular discos are a few doors farther out near the Sparkasse bank (T.G.I. Friday's at Ansbacher 15, in the alley next to the bank, open Wednesday, Friday, and Saturday; the other is Check Point, around the corner from the bank, open Wednesday and Friday–Sunday). A more central and touristy beer garden is behind Hotel Eisenhut (open nightly until 22:00 but may be closed in '98, access from Burggasse or through the hotel off Herrngasse). Next door (a block past the Criminal Museum on Burggasse, with the devil hanging out front) is the dark and foreboding Trinkstube Höll (Hell).

For a rare chance to mix it up with locals who aren't selling anything, bring your favorite slang and tongue-twisters to the English Conversation Club at Mario's Altfränkische Weinstube (Wednesday 18:30–24:00, Anneliese from the Friese shop is a regular). This dark and smoky pub is an atmospheric hangout any night but Tuesday, when it's closed (Klosterhof 7, off Klingengasse, behind St. Jacob's Church, tel. 09861/6404).

For mellow ambience, try the beautifully restored Alte Keller's Weinstube under walls festooned with old pots and jugs (closed Tuesday, Alter Keller 8). Wine lovers enjoy the Glocke Hotel's stube (Plonlein 1).

1998 Romantic Road Bus Schedule (Daily, April–October)

Frankfurt	8:00	—
Würzburg	9:45	—
Arrive Rothenburg	12:45	—
Depart Rothenburg	14:30	—
Arrive Dinkelsbühl	15:25	—
Depart Dinkelsbühl	16:15	16:15
Munich	19:50	—
Füssen	—	20:40
Füssen	8:00	—
Arrive Wieskirche	8:35	—
Depart Wieskirche	8:55	—
Munich	—	9:00
Arrive Dinkelsbühl	12:00	12:45
Depart Dinkelsbühl	—	14:00
Arrive Rothenburg	—	14:40
Depart Rothenburg	—	16:15
Würzburg	—	18:30
Frankfurt	—	20:30

The Romantic Road Bus

By Bus: The Europa Bus Company runs buses daily between Frankfurt and Munich in each direction (April–October). A second route goes between Dinkelsbühl and Füssen daily. Buses leave from train stations in towns served by a train. The 11-hour ride costs 120 DM but is only 10 DM with a Eurailpass (uses up a day of a flexipass). Each bus stops in Rothenburg (1.5–2 hours) and Dinkelsbühl (about an hour) and briefly at a few other attractions, and has a guide who hands out brochures and narrates the journey in English. While many claim Eva Braun survives as a Romantic Road bus-tour guide, there is no quicker or easier way to travel across Germany and get such a hearty dose of its countryside. Bus reservations are free, easy, and smart—without one you can lose your seat down the road to someone who does (especially on summer weekends; call 069/79030 one day in advance and leave your name). You can start, stop, and switch over where you like. If you plan to break your journey, you'll be guaranteed a seat only if you reserve each segment.

Transportation Connections—Rothenburg

The Romantic Road bus tour takes you in and out of Rothenburg each afternoon (April–October) heading to Munich, Frankfurt, or Füssen (your choice). See the Romantic Road bus schedule on page 172.

A tiny train line runs between Rothenburg and Steinach (almost hourly, 15 min). **Steinach by train to: Würzburg** (hrly, 30 min), **Munich** (hrly, 2 hrs), **Frankfurt** (hrly, 2 hrs, change in Würzburg). Rothenburg train info: tel. 079511/19419.

MUNICH (MÜNCHEN)

Munich, Germany's most livable and "yuppie" city, is also one of its most historic, artistic, and entertaining. It's big and growing, with a population of more than 1.4 million. Just a little more than a century ago, it was the capital of an independent Bavaria. Its imperial palaces, jewels, and grand boulevards constantly remind visitors that this was once a political and cultural powerhouse. And its recently-bombed-out feeling reminds us that 50 years ago it lost a war.

Orient yourself in Munich's old center with its colorful pedestrian mall. Immerse yourself in Munich's art and history—crown jewels, Baroque theater, Wittelsbach palaces, great art, and beautiful parks. Munich evenings are best spent in frothy beer halls, with their oompah bunny-hopping and belching Bavarian atmosphere. Pry big pretzels from the no-nonsense, buxom beer maids.

Planning Your Time
Munich is worth two days, including a half-day side trip to Dachau. If necessary, its essence can be nicely captured in a day (walk the center, tour a palace and a museum, and enjoy a beer-filled evening). Those without a car and in a hurry can do the castles of Ludwig as a day trip from Munich by tour. Even Salzburg can be done as a day trip from Munich.

Orientation (tel. code: 089)
The tourist's Munich is circled by a ring road (which was the town wall) marked by four old gates: Karlstor (near the train station), Sendlinger Tor, Isartor (near the river), and Odeonsplatz (near the palace). Marienplatz is the city center. A great pedestrian-only street cuts this circle in half, running nearly from Karlstor and the train station through Marienplatz to Isartor. Orient yourself along this east-west axis. Most sights are within a few blocks of this people-filled walk. Nearly all the sights and hotels I recommend are within about a 20-minute walk of Marienplatz and each other.

Tourist Information

Take advantage of the TI in the train station (Monday–Saturday 9:00–20:00, Sunday 10:00–18:00, Bahnhofplatz 2, tel. 089/233-30-256). Have a list of questions ready, confirm sightseeing plans, and pick up brochures, the excellent free city map, and a subway map. Consider buying the 2.50-DM *Monatsprogram* for a German-language list of sights and events calendar. The free twice-weekly magazine, *In München*, lists in German all the movies and entertainment in town (available at TI or any big cinema till supply runs out). The TI can refer you to hotels for a 10-DM fee, but you'll get a better value with my recommended hotels—contact them directly. If the line at the TI is bad, go to EurAide (below). The only essential item is the TI's great city map (also available at Euraide).

EurAide: The industrious, eager-to-help EurAide office in the train station is an American whirlpool of travel information ideal for Eurailers and budget travelers (daily 7:45–12:00, 13:00–18:00; closes at 16:00 summer weekdays, 12:00 on Saturday, and all day Sunday in winter; in Room 3 along track 11, tel. 089/593-889, fax 089/550-3965, Web site: www.cube.net/kmu/euraide.html, e-mail: euraide@compuserve.com). Alan Wissenberg and his staff know your train travel and accommodations questions and have answers in clear American English. The German rail company pays them to help you design your best train travels. They make reserva tions and sell train tickets, couchettes, and Eurailpasses (for $20 over U.S.A. price, next day service). They can find you a room for a 6-DM fee; and offer the city map and a free newsletter (which gets you the best exchange rate). They sell a "Czech Prague Out" train pass, convenient for Prague-bound Eurailers, which is good for train travel from any Czech border station to Prague and back to any border station within seven days (comes in first, second, and youth versions; to save money, buy in U.S.A.: call 630/420-2343, fax 630/420-2369). Every Wednesday in June and July, EurAide provides an excellent "Two Castle" tour of Neuschwanstein and Linderhof that includes Wieskirche (frustrating without a car).

Arrival in Munich

By Train: Munich's train station is a sight in itself—one of those places that can turn an accountant into a vagabond. For a quick orientation in the station, use the big wall maps of the train station, Munich, and Bavaria (through the center doorway as you leave the tracks on the left). For a quick rest stop, the Burger King upstairs has toilets as pleasant and accessible as its hamburgers. Next door, the post office (which has handy metered phones) is less crowded than the main post office across the street. Sussmann's Internationale Presse (across from track 24) is great for English-language books, papers, and magazines, including *Munich Found* (informative English-speaking residents' monthly, 4 DM). You'll also find two TIs (the city TI and EurAide, see above). The station is connected by U-Bahn, S-Bahn, and buses to the rest of the city (though many hotels listed in this book are within walking distance of the station).

By Plane: Munich's airport is an easy 40-minute ride on the S-Bahn (13 DM or free with train pass), or catch the Lufthansa airport bus to (or from) the train station (15 DM, 3/hr, 45 min, buy tickets on bus or from Euraide).

Getting Around Munich

Much of Munich is walkable. To reach sights away from the city center, use Munich's fine tram, bus, and subway system. Taxis are expensive and needless.

By Public Transit: Subways are called U- or S-Bahns. Subway lines are numbered (e.g., S-3 or U-5). Eurailpasses are good on the S-Bahn (actually an underground-while-in-the-city commuter railway). Regular tickets cost 3.40 DM and are good for two hours of changes in one direction. For the shortest rides (one or two stops) get the smallest 1.70-DM ticket (*Kurzstrecke*). The 8-DM all-day pass is a great deal (valid until 6:00 the next day). The Partner Daily Ticket (for 12 DM) is good for up to two adults, three kids, and a dog. Get a pass, validate it in a machine, and you have Munich-by-rail for a day (purchase at tourist offices, subway booths, and in machines at most stops). The entire system (bus/tram/subway) works on the same tickets. You must punch your own ticket before boarding. (Plainclothes ticket-checkers enforce this "honor system," rewarding freeloaders with stiff 60-DM fines.)

By Bike: Munich—level and compact, with plenty of bike paths—feels good on two wheels. Bikes can be rented quickly and easily at the train station at Radius Touristik (daily May–mid-October 10:00–18:00, near track 30, tel. 089/596-113). The owner, Englishman Patrick Holder, rents three-speed bikes (5 DM/hour, 25 DM/day, 30 DM/24 hours, 45 DM/48 hours; credit-card imprint, 100 DM, or passport for a deposit). Patrick dispenses all the necessary tourist information (city map, bike routes), including a do-it-yourself bike tour booklet full of information and history (3 DM).

Helpful Hints

Most Munich sights (including Dachau) are closed on Monday. If you're in Munich on Monday, you could visit the Deutsches Museum, BMW Museum, or churches; take a walking tour or bus tour; climb high for city views (below); stroll the pedestrian streets; have lunch at the Viktualien Markt (see Eating below); rent a bike for a spin through Englischer Garten; daytrip to Salzburg or Ludwig's castles; or hoist a beer at Oktoberfest (in fall, below) or any of the many beer gardens open year-round.

Munich Center

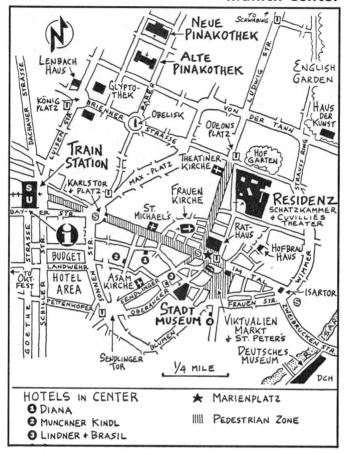

HOTELS IN CENTER
❶ DIANA
❷ MUNCHNER KINDL
❸ LINDNER + BRASIL

★ MARIENPLATZ
||||| PEDESTRIAN ZONE

Sights—Central Munich

▲▲**Marienplatz and das Pedestrian Zone**—The glory of
Munich will slap your face into a smile as you ride the escalator
out of the subway and into the sunlit Marienplatz (Mary's Place):
great buildings bombed flat and rebuilt, the ornate facades of the
new and old city halls (the Neues Rathaus, built in neo-Gothic
style from 1867 to 1910, and the Altes Rathaus), outdoor cafés,
and people bustling and lingering like the birds and breeze they
share this square with. From here the pedestrian mall (Kaufinger-
strasse and Neuhauserstrasse) leads you through a great shopping
area, past carnivals of street entertainers, the twin-towering
Frauenkirche (built in 1470, rebuilt after World War II), and

several fountains, to Karlstor and the train station. Europe's first pedestrian zone enraged shopkeepers when it was built in 1972. Today it is "Munich's living room." Nine thousand shoppers pass through it each hour . . . and the shopkeepers are very happy.

Drop into St. Michael's Church. One of the first great Renaissance buildings north of the Alps, its interior is decorated Baroque and has interesting photos of the bombed-out city center.

The twin onion domes of the 500-year-old Frauenkirche (Church of Our Lady) are the symbol of the city. While the church was destroyed in WWII, the towers survived. Gloriously rebuilt since, it's worth a visit. The church was built Gothic, but money problems meant the domes weren't added until Renaissance times. These domes were inspired by the typical arches of the Venetian Renaissance. And the church domes you'll see all over Bavaria were inspired by these.

Mary's Place is the city center surrounded by the 100-year-old "new town hall" (with the glockenspiel), the gray and pointy old town hall, and the oldest church in the city, St. Peter's. The not-very-old glockenspiel "jousts" on Marienplatz daily through the tourist season at 11:00, 12:00, 17:00, and at 21:00.

▲▲City Views—The highest viewpoint is from a 350-foot-high perch on top of the Frauenkirche (elevator, 4 DM, 10:00–17:00, closed Sunday). There is also a fine view from the Neues Rathaus (3 DM, elevator from under the Marienplatz glockenspiel, Monday–Friday 9:00–19:00, weekends 10:00–19:00). For a totally unobstructed view, but with no elevator, climb the St. Peter's Church tower just a block away. It's a long climb, much of it with two-way traffic on a one-way staircase, but the view is dynamite (2.50 DM, Monday–Saturday 9:00–18:00, Sunday 10:00–18:00). Try to be two flights from the top when the bells ring at the top of the hour (and when your friends ask you about your trip, you'll say, "What?"). The church, built upon the hill where the first monks founded the city in the 12th century, has a fine interior, with photos of the WWII bomb damage on a column near the entrance.

▲▲Residenz—For a long hike through rebuilt corridors of gilded imperial Bavarian grandeur, tour the family palace of the Wittelsbachs, who ruled Bavaria for more than 700 years (6 DM, Tuesday–Sunday 10:00–16:30, closed Monday, enter on Max-Joseph Platz, 3 blocks from Marienplatz). The Schatzkammer (treasury) shows off a thousand years of Wittelsbach crowns and knickknacks (same hours, another 6 DM from the same window). Vienna's palace and jewels are better, but this is Bavaria's best.

▲Cuvillies Theater—Attached to the Residenz, this national theater designed by Cuvillies is dazzling enough to send you back to the days of divine monarchs (3 DM, Monday–Saturday 14:00–17:00, Sunday 10:00–17:00).

▲▲Münchner Stadtmuseum—This Munich city museum is a pleasant surprise. Exhibits include life in Munich through the cen-

Munich Area

turies (including WWII) illustrated in paintings, photos, models, historic puppets, and carnival gadgets; a huge collection of musical instruments from around the world; old photography; and a medieval armory. No crowds, bored and playful guards (5 DM, 7.50 DM for families, Tuesday–Sunday 10:00–17:00, Wednesday until 20:30, closed Monday; 3 blocks off Marienplatz at St. Jakob's Platz 1, a fine children's playground faces the entry).

▲▲**Alte Pinakothek**—Bavaria's best collection of paintings is slated to reopen in August of 1998. If it doesn't happen on schedule, its top masterpieces will still be displayed in the neighboring Neue Pinakothek. This is art concentrate, a tourist's dream-come-true, with works by Fra Angelico, Botticelli, da Vinci, Raphael, Dürer, Rubens, Rembrandt, El Greco, Goya, Monet, and Renoir all in a row (7 DM, Tuesday and Thursday 10:00–20:00, Wednesday and Friday–Sunday 10:00–17:00, closed Monday, U-2 to Königsplatz or tram #27, tel. 089/238-05195).

▲**Haus der Kunst**—Built by Hitler as a temple of Nazi art, this bold and fascist building now houses modern art, much of which the Führer censored. It's a fun collection—Kandinsky, Picasso, Dali, and much more from this century (6 DM, Tuesday–Sunday 10:00–17:00, closed Monday, Prinzregentenstrasse 1).

Bayerisches Nationalmuseum—An interesting collection of Riemenschneider carvings, manger scenes, traditional living rooms, and old Bavarian houses (3 DM, Tuesday–Sunday

9:30–17:00, closed Monday; tram #20 or bus #53 or #55 to
Prinzregentenstrasse 3).

▲**Deutsches Museum**—Germany's answer to our Smithsonian
Institution has everything of scientific and technical interest, from
astronomy to zymurgy. With 10 miles of exhibits, even those on
roller skates will need to be selective. Technical types enjoy lots of
hands-on gadgetry, a state-of-the-art planetarium, and an IMAX
theater (10 DM, daily 9:00–17:00, self-serve cafeteria, S-Bahn to
Isartorplatz, tel. 089/217-9433). Save this for a Monday, when virtually all of Munich's museums are closed.

Schwabing—Munich's artsy, bohemian university district, or
"Greenwich Village," has been called "not a place but a state of
mind." All I experienced was a mental lapse. The bohemians run
the boutiques. I think the most colorful thing about Schwabing is
the road leading back downtown. U-3 or U-6 will take you to
the Münchener-Freiheit Center if you want to wander. Most of
the jazz and disco joints are near Occamstrasse. The Haidhausen
neighborhood (U-Bahn: Max Weber Platz) is becoming the "new
Schwabing."

▲**Englischer Garden**—Munich's "Central Park," the largest on
the Continent, was laid out in 1789 by an American. There's a
huge beer garden near the Chinese Pagoda. Caution: While a new
local law requires sun-worshipers to wear clothes on the tram, this
park is sprinkled with nude sunbathers. A rewarding respite from
the city, it's especially fun on a bike under the summer sun (bike
rental at train station).

Asam Church—Near the Stadtmuseum, this private church of the
Asam brothers is a gooey, drippy masterpiece by Bavaria's top two
Rococonuts, showing off their popular Baroque concentrate style.
A few blocks away, the small Damenstift church has a sculptural
rendition of the Last Supper so real you feel you're not alone (at
intersection of Altheimer Ecke and Damenstiftstrasse, a block
south of pedestrian street).

Sights—Outer Munich

▲▲**Nymphenburg Palace**—This royal summer palace is impressive, but if you've already seen the Residenz, it's only mediocre. If
you do tour it, don't miss King Ludwig's "Gallery of Beauties"—a
room stacked with portraits of Bavaria's loveliest women, according
to Ludwig (who had a thing about big noses). The palace park, good
for a royal stroll, contains the tiny, more-impressive-than-
the-palace Amalienburg hunting lodge, another Rococo jewel by
Cuvillies. The sleigh and coach collection (Marstallmuseum) is especially interesting for "Mad" Ludwig fans (8 DM for everything, less
for individual parts; Tuesday–Sunday 9:00–12:00 and 13:00–17:00,
closed Monday, shorter hours October–March, use the little English
guidebook; reasonable cafeteria; U-1 to Rotkreuzplatz, then tram or
bus #12, tel. 089/179-080).

BMW Museum—The BMW headquarters, located in a striking building across the street from the Olympic Grounds, offers a good museum popular with car buffs (5.50 DM, daily 9:00–17:00, last ticket sold at 16:00, ask about their rare factory tours, closed much of August, U-3 to the last stop: Olympic, tel. 089/382-23-307).

▲**Olympic Grounds**—Munich's great 1972 Olympic stadium and sports complex is now a lush park offering a tower (5 DM, commanding but so high it's a boring view from 820 feet, 8:00–24:00, last trip 23:30), an excellent swimming pool (5 DM, 7:00–22:30, Monday from 10:00, Thursday closed at 18:00), a good look at its striking "cobweb" style of architecture, and plenty of sun, grass, and picnic potential. Take U-3 to Olympiazentrum direct from Marienplatz.

Tours of Munich

Walking Tours—Original Munich Walks, run by the reputable people who started Berlin Walks, offers two tours: an introduction to the old town and "Infamous Third Reich Sites" (both tours are 15 DM, 2.5 hrs, tel. 0177/227-5901, e-mail: 106513.3461@compuserve.com). The old town tour starts daily at 10:00 (also at 15:00 May–October) and the Third Reich tour is offered at 10:00 Monday through Thursday and Saturday, June through October (less off-season). Both tours depart from the Euraide office (track 11) in the train station. There's no need to register; just show up. Bring along any type of Munich public transport ticket (like a Kurzstrecke) or buy one from your guide.

Radius-Turistik offers a wide variety of tours and guides (tel. 089/4366-0383, at train station). Renate Suerbaum is a good local guide (140 DM for two-hour walking tour, tel. 089/283-374).

City Bus Tour—Panorama Tours offers one-hour city orientation bus tours (17 DM; daily at 10:00, 11:30, 14:30, and 16:00; fewer off-season; near the train station, Arnulfstrasse 8, tel. 089/591-504).

Oktoberfest

When King Ludwig I had a marriage party in 1810, it was such a success that they made it an annual bash. These days the Oktoberfest lasts 16 days (Sept. 19–Oct. 4 in 1998), ending with the first full weekend in October. It starts (usually on the third Saturday in September) with an opening parade of more than 6,000 participants and fills eight huge beer tents with about 6,000 people each. A million gallons of beer later, they roast the last ox.

It's crowded, but if you arrive in the morning (except Friday or Saturday) and haven't called ahead for a room, the TI can normally find you a place. The fairground, known as the Wies'n (a few blocks south of the train station), erupts in a frenzy of rides, dancing, and strangers strolling arm-in-arm down rows of picnic tables while the beer god stirs tons of beer, pretzels, and wurst in a bubbling caldron of fun. The three-loops roller coaster must be the wildest on earth (best before the beer-drinking).

During the fair, the city functions even better than normal, and it's a good time to sightsee even if beer-hall rowdiness isn't your cup of tea. The Fasching carnival time (early January–mid-February) is nearly as crazy. And the Oktoberfest grounds are set up for a mini-Oktoberfest to celebrate spring for the two weeks around May Day.

Sights—Near Munich

Castle Tours—Two of King Ludwig's castles, Neuschwanstein and Linderhof, are an easy day trip by tour. Without a tour, only Neuschwanstein is easy (two hours by train to Füssen, ten-minute bus ride to Neuschwanstein). Panorama Tours offers all-day bus tours of the two castles (79 DM, castle admissions not included, near the train station, Arnulfstrasse 8, tel. 089/591-504). On Wednesdays in June and July, EurAide operates an all-day train/bus Neuschwanstein–Linderhof–Wies Church day tour (70 DM, 55 DM with a train pass, admissions not included, tel. 089/593-889), and also sells tickets for Panorama's castle tours (above) at a discount to railpass or ISIC holders. For info on Ludwig's castles, see the Bavaria and Tirol chapter.

Berchtesgaden—This resort, near Hitler's overrated "Eagle's Nest" getaway, is easier as a daytrip from Salzburg (just 20 km away). See Salzburg chapter.

▲**Andechs**—Where can you find a fine Baroque church in a rural Bavarian setting at a monastery that serves hearty food, and the best beer in Germany, in a carnival atmosphere full of partying locals? The Andechs Monastery, crouching quietly with a big smile between two lakes just south of Munich. Come ready to eat tender chunks of pork, huge and soft pretzels (best I've had), spiraled white radishes, savory sauerkraut, and Andecher monk-made beer that would almost make celibacy tolerable. Everything is served in medieval portions; two people can split a meal. Great picnic center offering first-class views and second-class prices (daily 9:00–21:00, TI tel. 08152/5227). To reach Andechs from Munich without a car, take the S-5 train to Herrsching and catch a "Rauner" shuttle bus (hourly) or walk 2 miles from there. Don't miss a stroll up to the church, where you can sit peacefully and ponder the striking contrasts a trip through Germany offers. . . .

▲▲**Dachau**—Dachau was the first Nazi concentration camp (1933). Today it's the most accessible camp to travelers and a very effective voice from our recent but grisly past, warning and pleading "Never Again," the memorial's theme. This is a valuable experience and, when approached thoughtfully, well worth the trouble. In fact, it may change your life. See it. Feel it. Read and think about it. After this most powerful sightseeing experience, many people gain more respect for history and the dangers of not keeping tabs on their government.

Dachau

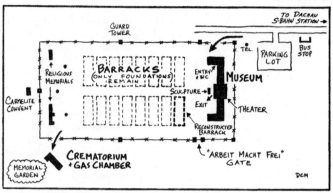

Upon arrival, pick up the mini-guide and note when the next documentary film in English will be shown (25 minutes, normally shown at 11:30 and 15:30). Both the museum and the movie are exceptional. Notice the Expressionist fascist-inspired art near the theater, where you'll also find English books, slides, and a WC. Outside, be sure to see the reconstructed barracks and the memorial shrines at the far end (Tuesday–Sunday 9:00–17:00, closed Monday). It's a 45-minute trip from downtown Munich: take S-2 (direction: Petershausen) to Dachau then, from the station, catch bus #724 or #726, Dachau-Ost, to Gedenkstätte (the camp). The two-zone 6.80-DM ticket covers the entire trip (one-way); with a train pass, just pay for the bus (1.80 DM one-way). If you're driving, follow Dachauerstrasse from downtown Munich to Dachau-Ost. Then follow the KZ-Gedenkstätte signs. The town of Dachau (TI tel. 08131/84566) is more pleasant than its unfortunate image.

Sleeping in Munich
(1.7 DM = about $1, tel. code: 089)
Sleep Code: **S**=Single, **D**=Double/Twin, **T**=Triple, **Q**=Quad, **b**=bathroom, **t**=toilet only, **s**=shower only, **CC**=Credit Card (**V**isa, **M**asterCard, **A**mex). English is nearly always spoken, unless otherwise noted. All prices include breakfast and increase with conventions and festivals. The cheapest rooms with no showers usually charge a few marks for one down the hall.

There are no cheap beds in Munich. Youth hostels strictly enforce their 26-year-old age limit, and side-tripping in is a bad value. But there are plenty of decent, moderately priced rooms. I've listed places in three areas: within a few blocks of the Hauptbahnhof (central train station), in the old center, and near the Deutsches Museum. Munich is packed during Oktoberfest (late September–early October) and room prices can triple. Call ahead and reserve one of my recommendations.

Sleeping near the Train Station

Budget hotels (90-DM doubles, no elevator, shower down the hall) cluster in the area immediately south of the station. It's seedy after dark (erotic cinemas, barnacles with lingerie tongues, men with moustaches in the shadows) but dangerous only to those in search of trouble. Still, I've listed places in more polite neighborhoods, generally a five- or ten-minute walk from the station and handy to the center. Places are listed in order of proximity to the station. Those farthest from the station are the most pleasant. The nearest laundromat is at Paul-Heyse Strasse 21, near the intersection with Landwehrstrasse (daily 6:00–22:00, 8-DM wash and dry).

Hotel Haberstock, less than a block from the station, is homey, a little worn, old-fashioned, and relatively quiet. It's a classic example of an older European hotel (S-58–72 DM, Ss-82 DM, Sb-102 DM, D-110 DM, Ds-130 DM, Db-170 DM, good breakfast, CC:VMA, Schillerstrasse 4, 80336 Munich, tel. 089/557-855, fax 089/550-3634). Ask about weekend and winter discounts.

4 You München, my only listing north of the station, is a newly opened hotel and hostel for travelers of any age. The hotel rooms are frayed but comfortable, in an unrenovated part of the building (Sb-79 DM, Db-119 DM, extra bed-49 DM). In the hostel, people over 26 pay an elder tax of 15 percent (regular prices: a bed in ten-bed room-24 DM, in four- to eight-bed room-29 DM, in D-38 DM, in S-54 DM, sheets-5 DM, no membership card required). Breakfast, not included for hostel guests, costs 7.50 DM (elevator, handicapped facilities available, CC:V, 1 block north of station, Hirtenstrasse 18, 80335 Munich, tel. 089/552-1660, fax 089/5521-6666). Web site: www.the4you.de, e-mail: infor@the4you.de).

Hotel Europäischer Hof München is a big hotel with fine rooms and cable TV (S-88 DM, Sb-122 DM, D-108 DM, Db-138 DM, Bayerstrasse 31, 80000 Munich, tel. 089/551-510, fax 089/5515-1222, e-mail: heh_munich@compuserve.com).

Hotel Odeon offers a combination of decent neighborhood, comfort, and price with a fine buffet breakfast and non-smoking rooms (Sb-95 DM, Db-130 DM, Tb-160 DM, 15-DM garage, elevator, CC:VMA, Goethestrasse 26, from the station walk 2 blocks down Goethestrasse, tel. 089/539-585, fax 089/550-4383).

Jugendhotel Marienherberge is a pleasant, friendly convent offering the best cheap beds in town to young women only (25-year age limit can flex upward a couple of years, S-40 DM, 35 DM per bed in D and T, 30 DM per bed in four- to seven-bed rooms, non-smoking, open 8:00–24:00, a block from the station down Goethestrasse at #9, tel. 089/555-805).

YMCA (CVJM), open to people of all ages and sexes, has clean, modern rooms (D-86 DM, T-120 DM, a bed in a shared triple-40 DM, those over 26 pay a 15 percent elder tax, free showers, elevator, Landwehrstrasse 13, 80336 Munich, tel. 089/552-1410, fax 089/550-4282, Web site: www.cvjm.org/ muenchen/

hotel/, e-mail: muenchen@cvjm.org). Reservations are accepted up
to six weeks in advance. The cafeteria offers 6-DM dinners (Tues-
day–Friday 18:30–22:00). When the Y is full, they recommend these
nearby hotels for cheap beds: **Hotel Pension Luna**, a dumpy build-
ing with cheery rooms (S-55 DM, Sb-65 DM, D/twin-80 DM,
D-95 DM, Db-110 DM, T-125 DM, Tb-135 DM, lots of stairs,
CC:V, Landwehrstrasse 5, tel. 089/597-833, fax 089/550-3761) and
Hotel Pension Erika, bright as dingy yellow can be (S-70 DM,
Ss-80 DM, D-100 DM, Ds-110 DM, Db-130 DM, CC:VMA,
Landwehrstrasse 8, tel. 089/554-327).

　　Hotel Pension Utzelmann has huge rooms, especially the
curiously cheap room #6. Each lacy room is richly furnished. It's
near a bakery, in an extremely decent neighborhood, a ten-minute
walk from the station a block off Sendlinger Tor (S-50 DM, Ss-85
DM, Sb-125 DM, D-90 DM, Ds-110 DM, Db-145 DM, T-125
DM, Ts-150 DM, Tb-175 DM, hall showers-5 DM, Pettenkofer-
strasse 6, enter through black iron gate, tel. 089/594-889, fax
089/596-228, Frau Earnst).

　　Hotel Bristol, nearly next door to Utzelmann, has renovated,
comfortable rooms (Sb-89 DM, Db-129 DM, Tb-155 DM; to get
these prices—which are 20–30 DM below the hotel's normal
rates—ask for Johannes and mention this book if you call, or show
this book if you walk in; non-smoking, hearty buffet breakfast on
terrace, bike rental-20 DM/day, free parking, CC:VMA, Pet-
tenkoferstrasse 2, 80336 Munich, one metro stop on U-1 or U-2
from station, tel. 089/595-151, fax 089/591-451). Johannes also
has an apartment (45 DM per person, up to four people).

　　Hotel Uhland, a veritable mansion, is a worthwhile splurge
(Sb-110 DM, Db-140 DM, Tb-180 DM, huge breakfast, elevator,
Internet access, free parking, Uhlandstrasse 1, 80336 Munich,
near the Theresienwiese Oktoberfest grounds, ten-minute walk
from the station, tel. 089/543-350, fax 089/5433-5250, e-mail:
Hotel_Uhland@compuserve.com, SE). Free use of computer,
e-mail, and photocopier.

　　Pension Westfalia overlooks the Oktoberfest grounds from
the top floor of a quiet and elegant old building. Well-run by Peter
and Mary Deiritz, this is a great value if you prefer sanity and personal touches to centrality (S-65 DM, Sb-90 DM, D-90 DM,
Db-110–125 DM, cheaper off-season, extra bed 25 DM, hallway
showers-3 DM, buffet breakfast, elevator, CC:VMA, Mozartstrasse
23, 80336 Munich, easy parking, U-3 or U-6 to Goetheplatz, tel.
089/530-377, fax 089/543-9120). Around the corner, **Pension
Schubert** rents four tidy and simple but elegant rooms (S-50 DM,
D-85 DM, Db-95 DM, Schubertstrasse 1, tel. 089/535-087.

Sleeping in the Old Center
Hotel Münchner Kindl is the most comfortable of my old-center
listings (15 rooms, S-80 DM, Sb-110 DM, D-120 DM, Ds-140 DM,

Db-160 DM, Tb-195 DM, Qs-200 DM, no elevator, easy telephone reservations, CC:VM, 2 blocks off main pedestrian drag from
"Thomas" sign at Damenstiftstrasse 16, 80331 Munich, tel.
089/264-349, fax 089/264-526, run by Gunter and English-speaking
Renate Dittert).

Pension Lindner is clean, quiet, and modern, with
pastel-bouquet rooms (S-55 DM, D-95 DM, Ds-120 DM, Db-135
DM, elevator, Dultstrasse 1, just off Sendlinger Strasse, 80331
Munich, tel. 089/263-413, fax 089/268-760, Marion Sinzinger).
One floor below, the quirky **Pension Brasil** isn't as homey, but
will do just fine if the Lindner is full (four Ds-120 DM, a tad
smoky, Dulstrasse 1, tel. 089/263-417, fax 089/267-548, some
English spoken).

Pension Seibel has cozy rooms and a family atmosphere a
block off the Viktualienmarkt in a fun neighborhood (S-70 DM,
Sb-89 DM, D-99 DM, Db-129 DM, Tb-150 DM, soft prices, some
non-smoking rooms, big breakfast, no elevator, CC:VMA, Reichenbachstrasse 8, 80469 Munich, tel. 089/264-043, fax 089/ 267-803).
You'll get these discounted prices if you call and ask for Moe or
Kirstin and mention this book, or show this book when you drop in.

Sleeping near Deutsches Museum
American **Audrey Bauchinger** rents quiet, pleasant rooms (though
some are cramped) and spacious apartments east of the Deutsches
Museum in a quiet residential area (Ss-45 DM, D-75 DM, one D
with private bath across hall-125 DM, Ds-80–105 DM, spacious
Db/Tb with kitchenette-160 DM/200 DM, no breakfast included,
CC:VMA accepted at 5 percent charge, Zeppelinstrasse 37, 81669
Munich, tel. 089/488-444, fax 089/489-1787, e-mail: 106437.3277
@compuserve.com). From the station, take any S-bahn to Marienplatz, then bus #52 to Schweigerstrasse.

Hostels and Cheap Beds
Munich's youth hostels charge 19 to 29 DM including breakfast
(sheets-5 DM) and strictly limit admission to YH members who
are under 27. **Burg Schwaneck Hostel** is a renovated castle (30
minutes from the center, S-7 to Pullach, then walk ten minutes to
Burgweg 4, tel. 089/793-0643).

Munich's **International Youth Camp Kapuzinerhölzl**
(a.k.a. "The Tent") offers 400 places on the wooden floor of a
huge circus tent with a mattress, blankets, good showers, and free
tea in the morning for 13 DM to anyone under 25 (flexible). Open
late June through August, it's a fun experience—kind of a cross
between a slumber party and Woodstock (if anyone under 25
knows what that was). Call 089/141-4300 (recorded message
before 17:00) before heading out. No curfew. Cool ping-pong-
and-frisbee atmosphere throughout the day. Take tram #17 from
the train station to Botanischer Garden (direction: Amalien-

burgstrasse), and follow the youthful crowd down Franz-Schrankstrasse to the big tent. This is near the Nymphenburg Palace. There is a theft problem, so sleep with your backpack or bring a lock and use one of the lockers.

Eating in Munich

Munich's most memorable budget food is in the beer halls. You have two basic choices: famous touristy places with music or mellower beer gardens with Germans.

The touristy ones have great beer, reasonable food, live music, and a central location. Germans go there for the entertainment—to sing "Country Roads," see how Texas girls party, and watch salarymen from Tokyo chug beer. The music-every-night atmosphere is thick; the fat and shiny-leather bands even get church mice to stand up and conductg three-quarter time withd breadsticks. Meals are inexpensive (for a light 10-DM meal, I like the local favorite, *Schweinswurst mit Kraut*); huge, liter beers called *Ein Mass* (or *"Ein* pitcher" in English) are 10 DM; white radishes are salted and cut in delicate spirals; and surly beermaids pull mustard packets from their cleavages. You can order your beer *Helles* (light, what you'll get if you say *"Ein* beer"), *Dunkel* (dark), or *Radler* (half lemonade, half light beer). Notice the vomitoriums in the WC.

The most famous beer hall, the **Hofbräuhaus**, is the most touristy (daily 9:30–24:00, Platzl 6, near Marienplatz, tel. 089/221-676, music for lunch and dinner). But check it out; it's fun to see 200 Japanese people drinking beer in a German beer hall. (They have a gimmicky folk evening upstairs in the *Festsaal* nightly at 19:00, 8 DM, tel. 089/290-13-610, food and drinks are sold from the same menu.) The tiny **Strudelstube**, less than a block south of the Hofbräuhaus, offers a rainbow array of strudel-to-go (daily 10:00–22:00, Orlandstrasse 4).

Weisses Bräuhaus is more local and features the region's fizzy "wheat beer" (daily 8:00–24:00, Tal 10, between Marienplatz and Isartor). Hitler met with fellow fascists here in 1920 when his Nazi party had yet to ferment. **Augustiner Beer Garden** is a sprawling haven for local beer-lovers on a balmy evening (10:00–23:00, across from the train tracks, three loooong blocks from the station, away from the center, on Arnulfstrasse 52). Upstairs in the tiny **Jodlerwirt** is a woodsy, smart-alecky, yodeling kind of pub (opens at 18:00, closed Sunday, Altenhofstrasse 4, between the Hofbräuhaus and Marienplatz). For a classier evening stewed in antlers and fiercely Bavarian, eat under a tree or inside at the **Nürnberger Bratwurst Glöckl am Dom** (daily 9:30–24:00, 20-DM dinners, Frauenplatz 9, at the rear of the twin-domed cathedral, tel. 089/220-385). Similarly stylish is the **Ratskeller Weinstuben**, with zither or *Akkordeon* music (daily 10:00–24:00, on Marienplatz, enter behind Rathaus and descend into the cellar, tel. 089/220-313). Locals enjoy the **Altes Hackerhaus** for traditional Bayerischer fare (Sendlingerstrasse 14, tel. 089/260-5026). On Marianplatz, the **Dom** has cheap 12-DM meals.

For outdoor atmosphere and a cheap meal, spend an evening at the Englischer Garden's **Chinesischer Turm** (Chinese Pagoda) **Biergarten**. You're welcome to BYO food and grab a table or buy from the picnic stall (*Brotzeit*) right there. Don't bother to phone ahead: they have 6,000 seats. For similar BYOF atmosphere right behind Marienplatz, eat at **Viktualien Markt's** beer garden. Lunch or dinner here taps you into about the best budget eating in town. Countless stalls surround the beer garden and sell wurst, sandwiches, produce, and so on. This BYOF tradition goes back to the days when monks were allowed to sell beer but not food. To picnic, choose a table without a tablecloth. This is a good place to grab the most typical meal in town: *Weisswurst* (white sausage) with *Süss* (sweet) mustard, a salty pretzel, and *Weissbier*. **Suppenkuche** is fine for a small, cozy, sit-down lunch (soup kitchen, 6–9 DM soup meals, in Viktualien Markt near intersection of Frauenkirche and Reichenbachstrasse, everyone knows where it is).

For an easy (though not cheap) cafeteria meal, try **Marche** on Neuhauser pedestrian street, across from St. Michael's Church (daily 8:00–23:00). Downstairs you get a card; as you load your tray, your card is stamped—pay after you eat.

The crown in its emblem indicates that the royal family assembled its picnics in the historic, and expensive **Alois Dallmayr** delicatessen at Dienerstrasse 14, behind the Rathaus (Monday–Friday 9:00–18:30, Saturday 9:00–16:00, closed Sunday). Explore this dieter's purgatory, put together a royal picnic, and eat it in the nearby, Hofgarten. To save money, browse at Dallmayr's but buy in the basement supermarkets of the Kaufhof stores across Marienplatz or at Karlsplatz.

Transportation Connections—Munich

Munich is a super transportation hub (one reason it was the target of so many WWII bombs).

By train to: Füssen (10/day, 2 hrs, the 8:53 departure is good for a Neuschwanstein castle day trip), **Berlin** (6/day, 8 hrs), **Würzburg** (hrly, 3 hrs), **Frankfurt** (14/day, 3.5 hrs), **Salzburg** (12/day, 2 hrs), **Vienna** (4/day, 5 hrs), **Venice** (2/day, 9 hrs), **Paris** (3/day, 9 hrs), **Prague** (3/day, 7–10 hrs), and just about every other point in western Europe. Munich is three hours from **Reutte** (hrly, 3 hrs, transfer in Garmisch).

BAVARIA
AND TIROL

Two hours south of Munich, between Germany's Bavaria and
Austria's Tirol, is a timeless land of fairy-tale castles, painted
buildings shared by cows and farmers, and locals who still yodel
when they're happy.

In Germany's Bavaria, tour "Mad" King Ludwig's ornate
Neuschwanstein Castle, Europe's most spectacular. Stop by the
Wies Church, a textbook example of Bavarian Rococo bursting with
curly curlicues, and browse through Oberammergau, Germany's
wood-carving capital and home of the famous *Passion Play*. In Austria's Tirol, hike to the Ehrenberg ruined castle, scream down a
nearby ski slope on an oversized skateboard, then catch your breath
for an evening of yodeling and slap-dancing.

In this chapter I'll cover Bavaria first, then Tirol. Austria's
Tirol is easier and cheaper than touristy Bavaria. My favorite
home base for exploring Bavaria's castles is actually in Austria, in
the town of Reutte. Füssen, in Germany, is a handier home base
for train travelers.

Planning Your Time

While locals come here for a week or two, the typical speedy
American traveler will find two days' worth of sightseeing. With
a car and some time you could enjoy the more remote corners,
but the basic visit ranges anywhere from a long day trip from
Munich to a three-night, two-day visit. If the weather's good and
you're not going to Switzerland, be sure to ride a lift to an
Alpine peak.

A good schedule for a one-day circular drive from Reutte is:
7:30-breakfast; 8:15-depart; 8:45-arrive at Neuschwanstein, park
and hike to the castle for a tour, possible visit to Hohenschwangau; 12:00-drive to the Wies Church (20-minute stop) and on to
Oberammergau for a stroll and lunch; 14:00-drive to Linderhof;
14:30-tour Linderhof; 16:30-drive along Plansee back into Austria;
17:30-back at hotel; 19:00-dinner at hotel and perhaps a folk

Highlights of Bavaria and Tirol

evening. In peak season you might arrive later at Linderhof to avoid the crowds. The next morning you could stroll Reutte, hike to the Ehrenberg ruins, and ride the luge on your way to Innsbruck, Munich, Venice, Switzerland, or wherever.

Getting Around Bavaria and Tirol

By Car: This region is ideal by car. All the sights are within an easy 60-mile loop from Reutte or Füssen.

By Train and Bus: It's frustrating by train. Local bus service in the region is spotty for sightseeing. Without wheels, Reutte, the luge ride, and Wies Church are probably not worth the trouble. Füssen (with a two-hour train ride to and from Munich every hour, transfer in Buchloe) is 3 miles from Neuschwanstein Castle with easy bus and bike connections. Oberammergau (hourly two-hour trains from Munich with one change) has decent bus

connections to nearby Linderhof Castle. Oberammergau to
Füssen is a pain.

By Tour: If you're interested only in Bavarian castles, consider an all-day organized bus tour of the Bavarian biggies as a side
trip from Munich (see Munich chapter).

By Bike: This is great biking country. Many train stations
(including Reutte) and many hotels rent bikes for about 15 DM a
day (tandems for 25 DM).

By Thumb: Hitchhiking, always risky, is a slow-but-
possible way to connect the public transportation gaps.

FÜSSEN, GERMANY

Füssen has been a strategic stop since ancient times. Its main street
sits on the Via Claudia Augusta, which crossed the Alps (over
Brenner Pass) in Roman times. The town was the southern terminus of the medieval trade route known among 20th-century
tourists as the "Romantic Road." Dramatically situated under a
renovated castle on the lively Lech River, Füssen just celebrated
its 700th birthday.

Unfortunately, in the summer it's entirely overrun by tourists.
Traffic can be exasperating, but by bike or on foot it's not bad.
Off-season, the town is a jester's delight.

Apart from Füssen's cobbled and arcaded town center, there's
little real sightseeing. The striking-from-a-distance castle houses a
boring picture gallery. The mediocre city museum in the
monastery below the castle exhibits lifestyles of 200 years ago and
the story of the monastery, and offers displays on the development
of the violin for which Füssen was famous (3 DM, Tuesday–
Sunday 11:00–16:00, closed Monday, explanations in German
only). Halfway between Füssen and the border (as you drive, or a
woodsy walk from the town) is the Lechfall, a thunderous waterfall
with a handy potty stop.

Orientation (tel. code: 08362)

Füssen's train station is within a few blocks of the TI, the town
center (a cobbled shopping mall), and all my hotel listings.

Tourist Information: The TI has a free room-finding service (look for Kurverwaltung, Monday–Friday 8:00–12:00 and
14:00–18:00, weekends 10:00–12:00, shorter hours off-season and
closed Sunday, tel. 08362/93850, fax 08362/938-520). After hours,
try the little self-service info pavilion, near the front of the TI. It
dispenses Füssen maps for 1 DM.

Arrival in Füssen: Exit left as you leave the train station and
walk a few straight blocks to the center of town and the TI.

Bike Rental: Rad Zucherl, nearly next door to the train station, rents road bikes for 14 DM/day (passport number for

deposit, Monday–Friday 9:00–12:00 and 14:00–18:00, Saturday 9:00–12:00, mountain bikes also available, Rupprechtstrasse 8).

Sights—Bavaria, near Füssen
These are listed in driving order from Füssen.)

▲▲▲**Neuschwanstein and Hohenschwangau Castles**—The fairy-tale castle Neuschwanstein looks medieval, but it's only about as old as the Eiffel Tower and feels like something you'd see at a home show for 19th-century royalty. It was built (1869–1886) to suit the whims of Bavaria's King Ludwig II and is a textbook example of the Romanticism that was popular in 19th-century Europe.

To beat the crowds, see Neuschwanstein, Germany's most popular castle, by 9:00 or late in the afternoon. The castle is open every morning at 8:30; by 11:00, it's packed. Rushed 35-minute English-language tours are less rushed early. Tours leave regularly, telling the sad story of Bavaria's "mad" king, who drowned under suspicious circumstances at age 41 after bankrupting Bavaria to build his castles. You'll go up and down more than 300 steps through lavish Wagnerian dream rooms, a royal state-of-the-19th-century-art kitchen, the king's gilded-lily bedroom, and his extravagant throne room. You'll see 15 rooms with their original furnishings and fanciful wall paintings. The rest of the castle is unfinished; the king lived here less than 200 days before he died.

After the tour, climb up to Mary's Bridge to marvel at Ludwig's castle, just as Ludwig did. This bridge was quite an engineering accomplishment 100 years ago. From the bridge, the frisky can hike even higher to the "Beware—Danger of Death" signs and an even more glorious castle view. For the most interesting (15 minutes longer and extremely slippery when wet) descent, follow signs to the Pöllat Gorge.

Nearby, the big yellow **Hohenschwangau Castle** was Ludwig's boyhood home. It's more lived-in and historic, and actually gives a better glimpse of Ludwig's life. There are only three ways to get an English tour: Gather 21 people together; wait in line until 20 English speakers join you; or politely ask your German guide to say a few words in English after her German spiels. (Each castle costs 10 DM and is open daily April–September 8:30–17:30, October–March 9:30–16:00, no photography inside, guided tours mandatory.)

The "village" at the foot of the castles lives off the hungry, shopping tourists who come in droves to Europe's "Disney" castle. The big yellow Bräustüberl restaurant by the lakeside parking lot is cheapest, with food that tastes that way. Next door is a little family-run, open-daily souvenir/grocery store with the makings for a skimpy picnic and a microwave fast-food machine. Picnic in the lakeside park or in one of the old-fashioned rent-by-the-hour rowboats. The bus stop, the post/telephone office, and a helpful TI cluster around the main intersection (TI open daily 9:00–18:00; till

Neuschwanstein

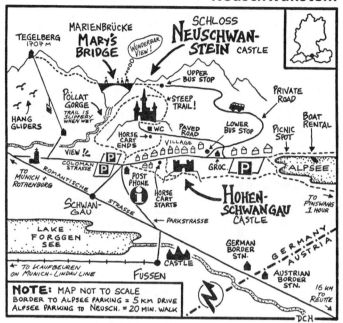

NOTE: MAP NOT TO SCALE
BORDER TO ALPSEE PARKING = 5 KM DRIVE
ALPSEE PARKING TO NEUSCH. = 20 MIN. WALK

17:00 off-season, tel. 08362/819-840).

It's a steep 20- to 30-minute hike to the castle. If you arrive by bus, the quickest (and steepest) way to the castle starts in parking lot D. A more gradual ascent starts at the parking lot near the lake (Parkplatz am Alpsee, best for drivers, all lots cost 6 DM). To minimize hiking, you can take advantage of the shuttle buses (3.50 DM up, 5 DM round-trip; drops you off at Mary's Bridge, a steep ten minutes above the castle) or horse carriages (8 DM up, 4 DM down; slower than walking, stops five minutes short of the castle) that go constantly (watch your step). Signposts and books often refer to these castles in the German, *Königsschlösser.*

To give your castle experience a romantic twist, hike or bike over from Austria (trailhead is at the recommended Hotel Schluxen in Pinswang). When the dirt road forks at the top of the hill, go right (downhill), cross the Austrian-German border (marked by a sign and deserted hut), and follow the paved road to the castles. It's an hour's hike one way (can return by bus) or a great circular bike trip.

Buses run between the Füssen train station and Neuschwanstein (2/hr, ten minutes, 4.80 DM round-trip), and between Füssen and Reutte (5/day, 30 min, never on Sunday; get schedule at either TI).

▲**Tegelberg Gondola**—Just north of Neuschwanstein, hang gliders hover like vultures. They jumped from the top of the Tegelberg Gondola. For 26 DM, you can ride high to the 5,500-foot summit and back down (daily from 9:00, last lift at 17:00, closes earlier in winter, tel. 08362/98360). On a clear day, you get great views of the Alps and Bavaria and the vicarious thrill of watching hang gliders and parasailers leap into airborne ecstasy. From there, it's a steep 2.5-hour hike down to Ludwig's castle.

Tegelberg Luge—About 2 kilometers west of Neuschwanstein Castle is a new luge (like a bobsled on wheels; for details see "Sights—Near Reutte" below). The track, made of stainless steel, is often open when rainy weather shuts other luges. It's not as fast or scenic as Bichlbach and Biberweir (below), but it's close and cheap (3 DM per trip, 10 percent less when using six-trip cards, can be crowded on sunny summer weekends, tel. 08362/98360).

▲▲**Wies Church (Wieskirche)**—Germany's greatest Rococo-style church, Wieskirche ("the church in the meadow") is newly restored and looking as brilliant as the day it floated down from heaven. With flames of decoration, overripe but bright and bursting with beauty, this church is a divine droplet, a curly curlicue, the final flowering of the Baroque movement. The ceiling depicts the Last Judgment.

This is a pilgrimage church. In the early 1700s, a carving of Christ too graphic to be accepted by that generation's church was the focus of worship in a peasant's private chapel. Miraculously, it wept. And pilgrims came from all around. Bavaria's top Rococo architects, the Zimmerman brothers, were then commissioned to build the Wieskirche, which features the amazing carving above its altar and still attracts countless pilgrims. Take a commune-with-nature-and-smell-the-farm detour back through the meadow to the car park.

Wieskirche (donation requested, daily 8:00–20:00, less off-season) is 30 minutes north of Neuschwanstein. The north-bound Romantic Road bus tour stops here for 15 minutes. Füssen-to-Wieskirche buses run several times a day. By car, head north from Füssen, turn right at Steingaden, and follow the signs. If you can't visit Wies, other churches that came out of the same heavenly spray can are Oberammergau's church, Munich's Asam Church, the Würzburg Residenz Chapel, or the splendid Ettal Monastery (free and near Oberammergau).

If you're driving from Wies Church to Oberammergau, you'll cross the Echelsbacher Bridge, arching 250 feet over the Pöllat Gorge. Drivers should let their passengers walk across and meet them at the other side. Any kayakers? Notice the painting of the traditional village woodcarver (who used to walk from town to town with his art on his back) on the first big house on the Oberammergau side, a shop called Almdorf Ammertal. It has a huge selection of overpriced carvings and commission-hungry tour guides.

▲**Oberammergau**—The Shirley Temple of Bavarian villages and exploited to the hilt by the tourist trade, Oberammergau wears way too much makeup. It's worth a wander only if you're passing through anyway. Browse through the woodcarvers' shops—small art galleries filled with very expensive whittled works—or see folk art at the local Heimat Museum (TI tel. 08822/1021; closed Saturday afternoon and Sunday off-season).

Visit the church, a poor cousin of the one at Wies. This church looks richer than it is. Put your hand on the "marble" columns. If they warm up, they're painted fakes. Wander through the graveyard. Ponder the deaths that two wars dealt Germany. Behind the church are the photos of three Schneller brothers, all killed within two years in World War II.

Still making good on a deal the townspeople made with God if they were spared devastation by the Black Plague 350 years ago, once each decade Oberammergau performs the *Passion Play*. The next show is in the year 2000, when 5,000 people a day for 100 summer days will attend Oberammergau's all-day dramatic story of Christ's crucifixion. For the rest of this millennium, you'll have to settle for browsing through the theater's exhibition hall (4 DM, daily 9:30–12:00 and 13:30–16:00, closed Monday off-season, tel. 08822/32278), seeing Nicodemus tool around town in his VW, or reading the *Book*.

Gasthaus zum Stern is friendly, serves good food (closed Tuesday in low season), and for this tourist town is a fine value (Sb-45 DM, Db-90 DM, closed November and December, Dorfstrasse 33, 82487 Oberammergau, tel. 08822/867, fax 08822/7027). Oberammergau's modern youth hostel is on the river a short walk from the center (20 DM beds, open all year, tel. 08822/4114).

Driving into town from the north, cross the bridge, take the second left, follow "Polizei" signs, and park by the huge grey Passionsspielhaus. Leaving town, head out past the church and turn toward Ettal on Road 23. You're 20 miles from Reutte via the scenic Plansee.

▲▲**Linderhof Castle**—This was Mad Ludwig's "home," his most intimate castle. It's small and comfortably exquisite, good enough for a minor god. Set in the woods, 15 minutes by car or bus (three per day) from Oberammergau, surrounded by fountains and sculpted, Italian-style gardens, it's the only palace I've toured that actually had me feeling envious. Don't miss the grotto (9 DM, daily April–September 9:00–17:30, off-season 10:00–16:00 with lunch break, fountains often erupt on the hour, English tours constantly, tel. 08822/3512). Plan for lots of crowds, lots of walking, and a two-hour stop. From mid-July through August, you can take a bus from Reutte to Linderhof in the morning and return in the afternoon (one-hour trip).

▲▲**Zugspitze**—The tallest point in Germany is a border crossing. Lifts from Austria and Germany go to the 10,000-foot summit of the Zugspitze. Straddle two great nations while enjoying an incredible view. There are restaurants, shops, and telescopes at the summit. The 75-minute trip from Garmisch on the German side costs 74 DM round-trip, with family discounts available (by direct lift or a combo cogwheel train and cable car ride, tel. 08821/7970). On the Austrian side, from the less crowded Talstation Obermoos, above the village of Erwald, the tram zips you to the top in ten minutes (420 AS or 61 DM round-trip, daily late May–October 8:30–16:30, tel. in Austria 05673/2309). The German ascent is easier for those without a car, but buses do connect the Erwald train station and the Austrian lift about hourly.

Sleeping in Füssen, Germany
(1.7 DM = about $1, tel. code: 08362, zip code: 87629)

Sleep Code: S=Single, D=Double/Twin, T=Triple, Q=Quad, b=bathroom, t=toilet only, s=shower only, CC=Credit Card (Visa, MasterCard, Amex).

Unless otherwise noted, breakfast is included, hall showers are free, and English is spoken. Prices listed are for one-night stays. Some places give a discount for longer stays. Always ask. Competition is fierce, and off-season prices are soft.

Füssen, 2 miles from Ludwig's castles, is a cobbled, crenelated, riverside oompah treat, but very touristy (notice the sushi bar). It has just about as many rooms as tourists, though, and the TI has a free room-finding service. All places I've listed (except the hostel) are within 2 or 3 blocks of the train station and the town center. They are used to travelers getting in after the Romantic Road bus arrives (20:40) and will hold rooms for a telephone promise.

Hotel Kurcafé is deluxe, with spacious rooms and all the modern conveniences, including cable TV and double-paned windows. Prices vary wildly with the season (July and August are sky-high), but the hotel's bakery can enjoyably ruin your budget, even in the off-season (Sb-89–129 DM depending on season, Db-119–189 DM, third or fourth person pays 30 DM extra, older rooms about 10 DM less, CC:VMA, on the tiny traffic circle a block in front of the train station at Bahnhofstrasse 4, tel. 08362/6369, fax 08362/39424, e-mail: hotel.kurcafe@t-online.de). The attached restaurant has good, reasonable daily specials.

Hotel Gasthaus zum Hechten offers all the modern comforts in a friendly, traditional shell right under the Füssen Castle in the old-town pedestrian zone (S-60 DM, Sb-75 DM, D-95 DM, Db-110–120 DM, Tb-150 DM, Qb-180 DM, prices promised with this book in 1998, cheaper off-season and for stays of more than one night, attached popular restaurant, Ritterstrasse 6, tel. 08362/91600, fax 08362/916099). The sound of the nearby bell tower, ringing four times hourly through the night, is muffled by the hotel's double-paned windows. To get to the hotel from the TI, walk down the pedestrian street and take the second right.

Gasthof Krone, a rare bit of pre-glitz Füssen also in the pedestrian zone, has dumpy halls and stairs but bright, cheery, comfy rooms (S-53 DM, D-96 DM, extra bed-48 DM, prices drop 6 DM for two-night stays, CC:VMA, Schrannenplatz 17, tel. 08362/7824, fax 08362/37505). From the TI, head down the pedestrian street and take the first left.

Hotel Bräustüberl has clean, bright, newly renovated rooms in a musty old beer-hall-type place (Db-90–110 DM, depending on season, Rupprechtstrasse 5, a block from the station, tel. 08362/7843, fax 08362/38781).

Haus Peters, Füssen's best value, is a comfy, smoke-free home renting four rooms, 2 blocks from the station (toward town, second left). Herr and Frau Peters are friendly, speak English, and know what travelers like: a peaceful garden, self-serve kitchen, and good prices (Db-86 DM, Tb-120 DM, Augustenstrasse 5, tel. 08362/7171). The funky, old, ornately furnished **Pension Garni Elisabeth**, in a garden just across the street, exudes an Addams-family friendliness (S-45 DM, D-80–90 DM, Db-100–170 DM, T-120 DM, Tb-150–180 DM, showers-6 DM, Augustenstrasse 10, tel. 08362/6275). Floors creak, dust balls wander, and the piano is never played. Consider the handy American-run **Suzanne's B&B** (Ds-80DM, large Ds with blacony and fridge—100 DM for two; 135 DM for three; 160 DM for four; non-smoking, bike rental, backtrack 2 blocks from station, Venetianerwinkel 3, tel & fax 08362/38485, e-mail: svorbrugg@t-online.de. a half-block from the train station, just opened by an American.

Füssen Youth Hostel, a fine, Germanly run youth hostel welcomes travelers under 27 (four- to six-bed rooms, 20 DM for bed and breakfast, 8 DM for dinner, 5.50 DM for sheets, laundry facilities—7 DM/load, non-smoking, Mariahilferstrasse 5, tel. 08362/7754, fax 08362/2770). From the station, backtrack ten minutes along the tracks.

Sleeping near Neuschwanstein Castle
(code: 87645 Hohenschwangau)

Inexpensive farmhouse Zimmer (B&Bs) abound in the Bavarian countryside around Neuschwanstein and are a good value. Look for signs that say "Zimmer Frei" ("room free," or vacancy). The going rate is about 80 DM per double including breakfast. For a Zimmer in a classic Bavarian home within walking distance of Mad Ludwig's place, try **Haus Magdalena** (Ss-48 DM, D-76 DM, Db-87 DM, extra bed-30 DM, free parking; from the castle inter-section, about 2 blocks down the road toward Schwangau at Schwangauerstrasse 11, tel. 08362/81126, run by Brumme Family) or **Pension Weiher**, with lots of balconies and a flood-lit Neuschwanstein view (S-35–38 DM, D-77 DM, Db-90 DM, Hofwiesenweg 11, tel. & fax 08362/81161).

For more of a hotel, try **Alpenhotel Meier**. Within walking distance of the castle, in a rural setting, with rooms that have new furnishings and porches, it's a joy (Sb-78 DM, Db-130 DM, extra person-40 DM, easy parking, Schwangauerstrasse 37, tel. 08362/81152, fax 08362/987-028).

Eating in Füssen

Infooday is a clever, modern self-service eatery that sells its hot meals and salad bar by weight and offers English newspapers (Monday–Friday 10:30–18:30, Saturday till 14:30, closed Sunday, 8 DM/filling salad, 12-DM meals; under the Füssen castle in Hotel zum Hechten, Ritterstrasse 6). A couple of blocks away, **Pizza Blitz** offers good take-out or eat-at-counter pizzas and hearty salads for about 8 DM apiece (Monday–Saturday 11:00–23:00, Sunday 12:00–23:00, Luitpoldstrasse 4). For more traditional fare, **Hotel Bräustüberl** (listed above) has famous home-brewed beer and a popular kitchen (11:30–14:00 and 16:00–22:00, closed Sunday evening and all day Monday). For picnicking, try the **Plus** supermarket on the tiny traffic circle a block from the train station (Monday–Friday 8:30–18:30, Saturday 8:00–13:00, closed Sunday, basement level of shopping complex).

Transportation Connections—Füssen

To: Neuschwanstein (2 buses/hr, 10 min, 4.8 DM round-trip; taxis cost 14 DM), **Reutte** (5 buses/day, 30 min, no service on Sunday; taxis cost 35 DM), **Munich** (hrly, 2 hrs, transfer in Buchloe).

Romantic Road Buses: The northbound Romantic Road bus departs Füssen at 8:00, and the southbound bus arrives at Füssen at 20:40 (bus stops at train station).

REUTTE, AUSTRIA
(12 AS=about $1)

Reutte (ROY-teh, rolled "r"), population 5,500, is a relaxed town, far from the international tourist crowd but popular with Germans and Austrians for its climate. Doctors recommend its "grade 1" air.

Reutte isn't in any other American guidebook. Its charms are subtle. It never was rich or important. Its castle is ruined, its buildings have paint-on "carvings," its churches are full, its men yodel for each other on birthdays, and lately its energy is spent soaking its Austrian and German guests in *Gemütlichkeit*. Most guests stay for a week, so the town's attractions are more time-consuming than thrilling. If the weather's good, hike to the mysterious Ehrenberg ruins or ride the luge. For a slap-dancing bang, enjoy a Tirolean folk evening.

Orientation (tel. code: 05672)

Tourist Information: Reutte's helpful TI is a block in front of the train station (Monday–Friday 8:00–12:00 and 13:00–17:00, Saturday 8:30–12:00, tel. 05672/62336 or, from Germany,

0043-5672/62336). Go over your sightseeing plans, ask about a folk evening, pick up a city map, and ask about discounts with the hotel guest cards.

Arrival in Reutte: Head straight out of the station 1 long block to the TI. At the TI, turn left to reach the center of town.

Bike Rental: The train station rents bikes for 100 AS, mountain bikes for 200 AS (50 AS discount if you have a railpass or train ticket).

Laundry: Don't ask the TI about a laundromat. Unless you can infiltrate the local campground, Hotel Maximilian, or Gasthof zum Schluxen (see Sleeping, below), the town has none.

Sights—Reutte

▲▲**Ehrenberg Ruins**—The brooding ruins of Ehrenberg Castle are a mile outside of Reutte on the road to Lermoos and Innsbruck. This 13th-century rock pile, a great contrast to King Ludwig's "modern" castles, is a super opportunity to let your imagination off its leash. Hike up from the parking lot at the base of the hill; it's a 25-minute walk to the castle for a great view from your own private ruins. (Facing the hill from the parking lot, the steeper trail is to the right, the easy gravelly road is to the left.) Imagine how proud Count Meinrad II of Tirol (who built the castle in 1290) would be to know that his castle repelled 16,000 Swedish soldiers in the defense of Catholicism in 1632.

The easiest way down is via the small road leading from the gully. The car park, with a café/guest house (closed Wednesday, offers a German-language flyer about the castle), is just off the Lermoos/Reutte road. Reutte is a pleasant one-hour walk away. In Reutte, Café Valier has a wall painting of the intact castle.

Folk Museum—Reutte's Heimatmuseum, offering a quick look at the local folk culture and the story of the castle, is more cute than impressive (20 AS, Tuesday–Sunday 10:00–12:00 and 14:00–17:00, closed Monday and off-season, in the Green House on Untermarkt, around the corner from Hotel Goldener Hirsch).

▲▲**Tirolean Folk Evening**—Ask the TI or your hotel if there's a Tirolean folk evening scheduled. About once a week in the summer, Reutte or a nearby town puts on an evening of yodeling, slap-dancing, and Tirolean frolic—usually worth the 80 AS and short drive. Off-season, you'll have to do your own yodeling. There are also weekly folk concerts in the park (ask at TI).

Swimming—Plunge into Reutte's Olympic-sized swimming pool to cool off after your castle hikes (60 AS, daily 10:00–21:00, off-season 14:00–21:00 and closed Monday).

Reuttener Bergbahn—This mountain lift swoops you high above the tree line to a starting point for several hikes and an Alpine flower park with special paths leading you past countless local varieties.

Flying and Gliding—For a major thrill on a sunny day, drop by the tiny airport in Hofen across the river and fly. A small single-prop plane can buzz the Zugspitze and Ludwig's castles and give you a bird's-eye peek at Reutte's Ehrenberg ruins (two people for 30 minutes, 1,350 AS; one hour, 2,700 AS; tel. 05672/63207). Or, for something more angelic, how about *Segelfliegen*? For 500 AS, you get 30 minutes in a glider for two (you and the pilot). Just watching the tow-rope launch the graceful glider like a giant slow-motion rubber-band gun is thrilling (late May–October 11:00–19:00, in good weather only, tel. 05672/71550).

Sights—Tirol, Near Reutte

▲▲**Sommerrodelbahn, the Luge**—Near Lermoos, on the Innsbruck–Lermoos–Reutte road, you'll find two rare and exciting luge courses or *Sommerrodelbahn*. To try one of Europe's great $5 thrills take the lift up, grab a sled-like go-cart, and luge down. The concrete course banks on the corners, and even a novice can go very, very fast. Most are cautious on their first run and speed demons on their second. (A woman once showed me her journal illustrated with her husband's dried 5-inch-long luge scab. He disobeyed the only essential rule of luging: Keep both hands on your stick.) No one emerges from the course without a windblown hairdo and a smile-creased face. Both places charge a steep 70 AS per run, with five-trip or ten-trip discount cards, and are open weekends from late May and daily from about mid-June through September or October, weather permitting, from 9:00 until about 17:00. They're closed in wet weather, so call before going out.

The small and steep luge: Bichlbach, the first course (100-meter drop over 800-meter course), is 6 kilometers beyond Reutte's castle ruins. Look for a chairlift on the right and exit on the tiny road at the yellow "Riesenrutschbahn" sign (call ahead, tel. 05674/5350, or contact the local TI at 05674/5354). If you're without wheels, catch the train from Reutte to Bichlbach (6/day, 20 min) and walk 1 kilometer to the luge.

The longest luge: The Biberwier Sommerrodelbahn, 15 minutes closer to Innsbruck, just past Lermoos in Biberwier (the first exit after a long tunnel), is a better luge and, at 1,300 meters, the longest in Austria. The only drawback is its shorter season (9:00–16:30, tel. 05673/2111, local TI tel. 05673/2922). One or 2 blocks downhill from this luge, behind the Sport und Trachten-stüberl shop, is a wooden church dome with a striking Zugspitze backdrop. If you have sunshine and a camera, don't miss it. Without a car, the bus from Reutte to Biberwier is your best bet (8/day, fewer on Sunday, 45 min; bus stop and posted schedule near Reutte's Hotel Goldener Hirsch on Untermarkt). The nearest train station is Lermoos, 4 kilometers from the luge.

▲**Fallerschein**—Easy for drivers and a special treat for those who may have been Kit Carson in a previous life, this extremely

Reutte

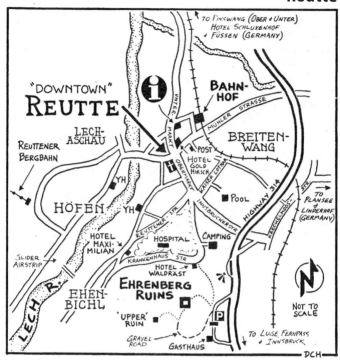

remote log-cabin village is a 4,000-foot-high, flower-speckled world of serene slopes and cowbells. Thunderstorms roll down the valley like it's God's bowling alley, but the pint-sized church on the high ground, blissfully simple in a land of Baroque, seems to promise that this huddle of houses will survive and the river and breeze will just keep flowing. The couples sitting on benches are mostly Austrian vacationers who've rented cabins here. Many of them, appreciating the remoteness of Fallerschein, are having affairs.

For a rugged chunk of local Alpine peace, spend a night in the local Matratzenlager Almwirtschaft Fallerschein, run by Kerle Erwin (120 AS per person with breakfast, open—weather permitting—mid-May–October, 27 cheap beds in a very simple loft dorm, meager plumbing, good, inexpensive meals, 6671 Weissenbach Pfarrweg 18, b/Reutte, tel. 05678/5142, rarely answered, and then not in English). It's crowded only on weekends. Fallerschein is at the end of a miserable 2-kilometer fit-for-jeep-or-rental-car-only paved road that looks more closed than it is, near Namlos on the Berwang Road southwest of Reutte.

Sleeping in Reutte, Austria
(12 AS = about $1, tel. code: 05672, zip code: 6600)
For fewer crowds, easygoing locals with a contagious love of life, and a good dose of Austrian ambience, those with a car should home-base in nearby Reutte. (To call Reutte from Germany, dial 0043-5672 and the local number.) You'll drive across the border but probably won't even have to stop.

Hotels
Reutte is popular with Austrians and Germans who come here year after year for a one- or two-week vacation. The hotels are big and elegant, full of comfy, carved furnishings and creative ways to spend so much time in one spot. They take great pride in their restaurants, and the owners send their children away to hotel management schools.

Hotel Goldener Hirsch, a grand old hotel renovated with a mod Tirolean Jugendstil flair, has sliding automatic doors, mini-bars, TV with cable in the room, and one lonely set of antlers. The hotel is located right downtown (2 long blocks from the station). For those without a car, this is the most convenient hotel (Sb-540 AS, Db-860 AS, decent attached restaurant, CC:VMA, 6600 Reutte-Tirol, tel. 05672/62508 and ask for Monika or grumpy Helmut, fax 05672/625-087).

Hotel Maximilian, up the river a mile or so in the village of Ehenbichl, is a fine splurge that includes the use of bicycles, ping-pong, a children's playroom, and the friendly service of the Koch family. Daughter Gabi speaks fine English. There always seems to be a special event here, and the Kochs host many Tirolean folk evenings (Sb-450 AS, Db-840–880 AS, Tb-1260 AS, cheaper for families, laundry service, far from the train station in the next village, A-6600 Ehenbichl-Reutte, tel. 05672/62585, fax 05672/625-8554, e-mail: maxhotel@ping.at). You can use their laundry service even if you're not staying at the hotel.

Gutshof zum Schluxen gets the "remote-old-hotel-in-an idyllic-setting" award. This working farm offers good food, modern rustic elegance draped in goose down and pastels, and a chance to pet the rabbit. Its picturesque meadow setting will turn you into a dandelion-picker (Sb-460–540 AS, Db-920–1,080 AS, extra person-220 AS, through 1998 only with this book, discounts for stays of at least two nights, excellent breakfast, self-service laundry, bikes free of charge for hotel guests, free parking, free e-mail service, no credit cards but traveler's checks accepted without commission, A-6600 Pinswang-Reutte, between Reutte and Füssen in the village of Unterpinswang, tel. 05677/8903, fax 05677/890-323, e-mail: schluxen@eunet.at). Schluxen is in the village of Pinswang, barely in Austria, midway between Reutte and Füssen.

Gasthof-Pension Waldrast, separating a forest and a meadow, is warmly run by the Huter family. It has big rooms like living rooms, many with fine castle views, and it's a good coffee stop if you're hiking into town from the Ehrenberg ruins (640–700 AS per double, 6600 Ehenbichl, on Ehrenbergstrasse, a half-mile out of town toward Innsbruck, past the campground, just under the castle, tel. & fax 05672/62443).

Zimmer

The tourist office has a list of over 50 private homes that rent out generally elegant rooms with facilities down the hall, pleasant communal living rooms, and breakfast. Most charge 200 AS per person per night, don't like to rent to people staying less than three nights, and speak little if any English. Reservations are nearly impossible for one- or two-night stays. But short stops are welcome if you just drop in and fill in available gaps. The TI can always find you a room when you arrive (free service).

The tiny village of Breitenwang is older and quieter than Reutte and has all the best Zimmer (a 20-minute walk from the Reutte train station: at the post office roundabout, follow Plannseestrasse past the onion dome to the pointy straight dome; unmarked Kaiser Lothar Strasse is the first right past this church). These four places are comfortable, quiet, and kid-friendly, have few stairs, speak some English, and are within 2 blocks of the Breitenwang church steeple: **Inge Hosp** (an old-fashioned place, S-200 AS, D-380 AS, one night OK, includes antlers over the breakfast table, Kaiser Lothar Strasse 36, tel. 05672/62401); her cousins **Walter and Emilie Hosp** across the street (D-380 AS for one night, D-350 AS for two or more, third or fourth person pays 150 AS, Kaiser Lothar Strasse 29, tel. 05672/65377); and **Maria Auer** (D-350 AS, minimum stay two nights, Kaiser Lothar Strasse 25, tel. 05672/67166); and **Helene Haissl** (fine rooms, S-180 AS, D-360 AS, 320 AS for a two-night stay, Planseestrasse 63, tel. 05672/67913). Zimmer charge 15 to 20 AS extra for heat in winter—worth it.

Hostels

Reutte has two excellent little hostels. If you've never hosteled and are curious, try one of these. They accept non-members of any age. The downtown hostel is a minimal place: clean, rarely full, and lacking in personality. It serves no meals but has a members' kitchen (68 AS per bed, open mid-June–late August, a pleasant ten-minute walk from the town center, follow the Jugendherberge signs to the Kindergarten sign, 6600 Reutte, Prof. Dengelstrasse 20, Tirol, tel. 05672/72309).

The homey, newly renovated **Jugendgastehaus Graben** has two to six beds per room and includes breakfast and sheets (160 AS per bed, Db-400 AS, self-service laundry; from downtown Reutte, cross the bridge and follow the road left along the river, about 2 miles from station; A-6600 Reutte-Höfen, Graben 1, tel. 05672/62644, fax 05672/626-444). Frau Reyman keeps the place traditional, clean, and friendly and serves a great 80 AS dinner. No curfew, open all year, bus connection to Neuschwanstein. This is a super value.

Eating in Reutte
Each of the hotels takes great pleasure in serving fine Austrian food at reasonable prices. Rather than go to a cheap restaurant, I'd order low on a hotel menu. For cheap food, the **Prima** self-serve cafeteria near the station (Monday–Friday 9:00–18:30, Mühler Strasse 20) and the **Metzgerei Storf Imbiss** (better but open only Monday–Friday 8:30–15:00), above the deli across from the Heimatmuseum on Untermarkt Street, are the best in town. For a late dinner, try **Zum Mohren** on the main street (serving until 22:30, across from #31, tel. 05672/2345). **Carina** in Breitenwang is a fine Italian restaurant with decent prices (near Zimmer, Bachweg 17).

Transportation Connections—Reutte
To: Füssen (5 buses/day, 30 min; departures at 7:10, 8:30, 12:10, 13:45, 16:45; returning from Füssen to Reutte at 8:00, 13:10, 15:30, 17:10, 19:02, no service on Sunday, confirm schedule; taxis cost 35 DM), **Linderhof** (1 bus/day, 60 min, mid-July–August only), **Garmisch** (2 trains/hr, 60 min), **Munich** (hrly trains, 3 hrs; transfer in Garmisch).

LONDON

London, more than 600 square miles of urban jungle with 7 million struggling people, many of whom speak English, is a world in itself, a barrage on all the senses. On my first visit, I felt very, very small. London is much more than its museums and famous landmarks. It's a living, breathing, thriving organism.

London has changed dramatically in recent years, and many visitors are surprised to find how "un-English" it is. Whites are now a minority in major parts of the city that once symbolized white imperialism. Arabs have nearly bought out the area north of Hyde Park. Chinese take-outs outnumber fish-and-chips shops. Many hotels are run by people with foreign accents (who hire English chambermaids), while outlying suburbs are home to huge communities of Indians and Pakistanis. London is learning—sometimes fitfully—to live as a microcosm of its formerly vast empire. With the English Channel Tunnel complete, many see more foreign threats to the Britishness of Britain.

With just a few days here, you'll get no more than a quick splash in this teeming human tidepool. But, with a quick orientation, you'll get a good taste of its top sights, history, and cultural entertainment, as well as its ever-changing human face.

Have fun in London. Blow through the city on the open deck of a double-decker orientation tour bus, and take a pinch-me-I'm-in-Britain walk through downtown. Ogle the crown jewels at the Tower of London, hear the chimes of Big Ben, and see the Halls of Parliament in action. Hobnob with the tombstones in Westminster Abbey, duck WWII bombs in Churchill's underground Cabinet War Rooms, and brave the earth-shaking Imperial War Museum. Overfeed the pigeons at Trafalgar Square. Visit with Leonardo, Botticelli, and Rembrandt in the National Gallery. Whisper across the dome of St. Paul's Cathedral and

rummage through our civilization's attic at the British Museum.
Cruise down the Thames River. You'll enjoy some of Europe's
best people-watching at Covent Garden and the Buckingham
Palace Changing of the Guard. Just sit in Victoria Station, at a
major tube station, at Piccadilly Circus, or in Trafalgar Square,
and observe. Spend one evening at a theater and the others
catching your breath.

Planning Your Time

The sights of London alone could easily fill a trip to Britain. I'd give
it three busy days. If you're flying in, consider starting your trip in
Bath and making London your British finale. Especially if you hope
to enjoy a play or concert, a night or two of jet lag is bad news.

Here's a suggested three-day schedule:

Day 1: 9:00, Tower of London (Beefeater tour, crown jewels);
12:00, Picnic on Thames while cruising from Tower to Westminster Bridge; 13:00, Big Ben, Halls of Parliament, Westminster
Abbey, walk up Whitehall, and visit the Cabinet War Rooms;
16:00, Trafalgar Square and National Gallery; 17:30, visit
National Tourist Information Centre near Piccadilly, planning
ahead for your trip; 18:30, Dinner near Piccadilly. Take in a play?

Day 2: 9:00, Spend 30 minutes in a phone booth getting all
essential elements of your trip nailed down. If you know where
you'll be and when, call those B&Bs now; 9:30, Take the Round
London bus tour (consider hopping off for the 11:30, Changing
of the Guard at Buckingham Palace); 12:30, Covent Gardens for
lunch and people-watching; 14:00, Tour British Museum; 17:30,
Visitor's Gallery in Houses of Parliament (if in session); 19:00,
Take in a play, concert, or evening walking tour.

Day 3: Choose among these activities for the day: some serious
shopping at Harrods or open-air markets, Museum of the Moving
Image, Imperial War Museum, Tate Gallery, cruise to Greenwich
or Kew, tour St. Paul's Cathedral, Museum of London, a walking
tour, or an early train to your next destination. If heading to Bath
on the 18:15 train, you'll check into your B&B at about 19:30.

After considering nearly all of London's tourist sights, I have
pruned them down to include only the most important (or fun) for
a first visit. You won't be able to see all of these, so don't try.
You'll keep coming back to London. After 20 visits myself, I still
enjoy a healthy list of excuses to return.

Orientation
(downtown tel. code: 0171, suburban: 0181)

To grasp London comfortably, see it as the old town without
the modern, congested sprawl. Most of the visitor's London
lies between the Tower of London and Hyde Park—about a
3-mile walk.

Tourist Information

London Tourist Information Centres are located at Heathrow Airport's Terminal 3 (daily 8:00–18:00, most convenient and least crowded), at Victoria Station (daily 8:00–19:00, shorter hours in winter, crowded and commercial), and at Waterloo International Terminal Arrivals Hall (daily 8:30–22:30). Like the LTICs, the handier National Tourist Info Centre (described below) covers London.

Bring your itinerary and a checklist of questions. Pick up these publications: *London Planner* (a great, free BTA monthly listing all the sights with latest hours and events), walking-tour brochures, the "Silver Jubilee Walkway" (a free map charting a 12-mile walk past 400 historic sights in London), theater guide, Thames River cruise schedules, a Britain map (£1.20), and a London map (£1.20). The fine £1.20 London map rivals the £4 maps sold in newsstands (free from BTA in the U.S.A., tel. 800/462-2748 or 212/986-2200, 551 5th Ave., 7th floor, New York, NY 10176-0799, Web site: www.bta.org.uk). The TIs sell BT phone cards, passes for the tube (subway), long-distance bus tickets and passes, Great British Heritage Passes, individual admissions to various London sights (saving a wait in line at the sight), and tickets to plays (if you don't mind a booking fee of 15 percent or more, depending on the play). They'll book you a room for a £5 booking fee—save money and call direct. Smelling a new source of profit, London TIs are pushing a 50p-per-minute telephone information service. Avoid it.

The National Tourist Information Centre makes gathering information easy (9:00–18:30, Saturday and Sunday 10:00–16:00). It's just off Picadilly Circus—to the southwest—on Lower Regent Street (tel. 0181/846-9000). The Scottish Tourist Centre, a block away at 19 Cockspur Street, will be moving nearby; call for new address before heading out (tel. 0171/930-8661).

Check out the National Tourist Information Centre's well-equipped London/England desk, Wales desk (tel. 0171/409-0969), and Ireland desk (tel. 0171/839-8416 or 0171/493-3201). At the center's extensive book shop, gather whatever books, maps, and information you'll need for your entire trip. Consider getting the *Michelin Green Guide to Britain* (£9). Train travelers can pick up *Let's Go: Britain and Ireland* (£15, 50 percent higher than the U.S. price), and hostelers may want the *Youth Hostel Association 1998 Guide* (£5). Drivers will need a *Britain Road Atlas* (£10). Stock up. You are your own guide. Be a good one.

Helpful Hints

Theft Alert: Be on guard in London more than anywhere else in Britain for pickpockets and thieves, particularly on public transportation and in places crowded with tourists. Tourists, considered naive and rich, are targeted.

Changing Money: Standard transaction fees at banks and exchange desks are £3 to £4. American Express Offices offer a good rate and change any brand of traveler's checks for no fee. There are several offices (Heathrow Terminal 4 tube station and at 6 Haymarket near Piccadilly, Monday–Friday 9:00–17:30, Saturday 9:00–16:00, Sunday 10:00–16:00, tel. 0171/930-4411).

Telephones: In London dial 999 for emergency help and 192 for directory assistance (free from phone booths only). The area code for any downtown London phone number is 0171, for suburban London, 0181. All numbers listed in this chapter with an area code of 0171 can be dialed directly (without the area code) within London. Beware of the many 0839 toll numbers. These will connect you to recorded information—usually slow moving and very expensive. At any newsstand, TI, or post office, buy a handy BT phone card (£2, £5, or £10). It's a big city. If you call sights before heading out, you'll travel more smooth and plan for special events or tours.

What's Up: For the best listing of what's happening (plays, movies, restaurants, concerts, exhibitions, protests, walking tours, shopping, and children's activities), pick up a current copy of *What's On* (£1.30, fine for tourists) or *Time Out* (50p more, more theater reviews, more hip) at any newsstand. The TI's free monthly *London Planner* lists sights, plays, and events at least as well.

Children: Call 0171/222-8070 for a taped rundown on "Children's London" (Monday–Friday 16:00–18:00). The TI has a free brochure "Where to Take Children in London."

Sunday Morning Activities: Few London sights are open on Sunday before 14:00. (Major museums are usually open Sunday afternoons.) Some Sunday morning activities: a church service at St. Paul's, Westminster Abbey, or the Tower of London chapel; Original London Sightseeing Tour by bus; a Thames cruise; Tate Gallery; Cabinet War Rooms; Imperial War Museum; Museum of the Moving Image; Kew Gardens and Palace; Madame Tussaud's; a walking tour; open-air markets at Petticoat Lane and Campden Market; and the Victoria and Albert Museum. "Speaker's Corner" in Hyde Park gets going at noon.

Arrival in London

By Train: London has eight train stations, all connected by the tube (subway), all with exchange offices and luggage storage. From any station, enter the tube and head to the stop nearest your hotel.

By Bus: The bus station is next to Victoria Station, which has a TI and tube entrance.

By Plane: For detailed information on getting from London's airports to downtown London, see Transportation Connections near the end of the chapter.

Getting Around London

London's taxis, buses, and subway system make a private car unnecessary. In a city this size, you must get comfortable with public transportation. Don't be timid.

By Taxi: Big, black, carefully regulated cabs are everywhere. I never met a crabby cabbie in London. They love to talk and know every nook and cranny in town. Rides start at £1.40 and cost about £1.50 per tube stop. Often legitimate charges are added on, but for a short ride, three people in a cab travel at tube prices. If a cab's top light is on, just wave it down. If that doesn't work, ask for directions to a nearby taxi stand. Telephoning is unnecessary; taxis are everywhere. Stick with the metered cabs. I take a cab a day just to get my general London questions answered.

By Bus: London's extensive bus system is easy to follow if you have a map listing the routes. Get a free map from a TI or tube station. Signs at stops list routes clearly. Conductors are terse but helpful. Ask to be reminded when it's your stop. Just hop on, tell the driver where you're going, pay what he says, grab a ticket, take a seat, and relax. (Go upstairs for the best view.) Rides start at 90p. If the driver is not taking money, hop in, grab a seat, and the conductor will eventually sell you a ticket. If you have a transit pass, get in the habit of hopping buses for quick little straight shots (even just to get to a metro stop). Buses and taxis are miserable during rush hours: 8:00 to 10:00 and 16:00 to 19:00.

By Tube: London's subway is one of the planet's great people-movers and the fastest (and cheapest) long-distance transport in town. Any ride in the Central Zone (on or within the Circle Line, including virtually all my recommended sights and hotels) costs £1.20. You can avoid ticket-window lines in metro stations by buying tickets from coin-op machines; practice a few fares on the punchboard to see how the system works. (Note: These tickets are valid only on the day of purchase.)

Every city map includes a tube map with color-coded lines and names. Pick up a free tube map at any station window and keep it handy. The lines each have a name (such as Circle, Northern, or Bakerloo). At every metro station, you'll have a choice of two platforms per line, served by trains heading in opposite directions. Navigate by signs leading to the platforms (usually labeled north, south, east, or west) that clearly list the stops served by each line, or ask a local or an orange-vested staff person for help. Some tracks are shared by several lines, and electronic signboards announce which train is next. Each train has its final destination or line name above its windshield. Read the system notices clearly posted at the platform; they explain the tube's latest flood, construction, or bomb scare. Ask questions of locals and watch your wallet. Bring something to do to pass the waits productively, especially on the notoriously tardy Circle Line. And always . . . mind the gap.

London Underground

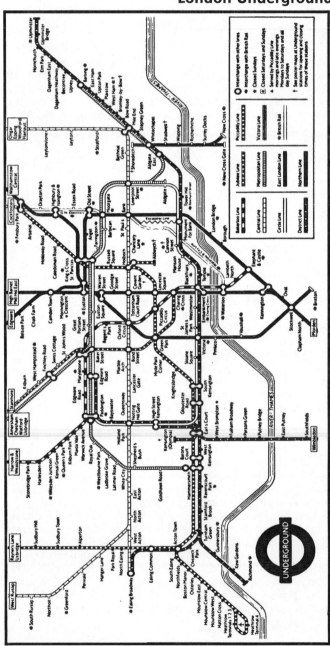

When leaving the system you'll need your ticket to get through the turnstiles. Save time by choosing the best street exit (look at the maps on the walls). Remember, "subway" means pedestrian underpass in "English." For tube and bus information, call 0171/222-1234.

London Tube and Bus Passes: These deals, valid on both the tube and buses, are worth considering. The "Travel Card," covering Zones 1 and 2, gives you unlimited travel for a day, starting after 9:30, for £3.20. The "LT Card" offers the same benefits, without any time restriction, for £4.30. Families should ask about the one-day "Family Travel Card." The "Weekend Travel Card," for £4.80, costs 25 percent less than two one-day cards. The "7 Day Travel Card" costs £13, covers Zone 1, and requires a passport-type photo (cut one out of any snapshot and bring it from home). All passes are available for more zones, and are purchased as easily as a normal ticket from any station. If you figure you'll take three rides in a day, get a day pass.

If you want to travel a little each day or if you're part of a group, consider buying a "carnet" for £10: You get ten separate tickets for tube travel in Zone 1 and you save 20 percent over the cost of buying individual tickets.

Tours of London

▲▲**Hello London Walk**—Catch a bus to Westminster Bridge (#12 from Notting Hill Gate or #211 from Victoria Station). Sit on the top deck and relax until the first stop east of the bridge. Allow an hour for the following 1.5-mile walk from Westminster Bridge to Piccadilly Circus (includes walking and gawking, not eating or sightseeing).

From Westminster Bridge, walk downstream along the Jubilee Promenade (along the eastern riverbank) for a capital view. Then, for that "Wow, I'm really in London!" feeling, cross the bridge for a close-up view of the Houses of Parliament and Big Ben (floodlit at night). If you ride the tube instead of the bus, the Westminster stop is right at Big Ben. Walk halfway across the bridge for the great view. (Then look for Westminster Pier, offering Thames River cruises, north of the bridge on the Big Ben side.)

To thrill your loved ones (or bug the envious), call home from a pay phone near Big Ben at about three minutes before the hour. You'll find a phone on Great George Street, across from Parliament Square. As Big Ben chimes, stick the receiver outside the booth and prove you're in London: ding dong ding dong . . . dong ding ding dong.

Cross Parliament Street to say hello to Churchill in the park. (He's electrified to avoid the pigeon problem that stains so many other great statues.) To his right is Westminster Abbey with its two stubby, elegant towers.

Walk north up Parliament Street (which turns into Whitehall) toward Trafalgar Square. As you stroll along this center-of-government boulevard, you'll see the thought-provoking cenotaph in the middle of the street, reminding passersby of Britain's many war dead.

Stop at the barricaded and guarded little Downing Street to see the British "White House" at #10, home of the prime minister. Break the bobby's boredom—ask him a question.

Nearing Trafalgar Square, look for the "Queen's Life Guard" (horse guards) behind the gated fence, and the 17th-century Banqueting Hall across the street (details below).

Just before Trafalgar Square, drop into the Clarence Pub for a reasonable meal or pint of whatever you fancy. (Cheaper cafeterias and eateries are on the same block.)

The column topped by Lord Nelson marks Trafalgar Square. The stately domed building on the far side of the square is the National Gallery (free) with its classy café (upstairs in the Sainsbury wing). To the right of the National Gallery is St. Martin-in-the-Fields Church and its Café in the Crypt (see Eating, below).

To get to Piccadilly from Trafalgar Square, take Cockspur Street to Haymarket (passing American Express at 6 Haymarket) then take a short left on Coventry Street.

On colorful Piccadilly, the classy Criterion Brasserie is an affordable splurge for lunch. The National Tourist Information Centre and theaters are nearby, and the Rock Circus and frenetic Pepsi Trocadero Center are within a block. Leicester Square (with its half-price ticket booth for plays) thrives just a few blocks away. For seediness, walk through Soho (north of Shaftesbury Avenue) up to Oxford Street. From Piccadilly or Oxford Circus, you can taxi, bus, or tube home.

▲▲▲**Original London Sightseeing Tour**—This 90-minute, once-over-lightly, double-decker bus tour drives by all the most famous sights, providing a stressless way to get your bearings and at least see the biggies. You "hop on and hop off" at any of the 25 stops and catch a later bus (runs about every ten minutes in summer, every 20 minutes in winter). Some buses have a tape-recorded narration (your choice of eight languages), and others come with a much-more-fun, English-only, live guide (roughly every third bus has a guide). An inexpensive form of transport as well as an informative tour, it's worth the £12. There are daily departures from 9:30 until early evening from Victoria Street (1 block north of Victoria Station), Marble Arch, Piccadilly Circus, Trafalgar Square, and so on (reservations unnecessary; ticket good for all the next day if purchased after 14:00, tel. 0181/877-1722). Bring a sweater and extra film. Note: If you pick up the bus at Victoria at 9:30, you can hop off near the end of the 90-minute loop at the Buckingham Palace stop, a five-minute walk from the

Central London

Palace and the Changing of the Guard at 11:30. The many copy-cat tours offer about the same service and value.

▲▲**Walking Tours**—Several times every day top-notch local guides lead small groups through specific slices of London's past. While the TI and many hotels have the various fliers, only *Time Out* and *What's On* list all scheduled walks, enabling you to choose according to your schedule and interests. Simply show up at the announced location, pay £4.50, and enjoy two chatty hours of Dickens, the Plague, Shakespeare, Legal London, the Beatles, Jack the Ripper, or whatever is on the agenda. Evenings feature organized pub crawls and ghost walks. "London Walks" is the dominant company (for recorded schedule, tel. 0171/624-3978, Web site: london.walks.com.) Chris Salaman offers private walking tours for as little as £3 per person (tel. 0181/871-9048).

▲▲**Cruise the Thames**—Boat tours with an entertaining commentary sail regularly between Westminster Pier (north of the base of Westminster Bridge on the Big Ben side) and the Tower of London (£4.20, round-trip £5.40, three tours hourly from 10:20–21:00 in peak season, 30-minute cruise, tel. 0171/930-4097). Similar boats leave the Westminster Pier for Greenwich (£5.60, round-trip £6.70, two hourly from 10:00–17:00, 50 minutes) and Kew Gardens (£6, round-trip £10, seven tours per day, 90 minutes, tel. 0171/930-2062). For pleasure and efficiency, consider combining a one-way cruise with a tube ride back.

Sights—Central London

Note: Summer hours are listed. Sights close early off-season. Students and seniors should ask for "concessions" (discounts). Since many places run sporadic tours, make a habit of telephoning first.

▲▲**Westminster Abbey**—England's historic coronation church is a crowded collection of famous tombs (including the tomb of the unknown soldier). Like a stony refugee camp waiting outside St. Peter's gates, this English hall of fame is thought-provoking but a bit overrated. Its tombstone history is thick with Richards, Annes, Henrys, Marys, Elizabeths, Poet's Corner, and so on. The most Gothic-looking decor (like the fine choir in the center) is 19th-century neo-Gothic. At the high altar you'll see the historic coronation throne (£4, Monday 9:30–16:45, Tuesday–Friday 9:00–16:45, Saturday 9:00–14:45 and 15:45–17:45, additional hours on Wednesday 18:00–19:45—the only time photography is allowed; last admission 45 minutes before closing; tube: Westminster, tel. 0171/222-5152). Praying is free—use separate entrance.

Walkman tours of the abbey cost £6 (offered until 15:15 weekdays or until 13:15 Saturday). Guided "super tours" are £7 and must be booked in advance (up to six per day, 90 minutes, tel. 0171/222-7110 to book and get times). These "super tours," a historic rundown on the tombs and memorials, are led by a verger (church equivalent of a bat boy). While the £4 entry gets you a brochure with all the basics for a self-guided tour, if you have 90 minutes to spare the live tour is worth the extra £3.

Evensong is on Monday, Tuesday, Thursday, and Friday at 17:00, Saturday and Sunday at 15:00; and an organ recital is held Sunday at 17:45. If you've got that urge to rub a knight, the cloister sports a brass-rubbing center.

▲▲**Houses of Parliament** (Commons and Lords)—These are too tempting to terrorists to be opened wide to tourists, but if Parliament is in session you can view debates in either house (Monday, Tuesday, and Thursday 14:30–22:00 with long waits until 18:00, Wednesday and Friday 9:30–14:00, use St. Stephen's entrance, tube: Westminster, tel. 0171/219-4272). The House of Lords has more pageantry, shorter lines, shorter hours, and less-interesting debates (tel. 0171/219-3107 for schedule).

If you request a "card of entry" from the American Embassy three to four months in advance, you can avoid the line (or "jump the queue") at the House of Commons and see the opening ceremony. Write to: American Embassy, 24 Grosvenor Square, W1A 1AE London; then pick up your card(s) at the American Embassy in London. You can request up to four cards (free). For more information call the embassy at 0171/499-9000; once in their phone tree press 0 to get an operator, then ask for Protocol.

Notice Westminster Hall on the left as you go through security. The Houses of Parliament are located in what was once the Palace of Westminster, long the palace of England's medieval kings before it was largely destroyed by fire in 1834. The impressive Westminster Hall dates from the 11th century (its famous hammer-beam roof was added in 1397). The palace was rebuilt in Victorian Gothic style after the fire (a move away from neoclassicism back to England's Christian and medieval heritage, true to the Romantic Age). Completed in 1860, only a few of its 1,000 rooms are open to the public.

The clock tower (315 feet high) is named for its 13-ton bell, Ben. The light above the clock is lit when the House of Commons is sitting. For a hip HOP view, walk halfway over Westminster Bridge.

▲▲**Cabinet War Rooms**—This is a fascinating walk through the underground headquarters of the British government's fight against the Nazis in the darkest days of the Battle for Britain. The nerve center of the British war effort was used from 1939 through 1945. Churchill's room, the map room, and so on, are just as they were in 1945. For all the blood, sweat, toil, and tears details, pick-up the headsets at the entrance and follow the included 45-minute Walkman tour (£4.40, daily 9:30–18:00, on King Charles Street just off Whitehall, follow the signs, tube: Westminster, tel. 0171/930-6961).

Horse Guards—The Horse Guards have a 11:00 inspection Monday through Saturday (at 10:00 on Sunday) and a colorful dismounting ceremony daily at 16:00. The rest of the day is terrible for camcorders (on Whitehall, between Trafalgar and #10 Downing Street, tube: Westminster).

▲**Banqueting Hall**—England's first Renaissance building (designed by Inigo Jones around 1620) and one of the few London landmarks spared by the 1666 fire, the Hall is the only surviving part of the original Palace of Whitehall. Don't miss its Rubens ceiling which, at Charles I's request, drove home the doctrine of the legitimacy of the divine right of kings. In 1649, divine right ignored, Charles I was beheaded on the balcony of this building by a Cromwellian parliament. Admission includes a fine 20-minute audiovisual history, an interesting-only-to-history-buffs 35-minute tape-recorded tour, and a look at a fancy banqueting hall (£3.25, Monday–Saturday 10:00–17:00, last entry at 16:30, subject to closure for government functions, aristocratic WC, immediately across Whitehall from the Horse Guards, tube: Westminster, tel. 0171/930-4179).

▲▲**Trafalgar Square**—London's central square is a thrilling place to just hang out. Lord Nelson stands atop his 185-foot-tall fluted granite column, gazing out to Trafalgar where he lost his life but defeated the French fleet (part of the 1842 memorial is

London

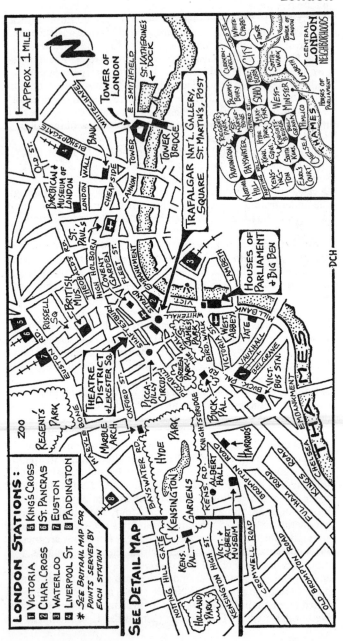

APPROX. 1 MILE

TOWER OF LONDON

ST. KATHERINE'S DOCK

E. SMITHFIELD

TOWER BRIDGE

TOWER

BANK

BISHOPSGATE

OLD ST.

BARBICAN + MUSEUM OF LONDON

LONDON WALL

CHEAPSIDE

CANNON

TRAFALGAR NAT'L. GALLERY, ST. MARTIN'S, POST SQUARE

ST. PAUL'S

THEOBALD'S RD.

HIGH HOLBORN

FLEET ST.

EMBANKMENT

STRAND

BRITISH MUS.

COVENT GARDEN

HOUSES OF PARLIAMENT + BIG BEN

RUSSELL SQ.

WHITEHALL

LAMBETH

THEATRE DISTRICT + LEICESTER SQ.

EUSTON RD.

SHAFTESBURY

OXFORD ST.

PICCADILLY CIRCUS

ST. JAMES PARK

GREEN PK.

BIRD WALK

WEST. ABBEY

TATE

MILLBANK

VAUXHALL

VICT. BUS STN.

BELGRAVE

VICTORIA

MARYLEBONE

ZOO

REGENT'S PARK

MARBLE ARCH

BAYSWATER RD.

HYDE PARK

KENSINGTON PK. RD.

KNIGHTSBRIDGE

BUCK. PAL.

BUCK. PAL. RD.

HARRODS

THAMES

CHELSEA EMBANKMENT

KING'S ROAD

FULHAM ROAD

KENSINGTON GARDENS

ALBERT HALL

ALBERT RD.

BROMPTON ROAD

CROMWELL ROAD

NOTTING HILL GATE

HOLLAND PARK

KENSINGTON HIGH ST.

KENS. PAL.

VICT. + ALBERT MUSEUM

OLD BROMPTON ROAD

SEE DETAIL MAP

LONDON STATIONS:

1 VICTORIA   5 KING'S CROSS
2 CHAR. CROSS   6 ST. PANCRAS
3 WATERLOO   7 EUSTON
4 LIVERPOOL ST.   8 PADDINGTON

* SEE BRITRAIL MAP FOR POINTS SERVED BY EACH STATION

CENTRAL LONDON NEIGHBORHOODS

WHITE CHAPEL

OLD ST.

TOWER OF LONDON

CITY

CLERKEN-WELL

BLOOMS-BURY

SOHO

HOLBORN

SOUTH-WARK

WEST-MINSTER

Houses of Parliament

LAMBETH

REGENT'S PARK

MARYLEBONE

OXFORD ST.

MAN-CHESTER SQ.

HYDE PARK

KENS. GDNS.

KNIGHTS-BRIDGE

SOUTH KENS.

GRANK.

CHELSEA

PIMLICO

THAMES

PADDINGTON

BAYSWATER

NOTTING HILL

KENS-ING-TON

EARL'S COURT

—— DCH ——

made from the melted-down cannons of his victims at Trafalgar). He's surrounded by giant lions, hordes of people, and even more pigeons. The square is the climax of most marches and demonstrations (tube: Charing Cross).

▲▲**National Gallery**—Newly renovated, displaying Britain's top collection of European paintings from 1250 to 1900—works by Leonardo, Botticelli, Velazquez, Rembrandt, Turner, van Gogh, and the Impressionists—this is one of Europe's classiest galleries. Don't miss the "Micro Gallery," a computer room even your dad could have fun in (closes 30 minutes earlier than museum). You can study any artist, style, or topic in the museum and even print out a tailor-made tour map. (Free, Monday–Saturday 10:00–18:00, Wednesday until 20:00, Sunday 2:00–18:00, free one-hour tours weekdays at 11:30 and 14:30 and Saturday at 14:00 and 15:30, on Trafalgar Square, tube: Charing Cross or Leicester Square, tel. 0171/839-3321.) Ask about the Walkman tours (free, but donation requested).

The National Portrait Gallery, just around the corner, is as exciting as somebody else's yearbook (free, Monday–Saturday 10:00–18:00, Sunday 12:00–18:00, tel. 0171/306-0055).

▲▲**Piccadilly Circus**—London's touristy "Town Square" is surrounded by fascinating streets and swimming with youth on the rampage. The new Rock Circus offers a very commercial but serious history of rock music with Madame Tussaud wax stars. It's an entertaining hour under radio earphones for rock 'n' roll romantics (£8, daily 10:00–20:00, plenty of photo ops, many enter with a beer-buzz and sing happily off-key under their headphones—nearly as entertaining as the exhibit itself, tube: Piccadilly Circus). For overstimulation, drop by the shiny new Pepsi Trocadero Center's "theme park of the future" for its virtual reality games, including SegaWorld, Imaginator, and Virtuality, along with a nine-screen cinema (admission to Trocadero is free; individual attractions cost £2–8; combined "Adrenalin Ticket"-£10; between Coventry and Shaftesbury, just off Piccadilly). Chinatown, to the east, has swollen since Hong Kong lost its independence. Nearby Shaftesbury Avenue and Leicester Square teem with fun-seekers, theaters, Chinese restaurants, and street singers.

Soho—North of Piccadilly, Soho isn't as sleazy as it used to be, but it's still worth a gawk. This is London's red-light district where "friendly models" wait in tiny rooms up dreary stairways and scantily clad con artists sell strip shows. Anyone who goes into any one of these shows will be ripped off. Every time. Even a £3 show comes with a £100 cover or minimum (as it's printed on the drink menu) and a "security man." The door has no handle until you pay.

▲**Covent Gardens**—This boutique-ish shopping district is a people-watcher's delight with cigarette-eaters, Punch 'n' Judy acts, food that's good for you (but not your wallet), trendy crafts, sweet whiffs of pot, hair that's two-tone (neither natural), and

National Gallery Highlights

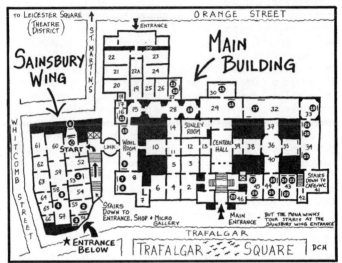

Medieval and Early Renaissance
1. Wilton Diptych
2. UCCELLO—Battle of San Romano
3. VAN EYCK—Arnolfini Marriage
4. CRIVELLI—Annunciation With St. Emidius
5. BOTTICELLI—Venus and Mars

High Renaissance
6. LEONARDO DA VINCI—Virgin and Child (cartoon)
7. MICHELANGELO—Entombment
8. RAPHAEL—Pope Julius II

Venetian Renaissance
9. TINTORETTO—Origin of the Milky Way
10. TITIAN—Bacchus and Ariadne

Northern Protestant Art
11. VERMEER—Young Woman Standing at a Virginal
12. Hoogstraten Peepshow
13. REMBRANDT—Self-Portrait

Baroque
14. RUBENS—The Judgment of Paris
15. VAN DYCK—Charles I on Horseback

faces that could set off a metal detector. For the best lunch deals walk a block or two away from the eye of this touristic tornado. It's hard to go wrong in a little tea-and-sandwich deli (vegetarians like #2 Neal's Yard, off Neal Street, tube: Covent Gardens). ▲▲▲**British Museum**—This is the greatest chronicle of our civilization anywhere. Visiting this immense museum is like hiking through Encyclopedia Britannica National Park. After an overview ramble, cover just two or three sections of your choice more thoroughly. The Egyptian, Mesopotamian (Assyrian), and Greek (Parthenon) sections are highlights. The huge winged lions (which guarded Assyrian palaces 800 years before Christ) guard the museum's three great ancient galleries. For a brief tour, connect these ancient dots:

Start with the Egyptian. Wander from the Rosetta Stone past the many statues, side-tripping into small rooms on the right for more intimate peeks at pharoahs' art. At the end of the hall, climb the stairs to mummyland.

Back at the winged lions, wander through the dark, violent, and mysterious Assyrian rooms. The Nimrud Gallery is lined with royal propaganda reliefs and wounded lions.

The most modern of the ancient art fills the Greek section. Find room #1 behind the winged lions and start your walk through Greek art history with the simple and primitive Cycladian fertility figures. Later, painted vases show a culture really into partying. The finale is the Elgin Marbles. The much wrangled over bits of the Athenian Parthenon (from 450 B.C.) are much more impressive than they look. To better appreciate these ancient carvings, read through the orientation material in the tiny intro rooms between rooms 7 and 8. (Free, Monday–Saturday 10:00–17:00, Sunday 14:30–18:00, least crowded weekday mornings, tube: Tottenham Court Road; guided 90-minute £6 tours offered daily—three per day on Sunday, two per day in winter—call museum for times, tel. 0171/636-1555.) As of March '98, the British Library (notable for its manuscripts) will no longer be in the British Museum (see below).

British Library—Wander through the manuscripts that have enlightened and brightened our lives for centuries, from the Magna Carta, Bibles, and Beethoven, to the Beatles (free, Monday–Saturday 9:30–18:00, Sunday 11:00–17:00, 96 Euston Road, tube: King's Cross or Euston, tel. 0171/412-7000). Note: The library will open in March '98.

▲**Buckingham Palace**—In order to pay for the restoration of the fire-damaged Windsor Castle, the royal family is opening its lavish home to the public until 2000 (£9 to see the state apartments and throne room; open August and September only; daily from 9:30–16:30; limited to 8,000 visitors a day—come early to get an appointed visit time; tube: Victoria, tel. 0171/930-4832). If the flag is flying (or you see her yellow Toyota), the queen is home.

▲**Changing of the Guard at Buckingham Palace**—Overrated but almost required. The guard changes daily from April through July at 11:30 and every other day August through March (no band when wet). Join the mob at the back side of the palace (the front faces a huge and very private park). The pageantry and parading are colorful and even stirring, but the actual changing of the guard is a non-event. It is interesting to see nearly every tourist in London gathered in one place at the same time. Hop into a big black taxi and say, "To Buckingham Palace, please." For all the color with none of the crowds, see the Inspection of the Guard Ceremony at 11:00 in front of the Wellington Barracks, east of the palace on Birdcage Walk. Afterwards, stroll through nearby St. James' Park. For today's schedule, call 0171/930-4832. (Tube: Victoria, St. James' Park, or Green Park.)

▲▲**Tate Gallery**—One of Europe's great art houses, the Tate specializes in British painting (14th-century through contemporary), pre-Raphaelites, Impressionism, and modern art (Matisse, van Gogh, Monet, Picasso). Learn about the mystical watercolorist Blake and the romantic, nature-worship art of Turner (free, daily 10:00–18:00; free tours weekdays 11:00, 12:00, 14:00, and 15:00; Saturday at 15:00; tube: Pimlico; call to confirm schedule, tel. 0171/887-8000).

Sights—West London

▲**Hyde Park**—London's "Central Park" has more than 600 acres of lush greenery, a huge man-made lake, the royal Kensington Palace (not worth touring), and the ornate neo-Gothic Albert Memorial across from the Royal Albert Hall. Early afternoons on Sunday, Speaker's Corner (tube: Marble Arch) offers soapbox oratory at its best. "The grass roots of democracy" is actually a holdover from when the gallows stood here and the criminal was allowed to say just about anything he wanted to before he swung. I dare you to raise your voice and gather a crowd—it's easy to do.

▲**Victoria and Albert Museum**—A gangly but surprisingly interesting collection of costumes, armor, furniture, decorative arts, and much more from the West as well as from Asia and Islam. Walk through centuries of aristocratic living rooms and follow the evolution of fashion in England (through 40 fascinating and well-described display cases) from 1600 to today (£5, Monday 12:00–18:00, Tuesday–Sunday 10:00–18:00, tube: So. Kensington, pleasant garden café, tel. 0171/938-8500).

Kew Gardens—For a fine park and a palatial greenhouse jungle to swing through, take the tube or the boat to every botanist's favorite escape, Kew Gardens (£4.50, Monday–Saturday 9:30–18:00, Sunday 9:30–19:00, galleries and conservatories close a half-hour earlier, tube: Kew Gardens, tel. 0181/940-1171). For tea, consider the Maids of Honor (280 Kew Road, near garden entrance, tel. 0181/940-2752).

Sights—East London, "The City"

▲▲**The City of London**—When Londoners say "the City," they mean the 1-square-mile business, banking, and journalism center that 2,000 years ago was Roman Londinium. The outline of the Roman city walls can still be seen in the arc of roads from Blackfriars Bridge to Tower Bridge. Within the City are 24 churches designed by Christopher Wren. It's a fascinating district to wander, but since nobody actually lives there, it's a ghost town on Saturday and Sunday. An hour in the city's Central Criminal Courts, known as "Old Bailey," is always interesting (Monday–Friday 10:30–13:00 and 14:00–16:00, quiet in August, no cameras or bags, no cloakroom, at Old Bailey and Newgate St., tube: St. Paul's, tel. 0171/248-3277).

▲▲**St. Paul's Cathedral**—Wren's most famous church is the great St. Paul's, its elaborate interior capped by a 365-foot dome. St. Paul's was Britain's World War II symbol of resistance, as Nazi bombs failed to blow it up. (There's a memorial chapel to the heroic firefighters who kept watch over it with hoses cocked.) The crypt (free with admission) is a world of historic bones and memorials, including Admiral Nelson's tomb and interesting cathedral models. This was the wedding church of Prince Charles and the late Princess Diana. Climb the dome for a great city view and some fun in the whispering gallery. Whisper sweet nothings into the wall and your partner (and anyone else) on the far side can hear you. (£4 entry, £3.50 extra to climb dome; daily 9:30–16:30; free on Sunday but restricted viewing due to services; allow an hour to climb up and down the dome; £3.50 for 90-minute cathedral and crypt tours: with a guide at 11:00, 11:30, 13:30, and 14:00 or £3 for a Walkman anytime; Sunday services at 8:00, 8:45, 11:00, and 15:15; tube: St. Paul's, tel. 0171/236-4128.)

▲**Museum of London**—Stroll through London history—from pre-Roman times to the Blitz up through today (£4, free after 16:30; Tuesday–Saturday 10:00–18:00, Sunday 12:00–18:00, usually closed Monday but open on bank-holiday Mondays; tube: Barbican or St. Paul's, tel. 0171/600-3699). This regular stop for the local schoolkids gives the best overview of London history in town.

▲▲**Tower of London**—William I, still getting used to his new title of "the Conqueror," built the stone "White Tower" (1077–1097) to keep the Londoners in line. The tower served as an effective lookout for invaders coming up the Thames. His successors enlarged it to its present 18-acre size. Because of the security it provided, over the centuries it has served as the Royal Mint, the Royal Jewel House, and a prison. You'll find more bloody history per square inch in this original tower of power than anywhere in Britain. Don't miss the entertaining 50-minute Beefeater tour (free, leaving regularly from inside the gate, last one usually at 15:30) of this historic fortress, palace, prison, and host to more than 3 million visitors a year. Britain's best armory and most lovely Norman chapel (St. John's Chapel, 1080) are in the White Tower. The crown jewels, which date from the Restoration (Cromwell sold or melted down the earlier jewels), are the best on earth. The long midday summer lines are made almost enjoyable

by museum displays along the way. To avoid the crowds arrive at
9:00 and go straight for the jewels, doing the tour and tower later.
(£8.50; tower hours: Monday–Saturday 9:00–18:00, with last entry
at 17:00, Sunday 10:00–18:00; the long but fast-moving line is
worst on Sundays; tube: Tower Hill, tel. 0171/709-0765.) Visitors
are welcome on the grounds to worship in the Royal Chapel on
Sunday (free, 11:00 service with fine choral music).

Every night at 21:30, with pageantry-filled ceremony, the
Tower of London is locked up (as it has been every night for the
last 700 years). To attend this free event, you need to request an
invitation at least five weeks before your visit. Write to: Ceremony
of Keys, H.M. Tower of London, London EC3N 4AB. Include
your name, number of people (up to seven), requested date, alternative dates, and an international reply coupon (buy at a U.S. post
office). Although five week's notice is requested, you might try for
an appointment near the end of your trip by sending a stamped
envelope addressed to your London hotel once you arrive.

Sights Next to the Tower—The best remaining bit of London's Roman Wall is just north of the tower (at the Tower Hill
tube station). **Tower Hill Pageant**, a 15-minute, high-tech, historical amusement ride, takes you through 20 centuries of London
history followed by a small but fine exhibition of Roman and
Saxon artifacts uncovered during the recent riverside development.
It's worthwhile for rich kids with time to kill (£6.95, daily
9:30–17:30, until 16:30 off-season, across the street from the
Tower turnstile, tel. 0171/709-0081). Freshly painted and
restored, **Tower Bridge** has an 1894–1994 history exhibit (£5.70,
daily 10:00–18:30, last entry at 17:15, good view, poor value, tel.
0171/403-3761). **St. Katherine Yacht Harbor**, chic and newly
renovated, just east of the Tower Bridge, has mod shops and the
classic old Dickens Inn, fun for a drink or pub lunch.

Sights—South London

▲▲Imperial War Museum—This impressive museum covers
the wars of this century, from heavy weaponry to love notes and
Varga Girls, from Monty's Africa campaign tank to Schwarzkopf's
Desert Storm uniform. You can trace the development of the
machine gun, watch footage of the first tank battles, hold your
breath through the gruesome WWI trench experience, and buy
WWII-era toys in the fun museum shop. Rather than glorify war,
the museum does its best to shine a light on the powerful human
side of one of mankind's most persistent traits (£4.70, daily
10:00–18:00, free after 16:30, 90 minutes is enough time for most
visitors, tube: Lambeth North, tel. 0171/416-5000).

▲▲Museum of the Moving Image—This high-tech, interac-
tive, hands-on museum traces the story of moving images from a
caveman's flickering fire to modern TV. There's great footage of
the earliest movies and TV shows. Turn-of-the-century-clad

staff speak as if silent films are the latest marvel. You can make your own animated cartoon. Don't miss the speedy 50-year montage of magic MGM moments. Brit movie buffs will enjoy the 90-minute film of British cinematic highlights (£5.95, daily 10:00–18:00, tube: Waterloo; or tube: Embankment, then walk across the Thames pedestrian bridge, tel. 0171/928-3535).

More Sights

▲▲**National Maritime Museum in Greenwich**—Today's museums are contained in a royal shell. The Tudor kings preferred Greenwich to their other palaces. Henry VIII was born here. Later kings commissioned Inigo Jones and Chris Wren to beautify the place. In spite of its architectural and royal treats, this is England's maritime capital, and visitors go for things salty.

Crawl through the *Cutty Sark*, the last of the great clipper ships. Launched in 1869, she was queen of the seas. With 32,000 square feet of sail, she could blow with the wind 300 miles in a day (£3.50, daily 10:00–17:00, from noon on Sunday, tel. 0181/858-3445). Moored nearby, the little *Gipsy Moth IV* is the 53-foot sailboat Sir Francis Chichester used for his solo voyage around the world in 1967 (£1).

Straddle the zero meridian, set your wristwatch to Greenwich mean time at the Old Royal Observatory, and relive four centuries of Britannia-rules-the-waves history at the National Maritime Museum (£5.50, £4 for observatory only; daily 10:00–17:00; tel. 0181/858-4422). Only two galleries of the Maritime Museum are open (because the museum is being refurbished for the year 2000 celebration) so you'll likely be sold a combined ticket that includes the Maritime Museum, Royal Observatory, and Queen's House.

Getting to Greenwich is either a joy (cruise down the Thames from central London's piers at Westminster, Charing Cross, or Tower of London) or a snap (tube to Island Gardens in Zone 2, free with tube pass, then walk under pedestrian Thames tunnel; or catch the train from Charing Cross station to Maze Hill). Greenwich tourist information: tel. 0181/858-6376.

Thames Barrier—East of Greenwich the world's largest movable flood barrier welcomes visitors with an informative and entertaining exhibition (£3.40, Monday–Friday 10:00–17:00, weekends 10:30–17:30; catch 70-minute boat from Westminster Pier, or take 30-minute boat from Greenwich pier, or train from London's Charing Cross station to Charlton then walk 15 minutes; tel. 0181/854-1373).

Honorable Mention—Madame Tussaud's Waxworks is expensive but dang good (£8.95, children £5.95, daily 9:00–17:30, buy ticket at TI to save a little money and get in with no wait, Marylebone Road, tube: Baker Street, tel. 0171/935-6861; combined ticket for Tussaud's and Planetarium is £10.95 for adults, £6.95 for

kids). At **Geffrye Decorative Arts Museum** you can walk
through British front rooms from 1600 to 1960 (free, Tuesday–
Saturday 10:00–17:00, Sunday 14:00–17:00, closed Monday, tube:
Liverpool Street, then bus 22A or 22B north, tel. 0171/739-9893).
Architects love the quirky **Sir John Soane's Museum** (free,
10:00–17:00, closed Sunday and Monday, tube: Holborn).

Shopping in London

▲**Harrods**—Artfully mixing big and classy, Harrods is filled
with wonderful displays, elegant high teas, and fingernail-
ripping riots during its July sales. Harrods has everything from
elephants to toothbrushes. Need some peanut butter? The food
halls are sights to savor (with reasonable cafeterias; 10:00–18:00;
until 19:00 on Wednesday, Thursday, and Friday; closed Sunday;
tel. 0171/730-1234). For royal window-shopping, cruise nearby
King's Road in Chelsea. Most stores close around 18:00 but stay
open until 20:00 on Wednesday or Thursday, depending on the
neighborhood.

▲**Street Markets**—If you like garage sales and people-
watching, hit a London street market. The tourist office has a
complete, up-to-date list. The best are Portobello Road (Saturday 8:30–17:00, antique and flea market, near recommended
B&Bs, tube: Notting Hill Gate) and Camden Market (Saturday
and Sunday 10:00–17:00; a huge, trendy arts and crafts festival;
tube: Camden Town). There's some good early morning market
activity somewhere any day of the week. Warning: Street markets attract two kinds of people—tourists and pickpockets.

Famous Auctions—London's famous auctioneers welcome
the curious public. For schedules (most weekdays, closed mid-
summer), telephone Sotheby's (tel. 0171/493-8080, tube: Oxford
Circus) or Christie's (tel. 0171/839-9060, tube: Green Park).

Entertainment and Theater in London

London bubbles with top-notch entertainment seven nights a week.
Everything's listed in the monthly *Time Out* or *What's On* magazines, available at most newsstands. You'll choose from classical,
jazz, rock, and far-out music, Gilbert and Sullivan, dance, comedy,
Bahai meetings, poetry readings, spectator sports, film, and theater.

London's theater rivals Broadway's in quality and beats it in
price. Choose from the Royal Shakespeare Company, top musicals,
comedy, thrillers, sex farces, and more. Performances are nightly
except Sunday, usually with one matinee a week. Matinees
(Wednesday, Thursday, or Saturday, listed in a box in *What's On*)
are cheaper and rarely sold out. Tickets range from about £8 to £25.

Most theaters, marked on tourist maps, are in the Piccadilly–
Trafalgar area. Box offices, hotels, and TIs have a handy "Theater
Guide" brochure listing what's playing.

London Area

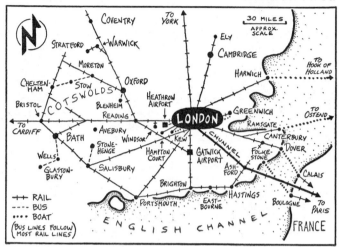

The best and cheapest way to book a ticket is simply to call the theater box office directly, ask about seats and dates available, and book by credit card. You can call from the U.S.A. as easily as from England (photocopy your hometown library's London newspaper theater section). Pick up your ticket 15 minutes before the show.

Getting a ticket through a ticket agency (at most tourist offices or scattered throughout London) is quick and easy but prices are inflated by a standard 20 to 25 percent booking fee. Ticket agencies are scalpers with an address. Agencies are worthwhile only if a show you've got to see is sold out at the box office. They scarf up hot tickets, planning to make a killing after the show is sold out. U.S.A. booking agencies get their tickets from another agency, adding even more to your expense by involving yet another middleman.

Cheap theater tricks: Most theaters offer cheap returned tickets, standing room, matinee, and senior or student stand-by deals. These "concessions" are indicated with a "conc" or "s" in the listings. Picking up a late return can get you a great seat at a cheap-seat price. Standing room costs only a few pounds. If a show is "sold out," there's usually a way to get a seat. Call and ask how. The famous (but overrated) "half-price booth" in Leicester (pronounced "Lester") Square sells cheap tickets to shows on the push list the day of the show only (Monday–Saturday, 14:30–18:30). I usually buy the second-cheapest tickets directly from the theater box office. Many theaters are so small that there's hardly a bad seat. After the lights go down, "scooting up" is less than a capital offense. Shakespeare did it.

Royal Shakespeare Company—If you'll ever enjoy Shake-speare, it'll be here. (But lo, I've tried and failed.) The RSC splits its season between the Royal Shakespeare Theatre in Stratford (tel. 01789/295-623) and the Barbican Centre in London (daily 9:00–20:00; credit-card booking, they mail out schedules; tel. 0171/638-8891, or for recorded information call 0171/628-9760). Tickets range in price from £5 (preview) to £24. The best way to buy is direct, by telephone and credit card. You can pick up your ticket at the door; £6 stand-by tickets are sold at 9:00 the day of the show. For a complete schedule, write to the Royal Shakespeare Theatre, Stratford-upon-Avon, Warwickshire, CV37 6BB.

Shakespeare at the New Globe Theater—To see Shake-speare in an exact replica of the theater for which he wrote his plays, check out the Globe. This thatch-roofed, open-air, round theater does the plays as Shakespeare intended (with no amplifi-cation). Curtain times are usually at 14:00 and 19:30, May through September. You'll pay £5 to stand and up to £20 to sit (on a backless bench). Allow time to explore the historic exhibit about the bard and his work. The theater and exhibit are open to tour when there are no plays (£5, daily 10:00–17:00, includes guided 30-minute tour offered on the half hour; if a play is scheduled, the museum is open only 9:00–12:30; on the south bank directly across the Thames from St. Paul's, tube: Mansion House, tel. 0171/928-6406).

Music—For a fun classical event, attend a "Prom Concert." This is an annual music festival with almost nightly concerts in the Royal Albert Hall from July through September at give-a-peasant-some-culture prices (£3 standing-room spots sold at the door, tel. 0171/589-8212). Look into the free lunchtime concerts popular in churches (especially Wren's St. Bride's Church, tel. 0171/353-1301; and St. Martin-in-the-Fields, weekdays except Thursday at 13:00, tel. 0171/930-1862).

Day Trips from London

You could fill a book with the many easy and exciting day trips from London (Earl Steinbicker did: *Daytrips in Britain by Rail, Bus or Car from London and Edinburgh*). Several tour companies take London-based travelers out and back every day. Some offer bus tours that can be used by those without a car as a "free" way to get to Bath or Stow-on-the-Wold (saving you, for instance, the £28.50 London–Bath train ticket). Evan Evans' tours leave from behind Victoria Station at 9:00 (with your bag stowed under the bus), include a full day of sightseeing with £5 to £10 worth of admissions, and leave you in Bath or Stow before returning to London (£29.50 for Stonehenge and Bath; £45 for Salisbury, Stonehenge, and Bath; and £42.50 for Oxford, Blenheim, Bur-ford, and Stow; tel. 0181/332-2222). Greenline does a tour of Bath and Stonehenge for £24 (tel. 0181/668-7261 or stop by the

Greenline office in Fountain Square directly south of Victoria Station).

The British rail system uses London as a hub and normally offers round-trip fares (after 9:30) that cost virtually the same as one-way fares. "Day return" tickets are best (and cheapest) for day trips. Sometimes you can save money if you purchase "Super Advance" tickets before 14:00 on the day before your trip.

For more ideas, see BritRail's handy "Day Trips from London" booklet (available in the U.S.A. for $17 postpaid, CC:VMA, tel. 800/677-8585). But given the high cost of big-city living and the charm of small-town England, I'd see London and get out.

Sleeping in London
(£1 = about $1.60, tel. code: 0171)
Sleep Code: **S**=Single, **D**=Double/Twin, **T**=Triple, **Q**=Quad, **b**=bathroom, **t**=toilet only, **s**=shower only, **CC**=Credit Card (**V**isa, **M**asterCard, **A**mex). Unless otherwise noted, prices include a big English breakfast.

London is expensive but there's no need to spend a fortune or stay in a depressing dump. Plan on spending £50 to £60 ($80–95) for a basic, clean, reasonably cheery double in a usually cramped, cracked-plaster building, with a hearty English (as opposed to continental) breakfast. Rather than mess with a dorm or hostel, I'd spend £35 for a sleepable double with breakfast in a safe, clean, tiny, dreary place where the landlords are absent and service is minimal. (Hang up your towel to dry and reuse). My London splurges, at £70 to £130, are spacious, thoughtfully appointed places you'd be happy to entertain or make love in. TVs are nearly standard in rooms (those without usually have an inviting TV lounge).

I reserve my London room in advance with a phone call direct from the States. Assure the manager you'll arrive before 16:00, and leave your credit-card number as security. If you must send a deposit, ask if you can send a signed $100 traveler's check. (Leave the "pay to" line blank and include a note explaining that you'll be happy to pay cash upon arrival. That way they can avoid bank charges.)

Sleeping in Victoria Station Neighborhood, Belgravia
The streets behind Victoria Station teem with budget B&Bs. It's a safe, surprisingly tidy and decent area without a hint of the trashy touristy glitz of the streets in front of the station. The first three listings are on Ebury Street, between the train and coach stations, proudly part of Belgravia. Even with Margaret Thatcher living around the corner (you'll see the policeman standing outside #73 Chester Square), this is a classy and peaceful place to call home in London. Decent eateries abound (see Eating below). The cheaper listings are relatively dumpy.

London, Victoria Neighborhood

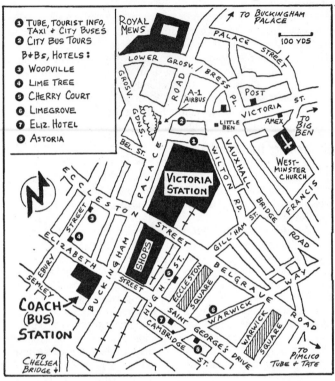

Legend:
- ❶ TUBE, TOURIST INFO, TAXI + CITY BUSES
- ❷ CITY BUS TOURS

B+Bs, HOTELS:
- ❸ WOODVILLE
- ❹ LIME TREE
- ❺ CHERRY COURT
- ❻ LIMEGROVE
- ❼ ELIZ. HOTEL
- ❽ ASTORIA

Don't expect £50 cheeriness in a £34 room. Those traveling on a shoestring off-season save a few pounds by arriving late without a reservation and checking around. Competition is fierce and prices in this area are often soft (especially for multi-night stays). Especially for Warwick Way hotels (and in the summer when you'll want the window open at night), request a quiet back room. All hotels are within a five-minute walk of the Victoria tube, bus, and train stations. There's a £8-per-day garage and a nearby launderette (self-serve or full-serve, 3 Westmoreland Terrace, tel. 0171/821-8692).

At **Woodville House** the quarters are tight, showers are down the hall, and several rooms are noisy on the street, but this well-worn place is a good value with lots of travel tips and endless tea, coffee, and friendly chat (especially about the local rich and famous) from Rachel Joplin (S-£39, D-£58; bunky family deals for three, four, or five in a room; easy credit-card reservations, 107 Ebury Street, SW1W 9QU; tel. 0171/730-1048, fax 0171/730-2574).

Lime Tree Hotel is enthusiastically run by David and Marilyn Davies. The thoughtfully decorated public areas and rooms are more spacious than most in this area and guests are welcome in the peaceful garden—ask where the entrance is. The renovated rooms offer the best value (Sb-£65–75, Db-£85–100, Tb £110–120, family room-£120–140, David will deal in slow times, CC:VMA, 135 Ebury Street, SW1W 9RA, tel. 0171/730-8191, fax 0171/730-7865). Each room comes with a TV, phone, hair dryer, safe, and coffee pot.

Cherry Court Hotel, run by the friendly Patel family, offers small rooms and good prices on a quiet street very close to the station (Sb-£35, Db-£40, Tb-£60, CC:VMA, pleasant garden, 23 Hugh Street, SW1V 1QJ, tel. 0171/828-2840, fax 0171/828-0393, e-mail: cherryc@globalnet.co.uk).

Cedar Guest House, across the street, is a minimal place with eight rooms at near-youth-hostel prices. It's run by a Polish organization to help Poles afford London, but all are welcome (D-£30–32, T-£46, 30 Hugh Street, SW1V 1RP, tel. 0171/828-2625).

Elizabeth Hotel has a gracious feel, offering a large lobby, small but pleasant rooms, and free access to the private park overlooks (S-£36–40, Sb-£55, D-£62, Ds-£66, small Db-£70, Db-£80, Tb-£96, Qb-£106, Quint/b-£115, 37 Eccleston Square, SW1V 1PB, tel. 0171/828-6812). Either traveler's checks or personal checks are accepted as a deposit.

Limegrove Hotel, run by harried Joyce, is a little smoky and has only two toilets and two showers for seven rooms, but is a fine value with full English breakfast served in your room (S-£28, small D-£36, D-£38, Db-£50, T-£48, Tb-from £60, cheaper off-season or for stays of six days or more, 101 Warwick Way, SW1V 4HT, tel. 0171/828-0458). Back rooms are quieter.

Astoria Hotel, a formerly elegant 1835 building, has faded but spacious rooms with soft prices for longer stays (Sb-£60, Db-£70, Tb-£75, Qb-£85, CC:VM, all with CNN on the TV, 39 St. Georges Drive, SW1V 4DG, tel. 0171/834-1965, fax 0171/834-1977, run by Ahmed).

Rubens at the Palace has a classy lobby and comfortable, if slightly worn, rooms. The American owners plan to remodel. Prices are soft—ask (Sb-£125, Db-£145, Tb-£185, suites available, CC:VMA, 2 blocks north of the station, close to Buckingham Palace, tel. 0171/834-6600, fax 0171/828-5401; from the U.S.A., tel. 800/424-2862).

"South Kensington," She Said, Loosening His Cummerbund

For the chance to live on a quiet street so classy it doesn't allow hotel signs, surrounded by trendy shops and colorful restaurants, call South Kensington home in London. Many locals just call it "South Ken." Shoppers will enjoy the location, a short walk from

Harrods and the designer shops of King's Road and Chelsea. You'll find plenty of budget ethnic eateries around the corner on Brompton Road (each hotel has restaurant scrapbooks or wall charts). This has got to be the ultimate fairy-tale London home-away-from-home. Of course, you'll pay for it. But these places are a fine value. A splendid splurge. Sumner Place is 200 yards from the South Kensington tube station (on the Circle Line, direct connection to Heathrow, two stops from Victoria Station—top of tube stairs, exit left, cross the doubled street, go right 2 blocks down Old Brompton Road, left onto Sumner Place).

Five Sumner Place Hotel is informal but professional, "highly commended" and recently voted "the best small hotel in London." You'll talk softly but not feel like you have to dress up as you wander, with your free daily newspaper, under the chandeliers out to the Victorian-style conservatory, a greenhouse dressed in blue, for breakfast. Each room is tastefully decorated with traditional period furnishings in a 150-year-old building (Sb-£88, Db-£129, Tb-£155, elevator, easy CC reservations, non-smoking, CC:VMA, 5 Sumner Place, South Kensington, SW7 3EE, tel. 0171/584-7586, fax 0171/823-9962, e-mail: no.5@dial.pipex.com).

Aster House Hotel has classy rooms, each with a TV, telephone, and fridge. Enjoy breakfast in the whisper-elegant Orangerie, a Victorian greenhouse and lounge in the tidy backgarden (S-£60, Sb-£80, third floor Db-£110, Db-£120, deluxe four-poster Db with both bath and shower-£135, entirely non-smoking, CC:VM, 3 Sumner Place, SW7 3EE, tel. 0171/581-5888, fax 0171/584-4925, e-mail: asterhouse@binternet.com, run by manager Simon Tan). Note: credit-card deposits are non-refundable if you cancel with less than two weeks' notice. A couple of blocks away, the big, stately **Kensington Juries Hotel** offers fine rooms for classier travelers (Db-£99–145 depending upon "availability," Queen's Gate, South Kensington, SW7 5LR, tel. 0171/589-6300, fax 0171/581-1492). If you happen to be visiting during a slow period (which could be any month) and can score a £99 room, this is an excellent value.

The Claverly, just a couple of blocks from Harrods, is on a quiet street insulated from the downtown chaos. The rooms are small but warmly furnished with elegant drapery and all the comforts (S-£70, Sb-£75–115, Db-£110–190, Tb-£160–215, some balconies, CC:VMA, 13-14 Beaufort Gardens, SW3 1PS, tube: Knightsbridge, tel. 0171/589-8541, fax 0171/584-3410, from the U.S.A., tel. 800/747-0398).

Sleeping in Notting Hill Gate Neighborhood

Residential Notting Hill Gate is the perfect traveler's neighborhood. It has quick and easy bus or tube access to downtown, it's on the A2 Airbus line from Heathrow (second stop from airport, after Kensington Hilton), is relatively safe (except during the dangerous,

London, Notting Hill Gate Neighborhood

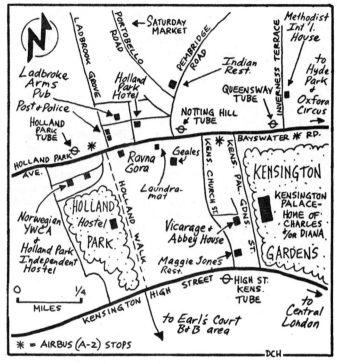

riot-plagued Notting Hill Carnival, the last weekend of August), and, for London, is very "homely." Notting Hill Gate has a self-serve launderette, an artsy theater, a late-hours supermarket, and lots of fun budget eateries (see below). All recommended accommodations are near the Holland Park or Notting Hill Gate tube stations. (Notting Hill Gate is in the central zone and on the Circle Line, handier and 40p cheaper from anywhere in the center than the Holland Park station.)

Vicarage Private Hotel is understandably popular. Family-run and elegantly British in a quiet, classy neighborhood, it has 19 rooms furnished with taste and quality, lots of stairs, a TV lounge, and facilities on each floor. Martin, Mandy, and Jim maintain a homey and caring atmosphere. Reserve long in advance with a one-night deposit. You won't find a better room for the price (S-£40, D-£62, T-£77, Q-£86, a six-minute walk from the Notting Hill Gate and High Street Kensington tube stations, near Kensington Palace at 10 Vicarage Gate, Kensington, W8 4AG, tel. 0171/229-4030, fax 0171/792-5989, Web site:

http://deadlock.com /hotels/vicarage). **Abbey House Hotel**, next door, is similar but has no lounge and is a bit less cozy (S-£38, D-£60, T-£74, Q-£86, Quint-£96, 11 Vicarage Gate, Kensington, W8 4AG, tel. 0171/727-2594).

The Ravna Gora Hotel was formerly the mansion of 18th-century architect Henry Holland. Now it's a large Slavic-run B&B—eccentric and well-worn, but handy for the price. Manda and Rijko offer a royal TV room and a good English breakfast. It has plain, tired rooms, bags of laundry in the halls, a creaky spiral staircase, easy parking, and a Balkan ambience (S-£30, D-£50, Db-£60, T-£60, Tb-£72, Q-£76, Qb-£88, CC:VM, 50 yards from Holland Park tube station, facing but set back from a busy road, 29 Holland Park Avenue, W11 3RW, tel. 0171/727-7725, fax 0171/221-4282).

Westland Hotel is comfortable, convenient, and hotelesque. The spacious rooms come with a phone, hair dryer, and coffee-maker (Sb-£80, Db-£95, Tb-£120, Qb-£135, elevator, free garage, CC:VMA, reserve with a credit card, 154 Bayswater Road, W2 4HP, tel. 0171/229-9191, fax 0171/727-1054). A block away, their **Westland Annex** offers bigger, plainer, quieter, cheaper rooms (Sb-£66, Db-£81, family deals also, same front desk and breakfast room as hotel).

Norwegian YWCA (Norsk K.F.U.K.) is for women under 30 only (and men with Norwegian passports). It's an incredible value. Located on a quiet, stately street, it offers smoke-free rooms, a study, TV room, piano lounge, and Norwegian atmosphere. All rooms (except singles) have private showers. They have mostly quads, so those willing to share with strangers are most likely to get a place (July–August: Ss-£27, bed in shared double-£25, shared triple-£21, shared quad-£18, with breakfast. September–June: same prices but with dinner included. 52 Holland Park, W11 3R5, tel. & fax 0171/727-9897). With each visit I wonder which is easier—getting a sex change or a Norwegian passport?

Sleeping in Other Neighborhoods
Bloomsbury District (near the British Museum): Cambria House, a fine value, is run by the Salvation Army (a plus when it comes to cheap big-city hotels). This smoke-free old building with a narrow maze of halls is newly painted and super clean, if institutional. The rooms are large and perfectly good. There are ample showers and toilets on each floor, and a TV lounge (S-£25.50, D-£40, Db-£50, T-£60, CC:VM, north of Russell Square at 37 Hunter Street, WC1N 1BJ, tel. 0171/837-1654, fax 0171/837-1229).

Near St. Paul's: The **City of London Youth Hostel** is clean, modern, friendly, and well-run. You'll pay about £22 for a bed in two- to five-bed rooms (CC:VM, cheap meals, 36 Carter Lane, EC4V 5AD, tube: St. Paul's, tel. 0171/236-4965, fax 0171/236-7681).

South of town: Hotel Oakley is like a B&B in a fine neighborhood (S-£29, D-£39, Db-£49, CC:VMA, 73 Oakley Street, just off King's Road, bus to Sloane Square and then walk, tel. 0171/352-5599). **Mary Ward's Guest House** is sleepable but very simple. On a quiet street in a well-worn neighborhood south of Victoria near Clapham Common, this beats the hostel. Friendly Mary Ward (Edith Bunker's English aunt) has been renting her five super-cheap rooms to budget travelers for 25 years (S-£12.5, D-£25 with English breakfast, 98 Hambalt Road, Clapham Common, SW4 9EJ London, tel. 0181/673-1077). It's 15 minutes by tube to Clapham Common, then a short bus ride or a 12-minute walk—exit left down Clapham South Road, left on Elms, right on Abbeville Road, left on Hambalt.

Near Gatwick: The peaceful **Crutchfield Inn B&B** offers three comfortable rooms in a 500-year-old renovated farmhouse. Friendly Mrs. Blok includes a ride to and from the airport (Db-£60, 2 miles from Gatwick Airport, 30 minutes by train from London, at Hookwood, Surrey, RH6 OHT, tel. 01293/863-110, fax 01293/863-233). **Barn Cottage**, a converted 17th-century barn in a large garden, has quiet rooms ten minutes from Gatwick (S-£25, D-£44, Leigh/Reigate/Surrey RH2 8RF, tel. 01306/611-347, run by friendly Pat and Mike Comer). **Lynwood Guest House** is ten minutes by train from Gatwick Airport (and 30 minutes by train from London). It offers a cozy, friendly alternative to big-city lodging in Redhill, a normal workaday English town. It's just a five-minute walk from the train station, but the gracious owner Shanta may pick you up if she's got the car. Ask for a quiet room off the street (Ss-£24–28, Ds-£38–42, Db-£40–45, Tb-£54–58, Qb-£55–65, cheaper off-season, 50 London Road, Redhill, Surrey RH1 1LN, tel. 01737/766-894).

Eating in London

If you want to dine (as opposed to eat), check out the extensive listings in *What's On* (or the train schedule for Paris). The thought of a £25 meal in Britain generally ruins my appetite, so my London dining is limited mostly to unremarkable but inexpensive alternatives. I've listed places by neighborhood—handy to your sightseeing or hotel.

Your £5 budget choices are pub grub, a café, fish and chips, pizza, ethnic, or picnic. Pub grub is the most atmospheric budget option. Many of London's 7,000 pubs serve fresh, tasty buffets under ancient timbers, with hearty lunches and dinners priced around £5. Ethnic restaurants from all over the world more than make up for England's lackluster cuisine. Eating Indian or Chinese is "going local" in London. It's also going cheap (cheaper if you take out). Pizza places all over town offer £3.50 all-you-can-stomach buffets. Most large museums (and many churches) have reasonable and handy cafeterias. Of course, picnicking is the fastest and cheapest way to go. Good grocery stores and sandwich shops, fine park benches, and polite pigeons abound in Britain's most expensive city.

Eating near Trafalgar Square

For a tasty meal on a monk's budget in an ancient crypt sitting on somebody's tomb, climb down into the **St. Martin-in-the-Fields Café in the Crypt** (Monday–Saturday 10:00–19:30, Sunday 12:00–18:00, £5–7 cafeteria plates, cheaper sandwich bar, profits go to the church; underneath St. Martin-in-the-Fields on Trafalgar Square, tel. 0171/839-4342). Down Whitehall (toward Big Ben), a block from Trafalgar Square, you'll find the touristy but atmospheric **Clarence Pub** (decent grub) and several cheaper cafeterias and pizza joints. For a classy lunch, treat your palate to the pricier **Brasserie** (open daily, on first floor of Sainsbury Wing of the National Gallery).

Eating near Piccadilly

Hungry in the theater district? Head for Panton Street (just off Haymarket, about 2 blocks southeast of Picadilly Circus) where you'll find a line of decent eateries. **Stockpot** is a mushy peas kind of place and rightly popular for its edible, cheap meals (Monday–Saturday 8:00–23:00, Sunday 8:00–22:00, 40 Panton Street). I prefer the **West End Kitchen** (across the street at #5, same hours and menu, fine seating downstairs).

The palatial **Criterion Brasserie**, serving a two-course lunch menu for £15 under gilded tiles and chandeliers, is right on Piccadilly Circus but a world away from the punk junk (opens daily at noon for lunch—a better value—and again at 18:00 for dinner at splurge prices, tel. 0171/930-0488). The **Carvery** serves a £15, all-you-can-eat meaty buffet with plenty of vegetables and a salad bar, Yorkshire and bread pudding, dessert, and coffee included—a carnivore's delight with concessions to vegetarians. Puffy-hatted carvers help you slice (daily 17:15–21:00, save £2 by arriving before 19:00, Regent Palace Hotel on Glasshouse Street, a few steps northwest of Piccadilly Circus, may close in 1998, call first at 0171/734-7000). The **Wren Café** at St. James Church is exclusively vegetarian, wonderfully green, and in a pleasant garden next to one of Wren's best churches—peek in (Monday–Saturday 9:00–17:00, Sunday 10:00–16:00, two minutes southwest of Piccadilly at 35 Jermyn Street, tel. 0171/437-9419).

Eating near Recommended Victoria Station Neighborhood Accommodations

A cluster of places a couple of blocks southeast of Victoria Station offers good values. **Jenny Lo's Tea House** is a simple, for-the-joy-of-good-food kind of place serving up £5 Cantonese meals to locals in the know (Monday–Saturday 12:00–15:00 and

18:00–20:00, 14 Eccleston Street, tel. 0171/259-0399). Her father runs a classy Chinese place around the corner. For pub grub with good local atmosphere, go down the street to the **Plumbers Arms** (serves filling £5 hot meals and cheaper sandwiches, closed Saturday and Sunday nights, indoor/outdoor seating, 14 Lower Belgrave Street, tel. 0171/730-4067; ask about the murdered nanny and the distraught wife who ran into the plumber's arms). Next door, the small but classy **La Campagnola** is Belgravia's favorite budget Italian restaurant (£10 meals, closed Sunday, reservations smart on Thursday and Friday, 10 Lower Belgrave Street, tel. 0171/730-2057). Across the street, the **Maestro Bar** is the closest thing to an English tapas bar I've seen with salads, sandwiches, and ten bar stools (very cheap).

Farther down Ebury Street, the **Ebury Wine Bar** offers a French, smoky ambience with the slight splurge (£10 meals, daily 12:00–14:30 and 18:00–22:30, 139 Ebury Street, at intersection with Elizabeth Street, near the coach station, tel. 0171/730-5447). Several cheap places are around the corner on Elizabeth Street (#23 for take-out or eat-in fish and chips).

The **Duke of Wellington** pub is good, if smoky, for dinner (£5 meals, 12:00–15:00 and 18:00–21:30, closed Sunday evening, 63 Eaton Terrace). **Peter's Restaurant** is the cabbie's hangout—cheap food, smoke, and chatter (end of Ebury, at intersection with Pimlico). Nearby, the **Flamenco** has decent, if pricey, Spanish tapas (54 Pimlico).

For picnics, the nearest supermarket is **J. Sainsbury**, a five-minute walk from Victoria Station (Monday–Saturday 7:30–20:00, Sunday 10:00–16:00, on Victoria Street just after the intersection with Palace Street). The late-hours **Whistle Stop** grocery at the station has decent sandwiches and a fine salad bar. The **Marche** is an easy cafeteria a couple of blocks north of Victoria Station at Bressenden Place.

Halfway between Victoria and the Halls of Parliament, the venerable **Albert Pub** serves a traditional three-course carvery buffet in rare cut-glass Victorian splendor (£15 appetizer, lunch or dinner, all the meat and vegetables you want, dessert, and tea or coffee, 52 Victoria Street, tel. 0171/222-5577).

Eating near Recommended Notting Hill Gate B&Bs

Costas has Greek food and eat-in or take-out fish and chips (£5 meals, Tuesday–Saturday 12:00–14:30 and 17:30–10:30, near the Coronet Theatre at 18 Hillgate Street). Next door, the **Hillgate Pub** has good food and famous hot saltbeef sandwiches (daily 11:00–23:00, indoor/outdoor seating, tel. 0171/727-8543). The **Modhubon** Indian restaurant is not too spicy and has cheap lunch specials (Sunday–Friday 12:00–15:00 and 18:00–24:00, Saturday 12:00–24:00, 29 Pembridge Road, tel. 0171/727-3399). Next door is a cheap Chinese take-out (daily 17:30–24:00, 19 Pembridge Road) and the tiny **Prost Restaurant and Schnapps Bar** which busily keeps yuppie vegetarians as well as carnivores happy (£10 meals, Monday–Friday 17:30–23:00, weekends 10:30–23:00, 35 Pembridge Road, tel. 0171/727-9620).

The small and woodsy **Arc** at 122 Palace Gardens Terrace is popular and worth the moderate splurge (£10–15 meals, Monday–Saturday 19:00–23:15, indoor/outdoor seating, call ahead, tel. 0171/229-4024). The **Churchill Arms** pub is a local hangout with good beer and old English ambience in front and hearty £5 Thai plates on an enclosed patio in the back (Monday–Saturday 11:00–23:00, Sunday from noon on, 119 Kensington Church Street, tel. 0171/727-4242). **Pizza & Pasta** does basic Italian at 145 Notting Hill Gate. The **Ladbroke Arms Pub** serves country-style meals that are one step above pub grub in quality and price (daily 12:00–14:30 and 19:00–22:00, great indoor/outdoor ambience, 54 Ladbroke Road, behind Holland Park tube station, tel. 0171/727-6648).

The almost-too-popular **Geale's** has long been considered one of London's best fish-and-chips joints (£8 meals, Tuesday–Saturday 12:00–15:00 and 18:00–23:00, 2 Farmer Street, just off Notting Hill Gate behind the Gate Cinema, tel. 0171/727-7969). Get there early for a place to sit and the best selection of fish.

The very English **Maggie Jones** serves my favorite £20 London dinner. You'll get solid English cuisine with huge plates of vegetables by candlelight (daily 18:30–23:00, CC:VMA, 6 Old Court Place, just east of Kensington Church Street, near the High Street Kensington tube stop; reservations smart, tel. 0171/937-6462). If you're going to eat well in London, eat here.

For a picnic dinner, shop at the **Europe Superstore** (Monday–Saturday 8:30–23:00, Sunday 12:00–18:00, 50 yards west of Notting Hill tube station on Notting Hill Gate).

Transportation Connections—London

Flying into London's Heathrow Airport
Heathrow Airport is user-friendly. Read signs, ask questions. Most flights land at Terminal 3, but British Air lands at Terminal 4 (same services as Terminal 3, but no Tourist Information office). In Terminal 3 you'll find exchange bureaus (24 hours daily, okay rates, £3 fees), an airport terminal information desk (pick up a map and ask questions, but for the official TI, see below), car rental agencies (if you're renting a car, stop to confirm your plans), a £3-a-day baggage check desk, and a TI. The American Express desk, with better rates than the banks, is in the underground at Terminal 4.

Heathrow's TI gives you all the help that London's Victoria Station does, with none of the crowds (daily 8:30–18:00, a five-

Heathrow and the Four Terminals

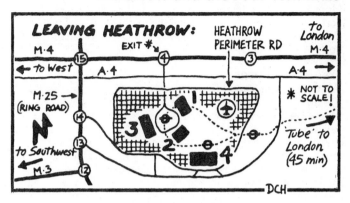

minute walk from Terminal 3, TI next to tube station, follow signs to the "underground"). If you're riding the Airbus into London, have your partner stay with the bags at the terminal. At the TI get a free map and brochures and buy a subway pass if you're riding the tube into London.

Buses from Heathrow: The National Express Central Bus Station offers direct bus connections to **Cambridge** (hrly, 3.5 hrs, £16), **Cheltenham** (6/day, 2 hrs, £19), **York** (3/day, 6 hrs, £32), **Gatwick** (2/hr, 1 hr), and **Bath** (9/day, starting at 8:35, 10:35, and so on; direct 2.5 hrs, £19, tel. 0990-808-080). Or try the slick 2.5-hour Heathrow–Bath bus/train connection via Reading. Buy the £26 ticket at the desk in the terminal (credit cards accepted), then catch the twice-hourly shuttle bus to Reading (RED-ding) to hop on the express train to Bath.

Transportation to London from Heathrow Airport
By Tube: For £3.20 ("free" with £3.20 all-day-after-9:30 tube pass), the tube takes you 14 miles to Victoria Station in 45 minutes (6/hr, one change).

By Airbus: All my recommended hotel neighborhoods are on one of the two airbus lines (serving each terminal, £6, 2/hr, 5:00–20:00, buy ticket on bus, tel. 0181/400-6655). If you take A1, South Kensington is the third stop and Victoria Station is the last stop. On A2, the second and third stops cover Notting Hill Gate. The tube works fine, but with baggage I prefer the airbus—no connections underground and a lovely view from the top of the double-decker bus. Ask the driver to remind you when to get off.

By Taxi: Taxis from the airport cost about £30. For four traveling together this can be a deal.

Flying into London's Gatwick Airport

More and more flights, especially charters, land at Gatwick Airport, halfway between London and the southern coast. Trains shuttle conveniently between Gatwick and London's Victoria Station (4/hr, 30 min, £9).

Trains and Buses

For train schedules and fares for any journey in Britain, call 0345/484-950 from anywhere in Britain (from the States, tel. 011/44/345-484-950). Ask for the cheapest fare for your journey; if you want to book with a credit card, you'll be referred to the appropriate rail company's phone number. You'll save money on point-to-point train tickets if you purchase in advance: To get Apex fares buy seven days ahead (available for moderate-length or longer journeys); for Super Apex fares, buy 14 days in advance (for long journeys only). For more information, see Transportation in the Introduction. This is worth the savings and trouble only if you're willing to pin down dates for your longer trips.

London, a major transportation hub in Britain, has a different train station for each region. The train station you arrive at (or leave from) depends on where you came from (or where you're going). King's Cross covers northeast England and Scotland (tel. 0171/278-2477). Paddington covers west and southwest England and South Wales (tel. 0171/262-6767). For the others, call 0171/928-5100.

National Express buses are considerably cheaper than trains. (For a busy signal call 0990-808080, or visit the bus station a block south of Victoria train station.)

To Bath: Trains leave London's Paddington Station every hour (at a quarter after) for the £28.50, 75-minute ride to Bath. Consider taking a guided bus tour from London to Stonehenge and Bath, and simply leaving the tour in Bath. Both Evan Evans (tel. 0181/332-2222) and Greenline (tel. 0181/668-7261) offer Stonehenge/Bath day trips from London.

To points north: Trains run hourly from London's King's Cross Station stopping in York (2 hrs), Durham (3 hrs), and Edinburgh (5 hrs). For Cambridge connections, see below.

To Dublin, Ireland: The boat/rail journey takes ten hours, all day or all night (£40–60). Consider a British Midland flight (Heathrow–Dublin, 10/day, 70 min, £95, cheaper Monday–Thursday, tel. 0345/554-554 or, in the U.S.A., 800/788-0555).

Crossing the English Channel

By Eurostar Train: The fastest and most convenient way to get from Big Ben to the Eiffel Tower is by rail. Eurostar is the speedy passenger train which zips you (and up to 800 others in 18 sleek, TGV-type cars) from downtown London to downtown

Paris (9/day, 3 hrs) or Brussels (5/day, 3 hrs) faster and easier than flying. The train goes 100 mph in England and 160 mph on the Continent. The actual tunnel crossing is a 20-minute black, silent, 100-mph non-event. Your ears won't even pop. You can change at Lille to catch a TGV directly to Paris' De Gaulle Airport or Disneyland Paris. Yes!

Channel fares (essentially the same to Paris or Brussels) are good. The following prices are from 1997—for the latest fares, call 1-800-EUROSTAR. The "Leisure" ticket is cheap ($99), but you're out of luck if you miss the train (50 percent refundable up to two days before departure). The pricier "Full-fare" tickets are fully refundable up to 120 days after the purchase date. "Full-fare" first class costs $199 including a meal (a dinner departure nets you more grub than breakfast); second class (or "standard") costs $139.

While basic round-trip tickets cost double, round-trips over a Saturday cost $178 (50 percent refundable up to two days before departure). Discounts are available for travelers holding railpasses that include France, Belgium, or Britain (about $50 off), youths under 26 ($60 off), and children under 12 (half fare). Cheaper seats can sell out. You can book your ticket from the U.S.A. When you're ready to commit to a date and time, book an "instant reservation" through your travel agent. Prices do not include FedEx delivery.

In Europe, get your Eurostar ticket at any major train station (in any country) or at any travel agency that handles train tickets (expect a booking fee). In Britain, you can order your tickets over the phone with a credit card by calling 0345/303-030; pick up your tickets at London's Waterloo station an hour before the Eurostar departure.

By Train, Bus, and Boat: The old-fashioned way of crossing the Channel is very competitive and cheaper than Eurostar; it's also twice as romantic, twice as complicated, and twice as time-consuming. You'll get better prices arranging your trip in London than you would in the U.S.A. Taking the bus is cheapest, and round-trips are a bargain. By bus: £33 one-way, £49 round-trip, ten hours, day or overnight, on Eurolines (tel. 0990/143-219) or CitySprint (tel. 0990/240-241). By train and ship: £42 one-way overnight, £59 by day, seven hours.

By Plane: Typical fares are £90 regular, £40 student standby. Call in London for the latest fares.

BATH

Any tour of Britain that skips Bath stinks. Two hundred years ago this city of 80,000 was the trend-setting Hollywood of Britain. If ever a city enjoyed looking in the mirror, Bath's the one. It has more "government-listed" or protected historic buildings per capita than any other town in England. The entire city, built of the creamy warm-tone limestone called "Bath stone," beams in its cover-girl complexion. An architectural chorus line, it's a triumph of the Georgian style. Proud locals remind visitors that the town is routinely banned from the "Britain in Bloom" contest to give other towns a chance to win. Bath's narcissism is justified. Even with its mobs of tourists, it's a joy to visit.

Long before the Romans arrived in the first century, Bath was known for its hot springs. What became the Roman spa town of Aquae Sulis has always been fueled by the healing allure of its 116-degree mineral hot springs. The town's importance carried through Saxon times when it had a huge church on the site of the present-day Abbey and was considered the religious capital of Britain. Things peaked in 973 when England's first king, Edgar, was crowned in the Abbey. Bath prospered as a wool town.

Bath then declined until the mid-1600s, when it was just a huddle of huts around the Abbey and a hot springs with 3,000 residents oblivious to the Roman ruins 18 feet below their dirt floors. Then, in 1687, Queen Mary, fighting infertility, bathed here. Within ten months she gave birth to a son . . . and a new age of popularity for Bath.

The town boomed as a spa resort. Ninety percent of the buildings you'll see today are from the 18th century. Local architect John Wood was inspired by the Italian architect Palladio to build a "new Rome." The town bloomed in the neoclassical style and streets were lined not with scrawny sidewalks but with wide "parades," upon which the women in their stylishly wide dresses could spread their fashionable tails.

Beau Nash (1673–1762) was Bath's "master of ceremonies." He organized both the daily regimen of the aristocratic visitors and the city—lighting and improving security on the streets, banning swords, and opening the Pump Room. Under his fashionable baton, Bath became a city of balls, gaming, concerts, and the place to see and be seen in England. This most civilized place became even more so with the great neoclassical building spree that followed.

Planning Your Time

Bath needs two nights even on a quick trip. There's plenty to do and it's a joy to do it. Bath could easily fill another day. Ideally, you would use Bath as your jet-lag recovery pillow and do London at the end of your trip.

Here's a suggested schedule:

Day 1: Land at Heathrow. Catch the National Express bus to Bath (departs nearly every hour, 2.5-hr trip). While you don't need or want a car in Bath, and most rental companies have an office there, those who pick up their cars at the airport can do Stonehenge (and maybe Salisbury) on their way to Bath on this day.

Day 2: 9:00, Tour the Roman Baths; 10:30, Catch the free city walking tour; 12:30, Picnic on the open deck of a Guide Friday bus tour; 14:30, Free time in the shopping center of old Bath; 16:00, Tour the Costume Museum.

Orientation (tel. code: 01225)

Bath's town square, 3 blocks in front of the bus and train station, is a bouquet of tourist landmarks including the Abbey, Roman and medieval baths, and royal Pump Room.

Tourist Information: The TI is in the Abbey churchyard (walk 2 blocks up Manvers Street from the bus or train station and turn left, Monday–Saturday 9:30–19:00, Sunday 10:00–18:00, shorter hours off-season, tel. 01225/477-101). Pick up the 25p Bath map/mini-guide and the free, packed-with-info *This Month in Bath*, and browse through scads of flyers. There's an American Express outlet in the TI (decent rates, no commission on any checks, open seven days a week).

Arrival in Bath: The Bath train station is a pleasure (small-town charm, an international tickets desk, and a Guide Friday office masquerading as a tourist information service). The bus station is immediately in front of the train station. My recommended B&Bs are all within a ten- or 15-minute walk or a £3 taxi ride. For Brock House and the B&Bs on Marlborough Lane, consider using the Guide Friday city bus tour (described below) as transportation (5/hr, from Lane 1 of the bus station). Start the tour, jump out, check into your B&B, and hop back on to finish the circle. If you're driving, streets with no lines allow free unlimited parking.

Car Rental: Avis (behind the station and over the river at Unit 4B Riverside Business Park, Lower Bristol Road, tel. 01225/446-680), Budget (Brassmill Lane, tel. 01225/482-211), and Hertz (at the train station, tel. 01225/442-911) are all trying harder (consider hotel delivery, usually £8). Take the train or bus from London to Bath and rent a car as you leave Bath rather than in London.

Tours of Bath

▲▲**City Bus Tours**—The Guide Friday green-and-cream, open-top tour bus makes a 70-minute figure-eight circuit of Bath's main sights with an exhaustingly informative running commentary. For one £7 ticket, tourists can stop and go at will for a whole day. The buses cover the city center and the surrounding hills (14 sign-posted pick-up points, 5/hr in summer, hrly in winter, about 9:25–17:00, tel. 01225/464-446). This is great in sunny weather and a feast for photographers. You can munch a sandwich, work on a tan, and sightsee at the same time. The competing red City-tour buses (£5, family of five for £12, tel. 01225/424-157) do basically the same tour but in 45 minutes and without the swing through the countryside, and pose the hard-to-answer question, "Why pay more?" Environmentalists ask an equally hard-to-answer question, "Why patronize these noisy hordes of street-clogging buses?"

▲▲▲**Walking Tours**—These two-hour tours, offered free by trained local volunteers who want to share their love of Bath with its many visitors, are a chatty, historical gossip-filled joy, essential for your understanding of this town's amazing Georgian social scene. How else will you learn that the old "chair ho" call for your sedan chair evolved into today's "cheerio" greeting? Tours leave from in front of the Pump Room daily at 10:30 (often at 14:00 and 19:00, May–October). For Ghost Walks and Bizarre Bath Comedy Walks, see Evening Entertainment, below.

Sights—Bath

▲▲▲**Roman and Medieval Baths**—Back in ancient Roman times, high society enjoyed the mineral springs at Bath. From Londinium, Romans traveled so often to Aquae Sulis, as the city was called, to "take a bath" that finally it became known simply as Bath. Today a fine Roman museum surrounds the ancient bath. The museum, with its well-documented displays, is a one-way system leading you past Roman artifacts, mosaics, a temple pediment, and the actual mouth of the spring piled high with Roman pennies. Enjoy some quality time looking into the eyes of Minerva, goddess of the hot springs. The included self-guided tour audio-wand makes the visit easy and plenty informative. Indepth 40-

Bath

minute tours leave from the end of the museum at the edge of the actual bath for those with a big appetite for Roman history (included, on the hour, a poolside clock is set for the next departure time). You can revisit the museum after the tour. (£6, £8 "combo" ticket includes Costume Museum, a family combo costs £20, daily 9:00–18:00; in August also 20:00–22:00; slightly shorter hours off-season, tel. 01225/477-000.)

▲**Pump Room**—After a centuries-long cold spell, Bath was reheated when the previously barren Queen Mary bathed here and in due course bore a male heir to the throne (1687). Once Bath was back on the aristocratic map, high society soon turned the place into one big pleasure palace. The Pump Room, an elegant Georgian hall just above the Roman baths, offers the visitor's best chance to raise a pinky in this Chippendale elegance. Drop by to sip coffee or tea to the rhythm of a string trio (tea/coffee and pastry for £3, live music all year 10:30–13:00, summers until 17:00). Above the newspaper table and sedan chairs a statue of Beau Nash himself sniffles down at you. Now's your chance to have a famous (but forgettable) "Bath bun" and split (and spit) a 45p drink of the awfully curative water. The Pump Room's toilets are open to the discreet public.

A quarter of a million gallons of mineral water still bubble through the spa daily. And in 2001 a new spa facility will be opened for the public to once again bathe in Bath.

▲ **Abbey**—Bath town wasn't much in the Middle Ages. But an important church has stood on this spot since Anglo-Saxon times. In 973, Edgar, the first king of England, was crowned here. Dominating the town center, the present church—the last great medieval church of England—is 500 years old and a fine example of Late Perpendicular Gothic, with breezy fan vaulting and enough stained glass to earn it the nickname "Lantern of the West" (Monday–Saturday 9:00–18:00, shorter hours on Sunday, concert and evensong schedule posted on the door, worth the £1.50 donation, handy flier narrates a 19-stop tour). **The Heritage Vaults**, within the abbey, is a small but interesting exhibit telling the story of Christianity in Bath since Roman times (£2, Monday–Saturday 10:00–16:00, closed Sunday). From the Abbey Green square, take a moment to really appreciate the Abbey's architecture.

Pulteney Bridge and Boats—Bath is inclined to compare its shop-lined bridge to Florence's Ponte Vecchio. That's pushing it. But to best enjoy a sunny Bath kind of day, pay £1 to go into the Parade Gardens below the bridge (free after 20:00). Across the bridge at Pulteney Weir, tour boats run cruises from under the bridge (£3.50, 50 minutes to Bathampton and back, one boat stops there if you'd like to walk back, the other company has a sundeck ideal for picnics).

▲▲**Royal Crescent and the Circus**—If Bath is an architectural cancan, these are the kickers. These first elegant Georgian (that's British for "neoclassical," from the 1770s) "condos" by John Wood (the Elder and the Younger) are well-explained in the city walking tours. The museum at #1 Royal Crescent offers the best look into a period house. It's worth the £3.50 admission to get behind one of those classy exteriors (Tuesday–Sunday 10:30–17:00, closed Monday, "no stiletto heels, please," tel. 01225/428-126). Stroll the Crescent after dark. Pretend you're rich. Pretend you're poor. Poke into the unmarked Royal Crescent Hotel (center door, big-name paintings in lounges near entry) consider a splurge in its elegant Old World restaurant. Study the cute little rooms below each entry walk. Notice the "ha ha fence," a drop in the front yard offering an invisible (from the windows) barrier to sheep and peasants.

▲▲▲**Costume Museum**—One of Europe's great museums, displaying 400 years of fashion—from Anne Boleyn to Twiigy—one frilly decade at a time, is housed in Bath's elegant Assembly Rooms. Follow the included and excellent radio phone "wand" self-guided tour. Learn why Yankee Doodle "stuck a feather in his cap and called it macaroni," and much more (£3.70, cheaper on combo ticket with Roman Baths, Monday–Saturday 10:00–17:00, Sunday 11:00–17:00, last admission at 16:30, tel. 01225/477-789).

▲▲**Industrial Heritage Centre**—This is the grand title for Mr. Bowler's Business, a turn-of-the-century engineer's shop, brass foundry, and fizzy-drink factory with a Dickensian office. It's just a pile of meaningless old gadgets until a volunteer guide lovingly resurrects Mr. Bowler's creative genius. Fascinating hour-long tours go regularly; you can join one in session. (£3.50, plus a few pence for a glass of genuine Victorian lemonade, daily 10:00–17:00, weekends only in winter, 2 blocks up Russel Street from the Assembly Rooms, call to be sure a volunteer is available to give a tour, tel. 01225/318-348.) There's a Bath stone exhibit downstairs and a café/shop upstairs.

Small Special-Interest Museums—The **Building of Bath Museum** offers a fascinating look behind the scenes at how the Georgian city was actually built. This is just one large room of exhibits but those interested in construction will find it worth the £3 (Tuesday–Sunday 10:30–17:00, closed Monday, near the Circus on a street called "the Paragon," tel. 01225/333-895). **Royal Photographic Society**, a hit with shutterbugs, exhibits the earliest cameras and photos and their development, along with temporary contemporary exhibits (£3, daily 9:30–17:30, tel. 01225/462-841).

▲**American Museum**—I know, you need this in Bath like you need a Big Mac. But this museum offers a fascinating look at Colonial and early-American lifestyles. Each of 18 completely furnished rooms (from the 1600s to the 1800s) is hosted by an eager guide waiting to fill you in on the candles, maps, bedpans, and various religious sects that make domestic Yankee history surprisingly interesting. One room is a quilter's nirvana (£5, Tuesday–Sunday 14:00–17:00, closed Monday and November–March, at Claverton Manor, tel. 01225/460-503). The museum is outside of town and a headache to reach if you don't have a car (15-minute walk from the Guide Friday stop or a ten-minute walk from bus #18).

Walking, Biking, and Swimming—The TI has a brochure describing options. Consider the idyllic walk up the canal path to Bathampton (from downtown, walk over Pulteney Bridge, through Sydney Gardens, turn left on canal, and in 30 minutes you'll hit Bathampton with its much-loved old George pub). The Bath skyline walk is a 6-mile wander around the hills surrounding Bath (75p leaflet available at TI). Consider taking the river cruise up to Bathampton and walking back (see Pulteney Bridge and Boats, above). From Bathampton it's another two hours along the canal to the fine old town of Bradford-on-Avon, from which a train can zip you back to Bath. You could rent a bike from behind the Bath train station (£9/half day, £14/all day, tel. 01225/442-442) and bike this route. The scenic 12-mile bridle/biking/walking path along the old Bath–Bristol train tracks is also popular. The Bath Sports and Leisure Centre has a swimming pool and more (£2, just across the North Parade Bridge, 8:00–22:00, call for free swim times, tel. 01225/462-563).

Shopping—There's great browsing between the Abbey and the Assembly Rooms. Shops close at 17:30, later on Thursday.

Interested in antiques? You'll find the most stalls open on
Wednesday. For the best deal, pick up the local paper (usually
out on Friday) and shop with the dealers at estate sales and
auctions listed in the "What's On" section.

Evening Entertainment
This Month in Bath (available at the TI and many B&Bs) lists
events and evening entertainment.

Plays: The Theatre Royal, newly restored and one of England's loveliest, offers a busy schedule of London West End–type
plays, including many "pre-London" dress rehearsal runs (£7–14,
cheap stand-by tickets, tel. 01225/448-844). You can often get late
cancellation seats for sold-out performances (drop by around 18:00).

Bizarre Bath and other walks: For a walking comedy act—
street theater at its best "with absolutely no history or culture"—
follow JJ or Noel Britten on their very creative and entertaining
Bizarre Bath walk. Their 90-minute "tour," which plays off local
passersby as well as tour members, is a kick (£3.50, 20:00 nightly;
heavy on magic, careful to insult all kinds of minorities and sensi-
tivities, just racy enough but still good family fun; from the Huntsman pub near the Abbey, confirm time and starting place at TI or
call 01225/335-124). Ghost Walks are another way to pass the
after-dark hours (£3, 20:00, 2 hrs, unreliably Monday–Friday, tel.
01225/463-618). And for the scholarly types, there are almost
nightly historical walks (19:00, 2 hrs, ask at TI).

Drinks: For a good spit-and-sawdust pub, drink real ale at
the Star Pub (top of Paragon Street, Bass sold by the jug if you
don't want to mess with pints). Or, for maximum entertainment,
look up two particularly musical local residents, Van Morrison and
Peter Gabriel.

Sleeping in Bath
(£1 = about $1.60, tel. code: 01225)
Sleep Code: S=Single, D=Double/Twin, T=Triple, Q=Quad,
b=bathroom, t=toilet only, s=shower only, CC=Credit Card (Visa,
MasterCard, Amex).

Bath is one of England's busiest tourist towns. To get a good
B&B, make a telephone reservation in advance. Competition is
stiff, and it's worth asking any of these places for a non-weekend,
three nights-in-a-row, or off-season deal. Friday and Saturday
nights are tightest (especially if you're staying only one night,
since B&Bs favor those staying longer). There's a laundrette
around the corner from Brock's Guest House on the cute pedestrian lane called Margaret's Buildings.

Sleeping near the Royal Crescent
Brock's Guest House will put bubbles in your Bath experience.
Marion Dodd and her husband Geoffrey have redone their Geor-

gian townhouse (built by John Wood in 1765) in a way that would nake the famous architect proud. This charming house couldn't be in a better location, between the prestigious Royal Crescent and the elegant Circus (Db-£55–65, Tb-£75–80, family deals in a quad, reserve with a credit-card number far in advance, 32 Brock Street, BA1 2LN, tel. 01225/338-374, fax 01225/334-245). If you can't find a sedan chair, Brock's is a 15-minute uphill walk, £3 taxi, or short bus ride (to Assembly Rooms and short walk) from the station. Guide Friday buses stop on Brock Street. If you're in a transportation jam, Marion can occasionally arrange a reasonable private car hire.

At the **Woodville House,** Anne and Tom Toalster offer Bath's best cheap beds. This grandmotherly little house has three charming rooms, one shared shower, and a TV lounge. Breakfast is a help-yourself buffet around a big, family-style table (D-£33, minimum two nights, anyone who smokes at all is not welcome, closed January–mid-February below the Royal Crescent at 4 Marlborough Lane, BA1 2NQ, tel. 01225/319-335).

Elgin Villa, run by Richard and Christina Robinson, is also a fine value (Ds-£36, Db-£40, minimum two nights, kids £10 extra, four rooms, parking, non-smoking, 6 Marlborough Lane, BA1 2NQ Bath, tel. 01225/424-557, fax 01225/425-633). They serve a big continental breakfast in your bedroom.

Other recommended B&Bs on Marlborough Lane: Athelney Guest House (D-£36, three rooms, continental breakfast, non-smoking, parking, 5 Marlborough Lane, tel. & fax 01225/312-031, Sue and Colin Davies). **Parkside Guest House** rents five classy Edwardian rooms (Db-£58, non-smoking, 11 Marlborough Lane, tel. & fax 01225/429-444, Erica and Inga Lynam). The **Marlborough House** is a Victorian place renting five rooms (tel. 01225/318-175, fax 01225/466-127).

Sleeping near the Train Station

Holly Villa Guest House, with a cheery garden and a cozy TV lounge, an eight-minute walk from the station and center, is enthusiastically and thoughtfully run by Jill McGarrigle (D-£35, Ds-£40, Db-£46, T-£48, Tb-£60, Q-family deals, seven rooms, strictly non-smoking, easy parking, cheap rooms get the famous "loo with a view," 14 Pulteney Gardens, BA2 4HG, tel. 01225/310-331, fax 01225/339-334). From the city center, walk over North Parade Bridge, take the first right, then the second left. It's 1 block from a Guide Friday bus stop. **Ashley House B&B,** two doors down, rents eight basic, smoke-free rooms (small D-£32, D-£40, Db-£45, 8 Pulteney Gardens, tel. 01225/425-027, Vanessa and Ron Pharo).

Sleeping in the Town Center

Henry Guest House is a clean, cheery, and vertical little eight-room, family-run place 2 blocks in front of the train station on a quiet side street (S-£17, D-£34, T-£51, TVs in rooms, lots of narrow stairs, one shower and one bath for all, 6 Henry Street, BA1 1JT, tel. 01225/424-052, Mrs. Cox). This kind of decency at this price, centrally located, is found nowhere else in Bath. **Harington's of Bath Hotel**, with 13 newly renovated rooms on a quiet street in the town center, is run by Susan Pow (Db-£65–85, family room deal, Sunday discounts, non-smoking, lots of stairs, CC:VMA, extremely central at 10 Queen Street, tel. 01225/461-728, fax 01225/444-804). **Parade Park Hotel**, with clean rooms and helpful owners, is centrally located (S-£30, Sb-£45–50, Db-£55–65, family deals, non-smoking rooms available, 10 North Parade, BA2 4AL, tel. 01225/463-384, fax 01225/442-322, Nita and David Derrick).

Sleeping near Pulteney Bridge

Kennard Hotel is a comfortable, hotel with 14 charming Georgian rooms. Richard Ambler runs this place warmly, with careful attention to detail (S-£45, Db-£74–84, non-smoking, CC:VMA, just over Pulteney Bridge at 11 Henrietta Street, BA2 6LL, tel. 01225/310-472, fax 01225/460-054, e-mail: kennard@dircon.co.uk). **Laura Place Hotel** is another elegant Georgian place (eight rooms, two on the ground floor, Db-£60–90 from small and high up to huge and palatial, 10 percent discount with cash and this book, family suite, non-smoking, easy parking, CC:VMA, 3 Laura Place, Great Pulteney Street, just over Pulteney Bridge, tel. 01225/463-815, fax 01225/310-222, Patricia Bull). **Henrietta Hotel** is a very plain place in the same elegant neighborhood but with nearly no character (Db-£42–55, 32 Henrietta Street, tel. 01225/447-779, fax 01225/466-916).

Cheap Dorm Beds

The **YMCA**, institutional but friendly, and wonderfully central on a leafy square down a tiny alley off Broad Street, has industrial strength rooms and scuff-proof halls (S-£14.50, D-£26, T-£39, beds in huge dorms-£10, includes breakfast, discounts for two nights, families offered a day nursery for kids over five, cheap dinners, CC:VM, tel. 01225/460-471, fax 01225/462-065). **Bath Backpackers Hostel**, billing itself as a totally fun-packed mad place to stay, is an Aussie-run hostel 3 blocks up from the station renting bunk beds in six- to ten-bed co-ed rooms (£11 per bed with continental breakfast, non-smoking, no lockers, 13 Pierrepont Street, tel. 01225/446-787, fax 01225/446-305). The **Youth Hostel** is in a grand old building outside of town (£10 per bed without breakfast in two- to 14-bed rooms, bus #18 from the station, tel. 01225/465-674).

Eating in Bath

While not a great pub grub town, Bath is bursting with quaint eateries. There's something for every appetite and budget—just stroll around the center of town. A picnic dinner of take-out fish and chips in the Royal Crescent Park is ideal for aristocratic hoboes.

Eating between the Abbey and the Station

Evans Self-Service Fish Restaurant is the best eat-in or take-out fish-and-chips deal in town (Monday–Wednesday 11:30–18:30, Thursday–Saturday 11:30–20:30, closed Sunday, student discounts, 7 Abbeygate, tel. 01225/463-981). **Crystal Palace Pub,** with hearty meals under rustic timbers or in the sunny courtyard, is a handy standby (meals under £5, daily from 12:00–14:30 and 18:00–20:30, closed Sunday; children welcome on the patio, not indoors; 11 Abbey Green, tel. 01225/423-944). **Sally Lunn's House** is a cutesy, quasi-historic place for expensive doily meals, tea, pink pillows, and lots of lace (4 North Parade Passage). **Demuth's Vegetarian Restaurant** (next door, nightly, tel. 01225/446-059) serves good, three-course, £10 meals. **Eastern Eye** has tasty Indian food (daily 12:00–14:30 and 18:00–23:30, 8a Quiet Street, tel. 01225/422-323). **The Huntsman,** which was greasy before there were spoons, offers good, filling meals in a handy if tired setting (next to Sally Lunn's buns, tel. 01225/460-100). For very cheap meals, try **Spike's Fish and Chips** (open very late) and the neighboring café just behind the bus station.

Eating between the Abbey and the Circus

George Street is lined with cheery eateries (Thai, Italian, wine bars, and so on). **Guildhall Market,** across from Pulteney Bridge, is fun for browsing and picnic shopping, with a very cheap cafeteria if you'd like to sip tea surrounded by stacks of used books, bananas on the push list, and honest-to-goodness old-time locals. **Lovejoy's Café** serves light and veggie lunches (closed Sunday, upstairs in the Bartlett Street Antiques Centre). The **Green Tree Pub** is a rare pub with good grub and a non-smoking room, on Green Street (lunch only). **Pasta Galore** puts more energy into its fine Italian food than its ambience (daily 18:00–22:30, 31 Barton Street, good homemade pasta, call to reserve a table—avoid the basement, tel. 01225/463-861). Next door is a cheap and fast Mexican joint. **Devon Savouries** serves greasy, delicious take-out pasties, sausage rolls, and vegetable pies (on the main walkway between New Bond Street and Upper Borough Walls). The **Waitrose** supermarket, at the Podium shopping center, is great for groceries (open until 19:00 or 20:00, across from the post office on High Street). For a classy, intimate setting and "new English" cuisine worth the splurge, dine at **No. 5 Bistro** (main courses with vegetables £12–15, Monday and Tuesday are "bring your own bottle of wine" nights—no corkage charge, Monday–Saturday 18:30–22:00, closed Sunday, just over Pulteney Bridge at 5 Argyle Street, tel. 01225/444-499). The **Bathtub Restaurant,** just around the corner on Grove Street, is cheaper (£8 meals) and funkier, serving international vegetarian cuisine (Monday–Friday 18:00–23:00).

Eating near the Circus and Brock's Guest House

Circus Restaurant is intimate and a good value with Mozartian ambience and candlelit prices: £15 for a three-course dinner special including great vegetables and a selection of fine desserts (daily, 34 Brock Street, tel. 01225/318-918, Felix Rosenow). **Woods Restaurant** serves modern English cuisine to well-dressed locals in a sprawling candlelit brasserie (£6 lunches, £16 three-course dinners, closed Sunday, 9-13 Alfred Street near Assembly Rooms, tel. 01225/314-812). If you want to dress up to eat, the **Royal Crescent Hotel Restaurant** is the classiest address in town (£15 lunch, £35 dinner, center of Royal Crescent, tel. 01225/739-955). On the opposite end of the decency spectrum, the **Chequers Inn** (2 blocks up the hill, 50 Rivers Street) is a smoky dive of a pub with cheap, finger-sticking, disgusting grub and darts.

Transportation Connections—Bath

To: London's Paddington station by train (hrly, 75 min, £28.50 one-way or round-trip) or cheaper by National Express bus (hrly, 3 hrs, £19 round-trip, £18 one-way, ask about £8 day returns). To get from London to Bath, consider using an all-day Stonehenge and Bath organized bus tour from London. For about the same cost as the train ticket, you can see Stonehenge, tour Bath, and leave the tour before it returns to London (they'll let you stow your bag underneath). Evan Evans (£29.50, tel. 0181/332-2222) and Greenline (£24, tel. 0181/668-7261) offer Stonehenge/Bath day trips from London. Train info tel. 0345/484-950.

   London's airports: By National Express bus to **Heathrow Airport** (9/day, at 10:35, 12:35, 13:35, 14:35, 16:35, and so on, 2.5 hrs, £10, tel. 0990/808-080), and **Gatwick** (8/day, 4.5 hrs, change at Heathrow). Trains are faster but more expensive (hrly, 2.5 hrs, £22.50, see London Connections section for details). You can also take the tube from the airport to London's Paddington station, then catch the Exeter train to Bath.

YORK

Historical York is loaded with world-class sights. Marvel at the York Minster, the finest Gothic church in England. Ramble through the Shambles, York's wonderfully preserved medieval quarter. Enjoy a walking tour led by an old Yorker. Hop a train at Europe's greatest Railway Museum, travel to the 1800s in the York Castle Museum, and head back to Viking York at the Jorvik exhibit.

York has a rich history. In A.D. 71 it was Eboracum, a Roman provincial capital. Constantine was proclaimed emperor here in A.D. 306. In the fifth century, as Rome was toppling, a Roman emperor sent a letter telling England it was on its own, and York became Eoforwic, the capital of the Anglo-Saxon kingdom of Northumbria. A church was built here in 627, and the town was an early Christian center of learning. The Vikings later took the town and from about 860 to 950 it was a Danish trading center called Jorvik. The invading and conquering Normans destroyed, then rebuilt the city, giving it a castle and the walls you see today. Medieval York, with 9,000 inhabitants, grew rich on the wool trade and became England's second city. Henry VIII spared the city's fine minster in order to use York as his Anglican church's northern capital. The Archbishop of York is second only to the Archbishop of Canterbury in the Anglican church. In the Industrial Age, York was the railway hub of north England. When it was built, York's train station was the world's largest. Today, except for its huge chocolate factory (Kit-Kats are made here), York's leading industry is tourism.

Planning Your Time
York rivals Edinburgh as the best sightseeing city in Britain after London. It deserves two nights and a day. For the best 36 hours,

follow this plan: Catch the 19:00 city walking tour on the evening of your arrival. The next morning be at Jorvik at 9:00 when it opens (to avoid the midday crowds). The nearby Castle Museum is worth the rest of the morning (10:00–noon, I could even spend more time here). If you're rough, have lunch in the Golden Fleece pub. If you're fancy, lunch in a teahouse. Three options for your early afternoon: shoppers browse the Shambles, train buffs tour the National Railway Museum, and scholars do the Yorkshire Museum. Tour the minster at 16:00 before catching the 17:00 evensong service. Finish your day with an early evening stroll along the wall and perhaps through the abbey gardens. This schedule assumes you're there in the summer (evening orientation walk) and that there's an evensong on. Confirm your plans with the TI first.

Orientation (tel. code: 01904)

The sightseer's York is small. Virtually everything is within a few minutes' walk: the sights, train station, tourist information, and B&Bs. The longest walk a visitor might take (from a B&B across town to the Castle Museum) is 15 minutes.

Bootham Bar, a gate in the medieval town wall, is the hub of your York visit. At Bootham Bar (and on Exhibition Square facing it) you'll find the TI, the starting points for most walking tours and bus tours, handy access to the medieval town wall, Gillygate (lined with good eateries), and streets leading to my recommended B&Bs. (In York, a "bar" is a gate and a "gate" is a street. Go ahead, blame the Vikings.)

Tourist Information: The TI at Bootham Bar sells a 65p map. Ask for the free *What's On* guide (July–August Monday–Saturday 9:00–19:00, Sunday 10:00–18:00; September–June Monday–Saturday 9:00–17:00, tel. 01904/621-756).

Arrival in York: Upon arrival, grab a bench at the station and enjoy the enchanting voice of the woman announcer singing the train arrivals. The station is a five-minute walk from town; turn left down Station Road and follow the crowd toward the Gothic towers of the minster. After the bridge a block before the minster, signs to the TI send you left. Buses #30, #31, and #32 go from the station to my recommended B&Bs. Otherwise, they are a ten-minute walk or a £3 taxi ride.

Tours of York

▲▲▲**Walking Tours**—Charming local volunteer guides give energetic, entertaining, and free two-hour walks through York (daily, 10:15 all year and 14:15 April–October, plus 19:00 June–August, from Exhibition Square across from the TI). There are many other commercial York walking tours. YorkWalk Tours have reliable guides and many themes (£2, TI has schedule). The ghost tours, offered after nightfall, are more entertaining than

York

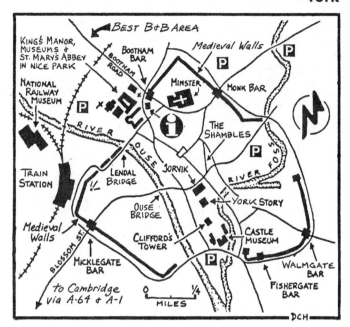

BEST B&B AREA

KING'S MANOR, MUSEUMS & ST. MARY'S ABBEY IN NICE PARK

NATIONAL RAILWAY MUSEUM

BOOTHAM ROAD

BOOTHAM BAR

MINSTER

Medieval Walls

MONK BAR

P

P

TRAIN STATION

RIVER

OUSE

LENDAL BRIDGE

JORVIK

THE SHAMBLES

P

RIVER FOSS

YORK STORY

OUSE BRIDGE

Medieval Walls

BLOSSOM ST.

MICKLEGATE BAR

CLIFFORD'S TOWER

CASTLE MUSEUM

P

to Cambridge via A-64 & A-1

0   ¼

MILES

WALMGATE BAR

FISHERGATE BAR

DCH

informative. Of the many ghost tours from which to choose, the "Original" and the "Haunted" are least gimmicky. But even their featured characters are pretty lame.

▲**Guide Friday Hop-on and Hop-off Bus Tours**—York's Guide Friday offers tour guides on speed who can talk enthusiastically to three sleeping tourists in a gale on a topless double-decker bus for an hour without stopping. Buses make the hour-long circuit, covering secondary York sights that the city walking tours skip. Tickets cost £7 on the bus, £6 from the TI (hop on and off all day, departures every ten or 15 minutes from 9:20 until around 18:00, tel. 01904/640-896). While you can hop on and off where you like, the York route is of no value from a transportation-to-the-sights point of view. I'd catch it at the TI and ride it for an orientation all the way around (1 hr) or get off at the Railway Museum, skipping the last five minutes. Many figure the information is kids' stuff after doing the free city walk. Guide Friday's competitors give you a little less for a little less.

Sights—York
▲**City Walls**—The historic walls of York provide a fine 2-mile walk. Walk from Bootham Bar (gate) to Monk Bar for outstanding cathedral views. Open until dusk (barring attacks) and free.

▲▲▲**York Minster**—The pride of York, this largest Gothic church north of the Alps (540 feet long, 200 feet tall) is a brilliant example of how the High Middle Ages were far from dark.

Your first impression might be the spaciousness and brightness of the nave (built 1280–1350). This is from the middle period of Gothic, called "Decorated Gothic," and it is one of the widest Gothic naves in Europe. Notice the Great West Window (1338) above the entry. The heart in the tracery is called "the heart of Yorkshire." The mysterious dragon's head (sticking out over the nave) was probably used as a crane to lift a font cover.

The north and south transepts are the oldest part of today's church (1220–1270). The oldest complete window in the minster, with the modern-looking "grisaille" pattern, is the Five Sisters' Window in the north transept (1260).

The fanciful choir and the east end (high altar) is from the last stage of Gothic, Perpendicular (1360–1470). The Great East Window (1405), the largest medieval glass window in existence, shows the beginning and the end of the world with scenes from Genesis and the Book of Revelation. A chart (on the right, with a tiny, more helpful chart within) highlights the core Old Testament scenes in this hard-to-read masterpiece.

The "foundations" (£2) give you a chance to climb down, archaeologically and physically, through the centuries to see the roots of the much smaller but still huge Norman church (Romanesque, 1100) which stood on this spot, and below that, to the Roman excavations. Constantine was proclaimed Roman emperor here in A.D. 306. Peek also at the modern concrete save-the-church foundations and the church treasury.

There are three more extra visits to consider: The chapter house, an elaborately decorated 13th-century Gothic dome, features playful details carved in the stonework (pointed out in the flier that comes with the 70p admission). You can step into the crypt which features 12th-century Romanesque art (70p), or scale the tower (£2, long climb, great view).

The cathedral is open daily 7:30–20:30 (tel. 01904/624-426). The chapter house, tower, and "foundations" have shorter hours, usually 10:00 to 18:00. Follow the *Welcome to the York Minster* flyer and ask about a free guided tour (they go frequently, you can join one in progress). The helpful blue-armbanded minster guides are happy to answer your questions. While a donation of £1.50 is reasonably requested, if I'm visiting the foundations or climbing the tower, I give it (and more) in the form of those admissions.

Evensong is a chance to experience the cathedral in musical and spiritual action. Evensong services are held daily at 17:00 (16:00 on Saturday and Sunday, but usually spoken on Monday and when the choir is off).

▲**The Shambles**—This is the most colorful old York street in the half-timbered, traffic-free core of town. Ye olde downtown York, while very touristy, is a window-shopping, busker-filled, people-watcher's delight. Don't miss the more frumpy Newgate Market or the old-time candy store just opposite the bottom end of the Shambles.

▲▲▲**York Castle Museum**—Truly one of Europe's top museums, this is a walk with Dickens, the closest thing to a time-tunnel experience England has to offer. It includes the Victorian Kirkgate: a fine collection of old shops well-stocked exactly as they were 150 years ago, along with costumes, armor, an eye-opening Anglo-Saxon helmet (from A.D. 750), and the entertaining "every home should have one" exhibit showing the evolution of vacuum cleaners, toilets, TVs, bicycles, stoves, and so on, from their crude beginnings to now. (£4.50, Monday–Saturday 9:30–17:30, Sunday 10:00–17:30, 1960s cafeteria, shop, car park; the £2.50 guidebook, while not necessary, makes a nice souvenir, tel. 01904/653-611.) Clifford's Tower (across from the Castle Museum) is all that's left of York's castle (13th century, site of a 1190 massacre of local Jews).

▲**Jorvik**—Sail the "Pirates of the Caribbean" north and back 800 years and you get Jorvik—more a ride than a museum. Innovative ten years ago, the commercial success of Jorvik inspired copycat ride/museums all over England. You'll ride a little Disney-type train car for 13 minutes through the re-created Viking street of Coppergate. It's the year 948 and you're in the village of Jorvik. Next your little train takes you through the actual excavation sight that inspired this. Finally you'll browse through a small gallery of Viking shoes, combs, locks, and other intimate glimpses of that redheaded culture (£4.50; daily from 9:00, last entry at 17:30; November–March last entry, at 15:30; tel. 01904/643-211). Avoid hour-long midday waits by going very early or very late. Some love this "ride"; others call it a gimmicky rip-off. If you're looking for a serious museum, see the Viking exhibit at the Yorkshire Museum. It's better. If you're thinking Disneyland with a splash of history, Jorvik's great. I like Jorvik, but it's not worth a long line.

▲▲**National Railway Museum**—This thunderous museum shows 150 fascinating years of British railroad history. Fanning out from a grand roundhouse are an array of historic cars and engines, including Queen Victoria's lavish royal car and the very first "stagecoaches on rails." There's much more, including exhibits on dining cars, post cars, sleeping cars, train posters, and videos. This biggest and best railroad museum anywhere is interesting even to people who think "Pullman" is Japanese for "tug-o-war" (£5, daily 10:00–18:00, tel. 01904/621-261).

▲**Yorkshire Museum**—Located in a lush and lazy park next to the stately ruins of St. Mary's Abbey, the Yorkshire Museum is the city's forgotten serious "archaeology of York" museum. While the hordes line up at Jorvik, the best Viking artifacts are here—with no crowds and in a better historical context. You have to walk through this museum, but the stroll takes you through Roman,

Saxon, Viking, Norman, and Gothic York. Its prize piece is the delicately etched 15th-century pendant called the "Middleham Jewel." The video about the creation of the abbey is worth a look (£3.50, open daily 10:00–17:00).

Honorable Mention—York has a number of other sights and activities (described in TI material) which pale in comparison to the biggies. The Fairfax House is perfectly Georgian inside (£3.50, Monday–Saturday 11:00–16:30, Sunday 13:30–16:30). The York Story offers a 45-minute video on the history of York—it's good, straight history (£2, associated with, across the street from, and pushed by the Castle Museum). The Richard III "museum" at Monk Bar is interesting only for Richard III enthusiasts (£1). The Antiques Centre is a fun browse (41 Stonegate near minster).

Sleeping in York
(£1 = about $1.60, tel. code: 01904)
Sleep Code: **S**=Single, **D**=Double/Twin, **T**=Triple, **Q**=Quad, **b**=bathroom, **t**=toilet only, **s**=shower only, **CC**=Credit Card (Visa, MasterCard, Amex).

I've listed peak-season book-direct prices. Don't use the TI. Outside of July and August some prices go soft. My recommendations are in the handiest B&B neighborhood, just outside the old-town wall's Bootham gate, along the road called Bootham. All are within a five-minute walk of the minster and TI and a ten-minute walk or £3 taxi ride from the station. If driving, head for the cathedral and follow the medieval wall to the gate called Bootham Bar. Bootham "street" leads away from Bootham Bar. The B&Bs are within 3 blocks on the left. These B&Bs are small and family-run. They will generally hold a room with a phone call, work hard to help their guests sightsee and eat smartly, have lots of fairly steep stairs, and are all on quiet, residential side streets. Most have permits for street parking. And most take no credit cards.

Airden House, the most central of my Bootham-area listings, has eight spacious rooms, a grandfather clock–cozy TV lounge, and brightness and warmth throughout. Susan and Keith Burrows keep their place simple, comfortable, and friendly. They are a great source of local travel tips (D-£38, Db-£46, non-smoking, 1 St. Mary's, York YO3 7DD, tel. 01904/638-915).

The Sycamore, run by Margaret and David Tyce, is a fine value with homey rooms and piles of personal touches, at the end of a dead-end opposite a fun-to-watch bowling green (D-£32, Db-£40, family deals, no lounge but TVs in the rooms, non-smoking, 19 Sycamore Place off Bootham Terrace, YO3 7DW, tel. & fax 01904/624-712).

The Hazelwood is my most hotelesque listing. Ian and Carolyn McNabb run this elegant and spacious old 14-room place in a stately, proper way, paying careful attention to details

York, Our Neighborhood

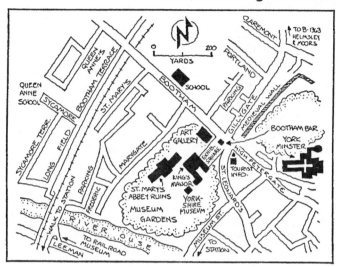

and serving a classy breakfast (Db-£50–53, Db with four-poster-£5 extra, family deals, non-smoking; a fridge, ice, and great travel library in the basement lounge; CC:VM, 24 Portland Street, Gillygate, YO3 7EH, tel. 01904/626-548, fax 01904/628-032).

Abbeyfields Guest House has cozy, freshly decorated rooms and lots of stairs (S-£18, Sb-£26, Db-£44, 19 Bootham Terrace, YO3 7DD, tel. 01904/636-471, Richard and Gwen).

Claremont Guest House is a friendly, non-smoking house offering two rooms, thoughtful touches, and solid beds. Gill and Martyn Cornell offer laundry service and will cook an evening meal (D-£32, Db-£42, 18 Claremont Terrace off Gillygate, YO3 7EJ, tel. 01904/625-158).

White Doves is a cheery little place with four comfy rooms (Db-£40, family deals, 20 Claremont Terrace off Gillygate, YO3 7EJ, tel. 01904/625-957, Pauline and David Pearce).

23 St. Mary's is a rococo riot. Mrs. Hudson has done everything super-correctly, and offers nine rooms with strong beds, modern facilities, a classy lounge, and all the doily touches (Sb-£30–34, Db-£56–66 depending on season and size, non-smoking, 23 St. Mary's, YO3 7DD, tel. 01904/622-738).

Queen Anne's Guest House has six compact, clean, and cheery rooms (D-£30, Db-£34, family deals, non-smoking, 24 Queen Anne's Road, tel. 01904/629-389, Judy and David West).

Arrow Lodge B&B is also good (S or D-£13–16 per person, family room, non-smoking, 8 Queen Anne's Road, tel. 01904/642-344, Edith and Dave Mowbray).

The Golden Fleece, a "haunted" 400-year-old pub, offers five rooms and a funky, murky, creaky experience right in the center of the old town. The floors aren't level, the beds are four-posters, and the local crowd fills the ground-floor pub with smoke and belly laughs (pub closes at 23:00, D-£40, huge family room with a four-poster and bunks, small Jacuzzi in the shared bath-room, private car park, at the bottom end of the Shambles, 16 Pavement, York, YO1 2ND, tel. 01904/625-171, Sally and Dave Pyne).

York's Youth Hotel is well run, with lots of extras like a kitchen, laundromat, games, and bar (D-£26, £11 in four- to six-bed dorms, sheets and breakfast extra, £1 less for multinight stays, CC:VM, ten-minute walk from station at 11 Bishophill Senior Road, York YO1 1EF, tel. 01904/625-904 or 01904/630-613).

Eating in York

Good Meals Downtown
The old center is slathered with cute eateries. Consider one of several places along the street called Pavement. **The Golden Fleece** pub is a hopping place for lunch, serving famous Yorkshire pudding and hearty meals with the highest-priced beer in town (see Sleeping, above). **Kites,** closer to the center, on Grape Lane, serves tasty, fresh, and unusual French and English meals at good prices. **Ye Olde Starre Inn,** the oldest pub in town, has yet to learn the art of cooking.

York is famous for its elegant teahouses. Drop into one around 16:00 for tea and cakes. Ladies love **Betty's** (£4, daily 9:00–21:00, mostly non-smoking, St. Helen's Square, fine people-watching from a window seat, usually a line, wait for a main floor table), but several others can satisfy your king- or queen-for-a-day desires.

Eating near Bootham Bar and Your B&B
Walk along Gillygate and choose from a fun array of eateries including **Mama Mia's** (authentic Italian, indoor/outdoor patio, daily 11:30–14:00 and 17:30–23:00, 20 Gillygate, tel. 01904/622-020), **Miller's Yard** (extremely vegetarian take-out, good desserts, Monday–Saturday 10:00–17:00, closed Sunday, in a courtyard opposite Mama Mia's, tel. 01904/610-676), **Cafe 8** (classy and good food), **Wagon and Horse** (basic pub grub with non-smoking section), **Rahima Indian Restaurant** (just beyond Gillygate on Clarance Street), the **Phoenix** (pricey Chinese, eat-in or take-out), and a traditional little fish-and-chips joint, **Gillygate Fisheries,** at #59 where tattooed people eat in and housebound mothers take out. For the closest you'll get to Mexico in Britain, try **Fiesta Mehicana** (17:30–19:00, sit-down or take-out, 14 Clifford Street, tel. 01904/610-243). **Cafe Concerto** has a loyal following (on Petergate, under Bootham Bar). For pub dinners, consider the

Coach House (nightly 18:30–21:30, 20 Marygate, tel. 01904/652-780). The people who run your B&B know what's good.

Transportation Connections—York

By train to: Durham (2/hr, 40 min), **Edinburgh** (hrly, 2 hrs, £39), **London** (2/hr, 2 hrs, £44), **Bath** (via Bristol, hrly, 5 hrs), **Cambridge** (nearly hrly, 2 hrs with a change in Petersborough), **Birmingham** (8/day, 3 hrs). Train info tel. 0345/484-950.

EDINBURGH

Edinburgh, the colorful city of Robert Louis Stevenson, Walter Scott, and Robert Burns, is Scotland's showpiece and one of Europe's most entertaining cities. Historical, monumental, fun, and well-organized, it's a tourist's delight.

Take a royal hike down the Royal Mile through the Old Town. Historic buildings pack the Royal Mile between the castle (on the top) and Holyrood Palace (on the bottom). Medieval skyscrapers stand shoulder-to-shoulder, hiding peaceful court-yards connected to High Street by narrow lanes or even tunnels. This colorful jumble, in its day the most crowded city in the world, is the tourist's Edinburgh.

Edinburgh (ED'n-burah) was once two towns divided by a lake. To alleviate crowding, the lake was drained and a magnificent Georgian city, today's New Town, was laid out to the north. Georgian Edinburgh, like the city of Bath, shines with broad boulevards, straight streets, square squares, circular circuses, and elegant mansions decked out in colonnades, pediments, and sphinxes in the proud, neoclassical style of 200 years ago.

Planning Your Time
While the major sights can be seen in a day, on a three-week tour of Britain, I'd give Edinburgh two days.
Day 1: Orient yourself with a Guide Friday bus tour. Do the whole loop, getting off only to tour the Georgian House. After lunch catch a 14:00 walking tour of the Royal Mile. If you tour Holyrood Palace, do it after your walk, at about 16:00. Evening: Scottish show, folk pub, or haunted walk.

Day 2: Climb Sir Walter Scott Memorial for a city view, then take the 10:30 "City, Sea, and Hills" bus tour (or tour the National Gallery). Visit the castle and spend the rest of the afternoon on the Royal Mile museum-going or shopping.

Orientation (tel. code: 0131)
The center of Edinburgh holds the Princes Street Gardens park and Waverley Bridge, where you'll find the TI, Waverley Shopping and Eating Center, train station, bus info office, the starting point for most city bus tours, festival office, the National Gallery, and a covered dance-and-music pavilion. Weather blows in and out—bring your sweater.

Tourist Information: The crowded TI has become a profit-seeking business with advice colored by who gives the best commissions. It's central as can be atop the Waverley Market on Princes Street (Monday–Saturday 9:00–20:00, Sunday 11:00–20:00, shorter hours and closed Sunday in off-season, tel. 0131/557-1700, airport TI tel. 0131/333-2167). Ideally, skip it and telephone if you have questions. Their misnamed *Essential Guide to Edinburgh* (which costs 25p and shuffles a little information between lots of ads) has a cruddy little map. *The List*, the best monthly entertainment listing, is sold for £1.50 at newsstands. Book your room direct without the TI's help.

For real info sans the sales push, visit the **Old Town Information Centre** at Tron Church, South Bridge at the Royal Mile, for a great free map of the Royal Mile. A couple of blocks down the Mile, at 5 Blackfriars Street, the Backpackers' Centre is a good source of budget travel information.

Banking: Barclays has decent rates without the typical 2 percent service charge if you have Barclays or Visa checks (daily 9:30–17:00, 50 meters into New Town from TI and station at 18 South Andrew Street).

Sunday Activities: Many sights close on Sunday, but there's still a lot to do: Royal Mile walking tour, city bus tour, Edinburgh Castle, St. Giles Cathedral, Holyrood Palace, Royal Botanic Gardens, Arthur Seat hike, shopping, and people-watching at Princes Street Gardens. The Georgian House and National Gallery open Sunday afternoon.

Arrival in Edinburgh: Arriving by train puts you in the city center, a few steps from the TI and the city bus to my recommended B&Bs. Both National Express and Scottish Citylink buses use the bus station a block from the train station in the Georgian town on St. Andrew Square.

Edinburgh's slingshot-of-an-airport is 10 miles northwest of the center and well connected by shuttle buses (4/hr from Waverley Bridge, £3.40, flight info: tel. 0131/333-1000, British Midlands tel. 0345/554-554, British Air tel. 0345/222-111). Taxi to airport: £14.

Getting Around Edinburgh

Nearly all Edinburgh sights are within walking distance.

City buses are handy and inexpensive (average fare-60p, LRT info office, corner of Waverley Bridge and Market Street, tel. 0131/555-6363). Tell the driver where you're going, drop exact change into the box or lose the excess, grab your ticket as you board, push the stop button as you near your stop (so your stop isn't skipped), and exit from the middle door. All-day "Freedom Ticket" passes (£2.20) are sold at the LRT office on Waverley Bridge. Taxis are reasonable (easy to flag down, several handy pickup points, 90p drop charge, 60p extra after 18:00, average ride between downtown and B&B district—£3).

Bus Tours of Edinburgh

▲**Hop-on and Hop-off City Bus Tours**—Two companies, Guide Friday and LRT's "Edinburgh Classic Tour," offer buses that circle the town center—Waverley Bridge, around the castle, Royal Mile, Calton Hill, Georgian New Town, and Princes Street—in about an hour, with pick-ups about every 15 minutes and an informative narration. You can stop and go all day on one ticket. Overlapping can be interesting, since each guide has her own story to tell. On sunny days they go topless (the buses), but can suffer from traffic noise and congestion. (Guide Friday, £7, tel. 0131/556-2244; Classic Tour, £5.50, tel. 0131/555-6363.)

▲**City Bus Tours**—"City, Sea, and Hills" is the best 90-minute tour of greater Edinburgh (£3.50, daily at 10:30, information at LRT office, on Waverley Bridge, tel. 0131/555-6363). Several all-day bus tours can take you as far as Loch Ness. Tours leave from near the train station.

Sights—Along the Royal Mile

(In walking order from top to bottom.)

▲▲▲**Royal Mile**—This is one of Europe's most interesting historic walks. Each step of the way is entertaining. Start at the top and amble down to the palace. I've listed the top sights of the Royal Mile—working downhill.

The Royal Mile is actually a series of different streets in a straight line. All along, you'll find interesting shops, cafés, and *closes* (lanes leading to tiny squares), providing the thoughtful visitor a few rough edges of a town well on its way to becoming a touristic mall. See it now. In a few years, tourists will be riding down it on bagpipe skateboards.

Royal Mile Walking Tours: Follow a local guide along the Royal Mile (£4, free during Edinburgh Festival, daily usually at 10:00, 11:00, and 14:00, about 2 hrs long). Of the competitive, hardworking little companies that offer these entertaining tours, Robin's is most historic (start at TI, tel. 0131/661-0125) and

Edinburgh

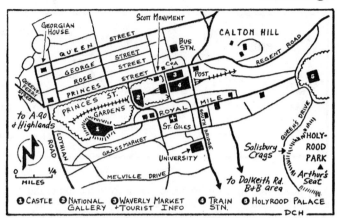

① CASTLE ② NATIONAL GALLERY ③ WAVERLY MARKET + TOURIST INFO ④ TRAIN STN. ⑤ HOLYROOD PALACE

Mercat is chattier (Mercat Cross on the Royal Mile, tel. 0131/661-4541). The guides, who enjoy making a short story long, ignore the big sights, taking you behind the scenes with piles of barely historic gossip, bully-pulpit Scottish pride, and fun but forgettable trivia.

▲▲**Edinburgh Castle**—The fortified birthplace of the city 1,300 years ago, this is the imposing symbol of Edinburgh. While the castle has been a royal residence since the 11th century, most of the buildings today are from its more recent use as a military garrison. Start with the free and wonderfully droll 30-minute guided introduction tour (3/hr, departs from entry, see clock for the next departure). Then see the Scottish National War Memorial, Great Hall, Scottish Crown Jewels, the room full of Battle of Culloden mementos, St. Margaret's Chapel (oldest building in town), the giant cannon, and the city view from the ramparts (in that order). There's also a 20th-century military museum and a daily "one-o'clock gun." Allow two hours, including the tour. (£5.50, daily 9:30–18:00, until 17:00 in winter and on holidays, cafeteria; tel. 0131/225-9846.)

Scotch Whiskey Heritage Centre—This touristy ambush is designed to distill £4.20 out of your pocket. You get a video history, a little whiskey-keg train-car ride, and a free sample before finding yourself in the shop. People do seem to enjoy it, but that might have something to do with the sample (tel. 0131/220-0441). The Camera Obscura, across the street, is just as rewarding.

▲▲**Gladstone's Land**—Take a good look at this typical 16th- to 17th-century house, complete with a lived-in furnished interior and guides in each room who love to talk (£2.60, April–October Monday–Saturday 10:00–17:00, Sunday 14:00–17:00, good Royal

Royal Mile

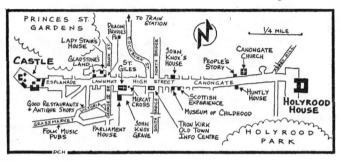

Mile photo from the top-floor window or from the top of the entry stairway through the golden eagle).

▲Lady Stair's House/Writers' Museum—This interesting house, which dates back to 1622, is filled with manuscripts and knickknacks of Scotland's three greatest literary figures: Robert Burns, Sir Walter Scott, and Robert Louis Stevenson. Worth a few minutes for anyone, fascinating for fans (free, Monday–Saturday 10:00–18:00, till 17:00 off-season, closed Sunday).

Deacon Brodie's Tavern—A decent place for a light meal (see Eating, below); read the story of its notorious namesake on the wall facing Bank Street.

▲St. Giles Cathedral—Wander through Scotland's most important church. Don't miss this engaging Gothic church's ornate, neo-Gothic—from 1911—thistle chapel (£1 donation, to the right of the altar, find the angels playing bagpipes) or the Scottish crown steeple on top (daily 9:00–19:00, until 17:00 off-season, fine café downstairs). John Knox (whose statue is in the back of the church), founder of austere Scottish Presbyterianism, is buried out back, austerely, under the parking lot (spot 44).

Parliament House—Stop in to see the grand hall with its fine hammer-beamed ceiling and stained glass. For a trip into the 18th century, Tuesday through Friday around 10:00 or 10:30 is the best time to see all the wigged and robed legal beagles hard at work pacing the hall deep in discussion. Greater eminence . . . longer wig. The doorman is helpful (free, public welcome Monday–Friday 9:00–16:30, open-to-the-public trials 10:00–16:00, entry behind St. Giles Cathedral near parking spot 21).

▲Tron Kirk—This fine old building houses an interesting (free) Old Town history display and the genuinely helpful Old Town tourist information center. No crowds, just caring help by an outfit working to better organize and show off Edinburgh's historic Old Town.

Museum of Childhood—This is a 5-story playground of historical toys and games (free, Monday–Friday 10:00–18:00, till 17:00 off-season, closed Sunday).

▲**John Knox's House**—Fascinating for Reformation buffs, this fine 16th-century house offers a well-explained look at the life of the great reformer (£1.75, Monday–Saturday 10:00–16:30, closed on Sunday).

Scottish Experience—This touristy little side trip (free but commercial) is where you can reserve a spot for a Scottish Folk Evening (see below). The video and historic kilt room are free before the show.

People's Story—This interesting exhibition traces the lot of the working class through the 18th, 19th, and 20th centuries (free, Monday–Saturday 10:00–18:00, till 17:00 off-season, closed Sunday).

▲**Huntly House**—Another old house full of old stuff, worth a look for its early Edinburgh history and handy ground-floor WC. Don't miss the copy of the National Covenant written on an animal skin or the sketches of pre-Georgian Edinburgh with its lake still wet (free, Monday–Saturday 10:00–18:00, closed Sunday). Just a toot farther downhill is Bagpipes Galore.

▲**Holyrood Palace**—At the bottom end of the Royal Mile, this is where the queen stays when she's in town. The building is rich in history and decor, but without information or a guided tour ("there's none of either," snickered the guy who sells the £3.50 museum guidebooks) you're just another peasant in the dark. Docents in each room are happy to give you the answer if you know the question. After wandering through the elegantly furnished rooms and a few dark older rooms filled with glass cases of historic bits and Scottish pieces, you're free to wander through the ruined abbey and the queen's gardens (£5.30, Monday–Saturday 9:30–18:00, Sunday 10:30–16:30, closed when the queen's home, tel. 0131/556-7371).

More Bonnie Wee Sights

▲**Walter Scott Monument**—Built in 1840, this elaborate, neo-Gothic monument honors the great author, one of Edinburgh's many illustrious sons. The 200-foot monument shelters a marble statue of Scott. He is surrounded by busts of 16 great Scottish poets and 64 characters from his books. Climb 287 steps for a fine view of the city (£1, Monday–Saturday 9:00–18:00, until 17:00 off-season, closed Sunday).

▲▲**Georgian House**—This refurbished Georgian house, set on Edinburgh's finest Georgian square, is a trip back to 1796. A volunteer guide in each room is trained in the force-feeding of stories and trivia. Start your visit with the interesting video (£4, Monday–Saturday 10:00–17:00, Sunday 14:00–17:00, 7 Charlotte Square, tel. 0131/225-2160). From this museum, walk through Georgian

Edinburgh. The grand George Street, connecting St. Andrew and Charlotte Squares, was the centerpiece of the elegantly planned New Town.

Princes Street Gardens—This grassy park, a former lake-bed, separates Edinburgh's New and Old Towns and offers a wonderful escape from the city. There are plenty of free concerts and country dances in the summer, and the oldest floral clock in the world. Join the local office workers for a picnic-lunch break.

National Gallery—An elegant neoclassical building with a small but impressive collection of European masterpieces and the best look you'll get at Scottish paintings (free, Monday–Saturday 10:00–17:00, Sunday 14:00–17:00, tel. 0131/556-8921).

Royal Botanic Garden—Britain's second-oldest botanical garden (established in 1670 for medicinal herbs) is now one of Europe's best (free, daily 10:00–20:00 in season, £2 "rainforest to desert" tours daily at 11:00 and 14:00, 1 mile north of the center at Inverleith, tel. 0131/552-7171).

▲▲Arthur's Seat Hike—A 30-minute hike up the 822-foot volcanic mountain (surrounded by a fine park overlooking Edinburgh), starting from the Holyrood Palace, Commonwealth Pool, or your B&B, gives you a rewarding view. It's the easiest "I climbed a mountain" feeling I've ever had. You can drive up most of the way from behind (follow the one-way street from the palace, park by the little lake) or run up like they did in *Chariots of Fire*. Ask a local for the best way up.

Brush Skiing—If you'd rather be skiing, the Hillend Ski Centre is an open-all-year hill covered with brush, with a chairlift, T-bar, and rentable skis, boots, and poles, on the edge of town (£6/hr with gear, daily 9:30–21:00, less on weekends, probably canceled if it snows, tel. 0131/445-4433).

Royal Commonwealth Games Swimming Pool—The biggest pool I've ever seen is open to the public, with Café Aqua (overlooking the pool), weights, saunas, and plenty of water rides, including Europe's biggest "flume," or water slide (£2, Monday–Friday 9:00–21:00, Saturday and Sunday 8:00–19:00, tel. 0131/667-7211).

Greyhound Races—This is a pretty lowbrow scene. But if you've never seen dog racing, this is a memorable night out combining great dog- and people-watching with a chance to lose some money gambling. Races are held about two nights a week at Powderhall Stadium.

Edinburgh Crystal—Blowing, molding, cutting, polishing, and engraving, the Edinburgh Crystal Company glassworks tour smashes anything you'll see in Venice. The 35-minute tours start at regular intervals between 9:15 and 15:30, Monday through Friday and summer weekends (£2, children under age 8 and large dogs are not allowed in for safety reasons). There is a shop full of "bargain" second-quality pieces, a video show, and a cafeteria. A free red minibus shuttle service from Waverley Bridge departs hourly (10:00–15:00) in summer, or drive 10 miles south of town on A701 to Penicuik. You can schedule a more expensive super tour where you actually blow and cut glass (tel. 01968/675-128).

Shopping—The best shopping is along Princes Street (don't miss elegant old Jenner's Department Store), Victoria Street (antiques galore), and the Royal Mile (touristy but competitively priced, shops usually open 9:00–17:30, later on Thursday).

Edinburgh Festival

One of Europe's great cultural events, Edinburgh's annual festival turns the city into a carnival of culture. There are enough music, dance, art, drama, and multicultural events to make even the most jaded traveler drool with excitement. Every day is jammed with formal and spontaneous fun. The official and fringe festivals rage through much of August (August 16–September 5 in 1998), with the Military Tattoo starting a week earlier. Many city sights run on extended hours and those that normally close on Sunday, don't. It's a glorious time to be in Edinburgh.

The official festival is more formal and serious, with entertainment by festival invitation only. Major events sell out well in advance (show office at 21 Market Street, £4–45, CC:VMA, booking from April on, tel. 0131/225-5756).

The less-formal **Fringe Festival** features "on the edge" comedy/theater (ticket/info office just below St. Giles Cathedral on the Royal Mile, tel. 0131/226-5259, bookings tel. 0131/226-5138). Its many events have, it seems, more performers than viewers. Tickets are usually available at the door (or strewn on the streets).

The **Military Tattoo** is a massing of the bands, drums, and bagpipes with groups from all over what was the British Empire. Displaying military finesse with a stirring lone-piper finale, this grand spectacle fills the castle esplanade nightly except Sunday, normally from a week before the festival starts until a week before it finishes: August 7 to 29 in 1998 (£8–16, CC:VMA, booking starts in January, tel. 0131/225-1188, Friday and Saturday shows sell out, Monday–Thursday shows rarely do). If nothing else, it is a really big show. The BBC airs the Tattoo in a grand TV spectacle throughout Britain once each season (worth watching).

If you do manage to hit Edinburgh during the festival, extend your stay by a day or two and book a room far in advance. While Fringe tickets and most Tattoo tickets are available the day of the show, you may want to book an official event or two in advance. Do it directly by telephone, leaving your credit-card number. You can pick up your ticket at the office the day of the show or at the door just before curtain time. Several publications list and evaluate festival events, including the festival's official schedule, the *Festival Times*, *The List*, *Fringe Program*, and the *Daily Diary*.

Entertainment in Edinburgh

▲▲**Evening Walking Tours**—These walks, more than a pile of ghost stories, are an entertaining and cheap night out (offered nightly, usually 19:00 and 21:00). The creatively staged Witchery Tours are the most established of the ghost tours (£5, 90 min, tel. 0131/225-6745). The new Literary Pub Tour leaves from the Beehive Pub on Grassmarket (£6, 2 hours, daily at 18:00 and 20:30 in season, tel. 0131/554-0777).

▲**Scottish Folk Evenings**—These £35 to £40 dinner shows, generally for tour groups, are held in huge halls of expensive hotels. (Prices are bloated to include 20 percent commissions, without which the show don't go on.) Your "traditional" meal is followed by a full slate of swirling kilts, blaring bagpipes, and Scottish folk-dancing with an "old-time music hall"–type emcee.

Prince Charlie's Extravaganza at the Edinburgh Old Town Weaving Company on the Royal Mile, is a fun show (just below the castle, near the Esplanade). You'll get a tasty four-course meal (Scotch broth, haggis with neeps and tatties, and a beef pastry with vegetables, wine, ice cream and coffee; salmon or vegetarian alternatives available). The dancing and music—piping, accordion, singing—are good, and if you book directly and show this book you get a 20 percent discount off the £36 price. The boss, Gavin Cruickshank, promised this discount for 1998. Shows are usually offered nightly. Come between 18:00 and 19:00 to see the "sheep to shop" display; try the tartan loom. You'll normally be seated with a wee band o' me bonnie readers. Dinner's at 19:00 and you sing "Auld Lang Syne" by 22:15 (180 seats, smoke-free, CC:VMA, tel. 0131/226-1555). During the day, you can rent a kilt at their shop.

Carlton Highland Hotel offers a Scottish folk evening without dinner (£12, at intersection of High Street and North Bridge).

▲▲ **Folk Music in Pubs**—Edinburgh is a good place for folk music. There's always a pub or two with a folk evening on. *The Gig* (a 50p monthly) lists all the live music action. Just off the Royal Mile on South Bridge, the **Tron Tavern and Ceilidh House** is home of the Tron Folk Club. They have nightly ad-lib traditional music from about 21:00 and a £3 folk concert on Saturday nights (tel. 0131/220-1550). **Whistle Binky** offers live folk music several nights a week (also near High Street) and **Finnigan's Wake** specializes in Irish folk music (a block off High Street on Victoria Street, tel. 0131/226-3816). On Grassmarket (below the castle), you'll find the **Fiddlers Arms** (fiddlers on Monday, tel. 0131/229-2665), **White Hart Inn**, and **Black Bull**, among others, all regularly featuring live folk music.

Theater—Even outside of festival time, Edinburgh is a fine place for lively and affordable theater. Pick up *The List* for a complete rundown of what's on.

Sleeping in Edinburgh
(£1 = about $1.60, tel. code: 0131)

Sleep Code: **S**=Single, **D**=Double/Twin, **T**=Triple, **Q**=Quad, **b**=bathroom, **t**=toilet only, **s**=shower only, **CC**=Credit Card (Visa, MasterCard, Amex).

The annual festival fills the city each August. Conventions, school holidays, and other surprises can make room-finding tough at almost any time. Call in advance or pay 30 percent extra for a relative dump. Downtown hotels are overpriced (minimum £70 doubles). For the best prices, book direct (rather than through the greedy TI) and, again, call in advance! "Standard" rooms, with toilets and showers a tissue-toss away, save you £8 a night.

My recommendations are south of town near the Royal Commonwealth Pool, just off Dalkeith Road. This comfortably safe neighborhood is a 20-minute walk or short bus ride from the Royal Mile. All listings are on quiet streets, a two-minute walk from a bus stop, and well-served by city buses. Near the B&Bs, you'll find plenty of eateries (see Eating, below), easy free parking, and a handy laundromat (Monday–Saturday 9:00–17:00, £5 for a self-serve load; £1 extra for B&B pick-up and drop-off service, 208 Dalkeith Road, tel. 0131/667-0825).

To reach the hotel neighborhood from the train station, TI, or Scott Monument, cross Princes Street and wait under the C&A sign (60p, buses #21, #33, #82, or #86, 60p, red bus: exact change or pay more, green bus: makes change, ride ten minutes to first stop 100 yards after the Pool, push the button, exit middle door). These buses also stop at the corner of North Bridge and High Street on the Royal Mile. Room prices are for peak-season 1998 (but not festival time when they can go sky high). Off-season prices go soft.

Millfield Guest House, run by Liz and Ed Broomfield, is thoughtfully furnished with antique class, a rare sit-and-chat ambience, and a comfy TV lounge. Since the showers are down the hall, you'll get spacious rooms and great prices (S-£21, D-£35–36, T-£48–52 for direct bookings only, good beds, absolutely non-smoking, quiet but friendly, CC:VM, easy reservation with CC which lets you arrive late, 12 Marchhall Road, EH16 5HR, tel. 0131/667-4428). Decipher the breakfast prayer by Robert Burns. Then try the "Taste of Scotland" breakfast option. See how many stone (14 lb) you weigh in the elegant throne room. This place is worth calling well in advance.

Kenvie Guest House offers lots of personal touches (one small twin-£35, D-£38, Db-£46 with this book in 1998, family deals, non-smoking, 16 Kilmaurs Road, EH16 5DA, tel.0131/668-1964, Dorothy Vidler).

Belford House is a tidy, simple, cheery place offering a warm welcome and a fine value (D-£34, T-£51, kid-friendly with family deals, CC:VM, a bit smoky, 13 Blacket Avenue, tel.

Edinburgh, Our Neighborhood

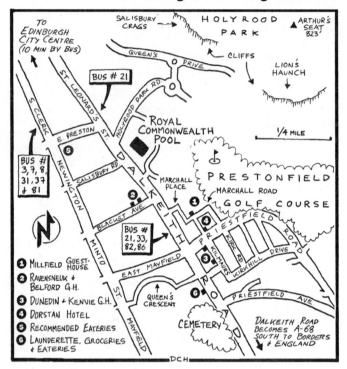

0131/667-2422, Isa and Tom Borthwick). They're adding baths to some rooms; ask the price.

Dunedin Guest House is bright and Scottish, non-smoking, and a good value for those who need a private bathroom (seven rooms, S-£22–27, Db-£44–54, family deals, handicapped-accessible, solid beds, strong showers, NASA lighting, TVs with satellite channels in rooms, Scotland and Edinburgh videos in lounge, 8 Priestfield Road, EH16 5HH, tel. 0131/668-1949, fax 0131/668-2181, Annette and Max Preston). The Prestons also offer mini-bus tours of Edinburgh.

Turret Guest House is teddy-on-the-beddie cozy with a great bay-windowed family room and a vast breakfast menu that includes haggis and vegetarian options (S-£18–24, D-£36–54 with this book through 1998, less off-season, 8 Kilmaurs Terrace, tel. 0131/667-6704, Mrs. Jackie Cameron).

Ravensneuk Guest House is also good—quiet, comfortable, and very Victorian (D-£40–50, Db-£50–60, prices vary with season and room size, family deals, great lounge, solid beds, all non-smoking rooms, 11 Blacket Avenue, EH9 1RR, tel. & fax 0131/667-5347, Chris and Toni Henry).

Dorstan Private Hotel is small and personable, but professional and hotelesque with all the comforts. Several of its 14 prim rooms are on the ground floor (Ds-£58, Db-£66, family rooms, CC:VM, 7 Priestfield Road, EH16 5HJ, tel. 0131/667-6721, fax 0131/668-4644, Mairae Campbell).

Priestville B&B is a big old place with charming rough edges and a friendly welcome (D-£36, Db-£44 with this book through 1998, family deals, non-smoking, 10 Priestfield Road, tel. 0131/667-2435, Audrey and Jim Christie).

Highland Park House is simple and bright (S-£20, D-£38 with this book, family deals, 16 Kilmaurs Terrace, tel. 0131/667-9204, Brian Love).

Eating in Edinburgh

Eating along the Royal Mile
Historic pubs and doily cafés with reasonable, unremarkable meals abound. **Deacon Brodie's Pub** serves soup, sandwiches, and snacks on the ground floor and good £6 meals upstairs (daily 12:00–22:00). Or munch prayerfully in the **Lower Aisle** restaurant under St. Giles Cathedral (Monday–Friday 10:00–16:30). At **The Brambles Tea Room** (next to Huntley House at 158 Cannongate), Shona serves light lunches and Starbucks coffee. **Food Plantation** has great, inexpensive fresh sandwiches to eat-in or take-out (274 Cannongate). **Clarinda's Tea Room**, near the bottom of the Royal Mile, is also good (daily 8:30–16:45). **Bann's Vegetarian Café** serves carnivore-pleasing veggie cuisine that goes way beyond tofu and granola (daily 10:00–23:00, just off South Bridge at 5 Hunter Square, tel. 0131/226-1112). **Dubh Prais Restaurant** offers decent Scottish food in a small, stone-walled basement (£15 and up, Tuesday–Saturday lunch and 18:30–22:30, closed Sunday and Monday, below St. Giles Cathedral at 123b High Street, reserve in advance, tel. 0131/557-5732, chef/owner James McWilliams). On Victoria Street, consider the very French **Pierre Victoire** (£5 lunch deals, closed Sunday, 9 Victoria Street, tel. 0131/225-1721) or the upstairs café in the Byzantium antique mall, across the street from Pierre Victoire. Gordon's Trattoria offers Italian cuisine, great service, and cheap prices (231 High Street). **Rafters**, upstairs from the Beehive Pub, serves fine three-course dinners for £11 (Grassmarket Street).

Eating in the New Town
Waverley Center Food Court, below the TI and above the station, is a food circus of flashy, trendy, fast-food joints (including The Scot's Pantry for quick traditional edibles) littered with paper plates and shoppers. Local office workers pile into

Lanterna for good Italian food (family-run, fresh and friendly, 83 Hanover Street, 2 blocks off Princes Street, tel. 0131/226-3090). For a generation, New Town vegetarians have munched salads at **Henderson's Salad Table and Wine Bar** (Monday–Saturday 8:00–22:45, closed Sunday, non-smoking section, strictly vegetarian, between Queen and George Streets at 94 Hanover Street, tel. 0131/225-2131). The bohemian but elegantly Georgian **Café 1812** must be holding a fine French cook prisoner (£6 lunch, £11 dinner deals, 29 Waterloo Place on Calton Hill, tel. 0131/556-5766). Rose Street has tons of pubs.

Eating in Dalkeith Road Area, near Your B&B

Within a block of the corner of Newington and Preston Streets are all kinds of eateries. For a fun local atmosphere that makes up for the food, the **Wine Glass Pub** serves filling "basket meals" (£4, Sunday–Thursday 18:00–20:30). **Chinatown**, next to the Wine Glass, is moderate and good. **Chatterbox** is fine for a light meal with tea (8:30–20:00, down East Preston from the pool). **Jade Palace** has tasty Chinese food (take-out only, closed Tuesday, 212 Dalkeith Road). **Jaipur Mansion** serves meals worth the £15 splurge in a maharajah's setting (across from the Wine Glass Pub at 10 Newington Road). **Brattisanis** is your basic chippie (lousy milkshakes, cheap haggis, 87 Newington Road). The huge **Commonwealth Pool** has a noisy cafeteria for hungry swimmers and budget travelers (pass the entry without paying, sit with a poolside view).

Transportation Connections—Edinburgh

By train to: Inverness (7/day, 4 hrs), **Oban** (3/day, change in Glasgow, 4.5 hrs), **York** (hrly, 2.5 hrs), **London** (hrly, 5 hrs), **Durham** (hrly, 2 hrs), **Lake District** (south past Carlisle to Penrith, catch bus to Keswick; 6/day, 40 min), **Birmingham** (6/day, 4.5 hrs), **Crewe** (6/day, 3.5 hrs). Train info tel. 0345/484-950.

   By bus to: Oban (3/day, 5 hrs) and **Fort William** (3/day, 5 hrs). For bus info, call National Express (tel. 0131/452-8777) or Scottish Citylink (tel. 0990/505-050).

DUBLIN

With reminders of its stirring history and rich culture on every corner, Ireland's capital and largest city is a sightseer's delight. Dublin's fair city will have you humming "Alive, alive-O."

Founded as a Viking trading settlement in the ninth century, Dublin grew to be a center of wealth and commerce second only to London in the United Kingdom. Dublin, the seat of English rule in Ireland for 700 years, was the heart of a "civilized" Anglo-Irish area (eastern Ireland) known as "the Pale." Anything "beyond the Pale" was considered uncultured and almost barbaric . . . purely Irish.

The Golden Age of English Dublin was the 18th century. Britain was on a roll and Dublin was Britain's second city. Largely rebuilt during this Georgian era, Dublin became an elegant and cultured capital. Everything was okay until nationalism and human rights got in the way. The ideas of the French Revolution inspired Irish intellectuals to buck British rule and, after the revolt of 1798, life in Dublin was never quite the same. But the 18th century left a lasting imprint on the city. Georgian (that's British for neoclassical) squares and boulevards gave the city a grand elegance. The National Museum, National Gallery, and many government buildings are in the Georgian section of town. Few buildings (notably St. Patrick's Cathedral and Christchurch Cathedral) pre-date this Georgian period.

In the 19th century, with the closing of the Irish Parliament, the famine, and the beginnings of the struggle for independence, Dublin was treated and felt more like a colony than a partner. The tension culminated in the Rising of 1916 and the battle that followed. While many of Dublin's grand streets were left in ruins, the city emerged as the capital of the only former colony in Europe.

While bullet-pocked buildings and dramatic statues keep memories of Ireland's recent struggle for independence alive, the city is looking to a bright future. Visitors enjoy a big-town cultural scene wrapped in a small-town smile.

Planning Your Time

Dublin deserves three nights and two days. Consider this sight-seeing plan:

Day 1: 9:30, Dublin Experience; 10:30, Trinity College walk; 11:00, Book of Kells and Old Library; 12:00, Browse Grafton Street, lunch there or picnic on St. Stephen's Green; 13:30, National Museum; 15:00, Historical town walk; 17:00, Return to hotel, rest, dinner; 19:30, Evening walk (literary or musical); 22:00, Irish music in Temple Bar area.

Day 2: 10:00, Kilmainham Jail; 12:00, Guinness Brewery tour; 13:30, Lunch (with a faint buzz); 15:00, Tour Dublin Castle; catch a play or concert in the evening.

Orientation (tel. code: 01)

Greater Dublin sprawls with about 1 million people—nearly a third of the country's population. But the center of touristic interest is a tight triangle between O'Connell Bridge, St. Stephen's Green, and Christchurch Cathedral. Within this triangle you'll find Trinity College (Book of Kells), Grafton Street (top pedestrian shopping zone), Temple Bar (trendy nightlife center), Dublin Castle, and the hub of most city tours and buses.

The River Liffey cuts the town in two. Focus on the southern half (where nearly all your sightseeing will take place). Dublin's main drag, O'Connell Street (near the Abbey Theater and outdoor pro-duce market) stretches from the very central O'Connell Bridge north of the river. Over the river, this main city axis continues—mostly as Grafton Street—to St. Stephen's Green. Only the Kil-mainham Jail and the Guinness Brewery (both west of the center) are outside your home triangle.

Tourist Information

The TI fills an old church on Suffolk Street (a block off Grafton Street). While packed with tourists, promotional brochures, an American Express office, a café, and traditional knickknacks, it's short on hard info. Less crowded but equally helpful TI branches are on Baggot Street and at the airport (daily 8:00–22:30). To talk to the TI on the phone you'll pay 60p per minute (550/112-233)—wel-come to Dublin. The TI gives a free newspaper with a lousy map, lots of advertisements, and the fliers that fill racks all over town. The best extensive publication they offer is *Dublin's Top Visitor Attractions* (which you can buy for £2.50 at the TI bookshop without any wait). This has a map and the latest on all the town's sights (many more than I list here). For a schedule of happenings in town, buy the excellent *In Dublin* at any newsstand (fortnightly, £1.50).

Arrival in Dublin

By Train: Trains arrive at Heuston Station (serving the west and southwest) on the west end of town. Dublin's second train station, Connolly Station (serving the north, northwest, and Rosslare), is closer to the center—a ten-minute walk from O'Connell Bridge. Each station has a luggage-check facility.

Bus 90 connects both train stations and the bus station and the city center (60p flat fee, 6/hr, runs along river).

By Bus: Bus Eireann, Ireland's national bus company, uses the Busaras Central Bus Station next to Connolly Station (catch bus 90 to the city center).

By Ferry: Irish Ferries dock at the mouth of the River Liffey (near the town center) while the Stena Line docks at Dun Laoghaire (easy DART train connections into Dublin, at least 3/hr, 15 min).

By Plane: From the airport, milk-run buses 41 and 41C go to O'Connell Bridge (£1.10, 3/hr). The faster Airlink direct bus connects the airport with the Heuston train station and Busaras bus station near Connolly Station (£3, 4/hr, 30 min). Taxis from the airport into Dublin cost about £10.

Getting Around Dublin

You'll do most of Dublin on foot. Big green buses are cheap and cover the city thoroughly. Most lines start at the four Quays nearest O'Connell Bridge. Tell the driver where you're going and he'll ask for 60p (one to five stops) or 80p (five to ten stops). The bus office at 59 Upper O'Connell Street has free "route network" maps and sells bus passes (one-day pass £3.30 adults, £5.50 per family, four-day adult pass-£10.00, bus information tel. 01/873-4222). DART trains connect Dublin with Dun Laoghaire (ferry terminal and recommended B&Bs, at least 3/hr, 15 min, £1.10). Taxis seem honest, and they are plentiful, friendly, and good sources of information (£3 for most downtown rides).

Tours of Dublin

While the physical treasures of Dublin are mediocre by European standards, the city has a fine story to tell and people with a natural knack for telling it. It's a good town for walking tours—and the competition is fierce for your business. You'll find pamphlets touting creative walks all over town. There are medieval walks, literary walks, Georgian Dublin walks, and more. The two evening walks are great ways to meet other travelers.

Historical Walking Tour of Dublin—This is your best introductory walk. A group of hardworking history graduates (many

Dublin

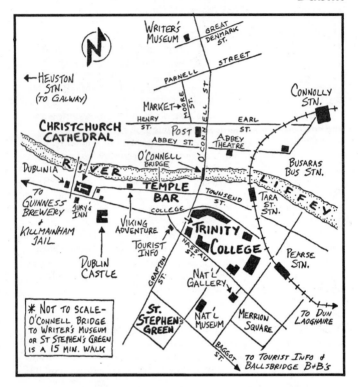

WRITER'S MUSEUM
GREAT DENMARK ST.
PARNELL STREET
←HEUSTON STN. (TO GALWAY)
CONNOLLY STN.
MARKET→
MOORE ST.
O'CONNELL ST.
HENRY ST.
EARL ST.
CHRISTCHURCH CATHEDRAL
POST
ABBEY ST.
ABBEY THEATRE
DUBLINIA
RIVER
O'CONNELL BRIDGE
LIFFEY
BUSARAS BUS STN.
TO GUINNESS BREWERY + KILLMAINHAM JAIL
JURY'S INN
TEMPLE BAR
COLLEGE
TOWNSEND ST.
TARA ST. STN.
VIKING ADVENTURE
TRINITY COLLEGE
DUBLIN CASTLE
TOURIST INFO
NASSAU ST.
PEARSE STN.
GRAFTON ST.
NAT'L GALLERY
* NOT TO SCALE— O'CONNELL BRIDGE TO WRITER'S MUSEUM OR ST STEPHEN'S GREEN IS A 15 MIN. WALK
ST. STEPHEN'S GREEN
NAT'L MUSEUM
MERRION SQUARE
TO DUN LAOGHAIRE
BAGGOT ST.
TO TOURIST INFO & BALLSBRIDGE B&B'S

who claim to have done more than just kiss the Blarney Stone) fill Dublin's basic historic strip—Trinity College-Old Parliament House-Dublin Castle-Christchurch Cathedral—with the story of their city from its Viking origin to the present. You stand in front of buildings that aren't much to see but are lots to talk about and listen to your guide's story. Guides talk at length about "the Troubles" and the roots of Ireland's struggle with Britain (£5, two hours, depart from gate of Trinity College, Monday–Saturday 11:00, 12:00, 15:00; Sunday 11:00, 12:00, 14:00, 15:00; winter schedule: Saturday and Sunday 12:00, tel. 01/845-0241).

Jameson Literary Pub Crawl—Two actors take 30 or so tourists on a walk stopping at four pubs. Half the time is spent enjoying their entertaining banter which introduces the novice to the high *craic* (conversation) of Joyce, O'Casey, and Yeats. The 2.5-hour tour is punctuated with 20-minute pub breaks (free time). It can be great fun socially, but the content suffers. Meet any night at 19:30

(or Sunday at noon) in the Duke Pub off Grafton on Duke Street (£6, runs three nights a week in winter, tel. 01/454-0228).

Traditional Irish-Music Pub Crawl—This is like the Literary pub crawl but features music. You meet at 19:30 at Gogarty's Pub (in the Temple Bar area) and spend 20 minutes in the upstairs rooms of four pubs listening to two musicians talk about, play, and sing traditional Irish music. While having only two musicians makes the music a bit thin and Irish music aficionados will tell you you're better off just finding a good session, the evening—while touristy—is not gimmicky. The musicians demonstrate four instruments and really enjoy introducing rookies to their art (£6 plus beer, nightly May–October except Friday, weekends only in winter, allow 2.5 hours, tel. 01/478-0191).

Hop On/Hop Off Bus Tours—Several companies offer the basic center-of-Dublin orientation. Dublin City Tour (£5, tel. 01/873-4222) and Guide Friday (£7, tel. 01/676-5377) do identical 90-minute circuits of the town allowing you to hop on and hop off at your choice of ten stops (two topless buses per hour with running commentaries; they go to Guinness Brewery but not to Kilmainham Jail). Just hop on and pay the driver. Your ticket's good for the entire day. Tours, which go from about 9:45 to 18:00, are especially enjoyable for photographers on sunny days. I see no reason to pay more for the Guide Friday tours.

Sights—Dublin's Trinity College

▲**Trinity College**—Started in 1592 by Queen Elizabeth I to establish a Protestant way of thinking about God, Trinity has long been Ireland's most prestigious college. Originally the student body was limited to rich, Protestant males. Women were admitted in 1903 and Catholics, while allowed entrance by the school much earlier, were given permission to study at Trinity in the 1970s. Today half of Trinity's 11,000 students are women and 70 percent are culturally Catholic (although only about 20 percent of Irish youth are churchgoing).

▲**Trinity College Tour**—Inside the gate of Trinity, students organize and lead 30-minute tours of their campus. You'll get a rundown on the mostly Georgian architecture, a peek at student life, both in the early days and today, and mostly enjoy a chance to hang out with a witty Irish college kid as he talks about his school (daily 10:15–15:30, the £4.50 tour fee includes the £3.50 fee to see the Book of Kells where the tour leaves you).

▲▲▲**Book of Kells/Trinity Old Library**—The 65-meter-long main chamber of the Old Library (from 1732) is home to an original copy of the 1916 Proclamation of the Irish Republic, the oldest Irish harp (from the 15th century), and stacked to its towering ceiling, 200,000 of the library's oldest books. The artistic prize of the library—and all Ireland—is the magnificent Book of Kells stored in the library's treasury. A first-class exhibit puts the

680-page illuminated manuscript in its historical and cultural context and prepares you for the original book and other precious manuscripts in the collection. Written on vellum (baby sheepskin) in the ninth century—probably by Irish monks in Iona (Scotland)—and taken to the Irish monastery at Kells in 806 after a series of Viking raids, this enthusiastically decorated copy of the four gospels is arguably the finest piece of art from what is generally called the Dark Ages. It shows how monastic life in this far fringe of Europe was far from dark. The book has been bound into four separate volumes. At any given time, two of the gospels are on display. You'll see four richly decorated 1,200-year-old pages—two text and two decorated cover pages—under glass (£3.50, Monday–Saturday 9:30–17:00, Sunday 9:30–16:30, shorter hours off-season, tel. 01/608-1171). The library also displays the Book of Armagh (A.D. 807) and the Book of Durrow (A.D. 680), neither of which can be checked out.

▲The Dublin Experience—Shown in a modern building next to the Trinity Old Library, this 40-minute video giving a historic introduction to Dublin is one more tourist movie with the sound turned up. It's good but pricey and riding on the coattails of the Book of Kells (£3, save a little with a combo Kells/video ticket, Trinity College Library, Monday–Saturday 9:30–17:00, Sunday 12:00–16:30).

More Sights—Dublin

▲▲Dublin Castle—Built on the spot of the first Viking fortress, this castle was the seat of British rule in Ireland for 700 years (until 1922). Located where the Poddle and Liffey Rivers came together making a black pool ("dubh linn" in Irish), Dublin Castle was the official residence of the Viceroy who implemented the will of the British royalty. Today it's used for fancy state and charity functions. The 45-minute tours offer a room-by-room walk through the lavish state apartments of this most English of Irish palaces (£2.50, about 4/hour, Monday–Friday 10:00–17:00, weekends 14:00–17:00, tel. 01/677-7129). The tour finishes with a look at the foundations of the Norman tower and the best remaining chunk of the 13th-century town wall.

▲Dublin's Viking Adventure—This really is an adventure. You start in a box of seats that transforms into a Viking ship. Your chieftain joins you and suddenly you're in a storm, waves splash, smoke rolls, and you land in a kind of Viking summer camp where you spend 30 minutes being shuttled from one friendly original Dubliner to the next (a trader, a sassy maiden, a monk building a church, and so on). A short film about the Vikings follows with a look at artifacts recently uncovered in the adjacent excavation sight. It feels hokey, but the cast is certainly hardworking and you leave feeling if not having visited a Viking town, at least having visited the set for a B-grade Viking movie.

This is on Essex Street a block off the riverside Essex Quay in Temple Bar—exactly where the Vikings established their first Dublin settlement in 841 (£4.75, Monday–Saturday 10:00–16:30, Sunday 11:30–17:30, tel. 01/679-6040).

Dublinia—This tries and fails to be a "bridge to Dublin's medieval past." The amateurish look at the medieval town starts with a goofy 12-minute Walkman tour followed by a few rooms of medieval exhibits and finishes with a hard-to-follow movie dramatizing medieval political wrangling. Possibly entertaining for a school field-trip, it just isn't worth the £4 or time (daily 10:00–17:00). The ticket does get you a tower-top city view and into Christchurch Cathedral (£1 otherwise).

Christchurch Cathedral—The oldest building in Dublin, the cathedral marks the spot where the Vikings established their town on the river. The first church here was built of wood in 1038 by King Sitric. The present structure dates from a mix of periods: Norman, Gothic, and mostly Victorian neo-Gothic (1870s restoration work). Because of its British past, neither of Dublin's two top churches are Catholic. Christchurch Cathedral and the nearby St. Patrick's Cathedral are both from the Church of Ireland. In Catholic Ireland they feel hollow and are more famous than visit-worthy.

▲▲▲**National Museum**—Showing off the treasures of Ireland from the Stone Age to the 20th century, this museum is wonderfully digestible under one dome. Ireland's Bronze Age gold fills the center. The prehistoric Ireland exhibit rings the gold, and in a corner you'll find the treasury with the most famous pieces (brooches, chalices, and other examples of Celtic metalwork) and an 18-minute video giving an overview of Irish art through the 13th century. Jumping way ahead, a special corridor features "The Road to Independence" with guns, letters, and death masks recalling the fitful birth of the "Terrible Beauty" (1900–1921 with a focus on the Easter Rising of 1916). The best Viking artifacts in town are upstairs (free, Tuesday–Saturday 10:00–17:00, Sunday 14:00–17:00, closed Monday, between Trinity College and St. Stephen's Green on Kildare Street, tel. 01/677-7444). Greatest-hits tours are given several times a day (£2, 45 minutes, call for schedule).

National Gallery—Along with a hall featuring the work of top Irish painters, this has Ireland's best collection of paintings by the European masters. It's impressive—unless you've been to London or Paris (free, Monday–Saturday 10:00–17:30, Thursday until 20:30, Sunday 14:00–17:00, tel. 01/661-5133).

Streets, Squares, and Parks—Dublin

▲**Grafton Street**—Once filled with noisy traffic, today Grafton Street is Dublin's liveliest pedestrian shopping mall. You'll find colorful pubs, fancy shops, singing buskers, and lots of browsers. The Powerscourt Townhouse Shopping Centre (nearby on William

Street South) is a hit with shoppers. Grafton Street connects Trinity College with St. Stephen's Green.

▲ **St. Stephen's Green**—This city park, originally a medieval commons, was enclosed in 1664 and gradually surrounded with fine Georgian buildings. Today it provides 22 acres of grassy refuge for Dubliners.

Merrion Square—This square offers an insider's look at Georgian Dublin. Tour the carefully restored house at **Number 29 Lower Fitzwilliam Street** for a walk through a Dublin home in 1790 (£2.50, Tuesday–Saturday 10:00–17:00, Sunday 14:00– 17:00, closed Monday). Notice the fine doors around the square—a Dublin trademark—and the elegant Georgian knobs and knockers.

▲ **O'Connell Street and surroundings**—Dublin's grandest street leads from O'Connell Bridge through the heart of north Dublin. Since the 1740s it's been a 45-meter-wide promenade. Ever since the first O'Connell Bridge connected it to the Trinity side of town in 1794, it's been Dublin's main drag. The street, while lined with fast-food and souvenir shops, echoes with history. Much of the fighting during the 1916 Easter Rising and the Civil War a few years later took place here. The imposing **General Post Office** is where Patrick Pearse read the Proclamation of Irish Independence. The GPO building itself—a kind of Irish Alamo—was the rebel headquarters and scene of a five-day bloody siege during the Rising. While there's little to see, its facade remains pockmarked with bullet holes.

The statues lining the street celebrate great figures in Ireland's fight for independence. One monument which didn't—a tall column crowned by a statue of the British hero of Trafalgar, Admiral Nelson—was blown up in 1966 as locals celebrated the 50th anniversary of the Rising.

Make a point to get away from tourists' Dublin. A good way to do that is to stroll the smaller streets north of the Liffey. Just a block west of O'Connell Street, the **Moore Street Market** is a colorful commotion of produce and hawkers. For workaday Dublin, the long pedestrian mall of Mary Street, Henry Street, and Talbot Street is a people-watchers' delight.

Explore. The prestigious **Abbey Theatre**, now a modern, ugly building, is still the much-loved home of the Irish National Theater (a block off the river on Abbey Street). **St. Mary's Pro-Cathedral** is the leading Catholic church in town, but curiously not a cathedral since Christchurch was made one in the 12th century (the pope chose to ignore the fact that it hasn't been Catholic for centuries). Georgian **Parnell Square** has a Garden of Remembrance honoring the victims of the 1916 Rising.

The **Dublin Writers' Museum** is a must for anyone interested in Irish literature, featuring the lives and works of Dublin's greats (£2.90, Monday–Saturday 10:00–17:00, Sunday 11:30– 18:00, 18 Parnell Square North, tel. 01/872-2077). With home-

town wits such as Swift, Yeats, Joyce, and Shaw, literary fans will
have a checklist of residences and memorials to see.

▲▲**Temple Bar**—For many visitors the heart of Dublin is its
hot and much-promoted nightlife center, the Temple Bar district.
While promoted as Dublin's "Left Bank," it's actually on the
right bank (as central as can be and just south of the river). It's a
pedestrians-only hive of creative energy day and night. The central
Meeting House Square (just off Essex Street) hosts free street theater and is surrounded by interesting cultural centers. For a listing
of events, visit the Temple Bar Information Centre (Eustace
Street, tel. 01/671-5717). Trendy shops, cafés, theaters, galleries,
pubs with live music, and restaurants (Italian, American, and even
Irish) vie for your attention. Rather than follow particular recommendations, simply wander the main drag and venture down a few
side lanes to see what looks good. Gallagher's Boxty House is a
good bet for traditional Irish food (call to reserve at 01/677-2762).
You'd eat their boxty (a stuffed dinner pancake) or Irish stew in
anticipation of a famine. The Bad Ass Café remains as popular as
can be (students-in-a-warehouse ambience, vegetarian and Italian).
Pub grub abounds. (To get some folk music away from the tourist
crowds, walk five minutes up the river to Merchants Quay where,
on Lower Bridge Street, you'll find the Merchants Pub and the
Brazen Head.) The pedestrian-only Ha' Penny Bridge, named for
the half-pence toll originally levied from those who walked it,
leads over the Liffey to Temple Bar. ("Bar" means a walkway
along the river.)

Sights—Outer Dublin

The Jail and the Guinness Brewery are the only sights outside of
the old center. Combine these in one visit.

▲▲▲**Kilmainham Gaol (Jail)**—Built in 1789 as a debtors'
prison and considered a model in its day, it was used for most of
its life as a political prison by the British. Many of those who
fought for Irish independence were held or executed here, including leaders of the rebellions of 1798, 1803, 1848, 1867, and 1916
(most notably Robert Emmett and Charles Stewart Parnell). The
last prisoner to be held here was Eamon de Valera (later president
of Ireland). He was released on July 16, 1924, the day Kilmainham
was finally shut down. The buildings, virtually in ruins, were
restored in the 1960s. Today it's a shrine to the Nathan Hales of
Ireland.

Your visit starts with an excellent exhibit on Ireland's fight
for independence, followed by a 30-minute video. Then a guide
shows you around for 30 minutes. Touring the cells and places
of execution while hearing tales of terrible colonialism and
heroic patriotism—alongside Irish schoolkids who know these
names well—is moving. Finally the museum explains Victorian
prison life and the battle for independence. Don't miss the dimly

lit hall off the second floor displaying the stirring last letters
patriots sent to loved ones hours before facing the firing squad
(£2, daily 9:30–18:00, last tour at 16:45; off-season Sunday–
Friday 10:00–17:00, closed Saturday; £4 taxi, bus 51 or 79 from
Aston Quay, tel. 01/453-5984).

▲**Guinness Brewery**—A visit to the Guinness Hop Store is
almost a pilgrimage for many. The home of Ireland's national
beer welcomes visitors (for £3) with a museum, video, and drink.
Arthur Guinness began brewing the famous stout here in 1759.
By 1868 it was the biggest brewery in the world. Today the
sprawling brewery fills several city blocks. Around the world
Guinness brews over 10 million glasses a day. You can learn as
much or as little about the brewing process as you like. Highlights are the cooperage (with old film clips showing the master
wood-kegmakers plying their now extinct trade) and a display of
the brewery's clever ads. The video is a well-done ad for the brew
that makes you feel almost patriotic as you run down to the sample bar to turn in your coupon for a half pint of the real thing
(£3, Monday–Saturday 9:30–17:00, Sunday 10:30–16:30, enter on
Crane Street off Thomas Street, bus 68A or 78A from Aston
Quay near O'Connell Bridge, tel. 01/453-6700 ext. 5155). Hop
on/hop off bus tours stop here. (Why is there no museum of Irish
alcoholism, which is a serious but rarely discussed problem in this
land where the social world seems to float in a sea of beer?)

Entertainment and Theater in Dublin
Ireland produced some of the finest writers in both English and
Gaelic, and Dublin houses some of Europe's finest theaters. While
Handel's *Messiah* was first performed in Dublin (1742), these days
Dublin is famous for its rock bands (U2, Thin Lizzie, and Sinead
O'Conner all got started here).

You have much to choose from: Abbey Theatre is Ireland's
National Theatre. Gate Theatre does foreign plays as well as Irish
classics. Point Theatre, once a railway terminus, is now the coun-
try's top live music venue. At the National Concert Hall, the
National Symphony Orchestra performs most Friday evenings.
Street theater takes the stage in Temple Bar on summer evenings.
Folk music rings in the pubs and street entertainers are every-
where. For the latest, pick up a copy of the twice-monthly *In
Dublin* (£1.50, any newsstand).

Irish Music in nearby Dun Laoghaire
For an evening of pure Irish music, song, and dance, check out
the **Comhaltas Ceoltoiri Eireann**, an association working to
preserve this traditional slice of Irish culture. It got started when
Elvis and company threatened to steal the musical heart of the
new generation. Judging by the pop status of traditional Irish
music these days, Comhaltas accomplished its mission. Their

"Fonntrai" evening is a costumed stage show mixing traditional music, song, and dance (£5, mid-June–August Monday–Thursday at 21:00). These are followed by an informal music session at 22:30. Fridays all year long they have a Cailidh where everyone dances (£5, 21:30–00:30). Saturday nights feature an informal session by the fireside. Performances are held in the Cuturlann na Eireann, near the Seapoint DART stop or a 20-minute walk from Dun Laoghaire, at 32 Belgrave Square, Monkstown (tel. 01/280-0295). Their bar is free, and often filled with music.

Sleeping in Dublin
(£1 = about $1.60, tel. code: 01)
Sleep Code: **S**=Single, **D**=Double/Twin, **T**=Triple, **Q**=Quad, **b**=bathroom, **t**=toilet only, **s**=shower only, **CC**=Credit Card (Visa, MasterCard, Amex).

Dublin is popular and rooms can be tight. Big and practical places (both cheap and moderate) are most central at Christchurch on the edge of Temple Bar. For classy, older Dublin accommodations you'll pay more and stay a bit farther out in the direction of Ballsbridge (embassy row). For a smalltown escape with the best budget values, side-trip by the convenient DART train (at least 3/hr, 15 min) from nearby Dun Laoghaire (see below).

Sleeping in Christchurch
These places each face Christchurch Cathedral, a great locale five minutes' walk from the best evening scene at Temple Bar and eight minutes from the sightseeing center (Trinity College). Buses 50, 54, 65, and 77 stop here. For an easy meal near your hotel, try Leo Burdocks Fish & Chips, popular with locals (2 Werburgh Street, off Christchurch).

Jurys Christchurch Inn, like its sister in Galway, is well-located offering business-class comfort in all its identical rooms. This no-nonsense, modern, American-style hotel has a winning keep-it-simple-and-affordable formula. If old is getting old (and you don't mind big bus-tour groups), you won't find a better value in town. All 190 rooms cost the same: £60 for one, two, or three adults, or two adults and two kids, breakfast not included. Each room has a modern bathroom, direct-dial telephone, and TV. Two floors are strictly non-smoking. Request a room far from the noisy elevator (CC:VMA Christchurch Place, Dublin 8, tel. 01/454-0000, fax 01/454-0012, in U.S.A. 800/843-3311). A 234-room **Jurys Custom House Inn** (£60, tel. 01/607-5000) has just opened on Custom House Quay in Dublin.

Kinlay House, across the square from Jurys, is its backpackers' equivalent—definitely the place to go for cheap beds with a good location, privacy, and an all-ages-welcome atmosphere. This huge, red-brick, 19th-century Victorian building has 120 metal, prison-style beds in spartan, smoke-free rooms: singles, doubles, and four- to six-bed dorms (generally co-ed). It fills up most days. Call well in advance especially for summer weekends (S-£18, D-£26, Db-£30, dorm beds-£12–13, includes continental breakfast, self-catering kitchen, launderette, left luggage, and so on, Christchurch, 2-12 Lord Edward Street, Dublin 2, tel. 01/679-6644, fax 01/679-7437). If Kinlay is full, a similar place is the well-located **Avalon House** (D-£24–28, dorm beds-£7.50–10.50, just south of Temple Bar at 55 Aungier Street, tel. 01/475-0001, fax 01/475-0303, e-mail: tkennedy@avalon.iol.ie).

Harding Hotel is a hardwood, 20th-century, Viking-style place with 53 hotelesque rooms. The hotel is as comfortable as Jurys but on a more intimate scale and without the tour-group scene (Sb-£45, Db or Tb-£55–60, breakfast extra, CC:VM, Copper Alley across the street from Christchurch, tel. 01/679-6500, fax 01/679-6504, Web site: www.iol.ie/usitaccm/, e-mail: harding@usit.ie).

Sleeping East of St. Stephen's Green

The Fitzwilliam rents 12 hotel-ish rooms in a classy guesthouse (Sb-£45, Db-£80, CC:VMA, 41 Upper Fitzwilliam Street, Dublin 2, tel. 01/662-5155, fax 01/676-7488).

Mespil Hotel is a huge, modern, business-class hotel renting 153 identical three-star rooms, each with all the comforts and at a very good price. Half the rooms overlook a canal greenbelt (Sb, Db, or Tb-£72, continental breakfast-£4, Irish breakfast-£7, elevator, one non-smoking floor, CC:VMA, Mespil Road, Dublin 4, tel. 01/667-1222, fax 01/667-1244, e-mail: mespil@leehotels.ie).

Albany House is Georgian style throughout and completely smoke-free. Each of the 29 rooms are tastefully designed with old elegance and modern comfort. Request the huge "superior" rooms which are the same price (Sb-£70, Db-£100, £70 in slow times, back rooms are generally bigger and quieter, the included breakfast is a healthy first-class continental buffet, CC:VMA, 1 block south of St. Stephen's Green at 84 Harcourt Street, Dublin 2, tel. 01/475-1092, fax 01/475-1093).

The next three listings are on Northumberland Road. While Trinity College is only a 15-minute walk away, buses 7, 7A, and 8 (to O'Connell Street) lumber down Northumberland Road to the city center every ten minutes.

Northumberland Lodge is a quiet, elegant mansion. Bridget and Tony Brady run a tight, comfortable, and friendly ship (Sb-from £55, Db-from £85, CC:VM, 68 Northumberland Road, Balls-bridge, Dublin 4, tel. 01/660-5270, fax 01/668-8679).

Bush House is small and homey with a pleasant lounge and six rooms mostly on the ground floor (Sb-£40, Db-£70, £60 for two nights or more, CC:VMA, 33 Northumberland Road, tel. & fax 01/668-3927, Diane Armstrong).

Glenveagh Town House, next door, has 13 classy rooms but is unreliable about reservations (Sb-£42, Db-£72, less in slow times, CC:VM, 31 Northumberland Road, tel. 01/668-4612, fax 01/668-4559).

Sleeping in nearby Dun Laoghaire
(tel. code: 01, mail: County Dublin)

The first three listings are a three-minute walk to the Sandycove DART station and a seven-minute walk to the Dun Laoghaire DART station/ferry landing. The rest are closest to the Dun Laoghaire DART station. Except for the first place, all are a bit tattered around the edges. While buses go into Dublin, the DART is much faster (6/hour in peak times, at least 3/hr otherwise, 15 min, £1.10; for a longer stay consider the four-day Rambler ticket covering DART and Dublin buses). The **Dun Laoghaire TI** is in the ferry terminal (daily 10:00–21:00 year-round). The Society of the Preservation of Irish Folk Music has a lively branch in Dun Laoghaire (see above).

Mrs. Kane's B&B is a modern house with three big, cheery rooms and a welcoming guests' lounge. While a few blocks farther out than the others, it's worth the walk for its great, bright, friendly feeling (Db-£45, completely smoke-free, past Rosmeen Gardens to 2 Granite Hall, tel. 01/280-9105).

Ferry House B&B is a stately old place facing a quiet square with a tennis court. It's warmly run by Mr. and Mrs. Field with seven huge rooms and a cozy lounge (S-£21, D-£36, Db-£40, CC:VM, 15 Clarinda Park North, tel. 01/280-8301, fax 01/284-6530).

Sandycove House, a comfortable old place overlooking a park and the harbor, is run in a no-nonsense kind of way. Its 12 rooms are generally large and fluffy (Sb-£29, Db-£45, Db overlooking the sea-£50, CC:VM, a £2 taxi or five-minute walk from the ferry landing and 2 blocks from the Sandycove DART station, Marine Parade, Sandycove, tel. 01/284-1600).

Lynden B&B, with a classy 150-year-old interior hiding behind a somber front, offers four big rooms run by the charming and energetic Maria Gavin (S-£23, D-£35, Db-£39, past Mulgrave Street to 2 Mulgrave Terrace, tel. 280-6404). Next door, the similar **Belmont B&B** rents three rooms (D-£33, Db-£37, tel. 01/280-1422).

Innisfree B&B is a well-worn place with a fine lounge and six big, bright rooms (D-£32, Db-£37, CC:VM, from George Street follow the "Yellow Fever Vaccination Centre" sign to 31 Northumberland Avenue, tel. 01/280-5598, Brendan and Mary Smith). **Duncree B&B** is similar with four mostly large rooms on a quiet street (S-£19.50, D-£35, Db-£39, 16 Northumberland Avenue, tel. 01/280-6118, Mrs. O'Sullivan).

The Old School House Hostel is a shoestring traveler's dream-come-true. It's just 2 blocks from the DART station and ferry landing with incredibly cheap beds in two- to six-bed rooms, and a hardworking and creative staff. The only problem is that it's

Dun Laoghaire

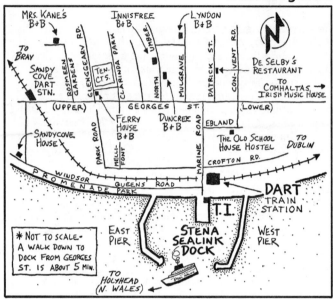

a hostel: old carpets, bare walls, and a general scruffiness. Having said that, it's clean with good beds and plenty of privacy and feels secure and safe (£9 bunks in six-bed dorms, £10 in a quad, £24 doubles, showers down the hall, or for 50p extra, in your room, breakfast not included, some non-smoking rooms, self-catering kitchen, restaurant, £3 laundry service, and 24-hour staff; CC:VMA, from ferry, go up Marine Road, take first left onto Eblana Avenue; tel. 01/280-8777, fax 01/284-2266, e-mail: osh@iol.ie).

Eating in Dun Laoghaire

George Street, the town's main drag and three blocks inland, has plenty of eateries and pubs, often with live music. Probably the best bet for a good mid-range meal is **De Selby's Restaurant**, serving traditional Irish food, stew, and seafood (£12 meals, nightly 17:30–23:00, a block off George Street at 17 Patrick Street, tel. 01/284-1761). The **Purty Kitchen Pub/Restaurant** has good seafood.

Transportation Connections—Dublin

By bus to: Belfast (7/day, 3 hrs), **Ennis** (7/day, 4.5 hrs), **Galway** (8/day, 4 hrs), **Limerick** (6/day, 3.5 hrs), **Tralee** (5/day, 6 hrs). Bus info tel. 01/836-6111.

By train to: Rosslare (3/day, 3 hrs), **Tralee** (5/day, 4 hrs), **Galway** (4/day, 3 hrs, talking timetable tel. 01/855-4422), **Ennis**

(4/day, 4 hrs), **Portrush** (5/day, 4 hrs, £19 one-way, £25 round-trip; stops in Belfast on the way south), **Belfast** (12/day, 1.5 hrs, talking timetable tel. 01/855-4477). The new Dublin–Belfast train will connect the two Irish capitals in 90 minutes at 90 mph on one continuous welded rail (£15 one-way, £23 round-trip, round-trip the same day Monday–Friday only £15, from the border to Belfast one-way £8.50, £10.50 round-trip). Train info tel. 01/836-6222.

The **Dublin Airport**, 12 miles from the city center, is well-connected to the center (see Arrival in Dublin). British Air flies to London's Gatwick Airport (4/day, £99, toll-free tel. 800/626747 in Ireland and 800/247-9297 in the U.S.A.), as do Aer Lingus (tel. 01/705-6705) and British Midland (tel. 01/283-8833 in Ireland and 800/788-0555 in the U.S.A.). Dublin airport info tel. 01/844-4900.

Transportation Connections—Ireland and Britain

Dublin and London: The boat/rail journey takes ten hours, all day or all night (£40–60). Dublin train info tel. 01/836-6222.

Dublin and Holyhead: Irish Ferries sails between Dublin and Holyhead in North Wales (5/day, 2.5 hrs, £20–29 one-way walk-on fare, Dublin tel. 01/661-0511, Holyhead tel. 01407/760-222).

Dun Laoghaire and Holyhead: Stena Line sails between Dun Laoghaire (near Dublin) and Holyhead in North Wales (5/day, 2.5 hrs, £22–30 one-way walk-on fare, £10 round-trip in a day if you have no baggage, plus £5 port tax, reserve by phone early—they book up long in advance on summer weekends, Dublin tel. 01/204-7777, recorded information 01/204-7799).

DINGLE PENINSULA

Dingle Peninsula, the westernmost tip of Ireland, offers just the right mix of far and away beauty, ancient archeological wonders, and desolate walks or bike rides all within convenient reach of its main town. Dingle Town is just big enough to have all the necessary tourist services and a steady nocturnal beat of Irish folk music.

While the big tour buses clog the neighboring Ring of Kerry before heading east to slobber all over the Blarney Stone, Dingle—while crowded in the summer—still feels like the fish and the farm matter. Fifty fishing boats sail from Dingle, and a faint whiff of peat still fills its nighttime streets.

For 15 years my Irish dreams have been set here on this sparse but lush peninsula where locals are fond of saying "The next parish is Boston." There's a closeness to the land on Dingle. When I asked a local if he was born here, he thought for a second and said, "No, it was about 6 miles down the road." When I told him where I was from, a faraway smile filled his eyes, he looked out to sea and sighed, "Ah, the shores of Americay."

Dingle feels so traditionally Irish because it's a Gaeltacht, a region where the government subsidizes the survival of the Irish language and culture. While English is always there, the signs, menus, and songs come in Gaelic. Even the local preschool brags "ALL Gaelic."

Of the peninsula's 10,000 residents, 1,300 live in Dingle Town. Its few streets, lined with ramshackle but gaily painted shops and pubs, run up from a rain-stung harbor always busy with fishing boats and yachts. During the day kids—already working on ruddy beer-glow cheeks—roll kegs up the streets and into the pubs in preparation for another night of music and *craic* (conversation).

Dingle Peninsula

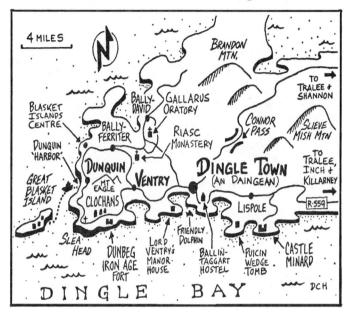

Dingle History

The wet sod of Dingle is soaked with medieval history. In the darkest depths of the Dark Ages, peace-loving, bookwormish monks fled the chaos of the Continent and its barbarian raids. They sailed to the drizzly fringe of the known world—places like Dingle. These monks kept literacy alive in Europe. Charlemagne, who ruled much of Europe in the year 800, imported Irish monks to be his scribes.

It was from this peninsula that the semi-mythical explorer monk, St. Brandon, is said to have set sail in the sixth century in search of a legendary western paradise. Some think he beat Columbus to North America by nearly a thousand years.

Dingle (An Daingean in Gaelic) was a busy seaport in the late Middle Ages. Along with Tralee, it was the only walled town in Kerry and a gateway to Northern Spain—a three-day sail due south. Many 14th- and 15th-century pilgrimages left from Dingle for Santiago di Compostela in Spain.

When its position as a medieval trading center ended, Dingle faded in importance. In the last century it was a linen-weaving center. Until 1970 fishing dominated. The only visitors were scholars and students of old Irish ways. In 1970, the movie *Ryan's Daughter* introduced the world to Dingle. The trickle of Dingle fans has grown to a flood in the 1990s as word of its musical, historical, gastronomical, and scenic charms—not to mention its friendly dolphin—has spread.

Planning Your Time

For the shortest visit, give Dingle two nights and a day. It takes about six hours to get there from Dublin, Galway, or the boat dock in Rosslare. I like two nights because you feel more like a local on your second evening in the pubs. You'll need the better part of a day to explore the 30-mile loop around the peninsula by bike, car, or tour bus (see Circular Tour, below). To do any serious walking or relaxing you'll need two or three days. It's not uncommon to find Americans slowing way, *way* down in Dingle.

Orientation (tel. code: 066)

Dingle is extremely comfortable on foot. The town hangs on a medieval grid of streets between the harborfront (where the Tralee bus stops) and Main Street (3 blocks inland). Nothing in town is more than a five-minute walk away.

Tourist Information: The Bord Failte (TI) is at the bottom of Main Street, 3 blocks off the water (April–October Monday–Saturday 9:30–18:00, Sunday in summer, tel. 066/51188). In the summer the TI organizes town walks. For more creative help, drop by the Mountain Man shop (on Strand Street, see below).

Helpful Hints

Crowds: Dingle gets so crowded during summer holiday weekends that the police actually close down the road access. July 15 to August 30 is bad (you might consider the less-discovered Beara Peninsula, south of the Ring of Kerry). The absolute craziest is St. Brandon's festival (three days in mid-July), Dingle Races (second weekend in August), and Dingle Regatta (third weekend in August). Dingle's dead before May 1: no music, activities, tours, or tourists.

Banking: There are two banks in town, both uphill from the TI on Main Street (Monday–Friday 10:00–12:30, 13:30–16:00). The Bank of Ireland has a cash machine.

Supermarket: The Super Valu supermarket/department store is at the base of town (Monday–Saturday 8:00–19:00, Sunday 8:00–13:00).

Launderette: At this full-service shop, you can drop off a load and pick it up three hours later (small–£3.50, large–£5.50, Monday–Saturday 9:15–17:15, on Green Street behind El Toro restaurant).

Bike Rental: Bike rental shops abound in Dingle. You can get good mountain bikes at Paddy's Bike Hire (daily 9:00–7:00, £5/day, £6 for a 24-hour period, on Dykegate), Sciuird Tours, the Mountain Man, and the Ballintaggert Hostel. Plan on leaving a credit card, driver's license, or passport as security.

Dingle Activities: The **Mountain Man**, a hiking shop run by two local guides, Con and Mike, is a clearinghouse for information, local tours, and excursions (located just off the harbor at Strand Street, tel. 066/51868, fax 066/51980). Pick up the free *Kerry Gems* booklet. For bike rentals and ideas on biking, hiking, horse riding, climbing, peninsula tours (which they offer), and trips to the Blaskets, stop by here.

Sights—Dingle Town

▲▲▲**Folk Music in Dingle Pubs**—Even if you're not into pubs, take a nap then give these a whirl. Dingle is renowned among traditional musicians as a place to get work ("£30 a day, tax-free, plus drink"). The town has 50 pubs. There's music every night (and never a cover charge). The scene is a decent mix of locals, Americans, and Germans. Music normally starts around 21:30 and the last call for drinks is "half eleven" (23:30). For a seat near the music, arrive early. If the place is chock-a-block, power in and find breathing room in the back. By midnight the door is closed and the chairs are stacked. While two pubs, the Small Bridge Bar and O'Flahertys, are the most famous for their good beer and folk music, make a point to wander the town and follow your ear. Smaller pubs may feel a bit foreboding to a tourist, but people—locals as well as travelers—are out for the *craic* (pronounced "crack," slang for the good time and fun conversation). Pubs are smoky and hot (leave your coat home). The more offbeat pubs are more likely to erupt into leprechaun karaoke.

The best pub crawl is along the Strand to O'Flaherty's (rough-and-tumble Murphy's is liveliest, offering rock as well as traditional music). Then head up Green Street. Dick Mack is a tiny leather shop by day/pub by night with two snugs (private booths), reliably good beer, and a strangely fascinating ambience; notice the Hollywood-type stars on the sidewalk recalling famous visitors. Wander up and down Main Street (Small Bridge Bar at the bottom is best) and then up Spa Road a few doors (often less crowded but with good music). During the day, music lovers will enjoy dropping by Danlann Gallery, a music shop on Dykegate Street (Monday–Saturday 10:00–18:00, Sunday 11:00–14:00).

More Evening Fun—Somewhere almost every night, a pub hosts "Set Dancing" with live music (Garvey's Bar does it on Monday after 21:30). The Hillgrove Hotel (up Spa Road a few hundred meters) is a mod hotel with traditional dances every Thursday (and pop dancing other nights in summer). Locals say the Hillgrove "is a good time if you're pissed." Dingle has a great little theater (The Phoenix on Dykegate). The film club (50 or

Dingle Town

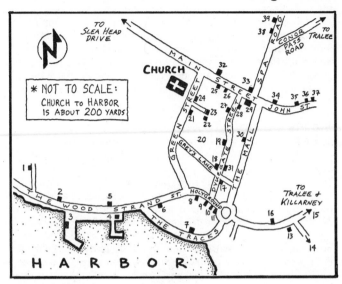

NOT TO SCALE: CHURCH TO HARBOR IS ABOUT 200 YARDS

1 Smeara Dubha
2 Oceanworld
3 Dingle Sailing Club
4 Cruiseboat offices
5 Maire De Barra Restaurant
6 Mountain Man
7 Bus Station
8 Greany's Restaurant
9 Super Value
10 Tig Lise
11 O'Flahertys
13 Bambury's B&B
14 Trail to lighthouse

15 Ballintaggert Hostel
16 Alpine House Guest House
17 Sciuird Tours/Kirrary B&B
18 Corner House B&B
19 Connors B&B
20 City park
21 Dick Mack
22 Café Ceo
23 Laundry
24 El Toro
25 Grapevine Hostel
26 Bank
27 Bike rental
28 An Cafe Litearta

29 Tourist information
30 Captain's House B&B
31 Cinema
32 Adam's Bar and Restaurant
33 Small Bridge Bar
34 Doyle's and Half Door Restaurants
35 Sraid Eoin B&B
36 Kellihers Ballyegan House
37 Greenmount House
38 Hillgrove Hotel
39 Ard Na Greine House B&B

60 locals) meets for coffee, cookies, and a film every Tuesday at 20:30.

▲**Oceanworld**—The only place charging admission in Dingle is worth considering. This new aquarium offers a little peninsula history, 160 different local fish and other sea creatures in thoughtfully described tanks (including a unique chance to walk under the fish in the "ocean tank"), and the easiest way to see Fungi the dolphin—on video (£4, £10 for families, daily 10:00–20:00 in summer, until 18:00 or earlier in off-season, just past the harbor on the west edge of town, tel. 066/52111).

Fungi—In 1983 a dolphin moved into Dingle Harbor and became a local celebrity. Fungi is now the darling of the town's tourist trade and one reason you'll find so many tour buses parked along the harbor. With a close look at Fungi as bait, tour boats are thriving. (While she's too cute to kill, I'll happily give a free copy of the next edition of this book to anyone who can make Fungi leave.)

▲**Short Harbor Walk from Dingle**—For an easy stroll along the harbor out of town (and a chance to see the dolphin) head east from the roundabout on R561. Just after Bambury's B&B, take a right following signs to Skelligs Hotel. At the beach, climb the steps over the wall and follow the seashore path to the mouth of Dingle harbor (marked by a tower—some 19th-century fatcat's folly). Ten minutes beyond that is a lighthouse. This is Fungi's neighborhood. If you see tourist boats out, you're likely to see her. If you continue walking you'll get to a dramatic cliff.

The Harbor—The harbor is on land reclaimed (with imported Dutch expertise) five years ago. The roundabout is new to let traffic skirt the town center. The string of old stone shops facing the harbor was the loading station for the narrow-gauge railway which hauled the fish from Dingle to Tralee (1891–1953). The Esk Tower on the distant hill is a marker built in 1847 during the famine as a make-work project. In pre-radar days, it helped ships locate Dingle's hidden harbor. The fancy mansion across the harbor is Lord Ventry's 17th-century Manor house.

Cruises—The SS *Merlin* takes £30 day-long cruises with commentary to the Skelligs (with a visit to early Christian ruins) and to the Blaskets (with a stop on the big island). Their harborside office has specifics (tel. 088/533-858 or 066/59876). The Dingle Sailing Club rents one-man sailboats (£15 per three hours) and larger boats. The *currachs* (Ireland's traditional lightweight fishing boats, easy to haul, easy to make: cover a wooden frame with canvas and paint with tar) stacked near the Sailing Club are owned by the Dingle rowing club and go out most evenings. The beaches nearby are popular in the summer.

Sleeping in Dingle Town
(£1 = about $1.60, tel. code: 066, mail: Dingle, Co. Kerry)
Sleep Code: **S**=Single, **D**=Double/Twin, **T**=Triple, **Q**=Quad, **b**=bathroom, **t**=toilet only, **s**=shower only, **CC**=Credit Card (Visa, MasterCard, Amex).

Sraid Eoin B&B, on the quiet end of town with four spacious pastel rooms and giant bathrooms, is warmly run by Kathleen and Maurice O'Connor (Sb-£25, Db-£32, family deals, CC:VM, John Street, tel. 066/51409, fax 066/52156). Maurice runs Galvin's Travel Agency on the ground floor (same phone number).

Kellihers Ballyegan House is a big, plain building with six comfortable rooms on the edge of town, run by friendly Mrs. Hannah Kelliher (£17.50, no CC, Upper John Street, tel. 066/51702).

Greenmount House sits among palm trees at the top of town, in the countryside with a commanding view of the bay and mountains, but just three minutes' walk from the town center. John and Mary Curran run one of Ireland's classiest B&Bs with six fine rooms (Db-£40) and six sprawling suites (Db-£60) in a modern building with lavish public areas and breakfast in a solarium (no singles or children under 8, lower prices off-season, CC:VM, up John Street to Gortonora, reserve in advance, tel. 066/51414, fax 066/51974).

Corner House B&B is my long-time Dingle home. It's a simple, traditional place with five rooms run with a twinkle and a smile by Kathleen Farrell (S-£16, D-£30, T-£42, plenty of plumbing but it's down the hall, no CC, reserve with a phone call and reconfirm a day or two ahead or risk losing your bed, central as can be on Dykegate Street, tel. 066/51516).

Captain's House B&B is a salty-feeling place in the town center with eight classy rooms (Sb-£30, Db-£44, CC:VMA, the Mall, tel. 066/51531, fax 066/51079, Jim and Mary Milhench).

Connors B&B, well-located and likely to have a room available, has 15 big, basic, uninspiring rooms (£18 per person in July and August, £14 other months, CC:VMA, in the center on Dykegate Street, tel. 066/51598, Mrs. Connor).

Ard Na Greine House B&B is a charming, windblown, modern house on the edge of town. Mrs Mary Houlihan rents four well-equipped, comfortable rooms to non-smokers (Sb-£22, Db-£36, Tb-£48, CC:VM, on the edge of town a ten-minute walk up Spa Road, three doors beyond the Hillgrove Hotel, tel. 066/51113, fax 066/51898).

Ballintaggert Hostel, a backpacker's complex, is housed in a stylish old manor house used by Protestants during the famine as a soup kitchen (for those hungry enough to renounce their Catholicism). It comes complete with horse riding, bike rental, laundry service, kitchen, café, classy study, family room with a fireplace, a shuttle into town, and a resident ghost (166 beds, £7 in eight- to 12-bed dorms, £10 in quads, £13 in singles and doubles, breakfast extra,

1 mile east of town on Tralee Road, tel. 066/51454, fax 066/52207, e-mail: btaggert@iol.ie).

Grapevine Hostel is a clean and friendly establishment with a cozy fireplace lounge and a fine members' kitchen. Each four- to eight-bed dorm has its own bathroom. Dorms are co-ed but there's usually a girls' room established. No curfew or lock-out (32 beds, £6.50 each, Dykegate Street, tel. 066/51434).

Alpine House Guest House (tel. 066/51250) and **Bambury's B&B** (tel. 066/51244), each big, modern buildings on the main Tralee Road a block or so from the roundabout, might have a reasonable bed when the others are full.

Eating in Dingle Town

For a rustic little village, Dingle is swimming in high and fun cuisine. Many of the best values close after 18:00. Most pubs also stop serving food early (to make room for maximum beer). The town's grocery stores stay open until about 21:00.

Adam's Bar and Restaurant serves traditional food at great prices. Try their corned beef and cabbage (last meal at 18:00, Upper Main Street).

Tig Lise offers a good, simple menu with a tasty lasagna-and-salad meal and good vegetarian selections (meals are £5, closed at 18:00, near the roundabout at Holyground).

An Cafe Litearta, a popular and friendly eatery hiding behind an inviting bookstore, has good sandwiches, salads, and hot food (10:00–17:30, Dykegate Street).

Greany's Restaurant, just off the roundabout, is a local hit serving good, basic food at decent prices in a cheery, modern atmosphere (12:30–21:00, Holyground).

El Toro offers a candlelit splash of Italy with good seafood, salads, and pizzas (12:30–15:00 and 17:30–20:30, Green Street, tel. 066/51820). **Maire De Barra** has simple traditional food and seafood (£5, the Pier).

Smeara Dubha is a small vegetarian restaurant down by the harbor (evenings only, 18:00–21:00, The Wood, Dingle). The funky **Café Ceo** is vegetarian-friendly (11:00–14:00 and 18:30 on, in the courtyard opposite the church).

Dingle's long-established top-notch restaurants are **Doyle's Seafood Bar** (more famous, John Street, tel. 066/51174) and the **Half Door** (heartier portions, John Street, tel. 066/51600). Both offer three-course early-dinner specials for £15 between 18:00 and 18:30 and more expensive dining after that. Reservations are necessary in both places.

Transportation Connections—Dingle Town

The nearest train station is in Tralee. Buses connect Dingle and Tralee nine times a day in summer, less off-season and on Sunday (75 min, £6). Dingle has no bus station and only one stop, on the

Dingle Peninsula Tour

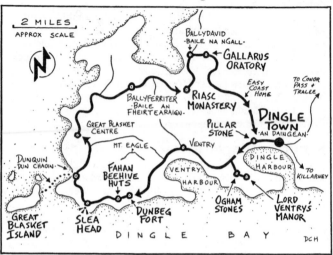

waterfront behind the Super Valu supermarket (bus info tel. 066/23566).

Dingle Peninsula: Circular Tour by Bike or Car

A ▲▲▲ sight, this loop trip is about 30 miles long (five hours by bike, three hours by car, including stops; do only in clockwise direction). While you can take a guided tour of the peninsula (below), it's not necessary with the route described in this section. A fancy map is also unnecessary with my instructions. I've keyed in mileage to help locate points of interest. If you're driving, as you leave Dingle reset your odometer at the Oceanworld. Even if you get off track or are biking, derive distances between points from these numbers. To get the most out of your circle, read through this entire section before departing. Then go step by step (staying on R559 and following the "The Slea Head Drive" signs). Note: Roads are very congested in August.

The Dingle Peninsula is 10 miles wide and runs 40 miles from Tralee to Slea Head. The top of its mountainous spine is Mount Brandon—at 3,300 feet, the second-tallest mountain in Ireland. While only tiny villages lie west of Dingle Town, the peninsula is home to 500,000 sheep.

Leave Dingle Town west along the waterfront (0.0 miles at Oceanworld). There's an 8-foot tide here. The seaweed was used to nourish reclaimed land. Across the water the fancy Milltown House B&B was Robert Mitchum's home for a year during the filming of *Ryan's Daughter*.

0.4 miles: Turn left over the bridge. The building on the right was a corn-grinding mill in the 18th century.

0.8 miles: The Milestone B&B is named for the **pillar stone** ("Gallaun" in Gaelic) in its front yard. This may have been a prehistoric grave marker or a boundary marker between two tribes. The stone goes down as far as it sticks up. Another pillar stone stands in the field across the street in the direction of the yellow manor house of Lord Ventry. The peninsula, literally an open-air museum, is dotted with more than 2,000 monuments dating from the Bronze Age through early Christian times.

2.1 miles: Pass through a rare grove of trees and turn left ("Leather Workshop" sign). After 100 yards, enter the **Lord Ventry Manor** taking the first left (unmarked, through white gate) and going up the long one-lane drive past small 18th-century estate houses and the palms, magnolias, fuschias, and exotic flora introduced to Dingle by Lord Ventry. Because of the mild climate (cradled by the gulf stream), fuschias line the roads all over the peninsula and fill the countryside with red from June to September. At the fork in the road, turn right. Fifty yards before the yellow mansion, stop at the six stones.

The **Ogham Stones** (third–seventh century, named for the Celtic goddess of writing) decorating the drive are rare examples of early Celtic writing. With variations on five straight lines, they could make 20 letters—the original bar code. Of the 300 known Ogham Stones, 100 are in Dingle. Lord Ventry, whose family came to Dingle as landlords in 1666, built this mansion in about 1750. Today it houses an all-Gaelic boarding school for 140 high school–age girls. Return to the main road and turn left (3.1 miles).

4.1 miles: Stay off the "soft margin" as you enjoy views of Ventry Bay and its 4-mile-long beach. Mt. Eagle (1,660 feet), the end of Ireland, is beyond. In the little town of Ventry, Gaelic is the first language.

6.0 miles: The rushes on either side of the road are the kind used to make the local thatched roofs. Thatching, which nearly died out because of the fire danger, is more popular now that anti-flame treatments are available. Magpies fly.

6.6 miles: The Irish football star Paidi O Se (Paddy O'Shea) is a household name in Ireland. He now trains the Kerry team and runs the pub on the left.

6.9 miles: The blue house hiding in the trees on the left (view through the white gate) was kept cozy by Tom Cruise and Nicole Kidman during the filming of *Far and Away*.

7.9 miles: "Taisteal go Mall" means "go slowly"; there's a yellow schoolhouse on the right.

8.2 miles: The circular mound on the right is a late–Stone Age ring fort. In 500 B.C. it was a petty Celtic chieftain's headquarters, a stone-and-earth stockade filled with little stone houses.

These survived untouched through the centuries because of superstitious beliefs that they were "fairy forts." While this is unexcavated, recent digging has shown that people have lived on this peninsula since 4000 B.C.

8.6 miles: The Hungarian red deer on the right are the work of the European community (easier on the land, but higher fences are needed). Grass-fed deer (venison) is in the Euro cards, not more sheep.

9.0 miles: **Dunbeg Fort**, a series of defensive ramparts and ditches around a central clochan, while ready to fall into the sea, is open to tourists. While there are no carvings to be seen, the small (beg) fort (dun) is dramatic (£1, daily 9:00–20:00, descriptive handout). Forts like this are the most important relics left from Ireland's Iron Age (500 B.C. to A.D. 500). Since erosion will someday take this fort, it has been excavated.

9.6 miles: The Fahan group of **beehive huts**, or clochans, is a short walk uphill. These mysterious stone igloos cluster together within a circular wall (£1; this is a better sight than the Fahan beehive huts a mile down the road). Farther on, you'll ford a stream. There has never been a bridge here; the road was designed as a ford.

10.6 miles: Pull off to the left at this second group of beehive huts. Look downhill at the scant remains of the scant home which was burned as the movie equivalent of Lord Ventry evicted the tenants in *Far and Away*. Even without Hollywood, this is bleak, godforsaken land. Look above at the patches of land slowly reclaimed by the inhabitants of this westernmost piece of Europe. Rocks were moved and piled into fences. Sand and seaweed were laid on the clay and in time it was good for grass. The created land was generally not tillable. Much has fallen out of use now.

11.4 miles: At **Slea Head**, marked by a crucifix, a pullout, and great views of the Blasket Islands (described below), you turn the corner on this tour.

11.9 miles: Pull out here to view the Blaskets and Dunmore Head (the westernmost point in Europe) and to review the roadside map (which traces your route) in the parking lot. The scattered village of Dunquin has many ruined rock homes—abandoned during the famine. They were built with small windows to minimize taxation. Some have been fixed up as this is a popular place these days for summer homes. (The lead singer of the Irish rock band The Cranberries just built a huge home a mile or so down the road.) You can see more good examples of land reclamation, patch by patch, climbing up the hillside.

13.4 miles: The Blasket Islanders had no church or cemetery on the island. This was their cemetery. The famous Blasket storyteller Peig Sayers (1873–1958) is buried in the center. Just past a washed-out bit of road, a lane leads left (100 yards) to a marker remembering the 1588 shipwreck of the *Santa Maria de la Rosa* of the Spanish Armada. Below that is the often tempestuous Dunquin Harbor from where the Blasket ferry departs.

13.5 miles: Back on the main road, follow signs to the Great Blasket Centre.

15 miles: Leave the Slea Head Road left for the modern Blasket Centre (described below).

15.7 miles: Back at the turnoff, head left (sign to Louis Mulcahy Pottery).

16.4 miles: Passing land which was never reclaimed, think of the work it took to pick out the stones, pile them into fences, and bring up sand and seaweed to nourish the clay and make soil for growing potatoes. On the left is a shadow of the main street of the fake poor village built to film *Far and Away*. Beyond that is the "Sleeping Giant" island—with hand resting happily on his beer belly.

16.8 miles: The view is spectacular, especially when the waves are "racing in like white horses." Ahead on the right study the top fields, untouched since the planting of 1845 when the potatoes rotted in the ground. The vertical ridges of the potato beds can still be seen—a reminder of the famine. Before the famine, 60,000 people lived on this peninsula.

20.2 miles: **Ballyferriter** (Baile an Fheirtearaigh), established by a Norman family in the 12th century, is the largest town on this end of the peninsula. The pubs serve grub and the schoolhouse is a museum (£1.50, daily in summer 10:00–17:30, off-season Monday–Friday 10:00–12:00, 14:00–16:00). The early Christian cross looks real. Tap it . . . it's a fiberglass prop from *Ryan's Daughter*.

21.0 miles: At the T-junction, signs direct you to Dingle (An Daingean 11 km) either way. Go left, via Gallarus. Take a right over the bridge, still following signs to Gallarus.

21.4 miles: Just beyond the bridge and a few yards before the sign to Mainistir Riaise (Riasc Monastic enclosure), detour right up the lane. After .2 miles (the unsigned turnout on your right) you find the scant remains of the walled **Riasc Monastery** (fifth–12th centuries). Step over the rocks and inside. The inner wall divided the community into work and religious sections. The layer of black felt marks where the original rocks stop and the excavators' reconstruction begins. The pillar stone is Celtic (from 1000 B.C.). When the Christians arrived in the fifth century they didn't throw out the Celtic society. Instead, they carved a Maltese-type cross over the Celtic scrollwork. The square building was an oratory (church). The round buildings would have been dwellings. The monasteries had cottage industries. Just outside the wall (opposite the oratory) find a stone hole with a passage facing the southwest wind. This was a kiln. Locals would bring their grain to be dried and ground. The monks would keep a "tithe." With the arrival of the Normans in the 12th century, these small religious communities were replaced by relatively big-time state and church governments.

21.9 miles: Back on the main road, continue to the right.

23.0 miles: At the big pink restaurant, turn left.

23.7 miles: At another restaurant, go right up an unmarked one-lane road.

24.0 miles: The **Gallarus Oratory** (£1), built about 1,200 years ago, is one of Ireland's best-preserved early-Christian churches. Its shape is reminiscent of an upturned boat, and the dry-stone walls are so perfectly fitted together that they are still waterproof. Notice the holes for some covering at the door and the fine alternating stonework on the corners. Continue up the rugged one-lane road.

24.6 miles: Turn left on the two-lane road, then right (to An Daingean, 7 km) where you'll crest and enjoy a 3-mile coast back into Dingle Town in the direction of the Esk Tower.

27.6 miles: At the intersection, just look for the happy dolphin. Head that way, over the bridge and back into Dingle Town (28.4 miles). Well done.

Dingle Peninsula Tours

Sciuird archaeology tours are offered by the Sciuirds, a family that has Dingle history—and a knack for sharing it—in its blood. Tim Coileain (a retired Dingle policeman), his son Tim Jr., and daughter Maura give serious 2.5-hour, £6.50 minibus tours one, twice, or three times a day depending upon demand. Drop by the Kirrary B&B (at intersection of Dykegate and Grey's Lane in Dingle Town) or call 066/51937 to put your name on the list. Call early. Tours fill quickly in summer. Off-season, you may have to call back to see if the necessary four people signed up to make a bus go. The running commentary gives an intimate peek into the history of Dingle. Sit as close to the driver as possible to get all the information. They do two completely different tours: west (Gallarus Oratory) and east (Minard castle and a wedge tomb). I enjoyed both. In summer they also offer a 75-minute historic town walk (£2.50). Dress for the weather. In a literal gale with horizontal winds, my guide kept saying "you'll survive it."

Moran's Tour does three-hour guided minibus trips around the peninsula with a more touristic slant (£6, normally at 10:30 and 14:00 from the Esso station near the roundabout in Dingle Town, tel. 066/51155). The **Mountain Man** also offers three-hour minibus tours of the peninsula (tel 066/51868).

ROME (ROMA)

Rome is magnificent and brutal at the same time. Your ears will ring, your nose will turn your hankie black, the careless will be run down or pickpocketed, you'll be frustrated by chaos that only an Italian can understand. You may even come to believe Mussolini was necessary. But Rome is required. If your hotel provides a comfortable refuge; if you pace yourself, accept and even partake in the siesta plan; if you're well-organized for sightseeing; and if you protect yourself and your valuables with extra caution and discretion, you'll do fine. You'll see the sights and leave satisfied.

Rome at its peak meant civilization itself. Everything was either civilized (part of the Roman Empire, Latin- or Greek-speaking) or barbarian. Today Rome is Italy's political capital, the capital of Catholicism, and a splendid . . . "junkpile" is not quite the right word . . . of western civilization. As you peel through its fascinating and jumbled layers, you'll find its buildings, people, cats, laundry, and traffic endlessly entertaining. And then, of course, there are its magnificent sights.

Tour St. Peter's, the greatest church on earth, and scale Michelangelo's 100-yard-tall dome, the world's largest. Learn something about eternity by touring the huge Vatican Museum. You'll find paradise—bright as the day it was painted—in the newly restored Sistine Chapel. Do the "Caesar shuffle" walk through ancient Rome's Forum and Colosseum. Take an early evening "Dolce Vita Stroll" down the Via del Corso with Rome's beautiful people. Enjoy an after-dark walk from Trastevere to the Spanish Steps, lacing together Rome's Baroque and bubbling night spots.

Rome Area

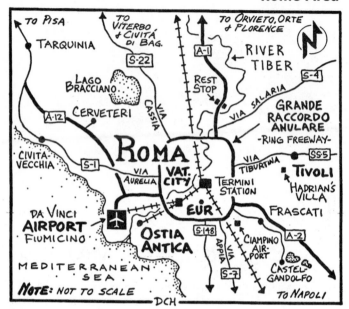

TO PISA
TARQUINIA
TO VITERBO & CIVITA DI BAG.
TO ORVIETO, ORTE & FLORENCE
A-1
S-22
RIVER TIBER
S-4
LAGO BRACCIANO
REST STOP
VIA CASSIA
VIA SALARIA
GRANDE RACCORDO ANULARE
-RING FREEWAY-
A-12
CERVETERI
ROMA
CIVITA-VECCHIA
S-1
VIA AURELIA
VAT. CITY
TERMINI STATION
VIA TIBURTINA
SS-5
TIVOLI
HADRIAN'S VILLA
FRASCATI
DA VINCI **AIRPORT** FIUMICINO
EUR
OSTIA ANTICA
S-148
VIA APPIA
CIAMPINO AIRPORT
A-2
CASTEL-GANDOLFO
MEDITERRANEAN SEA
NOTE: NOT TO SCALE
S-7
TO NAPOLI
DCH

Planning Your Time

For most, Rome is best done quickly. It's great, but exhausting. Time is normally short, and Italy is more charming elsewhere. To "do" Rome in a day, consider it as a side trip from Orvieto or Florence and maybe before the night train to Venice. Crazy as that sounds, if all you have is a day, it's a great one.

Rome in a day: Vatican (two hours in the Museum and Sistine Chapel, and one hour in St. Peter's), taxi over the river to the Pantheon (munch a bar snack picnic on its steps), then hike over Capitoline Hill, through the Forum, and to the Colosseum. Have dinner on Campo dei Fiori and dessert on Piazza Navona.

Rome in two days (the optimal first visit): Do the "Caesar Shuffle" from the Colosseum and Forum, over the Capitoline Hill to the Pantheon. After a siesta, join the locals strolling from Piazza del Popolo to the Spanish Steps. Have dinner near your hotel. On the second day, see the Vatican City (St. Peter's, climb the dome, tour the Vatican Museum). Spend the evening walking from Trastevere to Campo dei Fiori (atmospheric place for dinner) to the Spanish Steps. With a third day, consider adding another museum and a side trip to Ostia.

Orientation (tel. code: 06)

The modern sprawl of Rome is of no interest to us. Our Rome actually feels small when you know it. It's the old core—within the triangle formed by the train station, Colosseum, and Vatican. Get a handle on Rome by considering it in these chunks:

The ancient city had a million people. Tear it down to size by walking through just the core. The best of the classical sights stand in a line from the Colosseum to the Pantheon.

Medieval Rome was a little more than a hobo-camp of 50,000—thieves, mean dogs, and the pope, whose legitimacy required a Roman address. The medieval city, a colorful tangle of lanes, lies between the Pantheon and the river.

Window-shoppers' Rome twinkles with nightlife and ritzy shopping near medieval Rome, on or near Rome's main drag, the Via del Corso.

Vatican City is a compact world of its own with two great sights: a huge basilica and the museum.

Trastevere, the seedy/colorful wrong-side-of-the-river neighborhood-village, is Rome at its crustiest—and perhaps most "Roman."

Baroque Rome is an overleaf that embellishes great squares throughout the town with fountains and church facades.

Since no one is allowed to build taller than St. Peter's dome, the city has no modern skyline. And the Tiber River is ignored. It's not navigable and after the last floods (1870), the banks were built up very high and Rome turned its back on its naughty river.

Tourist Information
Few cities offer less tourist information per capita than Rome. There are three tourist information offices: airport, train station (near track #1, very crowded, the only one open on Sunday), and central office (open Monday–Friday 8:15–19:15, Saturday 8:15–13:45, next to the SAAB dealership, Via Parigi 5, tel. 06/488-99255 or 06/488-99253).

The central TI office, near Piazza della Republica's huge fountain, is a five-minute walk out the front of the train station. It's air-conditioned, less crowded and more helpful than the other TIs, and has comfortable sofas and a desk to plan on—or sit at to overcome your frustration. Ask for the better "long stay" city map and a quarterly periodical entertainment guide for evening events and fun. (If all you need is a map, forget the TI and pick one up at your hotel.) All hotels list an inflated rate to cover the hefty commission any TI room-finding service charges. Save money by booking direct.

Romanc'e is a cheap little weekly entertainment guide sold at newsstands with a helpful English section on musical events and the pope's schedule for the week. Fancy hotels carry a free English monthly, *Un Ospite a Roma* (A Guest in Rome).

Enjoy Rome is a free and friendly information service pro- viding maps, museum hours, a useful city guide (free), and a room-finding service, but you'll get better prices by going direct (8:30–13:30, 15:30–18:30, closed Saturday afternoon and on

Rome

Sunday, 3 blocks northeast of the station at Via Varese 39, tel. 06/445-1843, fax 06/445-0734, English-speaking). They offer several English-only city walking tours daily (L30,000 per three-hour tour, L25,000 for those under 26, children under 15 go free, tel. 06/397-28728).

Guided Walks Through Rome: Several companies do guided walks through Rome. Tom Rankin (an American in love with Rome and his Roman wife) runs **Scala Reale**, a small company committed to sorting out the rich layers of Rome for small groups of three to six people (with a longer-than-normal attention span). His excellent three-hour tours run around L50,000 per person and are well-explained on his web site (tel. & fax 06/447-00898, Web site: www.scalareale.org, e-mail: scalareale@mail.nexus.it,). You can book tours with Tom or one of his associates in advance or call upon arrival in Rome to see what's planned.

Helpful Hints

General Museum Hours: Most museums close on Monday (except the Vatican) and at 13:00 on Sunday. Outdoor sights like the Colosseum, Forum, and Ostia Antica are open 9:00 to 19:00 (or one hour before sunset). There are absolutely no absolutes in Italy. These hours will vary. Confirm sightseeing plans each morning with a quick L200 telephone call asking, "Are you open today?" ("*Aperto oggi?*") and "What time do you close?" ("*A che ora chiuso?*"). I've included telephone numbers for this purpose. The last pages of the daily *Messaggero* newspaper list current events, exhibits, and hours.

Churches: Churches open early, close for lunch, and reopen from about 16:00 to 19:00. Modest dress means no bare shoulders, miniskirts, or shorts (men or women). Kamikaze tourists maximize their sightseeing hours by visiting churches before 9:00 and seeing the major sights that stay open during the siesta (St. Peter's and the Forum) while all good Romans are taking it cool and easy.

Shop Hours: Usually 9:00 to 13:00 and 16:00 to 20:00. Groceries are often closed on Sunday. In the holiday month of August, many shops and restaurants close up for vacation and "*Chiuso per ferie*" signs decorate locked doors all over town.

Theft Alert: With sweet-talking con artists, pickpockets on buses and at the station, and thieving gangs at the ancient sights, Rome is a gauntlet of rip-offs. Other than getting run down, there's no great physical risk. But green tourists will be ripped off. Thieves strike when you're distracted. Don't trust kind strangers. Keep nothing important in your pockets. Assume you're being stalked. (Then relax and have fun.)

Buyer Beware: I carefully understand the final price before I order *anything* and I deliberately count my change. Expect the "slow count." Wait for the last bits of your change to straggle over to you.

There are legitimate extras (café prices skyrocket when you sit down, taxis get L5,000 extra after 22:00, and so on) to which paranoid tourists wrongly take offense. But the waiter who charges you L70,000 for the pizza and beer assumes you're too polite to involve the police. If you have any problem with a restaurant, hotel, or taxi, get a cop to arbitrate. Rome is trying to civilize itself.

Staying Healthy: The siesta is a key to survival in summer-time Rome. Lie down and contemplate the extraordinary power of gravity in the eternal city. I drink lots of cold, refreshing water from Rome's many drinking fountains (the Forum has three). If you get sick, call the International Medical Center (tel. 06/884-0113).

Arrival in Rome

By Train: The Termini train station is a minefield of tourist services: a late-hours bank, a day hotel, luggage lockers, 24-hour thievery, the city bus station, and a subway stop. Handy multi-lingual charts make locations very clear. The place is crawling with sleazy sharks with official-looking cards. Generally, avoid anybody selling anything at the station if you can. La Piazza, however, is a bright and cheery self-service restaurant (daily 11:00–22:30).

Most of my hotel listings are easily accessible by foot (near the train station) or by Metro (Colosseum and Vatican neighbor-hoods). The train station has its own Metro stop (Termini).

By Plane: If you arrive at the airport, catch a train (hourly, 30 min, L13,000) to Rome's train station or take a taxi to your hotel. For details, see Transportation Connections below.

Getting Around Rome

Sightsee on foot, by city bus, or by taxi. I've grouped your sight-seeing into walkable neighborhoods. Public transportation is efficient, cheap, and part of your Roman experience.

By Subway: The Roman subway system (Metropolitana) is simple, with two clean, cheap, fast lines. While much of Rome is not served by its skimpy subway, these stops are helpful: Termini (central train station, several recommended hotels, National Museum), Republica (main tourist office, several recommended hotels), Barberini (Cappuccin Crypt, Trevi Fountain), Spagna (Spanish Steps, Villa Borghese, classy shopping area), Flaminio (Piazza del Popolo, start of the Via del Corso Dolce Vita stroll), Ottaviano (the Vatican, recommended hotels), Colosseo (the Colosseum, Roman Forum, recommended hotels), and E.U.R. (Mussolini's futuristic suburb).

By Bus: Bus routes are clearly listed at the stops. Bus #64 is particularly useful, connecting the station, my recommended Via Nazionale hotels, Victor Emanuel Monument (near the Forum), Largo Argentina (near the Pantheon) and the Vatican. Ride it for a city overview and to watch pickpockets in action.

Metropolitana: Rome's Subway

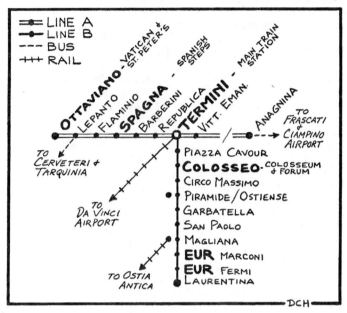

Buses and subways use the same ticket. You can buy tickets at newsstands, tobacco shops, or at major stations or bus stops but not on board (L1,500, good for 75 minutes—one Metro ride and unlimited buses, punch them yourself as you board—or you are cheating). Buy a bunch so you can hop a bus without searching for an open tobacco shop. (Riding without a ticket, while relatively safe, is stressful. Inspectors fine even innocent-looking tourists L50,000 if found on a bus or subway without a ticket that has been stamped.) If you hop a bus without a ticket, locals who use tickets rather than a monthly pass can sell you a ticket from their wallet bundle. All-day bus/Metro passes cost L6,000. Learn which buses serve your neighborhood.

Buses, especially the touristic #64, and the subway, are havens for thieves and pickpockets. Assume any commotion is a thief-created distraction. Bus #64 gets extremely crowded.

By Taxi: Taxis start at about L5,000 (L2,000 surcharge on Sunday and L5,000 surcharge after 22:00). Sample fares: train station to Vatican, L12,000; train station to Colosseum, L8,000; Colosseum to Trastevere, L10,000. Three or four companions with more money than time should taxi almost everywhere. Rather than wave and wave, ask in local shops for the nearest taxi stand (*"Dové*

[DOH-vay] *una fermata dei tassi?"*). Taxis with their telephone number on the door have fair meters—use them.

Sights—Rome, Near Forum

▲**St. Peter-in-Chains Church (San Pietro in Vincoli)**—The original chains and Michelangelo's able-to-stand-and-toss-those-tablets *Moses* are on exhibit in an otherwise unexceptional church, just a short walk uphill from the Colosseum (free, daily 6:30–12:30, 15:30–19:00, modest dress required).

▲▲**Colosseum**—This is the great example of Roman engineering, 2,000 years old. Using concrete, brick, and their trademark round arches, Romans constructed much larger buildings than the Greeks. But in deference to the higher Greek culture, notice how they finished their no-nonsense mega-structure by pasting all three orders of Greek columns (Doric, Ionic, and Corinthian) as exterior decorations. The Flavian Amphitheater's popular name "Colosseum" comes from the colossal statue of Nero that once stood in front of it.

Romans were into "big." By putting two theaters together, they created a circular amphitheater. They could fill and empty its 50,000 numbered seats as quickly and efficiently as we do our super-stadiums. Teams of sailors hoisted canvas awnings over the stadium to give fans shade. This was where ancient Romans, whose taste for violence was the equal of modern America's, enjoyed their Dirty Harry and *Terminator*. Gladiators, criminals, and wild animals fought to the death in every conceivable scenario. They even waged mock naval battles (L10,000 gets you inside and upstairs, Sunday and Wednesday 9:00–13:00, all other days 9:00–19:00, less off-season, tel. 06/700-4261).

▲▲▲**Roman Forum (Foro Romano)**—Ancient Rome's birthplace and civic center, the Forum was the common ground between Rome's famous seven hills (L12,000, Monday–Saturday 9:00–18:00, Sunday 9:00–13:00, off-season 9:00–15:00, last tickets sold an hour before closing, tel. 06/699-0110). Just past the entry, there's a WC and a handy headless statue for you to pose behind. To help resurrect this confusing pile of rubble, study the before-and-after pictures in the cheap city guidebooks sold on the streets. (Check out the small red *Rome, Past and Present* books with plastic overlays to un-ruin the ruins. They're priced at L25,000—pay no more than L15,000.) Follow this basic walk:

1. Start at the Basilica Aemilia (second century B.C., on your right as you walk down the entry ramp). Study the floor plan of the ancient palace. This pre-Christian "basilica" design was later adopted by medieval churches.

2. From the Basilica Aemilia, step out onto the Via Sacra (the Sacred Road), the main street of ancient Rome. It runs from the Arch of Septimus Severus on your right, past Basilica Aemilia, up to the Arch of Titus and the Colosseum on your left.

The Forum Area

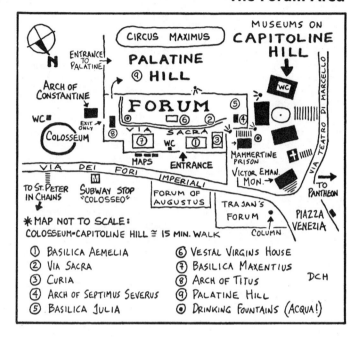

* MAP NOT TO SCALE:
COLOSSEUM=CAPITOLINE HILL ≅ 15 MIN. WALK

① BASILICA AEMELIA
② VIA SACRA
③ CURIA
④ ARCH OF SEPTIMUS SEVERUS
⑤ BASILICA JULIA
⑥ VESTAL VIRGINS HOUSE
⑦ BASILICA MAXENTIUS
⑧ ARCH OF TITUS
⑨ PALATINE HILL
⓪ DRINKING FOUNTAINS (ACQUA!)

DCH

3. The plain, intact brick building near the Arch of Septimus Severus was the Curia where the Roman senate sat. (Peek inside.) Roman buildings were brick and concrete, usually with a marble veneer, which in this case has been long lost.

4. The Arch of Septimus Severus, from about A.D. 200, celebrates that emperor's military victories. In front of it, a stone called the Lapis Niger covers the legendary tomb of Romulus. To the left of the arch, the stone bulkhead is the Rostra or speaker's platform. It's named for the ship's prows which used to decorate it as big shots hollered, "Friends, Romans, countrymen . . ."

5. The grand Basilica Julia, a first-century law court, fills the corner opposite the Curia. Ancient backgammon-type game boards are cut into the pavement.

6. Climb up toward the Palatine Hill, past the semi-circular Temple of Vesta to the House of the Vestal Virgins. Here, the VVs kept the eternal flame lit. A set of ponds and a marble chorus line of Vestal Virgins mark the courtyard of the house.

7. Climb down to the Via Sacra and turn right toward the Colosseum. A path on the left leads to up to the remains of the mammoth Basilica Maxentius. Only the giant barrel vaults remain, looming crumbly and weed-eaten. As you stand in the shadow of

the Bas Max, reconstruct it in your mind. The huge barrel vaults were just side niches. Extend the broken nub of an arch out over the vacant lot and finish your imaginary Roman basilica with rich marble and fountains. People it with plenty of toga-clad Romans. Yeow.

8. Back on Via Sacra, continue climbing to the small Arch of Titus (drinking fountain opposite). The arch is carved with propaganda celebrating the A.D. 70 defeat of the Jews, beginning the Diaspora that ended with the creation of Israel in 1947. Notice the gaggle of soldiers carrying the menorah.

9. From the Arch of Titus, walk up the Palatine Hill to the remains of the Imperial palaces. We get our word "palace" from this hill, where the emperors chose to live. The pleasant garden overlooks the Forum. On the far side, look down into an emperor's private stadium and then beyond at the dusty old Circus Maximus.

▲**Thief Gangs**—If you know what to look out for, the gangs of children picking the pockets and handbags of naive tourists are no threat but an interesting, albeit sad, spectacle. Gangs of city-stained children, too young to prosecute but old enough to rip you off, troll through the tourist crowds around the Forum, Colosseum, and train and Metro stations. Watch them target tourists distracted with a video camera or overloaded with bags. The kids look like beggars and use newspapers or cardboard signs to confuse their victims. They scram like stray cats if you're onto them. A fast-fingered mother with a baby is often nearby.

▲**Mammertine Prison**—The 2,500-year-old converted cistern that once imprisoned Saints Peter and Paul is worth a look. On the walls are lists of prisoners (Christian and non-Christian) and how they were executed: *Strangolati, Decapitato, Morto di Fame* . . . (donation requested, daily 9:00–12:00, 14:30–18:00). At the top of the stairs leading to Capitoline Hill, you'll find a refreshing water fountain. Block the spout with your fingers; it spurts up for drinking.

Sights—Rome's Capitoline Hill

▲▲**Capitoline Hill (Campidoglio)**—This hill was the religious and political center of ancient Rome. It's still the home of the city's government. Michelangelo's Renaissance square is bounded by two fine museums and the mayoral palace. Its centerpiece is a famous equestrian statue of Marcus Aurelius, a copy of the original (behind glass in the adjacent museum). There's a fine view of the Forum from the terrace just past the mayor's palace on the right.

The two **Capitoline Museums** (Musei Capitolino) are in two buildings (one L10,000 ticket is good for both museums, free for those over 60 and under 18, Tuesday–Saturday 9:00–19:00, Sunday 9:00–13:00, closed Monday, tel. 06/671-02071). The **Palazzo dei Conservatori** (the building nearest the river, on Marcus Aurelius' left side) is the world's oldest museum (500 years old). Outside the entrance, notice the marriage announcements (and, very likely, wedding-party photo ops). Inside the courtyard, have some photo fun with chunks of a giant statue of Emperor Constantine. (A rare public toilet hides near the museum ticket-taker.) The museum is worthwhile, with lavish rooms housing several great statues. Tops is the original (500 B.C.) Etruscan Capitoline Wolf (the little statues of Romulus and Remus were added in the Baroque age). Don't miss the *Boy Extracting a Thorn* or the enchanting *Commodus as Hercules*. The painting gallery (second floor) is forgettable except for one Carravagio.

Across the square, the **Palazzo Nuovo**, houses mostly portrait busts of forgotten emperors. But it has two must-sees: the *Dying Gaul* (first floor) and the restored gilded bronze equestrian statue of Marcus Aurelius (behind glass in the museum courtyard). This greatest surviving equestrian statue of antiquity was the original centerpiece of the square. While most such statues were destroyed by Dark Age Christians, Marcus was mistaken as Constantine (the first Christian emperor) and therefore spared.

To approach the great square the way Michelangelo wanted you to, walk halfway down the grand stairway toward Piazza Venezia, spin around, and walk back up. At the bottom of the stairs, look up the long stairway to your right (which pilgrims climb on their knees) for a good example of the earliest style of Christian church. While pilgrims find it worth the climb, sightseers can skip it.

From the bottom of the stairs, way down the street on your left, you'll see a condominium actually built around surviving ancient pillars and arches—perhaps the oldest inhabited building in Europe. Farther ahead (toward Piazza Venezia), look down into the ditch on your right, and see how everywhere modern Rome is built on the forgotten frescoes and mangled mosaics of ancient Rome.

Piazza Venezia—This vast square is the focal point of modern Rome. The Via del Corso, starting here, is the city's axis, surrounded by Rome's classiest shopping district. From the Palazzo Venezia's balcony above the square (to your left with back to Victor Emanuel Monument), Mussolini whipped up the nationalistic fervor of Italy. Fascist masses filled the square screaming, "Four more years!" or something like that. (Fifteen years later, they hung him from a meat hook in Milan.)

Victor Emanuel Monument—This oversized monument to an Italian king loved only by his relatives and the ignorant is known to most Romans as "the wedding cake," "the typewriter," or "the dentures." It wouldn't be so bad if it weren't sitting on a priceless acre of Ancient Rome. Soldiers guard Italy's Tomb of the Unknown Soldier as the eternal flame flickers. Stand directly in front of it and see how Via del Corso bisects Rome.

▲**Trajan's Column**—This is the grandest column and best example of "continuous narration" from antiquity. Study the propa-

ganda which winds up the column like a scroll, trumpeting
Trajan's wonderful military exploits. You can view this close-up
for free across Mussolini's busy Via dei Fori Imperiali from the
Victor Emanual Monument. In its day, for easier viewing, Trajan
fans could study the scenes from the balconies of buildings which
stood tall on either side.

Sights—Heart of Rome

▲▲▲**Pantheon**—For the greatest look at the splendor of Rome,
antiquity's best-preserved interior is a must (free, normally open
9:00–18:30, Sunday 9:00–13:00, less in winter, tel. 06/683-00230).
Since it became a church dedicated to the martyrs just after the fall
of Rome, the barbarians left it alone and the locals didn't use it as
a quarry. The portico is called Rome's umbrella—a fun local gathering in a rainstorm. Walk past its one-piece granite columns
(biggest in Italy, shipped from Egypt) and through the original
bronze doors. Sit inside under the glorious skylight and study it.

The dome, 140 feet high and wide, was Europe's biggest
until the 20th century. Michelangelo's dome at St. Peter's, while
much higher, is 1 meter smaller. The brilliance of its construction astounded architects through the ages. During the
Renaissance, Brunelleschi was given permission to cut into the
dome (see the little square hole above and to the right of the
entrance) to analyze the material. The concrete dome gets thin-
ner and lighter with height—the highest part is of volcanic
pumice.

This wonderfully harmonious architecture greatly inspired
the artists of the Renaissance, particularly Raphael. Raphael, along
with Italy's first two kings, chose to be buried here. As you walk
around the outside of the Pantheon, notice the "rise of Rome"—
about 15 feet since it was built.

▲▲**Curiosities near the Pantheon**—The only Gothic church
you'll see in Rome is **Santa Maria sopra Minerva**. On a little
square behind the Pantheon to the east, past the Bernini statue of
an elephant carrying an Egyptian obelisk, this Dominican church
was built *sopra* (over) a pre-Christian temple of Minerva. Before
stepping in, notice the high-water marks on the wall (right of
door). Inside, you'll see that the lower parts of the frescos were
lost to these floods.

Rome was at its low ebb, almost a ghost town, through much
of the Gothic period. Little was built from this time. (And much
of what was, was redone Baroque.) This church is a refreshing
exception. St. Catherine's body lies under the altar (her head is in
Siena). The patron saint of Italy, she convinced the pope to return
from France to Rome, thus saving Italy from untold chaos.

Left of the altar stands a little-known Michelangelo statue,
Christ Bearing the Cross. Michelangelo gave Jesus an athlete's
or warrior's body (a striking contrast to the more docile Christ of

Heart of Rome

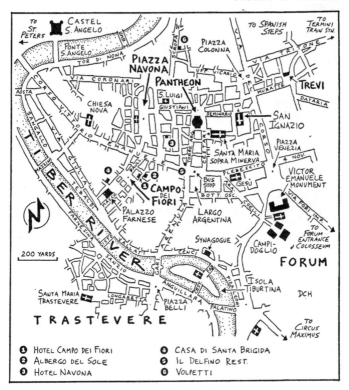

- ❶ Hotel Campo dei Fiori
- ❷ Albergo del Sole
- ❸ Hotel Navona
- ❹ Casa di Santa Brigida
- ❺ Il Delfino Rest.
- ❻ Volpetti

medieval art) but left the face to one of his pupils. Fra Angelico's simple tomb is farther to the left, on the way to the back door. Before leaving, head over to the right (south transept), pop in a L500 coin for light and enjoy a fine Filippo Lippi fresco showing scenes from the life of St. Thomas Aquinas—founder of the Dominicans.

Exit the church via its rear door (behind the Michelangelo statue), walk down Fra Angelico lane (spy any artisans at work), turn left, and walk to the next square. On your right you'll find the **Chiesa di St. Ignazio** church, a riot of Baroque illusions. Study the fresco over the door and the ceiling in the back of the nave. Then stand on the yellow disk on the floor between the two stars. Look at the central (black) dome. Keeping your eyes on the dome, walk under and past it. Church building project runs out of money? Hire a painter to paint a fake (and flat) dome. (Both churches stay open until 19:00, take a 12:30–16:00 siesta, and welcome modestly dressed visitors.)

A few blocks away, back across Corso Vittorio Emanuele, is the very rich and Baroque **Gesu Church**, headquarters of the Jesuits in Rome. The Jesuits powered the Church's Counter-Reformation. With Protestants teaching that all roads to heaven didn't pass through Rome, the Baroque churches of the late 1500s were painted with spiritual road maps that said they did.

Walk out the Gesu Church and 2 blocks down Corso V. Emanuele to the **Sacred Area** (Largo Argentina), an excavated square facing the boulevard, 2 blocks from the Pantheon. Walk around this square looking into the excavated pit at some of the oldest ruins in Rome. It was here that Caesar was assassinated. Today, this is a refuge for cats. Some 250 cats are cared for by volunteers. You'll see them (and their refuge) at the far (west) side of the square.

Self-guided Walks—Rome

▲▲▲**The Dolce Vita Stroll down Via del Corso**—This is the city's chic and hip "cruise" from the Piazza del Popolo (Metro: Flaminio) down a wonderfully traffic-free section of the Via del Corso and up Via Condotti to the Spanish Steps each evening around 18:00. Shoppers, take a left on Via Condotti for the Spanish Steps and Gucci (shops open after siesta, 16:30–19:30). Historians, start with a visit to the Baroque Church of Santa Maria del Popolo (with Raphael's Chigi Chapel and two Caravaggio paintings, on the far side of Piazza del Popolo), and continue down the Via del Corso to the Victor Emanuel Monument. Climb Michelangelo's stairway to his glorious Campidoglio Square, and catch the lovely view of the Forum (from past the mayor's palace on right) as the horizon reddens and cats prowl the unclaimed rubble of ancient Rome.

▲▲▲**Floodlit Rome Hike: Trastevere to the Spanish Steps**— Rome can be grueling. But a fine way to enjoy this historian's fertility rite is an evening walk lacing together Rome's floodlit night spots. Fine urban spaces, real-life theater vignettes, sitting close enough to the Bernini fountain to hear no traffic, water flickering its mirror on the marble, jostling with local teenagers to see all the gelato flavors, enjoying lovers straddling more than the bench, jaywalking past flak-vested *polizia*, marveling at the ramshackle elegance that softens this brutal city for those who were born here and can imagine living nowhere else—these are the flavors of Rome best tasted after dark.

Taxi or ride the bus (#23 from the Vatican area, #75 or #170 from Via Nazionale or Victor Emanuel) to Trastevere, the colorful neighborhood across (*tras*) the Tiber (*tevere*). Start your hike at Santa Maria in Trastevere. Trastevere offers the best look at medieval-village Rome. The action all marches to the chime of the church bells. Go there and wander. Wonder. Be a poet. This is Rome's Left Bank.

Santa Maria in Trastevere (free, daily 7:30–13:00, 15:00–19:00), one of Rome's oldest churches, was made a basilica in the fourth century when Christianity was legalized. It was the first church dedicated to the Virgin Mary. Most of what you see today is from around the 12th century, but the ancient basilica floor plan (and ambience) survives and the portico (covered area just outside the door) is decorated with fascinating ancient fragments filled with early Christian symbolism. The 12th-century mosaics behind the altar are striking and notable for their portrayal of Mary—the first showing her at the throne with Jesus in Heaven. The ahead-of-their-time paintings (by Cavallini, from 1300) below scenes from the life of Mary predate the Renaissance by 100 years.

Don't leave Trastevere until you've wandered the back streets. From the square (see Eating, below), Via del Moro leads to the river and Ponte Sisto, a pedestrian bridge with a good view of St. Peter's dome. Cross the bridge and continue straight ahead for 1 block. Take the first left, which leads down Via di Capo di Ferro through the scary and narrow darkness to Piazza Farnese, with the imposing Palazzo Farnese. Michelangelo contributed to the facade of this palace, now the French embassy. The fountains on the square feature huge one-piece granite hot tubs from the ancient Roman Baths of Caracalla.

One block from there (opposite the palace) is **Campo dei Fiori** (Field of Flowers), which is my favorite outdoor dining room after dark (see Eating, below). The statue of Giordano Bruno, a heretic who was burned in 1600 for believing the world was round and not the center of the universe, marks the center of this great and colorful square. Bruno overlooks a busy produce market in the morning and strollers after dark. This neighborhood is still known for its free spirit. When the statue of Bruno was erected in 1889, local riots overcame Vatican protests against honoring a heretic. Bruno faces his executioner, the Vatican Chancellory (the big white building in the corner a bit to his right), while on the pedestal the words say "and the flames rose up." The square is lined and surrounded by fun eateries. Bruno also faces La Carbonara, which gave birth to pasta Carbonara. The Forno, next door, is a popular place for hot and tasty take-out *pizza bianco*.

If Bruno did a hop, step, and jump forward and turned right, he'd cross the busy Corso Vittorio Emanuele and find **Piazza Navona**. Rome's most interesting night scene features street music, artists, fire-eaters, local Casanovas, ice cream, outdoor cafés (splurge-worthy if you've got time to sit and enjoy the human river of Italy), and three fountains by Bernini, the father of Baroque art. Its Tartufo "death by chocolate" ice cream (L5,000 to go, L11,000 at a table) made the Tre Scalini café world-famous among connoisseurs of ice cream and chocolate alike. This oblong square is molded around the long-gone stadium of Domitian, an ancient chariot racetrack that was often flooded so the masses could enjoy major water games.

Leave Piazza Navona directly across from the Tre Scalini café, go past rose peddlers and palm readers, jog left around the guarded building, and follow the yellow sign to the Pantheon straight down Via del Salvatore (cheap pizza place on left just before the Pantheon). Sit for a while under the flood- and moon-lit Pantheon's portico.

With your back to the Pantheon, head right, passing Bar Pantheon on your right. A blue-and-white arrow points down the street past the Tazza d'Oro Casa del Caffe. The Tazza d'Oro, one of Rome's top coffee shops, dates back to the days when this area was licensed to roast coffee beans. Look back at the fine view of the Pantheon from here.

Ahead is Piazza Capranica with the Florentine Renaissance-style Palazzo Capranica. Big shots, like the Capranica family, built stubby towers on their palaces—not of any military use . . . just to show off. Leave the piazza to the right of the palace, following another white arrow. (These arrows, which I put here for this tour in the late 1980s, are now accepted by local traffic.) Via in Aquino leads to another arrow pointing to a sixth-century B.C. Egyptian obelisk (taken as a trophy by Augustus after his victory in Egypt over Mark Antony and Cleopatra). Approaching the obelisk you'll find two arrows. Detour to the left for some of Rome's best gelato. **Gelateria Caffè Pasticceria Giolitti** (just behind Albergo Nazionale, Via Uffici del Vicario 40, open daily until very late) is cheap to go or elegant and splurge-worthy for a sit among classy locals. Or head right, walking down Via della Colonna Antonina to the big noisy main drag of downtown Rome, Via del Corso.

Piazza Colonna features a huge second-century column honoring Marcus Aurelius. The big important-looking palace is the prime minister's residence. While pink, this is the closest thing in Italy to a "White House." Cross the street, and take the right branch of the Y-shaped shopping gallery (1928) and exit, continuing straight down Via de Crociferi (or, if closed, head down Via dei Sabini) to the roar of the water, light, and people of the Trevi fountain.

The **Trevi fountain** is an example of how Rome took full advantage of the abundance of water brought into the city by its great aqueducts. This watery Baroque avalanche was built in 1762. Romantics toss two coins over their shoulder thinking it will give them a wish and assure their return to Rome. That may sound silly, but every year I go through this touristic ritual . . . and it actually seems to work.

Take some time to people-watch (whisper a few breathy *bellos* or *bellas*) before leaving. Facing the fountain, go past it on the right down Via delle Stamperia to Via del Triton. Cross the busy street and continue to the Spanish Steps (ask, *"Dové Piazza di*

Spagna?") a few blocks and thousands of dollars of shopping opportunities away.

The **Piazza di Spagna** (rhymes with "lasagna"), with the very popular Spanish Steps, got its name 300 years ago when this was the site of the Spanish Embassy. It's been the hangout of many romantics over the years (Keats, Wagner, Openshaw, Goethe, and others). The Boat Fountain at the foot of the steps was done by Bernini's father, Bernini. This is a thriving night scene.

Facing the steps, walk to your right about a block to tour one of the world's biggest and most lavish McDonald's. About a block on the other side of the steps is the subway, or Metropolitana, which (until 23:30) will zip you home.

Sights—Vatican City

This tiny independent country of just over 100 acres, contained entirely within Rome, has its own postal system, armed guard, helipad, mini-train station, and radio station (KPOP). Politically powerful, the Vatican is the religious capital of 800 million Roman Catholics. If you're not one already, become a Catholic for your visit. There's a helpful tourist office just to the left of St. Peter's Basilica (Monday–Saturday 8:30–19:00, tel. 06/698-84466). Check out the glossy L5,000 guidebooklet (crowded piazza on cover), which doubles as a classy souvenir. Telephone the Vatican TI if you're interested in their sporadic but very good tours of the Vatican grounds or the church interior, or the pope's schedule (see below). If you don't care to see the pope, minimize crowd problems by avoiding these times. Handy buses shuttle visitors between St. Peter's (in front of the tourist office) and the Vatican Museum (L2,000, twice an hour, 8:45 until 13:45, or 12:45 when museum closes early). This is far better than the exhausting 15-minute walk around the Vatican wall as it gives you a pleasant peek at the garden-filled Vatican grounds, and you bypass the line outside the Vatican Museum.

▲▲▲**St. Peter's Basilica**—There is no doubt: This is the richest and most impressive church on earth. To call it vast is like calling God smart. Marks on the floor show where the next largest churches would fit if they were put inside. The ornamental cherubs would dwarf a large man. Birds roost inside, and thousands of people wander about, heads craned heavenward, hardly noticing each other. Don't miss Michelangelo's pietà (behind bulletproof glass) to the right of the entrance. Bernini's altar work and seven-story tall bronze canopy (*baldacchino*) are brilliant.

For a quick self-guided walk through the basilica, follow these points:

1. The atrium is larger than most churches. Notice the historic doors (the Holy Door, on the right, will be opened in the year 2000—see point 13 below). Guided tours depart from the desk nearby.

St. Peter's Basilica

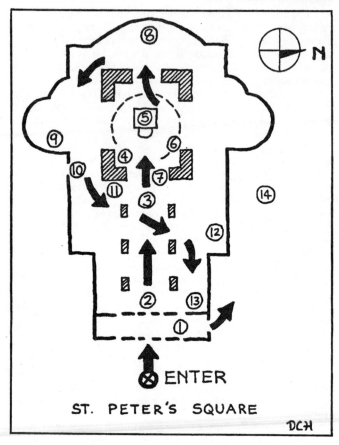

2. The purple circular porphyry stone marks the site of Charlemagne's coronation in A.D. 800. From here get a sense of the immensity of the church, which can accommodate 95,000 worshipers standing on its 6 acres.

3. Michelangelo planned to build a Greek Cross church plan. A Greek cross, symbolizing the perfection of God, and by association the goodness of man, was important to the humanist Michelangelo. But accommodating large crowds was important to the Church in the fancy Baroque age, so the original nave length was doubled. Stand halfway up the nave and imagine the stubbier design Michelangelo had in mind.

4. View the magnificent dome from the statue of St. Andrew. Check out the lofty vision of heaven above the windows: Jesus,

Mary, a ring of saints, rings of angels, and on the very top, God the Father.

5. The main altar sits directly over St. Peter's tomb and under Bernini's 70-foot-tall bronze canopy.

6. Take the stairs down to the crypt to see the foundation of St. Peter's chapels and tombs of popes.

7. The statue of St. Peter, with an irresistably kissable toe, is one of the few pieces of art which predate this church. It adorned the first St. Peter's church.

8. St. Peter's Throne and Bernini's star-burst dove window is the site of a daily Mass at 17:00.

9. St. Peter was crucified here (at the time the middle spot of a Roman race course) when this location was simply "the Vatican Hill."

10. For most, the treasury (in the sacristy) is not worth the admission.

11. The church is filled with mosaics, not paintings. Notice the mosaic version of Raphael's Transfiguration.

12. Blessed Sacrament Chapel.

13. Michelangelo sculpted this *Pietà* when he was 24 years old. A pietà is a work showing Mary with the dead body of Christ taken down from the cross. Michelangelo's mastery of the body is obvious in this powerfully beautiful masterpiece. Jesus is believably dead and Mary, the eternally youthful "handmaiden" of the Lord, still accepts God's will . . . even if it means giving up her son.

The Holy Door (piled high with plaster with a cross in its center, just to the right of the *Pietà*) will be opened in 2000, symbolizing the "Jubilee Year." Every 25 years the Church celebrates an especially festive year derived from the Old Testament idea of the Jubilee Year (originally every 50 years) which encourages new beginnings. Sins and debts are forgiven. The pope is tirelessly calling for this particularly monumental Jubilee year to be one in which the World Bank and the world's rich countries will usher in the new millennium by forgiving or relieving the crippling debt burden which keeps much of the Third World in squalor.

14. An elevator leads to the roof and the stairway up the dome. The dome, Michelangelo's last work, is (you guessed it) the biggest anywhere. Taller than a football field is long, it's well worth the sweaty climb for a great view of Rome, the Vatican grounds, and the inside of the Basilica—particularly heavenly while there is singing. Look around—Rome has no modern skyline. No building is allowed to exceed the height of St. Peter's. The elevator (just outside the church to the right as you face it) takes you to the rooftop of the nave. From there a few steps bring you to a balcony at the base of the dome looking down into the church interior. After that the one-way 300-step climb (for some people, claustrophobic) to the cupola begins. The rooftop level

Vatican City, St. Peter's, and the Museum

❶ Entrance to Vat. Museums
❷ Tourist Info, Post, W.C. + Bus Stop for Vat. Museum

(below the dome) has a gift shop, bathroom, drinking fountain, and a commanding view (L6,000 elevator, allow an hour to go up and down, closes 18:30).

The church strictly enforces its dress code. Dress modestly—a dress or long pants, shoulders covered (men and women). You are usually required to check any bags at a free cloakroom near the entry. St. Peter's is open daily 7:00–19:00, until 18:00 in winter; ticket booths to the treasury and dome close an hour early. All are welcome to join in the mass at the front altar (60 minutes, Monday–Saturday 17:00, Sunday 17:45).

The church is particularly moving at 7:00 while tourism is still sleeping. Volunteers who want you to understand and appreciate St. Peter's give free and excellent 90-minute "Pilgrim Service" tours in English at 15:00 (and occasionally at 10:00). Check for the day's schedule at the desk just after the dress code check as you're entering. Seeing the pietà is neat; understanding it is divine.

▲▲▲**The Vatican Museum**—Too often the immense Vatican Museum is treated as an obstacle course, with 4 nagging miles of displays, separating the tourist from the Sistine Chapel. Even without the Sistine, this is one of Europe's top three or four houses of art. It can be exhausting, so plan your visit carefully, focusing on a few themes. Allow two hours for a quick visit, three or four for time to enjoy it. The museum uses a nearly-impossible-not-to-follow, one-way system.

You'll start as civilization did, in Egypt and Mesopotamia. Next, the Pio Clementino collection features Greek and Roman statues. Decorating its courtyard are some of the very best Greek and Roman statues in captivity, including the Laocoon group (first century B.C., Hellenistic) and the *Apollo Belvedere* (a second-century Roman copy of a Greek original). The centerpiece of the next hall is the *Belvedere Torso* (just a 2,000-year-old torso, but one which had a great impact on the art of Michelangelo). Finishing off the classical statuary are two fine fourth-century porphyry sarcophagi (royal, purple stones for the coffins of Constantine's mother and daughter). Crafted in Egypt at a time when a declining Rome was unable to do such fine work, the details are fun to study.

After long halls of tapestries, old maps, broken penises, and fig-leaves, you'll come to what most people are looking for: the Raphael *stanza*, or rooms, and Michelangelo's Sistine Chapel.

These outstanding works are frescoes. A *fresco* (meaning "fresh" in Italian) is not actually a painting. The color is mixed into wet plaster and, when the plaster dries, the painting is actually part of the wall. This is a durable but difficult medium requiring speed and accuracy as the work is built slowly, one patch at a time.

After fancy rooms illustrating the "immaculate conception of Mary" (a hard-to-sell, 19th-century Vatican doctrine) and the triumph of Constantine (with divine guidance which led to his conversion to Christianity), you enter the first room completely done by Raphael and find the newly-restored *School of Athens*. This is remarkable for its blatant pre-Christian Classical orientation wallpapering the apartments of Pope Julius II. Raphael honors the great pre-Christian thinkers—Aristotle, Plato, and company—who are portrayed as the leading artists of Raphael's day. The bearded figure of Plato is Leonardo da Vinci. Diogenes, history's first hippie, sprawls alone in bright blue on the stairs reading a ripped-out chapter of *Mona Winks*, while Michelangelo broods in the foreground—supposedly added late. Apparently Raphael snuck a peek at the Sistine Chapel and decided that his arch-competitor was so good he had to put their personal differences aside and include him in this tribute to the artists of his generation. Today's St. Peter's was under construction as Raphael was working. In the *School of Athens*, he gives us a sneak preview of the unfinished church.

Next (unless you detour through the refreshingly modern
Catholic art section) is the brilliantly restored Sistine Chapel. The
Sistine Chapel, the pope's personal chapel, is where, upon the death
of the ruling pope, a new pope is elected. The College of Cardinals
meet here and vote four times a day until a two-thirds-plus-one
majority is reached and a new pope is elected.

The Sistine is famous for Michelangelo's pictorial culmination
of the Renaissance, showing the story of Creation with a powerful
God weaving in and out of each scene through that busy first week.
This is an optimistic and positive expression of the High Renaissance
and a powerful example of the artistic and theological maturity of the
33-year-old Michelangelo who spent four years at this work.

Later, after the Reformation wars had begun and after
the Catholic army of Spain had sacked the Vatican, the reeling
church began to fight back. As part of its Counter-Reformation, a
much-older Michelangelo was commissioned to paint the *Last
Judgment* (behind the altar). Newly restored, the message is as brilliant and clear as the day Michelangelo finished it: Christ is returning, some will go to hell and some to heaven, and some will be
saved by the power of the rosary.

In the recent (and controversial) restoration project no paint
was added. Centuries of dust, soot (from candles used for lighting
and Mass), and glue (added to make the art shine) were removed,
revealing the bright original colors of Michelangelo.

The Vatican's small but fine collection of paintings, the
Pinacoteca (with Raphael's *Transfiguration* and Caravaggio's
Entombment), is near the entry/exit. The underrated early
Christian art section is the final possible side trip before
exiting via the souvenir shop.

Vatican Museum nitty-gritty: Just inside the entrance
two huge elevators *(ascensore)* zip you past mobs climbing the
fancy staircase. (Museum admission L15,000, open late March,
April, May, early June, September, and October hours:
8:45–16:45, Saturday 8:45–14:00, closed Sunday, except last
Sunday of month when museum is free; the rest of the year it's
open 8:45–13:45. Last entry 45 minutes before closing. Many
minor rooms close 13:45–14:45 or from 13:30 on. The Sistine
Chapel is closed 30 minutes before the rest of the museum.)
The museum clearly marks out four color-coded visits of different lengths. The rentable CD-ROM tour (L8,000) is a great
new system, letting you dial whichever piece of art you'd like
commentary on as you come across numbered pieces in the
museum. It offers a fine coverage of the Raphael rooms and
Michelangelo's Sistine masterpiece. A small door at the rear of
the Sistine Chapel allows tour groups and speedy individuals
(without CD-ROM) to escape directly to St. Peter's Basilica
(ignore sign saying "Tour Groups Only"). If you squirt out here
you're done with the museum. The Pinacoteca is the only

important part left. Consider doing it at the start. Otherwise, it's a ten-minute heel-to-toe slalom through tourists from the Sistine to the entry/exit, tel. 06/698-83333. Closed May 1, June 29, August 15, November 1, December 8, and on church holidays.

The museum's excellent book-and-card shop offers a priceless (L12,000) black-and-white photo book (by Hupka) of the *Pietà*—great for gifts. The Vatican post, with an office in the museum and one on Piazza San Pietro (comfortable writing rooms, Monday–Friday 8:30–19:00, Saturday 8:30–18:00), is the only reliable mail service in Italy. The stamps are a collectible bonus (Vatican stamps are good throughout Rome, Italian stamps are not good at the Vatican). The Vatican bank has sinful rates. The modern cafeteria is handy but comes with long lines and mediocre food.

To see the pope: The pope reads a prayer and blesses the gathered masses from his library window overlooking Piazza San Pietro each Sunday at noon. During the summer (when he's in town), the Holy Father blesses the masses from St. Peter's Square each Wednesday morning at 11:00 (10:00 if it's really hot). In the winter this is done in the 7,000-seat Aula Paola VI Auditorium (free, Wednesday 11:00, call 06/698-83017 for reservations and details). Smaller ceremonies celebrated by the pope require reservations. The weekly entertainment guide *Romanc'e* always has a "Seeing the Pope" section.

More Sights—Rome

▲**National Museum of Rome (Museo Nazionale Romano delle Terme)**—Directly in front of the train station, the Palazzo Massimo houses much of the greatest ancient Roman sculpture (L12,000, 9:00–14:00, Sunday until 13:00, closed Monday, tel. 06/488-0530).

▲**Baths of Diocletian**—At the far side of the National Museum, facing Piazza Republica, the Aula Ottagona (or Rotunda of Diocletian, free, daily 10:00–19:00, borrow the English description booklet) is an impressive octagonal hall from A.D. 300 decorated with fine ancient statues and worth a quick peek.

▲**Cappuccin Crypt**—If you want bones, this is it: below Santa Maria della Immaculata Concezione on Via Veneto, just off Piazza Barberini, are thousands of skeletons, all artistically arranged for the delight—or disgust—of the always-wide-eyed visitor. The monastic message on the wall explains that this is more than just a macabre exercise. Pick up a few of Rome's most interesting postcards (L1,000 donation, daily 9:00–12:00, 15:00–18:30). A bank with long hours and good exchange rates is next door, and the American Embassy and Federal Express are just up the street.

▲**Villa Borghese**—Rome's unkempt "Central Park" is great for people-watching (plenty of modern-day Romeos and Juliets).

Take a row on the lake or visit its fine museums. The Borghese Gallery has some world-class Baroque art, including Bernini's *David* and his excited statue of Apollo chasing Daphne (L4,000, Tuesday–Saturday 9:00–19:00, Sunday 9:00–13:00, closed Monday, tel. 06/854-8577). The gallery's great painting collection (including works by Caravaggio, Giorgioni, Titian, and Rubens) is temporarily in the Complesso Monumentale San Michele a Ripa (L4,000, in Trastevere at Via de San Michele 22, Tuesday–Saturday 9:00–19:00, Sunday 9:00–13:00, closed Monday, tel. 06/581-6732). Also in the Villa Borghese, the **Museo di Villa Giulia** is a fine Etruscan museum (L8,000, Tuesday–Saturday 9:00–19:00, Sunday 9:00–13:30, closed Monday, tel. 06/320-1951).

▲**E.U.R.**—Mussolini's planned suburb of the future (65 years ago) is a ten-minute subway ride from the Colosseum to Metro: Magliana. From the Magliana subway stop, walk through the park uphill to the Palace of the Civilization of Labor (Pal. d. Civilta d. Concordia), the essence of Fascist architecture, with its giant, no-questions-asked, patriotic statues and its this-is-the-truth simplicity. On the far side is the **Museo della Civilta Romana**, a history museum which includes a large-scale model of ancient Rome (L5,000, Tuesday–Saturday 9:00–19:00, Sunday 9:00–13:30, closed Monday, Piazza G. Agnelli, Metro: E.U.R. Fermi, tel. 06/592-6041).

▲▲**Ostia Antica**—Rome's ancient seaport (80,000 people in the time of Christ, later a ghost town, now excavated), less than an hour from downtown, is the next best thing to Pompeii. Start at the 2,000-year-old theater, buy a map, explore the town, and finish with its fine little museum. To get there, take the subway's B Line to the Magliana stop, catch the Lido train to Ostia Antica (twice an hour), walk over the overpass, go straight to the end of that road, and follow the signs to (or ask for) "*scavi* Ostia Antica" (L8,000, Tuesday–Sunday 9:00–19:00 or one hour before sunset, closed Monday, museum closes at 14:00, tel. 06/563-58099). Just beyond is Rome's filthy beach (*lido*).

Overrated Sights—The Spanish Steps (with Italy's first, and one of the world's largest, McDonald's—McGrandeur at its greatest—just down the street) and the commercialized Catacombs, which contain no bones, are way out of the city and are not worth the time or trouble. The venerable old Villa d'Este garden of fountains near Hadrian's Villa outside of town at Tivoli is now run-down, overpriced, and disappointing.

Sleeping in Rome
(L1,600 = about $1, tel. code: 06)
Sleep Code: **S**=Single, **D**=Double/Twin, **T**=Triple, **Q**=Quad, **b**=bathroom, **t**=toilet only, **s**=shower only, **CC**=Credit Card (Visa, MasterCard, Amex), **SE**=Speaks English, **NSE**=No English. Breakfast is normally included in the expensive places.

The absolute cheapest doubles in Rome are L70,000, without shower or breakfast. You'll pay L25,000 in a sleazy dorm or hostel. A nicer hotel (L120,000 doubles, L150,000 with bath, L190,000 with air conditioning) provides an oasis and refuge, making it easier to enjoy this intense and grinding city. If you're going door-to-door, prices are soft—so bargain. Official prices that hotels list assume an agency or room-finding service kickback which, if you're coming direct, they avoid. Many hotels have high-season (mid-March through October) and low-season prices. Easter and September are the crowded times. In August, when temperatures climb, prices drop or get very soft. Most of my recommended hotels are small, with huge, murky entrances that make you feel like a Q-Tip in a gas station. Most places speak English, but the amount of English spoken drops with the price. While I've listed mostly places with minimal traffic noise, always ask for a *tranquillo* room. Many prices here are promised only to people who show this book, don't use a credit card, and come direct without using a room-finding service. On Easter, April 25, and May 1, the entire city gets booked up.

Sleeping North of the Train Station

The cheapest hotels in town are north of the station. Avoid places on the seedy south (Colosseum) side of the station. The first four listings are closest in a safe and decent area (which gets a little weird and spooky late at night). With your back to the train tracks, turn right and walk 2 blocks out of the station. A self-serve *lavanderia* (laundromat) is at 8 Via Milazzo (daily, 8:00–22:00, 6 kilos washed and dried for L12,000, friendly Maria Pia lets you drop off and pick up for no extra charge).

Albergo Sileo is a shiny-chandeliered, ten-room place with an elegant touch that has a contract to house train conductors who work the night shift. With maids doing double-time, they offer rooms from 19:00 to 9:00 only. If you can handle this, it's a great value (D-L65,000, Db-L75,000, Tb-L105,000, elevator; Via Magenta 39, tel. & fax 06/445-0246, Allesandro and Maria Savioli, NSE).

The **Fawlty Towers** is a backpacker-type place well-run by the Aussies from Enjoy Rome. It's young, hip, and English-speaking, with a rooftop terrace, lots of information, and no curfew (shared co-ed, four-bed dorms for L30,000 per bed, S-L50,000, Sb-L65,000, D-L75,000, Db-L90,000, Tb-L100,000, elevator; Via Magenta 39, tel. 06/445-0374, fax 06/445-0734, reservations by credit card but pay in cash).

Hotel Magic is a tiny, just-renovated place run by a mother-daughter team (Carmella and Rosanna). It's clean and it's high enough off the road to have no traffic problems (ten rooms, Sb-L70,000, Db-L110,000, Tb-L140,000 with this book, tiny breakfast included, thin walls, midnight curfew; Via Milazzo 20, third floor, 00185 Roma, tel. & fax 06/495-9880, little English spoken, unreliable for reservations).

Rome's Train Station Neighborhood

TO VILLA BORGHESE

TO SPANISH STEPS

SANTA MARIA VITTORIA

VENETO

CAPPUCCIN CRYPT

VIA BARBERINI

PIAZZA BARB

SANTA SUSANNA

QUATTRO

QUIRNALE PALACE

QUIRINALE

SAN CARLINO

FONTANE

TO TREVI FOUNTAIN + PANTHEON

VIA NAZIONALE

SERPENTI

PANISPERNA

DE PRETIS

VIA

CAVOUR

ANNIBALDI

FORI IMPERIALI

FORUM

ARCH OF CONSTANTINE

TO CIRCUS MAXIMUS

SETTEMBRE

PARGI

FIRENZE

TORINO

PIAZZA REP.

DE NICOLA

PIAZZA CINQUE-CENTO

DE PRETIS

VIA LANZA

ST PETER IN CHAINS

COLOSSEUM

DCH

1/4 MILE

NATIONAL MUSEUM

PIAZZA INDEP

MARSALA

GIOLITTI

PIAZZA CINQUE-CENTO

TERMINI STATION

SANTA MARIA MAGGIORE

LODGING:

1. SILEO / FAWLTY
2. MAGIC / FENECIA
3. OCEANIA / NARDIZZI
4. ADLER
5. ABERDEEN
6. CORTINA / IRISH PUB
7. ITALIA
8. YWCA
9. DUCA D' ALBA
10. FLAVIO
11. SUORE SANT ANNA
Ⓜ METRO STATIONS

In the same building, also with lots of stairs, **Hotel Fenicia** is eager for your business (Db-L120,000, third person pays L25,000, no breakfast, try café Gima across the street, CC:VM; Via Milazzo 20, tel. & fax 06/490-342, Anna and Georgio).

Sleeping near the Station on/near Via Firenze

The next listings are where I generally stay: tranquil, safe, handy, central, and a short walk from the central station, airport shuttle, 2 blocks beyond the Piazza Republica and the TI. The first four are family-run. Parking is actually workable on Via Firenze. Double-park below the hotel until a space without yellow lines becomes available and grab it (confirm locally that it's still legal). The defense ministry is nearby, and you've got heavily armed guards all night. All the orange buses which rumble down Via Nazionale take you to Piazza Venezia. Beyond that, #75 and #170 go to Trastevere (first stop after crossing the river), #64 to the Vatican (last stop—jammed with people and thieves), and #57 to Circus Maximus.

Hotel Nardizzi Americana is the best value in its price range. Traffic noise in the front rooms is a problem in the summer, when you'll want the window open (D-L100,000, Db-L120,000, T-L140,000, Tb-L160,000, prices promised through 1998 with this book, also four- and five-bed rooms, including breakfast; in summer and winter months they offer four nights for the price of three and discounts for longer stays, CC:VMA; Via Firenze 38, 00184 Roma, elevator, tel. 06/488-0368, fax 06/488-0035, helpful Nik speaks English).

Hotel Oceania (one floor below Nardizzi) is a peaceful slice of air-conditioned heaven. Its nine newly renovated rooms are spotless, spacious and quiet (Sb-L170,000, Db-L230,000, Tb-L295,000, Qb-L345,000, 10 percent off with this book, includes breakfast, CC:VMA; Via Firenze 38, 00184 Roma, tel. 06/482-4696, fax 06/488-5586, e-mail: hoceania@tin.it, the son Stefano SE).

Residence Adler, with its wide halls, garden patio, and 16 big, quiet, and elegant rooms in a great locale, is a good deal run by a charming family (D-L125,000, Db-L150,000, T-L145,000, Tb-L200,000, Q-L190,000, Qb-L240,000, including breakfast, CC:VMA, elevator; Via Modena 5, 00184 Roma, tel. 06/484-466, fax 06/488-0940, NSE).

Hotel Aberdeen is my classiest hotel listing and a good value for Rome. It has mini-bars, phones, TVs, and showers in its quiet, modern rooms; offers a first-class breakfast buffet; and is warmly run by Annamaria, with support from her cousins Sabrina and Cinzia, and trusty Reda on the late shift (Sb-L145,000, Db-L210,000, Tb-L250,000, with this book through 1998, L40,000 less per room in August and winter, including fine breakfast, air-con for an extra fee, CC:VMA, garage-L35,000; reach up and swing those knockers at Via Firenze 48, 00184 Roma, tel. 06/482-3920, fax 06/482-1092, SE).

Hotel Cortina, run by the Aberdeen folks, is similarly quiet, classy and comfortable. For the same prices as the Aberdeen, you get less soul but free air-conditioning (15 rooms, Db-L210,000 with breakfast in your room; Via Nazionale 18, 00184 Roma, tel. 06/481-9794, fax 06/481-9220, John Carlo SE).

Hotel Pensione Italia, in a busy, interesting, handy locale, placed safely on a quiet street next to the Ministry of the Interior, is comfortable, airy, bright, clean, and thoughtfully run by English-speaking Andrea and Abdul (23 rooms, Sb-L100,000,

Db-L150,000, Tb-L200,000, with breakfast, with cash and this book through 1998, all rooms one-third off in August, elevator; Via Venezia 18, just off Via Nazionale, tel. 06/482-8355, fax 06/474-5550).

The YWCA Casa Per Studentesse accepts women, couples, groups of men, and couples with children but not single men. It's an institutional place, filled with white-uniformed maids, more-colorful Third World travelers, and 75 single beds, closed from midnight to 7:00 (L35,000 per person in three- and four-bed rooms, S-L50,000, Sb-L70,000, D-L80,000, Db-L100,000, breakfast included; Via C. Balbo 4, 00184 Roma, 5 blocks toward the Colosseum from the station, tel. 06/488-0460, fax 06/487-1028).

Sleeping near the Colosseum *(zip code: 00184)*
One stop on the subway from the train station (to Metro: Cavour), these places are buried in a very Roman world of exhaust-stained medieval ambience.

Hotel Duca d'Alba is a classy, tight, and modern place just half a block from the metro station (Sb-L180,000, Db-L260,000, with this book through 1998, all air-con and with breakfast, extra bed–L40,000, CC:VMA; Via Leonina 14, 00184 Roma, tel. 06/484471, fax 06/488-4840, SE, e-mail: duca.d'alba@venere.it).

Hotel Flavio is a real hotel with an Old World TV-lounge/lobby, an elevator, and elegant furnishings throughout in a quiet setting. Its weakness is dim lights and lousy tub-showers down the hall for the five cheap doubles (S-L70,000, Sb-L80,000, D-L115,000, Db-L150,000, family rooms available, breakfast extra, CC:VMA; hiding almost torchlit under vines on a tiny street a block toward the Colosseum from Via Cavour at Via Frangipane 34, Metro: Cavour, tel. 06/679-7203, fax 06/679-6246, enough English). They also run the neary Holel Romano (same prices as Falvio, CC:VMA, Largo Corrado Ricci 32, tel. & fax 06/679-5851.

Suore di Sant Anna was built for Ukrainian pilgrims. The sisters are sweet, but the male staff doesn't seem to care. It's clumsy and difficult (23:00 curfew), but once you're in, you've got a comfortable home in a classic Roman village locale (SL42,000, D-L84,000, including breakfast, consider a monkish dinner for L26,000 more; off the corner of Via dei Serpenti and Via Baccina at Piazza Madonna dei Monti 3, Metro: Cavour, tel. 06/485-778, fax 06/487-1064).

Sleeping near the Campo dei Fiori *(zip code: 00186)*
Hotel Campo dei Fiori is an ideal location for wealthy bohemians who value centrality, just off the Campo dei Fiori, with comfortable rooms and an unreal rooftop terrace (D-L140,000, Db-L200,000, includes breakfast, CC:VM, lots of stairs and no elevator, Via del Biscione 6, tel. 06/6880-6865, fax 06/687-6003).

The **Albergo del Sole** is filled with German groups but well-located (D-L130,000, small Db-L150,000, Db-L170,000, no breakfast; Via del Biscione 76, tel. 06/688-06873, fax 06/689-3787).

Hotel Navona is a ramshackle 25-room hotel occupying an ancient building in a perfect locale a block off Piazza Navona and run by an Australian named Corry (S-L85,000, Sb-L95,000, D-L125,000, Db-L140,000 with breakfast, family rooms, lots of student groups; Via dei Sediari 8, tel. 06/686-4203, fax 06/688-03802, SE).

Casa di Santa Brigida is also near the characteristic Campo dei Fiori. With soft-spoken sisters gliding down polished hallways, and pearly gates instead of doors, this lavish convent makes the exhaust-stained Roman tourist feel like he's died and gone to heaven. If you're unsure of your destiny, this is worth the splurge (twins with all the comforts-L240,000; Piazza Farnese 96, tel. 06/688-92596, fax 06/688-91573, SE). Some of its 20 rooms overlook the Piazza Farnese.

Sleeping near the Vatican Museum (zip code: 00192)

Pension Alimandi is a good value, run by the friendly and entrepreneurial Alimandi brothers: Paolo, Enrico, Luigi, and Germano (35 rooms, Sb-L130,000, Db-L170,000, T bL200,000, 5 percent discount with this book and cash, CC:VMA, elevator, optional grand L15,000 breakfast, great roof garden, self-service washing machines, pool table, L27,000 garage, L70,000 airport pickup; down the stairs directly in front of the Vatican Museum, Via Tunisi 8, near metro: Ottaviano, tel. 06/397-26300, fax 06/397-23943, reserve by phone, no reply to fax means they are full, SE).

Hotel Spring House offers comfortable, clean, quiet rooms with balconies, TVs, refrigerators, and an impersonal staff (Db-L150,000–190,000, fancy Db with air-con, L230,000 is best value, with breakfast, CC:VMA; Via Mocenigo 7, a block from Alimandi, tel. 06/397-20948, fax 06/397-21047, e-mail: ~spring~@flashnet.it).

Hotel Gerber is sleek, modern, air-conditioned, business-like, and set in a quiet residential area (27 rooms, S-L110,000, Sb-L170,000, Db-L220,000, Tb-L260,000, Qb-L310,000, 10 percent discount with this book, includes breakfast buffet, CC:VMA; 1 block from Lepanto subway stop, Via degli Scipioni 24, tel. 06/321-6485, fax 06/321-7048, Peter SE).

Hotel Benjamin is a tiny family affair with seven simple but decent rooms on the third floor (D-L80,000, Db-L100,000, T-L90,000, Tb-L100,000 prices promised through 1998 with this book, no breakfast, no elevator, Metro: Ottaviano, corner of Via Terenzio at Via Boezio 31, tel. & fax 06/688-02437, Sra Franca Fondi NSE).

Suore Oblate dell'Assunzione, a convent, rents clean, peaceful and inexpensive rooms. No English is spoken and it's

hard to get in (S-L45,000, D-L90,000, T-L125,000; Via Andrea
Doria 42, 3 blocks from the Vatican Museum entrance, tel.
06/397-37567, fax 06/397-37020).

Sleeping in Hostels and Dorms

Rome has only one real youth hostel—big, institutional, not central or worth the trouble. For cheap dorm beds, consider Fawlty
Towers (above) or **Pensione Ottaviano** (25 beds in two- to six-
bed rooms, L25,000 per bed with sheets, no reservations, call from
the station). They offer free showers, lockers, a mini-fridge in each
room, a fun, laid-back clubhouse feel, and a good location (6
blocks from the Ottaviano Metro stop, near the Vatican, at Via
Ottaviano 6, tel. 06/397-37253). The same slum visionaries run
the dumpier **Pensione Sandy** (L25,000 beds, south of station, up
a million depressing stairs, Via Cavour 136, tel. 06/488-4585).

Eating in Rome

The cheapest meals in town are picnics (from *alimentari* shops or
open-air markets), self-serve rotisseries, and stand-up or take-out
meals from a **Pizza Rustica** (pizza slices sold by the weight, 100
grams is a hot cheap snack, 200 grams, or 2 *etti*, make a light meal).
Most alimentari will slice and stuff your sandwich (*panini*) for you, if
you buy the stuff there. For a fast/cheap/healthy lunch, find a bar
with a buffet spread of meat and vegetables and ask for a mixed plate
of vegetables with a hunk of mozzarella.

Eating in Trastevere or on the Campo dei Fiori

Trastevere: My best dinner tip is to go for Rome's Vespa street
ambience and find your own place in Trastevere or on Campo
dei Fiori. Guidebooks list Trastevere's famous places, but I'd
wander the fascinating maze of streets near the Piazza Santa
Maria in Trastevere and find a mom-and-pop place with barely a
menu. Check out the tiny streets north of the church. At Piazza
della Scala consider **Taverna della Scala** and the fine little gelateria. For the basic meal with lots of tourists, eat amazingly
cheap at **Mario's** (three courses with wine and service for
L17,000, near the Sisto bridge at Via del Moro 53, tel. 06/580-
3809, closed Sunday).

    Campo dei Fiori: For the ultimate romantic square
setting, eat at whichever place looks best on Campo dei Fiori.
Circle the square, considering each place. **La Carbonara** is the
birthplace of pasta carbonara. The **Forno,** next door, is popular for
hot greasy snacks. Meals on small nearby streets are a better value
but lack that Campo dei Fiori magic. Nearby, on Piazza Farnese,
Da Giovanni Ar Galletto has an ideal setting, moderate prices,
and fine food (Piazza Farnese 102, tel. 06/686-1714, closed
Sunday). Piazza Pasquino (a block off Piazza Navona, near Campo
dei Fiori) has a couple of interesting eateries (a trendy salad place

and **Cul de Sac** for bar munchies). **Trattoria Lilli** is a local favorite (on Via Tor di Nona, between the Tiber and Piazza Navona).

Eating near the Pantheon

Il Delfino is a handy self-service cafeteria on the Largo Argentina square (daily 7:00–21:00, closed Monday, not cheap but fast). Across the street, the **Frullati Bar** sells refreshing fruity frappés. The alimentari on the Pantheon square will make you a sandwich for a temple-porch picnic. **Volpetti** is a lively *tavola calda* (deli) selling hot food by the weight for take-out or to be eaten in their air-conditioned basement dining room (across the street from Alfreddo's, at Via della Scrofa 31, where the famous fettucine was born, tel. 06/686-1940).

Eating near Hotels Nardizzi, Adler, and Aberdeen

Snack Bar Gastronomia is a great local hole-in-the-wall for lunch or dinner (Via Firenze 34, really cheap hot meals dished up from under glass counter, tap water with a smile, open until 20:00, closed Sunday). There's an *alimentari* (grocery store) across the street. **Pasticceria Dagnino**, popular for its top quality Sicilian specialties—especially pastries and ice cream—is where those who work at my recommended hotels eat (in Galleria Esedra off Via Torino, a block from hotels, daily 7:00–22:00, tel. 06/481-8660). Their *arancino*, a rice, cheese and ham ball, is a greasy Sicilian favorite. Direct the construction of your meal at the bar, pay for your trayful at the cashier, and climb upstairs where you'll find the dancing Sicilian girls (free).

For an air-conditioned, classier, local favorite serving traditional Roman cuisine, run by a group of men who enjoy their work, eat at **Hostaria Romana** (midway between the Trevi fountain and Piazza Barberini, Via del Boccaccio 1, tel. 06/474-5284, closed Sunday). And locals line up for **Ristorante da Giovanni** (L22,000 menu, just off Via XX Septembre at Via Antonio Salandra 1, tel. 06/485-950, closed Sunday). **Lon Fon** serves reasonably priced Chinese food (18:30–23:00, closed Wednesday, Via Firenze 44, tel. 06/482-5261).

The **McDonald's** on Piazza della Republica (free piazza seating outside), Piazza Barberini, and Via Firenze offer air-conditioned interiors and a L7,000 salad bar that no American fast-food joint would recognize. **Greenpizz** is a fun and lively place for good pizza (Via Cernaia 16, tel. 06/474-1322). For pasta with Guinness or a late-night drink with live music, consider the lively **Irish Pub** (2 blocks from recommended hotels at Via Nazionale 18).

Eating near the Vatican Museum and Pension Alimandi

Viale Giulio Cesare is lined with cheap Pizza Rusticas and fun eateries (such as **Cipriani Self-Service Rosticceria** near the

Ottaviano subway stop at Via Vespasiano, with pleasant outdoor seating). Turn your nose loose in the wonderful **Via Andrea Doria** open-air market 2 blocks in front of the Vatican Museum (between Via Tunisi and Via Andrea Doria, Monday–Saturday, open late on Tuesday and Friday, otherwise closed by 13:30). Antonio's **Hostaria dei Bastioni** is tasty and friendly with good sit-down meals (L9,000–12,000 pastas, L15,000 *secondi*, no cover charge, at corner of Vatican wall, Via Leone IV 29, tel. 06/397-23034, closed Sunday). **La Rustichella** has a good antipasti buffet (L12,000, enough for a meal) and fine pasta dishes (arrive by 19:30 or wait to get in, closed Monday, opposite church at end of Via Candia, Via Angelo 1, tel. 06/3972-0649).

Transportation Connections—Rome
By train to: Venice (6/day, 5–8 hrs, overnight possible), **Florence** (12/day, 2 hrs), **Pisa** (8/day, 3–4 hrs), **Genova** (7/day, 6 hrs, overnight possible), **Milan** (12/day, 5 hrs, overnight possible), **Naples** (6/day, 2–3 hrs), **Brindisi** (2/day, 9 hrs), **Amsterdam** (2/day, 20 hrs), **Bern** (5/day, 10 hrs), **Frankfurt** (4/day, 14 hrs), **Munich** (5/day, 12 hrs), **Nice** (2/day, 10 hrs), **Paris** (5/day, 16 hrs), **Vienna** (3/day, 13–15 hrs). **Civita:** Take the Rome–Orvieto train (every 2 hrs, 75 min), catch the bus from Orvieto to Bagnoregio (8/day, 50 min, no service on Sundays), and walk to Civita. Train information: tel. 1478-88088.

Rome's Airport
A slick direct train link connects Rome's Leonardo da Vinci (a.k.a. Fiumicino) airport with the central Termini train station (L15,000 or free with first-class railpass, departures last year at 6:52, 7:22, then hourly at 22 minutes after each hour until 21:22, extra departures at 15:52, 17:52 and 19:52). Your hotel can arrange a taxi to the airport at any hour for about L75,000.

Airport information (tel. 06/65951) can connect you directly to your airline. (British Air tel. 06/6595-4190, Alitalia tel. 06/65642, American tel. 06/4274-1240, Delta tel. 06/1678-64114, KLM tel. 06/652-9286, SAS tel. 06/6501-0771, TWA tel. 06/47211, United tel. 06/1678-25181.)

Driving in Rome
Greater Rome is circled by the *Grande Raccordo Anulare*. This ring road has spokes that lead you into the center (much like the strings under the skin of a baseball). Entering from the north, leave the autostrada at the Settebagni exit. Following the ancient Via Salaria (and the black-and-white "Centro" signs), work your way doggedly into the Roman thick-of-things. This will take you along the Villa Borghese and dump you right on Via Veneto (where there's an Avis office). Avoid rush hour. Drive defensively:

Roman cars stay in their lanes like rocks in an avalanche. Parking in Rome is dangerous. Park near a police station or get advice at your hotel. The garage is L35,000 a day. The Villa Borghese underground garage (Metro: Spagna) is handy.

Consider this: Your car is a worthless headache in Rome. Avoid a pile of stress and save money by parking at the huge, easy, and relatively safe lot behind the Orvieto station (follow "P" signs from autostrada), and catch the train to Rome (every two hours, 75 min).

FLORENCE (FIRENZE)

Florence, the home of the Renaissance and birthplace of our modern world, is a "supermarket sweep," and the groceries are the best Renaissance art in Europe.

Get your bearings with a Renaissance walk. Florentine art goes beyond paintings and statues—there's food, fashion, and handicrafts. You can lick Italy's best gelato while enjoying Europe's best people-watching.

Planning Your Time

If you're in Europe for three weeks, Florence deserves a well-organized day. Siena, an easy hour away by bus, has no awesome sights but is a more enjoyable home base. For a day in Florence, see Michelangelo's *David*, tour the Uffizi Gallery (best Italian paintings), tour the underrated Bargello (best statues), and do the Renaissance ramble (explained below). Art lovers will want to chisel another day out of their itinerary for the many other cultural treasures Florence offers. Shoppers and ice-cream lovers may need to do the same. Plan your sightseeing hours carefully. Get an early start. Mondays and afternoons can be sparse. You may very likely lose an hour or two in lines. If the line at *David* depresses you, remind yourself that people think nothing of waiting an hour at Disneyland to see the Tiki Hut.

Orientation (tel. code: 055)

The Florence we're interested in lies mostly on the north bank of the Arno River. Everything is within a 20-minute walk of the train station, cathedral, or Ponte Vecchio (Old Bridge). The less impressive but more characteristic Oltrarno (south bank) area is just over the bridge. Orient yourself by the huge red-tiled dome of the cathedral (the Duomo) and its tall bell tower (Giotto's Tower). This is the center of historic Florence.

Tourist Information]

Normally overcrowded, under-informed, and understaffed, the train station's tourist information office is not worth a stop if you're a good student of this book. If there's no line, pick up a map (ask for the better "long stay" map), a current museum-hours listing, and the periodical entertainment guide or tourist magazine. The main TI (3 blocks north of Duomo at Via Cavour 1r, Monday–Saturday in summer 8:15–19:15, Sunday 8:15–13:45, tel. 055/290-832 or 055/290-833) is less crowded and more helpful. There's a fine international bookstore (with American guidebooks) across the street at Via Cavour 20r. The free monthly *Florence Concierge Information* magazine lists the latest museum hours, markets, bus and train connections, and events; it's stocked by the expensive hotels (pick one up, as if you're staying there).

Helpful Hints

Museums and Churches: See everyone's essential sight, *David*, right off. In Italy a masterpiece seen and enjoyed is worth two tomorrow; you never know when a place will unexpectedly close for a holiday, strike, or restoration. The Uffizi has one- to two-hour lines on busy days. During lunchtime (before 14:00), lines are shorter. By 17:00, lines are normally gone. Many museums close at 14:00 and stop selling tickets 30 minutes before that. Most close Monday and at 13:00 or 14:00 on Sunday. The *Concierge Information* magazine thoughtfully lists which sights are open afternoons, Sundays, and Mondays (best attractions open Monday: Michelangelo's Casa Buonarroti, Dante's House, Giotto's Belltower, Museo dell' Opera del Duomo, and Palazzo Vecchio). Churches usually close from 12:30 to 15:00 or 16:00. Local guidebooks are cheap and give you a map and a decent commentary on the sights.

Addresses: Street addresses list businesses in red and residences in black or blue (color-coded on the actual street number, and indicated by a letter following the number in printed addresses: n = black, r = red). Pensioni are usually black, but can be either.

Theft Alert: Florence has particularly hardworking thief gangs. They specialize in tourists and hang out where you do, near the train station and major sights. American tourists, especially older ones, are considered the easiest targets.

Medical Help: For a doctor who speaks English call 055/475-411 (reasonable hotel calls, cheaper if you go to the clinic, 24-hour pharmacy at the train station).

American Express is near the Palazzo Vecchio (Monday–Friday 9:00–17:30, Saturdays until 12:30, easy train tickets and reservations, Via Dante 22, tel. 055/50981).

Getting Around Florence

If you organize your sightseeing with some geographic logic, you'll do it all on foot. Taxis takes you from the train station to the Ponte Vecchio for about L8,000. A L1,500 ticket gives you 60 minutes on the buses, L2,500 gives you three hours, and L6,000 gets you 24 hours (tickets not sold on bus, buy in tobacco shop, validate on bus).

A Florentine Renaissance Walk

Even during the Dark Ages, people knew they were in a "middle time." It was especially obvious to the people of Italy—sitting on the rubble of Rome—that there was a brighter age before them. The long-awaited rebirth, or "Renaissance," happened in Florence for good reason. Wealthy because of its cloth industry, trade, and banking; powered by a fierce city-state pride (locals would pee into the Arno with gusto, knowing rival city-state Pisa was downstream); and fertile with more than its share of artistic genius (imagine guys like Michelangelo and Leonardo attending the same high school)—Florence was a natural home for this cultural explosion.

Take a walk through the core of Renaissance Florence by starting at the Accademia (home of Michelangelo's *David*) and cutting through the heart of the city to the Ponte Vecchio on the Arno River. (A ten-page, self-guided tour of this walk is outlined in my museum guidebook, *Mona Winks*. Otherwise, you'll find brief descriptions below.)

At the Accademia you'll look into the eyes of Renaissance man—humanism at its confident peak. Then walk to the cathedral (Duomo) to see the dome that kicked off the architectural Renaissance. Step inside the Baptistery to view a ceiling covered with preachy, flat, 2-D, medieval mosaic art. Then, to learn what happened when art met math, check out the realistic 3-D reliefs on the doors. The painter, Giotto, designed the bell tower—an early example of how a Renaissance genius excelled in many areas. Continue toward the river on Florence's great pedestrian mall, Via de' Calzaioli (or "Via Calz"), which was part of the original grid plan given the city by the ancient Romans. Down a few blocks, compare medieval and Renaissance statues on the exterior of the Orsanmichele Church. Via Calz connects the cathedral with the central square (Piazza della Signoria), the city palace (Palazzo Vecchio), and the Uffizi Gallery containing the greatest collection of Italian Renaissance paintings in captivity. Finally, walk through the Uffizi courtyard, a statuary think-tank of Renaissance greats, to the Arno River and the Ponte Vecchio.

Sights—Florence

▲▲▲**The Accademia (Galleria dell' Accademia)**—This museum houses Michelangelo's *David* and powerful (unfinished) *Prisoners*. Eavesdrop as tour guides explain these masterpieces. More than any other work of art, when you look into the eyes of *David*, you're looking into the eyes of Renaissance man. This was a radical break with the past. Man was now a confident individual, no longer a plaything of the supernatural. And life was now more than just a preparation for what happened after you died.

The Renaissance was the merging of art and science. In a humanist vein, *David* is looking at the crude giant of medieval darkness and thinking, "I can take this guy." Back on a religious track (and speaking of veins), notice David's large and overdeveloped right hand. This is symbolic of the hand of God that powered David to slay the giant . . . and enabled Florence to rise above its crude neighboring city-states.

Beyond the magic marble are two floors of interesting pre-Renaissance and Renaissance paintings, including a couple of dreamy Botticellis (L12,000, Tuesday–Saturday 8:30–19:00, Sunday 8:30–14:00, closed Monday, Via Ricasoli 60, tel. 055/238-8609).

Behind the Accademia, the Piazza Santissima Annunziata features lovely Renaissance harmony. Brunelleschi's Hospital of the Innocents (Spedale degli Innocenti, not worth going inside), with terra-cotta medallions by della Robbia, was built in the 1420s and is considered the first Renaissance building.

▲▲**Museum of San Marco**—One block north of the Accademia on Piazza San Marco, this museum houses the greatest collection anywhere of medieval frescoes and paintings by the early Renaissance master Fra Angelico. You'll see why he thought of painting as a form of prayer and couldn't paint a crucifix without shedding tears. Each of the monks' cells has a Fra Angelico fresco. Don't miss the cell of Savonarola, the charismatic monk who rode in from the Christian right, threw out the Medici, turned Florence into a theocracy, sponsored "bonfires of the vanities" (burning books, paintings, and so on), and was finally burned himself when Florence decided to change channels (L8,000, daily 8:30–14:00 but closed the second and fourth Monday of each month).

▲▲**The Duomo**—Florence's mediocre Gothic cathedral has the third-longest nave in Christendom (free, daily 9:00–18:00, with an occasional lunch break). The church's noisy neo-Gothic facade from the 1870s is covered with pink, green, and white Tuscan marble. Since nearly all of its great art is stored in the Museo dell' Opera del Duomo, behind the church, the best thing about the inside is the shade. The inside of the dome is decorated by what must be the largest painting of the Renaissance, a huge (and newly restored) *Last Judgment* by Vasari and Zuccari. The cathedral's claim to artistic fame is Brunelleschi's magnificent dome—the first

Florence

LODGING:

1. CASA RABATTI
2. PEZZATI
3. ENZA
4. MAGLIANI
5. LOGGIATO SERVITI
6. DUE FONTANE
7. UNIVERSO
8. ELITE
9. SOLE
10. CONCORDIA
11. CENTRALE
12. BURCHIANTI
13. MAXIM
14. ABACO
15. BRETAGNA
16. AILY HOME
17. SCALETTA
18. SORR. BANDINI
19. SILLA

Renaissance dome and the model for domes to follow (ascent L8,000, Monday–Saturday 9:30–18:20). When planning St. Peter's in Rome, Michelangelo said, "I can build a dome bigger, but not more beautiful, than the dome of Florence."

Giotto's Tower—Climbing Giotto's Tower (or Campanile) beats climbing the neighboring Duomo's dome because it's 50 fewer steps, faster, not so crowded, and offers the same view plus the dome (L8,000, daily 8:30–19:00, maybe later in summer).

▲▲**Museo dell' Opera del Duomo**—The underrated cathedral museum, behind the church at #9, is great if you like sculpture. It has masterpieces by Donatello (a gruesome wood carving of Mary Magdalene clothed in her matted hair, and the *cantoria*, a delightful choir loft bursting with happy children) and Luca della Robbia (another choir loft, lined with the dreamy faces of musicians praising the Lord); a late Michelangelo pietà (Nicodemus, on top, is a self-portrait); Brunelleschi's models for his dome; and the original restored panels of Ghiberti's doors to the Baptistery. To get the most out of your sightseeing hours, remember that this is one of the few museums in Florence that stays open late and is open on Monday (L8,000, Monday–Saturday 9:00–18:50, closed Sunday, tel. 055/230-2885).

▲**The Baptistery**—Michelangelo said its bronze doors were fit to be the gates of Paradise. Check out the gleaming copies of Ghiberti's bronze doors facing the Duomo, and the famous competition doors around to the right. Making a breakthrough in perspective, Ghiberti used mathematical laws to create the illusion of 3-D on a 2-D surface. Go inside Florence's oldest building and sit and savor the medieval mosaic ceiling. Compare that to the "new, improved" art of the Renaissance (L3,000 interior open 13:30–18:30, Sunday 9:00–12:30, bronze doors are on the outside so always "open"; original panels are in the Museo dell' Opera del Duomo).

▲**Orsanmichele**—Mirroring Florentine values, this was a combination church-granary. The best L200 deal in Florence is the machine which lights its glorious tabernacle. Notice the grain spouts on the pillars inside. Also study the sculpture on its outside walls. You can see man stepping out of the literal and figurative shadow of the church in the great Renaissance sculptor Donatello's *St. George* (free, daily 9:00–12:00, 16:00–18:00, on Via Calzaioli; if closed, as it often is due to staffing problems, try going through the back door).

▲**Palazzo Vecchio**—This fortified palace, once the home of the Medici family, is a Florentine landmark. But if you're visiting only one palace interior in town, the Pitti Palace is better. The Palazzo Vecchio interior is wallpapered with mediocre magnificence, worthwhile only if you're a real Florentine art and history fan (L10,000, 9:00–19:00, Sunday 8:00–13:00, closed Thursday, handy public WC inside on ground floor). Do step into the free courtyard (behind the fake *David*) just to feel the Medici. Until 1873, Michelangelo's *David* stood at the entrance, where the copy is today. While the huge statues in the square are important only as the whipping boys of art critics and as pigeon roosts, the nearby Loggia dei Lanzi has several important statues. Notice Cellini's bronze statue of Perseus (with the head of Medusa). The plaque

Florentines (free, Wednesday–Monday 7:15–12:30, 15:00–18:30, closed Tuesday). The loud 19th-century Victorian Gothic facade faces a huge square ringed with tempting touristy shops and littered with tired tourists (and ice-cream cups—Vivoli's is 2 blocks away). Escape into the church.

Working counterclockwise from the entrance you'll find: the tomb of Michelangelo (with the allegorical figures of painting, architecture and sculpture), a memorial to Dante (no body . . . he was banished by his hometown), tomb of Machaivelli, a relief by Donatello of the Annunciation, the tomb of the composer Rossini. To the right of the altar, step into the sacristy where you'll find the bit of St. Francis' cowl (he is supposed to have founded the church around 1290) and old sheets of music with the medieval and mobile C-clef (2 little blocks on either side of the line determined to be middle C). In the bookshop notice the photos high on the wall of the devastating flood of 1966. Beyond that is a touristy—but mildly interesting—"leather school." The chapels lining the front of the church are richly frescoed. The Bardi Chapel (far left of altar) is a masterpiece by Giotto featuring scenes from the life of St. Francis. On your way out you'll pass the tomb of Galileo (allowed in by the church long after his death). The neighboring Pazzi Chapel (by Brunelleschi) is considered one of the finest pieces of Florentine Renaissance architecture.

▲**Medici Chapel (Cappelle dei Medici)**—This chapel, containing two Medici tombs, is drenched in incredibly lavish High Renaissance architecture and sculpture by Michelangelo (L10,000, daily 8:30–14:00 but closed the first and third Monday of each month). Behind San Lorenzo on Piazza Madonna, it's surrounded by a lively market scene that I find more interesting. Don't miss a wander through the huge double-decker central market.

Science Museum (Museo di Storia della Scienza)—This is a fascinating collection of Renaissance and later clocks, telescopes, maps, and ingenious gadgets. One of the most talked-about bottles in Florence is the one here containing Galileo's finger. English guidebooklets are available. It's friendly, comfortably cool, never crowded, and just downstream from the Uffizi (L10,000, Monday, Wednesday, and Friday 9:30–13:00, 14:00–17:00, Tuesday and Thursday 9:30–13:00, closed Sunday, Piazza dei Giudici 1).

▲**Michelangelo's Home, Casa Buonarroti**—Fans enjoy Michelangelo's house, which has some of his early, much-less-monumental works (L10,000, Wednesday–Monday 9:30–13:30, closed Tuesday, Via Ghibellina 70).

▲▲**Gelato**—Gelato is a great Florentine edible art form. Italy's best ice cream is in Florence. Every year I repeat my taste test. And every year Vivoli's wins (on Via Stinche, see map, 8:00–01:00, closed Monday, the last three weeks in August, and January). Gelateria Carrozze (30 yards from the Ponte Vecchio towards the Uffizi, Via del Pesce 3), Festival del Gelato (Via del Corso) and Perche Non!

on the pavement in front of the fountain marks the spot where
Savonarola was burned in LCCCCXCVIII.

▲▲▲**Uffizi Gallery**—The greatest collection of Italian painting
anywhere is a must, with plenty of works by Giotto, Leonardo,
Raphael, Caravaggio, Rubens, Titian, and Michelangelo, and a
roomful of Botticellis, including his *Birth of Venus*. There are no
official tours, so buy a book on the street before entering (or follow
Mona Winks). The long entrance line is a reasonable cost for an
interior with no Louvre-style mob scenes. The museum is nowhere
near as big as it is great: few tourists spend more than two hours
inside. The paintings are displayed (behind obnoxious reflective
glass) on one comfortable floor in chronological order from the
13th through 17th centuries.

Essential stops are (in this order): the Gothic altarpieces (narrative, pre-realism, no real concern for believable depth); Giotto's
altarpiece in the same room, which progressed beyond "totem-
pole angels"; Uccello's *Battle of San Romano*, an early study in perspective (with a few obvious flubs); Fra Lippi's cuddly Madonnas;
the Botticelli room, filled with masterpieces including a pantheon
of classical fleshiness and the small *La Calumnia*, showing the glas-
nost of Renaissance free-thinking being clubbed back into the
darker age of Savonarola; two minor works by Leonardo; the
octagonal classical sculpture room with an early painting of Bob
Hope and a copy of Praxiteles' *Venus de Medici*, considered the
epitome of beauty in Elizabethan Europe; Michelangelo's only
surviving easel painting, the round *Holy Family*; Raphael's noble
Madonna of the Goldfinch; Titian's voluptuous *Venus of Urbino*; and
views from the café terrace at the end (L12,000, Tuesday–Saturday
8:30–19:00, Sunday 8:30–14:00, closed Monday, last ticket sold 45
minutes before closing, go very late to avoid crowds and heat, elevator available, tel. 055/234-7941). It is possible now to get a
reservation by paying in advance in Florence, or you can even
order online at www.weekendafirenze.com.

Enjoy the Uffizi square, full of artists and souvenir stalls. The
surrounding statues honor the earthshaking: artists, plus philosophers (Machiavelli), scientists (Galileo), writers (Dante), explorers
(Amerigo Vespucci), and the great patron of so much Renaissance
thinking, Lorenzo (the Magnificent) de Medici.

▲▲▲**Bargello (Museo Nazionale)**—This underrated sculpture
museum is behind Palazzo Vecchio in a former prison that looks
like a mini-Palazzo Vecchio. It has Donatello's *David* (the very
influential first male nude to be sculpted in a thousand years),
works by Michelangelo, and more (L8,000, daily 8:30–14:00 but
closed second and fourth Monday of each month, Via del
Proconsolo 4). Dante's house, across the street and around the
corner, is interesting only to his Italian-speaking fans.

▲▲**Santa Croce Church**—This 14th-century Franciscan church,
decorated by centuries of precious art, holds the tombs of great

(Via Tavolini), both just off Via Calzaioli, are also good. That's one souvenir that can't break and won't clutter your luggage. Get a free sample of Vivoli's *riso* (rice, my favorite) before ordering. (The Cinema Astro across the street from Vivoli's plays English/American movies in their original language, closed Mondays.)

Shopping—Florence is a great shopping town. Busy street scenes and markets abound, especially near San Lorenzo, on the Ponte Vecchio, and near Santa Croce. Leather, gold, silver, art prints, and tacky plaster "mini-*Davids*" are most popular.

Scenic City Bus Ride to Fiesole—For a candid peek at a Florentine suburb, ride bus #7 (from Piazza Adua, near the station, extra-urban ticket needed) for about 20 minutes through neighborhood gardens, vineyards, orchards, and large villas to the last stop—Fiesole. Fiesole is a popular excursion from Florence for its small eateries and good views of Florence. (Catch the sunset from the terrace just below the La Reggia restaurant; from the Fiesola bus stop, face the square and take the very steep road on your left to the terrace and good restaurant).

Sights—Florence, South of the Arno River

▲▲**The Pitti Palace**—From the Uffizi, follow the elevated passageway (closed to non-Medicis) across the river to the gargantuan Pitti Palace which has five separate museums. The **Palatine Gallery/Royal Apartments** (First floor, L12,000, Tuesday–Saturday 9:00–19:00, Sunday 9:00–13:00, closed Monday) features palatial room after chandeliered room, its walls sagging with paintings by the great masters. This Raphael collection is the biggest anywhere. The **Modern Art Gallery** (Second floor, L8,000, Tuesday–Sunday 9:00–14:00, closed Monday) features 19th- and 20th-century art (mostly Romanticism, Neo-classicism, Impressionism by Tuscan painters). The **Grand Ducal Treasures** (Il Museo degli Argenti, ground floor, L4,000, Tuesday–Sunday 8:30–14:00, closed Monday) is the Medici treasure chest entertaining fans of applied arts with jeweled crucifixes, exotic porcelain, gilded ostrich eggs, and so on). Behind the palace, the huge semi-landscaped Boboli Gardens offer a cool refuge from the city heat (L4,000, Tuesday–Sunday 9:00–17:30, closed Monday).

▲**Brancacci Chapel**—For the best look at the early Renaissance master Masaccio, see his restored frescoes here (L5,000, 10:00–17:00, Sunday 13:00–17:00, closed Tuesday; across the Ponte Vecchio and turn right a few blocks to Piazza del Carmine). The neighborhoods around here are considered the last surviving bits of old Florence.

▲**Piazzale Michelangelo**—Across the river overlooking the city (look for the huge statue of David), this square is worth the half-hour hike, drive, or bus ride (#13 from the train station) for the view. After dark it's packed with local schoolkids feeding their dates slices of watermelon. Just beyond it is the stark and beautiful, crowd-free, Romanesque San Miniato Church.

Evening Side Trip to Siena

Connoisseurs of peace and small towns who aren't into art or shopping (and who won't be seeing Siena otherwise), should consider riding the bus to Siena for the evening (75 min if you take the *"corse rapide"* via the autostrada). Florence has no after-dark magic. Siena *is* after-dark magic. Confirm when the last bus returns.

Sleeping in Florence
(L1,600 = about $1, tel. code: 055)

Sleep Code: **S**=Single, **D**=Double/Twin, **T**=Triple, **Q**=Quad, **b**=bathroom, **s**=shower only, **CC**=Credit Card (Visa, MasterCard, Amex), **SE**=Speaks English, **NSE**=No English. Unless otherwise noted, breakfast is included (but usually optional). English is generally spoken.

The hotel scene in generally crowded and overpriced Florence isn't bad. With good information and a phone call ahead, you can find a stark, clean, and comfortable double with breakfast for L90,000, with a private shower for L120,000. You get roof-garden elegance for L140,000. Most places listed are old and rickety. I can't imagine Florence any other way. Call direct to the hotel. Do not use the tourist office, which costs your host and jacks up the price. Except for Easter, Christmas, May and October, there are plenty of rooms in Florence (dead winter and August are easiest). Budget travelers can call around and find soft prices. If you're staying for three or more nights, ask for a discount. The optional and overpriced breakfast can be a bargaining chip. Call ahead. I repeat, *call ahead.* Places will hold a room until early afternoon. If they say they're full, mention you're using this book.

Sleeping East of the Train Station

East of the station, a handy modern launderette is just off Via Cavour at Via Guelfa 22 red (daily 8:00–22:00, 12 pounds wash and dry for L12,000).

Casa Rabatti is the ultimate if you always wanted to be a part of a Florentine family. It's simple, clean, friendly, and run with motherly warmth by Marcella and her husband Celestino, who speak minimal English (four rooms, D-L70,000, Db-L80,000, L30,000 per bed in shared quad or quint, prices good with this book, no breakfast; 5 blocks from station, Via San Zanobi 48 black, 50129 Florence, tel. 055/212-393).

Soggiorno Pezzati is another quiet little place with six homey rooms (Sb-L55,000, Db-L80,000, no breakfast; Via San Zanobi 22, tel. & fax 055/291-660, Daniela SE).

Hotel Enza has 16 rooms, run by English-speaking Eugenia, who clearly enjoys her work. While Eugenia's chihuahua, Tricky, is tiny, her singles are particularly spacious (S-L65,000, Sb-L70,000, D-L85,000, Db-L120,000, T-L120,000, Tb-L150,000, family loft, discounts for three nights, no breakfast; 6 blocks from station, Via San Zanobi 45 black, 50129 Florence, tel. 055/490-990, fax 055/292-192).

Soggiorno Magliani feels and smells like a great-grandmother's place, central and humble (seven rooms, D-L68,000; at the corner of Via Guelfa and Via Reparata, Via Reparata 1, tel. 055/287-378, run by Vicenza and her English-speaking daughter Christina).

Hotel Loggiato dei Serviti, at the most prestigious address in Florence on the most Renaissance (traffic-free) square in town, gives you Renaissance romance with a place to plug in your hair-dryer (29 rooms, Sb-L200,000, Db-L300,000, family suites, book a month ahead, deals in August, elevator, CC:VMA; Piazza S.S. Annunziata 3, 50122 Florence, tel. 055/289-592, fax 055/289-595). Stone stairways lead you under open-beam ceilings through this 16th-century monastery's elegantly appointed public rooms. The cells, with air conditioning, TVs, mini-bars, and telephones, wouldn't be recognized by their original inhabitants. This place is my kind of classy.

Le Due Fontane Hotel faces the same great square but fills its old building with a modern, business-class ambience. Its air-conditioned rooms are big, modern, and stylish—less memorable and less expensive (57 rooms, Sb-L150,000, Db-L240,000, Tb-L330,000, prices promised by Sr. Borgia through 1998, CC:VMA, elevator; Piazza S.S. Annunziata 14, 50122 Florence, tel. 055/210-185, fax 055/294-461, SE).

Sleeping South of the Station near Piazza Santa Maria Novella (zip code: 50123)

From the station, follow the underground tunnel to Piazza Santa Maria Novella, a pleasant square by day and a little sleazy after dark. (Theft alert where the tunnel surfaces.) It's handy: 3 blocks from the cathedral, near a good launderette (**La Serena,** Monday–Saturday 8:30–20:00, closed Sunday; Via della Scala 30 red; L20,000 for 11 pounds, tel. 055/218-183), cheap restaurants (on Via Palazzuolo, see below), and the bus and train station. There's a great Massaccio fresco (*The Trinity*) in the church on the square (free).

Hotel Universo, a big, group-friendly hotel with stark concrete hallways but fine rooms, is warmly run by a group of gentle men (D-L100,000, Db-L130,000, Tb-L175,000, Qb-L200,000, to get these discounted prices—promised through 1998—you must show this book, CC:VM, elevator; right on Piazza S. M. Novella at #20, tel. 055/281-951, fax 055/292-335, SE).

Hotel Pensione Elite, with eight comfortable rooms, is a good basic value, run warmly by Maurizio and Nadia (Ss-L85,000, Sb-L100,000, Ds-L100,000, Db-L130,000; at end of square with back to church, go right to Via della Scala 12, second floor, tel. & fax 055/215-395, SE).

The nearby **Albergo Montreal** is cheaper, with clean, airy and comfortable rooms but less character (14 rooms, Db-L90,000 with this book through 1998; Via della Scala 43, tel. 055/238-2331, fax 055/287-491, SE).

Pensione Sole, a clean, cozy, family-run place with seven bright rooms, is well-located just off Santa Maria Novella toward the river (S-L50,000, D-L70,000, Db-L90,000, Tb-L120,000, no breakfast; Via del Sole 8, third floor, lots of stairs, tel. & fax 055/239-6094, Anna NSE).

Albergo Concordia is a modern, well-run, and conveniently located place (16 rooms, one fine Sb-L65,000, Db-L100,000, Tb-L125,000, optional breakfast L15,000 extra, prices promised through 1998, CC:VMA, no elevator, filled with school groups February–April; Via dell'Amorino 14, 50123 Florence, tel. & fax 055/213-233, Fabrizio SE).

Pensione Centrale is very central, Old World-comfortable, and run by Marie Therese Blot and Franco, who make you feel right at home (D-L130,000, Db-L170,000 with an "American" breakfast, often filled with American students, CC:VMA; elevator near the Duomo at Via dei Conti 3, tel. 055/215-761, fax 055/215-216).

Pensione Burchianti is a spacious old noble house. Each of its 11 rooms has a bit of old Florence surviving on its walls or ceilings (Sb-L70,000, Ds-L110,000, Db-L120,000, extra bed-L30,000–40,000, L5,000 breakfast, prices promised with this book; midway between the station and the Duomo at Via del Giglio 6, tel. & fax 055/212-796). Friendly Gieuseppe SE.

Pensione Maxim is big, ramshackle, and as close to the sights as possible. You'll feel like a rat in a maze navigating its narrow, dingy halls (23 rooms, D-L100,000, Db-L125,000, T-L130,000, Tb-L160,000, Q-L180,000, Qb-L10,000, CC:VMA, in-house laundry service; Via dei Medici 4, elevator at Via deiCalzaiuoli 11, tel. 055/217-474, fax 055/283-729, e-mail: hotmaxim@tin.it).

Soggiorno Abaco is a bohemian, MTV-kind of place listed in most student guidebooks and run by friendly, guitar-strumming Bruno (seven rooms, S-L65,000, Sb-L80,000, Ds-L100,000, Db-L120,000, extra roommates-L20,000 each; Via Dei Banchi 1, tel. 055/238-1919, fax 055/282-289, SE).

Sleeping on or near the Arno River and Ponte Vecchio

Pensione Bretagna is a classy, Old World-elegant place with thoughtfully appointed rooms. The hotel is run by the very helpful, English-speaking Antonio, Maura, and Marco. Imagine eating breakfast under a painted, chandeliered ceiling overlooking the Arno River (S-L70,000, Ss-L75,000, Sb-L80,000,

D-L105,000, Ds-L120,000, Db-L145,000, Tb-L195,000, including optional L10,000 breakfast, family deals, prices special with this book through 1998, CC:VMA, elevator; just past Ponte San Trinita, at Lungarno Corsini 6, 50123 Firenze, tel. 055/289-618, fax 055/289-619, e-mail: hotelpens.bretagna@agora.stm.it).

Aily Home is a humble, homey, grandmotherly, five-room place tucked away on a peaceful square a block from the Ponte Vecchio (three-night minimum, S-L30,000, D-L60,000, showers-L3,000, elevator; Piazza San Stefano 1, tel. 055/239-6505, Rosaria Franchis NSE).

Sleeping in Oltrarno, South of the River *(zip code: 50125)*

Across the river in the Oltrarno area, between the Pitti Palace and the Ponte Vecchio, you'll still find small traditional crafts shops; neighborly piazzas hiding a few offbeat art treasures; family eateries; two distinctive, moderately priced hotels; two student dorms; and a youth hostel. Each of these places is only a few minutes walk from the Ponte Vecchio.

Hotel La Scaletta is elegant, friendly, and clean, with a dark, cool, labyrinthine floor plan and lots of Old World lounges. Owner Barbara, her son Manfredo, and daughters Bianca and Diana run this well-worn place. Your journal becomes poetry when written on the highest terrace of La Scaletta's panoramic roof garden. If Manfredo is cooking dinner, eat here (D-L120,000, Db-L155,000, T-L155,000, Tb-L190,000, Qb-L220,000, CC:VM, from L10,000–20,000 discount if you pay cash; elevator; Via Guicciardini 13 black, 150 yards up the street from the Ponte Vecchio, next to American Express, tel. 055/283-028, fax 055/289-562, Web site: www.alba.fi.it, e-mail: LaScaletta.htl@dada.it). Reserve well in advance by phone, then confirm your reservation with a fax and send a check.

Pensione Sorelle Bandini is a ramshackle 500-year-old palace on a perfectly Florentine square, with cavernous rooms, museum warehouse interiors, a musty youthfulness, cats, a balcony lounge-loggia with a view, and an ambience that, for romantic bohemians, can be a highlight of Florence. Mimmo or Sr. Romeo will hold a room until 16:00 with a phone call (D-L140,000, Db-L172,000, T-L210,000, Tb-L242,000, includes breakfast, elevator; Piazza Santo Spirito 9, tel. 055/215-308, fax 055/282-761).

Hotel Silla, a classic three-star hotel with cheery, spacious, pastel and modern rooms, is a fine splurge. It faces the river overlooking a park opposite the Santa Croce church (32 rooms, Db-L220,000, CC:VMA, some rooms with air-con; Via dei Renai 5, 50125 Florence, tel. 055/234-2888, fax 055/234-1437, manager Gabrielle SE).

Institute Gould is a Protestant church–run place with 72 beds in 27 rooms and clean, modern facilities (D-L66,000,

Db-L74,000, L37,000 beds in shared doubles, L30,000 in quads; 49 Via dei Serragli, tel. 055/212-576). You must arrive when office is open (Monday–Friday 9:00–13:00, 15:00–19:00, Saturday 9:00–13:00, no check-in on Sunday).

The Catholic-run **Pensionato Pio X-Artigianelli** is more freewheeling and rundown, with 54 beds in 20 rooms, and a midnight curfew (L24,000 beds in three- to five-bed rooms, minimum two nights; Via dei Serragli 106, tel. & fax 055/225-044).

Pension Ungherese, warmly run by Sergio, is good for drivers. It's outside the city center (near Stadio, on route to Fiesole) with easy free street parking and quick bus access into central Florence (Sb-L100,000, Db-L150,000, prices good with this book, extra 7 percent off if you pay cash, CC:VM; Via G. B. Amici 8, tel. & fax 055/573-474, NSE, e-mail: hotel.ungherese@dada.it). It has great singles, a backyard garden terrace, and just-renovated rooms (ask for one on the garden).

Last alternatives: **Ostello Santa Monaca** (L22,000 beds, ten-bed rooms, no breakfast, midnight curfew; very well located a few blocks past Ponte Alla Carraia, Via Santa Monaca 6, tel. 055/268-338, fax 055/280-185), and the classy **Villa Camerata IYHF** hostel (L23,000 per bed and breakfast, four- to ten-bed rooms; ride bus #17A or B then 500-meter walk, tel. 055/601-451) on the outskirts of Florence.

Eating in Florence

Eating in Oltrarno, South of the River
There are several good and colorful restaurants in Oltrarno on or near Piazza Santo Spirito. **Borgo Antico** serves hearty portions to a classy young and local clientele. It's right on a great square with indoor and outdoor seating and worth the extra lire (Piazza Santo Spirito 6 red, tel. 055/210-437). The **Ricchi** bar, #6 on the same square, has fine homemade gelati and outdoor tables shaded by trees (step inside to see the wallful of entries to finish the facade of the Brunelleschi church on the square).

Trattoria Casalinga is an inexpensive and popular standby, famous for its home-cooking (just off Piazza Santo Spirito, near the church at Via dei Michelozzi 9 red, closed Sunday, tel. 055/218-624).

Good food and ambience at reasonable prices are also served at **Trattoria Sabatino** at Borgo S. Frediano 17 blue and **Osteria del Cinghiale Bianco** at Borgo S. Jacopo 43 red (open at 19:00, closed Tuesday and Wednesday, arrive early or call 055/215-706 to reserve).

La Galleria Ristorante is a hard-working family affair with a passion for quality home-cooking in a small modern gallery a block off the Ponte Vecchio (good L20,000 menu, closed Monday, Via Guicciardini 48 red, tel. 055/218-545). Peek into the back to see mama cutting the pasta.

Trattoria Bordino is cozy and friendly, serving fine Florentine cuisine. Its prices aren't cheap, but it's an excellent value (L40,000 dinners, closed Sunday, Via Stracciatella 9 red). Take the second left after crossing Ponte Vecchio and walk under the arch.

Eating near Santa Maria Novella and the Train Station
Two similar chow houses, each offering a L16,000, hearty, family-style, fixed-price menu with a bustling working-class/budget-Yankee-traveler atmosphere, are **Trattoria il Contadino** (Via Palazzuolo 69 red, a few blocks south of the train station, Monday–Saturday 12:00–14:30, 18:15–21:30, closed Sunday, tel. 055/238-2673) and **Trattoria da Giorgio** (across the street at Via Palazzuolo 100 red, Monday–Saturday 12:00–15:00, 18:30–22:00, closed Sunday). Check each before choosing. Get there early or be ready to wait. The touristy **La Grotta di Leo** has a cheap, straightforward menu and edible food (Via della Scala 41 red, closed Wednesday, tel. 055/219-265). And near the recommended Hotel Enza and Via San Zanobi private homes: **Trattoria la Burrasca** is a small inexpensive place serving local-style dishes to Italians in a characteristic setting (12:00–15:00, 19:00–22:00, closed Thursday, near the market at Via Panicale 6r, tel. 055/215-827).

A Quick Lunch near the Sights
I keep lunch in Florence fast and simple, eating in one of count-less self-service places, Pizza Rusticas (holes-in-walls selling pizza by weight), or just picnicking (juice, yogurt, cheese, roll: L8,000). For mountains of picnic produce or just a cheap sandwich and piles of people-watching, visit the huge multi-storied **Mercato Centrale** (7:00–14:00, closed Sunday) in the middle of the San Lorenzo street market. Behind the Duomo, **Snack** (15 Pronconsolo) serves decent cheap lunches. For a reasonably priced pizza with a Medici-style view, try one of the pizzerias on Piazza della Signori. A few blocks behind the Palazzo Vecchio, the cozy **Rosticceria Guilano Centro** serves fine food to go or enjoy there (closed Monday, Via Dei Neri 74 red). **Osteria Vini e Vecchi Sapori** is a colorful hole-in-the-wall serving traditional food, including plates of mixed sandwiches, half a block from Palazzo Vecchio (Tuesday–Sunday 9:30–21:30, closed Monday, Via dei Magazzini 3 red). **Cantinetta dei Verrazzano** is a long established bakery/café/winebar which serves elegant sandwich plates and hot focaccia sandwiches in an elegant old-time setting (open until 21:00, closed Sunday, just off Via Calzaiuoli at Via dei Tavolini 18, tel. 055/268-590).

Transportation Connections—Florence
By train to: Assisi (10/day, 2.5 to 3 hrs), **Orvieto** (6/day, 2 hrs), **Pisa** (2/hr, 1 hr), **La Spezia** (for the Cinque Terre, 2/day direct, 2 hrs, or change in Pisa), **Venice** (7/day, 3 hrs), **Milan** (12/day, 3–5 hrs), **Rome** (hourly, 2.5 hrs), **Naples** (2/day, 4 hrs), **Brindisi** (3/day, 11 hrs with change in Bologna), **Frankfurt**

(3/day, 12 hrs), **Paris** (1/day, 12 hrs overnight), **Vienna** (4/day, 9–10 hrs). Train info: tel. 1478-88088.

Buses: The SITA bus station, a block from the Florence train station, offers service to **San Gimignano** (hourly, 1.75 hrs, L8,000) and **Siena** (hourly, 75-min fast buses or 2-hr slow buses, L10,000, faster than the train). Bus info: tel. 055/483-651; some schedules are in Florence's *Concierge* magazine.

PISA
Pisa was a regional superpower in her medieval heyday (11th, 12th, and 13th centuries), rivaling Florence and Genoa. Its Mediterranean empire, which included Corsica and Sardinia, helped make it a wealthy republic. But the Pisa fleet was beaten (1284, by Genoa) and its port silted up, leaving the city high and dry with only its Piazza of Miracles and its university keeping it on the map.

Pisa's three important sights (the cathedral, baptistery, and bell tower) float regally on the best lawn in Italy. Even as the church was being built, the Piazza del Duomo was nicknamed the Campo dei Miracoli, or "Field of Miracles," for the grandness of the undertaking. The style throughout is Pisa's very own "Pisan Romanesque" (surrounded by what may be Italy's tackiest ring of souvenir stands). This spectacle is tourism at its most crass. Wear gloves.

Orientation (tel. code: 050)
Tourist Information: TI offices are at the train station (daily 9:00–19:00, tel. 050/42291) and at the Leaning Tower. The Pisa tourist board has a scheme to get you into its neglected secondary sights. Various sight combination tickets run from L10,000 for any two sights to L15,000 for the works.

Arrival in Pisa: By Train—Train travelers bus easily from the station in the center, over the Arno River, and to the Duomo. Bus #1 (for Duomo) leaves from the bus circle to the right of the station every ten minutes. Buy your L1,300 ticket from the tobacco/magazine kiosk in the station's main hall.

Sights—Pisa
▲▲**Leaning Tower**—This most famous example of Pisan Romanesque architecture was leaning even before its completion. Notice how the architect, for lack of a better solution, kinked up the top section. The 294 tilted steps to the top are closed while engineers work to keep the bell tower from toppling. The formerly clean and tidy area around the tower is now a construction zone. Steam pipes drying out the subsoil and huge weights are working together to stop the leaning (but not straighten out the tower). For a quick lunch, the pizzeria/trattoria La Buca (near tower at Via S. Maria and Via G. Tassi) is a decent value.

▲▲**Cathedral**—The huge Pisan Romanesque cathedral, with its richly carved pulpit by Giovanni Pisano, is artistically more important than its more famous bell tower (L2,000, daily 8:00–13:00, 15:00–20:00).

Baptistery—The baptistery, the biggest in Italy, with a pulpit by Nicolo Pisano (1260) which inspired Renaissance art to follow, is interesting for its great acoustics (L5,000, daily 9:00–19:30, in front of the cathedral). If you ask nicely and leave a tip, the doorman uses the place's echo power to sing haunting harmonies with himself. Notice that even the baptistery leans about 5 feet. (The Nicolo Pisano pulpit and carvings in Siena were just as impressive to me—in a more enjoyable atmosphere.)

Transportation Connections—Pisa
By train to: Florence (hourly, 60 min), **La Spezia** (hourly, 60 min, milk-run from there into coastal villages), **Siena** (change at Empoli: Pisa–Empoli, hourly, 30 min; Empoli–Siena, hourly, 60 min). Even the fastest trains stop in Pisa, and you'll very likely be changing trains here whether you plan to stop or not. Train info: tel. 1478-88088.

VENICE (VENEZIA)

Soak all day in this puddle of elegant decay. Venice is Europe's best-preserved big city. It's a car-free urban wonderland of 100 islands, laced together by 400 bridges and 2,000 alleys, and doing well on the artificial respirator of tourism.

Born in a lagoon 1,500 years ago as a refuge from barbarians, Venice is overloaded with tourists and slowly sinking (unrelated facts). In the Middle Ages, the Venetians, becoming Europe's clever middleman for east-west trade, created a great trading empire. By smuggling in the bones of St. Mark (San Marco, in about 830), Venice gained religious importance as well. With the discovery of America and new trading routes to the Orient, Venetian power ebbed. But as Venice fell, her appetite for decadence grew. Through the 17th and 18th centuries Venice partied on the wealth accumulated through earlier centuries as a trading power.

Today Venice is home to about 75,000 people in its old city, down from a peak population of around 200,000. While there are about 500,000 in greater Venice (counting the mainland, not counting tourists), the old town has a small-town feel. Locals seem to know everyone. To see small-town Venice through the touristic flak, explore the back streets and try a Stand-Up Progressive Venetian Pub-Crawl Dinner.

Planning Your Time

Venice is worth at least a day on even the speediest tour. Hyper-efficient train travelers take the night train in and/or out. Sleep in the old center to experience Venice at its best: early and late. For a one-day visit: cruise the Grand Canal, do the major San Marco sights (the square, Doge's Palace, St. Mark's Basilica), see the

Venice

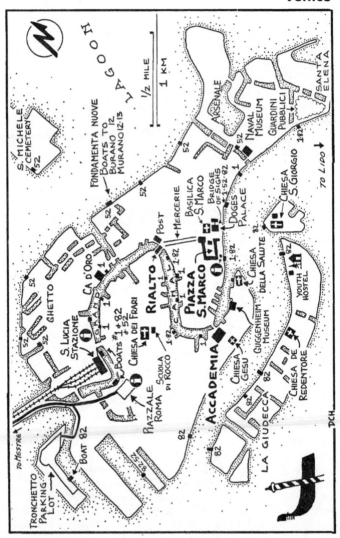

Church of the Frari for art, and wander the back streets on a pub crawl (see Eating, below). Venice's greatest sight is the city itself. Make time to simply wander. While doable in a day, Venice is worth two. It's a medieval cookie jar, and nobody's looking.

Orientation (tel. code: 041)

The island city of Venice is shaped like a fish. Its major thorough-fares are canals. The Grand Canal winds through the middle of the fish, starting at the mouth where all the people and food enter, passing under the Rialto Bridge, and ending at St. Mark's Square (San Marco). Park your 20th-century perspective at the mouth, and let Venice swallow you whole.

Venice is a car-less kaleidoscope of people, bridges, and odorless canals. The city has no real streets, and addresses are hopelessly confusing. There are six districts: San Marco (most touristy), Castello (behind San Marco), Cannaregio (from the station to the Rialto), San Polo (other side of the Rialto), Santa Croce, and Dorsoduro. Each district has about 6,000 address numbers. Luckily it's easy to find your way, since many street corners have a sign pointing you to the nearest major landmark, such as San Marco, Accademia, Rialto, and Ferrovia (the train station). To find your way, navigate by landmarks, not streets. Obedient visitors stick to the main thoroughfares as directed by these signs and miss the charm of back-street Venice.

Tourist Information

Tourist information offices are at the train station (8:00–19:00, crowded and surly) and near St. Mark's Square (much more help-ful, at the vaporetto stop; from the church go to the lagoon, turn right, walk about 150 yards, and you'll run into it, Monday–Saturday 9:00–19:00 in summer, closed Sunday, and early off-season, tel. 041/529-8730). Pick up a free city map, the week's events, the latest museum hours, and confirm your sightseeing plans. The free periodical entertainment guide, *Un Ospite de Venezia* (a monthly listing of events, nightlife, museum hours, train and vaporetto schedules, emergency telephone numbers, and so on) is at the TI or fancy hotel reception desks. The cheap Venice map on sale at postcard racks has much more detail than the TI map. Also consider the little sold-with-the-postcards guidebook, with a city map and explanations of the major sights.

Arrival in Venice

A 2-mile-long causeway (highway and train lines) connects Venice to the mainland. Mestre, the sprawling mainland industrial base of Venice, has fewer crowds, cheaper hotels, plenty of parking lots, but no charm. Don't stop here. Trains regularly connect Mestre with the Santa Lucia station (6/hr, 5 min).

By Train: Venice's Santa Lucia train station plops you right into the old town on the Grand Canal, an easy vaporetto ride or fascinating 40-minute walk from San Marco. Upon arrival, skip the station's TI (San Marco's is better), confirm your departure plan (good train info desk), consider stowing unnecessary heavy bags at *deposito*, then walk straight out of the station to the canal.

The dock for vaporettos #1 and #82 is on your left. Buy a L4500 ticket at the window and hop on a boat for downtown (direction Rialto or San Marco).

By Car: At Venice, the freeway ends like Medusa's head. Follow the green lights directing you to a parking lot with space. The standard place is Tronchetto (across the causeway and on the right) with a huge new multi-storied garage (L40,000 per day, half-price with a discount coupon from your hotel). From there you'll find travel agencies masquerading as tourist information offices and vaporetto docks for the boat connection (#82) to the town center. Don't let taxi boatmen con you out of the cheap vaporetto ride. Parking in Mestre is much cheaper (open-air lots L8,000 per day, L10,000-a-day garage across from the Mestre train station).

By Plane: A handy shuttle bus (30 minutes) or the cheaper L1500 bus #5 (60 minutes) connects the airport with the Tronchetto vaporetto stop. Those jetting in can get directly to San Marco by speedboat (L17,000).

Helpful Hints
The Venice fly-trap lures us in and takes our money any way it can. Count your change carefully. Accept the fact that Venice was a tourist town 400 years ago. It was, is, and always will be crowded. While 80 percent of Venice is actually an untouristy place, 80 percent of the tourists never notice. Hit the back streets.

Get Lost: Venice is the ideal town to explore on foot. Walk and walk to the far reaches of the town. Don't worry about getting lost. Get as lost as possible. Keep reminding yourself, "I'm on an island and I can't get off." When it comes time to find your way, just follow the directional arrows on building corners, or simply ask a local, *"Dové San Marco?"* ("Where is St. Mark's?") People in the tourist business (that's most Venetians) speak some English. If they don't, listen politely. Watch where their hands point. Then say *"Grazie"* and head off in that direction.

Rip-offs, Theft, and Help: While petty thieves work the crowded main streets, vaporetto boats, and docks, the dark, late-night streets of Venice are safe. A new service called *Venezia No Problem* aids tourists who've been mistreated by any Venetian business (tel. 041/167-355920).

Money: Bank rates vary. I like the Banco di Sicilia, a block toward San Marco from Campo San Bartolomeo. American Express, famous for its "no commission," makes up for that with mediocre rates. Non-bank exchange bureaus will cost you $10 more than a bank for a $200 exchange. A 24-hour cash machine near the Rialto vaporetto stop exchanges U.S. dollars and other currencies into lire at fair rates.

The "Rolling Venice" Youth Discount Pass: This L5,000 pass—giving those under 30 discounts on sights, transportation,

Downtown Venice

TO GHETTO, TRAIN STN,
& TRONCHETTO

TO FONDAMENTA
NUOVE &
BOATS TO
MURANO &
BURANO

STRADA
CA d'ORO
NOV
HOSP.

¼ MILE

TO TRAIN STN

FISH
MKT.

RIALTO
Post

FRARI

CAMPO
S. POLO

RUGA
VECCHIA

CAMPO
S. GIO.
PAOLO

SCUOLA
SAN
ROCCO

GRAND CANAL

CAMPO
S. LUCA

MERCE

S.
ZAC.

CAMPO S.
ANGELO

CAMPO
MANIN

MANDOL

FUSERI

CAMP.

DOGE'S
PAL.

CAMPO
S. STEFANO

LA
FENICE

WC

SCHIA

CAMPO
S. MAURIZIO

LARGA

S. MOISE

SAN
MARCO

ACCADEMIA

Acca-
demia
Museum

PEGGY
GUGGENHEIM
MUSEUM

SALUTE

DOGANA
(CUSTOM'S HOUSE)

TO
LIDO

S.
GIORGIO

DCH

ZATTERE

TO GUIADECCA
& HOSTEL

LODGING:

1. GUERATTO
2. STURION
3. CANADA
4. BRUNO
5. CANEVA
6. RIVA
7. PIAVA
8. TIEPOLO
9. DONI
10. CORONA

11. MASETTO
12. MARIN
13. GAMBERO
14. CAMPIELLO
15. PAGANELLI
16. ACCADEMIA
17. GALLERIA
18. ALBORETTI

● 1·82 VAPORETTI STOPS
   W/ LINE #'S
●····● TRAGHETTO ROUTES

information on cheap eating and sleeping—is worthwhile for a long stay (Monday–Friday 10:00–13:00, Tuesday and Thursday also open 15:00–18:00, closed Wednesday; behind American Express office, Corte Contarina 1529; tel. 041/274-7637).

Water: Venetians pride themselves on having pure, safe, and tasty tap water piped in from the foothills of the Alps (which you can actually see from Venice bell towers on crisp, clear winter days).

Pigeon Poop: If bombed by a pigeon, resist the initial response to wipe it off immediately—it'll just smear into your hair. Wait until it dries and flake it off cleanly.

Laundry: A handy *lavanderia* (Laundromat) near St. Mark's and near most of my hotel listings is the full-service Laundry Gabriella (Monday–Friday 8:00–19:00, 985 Rio Terra Colonne, one bridge off the Merceria near San Zulian church, down Calle dei Armeni, tel. 041/522-1758). The closest Laundromat to the Rialto is Lavanderia S.S. Apostoli (8:30–12:00, 15:00–19:00, closed Sunday, tel. 041/522-6650, on Campo S.S. Apostoli). At either place you can get 9 pounds of laundry washed and dried for L15,000. Drop it by in the morning, pick it up that afternoon. (Call to be sure they're open.)

Etiquette: Walk on the right and don't loiter on bridges. Picnicking is technically forbidden (keep a low profile). Dress modestly. Men should keep their shirts on. When visiting St. Mark's or other major churches, men and women should cover their knees and shoulders.

Getting Around Venice

The public transit system is a fleet of motorized bus-boats called *vaporetti*. They work like city buses except that they never get a flat, the stops are docks, and if you get off between stops, you may drown. For most, only two lines matter: #1 is the slow boat, taking 45 minutes to make every stop along the entire length of the Grand Canal; and #82 is the fast boat which zips down the Grand Canal in 20 minutes, stopping only at Tronchetto (car-park), Piazzale Roma (bus station), Ferrovia (train station), Rialto Bridge, and San Marco. Buy a L4,500 ticket before boarding or (for an extra fee) from a conductor on board. There are 24-hour (L15,000) and 72-hour (L30,000) passes, but I've never ferried enough to merit purchasing one (although it's fun to be able to hop on and off carelessly).

Only three bridges cross the Grand Canal, but *traghetti* (little L700 ferry gondolas, marked on better maps) shuttle locals and in-the-know tourists across the Grand Canal at seven handy locations (see downtown Venice map). Take advantage of these time-savers. They can also save money. For instance, while most tourists take the L4,500 vaporetto to connect St. Mark's with Salute Church, a L700 *traghetto* also does the job.

Grand Canal Tour of Venice

Grab a front seat on boat #82 (fast, 20 minutes) or #1 (slow, 45 minutes) to cruise the entire Canale Grande from Tronchetto (car-park) or Ferrovia (train station) to San Marco. If you can't snag a front seat, lurk nearby and take one when it becomes available, or find a seat outside at the very back of the boat. While Venice is a barrage on the senses that hardly needs a narration, these notes give the cruise a little meaning and help orient you to this great city. Some city maps (on sale at postcard racks) have a handy Grand Canal map on the back side.

Venice, built in a lagoon, sits on pilings: pine trees driven 15 feet into the mud. More than 100 canals—about 25 miles in length—drain the city, dumping like streams into the Grand Canal.

Venice is a city of palaces. The most lavish were built fronting this canal. This cruise is the only way to really appreciate the front doors of this unique and historic chorus line of mansions from the days when Venice was the world's richest city. Strict laws prohibit any changes in these buildings, so while landowners gnash their teeth, we can enjoy Europe's best-preserved medieval city—slowly rotting. Many of the grand buildings are now vacant. Others harbor chandeliered elegance above mossy ground floors.

Start at Tronchetto (the bus and car-park) or the train station (a good example of Fascist architecture built during Mussolini's time). F.S. stands for "Ferrovie dello Stato," the Italian state railway system. The bridge at the station is one of only three that cross the Canale Grande.

Vaporetto stop #4 (San Marcuola-Ghetto) is near the world's original ghetto, when this area was set aside as the local Jewish quarter in 1516. This urban island developed into one of the most closely knit business and cultural quarters of any Jewish community in Italy.

As you cruise, notice the traffic signs. Venice's main thoroughfare is busy with traffic. You'll see all kinds of boats: taxis, police boats, garbage, even brown-and-white UPS boats. Venice's 500 sleek, black, graceful gondolas are a symbol of the city. They cost up to $35,000 apiece and are built with a slight curve so that one oar propels them in a straight line.

At the Ca d'Oro stop (stop #6), notice the lacy Gothic palace of the same name. Named the "House of Gold," it's considered the most elegant Venetian Gothic palace on the canal. Unfortunately its art gallery interior shows nothing of its palatial origins.

After vaporetto stop #6, on the right, the outdoor produce market bustles with people in the morning, but is quiet with only a few grazing pigeons the rest of the day. Can you see the traghetto gondola ferrying shoppers—standing like Washington crossing the Delaware—back and forth? The huge post office, usually with a postal boat moored at its blue posts, is on the left just before the Rialto Bridge.

A major landmark of Venice, the Rialto Bridge, is lined with shops and tourists. Built in 1592, with a span of 42 meters, it was an impressive engineering feat in its day. Locals call the summit of this bridge the "icebox of Venice" for its cool breeze. But it's also a great place to kiss. *Rialto* means "high river." The restaurants lining the canal beyond the bridge feature high prices and low quality.

The Rialto, a separate town in the early days of Venice, has always been the commercial district, while San Marco was the religious and governmental center. Today a street called the Merceria connects the two, providing travelers with human traffic jams and a gauntlet of shopping temptations.

Take a deep whiff of Venice. What's all this nonsense about stinky canals? All I smell is my shirt. By the way, how's your captain? Smooth dockings? To get to know him, stand up in the bow and block his view.

Notice how the rich marble facades are just a veneer covering no-nonsense brick buildings. And notice the characteristic chimneys.

After the San Silvestro stop you'll see (on the right) a 13th-century admiral's palace. Venetian admirals marked their palaces with twin obelisks.

After the San Tomá stop look down the side canal (on the right) before the bridge to see the fire station and the fireboats ready to go.

The wooden Accademia Bridge crosses the Grand Canal and leads to the Accademia Gallery, filled with the best Venetian paintings. Put up in 1932 as a temporary fix for the original iron one, locals liked it, so it stayed.

Cruising under the bridge, you'll get a classic view of the Salute Church, built as a thanks to God when the devastating plague of 1630 passed. It's claimed that more than a million trees were used for the foundation alone. Much of the surrounding countryside was deforested by Venice. Trees were needed both to fuel the furnaces of its booming glass industry and to prop up this city in the mud.

The low white building on the right (before the church) is the Peggy Guggenheim Gallery. She willed the city a fine collection of modern art.

Just before the Salute stop (on the right), the house with the big view windows and the red and wild Andy Warhol painting on the living room wall was lived in by Mick Jagger. In the 1970s, this was famous as Venice's rock-and-roll-star party house.

The building on the right with the golden ball is the Dogana da Mar, a 16th-century customs house. Its two bronze Atlases hold a statue of Fortune riding the ball.

As you prepare to de-boat at stop #15—San Marco—look from left to right out over the lagoon. A wide harborfront walk leads past the town's most elegant hotels to the green area in the distance. This is the public garden, the only sizable park in town. Farther out is the Lido, Venice's beach. It's tempting with its sand and casinos, but its car traffic breaks into the medieval charm of Venice.

The dreamy church that seems to float is the architect Palladio's San Giorgio. It's just a scenic vaporetto ride away. Find the Tintoretto paintings in the church (such as the *Last Supper*) and take the elevator up the bell tower for a terrific, crowd-free view (L3000, daily 10:00–12:30, 14:30–17:30, tel. 041/522-7827). Beyond San Giorgio (to your right, if you're at San Marco) is a residential chunk of Venice called the Guidecca.

Get out at the San Marco stop. Directly ahead is Harry's Bar. Hemingway drank here when it was a characteristic no-name osteria and the gondoliers' hangout. Today, of course, it's the overpriced hangout of well-dressed Americans who don't mind paying triple for their drinks to make the scene. Piazza San Marco—a much better place to make the scene—is just around the corner.

For more vaporetto fun, ride a boat around the city (ask for the *circulare*, cheer-kew-lah-ray) and out into the lagoon. Plenty of boats leave from San Marco for the beach (Lido), and speedboats offer tours of nearby islands: Burano is a quiet, picturesque fishing and lace town, Murano is the glassblowing island, and Torcello has the oldest churches and mosaics, but is an otherwise dull and desolate island. Boat #12 takes you to these remote points slower and cheaper.

Sights—Venice, on St. Mark's Square

▲▲▲**St. Mark's Square (Piazza San Marco)**—Surrounded by splashy and historic buildings, Piazza San Marco is filled with music, lovers, pigeons, and tourists by day and is your private rendezvous with the Middle Ages late at night. Europe's greatest dance floor is the romantic place to be. This is the first place to flood, has Venice's best tourist information office (go to lagoon, turn right), and offers fine public restrooms (Albergo Diorno— "day hotel," L500 WC, shower, between Piazza San Marco and American Express office).

With your back to the church, survey one of Europe's great urban spaces and the only square in Venice to merit the title "Piazza." Nearly two football fields long, it's surrounded by the offices of the republic. On the right are the "old offices" (16th-century Renaissance). On the left are the "new offices" (17th-century Baroque). Napoleon enclosed the square with the more simple and austere neoclassical wing across the far end and called this "the most beautiful drawing room in Europe."

The clock tower, a Renaissance tower built in 1496, marks the entry to the Mercerie, the main shopping drag connecting San Marco with the Rialto. From the piazza you can see the bronze men (Moors) swing their huge clappers at the top of each hour. In the 17th century, one of them knocked an unsuspecting worker off the top and to his death—probably the first-ever killing by a robot. Notice the world's first "digital" clock on the tower facing the square (with dramatic flips every five minutes).

For a slow and pricey evening thrill, invest L10,000 (plus L5000 if the orchestra plays) in a beer or coffee in one of the elegant cafés with the dueling orchestras. If you're going to sit awhile and savor the scene, it's worth the splurge. For the most thrills L1500 can get you in Venice, buy a bag of pigeon seed and become popular in a flurry.

▲▲**St. Mark's Basilica**—Since about 830, it has housed the saint's bones. The mosaic above the door at the far left of the church shows two guys carrying Mark's coffin into the church. Mark looks pretty grumpy after the long voyage from Egypt. The church has 4,000 square meters of Byzantine mosaics. The best and oldest are in the atrium (turn right as you enter and stop under the last dome). Face the piazza, gape up (it's OK, no pigeons), and study the story of Noah, the Ark, and the flood (two by two, the wicked being drowned, Noah sending out the dove, a happy rainbow, and a sacrifice of thanks). Now face the church and read clockwise the story of Adam and Eve that rings the bottom of the dome. Step inside the church (stairs on right lead to bronze horses) and notice the rolling mosaic marble floor. Stop under the central dome and look up for the Ascension. (Modest dress, no shorts or bare shoulders, free, Monday–Saturday 9:45–19:30, Sunday 14:00–17:00, tel. 041/522-5205.) See the schedule board in the atrium listing two free English guided tours of the church each week. The church is particularly beautiful when lit at the 18:45 Mass on Saturday, 14:00–17:00 Sunday, and some middays.

In the museum upstairs (L4,000, daily 9:45–17:00), you can see an up-close mosaic exhibition, a fine view of the church interior, a view of the square from the horse balcony, and (inside, in their own room) the newly restored original bronze horses. These well-traveled horses, made during the days of Alexander the Great (fourth century B.C.), were taken to Rome by Nero, to Constantinople/Istanbul by Constantine, to Venice by crusaders, to Paris by Napoleon, back "home" to Venice when Napoleon fell, and finally indoors out of the acidic air.

The treasury and altarpiece of the church (requiring two L3,000 admissions) give you the best chance outside of Istanbul or Ravenna to see the glories of Byzantium. Venetian crusaders looted the Christian city of Constantinople and brought home piles of lavish loot (until the advent of TV evangelism, perhaps the lowest point in Christian history). Much of this plunder is stored in the treasury of San Marco (*tesoro*). As you view these treasures, remember most were made in A.D. 500, while western Europe was still rooting in the mud. Behind the high altar lies the body of St. Mark ("Marxus") and the Pala d'Oro, a golden altarpiece made (A.D. 1000–1300) with 80 Byzantine enamels. Each shows a religious scene set in gold and precious stones. Both of these sights are interesting and historic, but neither is as much fun as two bags of pigeon seed.

▲▲▲**Doge's Palace (Palazzo Ducale)**—The seat of the Venetian government and home of its ruling duke, or *doge*, this was the most powerful half-acre in Europe for 400 years (L14,000 combo-ticket

includes Correr museum also, daily 8:30–19:00, last entry at 17:30).
While each room has a short English description, the fast-moving
90-minute tape-recorded guided tour wand is wonderfully done and
worth the L7,000 if you don't have *Mona Winks* and you're planning
to really understand the palace. (Vagabond lovers, sightseeing cheek
to cheek, can crank up the volume and split one wand).

The palace was built to show off the power and wealth of the
republic and remind all visitors that Venice was number one. Built
in Venetian Gothic style, the bottom has pointy arches and the top
has an Eastern or Islamic flavor. Its columns sat on pedestals, but
in the thousand years since they were erected, the palace has settled into the mud, and they have vanished.

Enjoy the newly restored facades from the courtyard. Notice a
grand staircase (with nearly naked Moses and Paul Newman at the
top). Even the most powerful visitors climbed this to meet the doge.
This was the beginning of an architectural power trip. The doge, the
elected-for-life king of this "dictatorial republic," lived near the halls
of power with his family on the first floor. From his lavish quarters,
you'll follow the one-way tour through the public rooms of the top
floor, finishing with the Bridge of Sighs and the prison. The place is
wallpapered with masterpieces by Veronese and Tintoretto. Don't
worry much about the great art. Enjoy the building.

In room 12, the Senate Room, the 200 senators met,
debated, and passed laws. From the center of the ceiling, Tintoretto's *Triumph of Venice* shows the city in all her glory. Lady
Venice, in heaven with the Greek gods, stands high above the
lesser nations who swirl respectfully at her feet with gifts.

The armory shows remnants of the military might the empire
employed to keep the east-west trade lines open (and the local
economy booming). Squint out the window at the far end for a
fine view of Palladio's San Georgio Church and the Lido (cars,
casinos, crowded beaches) in the distance.

After the huge brown globes, you'll enter the giant Hall of
the Grand Council (180 feet long, capacity 2,000) where the entire
nobility met to elect the senate and doge. Ringing the room are
portraits of 76 doges (in chronological order). One, a doge who
opposed the will of the Grand Council, is blacked out. Behind the
doge's throne, you can't miss Tintoretto's monsterpiece, *Paradise*.
At 1,700 square feet, this is the world's largest oil painting. Christ
and Mary are surrounded by a heavenly host of 500 saints.

Walking over the Bridge of Sighs, you'll enter the prisons. The
doges could sentence, torture, and jail their opponents secretly
and in the privacy of their own homes. As you walk back over the
bridge, wave to the gang of tourists gawking at you.

▲**Museo Civico Correr**—The entire San Marco complex is
evolving into one grand sight. The until-lately rarely visited city
history museum is now included (whether you like it or not) with
the Doge's Palace admission. It offers dusty bits of Venice's

glory days (globes, flags, coins, paintings, and so on, all well-explained in English) and fine views of Piazza San Marco. The second floor is a lot of walking and worth a look only if you like musty old oil paintings (Pinacotek–English descriptions) and exhibits on the unification of Italy (Risorgimento–no English). Entry is on the square opposite the church (L14,000 combo ticket with Doge's Palace, daily 9:00–19:00, November–May 9:00–17:00).

▲Campanile di San Marco—Ride the elevator 300 feet to the top of the bell tower for the best view in Venice. Photos on the wall inside show how this bell tower crumbled into a pile of bricks in 1902, 1,000 years after it was built. For an ear-shattering experience, be on top when the bells ring (L6,000, daily 9:00–18:30). The golden angel at its top always faces into the wind.

More Sights—Venice

▲▲Galleria dell' Accademia—Venice's top art museum is packed with the painted highlights of the Venetian Renaissance (Bellini, Veronese, Tiepolo, Giorgione, Testosterone, and Canaletto). It's just over the wooden Accademia Bridge (L12,000, Monday–Saturday 9:00–19:00, Sunday 9:00–14:00; expect morning and midday delays, as they allow only 300 visitors at a time, come late to miss crowds, tel. 041/522-2247). There's a fine pizzeria at the bridge (Snack Bar Accademia Foscarini)

▲Peggy Guggenheim Collection—This popular collection of far-out art, including works by Picasso, Chagall, and Dali, offers one of Europe's best reviews of the art styles of the 20th century (L12,000, Wednesday–Monday 11:00–18:00, closed Tuesday, near the Accademia).

▲▲Chiesa dei Frari—This great Gothic Franciscan church, an artistic highlight of Venice featuring three great masters, offers more art per lira than any other Venetian sight. Freeload on English-language tours to get the most out of the Titian *Assumption* above the high altar. Then move one chapel to the right to see Donatello's wood carving of St. John the Baptist almost live. And for the climax, continue right through an arch into the sacristy to sit before Bellini's *Madonna and the Saints*. The genius of Bellini, perhaps the greatest Venetian painter, is obvious in the pristine clarity, believable depth, and reassuring calm of this three-paneled altarpiece. Notice the rich colors of Mary's clothing and how good it is to see a painting in its intended setting. For many, these three pieces of art make a visit to the Accademia Gallery unnecessary (or they may whet your appetite for more). Before leaving, check out the neoclassical pyramid-shaped tomb of Canova and (opposite that) the grandiose tomb of Titian, the Venetian. Compare the carved marble Assumption behind his tombstone portrait with the painted original above the high altar (L2,000, Monday–Saturday 9:00–12:00, 14:30–18:00, free on Sunday 15:00–18:00).

▲**Scuola di San Rocco**—Next to the Frari church, another lavish building bursts with art, including some 50 Tintorettos. The best paintings are upstairs, especially the *Crucifixion* in the smaller room. View the neck-breakingly splendid ceiling paintings with one of the mirrors (*specchio*) available at the entrance (L8,000, daily 9:00–17:30, last entrance 17:00). For *molto* Tiepolo (14 stations of the cross), drop by the nearby Church of San Polo.

Ca' Rezzonico—This 18th-century Grand Canal palazzo is now open as the Museo del '700 Veneziano, offering a good look at the life of Venice's rich and famous in the 1700s, along with frequent temporary exhibits for an additional admission fee (L12,000, Saturday–Thursday 10:00–16:00, closed Friday, at a vaporetto stop of the same name).

▲**Gondola Rides**—A rip-off for some but a traditional must for romantics; gondoliers charge about L100,000 for a 40-minute ride (less during the day). You can divide the cost—and the romance—by up to six people (some take seven if you beg and they're hungry). Glide through nighttime Venice with your head on someone else's shoulder. Follow the moon as it sails past otherwise unseen buildings. Silhouettes gaze down from bridges, while window glitter spills onto the black water. You're anonymous in the city of masks as the rhythmic thrust of your striped-shirted gondolier turns old crows into songbirds. For cheap gondola thrills, stick to the L700 one-minute ferry ride on a Grand Canal traghetto, or hang out on a bridge along the gondola route and wave at (or drop leftover pigeon seed on) romantics.

▲**Glassblowing**—Don't go all the way to Murano Island to see glassblowing demonstrations. A demo's a demo. For the handiest show, wait by one of several glassworks near St. Mark's Square and follow any tour group into the furnace room for a fun and free ten-minute show. You'll usually see a vase and a "leetle 'orse" made from molten glass. The commercial that always follows in the show-room is actually entertaining. Prices around St. Mark's have a sizable tour-guide commission built in. Serious glass-shoppers buy at small shops on Murano Island.

Santa Elena—For a pleasant peek into a completely untouristy residential side of Venice, catch the boat from San Marco to the neighborhood of Santa Elena (at the fish's tail). This 100-year-old suburb lives as if there were no tourism. You'll find a kid-friendly park, a few lazy restaurants, and beautiful sunsets over San Marco.

Old-Time Venetian Concerts—Vivaldi is as trendy here as Strauss in Vienna and Mozart in Salzburg. In fact you'll find frilly young Vivaldis all over town hawking concert tickets. The TI has a list of this week's concerts (tickets from L30,000 up). The Venice Orchestra plays traditional Vivaldi concerts in 18th-century attire at the Scuola Grande di San Giovanni Evengelista (L30,000–50,000, tel. 041/520-7823).

Sights—Venice Lagoon

Several interesting islands hide out in the Venice Lagoon. **Burano,**
famous for its lace-making, is a sleepy island with a sleepy community—village Venice without the glitz. Lace fans enjoy Burano's
Scuola di Merletti (L5000, Tuesday–Sunday 0:00–16:00, closed
Monday, tel. 041/730-034).
Torcello, another lagoon island, is dead except for its church,
which claims to be the oldest in Venice (L2,000, daily 10:00–
12:30, 14:00–17:00, tel. 041/730–084). It's impressive for its
mosaics, but not worth a look on a short visit unless you really
have your heart set on Ravenna but can't make it there. The island
of **Murano,** famous for its glass factories, has the Museo Vetrario,
which displays the very best of 700 years of Venetian glassmaking
(L8,000, Thursday–Tuesday 10:00–17:00, closed Wednesday, tel.
041/739-586). The islands are reached easily but slowly by
vaporetto (from the Fondamente Nuove dock). Four-hour speedboat tours of these three lagoon destinations leave twice a day
from the dock near the Doge's Palace.

Sleeping in Venice
(L1,600 = about $1, tel. code: 041)

Sleep Code: **S**=Single, **D**=Double/Twin, **T**=Triple, **Q**=Quad,
b=bathroom, **t**=toilet only, **s**=shower only, **CC**=Credit Card
(Visa, MasterCard, Amex), **SE**=Speaks English, **NSE**=No
English. Breakfast is included unless otherwise noted. I never met
an elevator in a Venetian hotel.
      Reserve a room as soon as you know when you'll be in town.
Call first to see what's available. Follow up with a fax unless
you're already on the road. Most places will take a credit card for
a deposit. If everything's full, don't despair. Call a day or two in
advance and fill in a cancellation. While many stay in a nearby
less-crowded place and side trip to Venice, I can't imagine not
sleeping downtown. If you arrive on an overnight train, your
room may not be ready. Drop your bag at the hotel and dive right
into Venice.
      Don't book (or confirm) through the tourist office (which pock-
ets a L15,000-per-person "deposit"). The prices I've listed here are
for those who book direct. Prices may be cheaper (or soft) off-season.
If on a budget, ask for a cheaper room or a discount. I've listed location
and character be my priorities. Rooms are clean, quiet, and generally
stark, with high ceilings, slick little modern pre-fabshower/toilet/sink
units, bare floors, and rickety freestanding furniture.

Sleeping near St. Mark's Square
(zip code: 30124)

Hotel Caneva is a funky, clean, vinyl-feeling place with plain,
big and bright rooms, lots of canal ambience and a wonderful
family-run feeling. Seventeen of its 23 rooms overlook a canal

Venice Lagoon

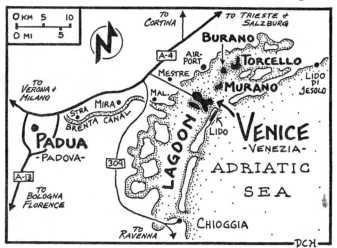

(S-L70,000, Sb-L100,000, D-L100,000, Db-L140,000, T-L135,000, Tb-L190,000, CC:VMA; midway between Rialto and San Marco near Chiesa la Fava but very quiet, Ramo Dietro La Fava #5515, 30122 Venezia, tel. 041/522-8118, fax 041/520-8676, Massimo and his family SE).

Hotel Riva, with gleaming marble hallways and bright modern rooms, is romantically situated on a canal along the gondola serenade route. You could actually dunk your breakfast rolls in the canal (but don't). Sandro may hold a corner (*angolo*) room if you ask. Reconfirm reservations you think you've made here. It's behind San Marco where the canals Rio di San Zulian and Rio del Mondo Nouvo hit Rio Canonica o Palazzo (two fourth-floor view D with adjacent showers-L120,000, Db-L150,000, Tb-L220,000; Ponte dell' Angelo, tel. 041/522-7034, fax 041/528-5551, unenthusiastic receptionists don't speak English).

Locanda Piave, with 12 fine rooms above a bright and classy lobby, is newly remodeled and very comfortable (D-L140,000, Db-L200,000, T-180,000, Tb-L260,000, family suites, air-con, CC:VMA; from Campo Santa Maria Formosa, go behind the church, over a bridge and 50 yards to Ruga Giuffa #4838/40, Castello, 30122 Venezia, tel. 041/528-5174, fax 041/523-8512, Mirella and Paolo SE).

Albergo Tiepolo, a simple old seven-room place tucked away down an alley just off Campo SS. Filippo e Giacomo, is pricey but well-located (D-L95,000, Db-L140,000, T-L130,000, Tb-L160,000, Q-160,000, Qb-L200,000; Campo SS. F e G #4510, tel. & fax 041/523-1315).

Albergo Doni is a dark, hardwood, clean, and quiet place with 12 dim-but-classy rooms run by a likable smart-aleck named Gina, who promises my readers one free down-the-hall shower each day (D-L100,000, Db-L140,000, Tb-L190,000, ceiling fans, prices with this book; use credit card to secure telephone reservations but must pay in cash; Riva Schiavoni, San Zaccaria N. #4656 Calle del Vin, tel. & fax 041/522-4267, Nick and Gina SE). From the Bridge of Sighs walk east along Riva Degli Schiavoni, over another bridge, take the first left (Calle del Vin), and follow the signs.

Albergo Corona is a squeaky-clean, confusing Old World place with nine hard-to-get basic rooms (D-L75,000, showers L3,000, lots of stairs; find Campo SS Filippo e Giacomo behind San Marco, go down Calle Sacristia, take first right then go left on Calle Corona to #4464, tel. 041/522-9174, SE).

Alloggi Masetto, well-located with four dirt-cheap rooms, is a homey place filled with birds, goldfish, and stacks of magazines, and run by Irvana Artico, a rude landlady who surprises you with pretty good English (D-L50,000, Db-L60,000, T-L70,000, Tb-75,000, confirm prices carefully two-night minimum, no breakfast, shower rapido or suffer Irvana's wrath; just off San Marco—from American Express head toward San Marco, first left, first left again through "Contarina" tunnel, follow yellow sign to Commmune di Venezia, jog left again and see her sign, Sotoportego Ramo Contarina, Frezzeria, tel. 041/523-0505).

Alloggi Alla Scala, a comfy and tidy seven-room place run by Senora Andreina della Fiorentina, is very central, tucked away on a quiet square with a famous spiral stairway called Corte Contarini del Bovolo (small Db-L100,000, big Db-L120,000, extra bed-L35,000, breakfast extra; near Campo Manin #4306, San Marco, tel. 041/521-0629, fax 041/522-8958).

Locanda Gambero, with 30 rooms, is the biggest one-star hotel in the San Marco area (S-L65,000–70,000, D-L110,000, Ds-L130,000, Db-L150,000, T-L160,000, Ts-L180,000, Tb-L200,000, CC:VM; a straight shot down Calle dei Fabbri from the Rialto vaporetto #1 dock; from Piazza San Marco walk down Calle dei Fabbri, over one bridge to #4685, tel. 041/522-4384, fax 041/520-0431, SE). These prices are as firm as ripe bananas. Gambero runs the pleasant art-deco "La Bistrot," serving old-time Venetian cuisine.

Sleeping near Waterfront and Doge's Palace

These places rub drainpipes with Venice's most palatial five-star hotels, about one canal down from the Bridge of Sighs on or just off the Riva degli Schiavoni waterfront promenade. Each, while pricey for the location and not particularly friendly, is professional and comfortable.

Hotel Campiello is a lacy and bright little 16-room place, ideally located 50 yards off the waterfront (Db-L200,000–250,000,

CC:VMA, all air-con; behind Hotel Savoia, Riva Schiavoni, San Zaccaria #4647, tel. 041/520-5764, fax 041/520-5798).

Albergo Paganelli is right on the Riva degli Schiavoni with a few incredible view rooms (D-L150,000, small Db-L190,000, Db-L220,000 or L250,000 with canal view, Tb-L275,000, request "*con vista*" for view, most rooms are air-con, CC:VMA; at the San Zaccaria vaporetto stop, Riva degli Schiavoni #4182, Campo S. Zaccaria 4687, Castello, 30122 Venezia, tel. 041/522-4324, fax 041/523-9267, SE). With spacious rooms, carved and gilded headboards, chandeliers, and hair-dryers, this very hotelesque place is a good value. Seven of their 22 rooms are in a less interesting *dependencia* a block off the canal.

Sleeping near the Rialto Bridge (zip code: 30125)

Locanda Sturion, with air-con and all the modern comforts, is pricey because it overlooks the Grand Canal (Db-L280,000, Tb-L360,000, Qb-L380,000, canal view rooms cost extra, CC:VMA, miles of stairs; 100 yards from the Rialto Bridge opposite the vaporetto dock, San Polo, Rialto, Calle Sturion #679, 30125 Venezia, tel. 041/523-6243, fax 041/522-8378, SE, e-mail: sturion@tin.it). They require a bank check for a deposit.

Hotel Canada has 25 small, bright rooms (two D with adjacent bath-L170,000, Db-L200,000, CC:VM; Castello San Lio #5659, 30122 Venezia, tel. 041/522-9912, fax 041/523-5852, SE). A "typical noble Venetian home," it's ideally located on a small, lively square, just off Campo San Lio between the Rialto and San Marco.

Hotel da Bruno, 100 yards from Hotel Canada, has a central location, nice rooms, and all the comforts (Db-L220,000, CC:VMA; Salizzada S. Lio #5726, Castello, 30122 Venezia, tel. 041/523-0452, fax 041/522-1157, SE).

Albergo Guerrato, overlooking a handy and colorful produce market, one minute from the Rialto action, is run by friendly, creative and hard-working Roberto and Piero Caruso. Georgio takes the night shift. Their 800-year-old building is Old World simple, airy, and wonderfully characteristic (D-L105,000, Db-L145,000, T-L140,000, Tb-L190,000, Q-L180,000, Qb-L230,000, including a L4000 city map, prices promised through 1998 with this book, CC:VM; walk over the Rialto away from San Marco, go straight about 3 blocks, turn right on Calle drio la Scimia—not Scimia, the block before— and you'll see the hotel sign, Calle drio la Scimia #240a, 30125 San Polo, tel. & fax 041/522-7131 or 528-5927, everyone speaks English). My tour groups completely book this place for 50 nights each year. Sorry. If you fax without calling first, no reply within three days means they are booked up. (It's best to call first.)

Sleeping near the Accademia

This quiet area, next to the best painting gallery in town, is a ten-minute walk from any other sightseeing action with three classy hotels and a cheap monastery.

Pension Accademia fills the 17th-century Villa Maravege. While its 27 comfortable and air-conditioned rooms are nothing extraordinary, you'll feel aristocratic gliding through its grand public spaces and lounging in its breezy garden (one S-L85,000, Sb-L160,000, Db-L270,000 or less off-season, family deals, CC:VMA, must send check to reserve; on corner of Rio della Toletta and Rio di San Trovaso 200 yards from gallery, Dorsoduro #1058, Venezia 30123, tel. 041/523-7846, fax 041/523-9152, SE).

Hotel Galleria is a compact and velvety little 10-room place (S-L80,000, Sb-L115,000, D-L115,000, Db-L140,000 to L170,000 depending on size and season; overlooking canal next to gallery, Dorsoduro #878a, 20123 Venezia, tel. & fax 041/520-4172).

Hotel Agli Alboretti is a cozy, family-run, 25-room place in a quiet neighborhood a block behind the Accademia Museum (Db-L220,000, air-con, CC:VMA; 100 yards from the Accademia vaporetto stop at #884 Accademia, tel. 041/523-0058, fax 041/521-0158, SE). You'll have breakfast in a shady patio.

Foresteria Domus Cavanis is a simple church-run dorm offering cheap beds (S-L50,000, D-L75,000, breakfast extra; next to Hotel Agli Alboretti at #912 on Rio Antonio Foscarini, tel. & fax 041/528-7374).

Sleeping near the Train Station

Hotel Marin is three minutes from the train station but completely out of the touristic bustle of the Lista di Spagna. Just renovated, cozy, and cheery, it seems like a 19-bedroom home the moment you cross the threshold (S-L70,000, D-L100,000, Db-L128,000, T-L135,000, Tb-L170,000, Q-L170,000, Qb-L200,000, prices good with this book and if you pay cash, CC:VMA; San Croce #670b, tel. & fax 041/718-022 or 041/721-485, e-mail: htl.marin@gpnet.it). It's family-run by helpful, friendly, English-speaking Bruno, Nadia, and son Samuel (they have city maps). It's across the canal from the train station behind the green dome (follow Rialto signs for 100 yards, look left).

Eating in Venice

Touristy restaurants are the scourge of Venice. I stick to small *cicchetti* bars (see Pub Crawl, below) or simple pizza-like dinners at scenic locations. You'll dine far better for less in other cities in Italy—go for the setting or the pub-crawl experience in Venice. For speed, value, and ambience, you can get a filling plate of local-style tapas at nearly any of the bars described below.

A key to cheap eating in Venice is bar snacks, especially stand-up mini-meals in out-of-the-way bars. Order by pointing. *Panini* (sandwiches) are sold fast and cheap at bars everywhere. Pizzerias are cheap and easy. Those that sell take-out by the slice or gram are cheapest. Fast food and self-serve places are easy to find.

The **produce market** that sprawls for a few blocks just past the Rialto Bridge (best 8:00–13:00, closed Sunday) is a great place to assemble a picnic. The nearby street, Ruga Vecchia, has good bakeries and cheese shops. Side lanes in this area are speckled with fine little hole-in-the-wall munchie bars.

The **Mensa DLF**, the public transportation workers' cafeteria, is cheap and open to the public (11:00–14:30, 18:00–21:30, tel. 041/716-242). Leaving the train station, turn right on the Grand Canal, walk about 150 yards, and you'll run into it.

The Stand-Up Progressive Venetian Pub-Crawl Dinner

A tradition unique to Venice in Italy is a *giro di ombre* (pub crawl)—ideal in a city with no cars. My favorite Venetian dinner is a pub crawl. I've listed plenty in walking order for a quick or extended crawl below. If you've crawled enough, most of the listed bars make a fine one-stop, sit-down dinner.

Venice's residential back streets hide plenty of characteristic bars with countless trays of interesting toothpick-munchie food (*cicchetti*). This is a great way to mingle and have fun with the Venetians. Real *cicchetti* pubs are getting rare in these fast-food days, but locals appreciate the ones that survive. As always, the best way to find a landmark is to ask locals, *"Dové . . . ?"* and go where they point. Since Venice is so quiet after dark, you can generally follow the crowds to these places.

Try fried mozzarella cheese, blue cheese, calamari, artichoke hearts, and anything ugly on a toothpick. Ask for a *piatto misto* (mixed plate). Or try *"Un classico piatto di cicchetti misti da cinque mila lire"* (a plate of assorted appetizers for L5,000) or go up to L10,000, depending upon how much food you want. Drink the house wines. A small glass of house red or white wine (*ombre rosso* or *ombre bianco*) or a small beer (*birrino*) costs about L1,000. *Vin bon,* Venetian for fine wine, may run you L2,000 to 3,000 per little glass. Meat and fish (*pesce:* PAY-shay) munchies are expensive; veggies (*verdura*) are cheap, around L4,000 for a meal-sized plate. Bread sticks (*grissini*) are free for the asking. A good last drink is *Fragolino,* the local sweet red wine. A liter of house wine costs around L7,000. Bars don't stay open very late, and the *cicchetti* selection is best early, so start your evening by 18:30. Most bars are closed on Sundays. You can stand around the bar or grab a table in the back for the same price. (I'd appreciate any feedback on this plan.)

Cicchetteria *near Rialto Bridge and* Campo San Bartolomeo

Start your crawl near the Rialto Bridge. The first places are on the San Polo side. Ai do Ladroni is a block past the bridge towards San Marco. And the last couple are a few blocks beyond the Campo.

Cantina "Do Mori" is famous with locals (since 1462) and savvy travelers (since 1962) as a classy place for fine wine and *frangobollo* (a spicy selection of 20 tiny sandwiches called "stamps"). Choose from the featured wines in the barrel on the bar. From Rialto bridge walk 200 yards down Ruga degli Orefici (opposite San Marco and ask, stand-up only, arrive early before *cicchetti* are gone, Monday–Saturday 17:00–20:30, closed Sunday, San Polo 429, tel 041/522-5401). The rough-and-tumble **Cantina All' Arco** across the lane is worth a quick *ombra*.

Antica Ostaria Ruga Rialto is less expensive than Do Mori and offers tables, a busier/younger crowd, and a better selection of munchies (near the bright yellow Chinese restaurant sign, just off corner of Ruga Rialto and Ruga degli Orefici, San Polo 692, closed Monday, tel. 041/521-1243). There are several other *cicchetti* bars within a block or two. You could track down: Cantina Do Spade, Vini da Pinto, and Osteria Enoteca Vivaldi (on Campo A. Aponal).

Osteria Ai do Ladroni is a great new place specializing in *"Veneziane piccola cucina"* and popular with locals, half a block off the main Rialto-Campo San Bartolomeo drag (Monday–Saturday 8:00–24:00, closed Sunday, tel. 041/522-7741). They also serve good L10,000 pasta plates.

Osteria "Alla Botte" Cicchetteria is an atmospheric place packed with a young, local, bohemian jazz clientele. It's good for a light meal or a *cicchetti* snack with wine (2 short blocks off Campo San Bartolomeo in the corner behind the statue, tel. 041/520-9775, notice the "day after" photo showing a debris-covered Venice after the notorious 1989 Pink Floyd open-air concert).

If the statue on the Campo San Bartolomeo walked backwards 20 yards, turned left and went under a passageway, he'd hit **Rosticceria San Bartolomeo**. This isn't a pub, but they have a likably surly staff, great fried *mozzarella e prosciutto* (L2,000), and L1,000 glasses of wine. Continue over a bridge to Campo San Lio (a good landmark), go left at the Hotel Canada, and walk straight over another bridge into Osteria Al Portego. This fine local-style bar has plenty of snacks and *cicchetti* (Monday–Saturday 9:00–22:00, closed Sunday, tel. 041/522-9038). From here, ask *"Dové Santa Maria di Formosa?"*

Cicchetteria *near Campo Santa Maria di Formosa*

Campo Santa Maria di Formosa is just plain atmospheric. For a balmy outdoor sit, you could split a pizza with wine on the square. **Piero's Bar all' Orologio**, opposite the canal, has the best setting and friendly service. *Capricciosa* means the house specialty. Or munch a slice of "pizza to go" on the square from **Cip Ciap Pizza Rustica** (over the bridge behind the SMF gelateria on Calle del Mondo Novo, open until 21:00, closed Tuesday). For your salad course, there's a fruit-and-vegetable stand on the square next to the water fountain (open until about 20:00).

Pub Crawl

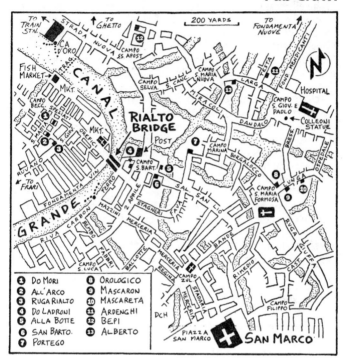

From Bar all' Orologio (on Campo S.M. di Formosa), with your back to the church (follow yellow sign to SS Giov e Paolo), head down the street to **Osteria Mascaron** (Gigi's bar, best selection by 19:30, closes at 24:00 and on Sunday).

Gigi also runs **Enoteca Mascareta**, with less food and more wine, 30 yards farther down the street (#5183, tel. 041/523-0744). The piano sounds like they dropped it in the canal, but the wine was saved. If you want more *cicchetti*, check out the two places described below in the Campo Santi Apostoli section. If you're feeling like the painting of Bacchus on the wall looks, it's time for . . .

Gelato: There's a decent *gelateria* on Campo di Formosa (closes at about 20:00 and on Thursday). There's a top-quality place 2 blocks away on the corner of Calle San Antonio and Calle Paradiso. Or head toward San Marco where the *gelaterias* stay open later (the best is opposite the Doge's Palace, by the two columns, on the bay). There's also a good late-hours *gelateria* midway between Campo San Bartolomeo and the Rialto Bridge selling cheap, small cones (on the left).

You're not a tourist, you're a living part of a soft Venetian night ... an alley cat with money. Streetlamp halos, live music, floodlit history, and a ceiling of stars make St. Mark's magic at midnight. Shine with the old lanterns on the gondola piers where the sloppy Grand Canal splashes at the Doge's Palace ... reminiscing. Comfort the four frightened tetrarchs (ancient Byzantine emperors) under the moon where the Doge's Palace hits the basilica. Cuddle history.

Eating near Campo San Bartolomeo
The very local, hustling **Rosticceria San Bartolomeo Gislon** is a cheap—if confusing—self-service restaurant on the ground floor (L7,000 pasta, L1000 wine, prices listed at door, no cover or service charge). It's on Calle della Bissa #5424 (starting from the statue in the San Bartolomeo square, it's 20 yards behind the statue to its left, under a passageway; 9:00–21:30, tel. 041/522-3569). While old "example" dishes are left on display, the kitchen whips up fine pastas. Good but pricier meals are served at the full-service restaurant upstairs. Take out or grab a table.

Eating near Campo Santi Apostoli
Trattoria da Bepi caters to a local crowd and specializes in good seafood and Venetian cuisine. Bepi's son, Loris, speaks English and makes a mean *licorice grappa* (midway between the Rialto Bridge and Ca d'Oro, next to the Santi Apostoli church and my recommended laundromat, tel. 041/528-5031, closed Tuesday).

Two colorful osterias are good for *cicchetti*, wine-tasting, or a simple, rustic, sit-down meal surrounded by a boistrous local ambience: **Osteria da Alberto** (18:00–21:30, closed Sunday, midway between Campo Santi Apostoli and Campo S.S. Giovanni e Paolo, next to Ponte de la Panada on Calle larga Giacinto Gallina) and **Osteria Candela** on Calle de l'Oca. You'll find local pubs such as Volante's (near Alberto's) and in the side streets opposite Campo St. Sofia across Strada Nuova.

Antiche Cantine Ardenghi de Lucia e Michael is a leap of local faith. Michael, an effervescent former Murano glass salesman, and his wife Lucia, cook for 20 people a night by reservation only. You must call first. You pay L60,000 and trust them to wine, dine, and serenade you in Venetian class. The evening can be quiet or raucous depending on who and how many are eating. There's no sign and the door's locked. Find #6369 and knock. From Campo S. Giovanni e Paolo, pass the church-looking hospital (notice the illusions painted on its facade), go over the bridge to the left, and take the first right to #6369 (8:30–2:00, closed Sunday, tel. 041/523-7691).

Transportation Connections—Venice
By train to: Verona (hourly, 90 min), **Florence** (6/day, 3 hrs), **Dolomites** (8/day to Bolzano, 4 hrs with one transfer; catch bus from Bolzano into mountains), **Milan** (hrly, 3–4 hrs), **Rome**

(6/day, 5 hrs, slower overnight), **Naples** (change in Rome), **Brindisi** (3/day, 11 hrs), **Cinque Terre** (two La Spezia trains go directly to Monterosso al Mare daily, 6 hrs, at 9:58 and 14:58), **Bern** (4/day, change in Milan, 8 hrs), **Munich** (5/day, 8 hrs), **Paris** (3/day, 11 hrs), **Vienna** (4/day, 9 hrs). Train and couchette reservations (L24,000) are easily made at the American Express office near San Marco. Venice train info: tel. 1478-88088.

HILL TOWNS OF
CENTRAL ITALY

Break out of the Venice-Florence-Rome syndrome. There's more
to Italy! Experience the slumber of Umbria, the texture of
Tuscany, and the lazy towns of Lazio. For starters, here are a few
of my favorites.

Siena seems to be every Italy connoisseur's pet town. In
my office whenever Siena is mentioned, someone moans, "Siena? I
luuuv Siena!" San Gimignano is the quintessential hill town, with
Italy's best surviving medieval skyline. Assisi—visited for its hometown boy, St. Francis, who made very good—is best after dark.
Orvieto, one of the most famous hill towns, is an ideal springboard for a trip to tiny Civita. Stranded alone on its pinnacle in a
vast canyon, Civita's the most lovable.

Planning Your Time

Siena, the must-see town, has the easiest train and bus connections. On a quick trip, consider spending three nights in Siena
(with a whole-day side trip into Florence and a day to relax and
enjoy Siena). Whatever you do, enjoy a sleepy medieval evening
in Siena. After an evening in Siena, its major sights can be seen
in half a day. San Gimignano is an overrun, pint-sized Siena.
Don't rush Siena for San Gimignano.

Civita di Bagnoregio is the great pinnacle town. A night in
Bagnoregio (via Orvieto bus) with time to hike to the town and
spend three hours makes the visit worthwhile. Two nights and
an entire day is a good way to keep your pain/pleasure ratio in
order.

Assisi is the third-most-visit-worthy town. It has half a day of
sightseeing and another half a day of wonder. While a zoo by day,
it's a delight at night.

Hill Towns of Central Italy

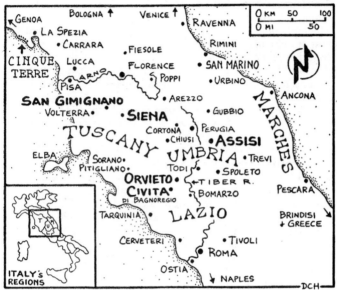

SIENA

Seven hundred years ago, Siena was a major military power in a class with Florence, Venice, and Genoa. With a population of 60,000, it was even bigger than Paris. The town was weakened by a disastrous plague in 1348. In the 1550s her bitter rival Florence really salted her, making Siena forever a non-threatening backwater. Siena's loss became our sightseeing gain, as its political and economic irrelevance pickled it purely Gothic. Today Siena's population is still 60,000 compared to Florence's 420,000.

Siena's thriving historic center, with traffic-free red-brick lanes cascading every which way, offers Italy's best Gothic city experience. Most people do Siena, just 30 miles south of Florence, as a day trip, but it's best experienced after dark. While Florence has the blockbuster museums, Siena has an easy-to-enjoy soul: courtyards sport flower-decked wells, alleys dead-end at rooftop views, and the sky is a rich blue dome. Right off the bat, Siena becomes an old friend.

For those who dream of a Fiat-free Italy, this is it. Sit at a café on the red-bricked main square. Take time to savor the first European city to eliminate automobile traffic (1966), and then, just to be silly, wonder what would happen if they did it in your city.

Orientation (tel. code: 0577)

Siena lounges atop a hill, stretching its three legs out from Il
Campo. This main square is the historic meeting point of Siena's
neighborhoods. The old center is nearly pedestrians-only. And
most of those pedestrians are students from the local university.
Everything I mention is within a 15-minute walk of the square.
Navigate by landmarks, following the excellent system of street-
corner signs. The typical visitor sticks to the San Domenico-Il
Campo axis.

Tourist Information: Pick up the excellent and free topo-
graphical town map from the main TI on Il Campo (#56, look
for the yellow Change sign, Monday–Saturday 8:30–19:30,
Sunday mornings in summer, tel. 0577/280-551).

Arrival in Siena: From Siena's train station, buy a L1,300
bus ticket from the yellow machine near the exit, cross the
square, and board any orange city bus heading for Piazza del
Sale. Your hotel is probably within a ten-minute walk.

From the autostrada, drivers take the Porta San Marco exit
and follow the Centro, then "Stadio" signs (stadium, soccer ball).
The soccer-ball signs take you to the stadium lot (L1,300/hour,
L15,000/day) at the huge bare-brick San Domenico church. You
can drive into the pedestrian zone (a pretty ballsy thing to do)
only to drop bags at your hotel. You can park free in the lot
below the Albergo Lea, white-striped spots behind Hotel Villa
Liberty, and behind the fortezza. (Note the L200,000 tow fee
incentive to learn the days of the week in Italian).

Sights—Siena

Siena is one big sight. Its essential individual sights come in two
little clusters: the square (city hall, museum, tower) and the cathedral (baptistery, cathedral museum with its surprise viewpoint).
Check these sights off, and you're free to wander.

▲▲▲**Il Campo**—Siena's great central piazza is urban harmony
at its best. Like a people-friendly stage set, its gently tilted floor
fans out from the tower and city hall backdrop. It's the perfect
invitation to loiter. Think of it as a trip to the beach without
sand or water. Il Campo was located at the historic junction of
Siena's various competing districts, or *contrada*, on the old marketplace. The brick surface is divided into nine sections, repre-
senting the council of nine merchants and city bigwigs who ruled
medieval Siena. Don't miss the Fountain of Joy at the square's
high point, with its pigeons politely waiting their turn to gin-
gerly tightrope down slippery snouts to slurp a drink, and with
the two naked guys about to be tossed in. At the base of the
tower, the Piazza's chapel was built in 1348 as a thanks to God
for ending the Black Plague (after it killed more than a third of
the population). The market area behind the city hall, a wide-

Siena

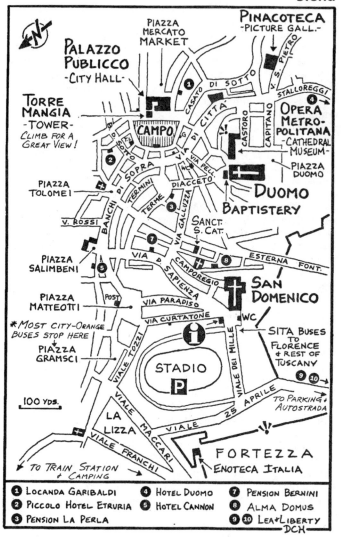

Legend:
1. LOCANDA GARIBALDI
2. PICCOLO HOTEL ETRURIA
3. PENSION LA PERLA
4. HOTEL DUOMO
5. HOTEL CANNON
7. PENSION BERNINI
8. ALMA DOMUS
9. 10. LEA+LIBERTY

open expanse since the Middle Ages, originated as a farming area within the city walls to feed the city in times of seige.

▲**Museo Civico**—The *Palazzo Pubblico* (City Hall), at the base of the tower, has a fine and manageable museum housing a good sample of Sienese art. You'll see, in the following order, the Sala

Risorgimento with dramatic scenes of Victor Emanuel's unification of Italy (surrounded by statues that don't seem to care); the
chapel with impressive inlaid wood chairs in the choir; and the
Sala del Mappamondo, with Simone Martini's *Maesta* (Enthroned
Virgin) facing the faded *Guidoriccio da Fogliano* (a mercenary providing a more concrete form of protection). Next is the Sala della
Pace, which has two interesting frescoes showing "The Effects of
Good and Bad Government." Notice the whistle-while-you-work
happiness of the utopian community ruled by the utopian government (in the best-preserved fresco) and the fate of a community ruled by politicians with more typical values (in a terrible
state of repair). The message: without justice there can be no
prosperity. Later you'll see a particularly gruesome *Slaughter of
the Innocents*. The big stairs lead to a loggia with a nothing-
special view (L6,000, Monday–Saturday 9:00–19:00, Sunday and
daily off-season 9:00–13:30, tel. 0577/292-111).

▲**City Tower (Torre del Mangia)**—Siena gathers around its
city hall, not its church. It was a proud republic and its "declara-
tion of independence" is the tallest secular medieval tower in
Italy, the 100-yard-tall Torre del Mangia (named after a hedo-
nistic watchman who consumed his earnings like a glutton con-
sumes food; his statue is in the courtyard, to the left as you
enter). Its 300 steps get pretty skinny at the top, but the reward
is one of Italy's best views (L5,000, daily 10:00–18:00 or 19:00,
limit of 30 towerists at a time, avoid the midday crowd).

The Palio—The feisty spirit of each of Siena's 17 *contrada*
lives on. These neighborhoods celebrate, worship, and compete
together. Each even has its own historical museum. Contrada
pride is evident any time of year in the colorful neighborhood
banners and parades. (If you hear distant drumming, run to it
for the medieval action). But *contrada* pride is most visible twice
a year (July 2 and August 16), when they have their world-
famous Palio di Siena. Ten of the 17 neighborhoods compete
(chosen by lot), hurling themselves with medieval abandon into
several days of trial races and traditional revelry. On the big day,
Il Campo is stuffed to the brim with locals and tourists, as the
horses charge wildly around the square in this literally no-holds-
barred race. Of course, the winning neighborhood is the scene
of grand celebrations afterward. The grand prize: Simply prov-
ing your *contrada* is *numero uno*. All over town, sketches and
posters depict the Palio. The TI has a free scrapbook-quality
Palio brochure with English explanations. While the actual
Palio really packs the city, you could side trip in from Florence
to see horse-race trials each of the three days before the big day
(usually at 9:00 and 19:45).

▲▲▲**The Duomo**—Siena's cathedral is as Baroque as Gothic
gets. The striped facade is piled with statues and ornamentation;
the interior is decorated from top to bottom. The heads of 172

popes peer down from the ceiling over the fine inlaid art on the floor. This is one busy interior.

To orient yourself in this *panforte* of Italian churches, stand under the dome and think of the church floor as a big clock—you're the middle, the altar is high noon. You'll find the *Slaughter of the Innocents* roped off on the floor at 10:00, Pisano's pulpit between two pillars at 11:00, Bernini's chapel at 3:00, two Michelangelo statues (next to snacks, shop, and WC) at 7:00, the library at 8:00, and a Donatello statue at 9:00. Take some time with the floor mosaics in the front. Nicolo Pisano's wonderful pulpit is crowded but delicate Gothic story-telling from 1268. To understand why Bernini is considered the greatest Baroque sculptor, step into his sumptuous *Cappella della Madonna del Voto.* This last work in the cathedral, from 1659, is enough to make a Lutheran light a candle. Move up to the altar and look back at the two Bernini statues: St. Jerome playing the crucifix like a violinist lost in beautiful music, and Mary Magdalene in a similar state of spiritual ecstasy. The Piccolomini altar is most interesting for its two Michelangelo statues (the lower big ones). Paul, on the left, may be a self-portrait. Peter, on the right, resembles Michelangelo's more famous statue of Moses. Originally contracted to do 15 statues, Michelangelo left the project early (1504) to do his great *David* in Florence. The Piccolomini Library (worth the L2,000 entry), brilliantly frescoed with scenes glorifying the works of a pope from 500 years ago, contains intricately decorated, or "illuminated," music scores and a Roman copy of three Greek graces. Donatello's statue of St. John the Baptist is being restored (church open 7:30–19:30, less in off-season, modest dress required).

Santa Maria della Scala—This newly opened and renovated old hospital (opposite the Duomo entrance) displays a rich treasury and a lavishly frescoed hall. The frescoes show medieval Siena's innovative healthcare and social welfare system in action. Unfortunately the high-tech gadgetry and signs are entirely in Italian (L5,000, daily 10:30–15:30).

▲**Baptistery**—Siena is so hilly that there wasn't enough flat ground to build a big church on. What to do? Build a big church and prop up the overhanging edge with the baptistery. This dark and quietly tucked-away cave of art is worth a look (and L3,000) for its cool tranquility and the bronze carvings of Donatello (the six women, or angels) and Ghiberti on the baptismal font (open same hours as the Duomo).

▲▲**Cathedral Museum (Opera Metropolitana)**—Siena's most enjoyable museum, on the Campo side of the church (look for the yellow signs), was built to house the cathedral's art. The ground floor is filled with the cathedral's original Gothic sculpture by Pisano (who spent ten years here carving and orchestrating the decoration of the cathedral in the late 1300s) and a fine Donatello *Madonna and Child.* Upstairs to the left awaits a private audience with Duccio's *Maesta* (Enthroned Virgin). Pull up a chair and study one of the great pieces of medieval art. What was the flip side of the *Maesta* (displayed on the opposite wall), with 26 panels—the medieval equivalent of pages—shows scenes from the passion of Christ. At the end of the top floor, a little sign directs you to the "panorama." Climb to the first landing, then take the skinnier second spiral for Siena's surprise view. Look back over the Duomo, then consider this: When rival republic Florence began its grand cathedral, proud Siena decided to build the biggest church in all Christendom. The existing cathedral would be used as a transept. You're atop what would have been the entry. The wall below you, connecting the Duomo with the museum of the cathedral, was as far as Siena got before a plague killed the city's ability to finish the project. Were it completed, you'd be looking straight down the nave (L6,000, daily 9:00–19:15, closing at 18:30 in spring and fall, 13:30 off-season, tel. 0577/283-048).

Church of San Domenico—This huge brick church is worth a quick look. The simple, bland interior fits the austere philosophy of the Dominicans. Walk up the steps in the rear of the church for a look at various paintings from the life of Saint Catherine, patron saint of Siena and, since 1939, of all Italy. Halfway up the church on the right, you'll find her head (free, daily 7:00–13:00, 15:00–17:30, less in winter).

Sanctuary of Saint Catherine—A few downhill blocks toward the center from San Domenico (follow signs to the Santuario di Santa Caterina), step into Catherine's cool and peaceful home. Siena remembers its favorite hometown girl, a simple, unschooled, but almost mystically devout girl who, in the mid-1300s, helped get the pope to return from France to Rome. Pilgrims have come here since 1464. Wander around to enjoy art depicting scenes from her life. Her room is downstairs (free, daily 9:00–12:30, 15:30–18:00, via Tiratoio).

▲The Pinacoteca (National Picture Gallery)—Siena was a power in Gothic art. But the average tourist, wrapped up in a love affair with the Renaissance, hardly notices. This museum takes you on a walk through Siena's art, chronologically from the 12th through 15th centuries. For the casual sightseer, the Sienese art in the city hall and cathedral museums is adequate. But art fans enjoy this opportunity to trace the evolution of Siena's delicate and elegant art (L8,000, Monday 8:30–13:30, Tuesday–Saturday 9:00–19:00, Sunday 8:00–13:00, tel. 0577/281-161). From the Campo, walk out Via di Citta to Piazza di Postierla and go left on San Pietro.

Tours by Roberto—Roberto Bechi is a hardworking Sienese tour guide who runs a tour business on the internet. Roberto, who ran a restaurant in the U.S.A. for years and is married to an American, communicates well with Americans. His passions are Sienese culture and local cuisine. He tailors half-day ($40 per person) and full-day ($80 per person, less for groups) tours of Siena and the region by mini-bus. For info and to book a tour, contact him at tel. 0577/704-789, fax 0577/48627, Web site: www.zaslon.si/roberto, e-mail: tourrob@box.tin.it.

Sleeping in Siena
(L1,600 = about $1, tel. code: 0577, zip code: 53100)

Sleep Code: **S**=Single, **D**=Double/Twin, **T**=Triple, **Q**=Quad, **b**=bathroom, **t**=toilet only, **s**=shower only, **CC**=Credit Card (**V**isa, **M**asterCard, **A**mex), **SE**=Speaks English, **NSE**=No English. Breakfast is generally not included. Have breakfast on Il Campo or in a nearby bar.

Finding a room is tough during Easter or for the Palio in early July and mid-August. Call ahead, as Siena's few budget places are listed in all the budget guidebooks. While day-tripping tour groups turn the town into a Gothic amusement park in mid-summer, Siena is basically yours in the evenings and off-season. Nearly all listed hotels lie between Il Campo and the church of San Domenico.

Lavarapido Wash and Dry is a modern coin-op self-service Laundromat (L12,000 per 8 kilo load in an hour, daily 8:00–22:00, near the Campo at Via di Pantaneto 38).

Sleeping near Il Campo

Each of these first listings is forgettable but inexpensive and just a horse-wreck away from one of Italy's most wonderful civic spaces.

Piccolo Hotel Etruria, a good bet for a real hotel with all the comforts but not much soul, is just off the square (S-L53,000, Sb-L63,000, Db-L100,000, Tb-L135,000, Qb-L170,000, breakfast-L6,000, CC:VMA; with back to the tower, leave Il Campo to the right, Via Donzelle 1-3, tel. 0577/288-088, fax 0577/288-461).

Albergo Tre Donzelle is a plain, institutional, but decent place next door that makes sense only if you think of Il Campo as your terrace (S-L40,000, D-L66,000, Db-L86,000; Via Donzelle 5, tel. 0577/280-358, fax 0577/223-933, Senora Iannini SE).

Pension La Perla is a funky, jumbled, 13-room place with a narrow maze of hallways, basic rooms, and a laissez-faire environ-ment (Sb-L60,000, Db-L90,000, Tb-L125,000, rooms have tiny box showers; a block off the square on Piazza Independenza at Via della Terme 25, tel. 0577/47144). Attilio and his American wife, Deborah, take reservations only a day or two ahead. Ideally, call the morning you'll arrive.

Hotel Duomo is the best in-the-old-town splurge, a classy place with spacious, elegant rooms (Sb-L130,000, Db-L200,000, Tb-L270,000, includes breakfast, CC:VMA, elevator; follow Via di Citta, which becomes Via Stalloreggi, to Via Stalloreggi 38; tel. 0577/289-088, fax 0577/43043, SE).

Hotel Cannon d'Oro, a few blocks up Via Banchi di Sopra, is spacious and group-friendly (30 rooms, Sb-L90,000, Db-L110,000, prices promised through 1998 with this book, family deals, CC:VMA; Via Montanini 28, tel. 0577/44321, fax 0577/280-868, SE).

Locanda Garibaldi is a modest, very Sienese restaurant-albergo. Gentle Marcello wears two hats, running a busy restaurant with seven neglected doubles upstairs. This is a fine place for dinner but a bit noisy and dirty for some to sleep in (D-L75,000, T-L100,000, no credit cards, takes reservations only a few days in advance; half a block downhill off the square at Via Giovanni Dupre 18, tel. 0577/284-204, NSE).

Sleeping closer to San Domenico Church

These hotels are listed in order of closeness to Il Campo—max ten minutes' walk. The first two enjoy views of the old town and cathedral (which sits floodlit before me as I type). The first three are the best values in town.

Albergo Bernini makes you part of a Sienese family in a modest, clean home with nine newly renovated rooms. Friendly Nadia and Mauro, who welcome you to picnic on their spectacular view terrace for breakfast or dinner, get the "we try hardest in Siena" award. The mynah bird (Romeo) actually says *"ciao"* as you come and go from the terrace (Sb-L95,000, D-L100,000, Db-L120,000, family deals, prices drop off season and for drop-ins; midnight curfew; on main San Domenico-Il Campo drag at Via Sapienza 15, tel. & fax 0577/289-047, NSE but has fun trying).

Alma Domus is ideal—unless nuns make you nervous, you need a double bed, or you plan on staying out past the 23:30 curfew. This quasi-hotel (not a convent) is run with firm but angelic smiles by sisters who offer clean, quiet, rooms for a steal and save the best views for foreigners. Bright lamps, quaint balconies, fine views, grand public rooms, top security, and a friendly atmosphere make this a great value. The checkout time is strictly 10:00, but they have a *deposito* for luggage (Db-L90,000, Tb-L110,000, Qb-L130,000; from San Domenico, walk downhill with church on your right toward the view, turn left down Via Camporegio, make a U-turn at the little chapel down the brick steps to Via Camporegio 37, tel. 0577/44177 and 0577/44487, fax 0577/47601, NSE).

Hotel Chiusarelli, a proper hotel in a fine location, is another wonderful value (50 rooms, S-L60,000, Sb-L90,000, Db-L130,000, CC:VMA, pleasant garden terrace, tiny free parking lot; just outside the old town, across from San Domenico and overlooking the stadium at Viale Curtone 15, tel. 0577/280-562, fax 0577/271-177, SE).

For a reasonable place in a classy residential neighborhood a few blocks away from the center (past San Domenico), with easy parking on the street, consider **Albergo Lea** (S-L70,000, Db-

L115,000, Tb-L150,000, Qb-L175,000, with breakfast, CC:VMA, Hertz desk in their lobby; Viale XXIV Maggio 10, tel. & fax 0577/283-207, SE). If you're traveling with rich relatives who want sterility near the action, the **Hotel Villa Liberty** has big bright and comfortable rooms (Db-L180,000 with breakfast, CC:VMA, elevator, air-con, TVs, mini-bars, etc.; facing the fortress at Viale V. Veneto 11, tel. 0577/44966, fax 0577/44770, SE).

The tourist office lists private homes that rent rooms for around L25,000 per person. Many require a stay of several days, but some are central and a fine value. Siena's **Guidoriccio Youth Hostel** has 120 cheap beds, but given the hassle of the bus ride and the charm of downtown Siena at night, I'd skip it (office open 7:00–9:00, 15:00–23:30; L21,000 beds in doubles, triples, and dorms with sheets and breakfast, cheap meals; bus #10 from Piazza Gramsci or the train station to Via Fiorentina 89 in the Stellino neighborhood, tel. 0577/52212, SE).

Eating in Siena

Restaurants are reasonable by Florentine and Venetian standards. Even with higher prices and lower quality food, consider eating on Il Campo. Eating in Il Campo ambience is a classic European experience. **Pizzeria Spadaforte** has a great setting, mediocre pizza, and tables steeper than its prices (daily 12:00–15:00, 19:00–22:00, tel. 0577/281-123).

Ristorante Gallo Nero is a friendly and inexpensive "grotto" for authentic Tuscan cuisine. This "black rooster" serves a mean *ribollita* (hearty Tuscan bean soup), offers a "medieval menu," and has cheap Chianti (3 blocks down Via del Porrione from the Campo at #65, tel. 0577/284-356).

Just around the corner, **Il Verrochio** serves a decent L22,000 menu (Logge del Papa 1). For authentic Sienese dining at a fair price, eat at the **Locanda Garibaldi**, down Via Giovanni Dupre a few steps from the square (L25,000 menu, open at 19:00, arrive early to get a table, closed Saturday). Marcello does a nice little L5,000 *piatto misto dolce*, featuring several local sweets with sweet wine. For a peasant's dessert, take your last glass of Chianti (borrow the *bicchiere* for *dieci minuti*) with a chunk of bread to the square, lean against a pillar, and sip Siena Classico. Picnics are royal on the Campo.

At **Antica Osteria Da Divo** the ambience is slippery as you climb deep into an Etruscan cellar to find your table. You'll pay a little extra here but the cuisine is local and good (daily 19:00–22:00, near Baptistry and Duomo, Via Franciosa 29, tel. 0577/284-381).

Osteria la Chiacchera is a wonderfully medieval, tasty, and affordable hole-in-the-brick-wall (12:00–15:00, 19:00–24:00, closed Tuesday, below Pension Bernini at Costa di San Antonio 4, tel. 0577/280-631). **Pizza Rustica** places, scattered throughout Siena, serve up cheap pizza-to-go, sold by the gram (100 grams for a snack, 200 grams for a filling meal). The **Enoteca Italia** is a good wine bar in the Fortezza.

For a chance to enjoy a treat on a balcony overlooking the Campo, stop by **Gelateria Artigiana La Costarella** (ice cream), **Bar Paninoteca** (sandwiches), **Bar Barbero d'Oro** (*panforte*—L3,500/100 grams—and cappuccino, best balcony open in summer), each on Via di Citta.

Siena's claim to caloric fame is its *panforte*, a rich, chewy concoction of nuts, honey, and candied fruits that impresses even fruitcake-haters (although locals I met prefer a white macaroon and lemon cookie called *ricciarelli*, and they were right). All over town Prodotti Tipici shops sell Sienese specialties.

Sala di Te, a local late night game and tea room with a curiously welcoming atmosphere, is popular with visiting American students (50 yards past recommended Gallo Nero restaurant, turn right off Via del Porrione down the Vicolo del Vannello, no sign, get close and ask).

Don't miss the evening *passeggiata* (peak strolling time is 19:00) along Via Banchi di Sopra with gelato in hand. **Nannini's** at Piazza Salimbeni has fine gelato (daily 10:30–24:00).

Transportation Connections—Siena

To: Rome (by bus, 1/day, 3 hrs, L20,000; by train, 8/day, 3.5 hrs, including a 20-minute connection in Chiusi), **Viterbo** (for Civita, 1/day).

To Florence: Take the *rapide* SITA bus from Siena's train station to downtown Florence (8/day, 70 min, L10,000, buy ticket before boarding at the *biglietteria* (tel. 0577/204-111 or 0577/204-245). Don't confuse the blue (intercity) and orange (city) buses. Fast buses are marked *"corse rapide."* Don't panic if there are too many people. They generally add buses when necessary. The milk-run bus is much slower but more scenic, offering an interesting glimpse of small-town and rural Tuscany. Trains, which take longer than SITA buses, require a change in Empoli. Shuttle buses connect the train station with the old town center.

SAN GIMIGNANO

The epitome of a Tuscan hill town with 14 medieval towers still standing (out of an original 72!), San Gimignano is a perfectly preserved tourist trap so easy to visit and visually pleasing that it's a good stop. In the 13th century, back in the days of Romeo and Juliet, towns were run by feuding noble families. And they'd periodically battle things out from the protective bases of their respective family towers. Pointy skylines were the norm in medieval Tuscany. But in San Gimignano, fabric was big business and many of its towers were built simply to hang dyed fabric out for drying.

While the basic three-star sight here is the town of San Gimignano itself, there are a few worthwhile stops. From the town gate, shop straight up the traffic-free town's cobbled main drag to the Piazza del Cisterna (with its 13th-century well). The town sights cluster around the adjoining Piazza del Duomo.

Tourist Information is in the old center on Piazza Duomo (daily 9:00–13:00, 15:00–19:00, tel. 0577/940-008).

Sights—San Gimignano

The **Collegiata,** with the round windows and wide steps, is a Romanesque church filled with fine Renaissance frescoes (free entry). In Palazzo del Popolo (facing the same piazza), you'll find the city museum and San Gimignano's tallest tower. The **Museo Civico** has a classy little painting collection with a 1422 altarpiece by Taddeo di Bartolo honoring Saint Gimignano. You can see him with the town in his hands surrounded by events from his life (L12,000 including the tower, Tuesday–Sunday 9:30–19:30, closed Monday). You can climb the 180-foot-tall **Torre Grossa** (9:30–19:30) but the free **Rocco** (castle), a short climb behind the church, offers a better view and a great picnic perch, especially at sunset. Thursday is market day (8:00–13:00), but for local merchants, every day is a sales frenzy.

Transportation Connections—San Gimignano

To: Florence (regular departures, 75 min, change in Poggibonsi; or catch the frequent 20-min shuttle bus to Poggibonsi, and train to Florence), **Siena** (16/day, 1.5 hr, change in Poggibonsi), **Volterra** (6/day, 2 hrs). Bus tickets are sold at the bar just inside the town gate. San Gimignano has no baggage-check service.

Drivers: You can't drive within the walled town of San Gimignano, but a car-park awaits just a few steps outside.

ASSISI

Around the year 1200, a simple monk from Assisi challenged the decadence of church government and society in general with a powerful message of nonmaterialism, simplicity, and a "slow down and smell God's roses" lifestyle. Like Jesus, Francis taught by example. A huge monastic order grew out of his teachings, which were gradually embraced (some would say co-opted) by the church. Clare, St. Francis' partner in poverty, founded the Order of the Poor Clares. Catholicism's purest example of simplicity is now glorified in beautiful churches. In 1939, Italy made Francis and Clare its patron saints.

Any pilgrimage site will be commercialized, and the legacy of St. Francis is Assisi's basic industry. In summer the town bursts with splash-in-the-pan Francis fans and Franciscan knickknacks. Those able to see past the tacky monk mementos can actually have a "travel on purpose" experience. Francis' message of love and simplicity and sensitivity to the environment has a broad appeal.

Orientation (tel. code: 075)

Assisi, crowned by a ruined castle, is beautifully preserved and has a basilica nearly wallpapered by Giotto. Most visitors are day-trippers. Assisi after dark is closer to a place Francis could call home.

Tourist Information: The TI is on Piazza del Comune (Monday–Saturday 9:00–13:00, 15:30–18:30, Sunday 9:00–13:00, tel. 075/812-534).

Arrival in Assisi: Buses connecting Assisi's train station (near Santa Maria degli Angeli) with the old town center (L1,200, 2/hr, 5 km) stop at Piazza Unita d'Italia (Basilica di San Francisco), Largo Properzio (Santa Chiara), and Piazza Matteotti (top of old town).

Excursions: If you want to visit the sights near Assisi, Gino's car and van taxi service can help: one hour is L12,000 per person (four minimum), two hours about L20,000 per person (tel. 033/764-7780).

Sights—Assisi

▲▲▲**The Basilica of St. Francis**—In 1230, at his request, St. Francis was buried outside of his town with the sinners on the "hill of the damned." Now called the "Hill of Paradise," this is one of the artistic highlights of medieval Europe. It's frescoed from top to bottom by Cimabue, Giotto, Simone Martini, and the leading artists of the day.

Note: The basilica, which suffered fresco damage during the earthquakes of October '97, may be closed or scaffolded for at least part of '98. Call the TI to confirm status.

The three-part basilica (upper and lower churches built over the saint's tomb) is a theological work of genius—but difficult for the 20th-century tourist/pilgrim to appreciate. Since the basilica is the reason most visit Assisi and the message of St. Francis has even the least devout blessing the town Vespas, I've designed a *Mona Winks*-type tour with the stress on the place's theology rather than art history. It's adapted from the excellent little *The Basilica of Saint Francis—A Spiritual Pilgrimage* by Goulet, McInally, and Wood (L4,000 in the bookshop).

Enter the church from the parking lot at the lower level. At the doorway look up and see St. Francis who (sounding a bit like John Wayne) greets you with the Latin inscription saying the equivalent of "Slow down and be joyful, pilgrim. You've reached the Hill of Paradise and this church will knock your spiritual socks off." Start with the tomb (turn left into the nave and go down the "Tomba" stairs). Grab a pew right in front of his tomb.

Assisi

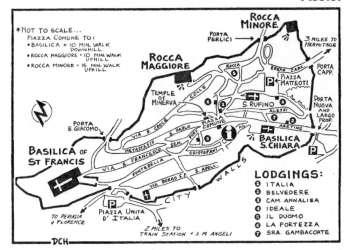

The message: Francis' message caused a stir. He traded a life of power and riches for one of obedience, poverty, and chastity. The Franciscan existence (Brother Sun, Sister Moon, and so on) is a space where God, man, and the natural world frolic harmoniously. Franciscan friars, known as the "Jugglers of God," were a joyful part of the community. In an Italy torn by fighting between towns and families, Francis promoted peace and the restoration of order. (He set an example by reconstructing a crumbled chapel.) While the Church was waging bloody Crusades, Francis pushed ecumenism and understanding. Even today, the leaders of the world's great religions meet here for summits.

This rich building seems to contradict the teachings of the poor monk it honors. But it was built as an act of religious and civic pride to remember the hometown saint. It was also designed and still functions as a pilgrimage center and a splendid classroom.

The tomb: Holy relics were the "ruby slippers" of medieval Europe. They gave you power—got your prayers answered and helped you win wars—and ultimately helped you get back to your eternal Kansas. For obvious reasons of security, you didn't flaunt your relics. In fact, Francis' tomb was hidden until 1818, when this crypt was opened to the public. The saint's remains are above the altar in the stone box with the iron ties. His four best friends are buried in the corners of the room. Opposite the altar, up four steps in between the entrance and exit, notice the remains of Francis' rich Roman patron, Jacopa dei Settesoli, in an urn behind the black metal grill.

The lower basilica is appropriately Franciscan, subdued and Romanesque. The nave was frescoed with parallel scenes from the lives of Christ and Francis—connected by a ceiling of stars. Unfortunately, after the church was built and decorated, the popularity of the Franciscans meant side chapels needed to be built. Huge arches were cut out of the scenes, but some scenes survive. The first panels show Jesus being stripped of his clothing, across the nave from the famous scene of Francis stripping off his clothes in front of his father. In the second arch fresco on the right wall, Christ is being taken down from the cross (just half his body can be seen) and it looks like the story is over. Defeat. But in the opposite fresco we see Francis preaching to the birds, reminding the faithful that through baptism, the message of the Gospel survives.

These stories directed the attention of the medieval pilgrim to the altar where, through the sacraments, he met God. The church was thought of as a community of believers sailing toward God. The prayers coming out of the nave (*navis*, or ship) fill the triangular sections of the ceiling—called *vele*, or sails—with spiritual wind. With a priest for a navigator and the altar for a helm, faith propelled the ship.

Stand behind the altar (toes to the bottom step) and look up. The three scenes in front of you are, to the right, "Obedience" (Francis wearing a yoke); to the left, "Chastity" (in a tower of purity held up by two angels); and straight ahead, "Poverty." Here, Jesus blesses the marriage as Francis slips a ring on Lady Poverty. In the foreground, two "self-sufficient" merchants (the new rich of a thriving North Italy) are throwing sticks and stones at the bride. But Poverty, in her patched wedding dress, is fertile and strong, and even those brambles blossom into a rosebush crown.

Putting your heels to the altar and bending back like a drum major, look up at Francis, who traded a life of earthly simplicity for glory in heaven. Turn to the right and march. . . .

St. Francis' patched robe is on display down the steps under the right transept. Back upstairs, look around at the painted scenes in this transept. In 1300, this was radical art—believable homespun scenes, landscapes, trees, real people. Check out the crucifix (by Giotto) with the eight sparrow-like angels. For the first time, holy people are expressing emotion—one angel turns her head sadly at the sight of Jesus; another scratches her hands down her cheeks, drawing blood. The up-until-now-in-control Mary has fainted in despair. The Franciscans, with their goal of bringing God to the people, found a natural partner in Europe's first modern painter, Giotto.

Francis' friend, "Sister Death," was really not all that terrible. In fact, Francis would like to introduce you to her now (to the right of the door leading into the bright courtyard). Go ahead, block the light and meet her. I'll wait for you in the courtyard.

From the courtyard you can enter the bookshop and the skipable Museum-Treasury (Gothic fine arts and paintings, no English explanations, L3,000). Monks in robes are not my idea of easy-to-approach people, but the Franciscans are still God's Jugglers (and most of them speak English). Climb the stairs to the upper basilica.

The upper basilica, built later than the lower, is brighter and Gothic. It's a gallery of frescoes by Giotto and his assistants showing 28 scenes from the life of St. Francis. Follow the great events of Francis' life, starting at the altar and working clockwise.

Immediately to the right of the altar, the first panel shows God looking over 20-year-old Francis, a dandy imprisoned in his selfishness. A medieval pilgrim, fluent in symbolism, would understand this because the Temple of Minerva (which you'll see today on Assisi's Piazza del Comune) was a prison at that time. The rose window never existed but symbolizes the eye of God. A common man, recognizing Francis as one who will do great things, spreads his cape before Francis as a sign of honor. In the next panel, after Francis was captured in battle, held as a prisoner of war, and then released, he offers his cape to a needy stranger. Next, he's visited by the Lord in a dream and told to leave the army and go home. Two scenes later is the sad scene of Francis giving his dad his clothes, his credit cards, and even his time-share condo on Capri. Naked Francis is covered by the bishop, symbolizing his transition from a man of the world to a man of the church. Next is a vision the pope had of a simple man propping up his teetering church. This led to the papal acceptance of the Franciscan reforms.

Skip to the other side (fourth panel from the door). Here, Christ appears to Francis being carried by a seraph (six-winged angel). For the strength of his faith, Francis is given the marks of his master, the "battle scars of love" . . . the stigmata. Throughout his life, Francis was interested in chivalry; now he's joined the spiritual knighthood. The weeds in the foreground were an herb which, in olden days, "drove away sadness and made men merry and joyful." Pilgrims smiled.

Turning to leave, notice the scene to the right of the door. Here Francis (sans seraph) is preaching to the birds. Francis was more than a nature lover. Notice that the birds are of different species. They represent the diverse flock of humanity and nature—all created and loved by God and worthy of each other's love.

This is the message that the basilica hopes the pilgrim will take home. Stepping out the door you see the Latin *Pax* (peace) and the Franciscan *Tau* cross in the grass. Tau, the last letter in the Hebrew alphabet, is symbolic of faithfulness to the end. Francis signed his name with this simple character. Tau and Pax. (For more pax, take the high lane back to town, up to the castle or into the countryside.)

The church is free (daily 7:00–19:00, sometimes closed for lunch or mass, tel. 075/812-238). (Tours are limited to 9:00–12:00 and 14:00–17:00—times you may want to avoid.) The modest dress code is strictly enforced.

▲**Basilica di Santa Chiara (Saint Clare)**—Dedicated to the founder of the order of the Poor Clares, this Umbrian Gothic church (1265, with the huge buttresses added in the next century) is simple, in keeping with the Poor Clares' dedication to a life of contemplation. The interior's fine frescoes were whitewashed in the Baroque days. The Chapel of St. George on the right (actually an earlier church incorporated into this one) has the crucifix which supposedly spoke to St. Francis, leading to his conversion in 1206. In the back of that chapel are some important Franciscan relics, including Clare's robe. Stairs lead from the nave down to the tomb of Saint Clare. The attached cloistered community of the Poor Clares has flourished for 700 years (church open 6:30–12:00, 14:00–19:00, Sunday till 18:00; 18:30 mass in English Saturday and Sunday, May–October, in the upper church). For a change of pace, cross the street behind the church at the arch and dip into the goofy mechanical and water-powered Biblical world of Silvano Gianbolina.

Piazza del Comune—This square (straight up Via San Francesco from the basilica) is the center of town. You'll find the Roman temple of Minerva, a Romanesque tower, banks, the post office, the Pinacoteca (pathetic art gallery, not worth the admission), and the tourist information office. For a look at Assisi's Roman roots, tour the **Roman Forum** (Foro Romano, L4,000, 10:00–13:00, 15:00–19:00) which is actually under the Piazza del Comune. The floor plan is sparse, and the odd bits and pieces obscure, but it's well explained in English, and it is ancient.

▲**Rocca Maggiore**—The "big castle" offers a good look at a 14th-century fortification and a fine view of Assisi and the Umbrian countryside (L5,000, daily 10:00–19:00). If you're counting lire, the view is just as good from outside the castle and the interior is pretty bare—except for a model of a guillotine with an interesting history in English. Inside, for an extra fee, there is a Torture Museum with four rooms filled with gruesome examples of medieval creativity—explained almost joyously in English. For a picnic with the same birds and views that inspired St. Francis, leave all the tourists and hike to the Rocca Minore (small castle) above Piazza Matteotti.

▲▲**Santa Maria degli Angeli**—This huge Baroque church, towering above the buildings below Assisi, was built around the tiny but historic Porziuncola chapel. St. Francis took Jesus literally when he told him to "go and restore my house." Twenty-four-year-old Francis put the ruined and abandoned chapel back together. It was in this chapel that Francis heard the command to organize his following into an order. As you enter St. Mary of the Angels, notice the sketch on the door showing the original little chapel with the monks' huts around it, and Assisi before it had its huge basilica. Francis lived here after he founded the Franciscan Order in 1208, and this was where he consecrated St. Clare as the Bride of Christ. The other "sights" in the church (a chapel on the spot where Francis died, the rose garden, a museum which has a few monastic cells upstairs) are not very interesting (daily 9:00–12:00 and 14:00–18:30).

Sleeping in Assisi
(L1,600 = about $1, tel. code: 075, zip code: 06081)
The town accommodates large numbers of pilgrims on religious holidays. Finding a room any other time should be easy.

Albergo Italia is clean and simple with great beds and delightful owners. Some of its 13 rooms overlook the town square (Ss-L37,000, D-L50,000, Db-L70,000, T-L63,000, Tb-L90,000, Qb-L100,000, CC:VM; just off the Piazza del Comune's fountain at Vicolo della Fortezza, tel. 075/812-625, fax 075/804-3749, SE).

Hotel Belvedere offers comfortable rooms and good views, and is run by friendly Enrico and his American wife, Mary (D-L70,000, Db-L100,000, breakfast-L10,000; 2 blocks past St. Clare's church at Via Borgo Aretino 13, tel. 075/812-460, fax 075/816-812, SE). Their attached restaurant is also good.

Camere Annalisa Martini is a cheery home swimming in vines, roses, and bricks in the town's medieval core. Annalisa speaks English and enthusiastically accommodates her guests with a picnic garden, washing machine, refrigerator, and homey, lived-in-feeling rooms (S-L38,000, Sb-L40,000, D-L58,000, Db-L60,000, T-L80,000, Q-L100,000, five rooms sharing three bathrooms; breakfast not included; 1 block below the Piazza del Comune, then left on Via S. Gregorio to #6, tel. 075/813-536).

Hotel Ideale is on the far edge of town, overlooking the valley, with a peaceful garden, free parking, view balconies, all the modern comforts, and an English-speaking welcome (Sb-L60,000–75,000, Db-L100,000–120,000 depending on season, breakfast buffet-L10,000, CC:VMA; Piazza Matteotti 1, tel. 075/813-570, fax 075/813-020, Lara SE).

Albergo Il Duomo is tidy and quiet on a stairstep lane 1 block up from San Ruffino (nine rooms, Sb-L45,000–55,000, D-L52,000–65,000, Db-L67,000–80,000 depending on season, L7,000 breakfast, CC:VM; Vicolo S. Lorenzo 2, tel. 075/812-742, fax 075/812-284, Carlo SE).

Hotel La Fortezza is small, very clean, tranquil, modern, and quite comfortable (Db-L90,000, Qb-L140,000, CC:VMA; just up the lane from the Piazza del Comune at Vicolo della Fortezza 19b, tel. 075/812-993, fax 075/812-418, SE).

La Pallotta has clean, bright rooms above its busy restaurant (see Eating, below). Ask for rooms #12 or #18 to get a great view

(Db-L85,000 including breakfast, CC:V; Via San Ruffino 4, tel. & fax 075/812-307, SE).

Senora Gambacorte rents several decent rooms on a quiet lane just above St. Clare's with a roof terrace, and no sign. Ask at the shop across the street if there's no answer at the door (L35,000 per person; 9 via Sermei, tel. 075/815-206 or 075/812-454, fax 075/813-186, NSE, Web site: www.umbrars.com/gambacorta, e-mail: geo@krenet.it). She also has an apartment for stays of one week or more.

Francis probably would have bunked with the peasants in Assisi's **Ostello della Pace** (L20,000 beds with breakfast, in four- to six-bed rooms; a 15-minute walk below town at Via di Valethye, at the San Pietro stop on the station-town bus, tel. & fax 075/816-767, SE).

Eating in Assisi

For the best Assisian perch and fine regional cooking, relax on a terrace overlooking the Piazza del Commune at the **Taverna dei Consoli** (L24,000 menu, two steps straight across from the Albergo Italia, laid-back owner Moreno SE, tel. 075/812-516).

La Pallotta, run by a friendly hardworking family, is locally popular and offers excellent regional specialties such as *piccione* (pigeon), *coniglio* (rabbit), and much more. (L26,000 menu, just 1 block up from the Piazza del Commune, Via San Ruffino 4, tel. 075/812-649, closed Tuesday).

The **Pozzo della Mensa** has a good L23,000 menu with simple, hearty cooking (1 block from Santa Chiara, hidden down a quiet alley at Via della Menza 11, tel. 075/816-247).

Transportation Connections—Assisi

By train to: Rome (9/day, 2.5 hrs with a change in Foligno), **Florence** (10/day, 2.5 hrs, sometimes changing at Terontola-Cortona), **Siena** (5/day, 4 hrs), **Orvieto** (4/day, 2–3 hrs). Train info: tel. 1478-88088. There are one or two buses a day to Rome and Florence.

ORVIETO

Umbria's grand hill town, while no secret, is still worth a quick look. Just off the freeway, with three popular gimmicks (its ceramics, cathedral, and Classico wine), it's loaded with tourists by day— quiet by night.

Ride the back streets of Orvieto into the Middle Ages. The town sits majestically on tufa rock. Streets lined with buildings made from the exhaust-stained volcanic stuff seem to grumble Dark Ages.

Piazza Cahen is only a transportation hub at the entry to the hilltop town. It has a ruined fortress with a garden, a commanding view, and a popular well which is an impressive (although over-priced) double helix carved into tufa rock.

Tourist Information: The TI is at #24 Piazza Duomo on the cathedral square (weekdays 8:00–13:45, 16:00–18:45, weekends from 10:00, tel. 0763/341-772).

Arrival in Orvieto: A handy funicular/bus shuttle takes visitors quickly from the train station and car-park to the top of the town (4/hr, L1,400 ticket includes Piazza Cahen-Piazza Duomo minibus transfer, where you'll find everything that matters). First buy your ticket at the train station tobacco shop, then cross the street to the funicular. At the top of the funicular, walk right onto the waiting orange bus. The shuttle bus drops you at the tourist office (last stop, in front of the Duomo). Drivers park at the base of the hill at the huge, free lot behind the Orvieto train station (follow the "P" and *funicolare* signs).

Sights—Orvieto

▲▲**Duomo**—Orvieto's cathedral has Italy's most striking facade (from 1330). Grab a gelato (to the left of the church) and study this fascinating mass of mosaics and sculpture (daily 7:30–12:45, 14:30–19:15, November–March closing at 17:15). Inside the cathedral notice how the downward-sloping floor diminishes the perspective, giving it an illusion of being shorter than it is. Notice also the alabaster windows.

To the right of the altar, the **Chapel of St. Brizio** features Signorelli's brilliantly lit and restored frescoes of the Apocalypse. Step into the chapel and you're surrounded by vivid scenes showing the Preaching of the Antichrist, the End of the World, the Resurrection of the Bodies, the Last Judgment, and a gripping pietà. For a bonus, check out Fra Angelico's painting of Jesus, the angels, and the prophets on the ceiling. This room is Orvieto's artistic must-see (get L3,000 ticket at the TI across the square, see TI hours above).

Near the striped cathedral are a fine **Etruscan Museum/ Archeological Museum** (L4,000, Monday–Saturday 9:00–13:30, 14:30–19:00, Sunday 9:00–13:00) and unusually clean public toilets (down the stairs from the left transept). Drinking a shot of wine in a ceramic cup as you gaze up at the cathedral lets you experience all of Orvieto's claims to fame at once.

Underground Orvieto Tours—Guides weave a good archeological history into an hour-long look at about 100 meters of caves (L10,000, tours twice daily at 11:00 and 16:00 from the TI, tel. 0763/375-084 or the TI). Orvieto is honeycombed with Etruscan and medieval caves. You'll see only the remains of an old olive press, two impressive 40-meter-deep Etruscan well shafts, and the remains of a primitive cement quarry, but if you want underground Orvieto, this is the place to get it.

Wine Tasting—Orvieto Classico wine is justly famous. For a peek into a local winery, visit **Tenuta Le Velette**, where English-speaking Corrado and Cecilia Bottai welcome those who call ahead

Orvieto

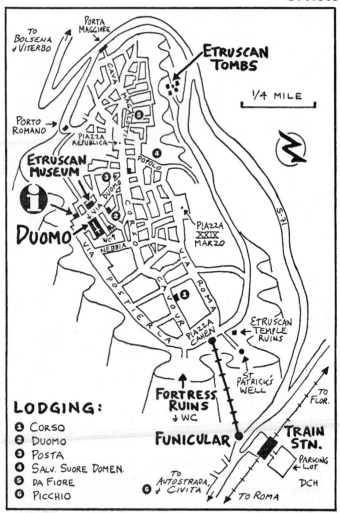

TO
BOLSENA
& VITERBO

PORTA
MAGGIORE

CAVA MAGGIORE

ETRUSCAN
TOMBS

1/4 MILE

PORTO
ROMANO

PIAZZA
REPUBLICA

POPOLO

ETRUSCAN
MUSEUM

VIA DUOMO

CORSO

DUOMO

WC

VIA NEBBIA

VIA POSTIERLA

CAVOUR

VIA ROMA

PIAZZA
XXIX
MARZO

PIAZZA
CAHEN

ETRUSCAN
TEMPLE
RUINS

ST
PATRICK'S
WELL

TO
FLOR.

**FORTRESS
RUINS**
& WC

FUNICULAR

**TRAIN
STN.**

PARKING
LOT

DCH

LODGING:

❶ CORSO
❷ DUOMO
❸ POSTA
❹ SALV. SUORE DOMEN.
❺ DA FIORE
❻ PICCHIO

❻ TO
AUTOSTRADA,
& CIVITA

TO ROMA

to set up an appointment for a look at their winery (Monday–Friday
8:30–12:00, 14:00–17:00, Saturday 8:30–12:00, closed Sunday, tel.
0763/29090 or 0763/29144). At their sign (five minutes past Orvieto
at the top of the switchbacks just before Canale, on the Bagnoregio
road) cruise down the long tree-lined drive and park at the striped
gate. Please call ahead; no drop-in visits.

Sleeping in Orvieto
(L1,600 = about $1, tel. code: 0763, zip code: 05018)
Here are six places in the old town, one in a more modern neighborhood near the station, and one on a local farm.

Hotel Virgilio is a decent hotel with bright modern—if overpriced—rooms shoe-horned into an old building ideally located on the main square facing the cathedral (Db-L150,000–165,000 including breakfast, CC:VM, elevator; Piazza Duomo 5, tel. 0763/341-882, fax 0763/343-797, SE). They also have a "dependence" with Db-L100,000 rooms.

Hotel Corso is small, clean, and friendly, with comfy modern rooms (Db-L135,000, CC:VM; on the main street up from the funicular toward the Duomo at Via Cavour 339, tel. & fax 0763/342-020).

Hotel Duomo is a funky, brightly colored, Old World place with not-quite-clean rooms and a great location (17 rooms, S-L40,000, D-L60,000, Db-L85,000; a block from the Duomo, behind the gelateria at Via di Maurizio 7, tel. 0763/341-887, fax 0763/341-105).

Albergo Posta is a five-minute walk from the cathedral into the medieval core. It's a big, old, formerly elegant, but well-cared-for-in-its-decline building with a breezy garden, a grand old lobby, and spacious, clean, plain rooms with vintage rickety furniture and springy beds (20 rooms, D-L68,000, Db-L88,000; Via Luca Signorelli 18, tel. 0763/341-909).

The sisters of the **Instituto Salvatore Suore Domenicane** rent 15 spotless twin rooms in their heavenly convent (Db-L80,000, loosely enforced two-night minimum; just off Piazza del Populo at Via del Populo 1, tel. & fax 0763/342-910).

At **Camere Da Fiora** (Bar Ricci), for the price of a dumpy room you get a dumpy room (three rooms, D-L40,000; Via Magalotti 22, tel. 0763/341-083, NSE).

Hotel Picchio is a concrete-and-marble place, more comfortable but with less character, and family-run by Marco and Picchio. It's in the lower, plain part of town, 300 yards from the train station (D-L50,000, Db-L70,000, Tb-L90,000; Via G. Salvatori 17, 05019 Orvieto Scalo, tel. 0763/301-144 or 0763/90246). A trail leads from here up to the old town.

Agriturismo Pomonte is a great farm-and-family experience (Db-L80,000, Canino N. 1, Corbara, Orvieto, house on a hilltop at curve in road 3 km before Corbara, tel. 0763/304-080, Cesari family).

Transportation Connections—Orvieto
By train to: Rome (14/day, 60 min, consider leaving your car at the large car-park behind the Orvieto station), **Florence** (14/day, 1.5 hrs), **Siena** (10/day, 2–3 hrs, change in Chiusi).

By bus to Bagnoregio: It's a 50-minute L3,000 bus ride (6:25, 7:20, 9:10, 12:40, 13:55, 15:45, 17:35, and 18:35 from Orvieto's Piazza Cahen and from its train station daily except Sunday, buy tickets from the "cafe snack bar" at the station, confirm return times from the conductor, tel. 0763/792-237). If the bus is empty, develop a relationship with your driver. He may let you jump out in Lubriano for a great photo of distant Civita. Note: While there is no bus service on Sunday the boys at Al Boschetto may be able to shuttle you to Orvieto.

CIVITA DI BAGNOREGIO

Perched on a pinnacle in a grand canyon, the traffic-free village of Civita is Italy's ultimate hill town. Curl your toes around its Etruscan roots.

Civita is terminally ill. Only 15 residents remain as, bit by bit, it's being purchased by rich big-city Italians who escape here. Apart from its permanent (and aging) residents and those who have weekend homes here, there is a group of Americans, introduced to the town through a small University of Washington architecture program, who have bought into the rare magic of Civita. When the program is in session, 15 students live with residents and study Italian culture and architecture.

Civita is connected to the world and the town of Bagnoregio by a long pedestrian bridge. While Bagnoregio lacks the pinnacle-town romance of Civita, it is a pure and lively bit of small-town Italy. It's actually a healthy, vibrant community (unlike Civita, the suburb it calls "the dead city"). Get a haircut, sip a coffee on the square, walk down to the old laundry (ask, *"Dové la lavanderia vecchia?"*). A lively market fills the parking lot each Monday.

From Bagnoregio, yellow signs direct you along its long, skinny spine to its older neighbor, Civita. Enjoy the view as you head up the bridge to Civita. A shuttle bus runs from the base of the Civita bridge to Bagnoregio and maybe to Al Boschetto (see Sleeping, below) about hourly in season (L1,000). Be prepared for the little old ladies of Civita who have become aggressive at getting lire out of visitors. Off season Civita, Bagnoregio, and Al Boschetto are all deadly quiet—and cold. I'd side trip in quickly from Orvieto or skip the area altogether.

Civita Orientation Walk

Civita was once connected to Bagnoregio. The saddle between the separate towns eroded away. Photographs around town show the old donkey path, the original bridge. It was bombed in WWII, and replaced in 1965 with the new bridge you'll climb today. The town's hearty old folks hang on the bridge's hand railing when fierce winter weather rolls through.

Entering the town you'll pass through a cut in the rock (made by Etruscans 2,500 years ago) and under a 12th-century Romanesque arch. This was the main Etruscan road leading to the Tiber Valley and Rome.

Inside the town gate, on the left, notice the old laundromat (in front of the WC). On the right, a fancy door and windows lead to thin air. This was the facade of a Renaissance palace—one of five which once graced Civita. It fell into the valley riding a chunk of the ever-eroding rock pinnacle. Today the door leads to a remaining chunk of the palace—complete with Civita's first hot tub—owned by the "Marchesa," a countess who married into Italy's biggest industrialist family.

Poke through the museum next door and check out the viewpoint around the corner near the long-gone home of Civita's one famous son, Saint Bonaventura.

Now wander to the town square in front of the church where you'll find Civita's only public phone, bar, restaurant—and a wild donkey race each August 15. The church marks the spot where an Etruscan temple, and then a Roman temple, once stood. The pillars which stand like giants' barstools are ancient—Roman or Etruscan.

Go into the church and find Anna. She'll give you a tour, proudly pointing out frescos and statues from "the school of Giotto" and "the school of Donatello," a portrait of the patron saint of your teeth (notice the scary-looking pincers), and an altar dedicated to Marlon Brando (or St. Ildebrando). Tip her and buy your postcards from her.

The basic grid street plan of the ancient town survives. Just around the corner from the church, on the main street, is Rossana and Antonio's cool and friendly wine cellar. Pull up a stump and let them or their children, Arianna and Antonella, serve you *panini* (sandwiches), *bruschetta* (garlic toast with tomato), wine, and a local cake called *ciambella*. Climb down into the cellar and note the traditional wine-making gear and the provisions for rolling huge kegs up the stairs. Tap on the kegs in the cool bottom level to see which are full.

The ground below Civita is honeycombed with ancient cellars (for keeping wine at the same temperature all year) and cisterns (for collecting rainwater, since there was no well in town). Many of these date from Etruscan times.

Explore farther down the street but remember, nothing is abandoned. Everything is still privately owned. After passing an ancient Roman tombstone on your left, you'll come to Victoria's **Antico Mulino**, an atmospheric collection of old olive-presses (give a donation of about L1,500). Her grandchildren, running the local equivalent of a lemonade stand, toast delicious *bruschetta* on weekends and holidays. For about L5,000 you get a fun light lunch featuring a *piatto misto* of *bruschetta*, local cheese, and salami with wine.

Farther down the way, Maria (for a donation of about L1,500) will show you through her garden with a grand view

Civita

(*Maria's Giardino*) and historical misinformation (she says Civita and Lubriano were once connected).

At the end of town the main drag peters out and a trail leads you down and around to the right to a tunnel that has cut through the hill under the town since Etruscan times. It was widened in the 1930s so farmers could get between their scattered fields easier.

Evenings on the town square are a bite of Italy. The same people sit on the same church steps under the same moon, night after night, year after year. I love my cool late evenings in Civita. If you visit in the cool of the early morning, have cappuccino and rolls at the small café on the town square.

Whenever you visit, stop halfway up the donkey path and listen to the sounds of rural Italy. Reach out and touch one of the monopoly houses. If you know how to turn the volume up on the crickets, do so.

Sleeping and Eating near Civita
(L1,600 = about $1, tel. code: 0761, zip code: 01022)
When you leave the tourist crush, life as a traveler in Italy becomes easy and prices tumble. Room-finding is easy in small-town Italy. Just outside Bagnoregio is **Al Boschetto**. The Catarcia family speaks no English. Have an English-speaking Italian call for you (D-L85,000–90,000, Db-L90,000–95,000, breakfast L6,000, CC:V; Strada Monterado, Bagnoregio/Viterbo, Italy, tel. 0761/792-369, walking and driving instructions below).

Most rooms, while very basic, have private showers (no curtains, slippery floors—be careful not to flood the place; sing in search of your shower's resonant frequency).

The Catarcia family (Angelino, his wife Perina, sons Gianfranco and Domenico, daughter-in-law Giuseppina, and the grandchildren) offer an honest look at rural Italian life. Giuseppina serves uninspired meals. If the boys invite you down deep into the gooey, fragrant bowels of the cantina, be warned: the theme song is "Trinka Trinka Trinka," and there are no rules unless the female participants set them.

The Orvieto bus drops you at the town gate. (Remember, no bus service at all on Sunday.) Al Boschetto is a 15-minute walk out of town past the old arch (follow Viterbo signs), turn left at the pyramid monument, and right at the first fork (follow Montefiascone sign). Civita is a pleasant 45-minute walk (back through Bagnoregio) from Al Boschetto.

Hotel Fidanza, in Bagnoregio near the bus stop—tired, with incredibly low blood pressure—is the only other hotel in town. Rooms 206 and 207 have views of Civita (Db-L90,000, breakfast-L20,000; Via Fidanza 25, Bagnoregio/Viterbo, tel. & fax 0761/793-444).

For information about a two-bedroom, fully furnished/equipped Civita apartment with terrace and cliffside garden, rentable May through October ($600/week, $2,000/month, one week minimum), call Carol Watts in Kansas (tel. 913/539-0815 evenings, or e-mail: cmwatts@ksu.edu).

The nearest cheap beds are back in Orvieto at Camere Da Fiora (near the station, see Orvieto section).

Casa San Martino, in the village of Lisciano Niccone (near Carona and Perugia), is a 250-year-old farmhouse run as a B&B by American Italophile Lois Martin. Using this comfortable hilltop countryside homebase, those with a car can tour Assisi, Orvieto, and Civita. While Lois reserves the summer for one week stays, she'll take guests staying a minimum of two nights for the rest of the year ($40 per person, Casa San Martino 19, Lisciano Niccone, tel. 075/844288, reserve in the U.S.A. via Tennessee tel. 423/928-8119, fax 423/928-8496).

Your best bets for dinner: Hearty country cooking at **Al Boschetto** (see above) or lighter more creative cuisine at the **Hostaria del Ponte** (at the car park at the base of the bridge to Civita, great view terrace, good food and prices, tel. 0761/793-565, closed Monday). For a simple meal in Civita, try **Trattoria al Forno** (serves a decent pasta-and-wine lunch or dinner, open daily for lunch at 12:30 and dinner at 19:30, June–September, sometimes October, tel. 0761/793-651). Or, for the best cooking in Bagnoregio, check out **Restorante Nello il Fumatore** (Piazza Fidanza, closed Friday).

Transportation Connections—Bagnoregio

To Civita: It's a 30-minute walk. Taking the shuttle bus (nearly hrly, 10 min; service halts during the 13:00–15:00 siesta) still involves a walk (15 min up the donkey path from the bus stop).

To Orvieto: Public buses (8/day, 50 min) connect Bagnoregio to the rest of the world via Orvieto (1997 departures from Bagnoregio: 6:50, 10:05, 13:00, 14:25, 17:20, see Connections—Orvieto, above). While there's no official baggage-check service in Bagnoregio, I've arranged with Laurenti Mauro, who runs the Bar Enoteca just outside the Bagnoregio old town gate (near the bus station), to let you leave your bags there (open 6:00–24:00 with a short lunch break, closed Thursday). Pay him L2,000 per bag or buy breakfast there (better than Al Boschetto's).

THE CINQUE TERRE

The Cinque Terre (CHINK-wuh TAY-ruh), a remote chunk of the Italian Riviera, is the traffic-free, low-brow, under-appreciated alternative to the French Riviera. There's not a museum in sight. Just sun, sea, sand (well, pebbles), wine, and pure unadulterated Italy. Enjoy the villages, swimming, hiking, and evening romance of one of God's great gifts to tourism. For a home base, choose among five villages, each of which fills a ravine with a lazy hive of human activity. Vernazza is my favorite.

The area was first described in medieval times as "the five castles." Tiny communities grew up in the protective shadows of the castles ready to run inside at the first hint of a Turkish "Saracen" pirate raid. Many locals were kidnapped and ransomed or sold into slavery somewhere far to the east. As the threat of pirates faded, the villages grew with economies based on fish and grapes. Until the advent of tourism in this generation, they were very remote. Even today, traditions survive and each of the five villages comes with a distinct dialect and proud heritage.

Planning Your Time
The ideal minimum stay is two nights and a completely uninterrupted day. The Cinque Terre is served by the milk-run train from Genoa and La Spezia. Speed demons arrive in the morning, check their bag in La Spezia, take the five-hour hike through all five towns, laze away the afternoon on the beach or rock of their choice, and zoom away on the overnight train to somewhere back in the real world. Each town has its own character, and all are a few minutes apart by an hourly train. There's no checklist of sights or experiences, just the hike, the towns, and your fondest vacation desires.

Cinque Terre

For a good Cinque Terre day consider this: Pack your beach and swimming gear, wear your walking shoes, and catch the train to town #1: Riomaggiore. (Since I still get the names mixed up, I think of the five Cinque Terre towns by number.) Walk the cliff-hanging Via dell' Amore to Manarola (#2) and buy food for a picnic, then hike to Corniglia (#3) for a rocky but pleasant beach. Swim here or in the more resorty Monterosso (#5, a ten-minute train ride away). From #5, hike or catch the boat home to Vernazza (#4).

If you're into *il dolce far niente* (the sweetness of doing *nada*) and don't want to hike, you could enjoy the blast of cool train-tunnel air that announces the arrival of every Cinque Terre train and go directly to Monterosso al Mare, where a sandy "front door"–style beach awaits. The Cinque Terre has a strange way of messing up momentum.

Getting Around the Cinque Terre

The city of La Spezia is the gateway to the Cinque Terre. In La Spezia's train station, the milk-run Cinque Terre train schedule is posted at the information window. Take the L2,000 half-hour train ride into the Cinque Terre town of your choice.

Cinque Terre Train Schedule: Since the train is the Cinque Terre lifeline, any shop or restaurant posts the current schedule (La Spezia train info: tel. 0187/714-960, Monterosso train info: tel. 0187/817-458).

Trains leave La Spezia for the Cinque Terre villages (last year's schedule) at 6:12, 7:17, 8:15, 10:06, 11:23, 12:30, 13:20, 14:24, 15:00, 16:30, 17:02, 17:48, 18:25, 19:06, 19:36, 21:19, and 22:36.

Trains leave Monterosso al Mare for La Spezia (departing Vernazza about three minutes later, last year's schedule) at 5:16, 6:33, 7:05, 8:44, 10:15, 11:02, 12:19, 13:31, 14:18, 15:01, 15:54, 17:05, 18:08, 19:09, 19:57, 20:07, 22:06, and 23:14.

To orient yourself, remember that directions are *"per* (to) *Genoa"* or *"per La Spezia,"* and any train that stops at any of the villages other than Monterosso will stop at all five. (Note that many trains leaving La Spezia skip them all or stop only in Monterosso.) The five towns are just minutes apart by train. Know your stop. After leaving the town before your destination, go to the door to slip out before mobs pack in. Since the stations are small and the trains are long, you might need to get off the train deep in a tunnel, and you might need to open the door yourself.

If the train station is not staffed, buy your ticket from the tobacco shop (in Vernazza, near the harbor) or on board from the conductor. If you buy from the conductor, explain, *"La stazione era chiusa"* (the station was closed); otherwise you'll pay a bit more.

Since a one-town hop costs the same as a five-town hop (L1,500), and every ticket is good all day with stopovers, save money and explore the region in one direction on one ticket. Stamp the ticket at the station machine before you board. Stations sell a L5,000 all day 5-Terre pass. Don't spend a railpass flexi-day on the Cinque Terre.

VERNAZZA

With the closest thing to a natural harbor, overseen by a ruined castle and an old church, and only the occasional noisy slurping up of the train by the mountain to remind you these are the 1990s, Vernazza is my Cinque Terre home base.

The action is at the harbor, where you'll find a kids' beach, plenty of sunning rocks, outdoor restaurants, a bar hanging on the edge of the castle (great for evening drinks), the tiny town soccer field, and a tailgate-party street market each Tuesday morning.

The town's 500 residents, proud of their Vernazzan heritage, brag that "Vernazza is locally owned. Portofino has sold out." Fearing the change it would bring, they stopped the construction of a major road into the town and region. Families are tight and go back centuries; several generations stay together. Leisure time is spent wandering lazily together up and down the

Vernazza

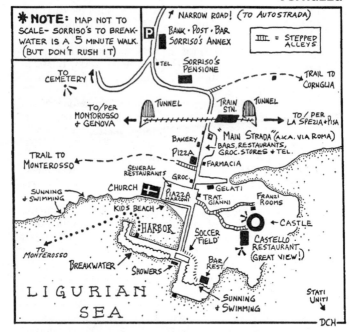

NOTE: MAP NOT TO SCALE- SORRISO'S TO BREAK-WATER IS A 5 MINUTE WALK. (BUT DON'T RUSH IT)

↑ NARROW ROAD! (TO AUTOSTRADA)
BANK · POST · BAR
SORRISO'S ANNEX

▥ = STEPPED ALLEYS

■TEL.
SORRISO'S PENSIONE

TO CEMETERY

TRAIL TO CORNIGLIA

TO/PER MONTOROSSO & GENOVA

TUNNEL   TRAIN STN.   TUNNEL

TO/PER LA SPEZIA + PISA

BAKERY   "MAIN STRADA" (A.K.A. VIA ROMA)
BARS, RESTAURANTS, GROC. STORES + TEL.

PIZZA   ■FARMACIA

TRAIL TO MONTEROSSO

SEVERAL RESTAURANTS   GROC.

SUNNING + SWIMMING

CHURCH   ■GELATI

PIAZZA MARCONI   TRAT. GIANNI   FRANZI ROOMS

KID'S BEACH ↗

HARBOR   SOCCER FIELD   ←CASTLE

TO MONTEROSSO   CASTELLO RESTAURANT (GREAT VIEW!)

BREAKWATER   SHOWERS   BAR/ REST.

L I G U R I A N   S E A   SUNNING + SWIMMING   STATI UNITI

— DCH

main street. Sit on a bench and study Vernazza's *passeggiata*. Then explore the characteristic alleys called *carugi*. In October the cantinas are draped with drying grapes. In the winter the population shrinks, as many people move to more comfortable big-city apartments.

An hourly boat service connects Vernazza and Monterosso (departures last year: 10:00, 11:00, 12:00, 14:30, 15:30, 16:30, 17:30, and 18:30, daily April–October, L4,000 one way, L6,000 round-trip, canceled when windy). A five-minute steep hike in either direction from Vernazza gives you a classic village photo op. Franco's Bar, with a panoramic terrace, is at the tower on the trail toward Corniglia.

The banks at the top of the town have decent rates. The nearest laundromat is a self-serve in La Spezia near its market square and full-service places in Monterosso.

Sights—Vernazza

▲▲**Vernazza Town Top Down Orientation Walk**—Walk uphill until you hit the parking lot, two banks, and post office. The tidy new square is called "Fontana Vecchia" after a long-gone fountain. Older locals remember the river filled with townswomen doing their washing. Begin your saunter downhill to the harbor.

Just before the "Pension Sorriso" sign you'll see the ambulance barn on the right. A group of volunteers are always on call for a dash to the hospital, 30 minutes away in La Spezia. Opposite that is a big empty lot behind Pension Sorriso. Like many landowners, Sr. Sorriso had plans to expand but the government said no. The old character of these towns is carefully protected.

Across from the "Pension Sorriso" sign is the honorary clubhouse for the ANPI (members of the local WWII resistance). Only five ANPI old-timers survive. Cynics consider them less than heroes. After 1943 Hitler called up any boy over 15. Like any reasonably smart person, they escaped to the hills rather than fight for Hitler on the front. Only to remain free did they become "resistance fighters."

A few steps farther you'll see a monument to those killed in WWII. Not a family was spared. The tiny monorail *"trenino"* is parked quietly here except in September and October when it's busy helping locals bring down the grapes. From here the path leads to Corniglia. The school bus picks up children from the many tiny neighboring villages. Today only about 25 children attend the Vernazza elementary school. At this point, Vernazza's tiny river goes underground.

Under tracks you'll find posters for various volunteer organizations. The second track was recently renovated to lessen the disruptive noise.

Until the 1950s, Vernazza's river ran open through the center of town from here to the gelateria. You can see where it once flowed.

Wandering through the main business center you'll pass many locals doing their *vasca* (laps) past the tiny Chapel of Santa Marta where mass is celebrated only on Palm Sunday, the Blue Marlin bar (a good breakfast place and the only night spot in town), the bakery, grocery, and pharmacy. Tiny lanes lead up in both directions (the best *carugi* are on the right).

To the left of the gelateria an arch leads to what was a beach and where the river used to flow out of town. Continue on down to the harbor square and breakwater or follow the trail (second path above the church toward Monterosso) to the classic view of Vernazza (best photos just before sunset).

▲▲▲**The Burned-Out Sightseer's Visual Tour of Vernazza**—Sit on the harbor breakwater (perhaps with a glass of local white wine from the Cantina del Molo, last door on left), face the town and see . . .

The harbor: In a moderate storm you'd be soaked as waves routinely crash over the *molo* (breakwater, built in 1972). The train line, built 130 years ago to tie a newly united Italy together, linked Turin and Genoa with Rome. A second line (hidden in a tunnel at this point) was built in the 1960s. The yellow building was Vernazza's first train station. You can see the four bricked-up waiting alcoves. Vernazza's fishing fleet is down to three small fishing boats (with the net spools)—the town's restaurants buy up everything they catch. Vernazzans are more likely to own a boat than a car. In the '70s tiny Vernazza had one of the top water polo teams in Italy and the harbor was their "pool." Later, when a real pool was required, Vernazza dropped out of the league.

The castle: On the far right, the castle (now a pleasant park, open daily 9:00 or 10:00–19:00, L2000) still guards the town. The Belforte Bar (the fort was named *"bea forte"* or "loud screams," for the warnings it made back in pirating days) is a great and grassy perch. The lowest deck (follow the rope) is great for a glass of wine. (Inside the submarine-strength door, a photo of a major storm shows the entire tower under a wave.) The highest umbrellas mark the recommended Castello restaurant (see Eating, below).

The town: From the lower castle, the houses were interconnected with an interior arcade—ideal for fleeing attacks. The pastel colors are regulated by a commissioner of good taste in the community government. The square before you is locally famous for some of the region's finest restaurants. The big red central house, the 12th-century site where Genoan ships were built, used to be a kind of guardhouse.

Above the town: The ivy-covered tower, another part of the city fortifications, reminds us of Vernazza's importance in the Middle Ages, when it was an important ally of Genoa (whose arch enemies were the other maritime republics of Pisa, Amalfi, and Venice). Franco's Bar (closed Tuesday), just behind the tower, welcomes hikers finishing (starting, or simply contemplating) the Corniglia–Vernazza hike with great town views. Vineyards fill the mountainside beyond the town. Wine production is down nowadays, as the younger residents choose less physical work. But locals still work their plots and proudly serve their family wine. A single steel train line winds up the gully behind the tower. This is for the vintner's *trenino*, the tiny service train.

The church and city hall: Vernazza's Ligurian Gothic church dates from 1318. The grey and red house above and to the left of the spire is the school. The red building to the right is the former monastery and present city hall. Vernazza and Corniglia function as one community. In 1995, they elected their popular mayor, a Communist, to his second five-year term. The party's banner (now the PDS or "people's democratic party of the left") decorates town walls. High school is in the "big city," La Spezia. Finally, on the top of the hill, with the best view of all, is the town cemetery where most locals plan to end up (*tutto completo* . . . but a new wing is under construction).

Sleeping in Vernazza
(L1,600 = about $1, tel. code: 0187, zip code: 19018)
Sleep Code: **S**=Single, **D**=Double/Twin, **T**=Triple, **Q**=Quad, **b**=bathroom, **t**=toilet only, **s**=shower only, **CC**=Credit Card (Visa,

MasterCard, Amex), **SE**=Speaks English, **NSE**=No English. Breakfast is included only in real hotels.

While the Cinque Terre is too rugged for the mobs that ravage the Spanish and French coasts, it's popular with Italians, Germans, and Americans in the know. Room-finding is difficult only on Easter, in August, and on summer Fridays and Saturdays. August weekends are worst. Important: Any other time, for the best value, arrive by midday, ask around, visit three private rooms and snare the best. Going direct cuts out a middleman and softens prices. Off-season, empty rooms abound. Private rooms are generally bigger and more comfortable than those offered by the pensions.

Vernazza, the essence of the Cinque Terre, is my favorite town. There is just one real pension, but two restaurants have about a dozen simple rooms each, and most locals rent extra rooms. Anywhere you stay here will require some climbing. Night noises can be a problem if you're near the station or the church bell tower. Address letters to 19018 Vernazza, Cinque Terre, La Spezia.

Trattoria Gianni rents 21 small rooms just under the castle. The funky ones are artfully decorated à la shipwreck, up lots of tight, winding, spiral stairs mostly with tiny balconies and grand views. The new more comfy rooms lack views but have modern bathrooms and a super-scenic, cliff-hanger private garden. The Franzi family splits the work: Gianni maintains the restaurant's good reputation, and stoic Marisa (who doles out smiles like a rich gambler on a losing streak) runs the rooms (they require a two-night minimum, S-L50,000, D-L85,000, Db-L100,000, Tb-L135,000, CC:VMA; Piazza Marconi 5, closed January–February, tel. & fax 0187/812-228, tel. 0187/821-003). Pick up your keys at the restaurant/reception on the harbor square and hike up the stairs to #41 (funky) or #47 (new) at the top. The nephew Alberto speaks English but communication can be difficult. No reply to your fax means they don't want to make a reservation (they get piles of requests and my tour company books this place out 50 nights of the season). Ideally, telephone three days in advance and leave your first name and time of arrival.

Pension Sorriso knows it's the only real pension in town. Don't expect an exuberant welcome (D-L75,000 per person with obligatory uninspired dinner and breakfast, Db-L90,000 per person with dinner and breakfast, cash only; 50 yards up from station; closed November–February; tel. 0187/812-224, fax 0187/821-198, no answer to your fax means Sorriso is full, some English spoken). While train sounds rumble through the front rooms of the main building, the annex up the street is quieter.

Locanda Barbara, on the harbor square, is run spittoon-style by Giacomo at the Taverna del Capitano (ten rooms with three public showers and WCs, S-L60,000, tiny loft D-L70,000, bigger D-L80,000, family deals; Piazza Marconi 21, tel. 0187/812-201, closed December–January, charming Valerio speaks English and loves the girls). The big doubles come with grand harbor views and are the best value (top two floors of the big red vacant-looking building facing the harbor). Guests get a free bottle of wine with dinner per couple at Trattoria del Capitano.

Affitta Camere: Vernazza is honeycombed year-round with pleasant, rentable private rooms and apartments (cheap for families, with kitchens). They are reluctant to reserve rooms ahead. To minimize frustration, call a day or two in advance, or simply show up by midday and look around. All are comfortable and inexpensive (L30,000–L40,000 per person depending on the view). Some are lavish with killer views, and cost the same as a small dark place on a back lane over the train tracks. Little or no English is spoken at these places. Any main street business has a line on rooms for rent.

Affitta Camere da Filippo is a good network of 15 rooms and apartments run by Antonio and his mother Rita (D-L70,000, Db-L80,000, apartments-L100,000; Via A. Del Santo 62 or ask at the Blue Marlin bar, tel. 0187/812-244). For rooms with some of the best harbor views in town, see the harborfront **Gambero Rosso** restaurant (closed Monday, tel. 0187/812-265). **Trattoria Il Baretto** also rents rooms (ask Francesca, tel. 0187/812-381). **Affitta Camere da Nicolina** has great views over the harbor, but is close to the noisy church bell tower (ask at the harborside Vulnetia restaurant/pizzeria, tel. 0187/821-193). Or try **Affitta Camere da Anna-Maria** (Db-L80,000 with view or terrace; turn left at pharmacy, climb via Carattino to #64, tel. 0187/821-082). Her German-speaking husband, Franco, runs the "Bar la Torre" and rents noisy rooms at the top of the town. The lady at the grocery store across from the gelateria has a line on rooms (Giuseppina's villa is a modern, deluxe apartment without view, Db-L80,000, Qb-L140,000; Via S. Giovanni Battista 5, tel. 0187/812-026). **Trattoria Sandro** also has rooms (Louisa's has great sea views).

Eating in Vernazza

If you're into Italian cuisine, Vernazza's restaurants are worth the splurge. All seem good and have similar prices. At about 20:00 wander around and compare the ambience. The **Castello,** run by gracious and English-speaking Monica and her family, serves good food just under the castle (12:00–22:00, closed Wednesday and November–April, also rents rooms, tel. 0187/812-296). On the harborfront, **Trattoria Franzi** and **Trattoria del Capitano** are more atmospheric and famous. **Gambero Rosso**, considered Vernazza's best restaurant, feels classy and costs only a few thousand lira more than the others. **Trattoria da Sandro** and the more off-beat and intimate **Trattoria Piva** (closed Monday) may come with late-night guitar-strumming.

You can get good pizza by the slice on the main street. Grocery stores (open 7:30–13:00, 17:00–19:30) make inexpensive sandwiches to order. The town's only gelateria is good, and most harborside bars will let you take your glass on a breakwater stroll.

Locals take breakfast about as seriously as flossing. A cappuccino and a pastry or a piece of focaccia bread does it. The two harborfront bars offer the most ambience. The bakery is open early and makes ham and cheese toast. The **Blue Marlin** bar, just below the station, offers the best selection and toasted cheese and ham sandwiches.

Cinque Terre Experiences

▲▲▲**Hiking**—All five towns are connected by good trails. Experience the area's best by hiking from one end to the other. The entire hike can be done in about four hours, but allow five for dawdling. While you can detour to hilltop sanctuaries, I'd keep it simple by following the easy red-and-white-marked low trails between the villages. A good L5,000 hiking map (sold in all the towns, not necessary for this described walk) covers the expanded version of this hike from Porto Venere through all five Cinque Terre towns to Levanto.

Riomaggiore–Manarola (20 min): From the train station in Riomaggiore (town #1), the Via del' Amore affords a film-gobbling promenade (wide enough for baby strollers) down the coast to Manarola. While there's no beach here, stairs lead down to sunbathing rocks.

Manarola–Corniglia (45 min): From the Manarola (#2) waterfront, it's easiest to take the high trail out of town. The broad and scenic low trail ends with steep stairs leading to the high road. The walk from #2 to #3 is a little longer, and a little more rugged, than from #1 to #2. The high alternative via the hamlet of Volastra takes two hours and offers sweeping views and a closer look at the vineyards. Ask locally about the more difficult 6-mile inland hike to Volastra. This tiny village, perched between Manarola and Corniglia, offers great views and the 5-Terre wine co-op; stop by the Cantina Sociale.

Corniglia–Vernazza (90 min): The hike from Corniglia (#3) to Vernazza (#4)—the wildest and greenest of the coast—is most rewarding. From the Corniglia station and beach, zigzag up to the town. Ten minutes past Corniglia toward Vernazza, you'll see the well-hung Guvano beach far below (see below). The trail leads past a bar and picnic tables, through lots of fragrant and flowery vegetation, and scenically into Vernazza.

Vernazza–Monterosso (90 min): The trail from Vernazza to Monterosso (#5) is a scenic, up-and-down-a-lot trek. Trails are rough (and some readers report "very dangerous") but easy to follow. Camping at the picnic tables midway is frowned upon. The views just out of Vernazza are spectacular.

▲**Swimming**—Wear your walking shoes and pack your swim gear. Each beach has showers that may work better than your hotel's.

(Bring soap and shampoo.) Monterosso's beaches, immediately in front of the train station, are easily the best (and most crowded). It's a sandy resort with everything rentable . . . lounge chairs, umbrellas, paddle boats, and usually even beach access (L2,000). Vernazza has a sandy children's cove, sunning rocks, and showers by the breakwater. The tiny "Acque Pendente" (waterfall) cove that locals call their *laguna blu* between Vernazza and Monterosso is accessible only by small hired boat. Forget Manarola or Riomaggiore for beaches. I do my Cinque Terre swimming on the pathetic but peaceful manmade beach below the Corniglia station. Unfortunately, much of it has washed away, and it's almost nonexistent when the surf's up. What's left is clean and less crowded than the Monterosso beach, and the beach bar has showers, drinks, and snacks.

The nude Guvano (GOO-vah-noh) beach (between Corniglia and Vernazza) made headlines in Italy in the 1970s, as clothed locals in a makeshift armada of dinghies and fishing boats retook their town beach. But big-city nudists still work on all-around tans in this remote setting. From the Corniglia train station (follow the road north, zigzag below the tracks, follow signs to tunnel) travelers buzz the intercom and the hydraulic *Get Smart*-type door is opened from the other end. After a 15-minute hike through a cool, moist, and dimly-lit unused old train tunnel, you'll emerge at the Guvano beach—and be charged L5,000 (L4,000 with this guidebook, water, no WC). A steep (free) trail also leads from the beach up to the Corniglia–Vernazza trail.

The crowd is Italian counterculture: pierced nipples, tattooed punks, hippie drummers in dreads, and nude exhibitionist men. The ratio of men to women is about three to two. About half the people on the pebbly beach keep their swimsuits on.

▲▲**Pesto**—This is the birthplace of pesto. Try it on spaghetti, *trofie*, or *trenette*. Basil, which loves the temperate Ligurian climate, is mixed with cheese (half *parmigiano* cow cheese and half *pecorino* sheep cheese), garlic, olive oil, and pine nuts, then poured over pasta. If you become addicted, small jars of it are sold in the local grocery stores.

▲▲**Wine**—The Vino delle Cinque Terre, famous throughout Italy, flows cheap and easy throughout the region. If you like sweet, sherry-like wine, the local Sciacchetrà wine is worth the splurge (L5,000 per glass, often served with a cookie). While 10 kilos of grapes yield 7 liters of local wine, Sciachetra is made from near-raisins, and 10 kilos of grapes makes only 1.5 liters of Sciachetra. If your room is up a lot of steps, be warned: Sciachetra is 18 percent alcohol, while regular wine is only 11 percent. In the cool, calm evening, sit on the Vernazza breakwater with a glass of wine and watch the phosphorous in the waves. While red wine is sold as Cinque Terre wine, it's a fantasy designed to please the tourists.

Cinque Terre Towns

(Note: Readers of this book fill Vernazza. For this reason, you might prefer to stay in another town with fewer Americans. See Sleeping, below.)

▲▲**Riomaggiore (town #1)**—The most substantial non-resort town of the group, Riomaggiore is a disappointment from the train station. But walk through the tunnel next to the train tracks (or take the scenic high road, straight up and to the right), and you land in a fascinating tangle of pastel homes leaning on each other as if someone stole their crutches. There's homemade gelato at the Bar Central and if Ivo is there, you'll feel right at home. A cliff-hanging trail leads out of town to a botanical garden and old WWII bunkers. Another climbs scenically to the Madonna di Montenero sanctuary high above the town.

▲**Manarola (town #2)**—Like town #1, #2 is attached to its station by a 200-yard-long tunnel. Manarola is tiny and rugged, a tumble of buildings bunny-hopping down its ravine to the tiny harbor. Buy a picnic (stores close from 13:00–17:00) before walking to the beaches of Corniglia.

▲▲**Corniglia (town #3)**—From the station, a footpath zigzags up 370 stairs to the only town of the five not on the water. Originally settled by a Roman farmer who named it for his mother, Cornelia, its ancient residents produced a wine so famous that vases found at Pompei touted its virtues. Today its wine is still its lifeblood. Follow the pungent smell of ripe grapes into an alley cellar and get a local to let you dip a straw into her keg. Remote and less visited, Corniglia has cooler temperatures, a windy belvedere, a few restaurants, and more than enough private rooms for rent. Past the train station is the Corniglia beach and Albergo Europa, a bungalow village filled with Italians doing the Cinque Terre in 14 days.

▲▲**Monterosso al Mare (town #5)**—This is a resort with cars, hotels, rentable beach umbrellas, and crowds. Walk east of the station through the tunnel for the Old World charm (and the nearly hourly boat to Vernazza, 1997 departures: 10:15, 11:15, 12:15, 14:15, 15:45, 16:45, 17:45, 18:45). If you want a sandy beach, this is it. Adventurers may want to rent a rowboat or paddleboat and find their own private cove. The TI is open from 10:00 to 12:00 and 15:30 to 19:30, and closed Sunday afternoon (tel. 0187/817-506).

Sleeping Elsewhere on the Cinque Terre
(L1,600 = about $1, tel. code: 0187)

If you're trying to avoid my readers, stay away from Vernazza and Mama Rosa's. Rich, sun-worshipping softies like Monterosso. Winos and mountain goats prefer Corniglia. Students sleep cheap in Riomaggiore. Sophisticated Italians and Germans take stuffy Manarola. (See "Sleeping in Vernazza," above, for room-finding tips.)

Sleeping in Riomaggiore
(tel. code: 0187, zip code: 19017)

Riomaggiore is bursting with private rooms. It's a very competitive scene. **Mar Mar Rooms** is a well-organized network of private rooms run by English-speaking Mario Franceschetti (Db-L70,000, bunky family deals, you can request kitchen, balcony, open year-round; Via Don Minzoni 6, tel. 0187/920-932, fax 0187/920-932, when full they will not return your fax). **Michielini Anna** rents good rooms (five D-L70,000 with kitchens; across from the Central Bar at Via Colombo 143, tel. 0187/920-950 for English-speaking Daniela). **Luciano and Roberto Fazioli** have five apartments, nine rooms, and a slummy seven-bed mini-hostel. Prices range from L25,000 to L50,000 per person (Via Colombo 94, tel. 0187/920-587 or 0187/920-904). **Edi** has a similar network of rooms (Via Colombo 111, tel. & fax 0187/920-325, cellular: 033-8619-0434). If friendly Ivo is on duty at the **Bar Central**, he'll help you find a room (tel. 0187/920-208). Ivo lived in San Francisco and speaks great English. His Bar Central is a good stop for breakfast and prize-winning gelato, and it's the only lively late-night place in town.

Youth Hostel **Mama Rosa** is run with a splash by Rosa Ricci (an agressively friendly character who snares backpackers at the train station), her husband, Carmine (a.k.a. "Papa Rosa"), and their English-speaking son, Silvio. This unique comedy of errors creates a special bond among the young, rugged, and poor who sleep here. Many consider it a slum. It's a chaotic but manageable jumble with the ambience of a YMCA locker room filled with bunk beds (L25,000 beds—price promised through 1998; 20 yards directly in front of the station; no curfew; just show up without a reservation—the earlier the better, no telephone). The nine coed rooms, with four to ten beds each, are plain, basic, and poorly ventilated. But a family atmosphere rages with hand-wash laundry facilities, trickle-down showers (best in afternoon), and Silvio's five cats. This is one of those rare places where perfect strangers become good friends with the slurp of spaghetti, and wine supersedes the concept of ownership. For sanity, sleep at the new Manarola hostel. For value, spend a few extra lire and find a private room. For new friends, the aroma of cat pee, and memories you'll be unable to forget, it's Mama Rosa's.

Eat well at **La Lampara** (check out their *frutti di mare* pizza, *trenete al pesto*, and the rice with seafood, closed Tuesday) on Via Colombo. The Pizzeria at Via Colombo 26 serves thick pizza by the delicious slice.

Sleeping and Eating in Manarola
(tel. code: 0187, zip code: 19010)

Marina Piccola has ten bright, modern rooms on the water, so they figure a warm welcome is unnecessary (Db-L120,000, requires dinner in July and August, CC:VMA, tel. 0187/920-103, fax 0187/920-966).

Up the hill, the utterly normal **Albergo ca' d'Andrean** is quiet, comfortable, modern, and very hotelesque, with ten big sunny rooms and a cool garden complete with orange trees. One-night drop-ins are OK, but not one-night reservations (Db L105,000, closed November; Via A. Discovolo 101, tel. 0187/920-040, fax 0187/920-452, Simone SE).

Farther up the street, **Casa Capellini** rents four rooms (D-L70,000, the *alta camera* on the top with a kitchen, private terrace, and knockout view-L80,000; take a hard right on the church square, then two doors down the hill on your right, Via Antonio Discovolo 6 or Via Ettore Cozzani 12, tel. 0187/920-823, run by a quiet older man and his daughter, who speak no English).

Manarola Ostello, Manarola's new youth hostel, is at the top of the town overlooking the church (beds-L25,000, 48 beds total; Via Riccobaldi 21, tel. 0187/920-113 fax 0187/920-866). While this is great news for travelers, the conservative people of Manarola are worried that the hostel crowd will disrupt the town's decency and tranquility. Please be sensitive to their concerns.

Sleeping in Corniglia
(tel. code: 0187, zip code: 19010)
At the town-end promontory, **Maria Guelfi** (tel. 0187/812-178) and **Senora Silvana** (tel. 0187/513-830) offer rooms. **Affittasi Vista Mare** has rooms scattered all over town (tel. 0187/812-293). **Pellegrini** has three rooms (D-L60,000, Via Solferino 34, tel. 0187/812-184) or try **Villa Sandra** (Via Fieschi 100, tel. 0187/812-384). The **Bar-Ristorante Dan Tinola** offers good meals and cheap rooms as does **Villa Cecio** (on main road 100 yards toward Vernazza, views, 0187/812-043). There is a good chance someone will be waiting for stray travelers at the station with a car to run you up to their place in the town.

Sleeping in Monterosso
(tel. code: 0187, zip code: 19016)
Monterosso al Mare, the most beach-resorty of the five Cinque Terre towns, offers maximum comfort and ease. There are plenty of hotels, rentable beach umbrellas, shops, and cars. The TI (Pro Loco) can find you a L40,000-per-person room in a private home (below station, open 10:00–12:00 and 15:30–19:30, closed Sunday afternoon, tel. 0187/817-506). If driving to Monterosso, leave the freeway at Carrodano exit (30 minutes from there to Monterosso) and park (L10,000/day) in the huge beachfront guarded lot.

The following hotel listings are listed in the order you'll see them as you head either right or left out of the station.

Turn right leaving the station to the **Hotel Baia**. Facing the beach, over half of the Baia's 30 comfortable rooms come with great beachfront balconies (Db-L150,000–180,000 including breakfast, CC:VM; Via Fegina 88, tel. 0187/817-512, fax 0187/818-322). Farther on, **Hotel Cinque Terre** is a slick new building with 54 similar rooms on the big road into (not out of) town near the beach (Db-L180,000, Db-L200,000, breakfast included, dinner is required in July and August, open April–October, CC:VMA, reconfirm reservations, signs say "Hotel 5 Terre," easy parking; Via IV Novembre 21, tel. 0187/817-543, fax 0187/818-380).

Turn left out of the station to the bright, airy **Pension Agavi** (eight rooms, some with balcony, Db-L110,000, tel. 0187/817-171, fax 0187/818-264, Claudia SE). The tunnel then leads to the old town and three unexceptional places that require dinner mid-June through mid-September: the neglected but cheap **Albergo Marina** (D-L95,000, Db-L110,000, open March–October; Via Buranco 40, tel. & fax 0187/817-242 or 0187/817-613); the big, fancy, and more expensive **Albergo degli Amici** (no views; next door at Via Buranco 36, tel. 0187/817-544, fax 0187/817-424); and **Ristorante/Pensione al Carugio** (D-L80,000, Db-L90,000, modern, blocky, no-view apartment at top of town; 15 Via S. Pietro, tel. 0187/817-453).

Farther on, the lovingly managed **Hotel Villa Steno** features great view balconies, private gardens off some rooms, TVs, telephones, all the comforts, and the friendly help of English-speaking Matteo. Of his 16 rooms, 12 have view balconies (Sb-L100,000, Db-L160,000, Tb-L190,000, Qb-L220,000, with hearty buffet breakfast, L10,000 discount per room per night if you pay with cash and show this book; ten-minute hike from the station at the top of the old town at Via Roma 109, tel. 0187/817-028 or 0187/818-336, fax 0187/817-056, Web site: www.pasini.com, e-mail: steno@pasini.com). Readers get a free glass of the local sweet wine, Sciacchetrà, when they check in—ask. The Steno has a tiny parking lot (free, but call to reserve a spot). The same family runs the **Albergo Pasquale**, a place with more stars but less soul on the beach (and train tracks). While Villa Steno is quieter, it's a climb from the beach and station. If Steno is full, they'll honor Steno prices at Pasquale (first place after tunnel; air-con, Via Fegina 4, tel. 0187/817-550 or 0187/817-477, fax 0187/817-056, Felicita SE).

Sleeping near the Cinque Terre

La Spezia: When all else fails, you can stay in a noisy, bigger town like La Spezia. Each of the following places is within a block of the train station. The elegant, old, newly restored **Hotel Firenze e Continentale** has all the classy comforts but no parking (Db-L190,000, maybe L160,000 in slow time, includes buffet breakfast, good group rates, CC:VMA, air-con, elevator; Via Paleocapa 7, 19122 La Spezia, tel. 0187/713-200, fax 0187/714-930, Maria Gabriella Liconti SE). **Albergo Parma,** bright and bleachy clean with TVs and folding metal furniture in the rooms, is located just below the station, down the stairs (D-L70,000, Db-L85,000, less for two nights, CC:VM; Via Fiume 143, 19100 La Spezia, tel. 0187/743-010, fax 0187/743-240). **Hotel Terminus** has filthy rooms with worn-out carpets, yellow walls, and old plumbing (D-L60,000, Db-L75,000; Via Paleocapa 21, just down from the station, tel. 0187/703-436). There's an automatic Laundromat nearby. Friday morning a huge open-air market sprawls for about a mile from the station.

Transportation Connections—Cinque Terre

The five towns of the Cinque Terre are on a milk-run train line described earlier in this chapter. Hourly trains connect each town with the others, La Spezia, and Genoa. While a few of the milk-run trains go to more distant points (Milan or Pisa), it's faster to change in La Spezia to a bigger train.

From La Spezia by train to: Rome (10/day, 4 hrs), Pisa (hrly, 60 min), Florence (hrly, 2.5 hrs, change at Pisa), Milan (hrly, 3 hrs, change in Genoa), Venice (2 direct 6-hr trains/ day—also from Monterosso).

Killing time in La Spezia's station? The station bar is OK, but 2 blocks down the street, C'est Bon Casa del Cioccolato serves crepes, gelati, and designer chocolates in turn-of-the-century splendor (15:00–23:00, closed Tuesday, Piazza Saint Bon 1, tel. 0185/705-850).

AMSTERDAM

Amsterdam is a progressive way of life housed in Europe's most 17th-century city. It's a city built on good living, cozy cafés, great art, street-corner jazz, stately history, and a spirit of live and let live. It has 800,000 people and as many bikes, with more canals than Venice—and as many tourists. While Amsterdam may box your Puritan ears, this great, historic city is an experiment in freedom.

Planning Your Time

While I'd sleep in nearby Haarlem, Amsterdam is worth a full day of sightseeing on even the busiest itinerary. While the city has a couple of must-see museums, its best sight is its own breezy ambience.

Amsterdam by tram and foot: You can see the top sights by foot, but a couple of hops on tram #20, which hits the biggies, makes it easier.

In the morning, tour the Anne Frank House (from the train station, catch tram #20B, which starts running at 9:00, or take tram #13 or #17 if you're running earlier; get off at the "Westerkerk" stop).

Next, for a dose of great art, tour the Rijksmuseum (has a café) and neighboring Van Gogh Museum (from Anne Frank House or train station, catch tram #20B to "Hobbemastraat"). The Leidesplein, a lively square with lots of people-watching and eateries (see Eating, below), is several blocks west.

Mid-afternoon, take a relaxing hour-long cruise from the dock at Spui (from the Rijksmuseum, it's either a 15-minute walk or a tram ride—#16 down Vijzelstraat or #20B on a circuitous route—to "Spui," rhymes with "cow").

Near Spui, choose from: the idyllic Begijnhof, Amsterdam Historical Museum, touristy flower market, or more food (see Eating, below).

Late afternoon, walk from Spui down the busy Kalverstraat pedestrian street to Dam Square, the heart of Amsterdam (palace, church, monument). From Dam Square, the Red Light District is several blocks northeast (see map), or walk down Damrak a few blocks to get back to the train station.

Orientation (tel. code: 020)

The central train station is your starting point (tourist information, bike rental, and trolleys and buses fanning out to all points). Damrak is the main street axis, connecting the station with Dam Square (people-watching and hangout center) and its Royal Palace. From this spine, the city spreads out like a fan, with 90 islands, hundreds of bridges, and a series of concentric canals (named "Princess," "Gentleman's," and "Emperor's") laid out in the 17th century, Holland's Golden Age. The city's major sights are within walking distance of Dam Square.

Tourist Information

Try to avoid Amsterdam's inefficient VVV office across from the train station. (VVV is Dutch for tourist-information office; daily 9:00–17:00 or later; TI in the train station open Monday–Saturday 8:00–20:00, Sunday until 17:00). Most people wait 30 minutes just to pick up the information brochures and get a room. Avoid this line by studying the wall display of publications for sale and going straight to the sales desk (where everyone ends up anyway, since any information of substance will cost you). Consider buying a city map (f3.50), *What's On* (f3.50, monthly entertainment calendar listing all the museum hours and much more), and any of the walking tour brochures (f4, "Voyage of Discovery Through the Center," "Jewish Amsterdam," "Stroll Through Jordaan," and "Jordaan: Three Walking Tours"). The "Amsterdam Culture & Leisure Pass," offering free or discounted admissions to some sights and boat rides, isn't worth the clutter or cost (f33.60, doesn't include Anne Frank House). Nor does it make sense to stand in line at the VVV to buy prepaid same-cost admissions to various Amsterdam sights.

The TI on Leidsestraat is much less crowded (daily 9:00–19:00, closing at 17:00 on Sunday). But for f75 cents a minute, you can save yourself a trip by calling the tourist information toll-line at 06-3403-4066 (Monday–Saturday 9:00–17:00). If you're staying in nearby Haarlem, use the helpful Haarlem TI (see Haarlem section, below) to answer most of your Amsterdam questions and provide you with the brochures.

Don't use the TI to book a room. The phone system is easy, everyone speaks English, and the listings in this book are a better value than the potluck booking you'd be charged for at the TI.

Helpful Hints

Many shops close all day Sunday and Monday morning. A *plein* is a square, *gracht* means canal, and most canals are lined by streets with the same name. Handy telephone cards (f10, f25, or f50) are sold at the TI, GVB public transit office, tobacco shops, post office, and train stations. The Dutch go "surfen" at the Internet Center a couple blocks east of the Rijksmuseum (9:00–18:00, closed Sunday, Monday morning, and Saturday by 17:00, Weteringschans 165, tel. 0800-0403, Web site: www.eteringschans.com). Beware of the bogus telephone offices dressed up like government outlets but ready to rip you off. Tourists are considered green and rich, and the city has more than its share of hungry thieves.

Arrival in Amsterdam

By Train: Amsterdam swings, and the hinge that connects it to the world is its perfectly central Central Station. Walk out the door and you're in the heart of the city. You'll nearly trip over trams ready to take you anywhere your feet won't. Straight ahead is Damrak street, leading to Dam Square. With your back to the entrance of the station, the TI and GVB public transit office are to your left, just across the bus lanes.

   By Plane: From Schiphol Airport, take the train to Amsterdam (4/hrly, 20 min, f6). If you'll be staying in Haarlem, take a direct express bus from the airport to Haarlem (#236 or #362, 2/hour, 30 min, f7).

Getting Around Amsterdam

The uncrowded and helpful transit-information office (GVB) is next to the TI (in front of the train station). Its free multilingual *Tourist Guide to Public Transport* includes a transit map and explains ticket options and tram connections to all the sights. Ask for the free "Circle Tram 20" brochure listing all of the stops (and nearby sights) of this handy tram that makes a loop around Amsterdam (#20A goes clockwise, #20B goes counterclockwise).

   By Bus, Tram, and Metro: Individual tickets cost f3.25 and give you an hour on the buses, trams, and metro system (on trams and buses pay as you board; on the metro buy tickets from machines before boarding). **Strip cards** are cheaper than buying individual tickets. Any downtown ride costs two strips (good for an hour of transfers). A card with 15 strips costs f11.25 at the GVB public transit office, train stations, post offices, airport, or tobacco shops throughout the country; shorter strip tickets (two, three, and eight strips) are also sold on some buses and trams. Strip cards are good on buses all over Holland (e.g., six strips for Haarlem to the airport), and you can share them with your partner. For f10, a **Day Card** gives you unlimited transportation on the buses and metro for a day in Amsterdam; you'll break even if you take three trips (valid until 6:00 the following morning; buy when you board or at GVB public transit office—which also sells a two-day version for f16). If you get lost in Amsterdam, ten of the city's 17 trams take you back to the central train station.

By Foot: The longest walk a tourist would take is 45 minutes from the station to the Rijksmuseum. Watch out for silent but potentially painful bikes, trams, and curb posts.

By Bike: One-speed bikes, with "brrringing" bells and two locks, rent for f8 per day at the central train station (Monday–Friday 6:00–22:00, weekends 8:00–22:00; deposit of f200, $150, or your credit-card imprint required; entrance to the left down the ramp as you leave the station, tel. 020/624-8391). In the summer, arrive early or make an easy telephone reservation. To take advantage of their (unadvertised) rate of four hours for f5, have the time of your checkout noted on the receipt.

By Boat: While the city is great on foot or bike, there is a "Museum Boat" and a similar "Canal Bus," with an all-day ticket that shuttles tourists from sight to sight. Tickets cost f22 (with discounts that'll save you about f5 on admissions). The sales booths, in front of the central train station (and the boats), offer handy free brochures with museum times and admission prices. The narrated ride takes 90 minutes if you don't get off (every 30 minutes in summer, every 45 minutes off-season, seven stops, live quadrilingual guide, 10:00–17:00, discounted after 13:00, tel. 020/622-2181).

Sights—Amsterdam

▲▲▲**Rijksmuseum**—Focus on the Dutch masters: Rembrandt, Hals, Vermeer, and Steen. For a list of the top 20 paintings, pick up the cheap (f1) leaflet "A Tour of the Golden Age" and plan your attack (or follow the self-guided tour, one of 20, in my *Mona Winks* guidebook). Audiotaped tours are available (f7.50, more than 200 paintings described, shortcuts advisable).

Follow the museum's chronological layout to see painting evolve from narrative religious art, to religious art starring the Dutch love of good living and eating, to the Golden Age, when secular art dominates. With no local church or royalty to commission big canvases in the post-1648 Protestant Dutch republic, artists specialized in portraits of the wealthy city class (Hals), pretty still lifes (Claesz), and nonpreachy slice-of-life art (Steen). The museum has four quietly wonderful Vermeers. And, of course, a thoughtful brown soup of Rembrandt, including the *Night Watch*. Works by Rembrandt show his excellence as a portraitist for hire (*De Staalmeesters*) and offer some powerful psychological studies, such as *St. Peter's Denial*—with Jesus in the murky background (f12.50, daily 10:00–17:00, great bookshop, decent cafeteria, tram #2, #5, or #20 from the station, Stadhouderskade 42, tel. 020/673-2121).

▲▲▲**Van Gogh Museum**—Next to the Rijksmuseum, this outstanding and user-friendly museum is a stroll through a beautifully displayed garden of van Gogh's work and life (f12.50, daily 10:00–17:00, Paulus Pitterstraat 7, tel. 020/570-5200). Note: This museum will be closed for renovation in September '98, and van

Gogh's art will gradually migrate to the south wing of the Rijksmuseum.

Stedelijk Modern Art Museum—Next to the Van Gogh Museum, this place is fun, far-out, and refreshing, with mostly post-1945 art, but also a permanent collection of Monet, van Gogh, Cézanne, Picasso, and Chagall (f9, daily 11:00–19:00, closes at 17:00 November–March, tel. 020/573-2911).

▲▲**Anne Frank House**—A fascinating look at the hideaway where young Anne hid when the Nazis occupied the Netherlands. Pick up the English pamphlet at the door and don't miss the thought-provoking neo-Nazi exhibit in the last room. Fascism smolders on (f10, June–August, Monday–Saturday 9:00–19:00, Sunday 10:00–19:00, September–May closes daily at 17:00, 263 Prinsengracht, tel. 020/556-7100). For an interesting glimpse of Holland under the Nazis, rent the powerful movie *Soldier of Orange* before you leave home.

Westerkerk—Near Anne Frank's House, this landmark church, with a barren interior and Amsterdam's tallest steeple, is worth climbing for the view (f3, ascend only with a guide, departures on the hour, April–September 10:00–16:00, closed Sunday, tel. 020/624-7766).

Royal Palace (Koninklijk Paleis)—It's right on Dam Square, built when Amsterdam was feeling its global oats, and worth a look (f5, open daily mid-May–early September, 12:30–17:00).

▲**Begijnhof**—Step into this tiny, idyllic courtyard in the city center to escape the crazy 1990s and feel the charm of old Amsterdam. Notice house #34, a 500-year-old wooden structure (rare since repeated fires taught city fathers a little trick called brick). Peek into the hidden Catholic church, opposite the English Reformed church, where the pilgrims worshiped while waiting for their voyage to the New World (marked by a plaque near door). Be considerate of the people who live here (free, on Begijnensteeg Lane, just off Kalverstraat between #130 and #132, pick up English info flier at office near entrance).

Amsterdam Historical Museum—Offering the town's best look into the age of the Dutch masters, this creative and hardworking museum features Rembrandt's paintings, fine English descriptions, and a carillon loft. The loft comes with push-button recordings of the town bell tower's greatest hits and a self-serve carillon "keyboard" to ring a few bells yourself. The museum is next to the Begijnhof, Kalverstraat 92 (f8, weekdays 10:00–17:00, Saturday and Sunday 11:00–17:00, good-value restaurant). Its free pedestrian corridor is a powerful teaser.

Rembrandt's House—Interesting only to his fans, with 250 etchings (f7.5, Monday–Saturday 10:00–17:00, Sunday 13:00–17:00, 15-minute English audiovisual presentation upon request, Jodenbreestraat 4).

Holland Experience—With the slogan "Experience Holland in 30 minutes," this show combines footage of Holland with multivi-

Amsterdam

sual effects (e.g., as you see a boat sailing, you feel wind on your face). It's fun but pricey, and focuses more on goofy tourists than on the wonders of Holland (f17.50, daily 19:00–21:00, Jodenbreestraat 8, near Rembrandt's House and Waterlooplein street market, metro: Waterlooplein, tel. 020/422-2233).

▲**Tropenmuseum (Tropical Museum)**—As close to the Third World as you'll get without lots of vaccinations, this imaginative museum offers wonderful re-creations of tropical-life scenes and explanations of Third World problems (f10, Monday–Friday 10:00–17:00, Saturday and Sunday 12:00–17:00, tram #9 to Linnaeusstraat 2).

Netherlands Maritime (Scheepvaart) Museum—This kid-friendly museum is fascinating if you're into Henry Hudson or *scheepvaarts* (f12.50, Monday–Saturday 10:00–17:00, Sunday 12:00–17:00, October–April closed Monday, English explanations, bus #22 or #28 to Kattenburgerplein 1).

▲**Herengracht Canal Mansion (Willet Holthuysen Museum)**—This 1687 patrician house offers a fine look at the old rich of Amsterdam, with a good 15-minute English introductory film and a 17th-century garden in back (f7.50, open weekdays 10:00–17:00, Saturday and Sunday 11:00–17:00, tram #4 or #9 to Herengracht 605).

Our Lord in the Attic (Amstelkring)—Near the station, in the red-light district, you'll find a 17th-century merchant's house turned museum, with a fascinating hidden church. This dates from 1661, when post-Reformation Dutch Catholics were not allowed to worship in public. The church fills the attics of several homes (f7.50, weekdays 10:00–17:00, Saturday and Sunday 13:00–17:00, O.Z. Voorburgwal 40).

▲**Red-Light District**—Europe's most high-profile ladies of the night shiver and shimmy in display-case windows along Voorburgwal, between the station and the Oudekerk. It's dangerous late at night but a fascinating walk at any other time after noon.

According to CNN statistics, more than 60 percent of Amsterdam's prostitutes are HIV-positive (but a naive tourist might see them as just hardworking girls from Latin America or Africa trying their best to build up a bank account—f50 at a time).

Amsterdam has two sex museums, one in the red-light district and one a block in front of the train station on Damrak. While visiting one can be called sightseeing, visiting both is a bit obsessive. Here's a comparison:

The red-light district sex museum is less offensive, with five sparsely decorated rooms relying heavily on badly-dressed dummies acting out the roles that women of the neighborhood play. It also has videos, phone-sex phones, and a lot of uninspired paintings, old photos, and sculpture (f5, along the canal at Oudezijds Achterburgwal 54).

The Damrak sex museum goes much deeper, with many more rooms. It tells the story of pornography from the 1860s through today, starting with early French pornographic photos. Every sexual deviation is uncovered in its various displays, and the nude and pornographic art is a cut above the other sex museum's. Also interesting is the international sex art and memorabilia from Europe, India, and Asia. You'll find a Marilyn Monroe tribute and some S&M displays, too (f4, Damrak 18, a block in front of the station).

Vondelpark—This huge and lively city park gives a fragrant look at today's Dutch youth, especially on sunny summer weekends.

Leidseplein—Brimming with cafés, this people- and pigeon-watching square is an impromptu stage for street artists, accordionists, jugglers, and unicyclists. Sunny afternoons are the liveliest. Stroll nearby Lange Leidsedwarsstraat (1 block north) for a taste-bud tour of ethnic eateries from Greece to Indonesia.

Shopping—Amsterdam brings out the browser even in those who were not born to shop. Ten general markets, open six days a week, keep folks who brake for garage sales pulling U-ies. Shopping highlights include Waterlooplein (flea market), the huge Albert Cuyp street market, various flower markets (daily along Singel Canal near the mint tower, or Munttoren), diamond dealers (free cutting and polishing demos at shops behind the Rijksmuseum and on Dam Square), and Kalverstraat, Amsterdam's teeming walking/shopping street (parallel to Damrak).

Tours of Amsterdam

▲▲**Canal-Boat Tour**—These long, low, tourist-laden boats leave continually from several docks around the town for a good, if uninspiring, 60-minute quadrilingual introduction to the city (f13, 2/hr, more frequent in summer). One very central company is at the corner of Spui and Rokin, about five minutes from Dam Square (9:30–22:00, tel. 020/623-3810). No fishing allowed but bring your camera for this relaxing orientation. Some prefer to cruise at night when the bridges are illuminated.

Biking and Walking Tours—The Yellow Bike Tour company offers bike tours (f29 for 3-hour city tour, f42.50 for 6.5-hour 35-kilometer countryside tour) as well as city walking tours (f15, 1.75 hours) daily April through November (Nieuwezijds Kolk 29, near train station, tel. 020/620-6940).

Brewery Tour—The infamous Heineken brewery tours are in full slosh Monday through Friday 9:30–11:00 (f2, Stadhouderskade 78).

Sleeping in Amsterdam
(f1=about 50 cents, tel. code: 020)

Sleep Code: **S**=Single, **D**=Double/Twin, **T**=Triple, **Q**=Quad, **b**=bathroom, **t**=toilet only, **s**=shower only, **CC**=Credit Card (**V**isa, **M**asterCard, **A**mex). Nearly everyone speaks English in the Netherlands, and prices include breakfast unless noted.

While I prefer sleeping in cozy Haarlem (see below), those into more urban charms will find that Amsterdam has plenty of beds. For a f5 fee, the VVV (tourist office) can find you a room in the price range of your choice.

Sleeping near the Station

Amstel Botel, the city's only remaining "boat hotel," is a shipshape, bright, and clean floating hotel with 175 rooms (Sb-f125, Db-f143, Tb-f190, f10 extra for canalside view and worth it, breakfast-f10, f30/day parking pass, CC:VMA, 400 yards from the station, on your left as you leave, you'll see the sign, Oosterdokskade 2-4, 1011 AE Amsterdam, tel. 020/626-4247, fax 020/639-1952).

Sleeping between Dam Square and Anne Frank's House

Hotel Toren is a chandeliered historic mansion in a pleasant, canalside setting in downtown Amsterdam. This splurge is classy, quiet, and 2 blocks northeast of Anne Frank's (S-f85, Sb-f165–85, three unadvertised D-f170, Db-f200–275, Tb-f240, bridal suites for f285–400 make you want to get married; prices vary according to season; CC:VMA, Keizersgracht 164, 1015 CZ Amsterdam, tel. 020/622-6352, fax 020/626-9705, e-mail: hotel.toren@tip.nl).

Well-heeled readers will prefer the pricier, fancier 17th-century **Canal House Hotel** a few doors down (Sb-from f210, Db-f225–270, CC:VMA, Keizersgracht 148, 1015 CX Amsterdam, tel. 020/622-5182, fax 020/624-1317, e-mail: canalhousehotel@compuserve.com).

Cheap hotels line the noisy main drag between the town hall and Anne Frank's House. Expect a long, steep, and depressing stairway, with quieter rooms in the back. **Hotel Aspen**, a good value for a budget hotel, is tidy, simple, and well-maintained, with firm beds (S-f50, D-f75, Db-f110, Tb-f120, Qb-f160, CC:MA, ideally reserve by fax using credit- card number, Raadhuisstraat 31, 1016 DC Amsterdam, tel. 020/626-6714, fax 020/620-0866). A few doors away, **Hotel Pax** has large, plain but airy rooms, carefully managed by Mr. and Mrs. Veldhuizen (tiny D-f75, D-f85, T-f105, showers down the hall, Raadhuisstraat 37, tel. 020/624-9735).

Sleeping in the Leidseplein Area

The area around Amsterdam's museum square (Museumplein) and the rip-roaring nightlife center (Leidseplein) is colorful, comfortable, convenient, and affordable. The first two hotels are on a quiet street, easy to reach from the central station (tram #1, #2, #5, or #20 to Leidseplein, then head west a block along the north side of canal), and within easy walking distance of the Rijksmuseum.

Hotel Maas, with a phone, TV, and coffeepot in every room, is a big, well-run, elegant, quiet, and hotelesque place (S-f100, one D-f125, Db-f195–295, prices vary with view and room size, extra person-f50, suite-f350, CC:VMA, hearty breakfast, air con, elevator, Leidsekade 91, 1017 PN Amsterdam, tel. 020/623-3868, fax 020/622-2613, e-mail: maas@worldaccess.nl).

Kooyk Hotel is a homey budget place with 17 rooms, four on the ground floor. Halls are narrow, some top rooms are dumpy, bedspreads and furnishings are faded, but the canalside rooms are bright (S-f75, D-f115, T-f155, Q-f190, Quint-f215, CC:VM, Leidsekade 82, 1017 PM Amsterdam, tel. 020/623-0295, fax 020/638-8337, run by Pierre).

Hotel Keizershof is a wonderfully Dutch place, with six bright, airy rooms in a 17th-century canal house. You'll climb a steep spiral staircase to rooms named after old-time Hollywood stars. The friendly De Vries family has made this place a treat for 38 years and offers its guests plenty of fine eating advice (S-f65, D-f120, Ds-f130, Db-f140, T-f150, family deals, includes classy breakfast, CC:VM, where Keizers canal crosses Spiegelstraat at Keizersgracht 618, 1017 ER Amsterdam, tel. 020/622-2855, fax 020/624-8412). It's a ten-minute walk from Leidseplein.

Hotel Seven Bridges, tastefully decorated with antiques, is a lot nicer than my house. The eleven rooms feature fine draperies, woven carpets, and beautifully crafted furniture (Sb-f170–230, two D-f150, Db-f190–270, prices vary with quality, ask for room #5 for a splurge, CC:VMA, near Rembrandtplein, Reguliersgracht 31, 1017 LK Amsterdam, reserve three–four weeks in advance, tel. 020/623-1329). Take trams #16, #24, or #25 from the station and get off at "Keizersgracht."

Hotel De Leydsche Hof has a fine canalside locale with simple, quiet rooms. Its peaceful demeanor almost helps you overlook the flimsy cots and old carpets (D-f85, Db-f95–110, Tb-f130, Qb-f170, no breakfast, Leidsegracht 14, 1016 CK Amsterdam, tel. 020/623-2148, run by friendly Mr. Piller). Also a ten-minute walk from Leidseplein.

Sleeping near Vondel Park

These options connect you with the sights via an easy tram ride or a pleasant 15-minute walk or short bike ride through Vondel Park.

Karen McCuster, a friendly Englishwoman, rents cozy rooms in her home as a B&B on weekends (Friday, Saturday, and Sunday; three-day stay required) and as a B without the breakfast the rest of the week (no minimum stay required). Rooms are clean, white, and bright with red carpeting and green plants; one room has a private rooftop patio. Advance reservations are necessary (D-f75–100 per night for B&B weekend, D-f70–90 weekdays). Tram #2 from the station gets you to Zeilstraat 22 (third floor, 1075 SH Amsterdam, tel. 020/679-2753); get off at "Amstelveenseweg" and cross street in same direction that tram runs (every ten minutes; buy ticket or day card on board).

Toro Hotel, in a peaceful residential area at the edge of Vondelpark, is your personal turn-of-the-century hotel/mansion, with an elegant dining hall and 22 rooms with TVs, safes, and phones. Rooms in the back overlook the park, canal, and terrace, yours for relaxing. Mr. Plooy fusses over his guests (Sb-f160, Db-f190, Tb-f280, CC:VMA, elevator, easy parking, Koningslaan 64, 1075 AG Amsterdam, tel. 020/673-7223, fax 020/675-0031). Take tram #2 from the station; get off at "Koningslaan."

Hotel Filosoof greets you with Aristotle and Plato in the foyer and classical music in its lobby. Its 25 rooms are subtly

decorated with themes; the Egyptian room has a frieze of hiero-
glyphics. Philosophers' sayings hang on walls, professors wander
down the halls, and on Thursday evenings in fall, guests meet to
discuss philosophy—in Dutch. The rooms are small (and split
between two buildings), but the hotel is endearing and the terrace
is made for pondering (Sb-f145, Db-f175, Tb-f235, Qb-f275,
cheaper off-season, all rooms with TV and phone, reserve three
weeks in advance for summer weekends, Anna Vondelstraat 6,
five-minute walk from tram #6 line, get off at "Constantyn Huy-
genstraat," tel. 020/683-3013, fax 020/685-3750).

Hostels
Christian Youth Hostel Eben Haezer is scruffy, with 20-bed
women's dorms and a 40-bed men's dorm. Friendly, well-run, in a
great neighborhood, it has Amsterdam's best rock-bottom budget
beds (f25 per bed with sheets and breakfast, maximum age 35, near
Anne Frank's House, Bloemstraat 179, tel. 020/624-4717). It serves
cheap, hot meals, runs a snack bar, offers lockers to all, leads
nightly Bible studies, and closes the dorms from 10:00 to 14:00.
The hostel will happily hold a room for a phone call (ideally three–
seven days in advance). Its sister Christian hostel, **The Shelter**
(in the red-light district, open to any traveler, f25 for a bed, tel.
020/625-3230), is similar but definitely not preaching to the choir.
    The city's two IYHF hostels are **Vondelpark**, Amsterdam's
top hostel (f29 with breakfast, S-f70, D-f90, non-members pay f5
extra, sheets-f6.50, lots of school groups, six–22 beds per dorm,
right on the park at Zandpad 5, tel. 020/683-1744, fax 020/616-
6591), and **Stadsdoelen YH** (f28 with breakfast, just past Dam
Square, open January–October, Kloveniersburgwal 97, tel.
020/624-6832, fax 020/639-1035).

Eating in Amsterdam
Dutch food is basic and hearty. *Eetcafés* are local cafés serving budget sandwiches, soup, eggs, and so on. Cafeterias, *broodje* (sandwich
shops), and automatic food shops are also good bets for budget
eaters. Picnics are cheap and easy. A central supermarket is **Albert
Heijn,** near the flower market, at the corner of Koningsplein and
Singel canal (Monday–Saturday 10:00–20:00, Sunday 12:00–18:00).

Eating near Spui in the Center
The city university's **Atrium** is a great, budget cafeteria (f9
meals, Monday–Friday 12:00–14:00 and 17:00–19:00, from Spui,
walk west down Landebrug Steeg past the canalside Café 't
Gasthuys 3 blocks to Oudezijds Achterburgwal 237, go through
arched doorway on the right, tel. 020/525-3999). **Café 't
Gasthuys,** one of Amsterdam's many "brown" cafés (named for
their smoke-stained walls), makes good sandwiches and offers

indoor or canalside seating (daily 12:00–01:00, walk west down Landebrug Steeg to Grimburgwal 7).

La Place, a cafeteria on the ground floor of the Vroom Dreesmann department store, has islands of entrées, veggies, fruits, desserts, and beverages (Monday–Saturday 10:00–21:00, Thursday until 22:00, Sunday 11:00–21:00, near Mint Tower, corner of Rokin and Muntplein). The locals splurge for Dutch food at **Restaurant Haesje Claes** (f25 entrees, daily 12:00–24:00, Spuistraat 275, tel. 020/624-9998). **Blincker Theatercafé** is popular with the younger crowd (open from 19:00, St. Barberenstraat 7-9, tel. 020/627-1938).

Eating in or near the Train Station
Keuken van 1870 has been cooking very simple, cheap cafeteria meals in a simple setting since, you guessed it, 1870 (Monday–Friday 12:30–20:00, weekends 16:00–21:00, Spuistraat 4, several blocks west of station, tel. 020/624-8965). The train station has a surprisingly classy budget self-service **Stationsrestauratie** on platform 1 (Monday–Saturday 7:00–22:00, Sunday from 8:00).

Eating near Anne Frank's House
For pancakes in a family atmosphere, try the **Pancake Bakery** (f11 pancakes, splitting is OK, offers an Indonesian pancake for those who want two experiences in one, daily 12:00–22:00, Prinsengracht 191, several blocks north of A.F. House, tel. 020/625-1333). Across the canal, **DeBolhoed** serves great vegetarian food (daily 12:00–22:00, Prinsengracht 60, tel. 020/626-1803).

Eating near the Rijksmuseum, on Leidseplein
The art deco **American Hotel** dining room serves an elegant all-you-can-eat f12 salad bar (available 12:00–14:30 and 18:00–20:30, where Leidseplein hits Singel Canal). **De Smoeshaan** offers classy and tasty f25 meals (next to Hotel Maas, 50 meters down Singel canal from the American Hotel). On the café-packed street called Lange Leidsedwarsstraat, **Bojo** is a reasonably-priced Indonesian restaurant at #51 (Monday–Wednesday 16:00–01:30, Thursday–Sunday 12:00–01:30, 020/622-7434). If hunger hits in the Rijksmuseum, head for the cafeteria in the west wing's ground floor.

Bars
Try a *jenever* (Dutch gin), the closest thing to an atomic bomb in a shot glass. While cheese gets harder and sharper with age, *jenever* grows smooth and soft. Old *jenever* is best.

Drugs
Amsterdam, Europe's counterculture Mecca, thinks the concept of a "victimless crime" is a contradiction. While hard drugs are definitely out, marijuana causes about as much excitement as a

bottle of beer. A "pot man" with a worldly menu of f25 baggies is a fixture in many bars (walk east from Dam Square on Damstraat for a few blocks, then down to Nieuwmarkt). While several touristy Bulldog cafés are very popular with tourists, less glitzy smaller places (farther from the tourists) offer a better value and a more comfortable atmosphere. Near the corner of Leidsestraat and Prinsengracht, the **Easy Times** coffee shop dangles its menu from a string at the bar. At the brighter **Tops** coffee shop next door, you can use the internet to say high to your friends back home. **Homegrown Fantasy**, about 2 blocks northwest of Dam Square, has a gentle atmosphere and cosmic restroom (daily 12:00–23:00, Nieuwe Zijds Voorburgwal 87a, tel. 020/627-5683). Another interesting place to get information on the marijuana scene in Amsterdam is the American-run **KGB** office (Kannabis Genetics Bureau), formerly the CIA office (Cannabis in Amsterdam), located in the Hempire State Building (Droogbak 1, afternoons, closed Tuesday, tel. 020/627-1646).

▲**Marijuana and Hemp Museum**—This is a collection of dope facts, history, science, and memorabilia (f6, daily 11:00–22:00, Sunday until 17:00, at Oudezijds Achterburgwal 148). While quite small, it has a shocker finale: the high-tech grow room in which tens of varieties of marijuana are cultivated in optimal hydroponic (among other) environments. Some plants stand 5 feet tall and shine under the intense grow lamps. The view is actually through glass walls into the neighboring "Sensi Seed Bank" Grow Shop (which sells carefully cultivated seeds and all the gear needed to grow them). Pot should never be bought on the street in Amsterdam. Well-established coffee shops are considered much safer. Up to 10 grams of marijuana can be possessed but not sold here—not the law but an accepted local standard.

Transportation Connections—Amsterdam

Amsterdam's train-information center requires a long wait. Save lots of time by getting train tickets and information in a small-town station or travel agency. For phone information, call 0900-9292 for local trains or 0900-9296 for international (75 cents/minute, daily 7:00–24:00, wait through recording and hold...hold...hold...).

By train to: Schiphol Airport (4/hr, 20 min, f6.25), **Haarlem** (6/hr, 15 min, f10.50 round-trip), **The Hague** (4/hr, 45 min), **Rotterdam** (2/hr, 1 hr), **Brussels** (hrly, 3 hrs), **Oostende** (hrly, 4 hrs, change in Roosendaal), **Paris** (5/day, 5 hrs, required fast train from Brussels with f21 supplement), **London** (4/day, 10–12 hrs), **Copenhagen** (5/day, 11 hrs), **Frankfurt** (10/day, 5 hrs), **Munich** (8/day, 8 hrs, change in Mannheim), **Bonn** (10/day, 3 hrs), **Bern** (8/day, 9 hrs, change in Basel).

Amsterdam's Schiphol Airport: The airport, like most of Holland, is English-speaking, user-friendly, and below sea level. Its banks offer fair rates (daily 6:00–24:00). Schiphol Airport has

easy bus and train connections (7 miles) into Amsterdam or Haarlem. The airport also has a train station of its own. (You can validate your Eurailpass and hit the rails immediately; or, to stretch
your train pass, buy the short ticket today and start the pass later.)
Schiphol flight information (tel. 06-350-34050 or 0900-503-4050)
can give you flight times and your airline's Amsterdam number for
reconfirmation before going home (75 cents a minute to climb
through its phone tree).

HAARLEM

Cute, cozy yet real, handy to the airport, and just 15 minutes by train from downtown Amsterdam, Haarlem is a fine home base, giving you small-town, overnight warmth with easy access to wild and crazy Amsterdam.

Haarlem is a busy Dutch market town, buzzing with shoppers biking home with fresh bouquets. Enjoy Saturday (general) and Monday (clothing) market days, when the square bustles like a Brueghel painting with cheese, fish, flowers, and families. You'll feel comfortable here. Buy some flowers to brighten your hotel room.

Orientation (tel. code 023)

Tourist Information: Haarlem's VVV, at the train station, is friendlier, more helpful, and less crowded than Amsterdam's. Ask your Amsterdam questions here (Monday–Friday 9:00–17:30, Saturday 11:00–17:00, closed Sunday; closes at 16:00 on off-season Saturdays, tel. 0900-616-1600, 75 cents a minute).

Arrival in Haarlem: As you walk out of the train station, the TI is on your right and the bus station is across the street. Two parallel streets flank the train station (Kruisweg and Jansweg). Head up either one and you'll reach the town square and church within ten minutes. If uncertain of the way, ask a local person, *"Grote Markt?"* ("Main Square?"), and you'll get pointed in the right direction.

Helpful Hints: The handy GWK change office at the station offers decent exchange rates (Monday–Friday 8:00–21:00, Saturday 8:00–20:00, Sunday 9:00–17:00). The train station rents bikes cheaply and easily (f5/4 hours, f8/day, f100 deposit, Monday–Saturday 6:00–24:00, Sunday 7:30–24:00). My Beautiful Laundrette is handy, self-service, and cheap (f10 wash and dry, daily

Haarlem

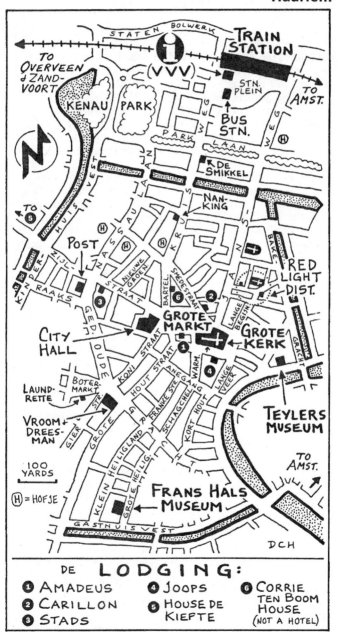

8:30–20:30, near Vroom Dreesman department store at Boter Markt 20). The VVV and local hotels have a helpful parking brochure.

Sights—Haarlem

▲▲**Frans Hals Museum**—Haarlem is the hometown of Frans Hals, and this delightful museum displays many of his greatest paintings in a glorious old building (f7.50, Monday–Saturday 11:00–17:00, Sunday 13:00–17:00, tel. 023/516-4200). Enjoy take-me-back paintings of old-time Haarlem. Peter Brueghel the Younger's painting *Proverbs* (outside room 24) shows 72 old Dutch proverbs; the handy English-language key gives you a fascinating peek into the Dutch old days. The museum across the street features the architecture of old Haarlem.

Corrie Ten Boom House—As many Americans (but few Dutch) know, Haarlem is also home to Corrie Ten Boom (popularized by *The Hiding Place*, an inspirational book and movie about the Ten Boom family's experience hiding Jews from the Nazis). The Ten Boom House, at Barteljorisstraat 19, is open for 45-minute English tours (donation requested; Tuesday–Saturday 10:00–16:00; November–April 11:00–15:00, same days; only one tour/day off-season; tel. 023/531-0823). Some of the guides do more preaching than teaching.

Grote Kerk (Church)—You'll see (and maybe hear) Holland's greatest pipe organ (regular free concerts mid-May–mid-October on Tuesdays at 20:15 and additional concerts in July and August on Thursdays at 15:00; confirm schedule at TI). The church is open and worth a look, if only to see its Oz-like organ (f2.50, Monday–Saturday 10:00–16:00; closes at 15:00 in winter). Note how the organ, which fills the west end, seems to steal the show from the altar. To enter the church, look for the small entrance marked "*Entree*" behind the church, kitty-corner from La Plume restaurant. (There is a handy public WC in the east end of the church.) The new church (Kathedrale Basiliek Sint Bavo at Leidsevaart 146) offers free concerts on Saturdays at 15:00 from April through September.

▲**Teylers Museum**—Famous as the oldest museum in Holland, it used to be interesting mainly as a look at a 200-year-old museum. New exhibition halls (with rotating exhibits) and a café have brought life to the dusty exhibits. Stop by if you enjoy mixing, say, Renaissance sketches with pickled coelecanths (f7.50, Tuesday–Saturday 10:00–17:00, Sunday 12:00–17:00, Spaarne 16).

Red Lights—For a little red-light district precious as a Barbie doll, wander around the church in Haarlem's cutest Begijnhof (2 blocks northeast of the big church, off Lange Begijnestraat, f50, no senior or student discounts). Don't miss the mall marked by the red neon sign, *t'Steegje*. The nearby *t'Poortje*, "office park," costs f7.50.

Nightlife in Haarlem

Haarlem's evening scene is great. The bars around the Grote Kerk and Lange Veerstraat are colorful, lively, and always full of music.

The **Studio** (next to the Hotel Carillon), jammed with Haarlem's 30-something crowd, has a pleasant ambience. **Café Brinkman**, on the square, is a good people-watching perch. **Café 1900** (across from the Corrie Ten Boom House) is classy by day and draws a young crowd with live music on Sunday nights. Lange Veerstraat (behind the church) is probably the best bar street in town. The **Crack** (Lange Veerstraat 32) is the wild and leathery place to go for loud music and smoking. Pot's for sale across the street (#47) at **High Times**. The **Imperial Café and Bar** has live music every night except Sunday (a few doors down from the Crack, at Korte Veerstraat 3).

Don't be shocked if locals drop into a bar, plunk down f25 for a baggie of marijuana, and casually roll a joint. (If you don't like the smell of pot, avoid "coffee shops" sporting Rastafarian yellow, red, and green colors; wildly painted walls; or plants in the windows.)

Sleeping in Haarlem
(f1 = about 50 cents, tel. code: 023)

The helpful Haarlem tourist office ("VVV" at the train station, Monday–Friday 9:00–17:30, Saturday 11:00–17:00, tel. 0900-616-1600, 75 cents/minute) can nearly always find you a f32.50 bed in a nearby private home (for a f9-per-person fee plus a cut of the hotel's money).

Haarlem is most crowded in April, on Easter weekend, May, and August, but if you phone ahead, my recommended hotels will happily hold a room without a deposit (though they may ask for a credit-card number). Nearly every Dutch person you'll encounter speaks English. The listed prices include breakfast (unless otherwise noted) and usually include the f3.50-per-person-per-day tourist tax. To avoid this town's louder than normal street noises, forego views for a room in the back. Don't needlessly use the TI's room-finding service.

Hotel Amadeus has 15 small, bright rooms, all with simple modern furnishings, TV, private shower, and toilet. Some have views of the square. This characteristic hotel, ideally located above a turn-of-the-century dinner café, is relatively quiet and has an elevator. The lush old lobby is on the second floor in a "pianola bar" (Sb-f85, Db-f110, Tb-f150, nicer rooms cost a little more, seconds-on-everything buffet breakfast, kid-friendly, a 12-minute walk from train station, CC:VMA, use credit card to secure reservations, Grote Markt 10, 2011 RD Haarlem, tel. 023/532-4530, fax 023/532-2328, Web site: www.euronet.nl/users/amadeus, or e-mail: amadeus@euronet.nl, brothers Dave and Mike run the place for their family).

Hotel Carillon, also right on the town square, has an ideal location. Many of the well-worn rooms are small, the stairs are ste-e-e-p, and front rooms come with great town square views, lots of street noise, and double-paned windows (22 rooms, tiny loft singles-f55, Db-f120, Tb-f170, no elevator, 12-minute walk from train station, CC:VMA, Grote Markt 27, 2011 RC Haarlem, tel. 023/531-0591, fax 023/531-4909). The Carillon also runs the nearby **Die Raeckse Hotel**, which has fewer stairs, less character, more traffic noise, smoky halls, and decent rooms (Sb-f90, Db-f130–150, CC:VMA, attached restaurant, Raaks 1, 2011 VA Haarlem, tel. 023/532-6629, fax 023/531-7937).

The rollicking **Stads Café** has 13 big, bright rooms, most with TV and solid modern wood furniture. Its restaurant hops at night (see Eating, below), but most of its rooms are in the back and quiet (S-f60, Sb-f80, D-f80, Db-f100, Tb-f130, Qb-f160, breakfast-f9, CC:VMA, 2 blocks off the marketplace, Zijlstraat 56-58, 2011 TP Haarlem, tel. 023/532-5202, fax 023/532-0504).

Hotel Joops is an innovative concept. A well-organized central office, just behind the church in the town center, administers a corral of 80 rooms in different buildings (all within 3 blocks of the church). They have cheap, run-down, spacious rooms (S-f55, D-f80, T-f120) and new, elegant suites with kitchenettes (Db-f125–145, Tb-f165–190, CC:V, get one day free if you stay a week, office at Oude Groenmarkt 20, 2011 HL Haarlem, tel. 023/532-2008, fax 023/532-9549, e-mail: joops@hotelinformation.com).

Bed and Breakfast House de Kiefte, your cozy, get-into-a-local-home budget option, epitomizes the goodness of B&Bs. Marjet (mar-yet) and Hans, a young Dutch couple who speak fluent English, rent four bright and cheery non-smoking rooms (with a good breakfast and plenty of travel advice) in their 100-year-old home on a quiet neighborhood street (S-f45, Ds-f85, T-f125, Qs-f160, Quint/s-f185, minimum two nights, family loft sleeps up to five, very steep stairs, kid-friendly, Coornhertstraat 3, 2013 EV Haarlem, tel. 023/532-2980, cellular phone 06/5474-5272). It's a 15-minute walk or f11-taxi ride from the train station, and a five-minute walk from the center. From Grote Markt (main square), walk straight out Zijlstraat, past Stads Café, over the bridge, and take a left on the fourth street.

Family Dekker B&B is in a fine, quiet neighborhood near the station. For 25 years Mrs. Dekker has given her guests a cheery welcome in her clean but well-worn place (small D-f60, D-f70, T-f105, Q-f140, 1 block from the station at Ripperdastraat 9, 2011 KG Haarlem, tel. 023/532-0554).

Hotel Lion D'Or is a classy business hotel with all the professional comforts, an attached restaurant, and a very handy location. Don't expect a warm welcome (Sb-f175–200, Db-f225–265, extra beds-f50, request a "weekend package" at least three days in advance to get substantial weekend discounts June–September and in winter months; CC:VMA; across the street from the station at Kruisweg 34, 2011 LC Haarlem, tel. 023/532-1750, fax 023/532-9543).

The 300-room, very American **Hotel Haarlem Zuid** is sterile but a good value for those interested only in sleeping and eating (Db-f95–115, Tb-f125, breakfast-f13, elevator, easy parking, inexpensive hotel restaurant, in an industrial zone, a 20-minute walk from the center on the road to the airport, CC:VMA, Toekenweg 2, 2035 LC Haarlem, tel. 023/536-7500, fax 023/536-7980). Buses #70, #72, and #75 connect the hotel to the station and town square every ten minutes.

Eating in Haarlem

Eating between Grote Markt (Main Square) and the Train Station

Enjoy an Indonesian *rijsttafel* feast at the **Nanking Chinese-Indonesian Restaurant** (Kruisweg 16, a few blocks off Grote Markt, tel. 023/532-0706, daily 12:30–22:00). Couples eat plenty, heartily, and more cheaply by splitting a f24.50 Indonesian rice table for one. (Each eater should order a drink.) Say hi to gracious Ai Ping and her daughter, Fan. Don't let them railroad you into a Chinese (their heritage) dinner. They also do cheap and tasty take-out.

Going Dutch? How about pancakes for dinner at **Pannekoek-huis "De Smikkel"**? Dinner and dessert pancakes cost f12 each; there's a f2.50 per person cover charge, so splitting pancakes is OK (daily until 20:00, 2 blocks in front of station, Kruisweg 57, tel. 023/532-0631).

For impressive meals, try the Indonesian **Mooi Java**. They don't mind diners splitting a f35 *rijsttafel* (daily 17:00–22:00, Kruisweg 32; with your back to the train station, it's to your right; tel. 023/532-3121).

Eat well, surrounded by trains, in the classy Old World **Stations Restaurant**, between tracks 5 and 6, in the Netherlands' oldest train station (daily 12:00–20:00).

Eating on or Near Zijlstraat

Stads Café has fun being a restaurant—it's a three-ring circus of reasonably-priced food (f9.75 dinner special, cheese or meat fondue buffet from f17, salad bar, or "meat on a hot rock sizzling at your table"), with a stained-glass, candlelit, honky-tonk atmosphere, and live piano music Friday through Sunday from 18:00 (Monday–Saturday 8:00–24:00, Sunday from 14:00, Zijlstraat 56-58, tel. 023/532-5202).

Eko Eet Café is great for a cheery, tasty vegetarian meal (f18 menu, daily 17:30–21:30, Zijlstraat 39).

For a "bread line" experience with basic/bland food, well-worn company, and the cheapest price in town (f9), eat at **Eethuis**

St. Vincent (Monday–Friday 12:00–13:30 and 17:00–19:00, Nieuwe Groenmarkt 22).

The friendly **De Buren** offers traditional Dutch food (such as *Draadjesvlees*—beef stew with applesauce and *Oma's kippetje*— Grandmother's chicken) to happy locals (daily 17:00–22:00, Brouwersvaart 146, near intersection with Zijlsingel, close to House de Kiefte B&B, tel. 023/534-3364).

Eating between the Church and Frans Hals Museum

For good food, classy atmosphere, and f30 dinners, try the **Bastiaan** (opens at 18:00, closed Monday, CC:VMA, Lange Veerstraat 8, off Grote Markt, behind the church). Nearby, **La Plume** is a less expensive steak house (open daily at 17:30, CC:VMA, Lange Veerstraat 1). Popular with locals, **Jacobus Pieck** offers a varied menu selection (daily 10:00–22:00, Warmoesstraat 18, tel. 023/532-6144). For a (f2) cone of old-fashioned local French fries, drop by **Friethuis de Vlaminck** on Warmoesstraat 3 (closed Sunday and Monday).

Dine at the Indonesian **De Lachende Javaan** ("The Laughing Javanese," opens at 17:00, closed Monday, Frankestraat 25, tel. 023/532-8792) or get Indonesian take-out from the **Toko Nina** deli (Koningstraat 48, just off Grote Markt).

For a candlelit dinner of cheese and wine, consider **In't Goede Uur** (opens at 17:30, closed Monday, Korte Houtstraat 1).

For a healthy budget lunch with Haarlem's best view, eat at **La Place**, on the top floor or roof garden of the Vroom Dreesman department store (Monday–Saturday 9:30–18:00, Thursday until 21:00, closed Sunday, on the corner of Grote Houtstraat and Gedempte Oude Gracht).

Picnic-shoppers head to the **DekaMarkt** supermarket (8:30–20:00, until 21:00 on Thursday, 18:00 on Saturday, closed Sunday, Gedemple Oude Gracht 54, near the Vroom Dreesmann).

Transportation Connections—Haarlem

By train to: Amsterdam (6/hr, 15 min, f10.50 same-day return), **Delft** (2/hr, 45 min), **Hoorn** (2/hr, 1 hr), **The Hague** (3/hr, 40 min), **Alkmaar** (2/hr, 30 min), **Schiphol Airport** (2/hr, 40 min, f10, transfer at suburban Amsterdam-Sloterdijk); the direct buses #236 and #362 to the airport are faster (2/hr, 30 min, f9); by taxi, it's a f70 ride.

Sights—Near Haarlem and Amsterdam

The Netherlands are tiny. The sights listed below are an easy day trip by bus or train from Haarlem or Amsterdam.

▲**Zaanse Schans**—At this 17th-century Dutch village turned open-air folk museum, you can see and learn about everything Dutch, from cheese-making to wooden-shoe carving. Take an inspiring climb to the top of a whirring windmill (get a group of people together and ask for a tour) and buy a small jar of fresh, windmill-ground mustard for your next picnic. Located in the town of Zaandijk, this is your easiest one-stop look at traditional Dutch culture and the Netherlands' best collection of windmills (free, daily 8:30–18:00, until 17:00 in winter, tel. 075/616-8218). Fifteen minutes by train north of Amsterdam: take the Alkmaar-bound train to Station Koog-Zaandijk, then walk following signs—past a fragrant chocolate factory—for ten minutes.

▲▲**Aalsmeer Flower Auction**—Get a bird's-eye view of the huge Dutch flower industry. Visitors are welcome to wander on elevated walkways (through what is claimed to be the biggest building on earth), over literally trainloads of fresh-cut flowers. About half of all the flowers exported from Holland are auctioned off here in six huge auditoriums (f7.5, Monday–Friday 7:30–11:00, it's pretty dead after 9:30 and on Thursday, gift shop, cafeteria, bus #140 from Amsterdam's station, 2/hr, 60 min; from Haarlem, take bus #191, 2/hr, 60 min; tel. 0297/393-939). Aalsmeer is close to the airport and a handy last fling before catching a morning weekday flight.

▲▲▲**Keukenhof**—The greatest bulb flower garden on earth—each spring 6 million flowers conspire to make even a total garden-hater enjoy them. This 70-acre park is packed with tour groups daily from about March 26–May 24 (f17.50, 8:00–19:30, last tickets sold at 18:00; if you bus from Haarlem, transfer at Lisse; tel. 0252/465-555). Go very late in the day for the best light and the fewest groups. At the Haarlem or Amsterdam train station, ask about a "Rail Idee" (rail ee-day) ticket to Keukenhof; it covers your transportation and admission.

▲**Delft**—Peaceful as a Vermeer painting (he was born here) and lovely as its porcelain, Delft is a typically Dutch town with a special soul. Enjoy it best by simply wandering around, watching people, munching local syrup-waffles, or daydreaming from the canal bridges. The town bustles during its Saturday antique market (9:00–17:00). Its colorful Thursday food and flower market (9:00–17:00) attracts many traditional villagers. The TI, on the main square, has a f3.50 brochure outlining Delft's sights, including a do-it-yourself "Historical Walk through Delft" (Monday–Friday 9:00–18:00, Saturday 9:00–17:30, Sunday 10:00–15:00, tel. 015/212-6100). The town is a museum in itself, but if you need a turnstile, it has an impressive Army Museum (f4.50, Monday–Saturday 10:00–17:00, Sunday 13:00–17:00). Or you can tour the Royal Porcelain Works to watch the famous 17th-century blue Delftware turn from clay into art (f5, Monday–Saturday 9:00–17:00, Sunday 9:30–17:00, tel. 015/256-9214).

▲**Alkmaar**—It's Holland's cheese capital—especially fun (and touristy) during its weekly cheese market (Friday 10:00–12:00).

▲▲**Edam**—For the ultimate in cuteness and peace, make tiny Edam your home base. It's very sweet but palatable, and 30 minutes by bus from Amsterdam (2/hour). Don't miss the Edam Museum, a small, quirky house offering a fun peek into a 400-year-old home and a floating cellar (Tuesday–Saturday 10:00–16:00, Sunday 14:00–16:00, on main square). Wednesday is the town's market day (9:00–1:00). In July and August, market day includes a traditional cheese market (10:00–12:00).

▲▲**The Hague** (Den Haag)—Locals say the money is made in Rotterdam, divided in the Hague, and spent in Amsterdam. The Hague is the Netherlands' seat of government and the home of several engaging museums. The Mauritshuis' delightful, easy-to-tour art collection stars Vermeer and Rembrandt (f10, Tuesday–Saturday 10:00–17:00, Sunday 11:00–17:00, Korte Vijverberg 8, tel. 070/302-3456). Across the pond, the Torture Museum (Gevangenpoort) shows the medieval mind at its worst (f6, Tuesday–Friday 10:00–16:00, weekends 13:00–17:00, closed Monday, required tours on the hour; confirm with ticket-taker if film and talk will be in English before committing, tel. 070/346-0861). For a look at the 19th century's attempt at virtual reality, tour Panorama Mesdag, a 360-degree painting of the nearby town of Scheveningen in the 1880s, with a 3-D sandy beach foreground (f6, Monday–Saturday 10:00–17:00, Sunday 12:00–17:00, Zeestraat 65, tel. 070/310-6665). The nearby Peace Palace, a gift from Andrew Carnegie, houses the International Court of Justice (f5, Monday–Friday 10:00–16:00, required guided tours at 10:00, 11:00, 14:00, or 15:00; tram #7 or #8 from the station; tel. 070/302-4137, closes without warning, call ahead or check at TI). Scheveningen, the Dutch Coney Island, is liveliest on sunny summer afternoons (take tram #7); and Madurodam, a mini-Holland amusement park, is a kid-pleaser (f19.50, discounts for kids, daily 9:00–17:00, until 20:00 in June, until 22:00 July and August, tram #1 or #9, tel. 070/355-3900). The Hague's TI is at the train station (Monday–Saturday 9:00–17:30, later in summer, Sunday 10:00–17:00, tel. 06-3403-5051, 75 cents a minute).

Trains make the 70-minute trip from Amsterdam to Arnhem twice an hour (likely transfer in Utrecht). At Arnhem station, take bus #3 or #13 (faster, 4/hr, 15 min) to the Openlucht Museum. By car from Haarlem, skirt Amsterdam to the south on E9, following signs to Utrecht, then take A12 east to Arnhem. Just before Arnhem, take the Arnhem Nord exit (you'll see the white "Openluchtmuseum" sign) and follow the signs to the nearby museum. For the Kröller-Müller Museum, follow the white signs to Hoge Veluwe.

▲▲**Kröller-Müller Museum and Hoge Veluwe National Park**—Also near Arnhem, the Hoge Veluwe National Park is Holland's largest (13,000 acres), and famous for its Kröller-Müller Museum. This huge and impressive modern-art collection, including 55 paintings by van Gogh, is set deep in the natural Dutch wilderness. The park has lots more to offer, including hundreds of white bikes you're free to use to make your explorations more fun.

After paying f8.50 at the park entrance, the museum is "free" (f8.50, Tuesday–Sunday 10:00–17:00, easy parking, tel. 055/378-1441). Pick up more information at the Amsterdam or Arnhem TI (tel. 026/442-6767). Bus #12 connects the Arnhem train station with the Kröller-Müller Museum (March–October). Consider combining a visit to the park and the open-air museum for a great day trip from Amsterdam.

LISBON

Lisbon is a wonderful, ramshackle mix of now and then. Old wooden trolleys shiver up and down its hills, bird-stained statues mark grand squares, taxis rattle and screech through cobbled lanes, and well-worn people sip coffee in Art Nouveau cafés. Lisbon, like Portugal in general, is underrated. The country seems somewhere just beyond Europe. The pace of life is noticeably slower than in Spain. Roads are rutted. Prices are cheaper. The economy is based on fishing, cork, wine, and manufacturing. Be sure to balance your look at Iberia with enough Portugal.

While Lisbon's history goes back to the Romans and the Moors, the glory days were the 15th and 16th centuries, when explorers like Vasco da Gama opened new trade routes around Africa to India, making Lisbon one of Europe's richest cities. The economic boom fueled the flamboyant art boom called the Manueline period, named after Portugal's King Manuel I. Later, in the early 18th century, the gold and diamonds of Brazil, one of Portugal's colonies, made Lisbon even wealthier.

Then, on All Saints' Day in 1755, while most of the population was in church, the city was hit by a tremendous earthquake. Candles quivered as far away as Ireland. Lisbon was dead center. Two-thirds of the city was leveled. Fires started by the many church candles raged throughout the city, and a huge tidal wave blasted the waterfront. Forty thousand of Lisbon's 270,000 people were killed.

Under the energetic and eventually dictatorial leadership of Prime Minister Marquis Pombal, Lisbon was rebuilt in a progressive grid plan with broad boulevards and square squares. Bits of pre-earthquake Lisbon charm survive in Belém, the Alfama, and the Baírro Alto district.

Portugal's vast colonial empire is virtually gone. Many remaining bits disappeared with the 1974 revolution that delivered her from the right-wing Salazar dictatorship. Emigrants from former colonies such as Mozambique and Angola have added diversity and flavor to the city, making it more likely that you'll hear African music than Portuguese *fado* these days.

But Lisbon's heritage survives. The city seems better organized, cleaner, and more prosperous and people-friendly now than in the 1980s. Square and elegant outdoor cafés, exciting art, entertaining museums, a hill-capping castle, the saltiest sailors' quarter in Europe, and much more, all at bargain-basement prices, make Lisbon a world-class city.

Lisbon will host EXPO '98 "The Ocean and the Seas" from June to September 1998, celebrating the 500th anniversary of Vasco da Gama's voyage to India and focusing on the importance of healthy, clean waters in our environment. The fairgrounds are along the river, east of the Santa Apolonia train station. Expect crowds, higher prices, and lots of excitement. Reserve your hotel early. The dramatic new Vasco da Gama bridge will link the fairgrounds to the south side of the river.

Planning Your Time

With three weeks in Iberia, Lisbon is worth two days: one for the city and one for day trips.

Day 1: Start by touring the castle São Jorge and surveying the city from its viewpoint. After a coffee break at the café next to Alfama viewpoint, Miradour de Santa Luzia, descend into the Alfama. Explore. Back in the Baixa (bai-shah, lower city), have lunch in the Rossio area and walk to the funicular near Praça dos Restauradores. Start the described walk through the Baírro Alto with a ride up the funicular. This afternoon might be a good time to joyride on trolley #28. If it's not later than 15:00, art-lovers can take the Metro or a taxi to the Gulbenkian Museum. After a break at the hotel, have dinner at Cervejaría da Trinidade. Finish off with a *fado* show in the Baírro Alto.

Day 2: Trolley to Belém, tour the tower, monastery, and coach museum. Have lunch in Belém (picnics are ideal). You could catch the train or drive to Sintra to tour the Pena Palace and explore the ruined Moorish castle. If you have a car, drive out to Cabo da Roca. Spend the evening in the resorts of Estoril or Cascais, or back in Lisbon. If you're itchy for the beach, you could drive five hours from Sintra to the Algarve.

A third day could easily be spent at the Museum of Ancient Art and browsing through the Rossio, Baírro Alto, and Alfama.

The Gulbenkian museum and the side trip to Sintra/Cabo da Roca are time-consuming and rush Lisbon. If you'd appreciate more time to absorb the general ambience of the city, spend a full two days in Lisbon and do the museum (the Gulbenkian is mediocre by Paris or Madrid standards) and side trip only if you have a third day.

Orientation (tel. code: 01)

Lisbon's center is a series of parks, boulevards, and squares bunny-hopping between two hills down to the waterfront. The main boulevard, Avenida da Liberdade, goes from the high-rent district downhill, ending at the Praça dos Restauradores (TI, Rossio train station), where an obelisk celebrates the restoration of Portuguese independence from Spain. The monumental Rossio and Figueira squares (with plenty of buses, subways, cheap taxis, and pigeons leaving in all directions) are just beyond that. Between the Rossio and the harbor is the flat lower city, the Baixa, with its many cafés, bustling shops, elegant architecture, and checkerboard street plan (rebuilt after the earthquake on a grid plan with uniform 5-story buildings). Several streets are pleasant pedestrian zones, making this area even more enjoyable. The mosaic-decorated Rua Augusta is every bit as delightful as Barcelona's Ramblas for strolling. Most of Lisbon's prime attractions are within walking distance of the Rossio.

The three characteristic neighborhoods that line the downtown harborfront are: Baixa (with its gridplan business district, in the middle), the Chiado/Baírro Alto (Lisbon's "Latin Quarter," on a hill to the west), and the tangled, medieval Alfama (topped by the castle on the hill to the east).

Avenida da Liberdade is the tree-lined Champs Elysées of Lisbon, connecting the Rossio with the newer upper town (airport, bullring, popular fairgrounds, Edward VII Park, and breezy botanical gardens).

Tourist Information

The main tourist information office gives out a map and free monthly magazines on events: *Lisboaem* and *What's on in Lisbon* (with more English) are both better than the *Cultural Agenda* (daily 9:00–20:00, free room-finding service, at the lower end of Avenida da Liberdade in the Palacio da Foz at Praça dos Restauradores, Metro: Restauradores, 3 blocks north of Rossio, tel. 01/346-6307). The TI's city map is nearly useless. The Falk Map, sold for 1,100$ at bookstores (*liveiros*), is excellent.

Arrival in Lisbon

By Train: Lisbon has four train stations. Rossio station is the most centrally located (within walking distance of most of my hotel listings) and handles trains from Sintra (and Óbidos and Nazaré, with transfers at Cacém). There's a handy train information office on the ground floor of the station (Monday–Friday 9:00–18:00, weekends 10:00–19:00). Lisbon's Santa Apolonia station covers Coimbra, nearly all of Portugal (except the south), Madrid, and other international trains. It's just past the Alfama, with foreign-currency change machines and good bus connections to the town center (buses #9, #39, #46, and #90 go from the station through the center and up Avenida da Liberdade). A taxi from Santa Apolonia to any hotel I recommend should cost around 700$ (including the luggage supplement). If there's a long taxi-stand lineup, walk a block away and hail one off the street. The Barreiro train station, a 30-minute ferry ride across the Tagus River (*Rio Tajo*) from Praça do Comércio, is for trains to the Algarve and points south (the 160$ ferry ticket is generally sold to you with a train ticket). Caís do Sodre station handles the 30-minute rides to Cascais and Estoril. If you'll be leaving Lisbon by train, check to see if your train requires a reservation (boxed "R" in timetable, or ask at train station); if so, reserve early.

By Bus: Lisbon's Rodoviara bus station is at Avenida Casal Ribeiro 18 (Metro: Saldanha, tel. 01/354-5439). Take a taxi to get downtown, or if you have more time than money, turn right out of the bus station on to Avenida Casal Ribeiro and walk to its end at the grand Avenida Republica, turn right there and walk 4 more blocks to the Metro. Take the Metro (70$, buy at machines) to the Rossio metro stop (transfer at Rotunda) and you've made it. The bus station is within walking distance of American Express (good place to cash traveler's checks; see Helpful Hints, below).

By Plane: Lisbon's easy-to-manage airport (tel. 01/840-2060), just 8 kilometers northeast of downtown, has a 24-hour bank, ATM and bill-changer machines, a tourist office, reasonable taxi service (1,500$–center), good city bus connections into town (#44 and #45, 150$), and an airport bus. The Aero-Bus runs between the airport and the Caís Sodre train station, with various stops including Restauradores, Rossio, and Praça do Comércio (430$, 3/hr, 30 min, operates 7:00–21:00, buy ticket on bus). Your ticket is actually a one-day Lisbon transit pass that covers bus, tram, and elevator rides. If you fly in on TAP airline, show your ticket at the TAP welcome desk on the arrivals level to get a free one-way voucher for the Aero-Bus (TAP tel. 01/841-6990). A Lisbon transit pass (sold in one-day and three-day versions) covers the Aero-Bus trip to the airport if you're flying out of Lisbon.

Getting Around Lisbon

By Metro: Lisbon's simple, fast, 70$-per-ride subway runs only north of Praça Rossio (Rossio Square) into the new town. You'll need it only for the Gulbenkian Museum, the fairgrounds, a bullfight, and the long-distance bus station. Bring change for the ticket machines, as many stations are un-staffed. Remember to validate your ticket. Metro stops are marked with a red "M." *Saida* means exit.

By Trolley, Funicular, and Elevator: For fun and practical public transport, use the trolley system, the funicular, and the

Eiffelesque elevator (tickets at the door, going every few minutes) that connect the lower and upper towns. One ride on any of these costs 150$. The 430$ day pass and the 1,000$ three-day transit pass cover all public transportation (including the extensive city bus system) except for the Metro.

The Bilhete Unico de Coroa gives you two trips on the tram, bus, or elevator for only 150$ (half the cost of two one-way tickets). Buy these tickets at Carris booths (on Praça Figueira or at the base of the Santa Justa elevator—up a few stairs and behind the elevator). Since they're not advertised, you'll have to ask for them. Each ticket is good for only one ride and does not include transfers.

By Taxi: Lisbon taxis are abundant and use their meters. Rides start at 250$ and you can go anywhere in the center for under 500$. Especially if there are two of you, Lisbon cabs are a great, cheap timesaver.

Helpful Hints

Most museums are free on Sunday until 14:00 and closed all day Monday (a good day to explore Lisbon's neighborhoods or Sintra's Pena Palace and Moorish ruins). Bullfights are occasionally on Thursday and more frequently on Sunday. Tuesday and Saturday are flea-market days in the Alfama.

Pedestrian Warning: Sidewalks are narrow and drivers are daring; cross streets with care.

Language: Remember to try to start conversations in Portuguese (see Survival Phrases, near the back of this book). Fortunately, many people in the tourist trade speak some English. Otherwise, try Portuguese (ideal), Spanish, or French, in that order.

Time Zone Change: Portuguese time is usually one hour earlier than Spanish time.

LisboaCard: This card covers all public transportation (including the Metro), allowing free entrance to many museums and discounts on others. If you plan to museum-hop, the card is a good value, particularly for a day in Belém (covers your transportation and every worthwhile sight in Belém). Do not buy it to use on a Monday, when virtually all sights are closed throughout Lisbon and Belém, or on a Sunday, when many sights are free until 14:00 (24-hour card/1,500$; 48-hour card/2,500$, 72-hour card/3,250$; includes explanatory guidebook, buy at Rua Jardím do Regedor 50, off the southeast corner of Praça dos Restauradores, across the square from TI, tel. 01/343-3672, or at the Monastery of Jerónimos in Belém). You can buy the card in advance; just say what date and time you want it to "start."

Banking: Bring a Visa or MasterCard with a pin code to take advantage of the omnipresent Multibanco cash machines. Traveler's checks cost a small fortune to cash at banks; the fee ranges from 1,000$ to 2,500$ (bank hours are generally Monday–Friday

8:30–11:45 and 13:00–15:00). Shop around and try to cash in all your checks at once. American Express, in the Top Tours office at Avenida Duque de Loule 108, cashes any kind of traveler's check at a decent rate without a commission, but is not very central (Monday–Friday 9:30–13:00 and 14:30–18:30, Metro: Rotunda, tel. 01/315-5885). Automatic bill-changing machines are available and seductive, offering fair rates but high fees.

Post Office and Telephones: The post office, at Praça dos Restauradores 58, has easy-to-use metered phones (Monday–Friday 8:00–22:00, weekends 9:00–18:00). The telephone center, on the northwest corner of Rossio Square, sells phone cards and also has metered phone booths (daily 8:00–23:00, accepts credit cards). Most of Lisbon's phone booths require a different kind of phone card than is used in the rest of Portugal. It's not worth buying one of Lisbon's "modern" cards (inserted sideways into a small slot) just before you leave Lisbon. The rest of Portugal uses the old-fashioned cards (inserted lengthwise into a long slot). If you have only a few calls to make in Lisbon, use a metered phone at the telephone office, post office, or bar.

Do-It-Yourself Walking Tours—Lisbon

▲▲**The Baírro Alto and Chiado Stroll**—This colorful upper-city walk starts at the funicular and ends with the elevator (each a funky 150$ experience in itself). Leave the lower town on the funicular (called Elevator da Gloria), near the obelisk at Praça dos Restauradores. Leaving the funicular on top, turn right to enjoy the city view from the San Pedro Park belvedere.

If you're into port (the fortified wine that takes its name from the city of Oporto), you'll find the world's greatest selection across the street from the lift at Solar do Vinho do Porto (run by the Port Wine Institute, Rua São Pedro de Alcantara 45, 10:00–23:30, closed Sunday). In a stuffy '60s-decor living-room atmosphere you can, for 150$ to 2,000$ per glass poured by an English-speaking bartender, taste any of 300 different ports, though you may want to try only 150 or so and save the rest for the next night. Fans of port describe it as "a liquid symphony playing on the palate."

Follow the main street (Rua São Pedro de Alcantara) downhill a couple of blocks (it turns into the Rua Misericordia). São Roque Church (open 8:00–17:00) is on your left at Largo Trinidade Coelho. It looks like just another church, but wander slowly under its flat, painted ceiling and notice the rich side chapels. The highlight is the Chapel of St. John the Baptist (left of altar, gold and blue), which looks like it came right out of the Vatican. It did. Made at the Vatican out of the most precious materials, it was the site of one papal mass; then it was taken down and shipped to Lisbon—probably the most costly chapel per square inch ever constructed. Notice the beautiful mosaic floor and the three paintings that are actually intricate mosaics, a Vatican specialty. The São

Lisbon

HOTELS:
1. INSULANA
2. DUAS NAÇÕES
3. ALJUBARROTA
4. METROPOLE
5. LISBOA E TEJO
6. GERES
7. 13 DA SORTE
8. SUISSO ATLANTICO
9. FLORESCENTE
10. NOVA SILVA
11. CAMOES
12. BORGES

Roque Museum has some impressive old paintings and church riches (150$, 10:00–17:00, closed Monday).

After a visit with the poor pigeon-drenched man in the church square, continue downhill along Rua da Misericordia into the Chiado (SHEE-ah-doo) district. Shoppers can duck into the chic Centro Comercial Espaço Chiado at Rua da Misericordia #14 (with chic public-enough toilets and classy bars; closed Sunday) en route to Praça Luis de Camões (named after Portugal's best-loved poet).

A left takes you to a small square (Largo Chiado, the torn-up site of a future Metro stop, which should be completed by the time you get here) past **A Brasileira** café and the classy Rua Garrett. Coffeehouse aficionados enjoy this grand old café, reeking with smoke and the 1930s (open daily). After 2 downhill blocks on Rua Garrett, take a left uphill along Calle Sacramento, which leads to another pleasant square, Largo dos Carmo, with the ruins of the Convento do Carmo (likely closed until some time in '98 due to the new Metro addition; if open, peek in to see the elegant, earthquake-ruined Gothic arches for free, or pay 300$ to get all the way in and see the museum, Monday–Saturday 10:00–17:30, closed Sunday). Follow the trolley tracks alongside the church to the Santa Justa elevator. Climb the spiral stairs one floor to the small observatory deck or to the top of this Eiffelian pimple for a great view café (daily, English spoken, reasonable coffee, expensive eats). The elevator takes you down into the Baixa.

▲▲▲**Alfama Stroll**—Europe's most colorful sailors' quarter goes back to Visigothic days. It was a rich district during the Arabic period and finally the home of Lisbon's fisherfolk (and of the poet Luis de Camões, who wrote, "our lips meet easily high across the narrow street"). One of the few areas to survive the 1755 earth-quake, the Alfama is a cobbled playground of Old World color. A visit is best during the busy midmorning market time or in the late afternoon/early evening, when the streets teem with locals.

Start at the top and work your way down. Take trolley #28 to the Largo Santa Luzia; admire the view from the small ter-race. Probably the most scenic cup of coffee in town is enjoyed from the nearby Cerca Moura bar/café terrace (Largo das Portas do Sol 4). Then follow the yellow signs (and tour groups) up to the Castelo São Jorge, the city castle, with a history going back to Roman days. It caps the highest hill above the Alfama and offers a pleasant garden and Lisbon's top viewpoint but nothing in the way of an interior. Orient yourself from this perch (daily until sunset, bus #37 from Praça Figueira).

Drop back down to Largo Santa Luzia and wander deep into the Alfama. Use the Beco Santa Helena stairway to connect the upper Alfama's Largo das Portas do Sol and the Santa Luzia view-point with the lower Alfama. (Descending from the viewpoint: Behind the Santa Luzia church, take Rua Norberto de Araujo down a few stairs, go left under the arch, and you'll hook up with Beco Santa Helena.) This urban jungle's roads are squeezed into tangled and confusing alleys, bent houses comfort each other in their romantic shabbiness, and the air drips with laundry and the smell of clams and raw fish. Get lost. Poke aimlessly, sample ample grapes, peek through windows, buy a fish. Don't miss Rua de São Pedro, the liveliest street around. On Tuesday and Saturday mornings, the fun Feira da Ladra flea market rages on the Campo de Santa Clara (a good 20-minute walk, worth it only if it's flea market day).

Tours—Lisbon

▲▲**Ride a Trolley**—Lisbon's vintage trolleys, most from the 1920s, shake and shiver all over town, somehow safely weaving within inches of parked cars, climbing steep hills, and offering sightseers breezy wide-open-window views of the city. Line #28 is a Rice-A-Roni Lisbon joyride. Starting at the Estrela basilica and park, it runs through the Chiado, Baixa, and Alfama to Santa Clara church near the flea market. Stops from west to east include the top of Bica funicular, Chiado square, top of Rua Victor Cordon, in Baixa on Rua da Conceicão between Augusta and Prata, at the cathedral (*Sè*), at the Alfama viewpoint (Santa Luzia Belvedere), at Portas do Sol, and at the Santa Clara church. Just pay the conductor as you board, sit down, and catch the pensioners as they lurch at each stop.

City Bus Tours—Two tours give tired tourists a lazy two-hour overview of the city. Neither is great, but both are handy, daily, and inexpensive. **Tagus Tour** lets you hop on and off their topless double-decker buses (2,000$, hourly departures start at 11:00 May–September, covers the town and Belém, taped commentary in English, Portuguese, and French). On the **Hills Tour** you follow the rails on restored turn-of-the-century trams through the Alfama and Baírro Alto (2,800$; live, trilingual guide; up to five departures in summer, two afternoon-only departures during offseason, runs March–October). Both tours leave from the same info kiosk on Praça do Comércio (tel. 01/363-9343). It's a stressfree way to see the town (though subject to traffic jams).

Sights—Lisbon

▲▲**Gulbenkian Museum**—This is the best of Lisbon's 40 museums. Gulbenkian, an Armenian oil tycoon, gave his art collection (or "harem," as he called it) to Portugal in gratitude for the hospitable asylum granted him there during World War II. Now this great collection, spanning 2,000 years, is displayed in a classy and comfortable modern building. Ask for the excellent English text explaining the collection.

You'll stroll chronologically through the ages past the great Egyptian, Greek, and Middle Eastern sections. There are masterpieces by Rembrandt, Rubens, Renoir, Rodin, and artists whose names start with other letters (500$, free all day Sunday; from June–September open Tuesday, Thursday, Friday, and Sunday 10:00–17:00, Wednesday and Saturday 14:00–19:30; off-season open 10:00–17:00; always closed Monday; pleasant gardens; good, air-con cafeteria; bus #46 from Rossio or Metro from Rossio to São Sebastião, Berna 45, tel. 01/793-5131).

▲▲Museum of Ancient Art (Museu Nacional de Arte Antiga)—This is the country's best for Portuguese paintings from her glory days, the 15th and 16th centuries. You'll also find the great European masters (such as Bosch, Jan van Eyck, and Raphael) and rich furniture, all in a grand palace (500$, Tuesday 14:00–18:00, Wednesday–Sunday 10:00–18:00, closed Monday, bus #40 or #60 from Praça Figueira, Rua das Janeles Verdes 9, tel. 01/397-6002).

▲Museu Nacional do Azulejo—This museum, filling the Convento da Madre de Deus, features piles of tiles which, as you've probably noticed, are an art form in Portugal (400$, Tuesday 14:00–18:00, Wednesday–Sunday 10:00–18:00, closed Monday; ten minutes on bus #59 or #105 from Praça Figueira, Rua da Madre de Deus 4, tel. 01/814-7747).

Sè (Cathedral)—Just a few blocks east of Praça do Comércio, it's not much on the inside, but its fortresslike exterior is a textbook example of a stark and powerful Romanesque fortress of God. Started in 1150, after the Christians reconquered Lisbon from the Islamic Moors, its crenelated towers made a powerful statement: The Reconquista was here to stay.

▲The 25th of April Bridge—At a mile long, this is the third-longest suspension bridge in the world. Built in 1966, it was originally named for the dictator Salazar but renamed for the date of Portugal's revolution and freedom.

Cristo Rei—A huge statue of Christ (à la Rio de Janeiro) overlooks Lisbon from across the Tagus River. While it's designed to be seen from a distance, a lift takes visitors to the top for a great view (250$, daily 10:00–18:00). Catch the ferry from downtown Lisbon (leaves every ten minutes from Praça do Comércio) to Cacilhas, then take a bus marked "Cristo Rei" (leaves from the ferry dock every 15 minutes). Taxis to or from the site are too expensive.

Sights—Lisbon's Belém District

Three miles from downtown Lisbon, the Belém District is a sprawling pincushion of important sights from Portugal's Golden Age, when Vasco da Gama and company made it Europe's richest power. This is the best possible look at the grandeur of pre-earthquake Lisbon. While the monastery is great, its several museums are somewhere between good and mediocre, depending upon your interests. The new Belém Cultural Center, filled with exhibition halls (check out what's showing), concert halls, and a snazzy good-value cafeteria with a salad bar, puts this area on the contemporary culture map. You can get to the sights of Belém by taxi or bus (#27, #28, #29, #43, #49, and #51), but I'd ride the sleek new tram #15 (how about those window screens?) from Praça do Comércio or Figueira (buy tickets from machine on-board, no change) to the second stop in Belém (Mosterio dos Jerónimos). The best picnic grounds are in the park near the Monument to the Discoveries. You'll find several good restaurants along Rua de Belém between the coach museum and the monastery. At **Pastel de Belém**, a handy dessert shop, have a *café com leite* with the house specialty, *pasties de Belém*.

▲ **Monument to the Discoveries**—This giant monument was built in 1960 to honor Prince Henry the Navigator on the 500th anniversary of his death. Huge statues of Henry and other of Portugal's leading explorers line the giant concrete prow. Note the marble map chronicling Portugal's empire-building, on the ground in front. Inside you can ride a lift to a fine view (320$, Tuesday–Sunday 9:30–18:00, closed Monday).

▲▲ **Monastery of Jerónimos**—This is, for me, Portugal's most exciting building. The giant church and its cloisters were built as a thanks for the discoveries. Vasco da Gama is buried here (from back of church facing altar, his tomb is on the left). Notice how nicely the Manueline style combines Gothic and Renaissance features with motifs from the sea, the source of wealth that made this art possible. Don't miss the elegant cloisters (church free, 400$ for cloisters, get the 200$ English pamphlet, Tuesday–Sunday 10:00–17:00, closed Monday). Go upstairs for a better view (and the women's toilet; men's downstairs).

▲**Belém Tower**— The only purely Manueline building in Portugal (built in 1515), this tower protected Lisbon's harbor and today symbolizes the voyages that made it powerful. This was the last sight sailors saw as they left and the first when they returned loaded with gold, spices, and social diseases. Its collection of 15th- and 16th-century armaments is barely worth the admission and the 15-minute walk from the Monastery, but if you do go in, climb up for the view (400$, Tuesday–Sunday 10:00–17:00, closed Monday, tel. 01/362-0034).

▲**Coach Museum (Museu dos Coches)**—Claiming to be the most visited sight in Portugal, it's impressive, with more than 70 dazzling 18th-century carriages (450$, Tuesday–Sunday 10:00–17:00, closed Monday, tel. 01/363-8022).

Popular Art Museum (Museu de Arte Popular)—This museum takes you through Portugal's folk art one province at a time (300$, Tuesday–Sunday 10:00–12:30 and 14:00–17:00, closed Monday, Avenida Brasilia).

Maritime Museum (Museu de Marinha)—A cut above the average European maritime museum. Sailors love it (300$, free on Wednesday, Tuesday–Sunday 10:00–18:00, closed Monday, Praça do Império).

Belém

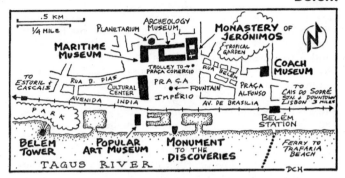

Evening Entertainment—Lisbon

From the Baixa, nighttime-Lisbon seems dead. But head up into the Baírro Alto and you'll find plenty of action. The Jardím do São Pedro is normally festive and the Rua Diario de Noticias is lined with busy bars.

▲**Fado**—Mournfully beautiful, haunting ballads about lost sailors, broken hearts, and sad romance are one of Lisbon's favorite late-night tourist traps. Be careful, this is one of those cultural clichés that all too often becomes a rip-off. The Alfama has many touristy *fado* bars, but the Baírro Alto (plenty of joints around Rua Diario de Noticias, Rua das Gaveas, and Rua Norte) is your best bet. **Canto do Camões** is great, run by friendly Gabriel (Travessa da Espera 38, call ahead to reserve, tel. & fax 01/346-5464). At *fado* bars, things don't start until 21:30 and then take an hour or two to warm up. A *fado* performance isn't cheap (expect a 2,500–3,000$ cover), but a good one is a great experience. Many *fado* joints require dinner (5,000–6,000$). Get advice from your hotel or the TI.

▲▲▲**Portuguese Bullfight**—If you always felt sorry for the bull, this is Toro's Revenge—in a Portuguese bullfight, the matador is brutalized along with the bull. After an exciting equestrian prelude in which the horseman (*cavaleiro*) skillfully plants barbs in the bull's back while trying to avoid the padded horns, a colorfully clad, eight-man team (suicide squad) enters the ring and lines up single file facing the bull. The leader prompts the bull to charge, then braces himself for a collision that can be heard all the way up in the cheap seats. As he hangs onto the bull's head, his buddies then pile on, trying to wrestle the bull to a standstill. Finally, one guy hangs on to *el toro's* tail and "water-skis" behind him. Unlike at the Spanish *corrida*, the bull is not killed in front of the crowd at the Portuguese *tourada* (yet it *is* killed later).

You're most likely to see a bullfight in Lisbon, Estoril, or on the Algarve. The season lasts from Easter through October.

Get schedules in the tourist office; fights start late in the evening. In Lisbon there are fights at Campo Pequeño on Thursday nights from mid-June through September at 22:00 (tickets from about 2,000$). Nearby arenas advertise fights on Sunday. Tickets are available at the door or at the green ABEP kiosk across the square from Lisbon's central tourist office.

▲**People's Fair (Feira Popular)**—Consider spending a lowbrow evening at Lisbon's Feira Popular, which bustles with Portuguese families at play. Pay the entry fee, then enjoy rides, munchies, great people-watching, entertainment, music—basic Portuguese fun. Have dinner among the chattering families, with endless food and wine paraded frantically in every direction. Food stalls dispense wine from the udders of porcelain cows. Fried ducks drip, barbecues spit, and dogs squirt the legs of chairs while, somehow, local lovers ignore everything but each other's eyes. (200$, nightly, May 1–September 30, 19:00–midnight, Saturday and Sunday 15:00–midnight. Located on Avenida da República at the Entre-Campos Metro stop.)

Movies—Lisbon reels with theaters, and unlike in Spain, most films are in the original language with subtitles. Many of Lisbon's theaters are classy, complete with assigned seats and ushers, and the normally cheap tickets go for half price on Monday. Check the cinema listings in the monthly magazine *Lisboaem* (free at TI).

Sleeping in Lisbon
(170$ = about $1, tel. code: 01)
Sleep Code: **S**=Single, **D**=Double/Twin, **T**=Triple, **Q**=Quad, **b**=bathroom, **t**=toilet only, **s**=shower only, **CC**=Credit Card (Visa, MasterCard, Amex), **SE**=Speaks English, **NSE**=No English. Breakfast is usually included.

Lisbon has plenty of cheap and handy rooms, but this is EXPO '98 (June–September), so reserve as early as you can. Off-season, prices are soft.

Physically, Lisbon is a tired and well-worn city; rooms in the center feel the same way. To sleep in a well-located place with local character, you'll be climbing dark stairways into a world of cracked plaster, taped handwritten signs, dingy carpets, cramped and confusing floor plans, and ramshackle plumbing. If you're on a tight budget, arrive without a reservation and bargain. If you have a room reserved, taxi there from the station if you arrive at night. While old Lisbon seems a little sleazy at night, with normal discretion my listings are safe.

Singles cost nearly the same as doubles. Rooms with bathtubs often cost more than rooms with showers. Addresses like 26-3 stand for street #26, third floor (which is fourth floor in American terms). Never judge a place by its entryway.

Sleeping Downtown in Baixa
(zip code: 1100)

Central as can be, this area bustles with lots of shops, traffic, people, buskers, pedestrian areas, and urban intensity. I've listed places that are in relatively quiet areas or on pedestrian streets.

Albergaria Residencial Insulana, on a pedestrian street, is very professional with 32 quiet and comfortable, if a bit smoky, rooms (Sb-7,500$, Db-8,500$, Tb-11,000$, includes breakfast, elevator, all with air-con, CC:VMA, Rua da Assuncão 52, tel. 01/342-3131, fax 01/342-3131, SE).

Residencial Duas Nacões is a hardworking old hotel in the heart of Rossio on a classy pedestrian street (S-3,500$, Sb-6,000$, D-4,500$, Db-7,500$, Tb-9,000$ with breakfast, elevator, CC:VMA, Rua Augusta e Rua da Vitoria 41, tel. 01/346-0710, fax 01/347-0206, SE). Some rooms smell musty, others are OK. Ask to see another if the first won't do.

Pensão Aljubarrota is just renovated and a fine value if you can handle the long climb up four floors and the bubbly black-vinyl flooring. Once on top you'll have spotless rooms and cute tiny balconies from which to survey the Rua Augusta scene (S-3,200$, D-5,200$, Ds-6,200$, T-6,900$, includes breakfast, Rua da Assuncão 53-4, tel. & fax 01/346-0112, SE).

Sleeping Downtown on Rossio and Praça da Figueira
(zip code: 1100)

Hotel Metropole, on Rossio Square, has 1920s elegance and beautiful rooms, some overlooking the square. If you're in the mood for a splurge, this is the place (Sb-17,900$, Db-19,800$, extra bed-3,500$, includes breakfast, air-con, elevator, double-paned windows, CC:VMA, Rossio 30, tel. 01/346-9164, fax 01/46-9166, SE).

Lisboa e Tejo is another oasis, newly and tastefully refurbished, with comfortable rooms and a welcoming staff (Sb-10,000–12,000$, Db-12,000–15,000$, prices vary according to room size, includes breakfast, air-con, CC:VMA, Rua do Poço do Borratém, from southeast corner of Praça da Figueira, walk 1 block down Rua Dos Condes de Monsanto and turn left, tel. 01/886-6182, fax 01/886-5163, SE).

Pensão Residencial Gerês, your best budget bet downtown, has bright, basic, cozy rooms (S-5,500$, Sb-7,000$, D-7,000$, Db-8,500$, T-9,000$, Ts-10,000$, CC:VMA, Calçada do Garcia 6, located off the northeast corner of Rossio—at the entrance of pedestrian street Rua das Portas de St. Antão, look uphill to see the sign 1 block away, tel. 01/881-0497, fax 01/888-2006, some English spoken). Recently remodeled, it lacks the dingy smokiness that pervades Lisbon's cheaper hotels.

Sleeping Uptown along Avenida da Liberdade

Pensão Residencial 13 da Sorte, a simple, but cheery place, has full bathrooms in each of its 23 rooms and bright, small-town tiles throughout (Sb-6,000$, Db-6,000–7,500$, Tb-7,500$, no breakfast, elevator, CC:VMA, Rua do Salitre 13, 1200 Lisbon, tel. 01/353-9746, fax 01/353-1851, SE). Coming from the Rossio Station up Avenida da Liberdade, turn left on Rua do Salitre at the big "Cerveja Sagres" sign (ten-minute walk). Back rooms are quieter.

Hotel Suisso Atlantico is formal, hotelish, and stuffy, with tour groups and drab carpets throughout, but it has decent rooms and a TV lounge. If you want a functional hotel and practical location, it's a good value (Sb-7,500$, Db-9,500$, Tb-11,300$, includes breakfast, parking available, CC:VMA, Rua da Gloria 3-19, 1200 Lisbon, behind the funicular station, around the corner from the tourist office on a quiet street 1 block off Praça dos Restauradores, tel. 01/346-1713, fax 01/346-9013, SE).

Residencial Florescente is a slumber mill with 100 rooms on a thriving pedestrian street a block off Praça dos Restauradores. It's institutional, but rooms are clean and some even approach charm (Ss-5,000$, Ds-5,500–6,500$, Db-6,000–8,500$, no breakfast, CC:VMA, Rua Portas S. Antão 99, 1100 Lisbon, tel. 01/346-3517, fax 01/342-7733, SE).

Sleeping in Baírro Alto
(zip code: 1200)

Just west of downtown, this area is more colorful, with less traffic. It's a bit seedy but full of ambience, good bars, local *fado* clubs, music, and markets. The area may not feel comfortable for women alone at night, but the hotels themselves are safe.

Residencial Nova Silva feels a little dumpy and unloved. Still, it's a quiet, ramshackle place on the crest of the Baírro Alto overlooking the river. The five rooms with grand little river-view balconies give you bird noises rather than traffic noises (priority for longer stays). It's 3 blocks from the heart of Chiado on the scenic #28 tram line, with the easiest street parking of all my listings (S-4,500$, Ss-5,000$, Sb-6,000$, D-5,000$, Ds-5,500$, Db-6,000–7,000$, breakfast-400$, no elevator, Rua Victor Cordón 11, tel. 01/342-4371, fax 01/342-7770, SE).

Residencial Camões lies right in the seedy thick of the Baírro Alto but offers fine rooms with a friendly, safe atmosphere (S-2,500$, Sb-3,500$, D-4,500$, Db-5,500$, includes breakfast, Travessa Poco da Cidade 38, 1 block south of São Roque Church and to the right, you'll see the sign a couple of blocks up, tel. 01/346-7510, fax 01/346-4048, some English spoken).

Hotel Borges is a big, dark, tired, smoky, formerly regal place with one of the old town's best addresses (Sb-9,000$, Db-10,500$, includes breakfast, cheaper off-season, elevator, CC:VMA, Rua Garrett 108, on the shopping street next to A

Brasiliera café, tel. 01/346-1951, fax 01/342-6617, SE). A Metro stop is scheduled to be at their doorstep in 1998.

Eating in Lisbon

Eating in the Alfama

This gritty chunk of pre-earthquake Lisbon is full of interesting eateries, especially along the Rua San Pedro (the lower main drag) and on Largo de São Miguel. For a seafood feast (2,600$ menu) after your Alfama exploration, consider dining high in the Alfama at the **Farol de Santa Luzia** restaurant (Largo Santa Luzia 5, across from the Santa Luzia patio viewpoint overlooking the Alfama, no sign but many window decals, closed Sunday, tel. 01/886-3884). For cheap and colorful dinners, walk past Portas do Sol (dip into a dark bar for a damp appetizer) and follow the trolley tracks along Rua da São Tome to a square called Largo Rodrigues Freitas, where **Nossa Churrasqueira** is busy feeding happy locals on rickety tables and meager budgets (closed Monday). If that's too touristy, walk from there down the steepest lane, Rua do Salvador, to the little eatery a few doors down at #81 (Restaurante Gema de Ova). This road continues downhill into the less touristed fringe of the Alfama. While in the Alfama, brighten a few dark bars. Have an *aperitif*, taste the *branco seco* (local dry white wine). Make a friend, pet a chicken, read the graffiti, pick at the humanity ground between the cobbles.

Eating in Baírro Alto

Lisbon's "high town" is full of small, fun, and cheap places. Fisher-men's bars abound. Just off São Roque's Square you'll find two fine eateries: the very simple and cheap **Casa Trans-Montana** (closed Sunday) down the steps of Calcada do Duque at #43; and the **Cervejaría da Trinidade** (1 block down from Sao Roque at Rua Nova da Trinidade 20C), a Portuguese-style beer hall covered with historic tiles and full of fish and locals (daily 12:00–24:00, CC:VMA, tel. 01/342-3506). You'll find many less-touched restaurants deeper into the Baírro Alto on the other (west) side of Rua Misericordia.

Eating in Rossio, Baixa, and Beyond

The "eating lane" is a galloping gourmet's heaven, a galaxy of eateries with small zoos hanging from their windows for you to choose from (opposite the Rossio station, just off Praça dos Restauradores down Rua do Jardím do Regedor and Rua das Por-tas de St. Antão). The seafood is some of Lisbon's best. For cod and vegetables prepared faster than a Big Mac and served with more energy than a soccer team, stand or sit at the **Restaurant/ Cervejaría Beira-Gare** (a greasy spoon in front of the Rossio sta-tion at the end of Rua 1 de Dezembro, 6:00–24:00, closed Sun-day). To get a simple fish sandwich, ask for a *filete pescada no pão*.

Farther down the same street is **Celerio**, a handy supermarket that's bigger than it looks (8:30–20:00, until 19:00 Saturday, closed Sunday, Rua 1 de Dezembro 67-68). On the next block, same street, same hours, Celerio runs a health-food store at #65.

Stand with the locals at **Pastelaria Tentacão**, on the east side of Praça Figueria, and munch one of their *prato do dia* (daily specials, all under 1,000$). The house specialty to try (or avoid) is *leitão*, a suckling pig sandwich.

The Rossio area is lined with local eateries (like **Restaurant X** at Rua dos Correeiros #116, look for the red X). The **Os Unidos** snack bar at Rua dos Fanqueiros 161 is fun and friendly (closed Sunday).

Just off the Avenida da Liberdade on the Rua do Salitre (near the Pensión Residencial da Sorte 13) are two locally popular and slightly upscale restaurants: **Cerevejaria Ribadouro**, at the corner of Avenida da Liberdade and Rua do Salitre, and **Forno Velho**, at Rua do Salitre 42.

And don't miss a chance to go purely local with hundreds of Portuguese families having salad, fries, chicken, and wine at the **Feira Popular** (nightly from 19:00, May–September, on Avenida da República, Metro: Entre-Campos).

Transportation Connections—Lisbon
Remember to reserve ahead if your train requires a reservation.

By train to: Madrid (2/day, 10–12 hrs, ideal overnight), **Faro** (4/day, 5 hrs), **Paris** (1/day, 26 hrs), **Porto** (12/day, 3.5 hrs), **Évora** (5/day, 3 hrs), **Lagos** (5/day, 5 hrs, overnight possible, likely transfer in Tunes), **Coimbra** (17/day, 2.5 hrs), **Nazaré Valado** (4/day, 2.5 hrs), **Sintra** and **Cascais** (4/hr, 45 min). Train information: tel. 01/888-4025 or 01/888-5092.

COPENHAGEN

Copenhagen (København) is Scandinavia's largest city. With over a million people, it's home to more than a quarter of all Danes. A busy day cruising the canals, wandering through the palace, taking a historic walking tour, and strolling the Strøget (Europe's greatest pedestrian shopping mall) will get you oriented, and you'll feel right at home. Copenhagen is Scandinavia's cheapest and most fun-loving capital, so live it up.

Planning Your Time

A first visit deserves two days.

Day 1: If staying in Christianshavn, start the day browsing through the neighborhood, called Copenhagen's "Little Amsterdam." Catch the 10:30 city walking tour. After a Riz-Raz lunch, visit the Use It information center and catch the relaxing canal boat tour out to *The Little Mermaid*. Spend the rest of the afternoon tracing Denmark's cultural roots in the National Museum and/or touring the Ny Carlsberg Glyptotek art gallery; the evening strolling or biking Strøget (follow "Heart and Soul" walk described below) or Christianshavn.

Day 2: At 10:00 explore the subterranean Christiansborg Castle ruins under today's palace. At 11:00 take the 50-minute guided tour of Denmark's royal Christiansborg Palace. The afternoon is free, with many options, including a smørrebrød lunch, tour of the Rosenborg Castle/crown jewels, brewery tour, or Nazi Resistance museum (free tour often at 14:00). Evening at Tivoli Gardens before catching a night train out.

Remember the efficiency of sleeping in-and-out by train. If flying in, most flights from the States arrive in the morning. After that, head for Stockholm and Oslo. Kamikaze sightseers see Copenhagen as a Scandinavian bottleneck. They sleep in-and-out heading north and in-and-out heading south, with two days and no nights in the city. Considering the joy of Oslo and Stockholm, this isn't that crazy if you have limited time. You can check your bag at the station and take a 10-kr shower in the Interail Center.

You can set yourself up in my best rooms for your Scandinavian tour with a quick trip to a pay phone. This is probably a wise thing to do.

Orientation

Nearly all of your sightseeing is in Copenhagen's compact old town. By doing things by bike or on foot you'll stumble into some surprisingly cozy corners, charming bits of Copenhagen that many miss. Study the map. The medieval walls are now roads that define the center: Vestervoldgade (literally, "western wall street"), Nørrevoldgade, and Østervoldgade. The fourth side is the harbor and the island of Slotsholmen where København ("merchants' harbor") was born in 1167. The next of the city's islands is Amager, where you'll find the local "Little Amsterdam" district of Christianshavn. What was Copenhagen's moat is now a string of pleasant lakes and parks, including Tivoli Gardens. To the north is the old "new town," where the Amalienborg Palace is surrounded by streets on a grid plan, and *The Little Mermaid* poses relentlessly, waiting for her sailor to return and the tourists to leave.

The core of the town, as far as most visitors are concerned, is the axis formed by the train station, Tivoli Gardens, the Rådhus (city hall) square, and the Strøget pedestrian street. It's a great walking town, bubbling with street life and colorful pedestrian zones. But be sure to get off the Strøget.

The character in Copenhagen's history who matters most is Christian IV, who ruled from 1588 to 1648. He was Denmark's Renaissance king, the royal Danish party animal whose personal energy kindled a Golden Age when Copenhagen prospered and many of the city's grandest buildings were built. Locals love to tell great stories of everyone's favorite king.

Tourist Information

The tourist office is now run by a for-profit consortium called "Wonderful Copenhagen." This colors the advice and information it provides. Still, it's worth a quick stop for the top-notch freebies it provides, such as a city map and *Copenhagen This Week* (a free, handy, and misnamed monthly guide to the city, worth reading for its good maps, museum hours with telephone numbers, sightseeing tour ideas, shopping suggestions, and calendar of events, including free English tours and concerts). The TI is across from the train station, near the corner of Vesterbrogade and Bernstorffsgade, next to the Tivoli entrance (daily May–mid-September 9:00–21:00; mid-September–April weekdays 9:00–17:00, Saturday 9:00–14:00, closed Sunday; tel. 33 11 13 25).

Copenhagen

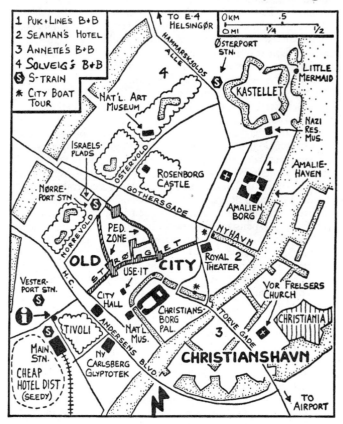

1 PUK+LINE'S B+B
2 SEAMAN'S HOTEL
3 ANNETTE'S B+B
4 SOLVEIG'S B+B
Ⓢ S-TRAIN
✳ CITY BOAT TOUR

TO E-4 HELSINGØR
ØSTERPORT STN.
LITTLE MERMAID
KASTELLET
NAZI RES. MUS.
NAT'L. ART MUSEUM
ISRAELS-PLADS
ROSENBORG CASTLE
AMALIE-HAVEN
NØRRE-PORT STN.
GOTHERSGADE
AMALIEN-BORG
PED. ZONE
NYHAVN
OLD   CITY
ROYAL THEATER
USE·IT
VESTER-PORT STN.
VOR FRELSERS CHURCH
CITY HALL
CHRISTIANS-BORG PAL.
CHRISTIANIA
NAT'L. MUS.
TIVOLI
MAIN STN.
CHRISTIANSHAVN
CHEAP HOTEL DIST (SEEDY)
NY CARLSBERG GLYPTOTEK
TO AIRPORT

Corporate dictates prohibit the TI from freely offering other brochures (such as walking-tour schedules and brochures on any sights of special interest), but ask and you shall receive. The TI's room-finding service charges you and the hotel a fee and cannot give hard opinions. Do not use it. Get on the phone and call direct—everyone speaks English.

Use It is a better information service. This "branch" of Huset, a hip, city government–sponsored, student-run cluster of cafés, theaters, and galleries, caters to Copenhagen's young but welcomes travelers of any age. It's a friendly, driven-to-help, energetic, no-nonsense source of budget travel information, with a free budget room-finding service, ride-finding board, free luggage lockers, pen-pals-wanted scrapbook, free condoms, and Copenhagen's best free city maps. Their free *Playtime* publication is full of Back Door–style travel articles on Copenhagen and the Danish culture, special budget tips, and events. They have brochures on just about everything, including self-guided tours for bikers, walkers, and those riding scenic bus #6. They have a list of private rooms (250-kr doubles without breakfast). Use It is a ten-minute walk from the station: head down Strøget, then turn right on Rådhustræde for 3 blocks to #13 (daily June–September 9:00–19:00; off-season open weekdays 10:00–16:00 and closed weekends; tel. 33 15 65 18, fax 33 15 75 18). After hours, their computer touch screen lists the cheapest rooms available in town.

The **Copenhagen Card** covers the public transportation system and admissions to nearly all the sights in greater Copenhagen, which stretches from Helsingør to Roskilde. It includes virtually all the city sights, Tivoli, and the bus from the airport. Available at any tourist office (including the airport's) and the central station: 24 hours, 140 kr; 48 hours, 230 kr; 72 hours, 295 kr. It's hard to break even, unless you're planning to side trip on the included (and otherwise expensive) rail service. It comes with a handy book explaining the 60 included sights, such as: Christiansborg Palace (normally 35 kr), Castle Ruins (20 kr), National Museum (30 kr), Ny Carlsberg Glyptotek (15 kr), Rosenborg Castle (40 kr), Tivoli (39 kr), Frederiksborg Castle (40 kr), and Roskilde Viking Ships (40 kr), plus round-trip train rides to Roskilde (70 kr) and Frederiksborg Castle (70 kr).

Arrival in Copenhagen

By Train: The main train station, Hovedbanegården (HOETH-ban-gorn; learn that word—you'll need to recognize it) is a temple of travel and a hive of travel-related activity. You'll find lockers (25 kr/day), a *garderobe* (35 kr/day per rucksack), a post office, a grocery store (daily 8:00–24:00), 24-hour thievery, and bike rentals. The Interail Center, a service the station offers to mostly young travelers (but anyone with a Eurailpass, Scanrail, student BIGE or Transalpino ticket, or Interail pass is welcome) is a pleasant lounge with 10-kr showers, free (if risky) luggage storage, city maps, snacks, and other young travelers (June– mid-September 6:30–22:00). If you just need the map and *Playtime*, a visit here is quicker than going to the TI.

Most travelers arrive in Copenhagen after an overnight train ride. The station has two long-hours money exchange desks. Den Danske Bank is fair—charging the standard 40-kr minimum or 20-kr-per-check fee for traveler's checks (daily 7:00–20:00). FOREX, which has a worse rate but charges only 10 kr per traveler's check with no minimum, is better for small exchanges (daily 8:00–21:00). On a $100 exchange, I saved 22 kr at FOREX. (The American Express office—a 20-minute walk away, off Strøget—may be even better; see Helpful Hints, below).

While you're in the station, reserve your overnight train seat or couchette out (at Rejse-bureau). International rides and all IC trains require reservations (usually 20 kr). Bus #8 (in front of the station on the station side of Bernstorffsgade) goes to Christian-shavn B&Bs. Note the time the bus departs, then stop by the TI (across the street on the left) and pick up a free Copenhagen city map that shows bus routes.

By Plane: Copenhagen's International Airport is a traveler's dream, with a tourist office, bank (standard rates), post office, telephone center, shopping mall, grocery store, and bakery. You can use American cash at the airport and get change back in kro-ner. (Phone service for all airline offices is split between two switchboards: SAS services—tel. 31 54 17 01, and Copenhagen Air Service—tel. 32 47 47 47. SAS ticket hotline—tel. 32 32 68 00.) If you need to kill a night at the airport, try the fetal rest cabins, the *hvilekabiner* (Sb-270 kr, Db-405 kr, rented by the eight-hour period; reception open 6:00–22:00; easy telephone reservations, CC:VMA, tel. 32 31 32 31, fax 32 31 31 09).

Getting Downtown from the Airport: Taxis are fast and easy, accept credit cards, and, at about 150 kr to the town center, are a good deal for foursomes. The SAS **shuttle bus** zips between the central train station and airport in 20 minutes for 35 kr. **City bus** #250s gets you downtown (City Hall Square, TI) in 30 minutes for 17 kr (12/hour, across the street and to the right as you exit the airport). If you're going from the airport to Christianshavn, ride #9 just past Christianshavn Torv to the last stop before Knippels Bridge.

Helpful Hints

Ferries: Book any ferries you plan to use in Scandinavia now. Any travel agent can book the boat rides you plan to take later on your trip, such as the Denmark–Norway ferry (ask for special discounts on this crossing) or the Stockholm–Helsinki–Stockholm cruise (the Silja Line office is directly across from the station at Nyhavn 43A, open Monday–Friday 9:00–17:00, tel. 33 14 40 80). Drivers heading to Sweden by ferry should call for a reservation (two com-peting Helsingør lines: 33 15 15 15 and 49 26 01 55, and the often cheaper Dragør line: 32 53 15 85). Reservations are free and easy and assure that you won't be stuck in a long line.

Jazz Festival: The Copenhagen Jazz Festival—ten days start-ing the first Friday in July (July 3–12 in 1998)—puts the town in a rollicking slide-trombone mood. The Danes are Europe's jazz enthusiasts and, more than most music festivals, this one fills the town with happiness. The TI prints up an extensive listing of each year's festival events (as well as a listing of other festivals).

Telephones: Use the telephone liberally. Everyone speaks English, and *This Week* and this book list phone numbers for everything you'll be doing. All telephone numbers in Denmark are eight digits, and there are no area codes. Calls anywhere in Denmark are cheap; calls to Norway and Sweden cost 6 kr per minute from a booth (half of that from a private home). Coin-op booths are often broken. Get a phone card (from newsstands, starting at 20 kr).

Traveler's Checks: The American Express Company does not charge any fee on their checks and only 15 kr per transaction on any other checks and cash (Strøget at Amagertorv 18, Monday–Friday 9:00–17:00, summer Saturdays 9:00–14:00, tel. 33 12 23 01).

Getting Around Copenhagen

By Bus and Subway: Take advantage of the fine bus (tel. 36 45 45 45) and subway system called S-tog (Eurail valid on S-tog, tel. 33 14 17 01). A joint fare system covers greater Copenhagen. You pay 11 kr as you board for an hour's travel within two zones, or buy a blue two-zone *klippekort* from the driver (75 kr for ten one-hour "rides"). A 24-hour pass costs 70 kr. Don't worry much about "zones." Assume you'll be within the middle two zones. Board at the front, tell the driver where you're going, and he'll sell you the appropriate ticket. Drivers are patient, have change, and speak English. City maps list bus and subway routes. Locals are friendly and helpful. Copenhagen is a bit torn up as it puts together a slick new subway system to celebrate the year 2000.

By Bus Tour: The city tour bus scene is in flux, but there are always tours leaving from the City Hall Square (under the statue of the two Lur Blowers, in front of Palace Hotel, one hour blitz overview—with a short stop only at the *Mermaid*, two departures per hour, 100 kr, also longer tours, tel. 31 54 06 06). There is a new "hop-on-hop-off" tour bus making a general circuit of the town's top sights (daily 9:00–18:00, 100 kr, tel. 36 77 77 66). Budget do-it-yourselfers simply ride city bus #6: from the Carlsberg Brewery, it stops at Tivoli, town hall, national museum, palace, Nyhavn, Amalienborg castle, the Kastellet, and the *Mermaid* (11 kr for one stop-and-go hour). The entire tour is clearly described in a free Use It brochure.

By Taxi: Taxis are plentiful and easy to call or flag down (22-kr drop charge, then 9 kr per km). For a short ride, four people can travel cheaper by taxi than by bus (e.g., 50 kr from train station to Christianshavn B&Bs). Taxis accept all major credit cards. Calling 31 35 35 35 will get you a taxi within minutes.

Free Bikes! Copenhagen's radical "city bike" program is great for sightseers. Two thousand clunky but practical little bikes are scattered around the old town center (basically the terrain covered in the Copenhagen map in this chapter). Simply locate one of the 150 racks, unlock a bike by popping a 20-kr coin into the handlebar, and pedal away. When you're done, park the bike at any other rack, pop in the lock and you get your deposit coin back (if you can't find a rack, leave the bike on the street anywhere and a bum will take it back and pocket your coin). These simple bikes come with "theft-proof" parts (unusable on regular bikes) and—they claim—computer tracer chips embedded in them so bike patrols can retrieve strays. These are constructed with prison labor and funded by advertisements painted on the wheels and by a progressive electorate. Try this once and you'll find Copenhagen suddenly a lot smaller and easier.

For a serious bike tour, rent a more comfortable bike. Use It has a great biking guide brochure and information about city bike tours (50 kr including bike, two hours, grunge approach). You can rent bikes at Central Station's Cykelcenter (50 kr/day, weekdays 8:00–18:00, Saturday 9:00–13:00, summer Sundays 10:00–13:00, closed Sunday off-season, tel. 33 33 86 13) and Dan Wheel (35 kr/day, 60 kr/2 days, weekdays 9:00–18:00, Saturday and Sunday 9:00–14:00, 2 blocks from the station at 3 Colbjørnsensgade, on the corner of Vesterbrogade, tel. 31 21 22 27).

Do-It-Yourself Orientation Walk: "Strøget and Copenhagen's Heart and Soul"

Start from Rådhuspladsen (City Hall Square), the bustling heart of Copenhagen, dominated by the city hall spire. This used to be the fortified west end of town. The king cleverly quelled a French Revolution–type thirst for democracy by giving his people Europe's first great public amusement park. Tivoli was built just outside the city walls in 1843. When the train lines came, the station was placed just beyond Tivoli. The golden girls high up on the building on the square opposite the Strøget's entrance tell the weather: on a bike (fair) or with an umbrella. These two have been called the only women in Copenhagen you can trust. Here in the traffic hub of this huge city you'll notice . . . not many cars. Denmark's 200 percent tax on car purchases makes the bus or bike a sweeter option.

Old Hans Christian Andersen sits to the right of the city hall, almost begging to be in another photo (as he did in real life). On a pedestal left of the city hall, note the Lur-Blowers sculpture. The *lur* is a horn that was used 3,500 years ago. The ancient originals (which still play) are displayed in the National Museum.

The American trio of Burger King, 7-Eleven, and McDonald's marks the start of the otherwise charming Strøget (stroy-et). Copenhagen's 25-year-old experimental, tremendously successful, and most-copied pedestrian shopping mall is a string of lively (and individually named) streets and lovely squares that bunny-hop through the old town from the city hall to Nyhavn, a 15-minute stroll (or *strøget*) away.

As you wander down this street, remember that the commercial focus of a historic street like Strøget drives up the land value, which generally tears down the old buildings. While Strøget has become quite hamburgerized, charm lurks in adjacent areas and many historic bits and pieces of old Copenhagen are just off this commercial cancan.

After 1 block you can side trip 2 blocks left up Larsbjørns-stræde into Copenhagen's colorful university district. Formerly the old brothel area, today this is Soho-chic.

Back on Strøget, the first segment, Frederiksberggade, ends at Gammel Torv and Nytorv (Old Square and New Square). This was the old town center. The Oriental-looking kiosk was one of the city's first community telephone centers before phones were privately owned. The squirting woman and boy on the very old fountain was so offensive to people from the Victorian age that the pedestal was added, raising it—they hoped—out of view. The brick church at the start of Amager Torv is the oldest building you'll see here.

Side trip 2 blocks north of Amager Torv to the leafy and caffeine-stained Gråbrødretorv (Grey Brothers' Square). At the next big intersection, Kobmagergade—an equally lively but less-touristy pedestrian street—is worth exploring.

The final stretch of Strøget leads past the American Express office, Pistolstræde (a cute street of shops in restored 18th-century buildings leading off Strøget to the right from Ostergade), McDonald's (good view from top floor), and major department stores (Illum and Magasin, see below) to a big square called Kongens Nytorv, where you'll find the Royal Theater.

Nyhavn, a recently gentrified sailors' quarter, is just opposite Kongens Nytorv. This formerly sleazy harbor is an interesting mix of tattoo parlors, taverns, and trendy (mostly expensive) cafés lining a canal filled with glamorous old sailboats of all sizes. Any historic sloop is welcome to moor here in Copenhagen's ever-changing boat museum. Hans Christian Andersen lived and wrote his first stories here.

Continuing north, along the harborside (from end of Nyhavn canal, turn left), you'll pass a huge ship that sails to Oslo every evening. Follow the water to the modern fountain of Amaliehave Park. The Amalienborg Palace and Square (a block inland, behind the fountain) is a good example of orderly Baroque planning. Queen Margrethe II and her family live in the palace to your immediate left as you enter the square from the harbor side. Her son and heir to the throne, Frederik, recently moved into the palace directly opposite his mother's. While the guards change with royal fanfare at noon only when the queen is in residence, they shower every morning.

Leave the square on Amaliegade, heading north to Kastellet (Citadel) Park and a small museum about Denmark's World War II resistance efforts. A short stroll, past the Gefion fountain (showing the mythological story of the goddess who was given one night to carve a chunk out of Sweden to make into Denmark's main island, Zealand—which you're on) and a church built of flint and

Central Copenhagen

along the water, brings you to the overrated, over-fondled, and over-photographed symbol of Copenhagen, *Den Lille Havfrue—The Little Mermaid*.

You can get back downtown on foot, by taxi, or on bus #1, #6, or #9 from Store Kongensgade on the other side of Kastellet Park (a special bus may run from the *Mermaid* in summer).

Tours of Copenhagen

▲**Walking Tours**—Once upon a time, American Richard Karpen visited Copenhagen and fell in love with the city (and one of its women). He gives daily two-hour walking tours of his adopted hometown covering its people, history, and contemporary scene. His entertaining walks (there are three—each about 1.5 miles with breaks—covering different parts of the city center) leave daily at 10:30 Monday–Saturday, May–September, from in front of the TI (40 kr, kids under 12 free, pick up schedule at the TI or call Richard at tel. 32 97 14 40). All of Richard's tours, while different, complement each other and are of equal "introduction" value. Richard and local historian Helge "Jack" Jacobsen (tel. 31 51 25 90) give reasonably priced private walks and tours. Use It also offers walking tours (40 kr, 15:30 on Wednesday).

▲▲**Harbor Cruise and Canal Tours**—Two companies offer basically the same live, four-language, 60-minute tours through the city canals (2/hour, daily 10:00–17:00, later in July; runs May to mid-September). They cruise around the palace and Christianshavn area, into the wide-open harbor, and out to the *Mermaid*. Both leave from near Christiansborg Palace. It's a pleasant way to see the *Mermaid* and take a load off those weary feet. Dress warmly; boats are open-top.

The low-overhead 20-kr Netto-Bådene Tour boats (tel. 31 87 21 33) leave from Holmens Kirke across from the Borsen (stock exchange), just over Knippels Bridge. The competition, Canal Tours Copenhagen, does a 40-kr harbor tour with a hop-on-and-hop-off version. It leaves from Gammel Strand near Christiansborg Palace and the National Museum (tel. 33 13 31 05). Don't be confused. If you don't plan to get off the boat, go with Netto. There's no reason to pay double. Tour boats also start at Nyhavn.

Sights—Copenhagen
▲**Copenhagen's Town Hall (*Rådhus*)**—This city landmark, between the station/Tivoli/TI and Strøget pedestrian mall, offers private tours and trips up its 350-foot-high tower. It's draped, inside and out, in Danish symbolism. Bishop Absalon (the city's founder) stands over the door. The polar bears climbing on the rooftop symbolize the giant Danish protectorate of Greenland. The city hall is free and open to the public (Monday–Friday 10:00–15:00). Tours are given in English and get you into otherwise-closed rooms (20 kr, 45 minutes, Monday–Friday at 15:00, Saturday at 10:00). Tourists are allowed to romp up the tower's 300 steps for the best aerial view of Copenhagen (10 kr, Monday–Friday 10:00, 12:00, and 14:00; Saturday 12:00; off-season Monday–Saturday 12:00, tel. 33 66 25 82).
▲**Christiansborg Palace**—This modern *slot*, or palace, built on the ruins of the original 12th-century castle, houses the parliament, supreme court, prime minister's headquarters, and royal reception rooms. Guided 40-minute English tours of the queen's reception rooms let you slip-slide on protect-the-floor slippers through 22 rooms and gain a good feel for Danish history, royalty, and politics in this 100-year-old, still-functioning palace (35 kr, June–August daily at 11:00, 13:00, 15:00; off-season Tuesday, Thursday, and Sunday 11:00 and 15:00; tel. 33 92 64 92). For a rundown on contemporary government, you can also tour the parliament building. From the equestrian statue in front, go through the wooden door, past the entrance to the Christiansborg Castle ruins, into the courtyard, and up the stairs on the right.
▲**Christiansborg Castle ruins**—An exhibit in the scant remains of the first castle built by Bishop Absalon—the 12th-century founder of Copenhagen—lies under the palace (20 kr, daily 9:30–15:30, closed off-season Monday and Saturday, good 1-kr

guide). Early birds note that this sight opens 30 minutes before other nearby sights.

▲▲▲**National Museum**—Focus on the excellent and curiously enjoyable Danish collection, which traces this civilization from its ancient beginnings. Exhibits are laid out chronologically and well-described in English. Pick up the museum map and consider the 10-kr mini-guide which highlights the top stops. Find room 1 opposite the new entrance and begin your walk following the numbers through the "prehistory" section on the ground floor—oak coffins with still-clothed and armed skeletons from 1300 B.C., ancient and still playable lur horns, the 200-year old Gunderstrup Cauldron of art textbook fame, lots of Viking stuff, and a bitchin' collection of well-translated rune stones. Then go upstairs, find room 101 and carry on—fascinating dirt on the Reformation, everyday town life in the 16th and 17th centuries and, in room 126, a unique "cylinder perspective" of the royal family (from 1656) and two peep shows. The next floor takes you into modern times (30 kr, Tuesday–Sunday 10:00–17:00, free on Wednesday, closed Monday, enter from Ny Vestergade 10, tel. 33 13 44 11). Occasional free English tours are offered in the summer—call first).

▲**Ny Carlsberg Glyptotek**—Scandinavia's top art gallery, with especially intoxicating Egyptian, Greek, and Etruscan collections, the best of Danish Golden Age (early 19th century) painting, and a heady, if small, exhibit of 19th-century French paintings (in the new "French Wing," including Géricault, Delacroix, Manet, Impressionists, Gauguin before and after Tahiti) is an impressive example of what beer money can do. Linger with marble gods under the palm leaves and glass dome of the very soothing winter garden. Designers, figuring Danes would be more interested in a lush garden than classical art, used this wonderful space as leafy bait to cleverly introduce locals to a few Greek and Roman statues. (It works for tourists too.) One of the original Rodin *Thinker*s (wondering how to scale the Tivoli fence?) can be seen for free in the museum's backyard. This collection is artfully displayed and thoughtfully described—good even after a visit to Rome (15 kr, Tuesday–Sunday 10:00–16:00, free on Wednesday and Sunday, 2-kr English brochure/guide, classy cafeteria under palms, behind Tivoli, Dantes Plads 7, tel. 33 41 81 41).

▲▲**Rosenborg Castle**—This impressively furnished Renaissance-style castle houses the Danish crown jewels and 500 years of royal knickknacks. It's musty with history (including some great Christian IV lore . . . like the shrapnel he pulled from his eye after a naval battle and made into earrings for his girlfriend) and would be fascinating if anything was explained in English. Consider purchasing the guide. The castle is surrounded by the royal gardens, a rare plant collection, and on sunny days, a minefield of sunbathing Danish beauties and picnickers (40 kr, daily June–August 10:00–16:00; May, September, and October 11:00–15:00; there's no electricity inside, so visit at a bright time; Richard Karpen—see Walking Tours, above—does two Rosenborg tours a week; S-train: Nørreport, tel. 33 15 32 86). There is a daily changing of the guard mini-parade from Rosenborg Castle (at 11:30) to Amalienborg Castle (at 12:00). The King's Rosegarden (across the canal from the palace) is a fine place for a picnic (for cheap open-face sandwiches to go, walk a couple of blocks to Lorraine's at the corner of Borgergade and Dronningenstværgade). The fine statue of Hans Christian Andersen in the park, actually erected in his lifetime (and approved by H.C.A.), is meant to symbolize how his stories had a message even for adults.

▲**Denmark's Resistance Museum** (*Frihedsmuseet*)—The fascinating story of a heroic Nazi resistance struggle (1940–1945) is well-explained in English (free, between the Queen's Palace and the *Mermaid*, daily May to mid-September 10:00–16:00, closed Monday; off-season 11:00–15:00; bus #1, #6, or #9, tel. 33 13 77 14). If prioritizing, the Resistance Museum in Oslo is more interesting.

▲**Our Savior's** (*Vor Frelsers*) **Church**—The church's bright Baroque interior is worth a look (free, daily June–August 9:00–16:30, Sunday 13:30–16:30; closes an hour early in spring and fall; closed in winter, bus #8, tel. 31 57 27 98). The unique spiral spire that you'll admire from afar can be climbed for a great city view and a good aerial view of the Christiania commune below. It's 311 feet high, claims to have 400 steps, and costs 20 kr.

Lille Mølle—This tiny intimate museum shows off a 1916 house in Christianshavn (Monday–Friday 11:00–14:00, just off south end of Torvgade, tel. 33 47 38 38). A fine café serves light lunches and dinners in its terrace garden.

Carlsberg Brewery Tour—Denmark's beloved source of legal intoxicants, Carlsberg, provides free one-hour brewery tours followed by 30-minute "tasting sessions" (Monday–Friday 11:00 and 14:00; bus #6 to 140 Ny Carlsberg Vej, tel. 33 27 13 14).

Museum of Erotica—This museum's focus: the love life of *Homo sapiens*. Better than the Amsterdam equivalents, it offers a chance to visit a porno shop and call it a museum. It took some digging, but they've documented a history of sex from Pompeii to present day. Visitors get a peep into the world of 19th-century Copenhagen prostitutes and a chance to read up on the sex lives of Martin Luther, Queen Elizabeth, Charlie Chaplin, and Casanova. After reviewing a lifetime of *Playboy* centerfolds, visitors sit down for the arguably artistic experience of watching the "electric *tabernakel*," a dozen silently slamming screens of porn seething to the gentle accompaniment of music (worth the 49-kr entry fee only if fascinated by sex, daily May–September 10:00–23:00; 11:00–20:00 the rest of the year, a block north of Strøget at Købmagergade 24, tel. 33 12 03 11). For the real thing—unsanitized but free—wander Copenhagen's dreary little red-light district along Istedgade behind the train station.

Hovedbanegården—The great Copenhagen train station is a fascinating mesh of Scandinanity and transportation efficiency. Even if you're not a train traveler, check it out.

Nightlife—For the latest on Copenhagen's hopping jazz scene, pick up the *Copenhagen Jazz Guide* at the TI or the more "alternative" *Playtime* magazine at Use It.

Tivoli Gardens

The world's grand old amusement park—which just turned 150 years old—is 20 acres, 110,000 lanterns, and countless ice-cream cones of fun. You pay one admission price and find yourself lost in a Hans Christian Andersen wonderland of rides, restaurants, games, marching bands, roulette wheels, and funny mirrors. Tivoli is wonderfully Danish. It doesn't try to be Disney (39 kr regular admission, 30 kr entry before 13:00 and after 22:00, open daily April– mid-September 10:00–24:00, closed off-season, tel. 33 15 10 01). Rides are 15 kr, or 1,148 kr for an all-day pass. All children's amusements are in full swing by 11:30; the rest of the amusements are open by 13:30.

Entertainment in Tivoli: Upon arrival, go right to the Tivoli Service Center (through main entry, on left) to pick up a map and events schedule. Take a moment to sit down and plan your entertainment for the evening (events on the half-hour 18:30–23:00; 19:30 concert in the concert hall can be free or cost up to 500 kr, depending on the performer). Free concerts, mime, ballet, acrobats, puppets, and other shows pop up all over the park, and a well-organized visitor can enjoy an exciting evening of entertainment without spending a single krone (though occasionally the schedule is a bit sparse). The children's theater, Valmuen, plays excellent traditional fairy tales (daily except Monday, 12:00, 13:00, and 14:00). If the Tivoli Symphony is playing, it's worth paying for. Friday evenings feature a 22:00 rock or pop show. On Wednesday and Saturday at 23:45, fireworks light up the sky. If you're taking an overnight train out of Copenhagen, Tivoli (across from the station) is the place to spend your last Copenhagen hours.

Eating at Tivoli: Generally, you'll pay amusement-park prices for amusement-park-quality food inside. **Søcafeen**, by the lake, allows picnics if you buy a drink. The *pølser* (sausage) stands are cheap. **Færgekroen** is a good lakeside place for a beer or some typical Danish food. The Croatian restaurant, **Hercegovina**, is a decent value (100-kr lunch buffet, 140-kr dinner buffet). For a cake and coffee, consider the **Viften** café.

Christiania

In 1971 the original 700 Christianians established squatters right in an abandoned military barracks just a ten-minute walk from the Danish parliament building. A generation later this "free city"—an ultra-human mishmash of 1,000 idealists, anarchists, hippies, dope fiends, non-materialists, and people who dream only of being a Danish bicycle seat—not only survives, it thrives. This is a communal cornucopia of dogs, dirt, soft drugs, and dazed people—or haven of peace, freedom, and no taboos, depending on your perspective. Locals will remind judgmental Americans that a society must make the choice: allow for alternative lifestyles . . . or build more prisons.

For 25 years Christiania was a political hot potato . . . no one in the Danish establishment wanted it—or had the nerve to mash it. Now that Christiania is no longer a teenager, it's making an effort to connect better with the rest of society. The community is paying its utilities and even offering daily walking tours (see below).

Passing under the city gate you'll find yourself on "Pusher Street" . . . the main drag. This is a line of stalls selling hash, pot, pipes, and souvenirs leading to the market square and a food circus beyond. Make a point of getting past this "touristy" side of Christiania. You'll find a fascinating ramshackle world of moats and earthen ramparts, alternative housing, unappetizing falafel stands, carpenter shops, hippie villas, children's playgrounds, and peaceful lanes. Be careful to distinguish between real Christianians and Christiania's uninvited guests—motley lowlife vagabonds from other countries who hang out here in the summer, skid row–type Greenlanders, and gawking tourists.

Soft Drugs: While hard drugs are out, hash and pot are sold openly (huge joints for 20 kr, senior discounts) and smoked happily. While locals will assure you you're safe within Christiania, they'll remind you that it's risky to take pot out—Denmark is required by Uncle Sam to make a token effort to snare tourists leaving the "free city" with pot. Beefy marijuana plants stand on proud pedestals at the market square. Beyond that an open-air food circus (or the canal-view perch above it, on the earthen ramparts) creates just the right ambience to lose track of time. Graffiti on the wall declares "a mind is a wonderful thing to waste."

Nitty-Gritty: Christiania is open all the time and visitors are welcome (follow the beer bottles and guitars down Prinsessegade behind Vor Frelsers' spiral church spire in Christianshavn). Photography is absolutely forbidden on Pusher Street (if you value your camera, don't even sneak a photo). Otherwise, you are welcome to snap photos, but ask residents before you photograph them. Christiania's free English/Dansk visitor's magazine, *Nitten* (available at Use It), is good reading, offering a serious explanation about how this unique community works and survives. It suggests several do-it-yourself walking tours. Guided tours leave from the front entrance of Christiania at 15:00 (daily June–August, 20 kr, in English and Danish, tel. 32 95 65 07 to confirm). Morgenstedet is a cheap and good vegetarian place (left after Pusher Street). Spiseloppen is the classy good-enough-for-Republicans restaurant (see Eating, below).

More Sights—Copenhagen

Thorvaldsen's Museum features the early 18th-century work of Denmark's greatest sculptor (free, Tuesday–Sunday 10:00–17:00, closed Monday, next to Christiansborg Palace). The noontime **changing of the guard** at the Amalienborg Palace is boring: All they change is places. **Nyhavn**, with its fine old ships, tattoo shops (pop into Tattoo Ole at #17—fun photos, very traditional), and jazz clubs, is a wonderful place to hang out. The **Round Tower**, built in 1642 by Christian IV, connects a church, library, and observatory (the oldest functioning observatory in Europe) with a ramp which spirals up to a fine view of Copenhagen (15 kr, daily 10:00–17:00, later in summer, less on Sunday, nothing to see but the ramp and the view, just off Strøget on Købmagergade).

Copenhagen's **Open Air Folk Museum** (*Frilandsmuseet*) is a park filled with traditional Danish architecture and folk culture (30 kr, Tuesday–Sunday April–October 10:00–17:00, closed Monday; shorter hours off-season, outside of town in the suburb of Lyngby, tel. 45 85 02 92). From Copenhagen, hop on the S-train to Sorgenfri; then either take a 20-minute walk to the museum (as you exit the station, turn right and walk about 1 kilometer to next traffic light, turn left and go 2 blocks to museum) or catch bus #184 from the north end of Nørreport station (this bus takes a cicuitous route through several towns before stopping at museum).

Danes gather at Copenhagen's other great amusement park, **Bakken** (free, daily April–August 14:00–24:00, 30 minutes by S-train to Klampenborg, then walk through the woods, tel. 39 63 35 44).

If you don't have time to get to Denmark's idyllic islands, consider a trip to the tiny fishing village of **Dragør** (30 minutes on bus #30 or #33 from Copenhagen's City Hall Square).

Shopping

Copenhagen's colorful flea market is small but feisty and surprisingly cheap (summer Saturdays 8:00–14:00 at Israels Plads). More flea markets are listed in *Copenhagen This Week*. An antique market enlivens Nybrogade (near the palace) every Friday and Saturday. For a streetful of shops selling "Scantiques," wander down Ravnsborggade from Nørrebrogade. The city's top department stores (Illum at 52 Østergade, tel. 33 14 40 02, and Magasin at 13 Kongens Nytorv, tel. 33 11 44 33) offer a good, if expensive, look at today's Denmark. Both are on Strøget and have fine cafeterias on their top floors.

Danes shop cheaper at Dælls Varehus (corner of Krystalgade and Fiolstræde). At UFF on Kultorvet you can buy nearly new

clothes for peanuts and support charity. Shops are open Monday
through Friday 10:00 to 19:00; Saturday 9:00 to 16:00.

The department stores and the Politiken Bookstore on the Rådhus Square have a good selection of maps and English travel guides.

If you buy more than 300 kr ($50) worth of stuff, you can get
80 percent of the 25 percent VAT (MOMS in Danish) back if you
buy from a shop displaying the Danish Tax-Free Shopping emblem.
If you have your purchase mailed, the tax can bededucted from your
bill. Call 32 52 55 66 (8:30–16:00 weekdays), see the shopping-
oriented *Copenhagen This Week*, or ask a merchant for specifics.

Sleeping in Copenhagen
(7 kr = about $1)
Sleep Code: **S**=Single, **D**=Double/Twin, **T**=Triple, **Q**=Quad,
b=bathroom, **CC**=Credit Card (Visa, MasterCard, Amex). Breakfast is often included at hotels and rarely included with private
rooms and hostels.

I've listed the best budget hotels in the center (with doubles
for 400–600 kr), rooms in private homes an easy bus ride or 15-
minute walk from the station (around 350 kr per double), and dor-
mitory options (100 kr per person).

Ibsen's Hotel is a rare, simple, bath-down-the-hall, cheery,
and central budget hotel, run by three women who treat you like
you're paying top dollar (S-450 kr, Sb-700 kr, D-600 kr, Db-950 kr,
third person-150 kr, lots of stairs, CC:VMA, Vendersgade 23,
DK-1363 Copenhagen, bus #5, #7E, #16, or #40 from the station,
or S-train: Nørreport, tel. 33 13 19 13, fax 33 13 19 16, e-mail:
hotel@nicholls.dk).

Hotel Sankt Jørgen has big, friendly-feeling rooms with
plain old wooden furnishings. Brigitte and Susan offer a warm
welcome and a great value (S-375 kr, D-475 kr with this book
through 1998, third person-125 kr extra, five-bed family rooms, 10
percent less in winter, breakfast served in your room, elevator, a
12-minute walk from the station or catch bus #13 to the first stop
after the lake, Julius Thomsensgade 22, DK-1632 Copenhagen V,
tel. 35 37 15 11, fax 35 37 11 97, Web site: www.m-p.dk). Unfortunately, each room smells musty from smokers.

Webers Best Western Hotel is my best fine hotel by the
train station. Just a five-minute walk down Vesterbrogade from
the station, it offers breakfast in a peaceful garden courtyard (if
sunny); a classy, modern but inviting interior; and generous
weekend/summer rates (May–September and Friday, Saturday,
and Sunday all year: Sb-695 kr, Db-995 kr, 1,095 kr, and 1,195 kr
depending on size/grade of room; high season: Sb-from 1,080 kr,
Db-from 1,280 kr, CC:VMA, sauna/exercise room, Vesterbrogade 11B, DK-1620 Copenhagen, tel. 31 31 14 32, fax 31 31 14
41, e-mail: webers.hotel @dk.online.dk).

Excelsior Hotel is a big, mod, normal, tour-group hotel a block behind the station, in a sleazy but safe area just half a block off the decent, bustling Vesterbrogade (small Db-770 kr, bigger Db-865 kr, CC:VMA, Colbjørnsensgade 4, DK-1652 Copenhagen, tel. 31 24 50 85, fax 31 24 50 87).

Hotel KFUM Soldaterhjem, originally for soldiers, rents eight singles and three doubles on the fifth floor, with no elevators (S-215 kr, S plus hideabed-315 kr, D-340 kr, no breakfast, Gothersgade 115, Copenhagen K, tel. 33 15 40 44). The reception is on the first floor up (weekdays 8:30–23:00, weekends 15:00–23:00) next to a budget cafeteria.

Cab-Inn is a radical innovation: 86 identical, mostly collapsible, tiny but comfy, cruise ship–type staterooms, all bright, molded, and shiny with TV, coffeepot, shower, and toilet. Each room has a single bed that expands into a twin with one or two fold-down bunks on the walls. The staff will hardly give you the time of day, but it's tough to argue with this efficiency (S-395 kr, D-495 kr, T-595 kr, Q-695 kr, breakfast-40 kr, easy parking-30 kr, CC:VMA). There are two virtually identical Cab-Inns in the same neighborhood: **Cab-Inn Copenhagen** has a bit nicer locale (Danasvej 32-34, 1910 Frederiksberg C, five minutes on bus #29 to center, tel. 31 21 04 00, fax 31 21 74 09). **Cab-Inn Scandinavia** has a bit bigger building with a bigger cafeteria. Some rooms come with a real double bed for 100 kr extra (Vodroffsvej 55, tel. 35 36 11 11, fax 35 36 11 14). E-mail either at cabinn@inet.inu-c.dk.

Sleeping in Rooms in Private Homes

Following are a few leads for Copenhagen's best accommodations values. Most are in the lively Christianshavn neighborhood. While each TI has its own list of B&Bs, by booking direct you'll save yourself and your host the tourist-office fee. *Always* call ahead; they book in advance. Most are run by single professional women supplementing their income. All speak English and afford a fine peek into Danish domestic life. Rooms generally have no sink. Don't count on breakfast.

In Christianshavn: This area—my Copenhagen home—is a never-a-dull-moment hodgepodge of the chic, artistic, hippie, and hobo, with beer-drinking Greenlanders littering streets in the shadow of fancy government ministries. Colorful with lots of shops, cafés, and canals, it's an easy ten-minute walk to the center, and has good bus connections to the airport and downtown.

Annette and Rudy Hollender enjoy sharing their 300-year-old home with my readers. Even with a long skinny staircase, sinkless rooms, and three rooms sharing one toilet/shower, it's a comfortable and cheery place to call home—which you will by day two (S-225 kr, D-300 kr, T-400 kr, Wildersgade 19, 1408 Copenhagen K, closed November–April, tel. 32 95 96 22, fax 31

57 24 86). Take bus #9 from the airport, bus #8 from the station, or bus #2 from the city hall. From downtown, push the button immediately after crossing Knippels Bridge, and turn right off Torvegade down Wildersgade.

Morten Frederiksen, a laid-back, ponytailed sort of guy, rents five spacious rooms and two four-bed suites in a mod-funky-pleasant old house. The furniture is old-time rustic but elegant. The posters are Mapplethorpe. It's a clean, comfy, good look at today's hip Danish lifestyle and has a great location right on Christianshavn's main drag (D-275 kr, T-375 kr, Q-475 kr, no breakfast, two minutes from Annette's, Torvegade 36, tel. 32 95 32 73, cell phone 20 41 92 73).

Britta Krogh-Lund rents two spacious doubles in an old Christianshavn house (S-225 kr, D-300 kr, T-400 kr, kitchen for self-serve breakfast only, Amagergade 1, C-1423 Copenhagen K, tel. 32 95 55 85). **Loni Føgh** rents two rooms in her modern apartment in the same area (D-300 kr, no breakfast, Strandgade 41, third floor, tel. 32 95 44 77).

South of Christianshavn, **Gitte Kongstad** rents two apartments, each taking up an entire spacious floor in her flat. You'll have a kitchenette, little garden, and your own bike (D-300 kr, family deals, no breakfast, bus #9 from airport, bus #12 or #13 from station, a ten-minute ride past Christianshavn to Badens-gade 2, 2300 Copenhagen, tel. and fax 32 97 71 97, cell phone 20 74 21 17). While the neighborhood is inconvenient, you'll feel very at home here and the bike ride into town is a snap.

Private Rooms in Central Copenhagen

Lone (loan-nuh) **Hardt** rents two white woody rooms, each with a double mattress on the floor and nearly no furniture, in a 300-year-old half-timbered building a stone's throw from the Round Tower in the old center of town. If you want to stow away in the very center of town, this can't be beat (D-300 kr, no breakfast, St. Kannikestræde 5, tel. 33 14 60 79).

Solveig Diderichsen rents three rooms in her comfortable, high-ceilinged, ground-floor apartment home. She serves no breakfast but offers kitchen facilities, and there's a good bakery around the corner. Located in a quiet embassy neighborhood next to a colorful residential area with fun shops and eateries behind the Østre Anlæg park (S-275 kr, D-325 kr, T-450 kr, bus #9 direct from the airport or three stops on the subway from the central station, to Østerport, then a three-minute walk to Upsalagade 26, 2100 Copenhagen Ø, tel. 35 43 39 58, fax 35 43 22 70, cell phone 40 11 39 58). If her place is full, she can find you a room in a B&B nearby. An avid sledder, Solveig shares her home with her sled-dog, Maya.

Annette Haugballe rents three modern, pleasant rooms in the quiet, green, residential Frederiksberg area (D-300 kr, no breakfast, easy parking, Hoffmeyersvej 33, 2000 Frederiksberg, on bus line #1 from station or City Hall Square, and near Peter Bangsvej S subway station, tel. 38 74 87 87). Her parents and her friends also rent rooms.

Near the Amalienborg Palace: This is a stately embassy neighborhood—no stress but a bit bland and up lots of stairs. You can look out your window to see the queen's palace (and the guards changing). It's a ten-minute walk north of Nyhavn and Strøget. **Puk** (pook) **De La Cour** rents two rooms in her mod, bright, and easygoing house (D-325 kr with no breakfast but tea, coffee, and a kitchen/family room available, Amaliegade 34, fourth floor, tel. 33 12 04 68). Puk's friend **Line** (lee-nuh) **Voutsinos** offers a similar deal June through September only (D-325 kr, 125 kr/extra bed, each room comes with a small double bed, no breakfast, long-term parking—5 kr/hour or 50 kr/day on street, Amaliegade 34, third floor, tel. 33 14 71 42).

Sleeping in Hostels

Copenhagen energetically accommodates the young vagabond on a shoestring. The Use It office is your best source of information. Each of these places charges about 100 kr per person for bed and breakfast. Some don't allow sleeping bags, and if you don't have your own hostel bedsheet, you'll normally have to rent one for around 30 kr. IYHF hostels normally sell non-cardholders a "guest pass" for 22 kr.

The modern **Copenhagen Hostel** (IYHF) is huge, with sixty 220-kr doubles, five-bed dorms at 80 kr/bed, sheets extra, no curfew, excellent facilities, cheap meals, and a self-serve laundry. Unfortunately, it's on the edge of town: bus #10 from the station to Mozartplads, then #37; or, daytime only, ride bus #46 direct from the station (breakfast not included, Vejlands Alle 200, 2300 Copenhagen S, tel. 32 52 29 08, fax 32 52 27 08).

The Danish **YMCA/YWCA,** open only in July and August, is a ten-minute walk from the train station or a short ride on bus #6 (dorm bed-65 kr, four- to ten-bed rooms, breakfast-30 kr, Valdemarsgade 15, tel. 31 31 15 74).

Eating in Copenhagen

Copenhagen's many good restaurants are well listed by category in *Copenhagen This Week*. Since restaurant prices include 25 percent tax, your budget may require alternatives. These survival ideas for the hungry budget traveler in Copenhagen will save lots of money.

Picnics

Irma (in arcade on Vesterbrogade next to Tivoli) and **Brugsen** are the two largest supermarket chains. **Netto** is a cut-rate outfit with the cheapest prices. The little grocery store in the central station is expensive but handy (daily 8:00–24:00).

Viktualiehandler (small delis) and bakeries, found on nearly every corner, sell fresh bread, tasty pastries (a *wienerbrød* is what we call a "Danish"), juice, milk, cheese, and yogurt (drinkable, in tall liter boxes). Liver paste (*leverpostej*) is cheap and a little better than it sounds.

Smørrebrød
While virgins no longer roll around carts filled with delicate sand-wiches, Denmark's 300-year-old tradition of open-face sandwiches survives. Open-face sandwiches cost a fortune in restaurants, but the many smørrebrød take-out shops sell them for 8 kr to 30 kr. Drop into one of these often-no-name, family-run budget savers, and get several elegant OFSs to go. The tradition calls for three sandwich courses: herring first, then meat, then cheese. It makes for a classy—and cheap—picnic. Downtown you'll find these handy local alterna-tives to Yankee fast-food chains: **Centrum** (open long hours, Vesterbrogade 6C, across from station), **Tria Cafe** (Monday–Friday 8:00–14:00, closed weekends, Gothersgade 12, near Kongens Nytorv), **Domhusets Smørrebrød** (Monday–Friday 7:00–14:30, Kattesundet 18), and one in Nyhavn, on the corner of Holbergsgade and Peder Skrams Gade.

The Pølse
The famous Danish hot dog, sold in *pølsevogn* (sausage wagons) throughout the city, is one of the few typically Danish institutions to resist the onslaught of our global fast-food culture. "Hot dog" is a Danish word for wienie—study the photo menu for varia-tions. These are fast, cheap, tasty, easy to order, and almost worthless nutritionally. Even so, the local "dead man's finger" is the dog kids love to bite.

By hanging around a pølsevogn you can study this institution. Denmark's "cold feet café" is a form of social care: Only people who have difficulty finding jobs, such as the handicapped, are licensed to run these wiener-mobiles. As they gain seniority they are promoted to work at more central locations. Danes like to gather here for munchies and *pølsesnak* ("sausage talk"), the local slang for empty chatter.

Inexpensive Restaurants
Riz-Raz, around the corner from Use It at Kompagnistræde 20, serves a healthy, all-you-can-eat, 49-kr Mediterranean/vegetarian buffet lunch (daily 11:30–17:00), and an even bigger 59-kr dinner buffet (until 24:00, tel. 33 15 05 75), which has to be the best deal in town. And they're happy to serve free water with your meal. Department stores serve cheery, reasonable meals in their cafete-rias (such as **Illum**, an elegant top-floor circus of reasonable food under a glass dome, just past the American Express office; **Maga-sin**; or **Dælls Varehus**, at Nørregade 12). At **El Porron**, you'll

find good Spanish tapas (Vendersgade 10, 1 block from Ibsen's Hotel).

Det Lille Apotek, the "little pharmacy," is a reasonable, candlelit place which has been popular with locals for 200 years (reasonable sandwich lunches, bigger dinners, just off Strøget, between the Frue Church and the Round Tower at St. Kannikestræde 15, tel. 33 12 56 06). The **Chicago Pizza Factory**, next door, serves a cheap and lousy pizza buffet and salad bar (49 kr).

To explore your way through a world of traditional Danish food, try a Danish *koldt bord* (an all-you-can-eat buffet). The central station's **Bistro Restaurant** is handy but touristy (154-kr dinner, served daily 11:30–21:30, tel. 33 14 12 32).

Good Eating in Christianshavn

This neighborhood is so cool, it's worth combining an evening wander with dinner even if you don't live here. **Café Wilder** serves creative and hearty dinner salads by candlelight to a trendy local clientele (corner of Wildersgade and Skt. Annæ Gade, a block off Torvegade, open until 22:00). To avoid having to choose just one of their interesting salads, try their three-salad plate (60 kr with bread). They also feature a budget dinner plate for around 75 kr and are happy to serve free water. Across the street, the **Luna Café** is also good and serves a slower-paced meal. Choose one of three good dinner salads and bread for 40 kr.

The **Ravelin Restaurant**, on a tiny island on the big road just south of Christianshavn, serves good traditional Danish-style food at reasonable prices to happy local crowds. Its lovely lakeside terrace is open on sunny days (100–170-kr dinners, Torvegade 79, tel. 32 96 20 45). A block away, at the little windmill (Lille Mølle), **Bastionen & Loven** serves Scandinavian nouveau cuisine on a Renoir terrace or in its Rembrandt interior (40-kr lunch specials, 50-kr dinner salads, 80–120-kr dinners, menu is small but fresh, Voldgade 54, up on the bastion off Torvegade at south end of Christianshavn, tel. 32 95 09 40).

In Christiania, the wonderfully classy **Spiseloppen** (meaning "the flea eats") serves great 100-kr vegetarian meals and 140-kr meaty ones by candlelight. Christiania is the free city/squatter town, located 3 blocks behind the spiral spire of Vor Frelser's church (restaurant open Tuesday–Sunday 17:00–22:00, closed Monday, on the top floor of an old brick warehouse, turn right just inside Christiania's gate, reservations often necessary on weekends, tel. 31 57 95 58).

Transportation Connections—Copenhagen

By train to: Hillerød/Frederiksborg (40/day, 30 min), **Louisiana Museum** (Helsingør train to Humlebæk, 40/day, 30 min), **Roskilde** (16/day, 30 min), **Odense** (16/day, 2 hrs), **Helsingør** (ferry to Sweden, 40/day, 50 min), **Stockholm** (8/day,

8 hrs), **Oslo** (4/day, 10 hrs), **Växjö** (via Alvesta, 6/day, 5 hrs),
Kalmar (6/day, via Alvesta and Växjö, 7 hrs), **Berlin** (via Gedser,
2/day, 9 hrs), **Amsterdam** (2/day, 11 hrs), **Frankfurt/Rhine**
(4/day, 10 hrs). National train info tel. 33 14 17 01. International
train info: tel. 70 13 14 16.

Cheaper **bus trips** are listed at Use It. All Norway- and
Sweden-bound trains go right onto the Helsingør–Helsingborg
ferry. (You get 20 minutes to romp on the deck, eat the wind,
grab a bite, and change money.) The crossing is included in any
train ticket. There are convenient overnight trains from Copenhagen directly to Stockholm, Oslo, Amsterdam, and Frankfurt.

A quickie cruise from Copenhagen to Oslo: A luxurious
cruise ship leaves daily from Copenhagen (departs 17:00, returns by
9:15 two days later; 16 hours sailing each way and seven hours in
Norway's capital). Special packages give you a bed in a double cabin,
a fine dinner, and two smørgåsbord breakfasts for around $170 in
summer ($200 for single, Friday and Saturday cost more). Call
DFDS Scandinavian Seaways (tel. 33 42 30 00). It's easy to make a
reservation in the U.S.A. (tel. 800/5DF-DS55).

STOCKHOLM

If I had to call one European city home, it would be Stockholm. Surrounded by water and woods, bubbling with energy and history, Sweden's stunning capital is green, clean, and underrated.

Crawl through Europe's best-preserved old warship and relax on a canal-boat tour. Browse the cobbles and antique shops of the lantern-lit Old Town and take a spin through Skansen, Europe's first and best open-air folk museum. Marvel at Stockholm's glittering city hall, modern department stores, and art museums.

While progressive and sleek, Stockholm respects its heritage. Throughout the summer, mounted bands parade each noontime through the heart of town to the royal palace, announcing the changing of the guard, and turning even the most dignified tourist into a scampering kid. The *Gamla Stan* (Old Town) celebrates the Midsummer festivities (late June) with the down-home vigor of a rural village, forgetting that it's the core of a gleaming 20th-century metropolis.

Stockholm is Europe's "Culture Capital" in 1998. The year will be filled with special events with this theme: "Culture holds a society together." All the details can be found at www.kulture98.stockholm.se or on the city's Web site: www.stoinfo.se.

Planning Your Time

Stockholm is worth two days. Efficient train travelers sleep in and out for two days in the city with only one night in a hotel. (Copenhagen and Oslo trains arrive at about 8:00 and depart at about 23:00.) To be even more economical and efficient, you could use the luxury Stockholm–Helsinki boat as your hotel for two nights (spending a day in Helsinki) and have two days in Stockholm without a hotel (e.g., Copenhagen; night train to

Stockholm, day in Stockholm; night boat to Helsinki, day in
Helsinki; night boat to Stockholm, day in Stockholm; night train
to Oslo). That may sound crazy, but it gives you three interesting and inexpensive days of travel fun.

Spend two days in Stockholm this way:

Day 1: Arrive by train (or the night before by car), do station
chores (reserve next ride, change money, pick up map, *Stockholm
This Week*, and a Stockholm Card at the Hotellcentralen TI),
check into hotel. At 10:00 catch one-hour bus tour from Opera;
11:00 tour *Vasa* warship and have a picnic; 13:00 tour Nordic
Museum; 15:00 Skansen (ask for an open-air folk museum tour);
19:00 folk dancing, possible smørgåsbord, and popular dancing, or
wander Gamla Stan.

Day 2: Do the 10:00 city hall tour and climb the city hall tower
for a fine view; 12:00 catch the changing of the guard at the
palace, tour royal palace and armory, explore Gamla Stan, or picnic on one-hour city boat tour; 16:00 browse the modern city center around Kungsträdgården, Sergels Torg, Hötorget market and
indoor food hall, and Drottninggatan area.

Orientation (tel. code: 08)

Greater Stockholm's 1.8 million residents live on 14 islands that
are woven together by 50 bridges. Visitors need only concern
themselves with five islands: **Normalm** is downtown, with most
of the hotels, shopping areas, and the train station. **Gamla Stan** is
the old city of winding lantern-lit streets, antique shops, and
classy, glassy cafés clustered around the royal palace. **Södermalm**,
aptly called Stockholm's Brooklyn, is residential and untouristy.
Skeppsholmen is the small, very central traffic-free park island
with the Museum of Modern Art and two fine youth hostels.
Djurgården, literally "deer garden" and now officially a national
city park, is Stockholm's wonderful green playground with many
of the city's top sights (bike rentals just over the bridge as you
enter the island).

Tourist Information

Hotellcentralen is primarily a room-finding service (in the central
train station), but its friendly staff adequately handles all your sightseeing and transportation questions. This is the place for anyone
arriving by train to arrange accommodations, buy the Tourist Card
or Stockholm Card (see below), and pick up a city map, *Stockholm
This Week* (which lists opening hours and directions to all the sights,
special events, and all the tedious details: lost and found, embassies,
post offices, etc.), and brochures on whatever else you need (city
walks, parking, jazz boats, excursions, bus routes, shopping, and so
on). While *This Week* has a decent map of the sightseeing zone, the
15-kr map covers more area and bus routes. It's worth the extra
money if you'll be using the buses (daily June–August 7:00–21:00;

Greater Stockholm

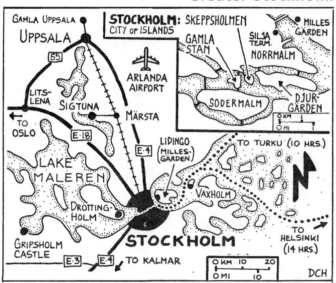

May and September 8:00–19:00; off-season 9:00–18:00; tel.
08/789-2425, fax 08/791-8666, e-mail: hotels@stoinfo.se).

Sverige Huset (Sweden House), Stockholm's official tourist
information office (a short walk from the station on Kungsträdgården), is very good but usually more crowded than Hotellcentralen. They've got pamphlets on everything; an "excursion shop"
for transportation, day-trip, and bus-tour information, and tickets; and an English library and reading room upstairs with racks
of 5-kr information on various aspects of Swedish culture and one
state's attempt at cradle-to-grave happiness (July–September
Monday–Friday 9:00–18:00, Saturday–Sunday 9:00–17:00; off-
season weekdays 9:00–18:00, weekends 9:00–15:00; Hamngatan
27, tel. 08/789-2490 for info, 08/789-2415 for tickets; T-bana:
Kungsträdgården).

The **City Hall TI** is smaller but with all the information and
a bit less chaos (daily 9:00–17:00, May–October only, at the Stadshuset or City Hall, tel. 08/5082-9000).

Arrival in Stockholm

By Train: Stockholm's central train station is a wonderland of
services, shops, and people going places. The Hotellcentralen TI
is as good as the city TI nearby. If you're sailing to Finland,
check out the Viking Line office. The FOREX long-hours
exchange counter changes traveler's checks for only a 15-kr fee
(two offices, upstairs and downstairs, in the station).

By Plane: Stockholm's Arlanda Airport is 45 kilometers north of town. Shuttle buses run between the airport and the City Terminal next to the station (6/hour, tel. 08/600-1000). Airport information tel. 08/797-6000 (SAS tel. 08/910-150, British Air tel. 08/679-7800).

Helpful Hints

The Kulturhus on Sergels Torg has a cyber café (Monday–Saturday 11:00–18:00, 20 kr for 30 minutes with assistance, 30 kr same with coffee and a roll). There are three kinds of public phones: coin-op, credit card, and phone card. For operator assistance, call 0018. Numbers starting with 020 are toll-free. For medical help, call 08/644-9200. There's a 24-hour pharmacy near the central station at Klarabergsgatan 64 (tel. 08/454-8100). To get a taxi within three minutes, call Taxi Stockholm (tel. 08/150-000) or Taxi Kurir (tel. 08/300-000).

Getting Around Stockholm

By Bus and Subway: Stockholm complements her many sightseeing charms with great information services, a fine bus and subway system, and special passes that take the bite out of the city's cost (or at least limit it to one vicious budgetary gash).

Buses and the subway work on the same tickets. Ignore the zones since everything I mention (except Drottningholm and Carl Millesgården) is in Zone One. Each 14-kr ticket is valid for one hour (ten-packs cost 95 kr). The subway, called T-bana or Tunnelbana, gets you where you want to go very quickly. Ride it just for the futuristic drama of being a human mole and to check out the modern public art (for instance, in the Kungsträdgården station, transit info tel. 08/600-1000). The **Tourist Card**, which gives you free use of all public transport and the harbor ferry (24 hours/60 kr, 72 hours/120 kr, sold at TIs and newsstands), is not necessary if you're getting the Stockholm Card (see below). The 72-hour pass includes admission to Skansen, Gröna Lund, and the Kaknäs Tower.

It seems too good to be true, but each year I pinch myself and the **Stockholm Card** is still there. This 24-hour, 185-kr pass (sold at TIs and ship terminals) gives you free run of all public transit, free entry to virtually every sight (70 places), free parking, a handy sightseeing handbook, and the substantial pleasure of doing everything without considering the cost (many of Stockholm's sights are worth the time but not the steep individual ticket costs). This pays for itself if you do Skansen, the *Vasa*, and the Royal Palace and Treasury tour. If you enter Skansen on your 24th hour (and head right for the 50-kr aquarium), you get a few extra hours. (Parents get an added bonus: Two children under age 18 go along for free with each adult pass.) The same pass comes in 48-hour (350-kr) and 72-hour (470-kr) versions.

By Harbor Shuttle Ferry: Throughout the summer, ferries connect Stockholm's two most interesting sightseeing districts. They sail from Nybroplan and Slussen to Djurgården, landing next to the *Vasa* and Skansen (15 kr, not covered by Stockholm Card, every 20 min).

Sights—Downtown Stockholm

▲**Kungsträdgården**—The King's Garden Square is the downtown people-watching center. Watch the life-sized game of chess and enjoy the free concerts at the bandstand. Surrounded by the Sweden House, the NK department store, the harborfront, and tour boats, it's the place to feel Stockholm's pulse (with discretion).

▲▲**Sergels Torg**—The heart of modern Stockholm, between Kungsträdgården and the station, is worth a wander. Enjoy the colorful, bustling underground mall and dip into the Gallerien mall. Visit the Kulturhuset, a center for reading, relaxing, and socializing designed for normal people (but welcoming tourists), with music, exhibits, hands-on fun, and an insight into contemporary Sweden (free, Tuesday–Sunday 11:00–17:00, often later, tel. 08/700-0100). From Sergels Torg, walk up the Drottninggatan pedestrian mall to Hötorget (see Eating, below).

▲▲**City Hall**—The Stadshuset is an impressive mix of 8 million bricks, 19 million chips of gilt mosaic, and lots of Stockholm pride. One of Europe's most impressive public buildings (b. 1923) and site of the annual Nobel Prize banquet, it's particularly enjoyable and worthwhile for its entertaining tours (30 kr, daily June–August at 10:00, 11:00, 12:00, and 14:00; off-season at 10:00 and 12:00; just behind the station, bus #48 or #62, tel. 08/5082-9059). Climb the 350-foot tower (an elevator takes you halfway) for the best possible city view (15 kr, daily 10:00–16:30, May–September only). The City Hall also has a TI and a good cafeteria with complete lunches for 60 kr (11:00–14:00, Monday–Friday).

▲**Orientation Views**—Try to get a bird's-eye perspective on this wonderful urban mix of water, parks, concrete, and people from the City Hall tower (see above), the Kaknäs Tower (at 500 feet, the tallest building in Scandinavia, 20 kr, daily May–August 9:00–22:00, daily September–April 10:00–21:00, bus #69 from Nybroplan or Sergels Torg, tel. 08/789-2435), the observatory in Skansen, or the Katarina elevator (5 kr, daily 7:30–21:00, circa 1930s, ride 40 meters to the top, near Slussen subway stop, then walk behind Katarinavagen for grand views, a classy residential neighborhood, and the lively Mosebacke evening scene—strolling, dancing, and beer gardens).

▲**Quickie Orientation Bus Tour**—Several different city-bus tours leave from the Royal Opera House: 50 minutes for 85 kr with a Swedish/English guide (mid-June–mid-August at 10:30, 11:30, 12:30, 13:30, 14:30) or 90 minutes for 130 kr (mid-April–October at 10:00, 12:00, 14:00, 17:00, tel. 08/411-7023). They also

Stockholm Center

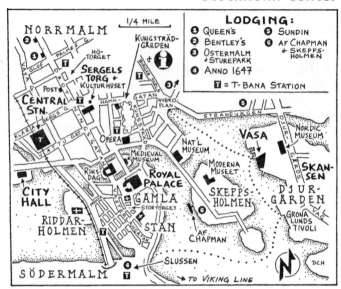

organize 75-minute Old Town walks (75 kr, daily in summer at
11:30 and 14:30). For a free self-guided tour, follow the Gamla
Stan walk laid out below.

▲**City Boat Tour**—For a good floating look at Stockholm, and a
pleasant break, consider a sightseeing cruise. Tour boats leave regularly from in front of the Grand Hotel (tel. 08/240-470). The
"Historical Canals of Stockholm" tour offers the best informative
introduction (80 kr, one hour, departing on the half-hour
10:30–16:30 mid-June–mid-August). The "Under the Bridges" tour
goes through two locks and under 15 bridges (live guide, 130 kr,
2 hours, hourly departures mid-April–mid-October). The "Royal
Canal" tour is a scenic joyride through lots of greenery (80 kr,
one-hour tape-recorded spiel, departs at half-past each hour
mid-May–August).

▲**National Museum**—Though mediocre by European standards,
this museum is small, central, uncrowded, and very user-friendly.
The highlights of the collection are several Rembrandts, Rubens, a
fine group of Impressionists, and works by the popular and good-
to-get-to-know local artists Carl Larsson and Anders Zorn (60 kr,
Tuesday–Sunday 11:00–17:00, Tuesday and Thursday until 20:00,
closed Monday, tel. 08/666-4250). A worthwhile audiotape (20 kr)
guides you through a 50-minute tour of the collection's highlights.
Museum of Modern Art—Newly reopened after a major renovation, this bright and cheery gallery is as far out as can be, with

Picasso, Braque, and lots of goofy Dada art (such as the *Urinal* and the *Goat with Tire*). It's in a pleasant park on Skeppsholmen (60 kr, Tuesday–Thursday 11:00–22:00, Friday–Sunday 11:00–18:00, closed Monday, tel. 08/666-4363).

Sights—Stockholm's Gamla Stan

▲▲**Gamla Stan self-guided walk**—Stockholm's old island core is charming, fit for a film, and full of antique shops, street lanterns, painted ceilings, and surprises. While many will happily just wander around, take this guided walk first:

Slottsbacken: Start at the base of the palace (bottom of Slottsbacken) where a statue of King Gustav III gazes at the palace, formerly the site of Stockholm's first castle. Walk up the broad cobbled boulevard. Behind the obelisk stands the Storkyrkan, Stockholm's cathedral (and most interesting church, which we'll visit later in the walk). Opposite the palace (orange building on left) is the Finnish church (Finska Kyrkan), which originated as the royal tennis hall. Walk behind the church into the shady churchyard where you'll find the 3-inch-tall "iron boy," the tiniest statue in Stockholm (often with a little gift). Continue through the yard onto Tradgardsgatan, which leads (turn right) to the old stock exchange.

Stortorget: Left of the stock exchange is the oldest square in town, Stortorget. The town well is now dry but this is still a popular meeting point. Scan the fine old facades. This square has a notorious history. It was the site of Stockholm's bloodbath of 1520—during a royal power-grab, most of the town's aristocracy was beheaded. Rivers of blood were said to have run through the streets. Later, this was the location of the town's pillory. At the far end of the square (under the finest gables) turn right and follow Trangsund toward the cathedral.

Cathedral: Just before the church you'll see my favorite phone booth (Rikstelefon) and the gate to the churchyard being guarded by statues of Caution and Hope. Enter the cathedral (10 kr, daily 9:00–18:00, until 16:00 off-season, pick up the free English flier describing interior). The fascinating interior is paved with centuries-old tombstones; more than 2,000 people are buried under the church. In front on the left is an impressive sculpture of *Saint George and the Dragon* made of oak, gilded metal, and elk horn (1489). Near the exit is a painting with the oldest existing depiction of Stockholm (from 1535, showing a walled city filling only today's Gamla Stan).

Prastgatan: Exiting through the churchyard, continue down Trangsund. At the next corner go downhill on Storkyrkobrinken and take the first left—where the priests used to—on Prastgatan. Enjoy a quiet wander down this peaceful lane. After 2 blocks (at Kakbrinken) you'll see a cannon on the corner guarding a prehistoric rune stone. (In case you can't read ancient Nordic script, it says: "Torsten and Trogun erected this stone in memory of their son.") Continue farther down Prastgatan until you see the German-strength brick steeple of the *Tyska Kyrkan* (German church). This is a reminder of the days when German merchants worked here. Wander through its churchyard and out the back onto Svartman-gatan. Follow it downhill to its end at a couple of benches and an iron railing overlooking Österlånggatan.

Österlånggatan: From this perch, survey the street to the left and right. Notice how it curves. This marks the old shoreline. In medieval times piers stretched out like many fingers into the harbor. Gradually, as land was reclaimed and developed, these piers were extended and what were originally piers became lanes leading to piers farther away. Walk left along Österlånggatan. At the cob-bled Y in the road head uphill (up Kopmanbrinken) past a copy of *George and the Dragon.* (Or, for a quick finish, Österlånggatan takes you back to your starting point at the palace.)

Shopping, Jazz, and Food: From Kopmantorget (the statue), Kopmangatan leads past fine antique shops (some with their medieval painted ceilings still visible) back to Stortorget. Crossing the square, follow the crowds downhill 2 blocks to Stora Nygatan. This is Gamla Stan's main commercial drag, a festival with all the distractions which keep most visitors from seeing the historic charms of the old town—which you just did. Now you can shop and eat.

▲▲**Military Parade and Changing of the Guard**—Starting at the Army Museum (daily at 12:00), the parade marches over either Nor-rbro bridge or Strombron bridge and up to the palace courtyard where the band plays and the guard changes (every other day the band is mounted . . . on horses). These days, the royal family lives out of town at Drottningholm, but the guards are for real. If the guard by the cannon in the semicircular courtyard looks a little lax, try wandering discreetly behind him.

▲▲**Royal Palace**—The palace is a complex of sights. Drop by the info booth in the semicircular courtyard (at the top where the guard changes) for an explanatory brochure with a map marking the different entrances. In a nutshell: The apartments of state are lavish, as worthwhile as any; the treasury is the best in Northern Europe; the chapel is no big deal; Gustav III's museum of antiqui-ties—skip it; and the Royal Armoury is awesome—plan to spend some time. An 80-kr combo ticket covers the apartments, treasury, and antiquities (more info below).

▲▲**Apartments of State**—The stately palace exterior encloses 608 rooms (one more than Britain's Buckingham Palace) of glit-tering Baroque and rococo decor. Clearly the palace of Scandi-navia's superpower, it's richly decorated (18th century) and steeped in royal history. The guided tour is heavy and tedious; the place is more interesting on your own—pick up English descriptions where they are available and don't miss the Berna-dotte rooms (45 kr, daily June–August 10:00–16:00; off-season

Tuesday–Sunday 12:00–15:00, closed Monday; free English-language tours at 12:00 and 13:15).

▲▲**Royal Treasury**—You'll find great crowns, scepters, jeweled robes, and plenty of glitter that's gold. Nothing is explained, so get the 2-kr description at the entry (40 kr, same hours as above, no samples, often tours at 11:00 and 14:15, tel. 08/402-6000).

Gustav III's Museum of Antiquities—In the 1700s, Gustav III traveled through Italy and brought home an impressive gallery of classical Roman statues. This was a huge deal if you'd never been out of Sweden. It's worth a look only if you've never been to the rest of Europe. Nothing is explained in English (40 kr, same hours).

▲▲▲**Royal Armoury (*Livrust Kammaren*)**—This, the oldest museum in Sweden, has the most interesting and best displayed collection of medieval royal armor I've seen anywhere in Europe. The incredible, original 17th-century gear includes royal baby wear, outfits kings wore when they were killed in battle or assassinated, and five centuries of royal Swedish armor—all wonderfully described in English. An added bonus is a basement lined with royal coaches, including coronation coaches, all beautifully preserved and richly decorated (40 kr, daily 11:00–16:00, closed winter Mondays, tours daily in summer at 13:00, entry at the bottom of Slottsbacken at the base of the palace, tel. 08/666-4475).

Riksdaghuset—You can tour Sweden's parliament buildings if you'd like a firsthand look at its government (free hourly tours in English from June through August, usually Monday–Friday at 11:00, 12:30, and 14:00, enter at Riksgatan 3a, but call 08/786-4000 to confirm times).

Museum of Medieval Stockholm (*Medeltidsmuseet*)—While grade-schoolish, this gives you a good look at medieval Stockholm (30 kr, daily July–August 11:00–16:00, Tuesday, Wednesday, Thursday until 18:00; Monday–Saturday September–June 11:00–16:00, closed Monday; free 30-minute English tours at 14:00 daily in summer enlivens the exhibits; enter from the park in front of the Parliament, tel. 08/700-0593). The Stromparterren park, with its Carl Milles statue of the *Sun Singer* greeting the day, is a pleasant place for a sightseeing break (but an expensive place for a potty break—use the free WC in the museum).

Riddarholm Church—This final resting place for about 600 years of Sweden's royalty is pretty lifeless (20 kr, daily June–August 11:00–16:00, less in May and September, closed in winter, tel. 08/402-6000). In a futile attempt to make this more interesting, they'll loan you the church guidebooklet. The cathedral next to the palace (see Gamla Stan walk, above) is far more interesting.

Sights—Stockholm's Djurgården

▲▲▲**Skansen**—Europe's original and best open-air folk museum, Skansen is a huge park gathering more than 150 historic buildings (homes, churches, shops, and schoolhouses) transplanted from all corners of Sweden. Tourists can explore this Swedish-culture-on-a-lazy-Susan, seeing folk crafts in action and wonderfully furnished old interiors (lively only in the summer). In the town quarter (top of the escalator), craftspeople such as potters are busy doing their traditional thing in a re-created Old World Stockholm. Don't miss the glassblowers if you'll be missing Sweden's Glass Country to the south.

Spreading out from there, the sprawling park is designed to show northern Swedish culture and architecture in the northern part of the park (top of park map) and southern Sweden in the south (bottom of map). Excellent, free one-hour guided walks (from Bollnästorget info stand at top of escalator) paint a fine picture of old Swedish lifestyles (usually daily at 14:00 and 16:00 June–August). There's fiddling nightly (except Sunday) at 18:15, folk dancing demonstrations daily in summer at 19:00, Sunday at 14:30 and 16:00, and public dancing to live bands weeknights (20:30–23:30, call for evening theme—jazz, folk, rock, or disco, nightly except Sunday). Admission to the aquarium is the only thing not covered on your entry ticket (45 kr, 10:00–20:00, shorter hours off-season).

Kids love Skansen, especially its zoo (ride a life-sized wooden Dala-horse and stare down a hedgehog) and Lill' Skansen (Punch 'n' Judy, mini-train, and pony ride fun daily from 11:00 till at least 16:00). There are lots of special events and several restaurants. The main restaurant serves a grand smørgåsbord (200 kr) and the Ekorren café offers the least expensive self-service lunches with a view. Tre Byttor (next to Ekorren) serves 18th-century-style food in a candlelit setting. Another cozy inn, the old-time Stora Gungan Krog, at the top of the escalator, has better food (60-kr indoor or outdoor lunches with a salad and cracker bar).

Skansen is great for people-watching and picnicking, with open and covered benches all over (especially at Torslunden and Bollnästorget, where peacenik local toddlers don't bump on the bumper cars). Get the map or the 30-kr museum guidebook that has the same map, and check the live crafts schedule at the information stand at Bollnästorget to confirm your Skansen plans.

Use the west entrance (Hazeliusporten) if you're heading to or from the Nordic Museum. (55-kr entry, 30-kr in winter; daily May–August 9:00–22:00, buildings 11:00–17:00; winter 9:00–17:00, some buildings 11:00–15:00; take bus #47 or #44 from the station; call 08/5789-0005 for a recording of the day's tour, music, and dance schedule, or 08/442-8000.) You can miss Gröna Lund, the second-rate amusement park across the street.

▲▲▲*Vasa*—Stockholm turned a titanic flop into one of Europe's great sightseeing attractions. This glamorous but unseaworthy warship—top-heavy with a tacked-on extra cannon deck—sank 20 minutes into her 1628 maiden voyage when a breeze caught the sails and blew her over in the Stockholm harbor. After 333 years she rose again from the deep (with the help of marine archeologists) and today is the best-preserved ship anywhere, housed in a state-of-the-art museum. The masts on the roof are placed to show their actual height.

Catch the 25-minute English-subtitled movie (at the top of each hour, dubbed versions often play at 11:30 and 13:30), and for more information, take the free 25-minute English tours (at the bottom of each hour from 10:30, every other hour off-season) to best enjoy and understand the ship. Learn about ship's rules (bread can't be older than eight years), why it sank (heavy bread?), how it's preserved, and so on. Private tours are easy to freeload on, but the displays are so well described that a tour is hardly necessary. (50 kr, daily mid-June–mid-August 9:30–19:00; off-season 10:00–17:00, winter on Wednesday until 20:00, tel. 08/666-4800.) Take bus #47 to the big brick Nordic Museum or catch the boat from Nybroplan or Slussen, or walk from Skansen.

▲▲**Nordic Museum**—This museum, built to look like a Danish palace, offers a look at how the Swedish lived over the last 500 years. Highlights include the Food and Drink section, with its stunning china and crystal table settings; the Nordic folk art (second and third floors); the huge statue of Gustav Vasa, father of modern Sweden, by Carl Milles (top of second flight of stairs); and the Sami (Lapp) exhibit in the basement (Tuesday–Sunday 11:00–17:00, summer Tuesdays and Thursdays until 21:00, closed Monday, tel. 08/666-4600). Worth your time if you have the Stockholm Card, but it's overpriced at 60-kr admission. The 30-kr guidebook isn't necessary, but pick up the English brochure at the entrance.

▲**Thielska Galleriet**—If you liked the Larsson and Zorn art in the National Gallery and/or if you're a Munch fan, this charming mansion on the water at the far end of the Djurgården park is worth the trip (40 kr, Monday–Saturday 12:00–16:00, Sunday 13:00–16:00; bus #69 from the central station, tel. 08/662-5884).

Sights—Outer Stockholm

▲▲**Carl Millesgården**—The home and garden housing a museum and the major work of Sweden's greatest sculptor is dramatically situated on a cliff overlooking Stockholm. Milles' entertaining, unique, and provocative art was influenced by Rodin. There's a classy café and a great picnic spot (50 kr, daily May–September 10:00–17:00; off-season Tuesday–Sunday 12:00–16:00, closed Monday; tel. 08/446-7590.) Catch the T-bana to Ropsten, then take any bus (except #203 and #213) to the first stop (Torsvik). It's a five-minute walk from there (follow the signs).

▲▲**Drottningholm**—The queen's 17th-century summer castle and present royal residence has been called, not surprisingly, Sweden's Versailles. The adjacent, uncannily well-preserved Baroque theater is the real highlight, especially with its 40-kr guided tours

(English theater tours normally depart 12:30, 13:30, 14:30, 15:30, and 16:30 May–September). Get there by a relaxing but over-priced boat ride (70 kr round-trip, two hours) or take the subway to Brommaplan and bus #301 or #323 to Drottningholm. (40-kr entry, palace open daily May–August 11:00–16:30; September weekdays 13:00–15:30, weekends 12:00–15:30; tel. 08/402-6280 for palace tours in English, scheduled often at 11:00.)

The 18th-century Drottningholm court theater performs perfectly authentic operas (about 30 performances each summer). Tickets to these very popular and unique shows go on sale each March. Prices for this time-tunnel musical and theatrical experience are 100 kr to 470 kr. For information, write to Drottningholm's Theater Museum, Box 27050, 10251 Stockholm, or phone 08/660-8225, fax 08/665-1473.

▲▲**Archipelago**—The world's most scenic islands (24,000 of them!) surround Stockholm. Europeans who spend entire vacations in and around Stockholm rave about them. If you cruise to Finland, you'll get a good dose of this island beauty. Otherwise, consider the pleasant hour-long cruise (90 kr each way) from Nybroplan downtown to the quiet town of Vaxholm. The tourist office has a free archipelago guide booklet.

Sauna

Sometime while you're in Sweden or Finland, you'll have to treat yourself to Scandinavia's answer to support hose and a face-lift. (A sauna is actually more Finnish than Swedish.) Simmer down with the local students, retired folks, and busy executives. Try to cook as calmly as the Swedes. Just before bursting, go into the shower room. There's no luke-cold, and the trickle-down theory doesn't apply—only one button, bringing a Niagara of liquid ice. Suddenly your shower stall becomes a Cape Canaveral launch pad, as your body scatters to every corner of the universe. A moment later you're back together. Rejoin the Swedes in the cooker, this time with their relaxed confidence; you now know that exhilaration is just around the corner. Only very rarely will you feel so good.

Any tourist office can point you toward the nearest birch twigs. Good opportunities include a Stockholm–Helsinki cruise, any major hotel you stay in, some hostels, or cheapest, a public swimming pool. In Stockholm, consider the Eriksdalsbadet (Hammarby Slussvag 8, near Skanstull T-bana, tel. 08/643-0673). Use of its 50-meter indoor/outdoor pool and first-rate sauna costs 35 kr.

For a classier experience, the newly refurbished Centralbadet lets you enjoy an extensive gym, "bubblepool," sauna, steam room, and an elegant Art Nouveau pool from 1904 (79 kr, long hours, last entry 20:30, closed Sunday, Drottningatan 88, five minutes up from Sergels Torg, tel. 24 24 03). Bring your towel into the sauna; the steam room is mixed, the sauna is not. Massage and solarium cost extra, and the pool is more for floating than for jumping and splashing. The leafy courtyard is an appropriately relaxing place to enjoy their restaurant (reasonable and healthy light meals).

Shopping

Modern design, glass, clogs, and wooden goods are popular targets for shoppers. Browsing is a free, delightful way to enjoy Sweden's brisk pulse. Cop a feel at the Nordiska Kompaniet (NK, also meaning "no kroner left") just across from the Sweden House or close by in the Gallerian mall. The nearby Åhlens is less expensive. Swedish stores are open 9:30 to 18:00, until 14:00 on Saturday, and closed Sunday. Some of the bigger stores (like Åhlens and NK) are open later on Saturday and on Sunday afternoon. Take a short walk to Norrmalms Torg to the new bank branch of Scandia Insurance for its ATMs, clean design, Internet access, and free coffee, tea, or chocolate.

For a smørgåsbord of Scanjunk, visit the Loppmarknaden (northern Europe's biggest flea market) at the planned suburb of Skarholmen (free on weekdays, 10 kr on weekends, Monday–Friday 11:00–18:00, Saturday 9:00–15:00, Sunday 10:00–15:00, busiest on weekends, T-bana: Skarholmen, tel. 08/710-0060).

Sleeping in Stockholm
(7 kr = about $1, tel. code: 08)

Sleep Code: **S**=Single, **D**=Double/Twin, **T**=Triple, **Q**=Quad, **b**=bathroom, **CC**=Credit Card (Visa, MasterCard, Amex). "Summer rates" mean mid-June to mid-August, and Friday and Saturday (sometimes Sunday) the rest of the year. Prices include breakfast unless otherwise noted.

Stockholm has plenty of money-saving deals for the savvy visitor. Its hostels are among Europe's best ($15 a bed), and plenty of people offer private accommodations ($50 doubles). Peak season for Stockholm's expensive hotels is business time—workdays outside of summer. Rates drop by 30 to 50 percent in the summer or on weekends, and if business is slow, occasionally any night—ask. To sort through all of this, the city has helpful, English-speaking room-finding services with handy locations and long hours (see Hotellcentralen and Sweden House, above).

The **Stockholm Package** offers business-class doubles with buffet breakfasts from 790 kr, includes two free Stockholm Cards, and lets two children up to 18 years old sleep for free. This is limited from mid-June to mid-August, and Friday and Saturday throughout the year. Assuming you'll be getting two Stockholm Cards anyway (370 kr), this gives you a $200 hotel room for about $50. This is for real (summertime is that dead for business hotels). The procedure (through either tourist office) is easy: a 100-kr advance booking fee (you can arrange by fax, pay when you arrive) or a 40-kr in-person booking fee if you just drop in. Arriving without reservations in July is never a problem. It gets tight during the

Water Festival (ten days in early August) and during a convention
stretch for a few days in late June.

My listings are a good value only outside of Stockholm Package time, or if the 790 kr for a double and two cards is out of your
range and you're hosteling. Every place listed here has staff who
speak English and will explain their special deals to you on the
phone. If money is limited, ask if they have cheaper rooms. It's not
often that a hotel will push their odd misfit room that's 100 kr
below all the others. And at any time of year, prices can be soft.

About the only Laundromat in central Stockholm is Tvätto-
maten, at Våstmannagatan 61 on Odenplan, bus route #53 from
Upplandsgaten to Central Station (60 kr, 80-kr full-serve, weekdays
8:30–18:30, Saturday 9:30–15:00, closed Sunday, across from Gustav
Vasa church, helpful manager, tel. 08/346-480).

Sleeping in Hotels

Queen's Hotel is cheery, clean, and just a ten-minute walk from
the station, located in a great pedestrian area across the street
from the Centralbadet (city baths, listed on all maps). With a fine
TV and piano lounge, coffee in the evenings, and a staff that
enjoys helping its guests, this is probably the best cheap hotel in
town (summer and Friday-Saturday rates: S-450 kr, Ss-480 kr, Sb-
595 kr, D-550 kr, Ds-580 kr, Db-695–895 kr, winter rates: D-
550–680 kr, Ds-580–780 kr, Db-1,050–1,150 kr, CC:VMA,
Drottninggatan 71A, tel. 08/249-460, fax 08/217-620, e-mail:
queenshotel@queenshotel.se, run by the Bergman family). Their
simple rooms have no sinks. If you're arriving early from the train
or boat, you're welcome to leave your bags and grab a 45-kr
breakfast.

Bentley's Hotel is an interesting option with old English
flair and renovated rooms (summer rates include winter Sundays:
very small Db-490 kr, Db-690 kr, suite Db-750–850 kr, winter
Db-1,090 kr, CC:VMA, a block up the street from Queen's at
Drottninggatan 77, 11160 Stockholm, tel. 08/141-395, fax 08/212-
492). Klas and Agi Kallstrom attempt to mix elegance, comfort,
and simplicity into an affordable package. Each room is tastefully
decorated with antique furniture but has a modern full bathroom.

The proud little **Stureparkens Gästvåning** is a carefully run,
traditional-feeling place with lots of class and ten thoughtfully
appointed rooms. It's a better value during the high season (July
rates: S-400 kr, D-600 kr, Db-700 kr; high season: S-460 kr,
D-660 kr, Db-760 kr, two-night minimum, elevator, CC:VM, near
T-bana: Stadion, across from Stureparken at Sturegatan 58, tel.
08/662-7230, fax 08/661-5713).

Hotel Gustav Vasa has classy Old World rooms in a listed
building with a family-run feel on a convenient square a 15-minute
walk from the center (Sb-550 kr, D-550 kr, Db-650 kr, rates
100–150 kr higher outside of summer and weekends, they have

some cheaper very small doubles, family deals, CC:VMA, elevator, subway to Odenplan, exit Våstmannagatan, to Våstmannagatan 61, tel. 08/343-801, fax 08/307-372).

Drottning Victorias Orlogshem, formerly a hotel for Navy personnel, now accepts the public, offering functional quiet rooms with hardwood floors and naval decor in a great neighborhood just a block off the central harbor behind the National Museum (35 rooms, Sb-450 kr, Db-650 kr, Tb-750 kr, Qb-1,000 kr, family deals, same prices all year, breakfast-35 kr, no double beds—only twins, Teatergatan 3, 11148 Stockholm, tel. 08/611-0113, fax 08/611-3150).

Prize Hotel is unique—a super-modern, happy place with tight 'n' tidy rooms 2 blocks from the station in Stockholm's World Trade Center. Designed for business travelers, it has mostly singles (with wall-beds which fold down to make doubles) and major summer and weekend discounts (not worth the high-season price, low prices Friday, Saturday, and June 8 through August 10: Sb-550 kr, Db-650 kr, they have a few real doubles for the same price as their wall-bed doubles—worth asking for, low rates offered during slow winter times—ask, breakfast-55 kr, CC:VMA, Kungsbron 1, tel. 08/566-2200, fax 08/5662-2444, Web site: www.prize.se, e-mail: prize.sth@prize.se).

City Hotel is also unique. Filling the top floors of a down-sized department store and a leader in environmental friendliness, this modern place offers hardwood floors and all the comforts in a "one-star delux" package (200 rooms, discount rates for Friday, Saturday, and June 20 through August 15: Sb-550 kr, Db-790 kr, Qb-990 kr, some Db with no windows but good ventilation-690 kr, all D are twins shoved together, high season Db-1,100 kr, breakfast included, CC:VMA, free loaner bikes, overlooking Hotorget market at Kungsgatan 47, tel. 08/723-7220, fax 08/723-7299).

Sleeping in Rooms in Private Homes

Stockholm's centrally located private rooms are nearly as expensive as discounted hotels—a deal only in the high season. More reasonable rooms are a few T-bana stops just minutes from the center. Stockholm's tourist offices refer those in search of a room in a private house to **Hotelljånst** (near station, Vasagatan 15, tel. 08/104-467, fax 08/213-716). They can set you up for about 430 kr per double without breakfast for a minimum two-night stay. Go direct—you'll save your host the listing service's fee. Be sure to get the front door security code when you call, as there's no intercom connection with front doors.

Else Mari Sundin is an effervescent retired actress who rents her homey apartment, beautifully located just 2 blocks from the bridge to Djurgården (D-600 kr for up to four people, bus #47 or #69 to Torstenssonsgatan 7, go through courtyard to "garden house" and up to second floor, tel. 08/665-3348, 0884 door code). Since she lives out of town, this can be complicated. But once you're set up, it's great.

Mrs. Lichtsteiner offers rooms with kitchenettes and has a family room with a loft (Sb-300 kr, Db-400 kr without breakfast, a block from T-bana: Rådhuset, exit T-bana direction Polishuset, at Bergsgatan 45, once inside go through door on left and up elevator to second floor, tel. 08/746-9166, call ahead to get the security code, e-mail: lichtsteiner@monitor-akuten.se).

Sleeping in Hostels

Stockholm has Europe's best selection of big-city hostels offering good beds in simple but interesting places for 100 kr. If your budget is tight, these are right. Each has a helpful English-speaking staff, pleasant family rooms, good facilities, and good leads on budget survival in Stockholm. All will hold rooms for a phone call. Hosteling is cheap only if you're a member (guest membership: 35 kr per night necessary only in IYHF places); bring your own sheet (paper sheets rent for 30 kr), and picnic for breakfast (breakfasts cost 40 kr). Several of the hostels are often booked up well in advance but hold a few beds for those who are left in the lurch.

Af Chapman (IYHF), Europe's most famous youth hostel, is a permanently moored cutter ship. Just a five-minute walk from downtown, this floating hostel has 140 beds—two to eight per stateroom. A popular but compassionate place, it's often booked far in advance, but saves some beds each morning for unreserved arrivals (given out at 7:00) and gives away unclaimed rooms each evening after 18:00. If you call at breakfast time and show up before 12:00, you may land a bed, even in summer (110 kr per bed, D-240 kr, open April–mid-December, sleeping bags allowed, has a lounge and cafeteria that welcomes non-hostelers, reception open 24 hours, rooms locked up 11:00–15:00, STF Vandrarhem *Af Chapman*, Skeppsholmen, 11149 Stockholm, tel. 08/679-5015 for advance booking or 08/679-5016).

Skeppsholmen Hostel (IYHF), just ashore from the *Af Chapman*, is open all year. It has better facilities and smaller rooms (120 kr per bed in doubles, triples, and quads, only 90 kr in dorms, nonmembers pay 40 kr extra, tel. 08/679-5016), but it isn't as romantic as its seagoing sister.

Zinken Hostel (IYHF) is a big, basic hostel in a busy suburb, with 120-kr dorm beds (40 kr extra for sheets and nonmembers), plenty of 355-kr doubles without sheets, a laundromat, and the best hostel kitchen facilities in town (STF Vandrarhem Zinken, open 24 hours all year, Zinkens Väg 20, T-bana: Zinkensdamm, tel. 08/616-8100 or 08/616-8188 in evenings). This is a great no-nonsense, user-friendly value.

Vandrarhemmet Brygghuset, in a former brewery near Odenplan, is small (57 beds in 12 spacious rooms), bright, clean, and quiet, with a laundromat and a kitchen. Since this is a private hostel, its two- to six-bed rooms are open to all for 125 kr per bed (no sleeping bags allowed, sheets rent for 35 kr). Sheetless doubles are 310 kr. (Open June–mid-September 7:00–12:00, 15:00–23:00, 02:00 curfew, good lockers, Norrtullsgatan 12 N, tel. 08/312-424.)

Café Bed and Breakfast is Stockholm's newest cozy hostel, with only 30 beds (130 kr per bed in eight- to 12-bed rooms, breakfast-30 kr, sheets-30 kr, near Radmansgatan T-bana stop, just off Sveavägen at Rehnsgatan 21, tel. & fax 08/152-838). Bjorn and Daniela also offer three 335-kr doubles and a free sauna.

Stockholm has 12 **campgrounds** (located south of town) that are a wonderful solution to your parking and budget problems. The TI's "Camping Stockholm" brochure has specifics.

Eating in Stockholm

Stockholm's elegant department stores (notably NK and Åhlens, near Sergels Torg) have cafeterias for the kroner-pinching local shopper. Look for the 50-kr "rodent of the day" (*dagens rett*) specials. Most museums have handy cafés. The café at the *Af Chapman* **hostel** (open to the public in summer daily 11:30–18:00) serves a good salad/roll/coffee lunch in an unbeatable deck-of-a-ship atmosphere (if the weather's good).

The Old Town (*Gamla Stan*) has lots of restaurants. Try the wonderfully atmospheric **Kristina Restaurang** (Västerlånggatan 68, Gamla Stan, tel. 08/200-529). In this 1632 building, under a leather ceiling steeped in a turn-of-the-century interior, you'll find good dinners from 145 kr, including a salad and cracker bar and a cheaper "summer" menu. They serve a great 55-kr lunch (from 11:00 to 15:00) that includes an entrée, salad bar, bread, and a drink. The place is best Wednesday through Saturday 20:00 to 23:00, when live jazz accompanies your meal (silent in July and August). You can enjoy the music over just a beer or coffee, too. **Hermans** has good vegetarian food and daily specials (Stora Nygatan 11, also in Gamla Stan).

Picnics

With higher taxes almost every year, Sweden's restaurant industry is suffering. You'll notice many fine places almost empty. Swedes joke that the "local" cuisine is now Chinese, Italian, and hamburgers. Here more than anywhere, budget travelers should picnic.

Stockholm's major department stores and the many small corner groceries are fine places to assemble a picnic. **Åhlens** department store has a great food section (open until 21:00, near Sergels Torg). The late-hours supermarket downstairs in the central train station is picnic-friendly, with fresh, ready-made sandwiches (weekdays 7:00–23:00, weekends 9:00–23:00).

The market at **Hötorget** is a fun place to picnic shop, especially in the indoor, exotic ethnic Hötorgshallen (fun café and restaurant in fish section). The outdoor market closes at 18:00, and many merchants put their unsold produce on the push list (earlier closing and more desperate merchants on Saturday).

For a classy vegetarian buffet lunch (70 kr, Monday–Friday until 17:00), often with a piano serenade, or dinner (85 kr, evenings and weekends), eat at **Örtagården** (literally, "the herb garden," Nybrogatan 31, tel. 08/662-1728), above the colorful old Östermalms food market at Östermalmstorg.

Transportation Connections—Stockholm

By train to: Uppsala (30/day, 45 min), **Kalmar** (12/day, 5 hrs, including evening service 18:18–23:06), **Copenhagen** (6/day, 8 hrs, night service 22:30–7:00), **Oslo** (3/day, 7 hrs, night service 23:40–7:30). For train information, call 020/757-575 (toll-free in Sweden) for domestic trains, 08/227-940 for international trains.

By boat to: Helsinki (daily/nightly boats, 14 hrs), **Turku** (daily/nightly boats, 10 hrs).

Estline runs a regular ferry from Stockholm to **Tallinn, Estonia** (every other night at 17:30, arriving at 9:00 the next morning, 445 kr each way, 590 kr round-trip with breakfasts and a bed in a quad, cheaper off-season). It offers a 36-hour tour (no visa necessary, round-trip, simple two-bed cabins, two breakfasts, two dinners) for 1,030 kr per person (tel. 08/667-0001).

OSLO

Oslo is the smallest and least earthshaking of the Nordic capitals, but this brisk little city offers more sightseeing thrills than you might expect. Sights of the Viking spirit—past and present—tell an exciting story. Prowl through the remains of ancient Viking ships and marvel at more peaceful but equally gutsy modern boats like the *Kon-Tiki*, *Ra*, and *Fram*. Dive into the country's folk culture at the open-air folk museum and get stirred up by Norway's heroic spirit at the Nazi resistance museum.

For a look at modern Oslo, browse through the new yuppie-style harbor shopping complex, tour the striking city hall, take a peek at sculptor Vigeland's people pillars, and climb the towering Holmenkollen ski jump.

Situated at the head of a 60-mile-long fjord, surrounded by forests, and populated by more than 500,000 people, Oslo is Norway's cultural hub and an all-you-can-see smørgåsbord of historic sights, trees, art, and Nordic fun.

Planning Your Time

Oslo offers an exciting two-day slate of sightseeing thrills. Ideally, arrive on the overnight train from Stockholm, spend two days, and leave on the night train to Copenhagen or on the scenic train to Bergen the third morning. Spend the two days like this:

Day 1: Set up. Visit the TI. Tour the Akershus Castle and Norwegian Resistance Museum. Take a picnic on the ferry to Bygdøy and enjoy a view of the city harbor. Tour the *Fram*, *Kon-Tiki*, and Viking ships. Finish the afternoon at the Norwegian Open Air Folk Museum. Boat home. For evening culture, consider the folk music and dance show (20:30 Monday and Thursday).

Day 2: At 10:00 catch the city hall tour, then browse through the National Gallery. Spend the afternoon at Vigeland Park and at the Holmenkollen ski jump and museum. Browse Karl Johans Gate (all the way to the station) and Aker Brygge harbor in the early evening for the Norwegian *paseo*. Consider munching a fast-food dinner on the harbor mini-cruise.

Orientation

Oslo is easy to manage, with nearly all its sights clustered around the central "barbell" street (Karl Johans Gate, with the Royal Palace on one end and the train station on the other), or in the Bygdøy district, a ten-minute ferry ride across the harbor.

Tourist Information

The **Norwegian Information Center** displays Norway as if it were a giant booth at a trade show (on the waterfront between the city hall and Aker Brygge, daily 9:00–20:00, shorter hours off-season, tel. 22 83 00 50). Stock up on brochures for Oslo and all of your Norwegian destinations, especially the *Bergen Guide*. Pick up the free Oslo map, Sporveiskart transit map, *What's on in Oslo* monthly (for the most accurate listing of museum hours and special events), *Streetwise* magazine (hip, fun to read, and full of offbeat ideas), and the free annual *Oslo Guide* (with plenty of details on sightseeing, shopping and eating). Consider buying the Oslo Card (unless your hotel provides it for free, see below). The info center has a rack of free pages on contemporary Norwegian issues and life (near the door); a 30-minute "multi-vision" slideshow taking you around Norway (free, top of the hour, in theater in the back); a 30-minute video called *Look to Norway* that runs all day; a handy public toilet; and rooms showcasing various crafts and ways you can spend your money. The tourist information window in the central station is much simpler and deals only with Oslo but can handle your needs just as well (daily in summer 8:00–23:00, less off-season).

Use It is a hardworking youth information center, providing solid, money-saving, experience-enhancing information to young, student, and vagabond travelers (mid-June–mid-August Monday–Friday 7:30–18:00, Saturday 9:00–14:00, closed Sunday; Monday–Friday 11:00–17:00 the rest of the year, Møllergata 3, tel. 22 41 51 32, Web site: www.unginfo.oslo.no). They have telephones and e-mail, and can find you the cheapest beds in town for no fee. Read their free *Streetwise* magazine for ideas on eating and sleeping cheap, good nightspots, best beaches, and so on.

The **Oslo Card** gives you free use of all city public transit and boats, free entry to all sights, a free harbor mini-cruise tour, free parking, and many more discounts—and is also a handy handbook (24 hours-130 kr, 48 hours-200 kr, or 72 hours-240 kr). Almost any two-day visit to Oslo will be cheaper with the Oslo

Card (which costs less than three Bygdøy museum admissions, the ski jump, and one city bus ride). Students with an ISIC card may be better off without the Oslo Card. The TI's special Oslo Package hotel deal (described under Sleeping, below) includes this card with your discounted hotel room.

Arrival in Oslo

Oslo S, the modern central train station, is slick and helpful, with a late-hours TI (daily in summer 8:00–23:00, less off-season), room-finding service, late-hours bank (fair rates, normal fee), supermarket (daily 6:30–23:30), and an **Interrail Center** that offers any traveler with a train pass 15-kr showers, free rucksack storage racks, a bright and clean lounge, cheap snacks, a bulletin board for cheap sleeping deals, and an information center (daily mid-June–September 7:00–23:00). Pick up information leaflets on the Flåm and Bergen Railway.

Getting Around Oslo

By Public Transit: Oslo's transit system is made up of buses, trams, ferries, and a subway. Tickets cost 18 kr and are good for one hour of use on any combination of the above. Flexicards give eight rides for 105 kr. Buy tickets as you board (bus info tel. 22 17 70 30, daily 8:00–23:00). **Trafikanten,** the public transit information center, is under the ugly tower immediately in front of the station. Their free "Sporveiskart for Oslo" transit map is the best city map around and makes the transit system easy. The similar but smaller "Visitor's Map Oslo" (available at TI) is easier to use and also free. The **Dagskort Tourist Ticket** is a 40-kr, 24-hour transit pass that pays for itself on the third ride. The Oslo Card (see Tourist Information, above) gives you free run of the entire transit system. Note how gracefully the subway lines fan out after huddling at Stortinget. Take advantage of the way they run like clockwork, with schedules clearly posted and followed.

By Bike: Oslo is a good biking town, especially if you'd like to get out into the woods or ride a tram uphill out of town and coast for miles back. Vestbanen organizes tours and rents bikes (three hours/90–130 kr, six hours/140–180 kr depending on bike, in-line skates three hours/100 kr, 20 percent discount for readers of this book; May–September weekdays 7:00–22:00, weekends 10:00–18:00, closes earlier off-season; on the harbor next to the Norway Information Center; tel. 23 11 51 00).

Helpful Hints

To get a taxi, call 22 38 80 70, then dial 1. To get on the Internet, try the new cyber café in the east hall of the train station and the Velvet café nearby (10 kr per hour, Monday–Thursday 14:00–20:00, Friday 14:00–18:00, Nedre Slottsgate 2). Jernbanetorgets Apotek is a 24-hour pharmacy directly across from the train station (on

Oslo Center

❶ CITY HOTEL
❷ RAINBOW HOTEL ASTORIA
❸ RAINBOW HOTEL SPECTRUM
❹ COCH'S PENSJONAT
❺ VEGETA VERTSHUS

Jernbanetorget, tel. 22 41 24 82). Kilroy Travel is everyone's favorite for student and discounted air tickets (Nedre Slottsgate 23, tel. 23 10 23 10).

Sights—Downtown Oslo

Note: Because of Norway's passion for minor differences in opening times from month to month, I've generally listed only the peak-season hours. Assume opening hours shorten as the days do. The high season in Oslo is mid-June to mid-August. (I'll call that "summer" in this chapter.)

▲▲**City Hall**—Construction on Oslo's richly decorated Rådhuset began in 1931. Finished in 1950 to celebrate the city's 900th birthday, Norway's leading artists (including Edvard Munch) all contributed to what was an avant-garde thrill in its day. The interior's 2,000 square yards of bold and colorful "socialist modernism" murals (which take you on a voyage through the collective psyche of Norway, from its simple rural beginnings through the scar tissue of the Nazi occupation and beyond) are meaningful only with the excellent, free guided tours (20 kr, tours offered Monday–Friday at 10:00, 12:00, and 14:00; open Monday–Saturday 9:00–17:00, Sunday 12:00–17:00, until 16:00 in off-season, entry on the Karl Johans side, tel. 22 86 16 00). Ever notice how city halls rather than churches are the dominant buildings in the your-government-loves-you northern corner of Europe? The main hall of Oslo's city hall actually feels like a temple to good government (the altar-like mural celebrates "work, play, and civic administration"). The Nobel Peace Prize is awarded each December in this room.

▲**Akershus Fortress Complex**—This park-like complex of sites scattered over Oslo's fortified center is still a military base. But dodging patrolling guards and vans filled with soldiers you'll see war memorials, the castle, prison, Nazi resistance museum, armed forces museum, and cannon-strewn ramparts affording fine harbor views and picnic perches. Immediately inside the gate is an information center with an interesting exhibit on medieval Oslo's fortifications. In summer, free 45-minute tours of the grounds leave from the center (10:00, 12:00, 14:00, 16:00, daily but not Sunday morning, tel. 23 09 39 17). There's a small changing of the guard daily at 13:30. The prison, which is visited on the guided walk, will open as a museum in 1998.

Akershus Fortress—One of the oldest buildings in town, this castle overlooking Oslo's harbor is mediocre by European standards. The big, empty rooms remind us of Norway's medieval poverty. Behind the chapel altar, steps lead down to the tombs of some Norwegian kings. The castle is interesting only with the tour (20 kr for castle entry, May–mid-September Monday–Saturday 10:00–16:00, Sunday 12:30–16:00; open Sunday only in spring and fall; closed in winter; free 50-minute English tours offered in summer Monday–Saturday at 11:00, 13:00, and 15:00, Sunday at 13:00 and 15:00; tel. 22 41 25 21).

▲▲**Norwegian Resistance Museum** (*Norges Hjemmefrontmuseum*)—A stirring story about the Nazi invasion and occupation is told with wonderful English descriptions. This is the best look in Europe at how national spirit endured total German occupation (20 kr, Monday–Saturday 10:00–17:00, Sunday 11:00–17:00, closes one hour earlier off-season, next to castle in building overlooking the harbor, tel. 23 09 31 38).

Armed Forces Museum—Across the fortress parade ground, a large museum traces Norwegian military from Viking days to post WWII. The early stuff is very sketchy but the WWII story is fascinating (free, Monday–Friday 10:00–18:00, weekends 11:00–16:00, shorter hours September–May, tel. 22 40 35 82).

▲**National Gallery**—Located downtown, this easy-to-handle museum gives you an effortless tour back in time and through Norway's most beautiful valleys, mountains, and villages, with the help of its romantic painters (especially Dahl). The gallery also has several Picassos, a noteworthy Impressionist collection, some Vigeland statues, and a representative roomful of Munch paintings, including the famous *Scream*. His paintings here make a trip to the Munch museum unnecessary for most. For an entertaining survey of 2,500 years of sculpture, go through the museum gift shop and down the stairs to the right for a room filled with plaster copies of famous works (free, Monday, Wednesday, Friday 10:00–18:00; Thursday 10:00–20:00; Saturday 10:00–16:00; Sunday 11:00–15:00; closed Tuesday; Universitets Gata 13, tel. 22 20 04 04).

▲▲**Browsing**—Oslo's pulse is best felt along and near the central Karl Johans Gate (from station to palace), between the city hall and the harbor, and in the trendy new harborside Aker Brygge Festival Market Mall—a glass-and-chrome collection of sharp cafés and polished produce stalls just west of the city hall (trams #10 and #15 to/from train station). The buskers are among the best in Europe. Aker Brygge is very lively late evenings.

▲▲▲**Vigeland Sculptures and the Vigeland Museum in Frogner Park**—The 75-acre park contains a lifetime of work by Norway's greatest sculptor, Gustav Vigeland. From 1924 through 1942, he sculpted 175 bronze and granite statues—each nude and unique. Walking over the statue-lined bridge you'll come to the main fountain. Trace the story of our lives in the series of humans intertwined with trees around the fountain. The maze in the pavement around the fountain starts opposite the monolith and comes out, 3 kilometers later, closest to the monolith. Try following it . . . you can't go wrong. Vigeland's 60-foot-high tangled tower of 121 bodies called "the monolith of life" is the centerpiece of the park. While it seems the lower figures are laden with earthly concerns and the higher ones are freed to pursue loftier, more spiritual adventures, Vigeland gives us permission to interpret it any way we like. Pick up the free map from the box on the kiosk wall as you enter. The park is more than great art. It's a city at play. Enjoy its urban Norwegian ambience. Then visit the Vigeland Museum to see the models for the statues and more in the artist's studio. Don't miss the photos on the wall showing the construction of the monolith (20 kr for museum, Tuesday–Saturday 10:00–18:00, Sunday 12:00–19:00, closed Monday; off-season Tuesday–Sunday 12:00–16:00 and free, tel. 22 44 11 36). The park is always open and free. Take T-bane #2, bus #20 or #45, or tram #12 or #15 to Frogner Plass.

Oslo City Museum—Located in the Frogner Manor farm in Frogner Park, this museum tells the story of Oslo. A helpful free English brochure guides you through the exhibits (20 kr, Tuesday–Friday 10:00–18:00, Saturday and Sunday 11:00–17:00, closed Monday; shorter hours off-season, tel. 22 43 06 45).

▲▲**Edvard Munch Museum**—The only Norwegian painter to have had a serious impact on European art, Munch (monk) is a surprise to many who visit this fine museum. The emotional, disturbing, and powerfully expressionist work of this strange and perplexing man is arranged chronologically. You'll see paintings, drawings, lithographs, and photographs. Don't miss *The Scream*, which captures the fright many feel as the human "race" does just that (50 kr, daily 10:00–18:00; off-season closes as early as 16:00 and all day Monday; take the T-bane from the station to "Tøyen," tel. 22 67 37 74). If the price or location is a problem, you can see a roomful of Munch paintings in the free National Gallery downtown.

Greater Oslo

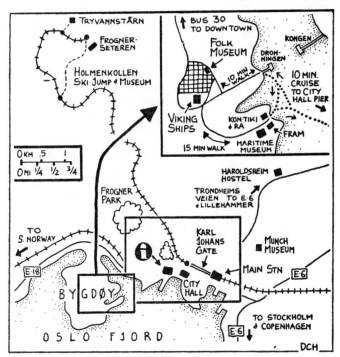

Sights—Oslo's Bygdøy Neighborhood

▲▲▲**Bygdøy**—This exciting cluster of sights is on a park-like peninsula just across the harbor from downtown. To get to Bygdøy, either take bus #30 from the station and National Theater or, more fun, catch the ferry from City Hall (18 kr, free with transit pass or Oslo Card, 3/hour, 8:30–21:00). The Folk Museum and Viking ships are a ten-minute walk from the ferry's first stop, Dronningen. The other museums are at the second stop, Bygdøynes. (See Bygdøy inset in "Greater Oslo" map in this chapter.) All Bygdøy sights are within a 15-minute walk of each other. While a handy tourist train shuttles visitors around Bygdøy (3/hour, 20 kr for an all-day pass) the *Fram*-Viking ships walk gives you a fine feel for rural Norway.

▲▲**Norwegian Folk Museum**—Brought from all corners of Norway, 150 buildings have been reassembled on these 35 acres. While Stockholm's Skansen was the first to open to the public, this museum is a bit older, starting in 1885 as the king's private collection. You'll find craftspeople doing their traditional things;

security guards disguised in cute, colorful, and traditional local costumes; endless creative ways to make do in a primitive log-cabin-and-goats-on-the-roof age; a 12th-century stave church; and a museum filled with toys and fine folk costumes. The place hops in the summer but is dead off-season. Catch the free one-hour guided walks at 10:00, 12:00, and 14:00 (call to confirm schedule). Otherwise, glean information from the 10-kr guidebook and the informative attendants who look like Rebecca Boone's Norwegian pen pals (50 kr, daily June–August 9:00– 18:00; off-season 10:00–17:00 or less). For folk dance performance, tour, and crafts demonstration schedules, call 22 12 37 00.

▲▲**Viking Ships**—Three great ninth-century Viking ships are surrounded by artifacts from the days of rape, pillage, and—ya sure, yu betcha—plunder. There are no museum tours, but everything is well described in English, and it's hard not to hear the English-speaking bus tour guides. There was a time when much of a frightened Europe closed every prayer with "And deliver us from the Vikings, Amen." Gazing up at the prow of one of these sleek, time-stained vessels, you can almost hear the screams and smell the armpits of those redheads on the rampage (30 kr, daily summer 9:00–18:00, off-season 11:00–15:00, tel. 22 43 83 79). To miss the tour-group crowds, come early, late, or at lunchtime.

▲▲**The *Fram***—This great ship took modern-day Vikings Amundsen and Nansen deep into the Arctic and Antarctic, farther north and south than any ship before. For three years the *Fram* was part of an Arctic ice drift. The exhibit is fascinating. Read the ground-floor displays, then explore the boat (20 kr, daily summer 9:00–18:45, shorter hours off-season). You can step into the lobby and see the ship's hull for free. The **Polar Sloop *Gjøa*** is dry-docked next to the ferry dock. This is the boat Amundsen and a crew of six used from 1903 to 1906 to "discover" the Northwest Passage (*Fram* ticket gets you aboard).

▲▲**The *Kon-Tiki* Museum**—Next to the *Fram* are the *Kon-Tiki* and the *Ra II*, the boats Thor Heyerdahl built and sailed 4,000 and 3,000 miles, respectively, to prove that early South Americans could have sailed to Polynesia and Africans could have populated Barbados. Both are well-displayed and described in English. A short "adventures of Thor Heyerdahl" movie plays constantly (25 kr, daily 9:30–17:45, off-season 10:30–16:45).

▲**Norwegian Maritime Museum**—If you like the sea, this museum is a salt lick, providing a fine look at Norway's maritime heritage (30 kr, 60 kr for a family, daily 10:00–19:00, off-season 10:30–16:00 and sometimes later). Consider viewing the wide-screen nature film on Norway's coast called *The Ocean, A Way of Life* (free, 20 min, on the half-hour).

Other Oslo Sights and Activities

▲**Henie-Onstad Art Center**—Norway's best private modern art collection, donated by the famous Norwegian Olympic skater/movie star Sonja Henie (and her husband), combines modern art, a stunning building, a beautiful fjord-side setting, and the great café/restaurant Pirouetten. Don't miss her glittering trophy room near the entrance of the center (40 kr, Monday 11:00–17:00, Tuesday–Friday 9:00–21:00, weekends 11:00–19:00, tel. 67 54 30 50). It's in Høvikodden, 8 miles southwest of Oslo (catch bus #151, #153, #251, or #252 from the Oslo train station or from Universitets Plass by the National Theater).

▲▲**Holmenkollen Ski Jump and Ski Museum**—Overlooking Oslo is a tremendous ski jump with a unique museum of skiing. The T-bane #1 gets you out of the city, into the hills and forests that surround Oslo, and to the jump. After touring the history of skiing in the museum, ride the elevator and climb the 100-step stairway to the thrilling top of the jump for the best possible view of Oslo—and a chance to look down the long and frightening ramp that has sent so many tumbling into the agony of defeat. The **ski museum** is a must for skiers—tracing the evolution of the sport from 4,000-year-old rock paintings, to crude 1,500-year-old skis, to the slick and quickly evolving skis of our century (50 kr, ski jump and museum open daily 9:00–20:00 in June, 9:00–22:00 in July and August, closes earlier off-season).

For a special thrill, step into the **Simulator** and fly down the French Alps in a Disneyland-style downhill ski-race simulator. My legs were exhausted after the four-minute terror. This stimulator, parked in front of the ski museum, costs 35 kr. (Japanese tourists, who wig out over this one, are usually given a free ride after paying for four.)

To get to the ski jump, ride the T-bane line #1 to the Holmenkollen stop and hike up the road ten minutes. For a longer walk, ride to the end of the line (Frognerseteren) and walk ten minutes down to the **Frognerseteren Hovedrestaurant**. This classy, traditional old place, with a terrace that offers a commanding view of the city, is a popular stop for apple-cake and coffee or a splurge dinner (daily 11:00–22:30, tel. 22 14 37 36). From the restaurant it's a 30-minute walk downhill through the woods on a gravel path that runs generally parallel to Holmenkollenveien.

The nearby **Tryvannstårnet observatory tower** offers a lofty 360-degree view of Oslo in the distance, the fjord, and endless forests, lakes, and soft hills. It's impressive but not necessary if you climbed the ski jump, which gives you a much better view of the city (daily 10:00–19:00 in June, 9:00–22:00 in July, and 9:00–20:00 in August, less off-season, ten-minute walk from Voksenkollen T-bane stop, tel. 22 14 67 11).

Harbor and Fjord Tours—Several tour boats leave regularly from Pier 3 in front of the city hall. A relaxing and scenic 50-minute mini-cruise with a boring three-language commentary departs hourly and costs only 70 kr (free with Oslo Card, daily 11:00–20:00, tel. 22 20 07 15). They won't scream if you bring something to Munch. The cheapest way to enjoy the scenic Oslo fjord is to simply ride the ferries that regularly connect the nearby islands with downtown (free with the Oslo Card or transit pass).

▲▲▲**Folk Entertainment**—A group of amateur musicians and dancers (called "Leikarringen Bondeungdomslaget"—Oslo's country youth society) gives a sweet, caring, and vibrant 90-minute show at the Oslo Concert Hall. Several traditional instruments are explained and demonstrated. While folk dancing seems hokey to many, if you think of it as medieval flirting set to music and ponder the complexities of village social life back then, the experience takes you away (140–180 kr, Monday and Thursday July–early September at 20:30; tel. 22 83 45 10 or 81 53 31 33). Look for the big, brown, glassy overpass on Munkedamsveien; the recommended Vegata Vertshus restaurant is just up the street. For their off-season concert schedule (different locales), call 22 41 40 70.

Tusenfryd/Vinkinglandet—A giant amusement complex just out of town offers a world of family fun—sort of a combo Norwegian Disneyland/Viking Knott's Berry Farm. It's one big company. While the Tusenfryd entry includes the Vikings, you can do just the Viking park if you like. Tusenfryd offers more than 50 rides, plenty of entertainment, family fun, and restaurants. Vikinglandet is a Viking theme park. A coach shuttles fun-seekers to the park from behind the train station (20 kr, 2/hr, 20-minute ride). The entry, 180 kr, is not covered by the Oslo Card (daily 10:30–19:00 in summer, closed in winter). For Viking Land only, tickets cost 95 kr (55 kr for kids under 4'7", tel. 64 94 63 63).

Wet Fun—Oslo offers lots of water fun for about 35 kr (kids half-price). In Frogner Park, the Frognerbadet has a sauna, outdoor pools, high dives, a cafeteria, and lots of young families (free with Oslo Card, daily mid-May–late August 11:00–17:45, Middelthunsgate 28, tel. 22 44 74 29). Kriskis and Svettis (tel. 22 83 25 40) organize free community exercise sessions at Frognerpark. Toyenbadet is a modern indoor pool complex with mini-golf and a 100-yard-long water slide (free with Oslo Card, open at odd hours throughout the year, Helgengate 90, a ten-minute walk from Munch Museum, tel. 22 68 24 23). Oslo's free botanical gardens are nearby. (For more ideas on swimming, pick up *Streetwise* magazine.)

Nightlife—They used to tell people who asked about nightlife in Oslo that Copenhagen was only an hour away by plane. Now Oslo has sprouted a nightlife of its own. The scene is always changing. The tourist office has information on Oslo's many cafés, discos, and jazz clubs. Use It is the best source of information for local hot spots.

Shopping—For a great selection (but high prices) in sweaters and other Norwegian crafts, shop at Husfliden, the retail center for the Norwegian Association of Home Arts and Crafts (Sunday–Friday 10:00–17:00, Saturday until 15:00, Den Norske Husflidsforening, Møllergata 4, behind the cathedral, tel. 22 42 10 75). Shops are generally open 10:00 to 18:00. Many stay open until 20:00 on Thursday and close early on Saturday and all day Sunday.

Sleeping in Oslo
(7 kr = about $1)
Sleep Code: **S**=Single, **D**=Double/Twin, **T**=Triple, **Q**=Quad, **b**=bathroom, **CC**=Credit Card (**V**isa, **M**asterCard, **A**mex).

Yes, Oslo is expensive. In Oslo, the season dictates the best deals. In low season (July–mid-August, and Friday, Saturday, and Sunday the rest of the year), fancy hotels are the best value for softies, with 600 kr for a double with breakfast. In high season (business days outside of summer), your affordable choices are dumpy-for-Scandinavia (but still nice by European standards) doubles for around 500 kr in hotels and 350 kr in private homes. For experience and economy (but not convenience), go for a private home. Oslo's new Albertine hostel (see below) is well-located and normally has space available (100 kr per bed, 300-kr doubles).

Like those in its sister Scandinavian capitals, Oslo's hotels are designed for business travelers. They're expensive during our off-season (fall through spring), full in May and June for conventions (get reservations), and empty otherwise. Only the TI can sort through all the confusing hotel "specials" and get you the best deal possible on a fancy hotel—push-list rooms at about half-price. Half-price is still 600 to 700 kr, but that includes a huge breakfast and a lot of extra comfort for a few extra kroner over the cost of a cheap hotel. Cheap hotels, whose rates are the same throughout the year, are a bad value in summer but offer real savings in low season.

The TI's **Oslo Package** advertises 700-kr discounted doubles in business-class (normally priced at 1,200 kr) rooms and includes a free Oslo Card (worth 130 kr/day). The Oslo Package is a good deal for couples and an incredible deal for families with children under 16 who are traveling in late-June through mid-August or on week-ends. Two kids under 16 sleep free, breakfast included, and up to four family members get Oslo Cards, covering free admission to sights and all public transportation. The clincher is that the cards are valid for four days, even if you only stay at the hotel for one night (technically, you should stay two nights, but this is not enforced). Buy this through your travel agent at home, ScanAm World Tour at 800/545-2204, or, easier, upon arrival in Oslo (at the tourist information office).

Use the TI only for these push-list deals, not for cheap hotels or private homes. Some of the cheaper hotels (my listings) tell the TI (which gets a 10 percent fee) they're full when they're not. Go direct. A hotel getting 100 percent of your payment is more likely to have a room. July and early August are easy, but June can be crammed by conventions and September can be tight.

Sleeping in Hotels near the Train Station
Each of these places is within a five-minute walk of the station, in a neighborhood your mom probably wouldn't want you hanging around in at night. The hotels themselves, however, are secure and comfortable. Leave nothing in your car. The Paleet parking garage is handy but not cheap—120 kr per 24 hours.

City Hotel, clean, basic, very homey, and with a wonderful lounge, originated 100 years ago as a cheap place for Norwegians to sleep while they waited to sail to their new homes in America. It now serves the opposite purpose with good if well-worn rooms and a great location (S-380 kr, Sb-495 kr, D-550 kr, Db-680 kr, includes breakfast, CC:VMA, Skippergata 19, enter from Prinsens Gate, tel. 22 41 36 10, fax 22 42 24 29).

Rainbow Hotel Astoria is a comfortable, modern place, and part of the quickly growing Rainbow Hotel chain that understands which comforts are worth paying for. There are umbrellas, televisions, telephones, and full modern bathrooms in each room. Ice machines! Designed for businessmen, the place has mostly singles. Most "twins" are actually "combi" rooms with a regular bed and a fold-out sofa bed (Sb-395–595 kr, Twin/Db-540–695 kr, Db-640–795 kr, rates vary with season, included buffet breakfast, CC:VMA, 3 blocks in front of the station, 50 yards off Karl Johans Gate, Dronningensgate 21, 0154 Oslo, tel. 22 42 00 10, fax 22 42 57 65).

Rainbow Hotel Spectrum is also conveniently located and a good value (discounted prices Friday, Saturday, Sunday, and throughout July: "combi" Twin/b-570–695 kr, full doubles—actually two twins shoved together—100 kr more, CC:VMA, 4 blocks to the right as you leave the station on Lilletorget, Brugata 7, 0186 Oslo, tel. 22 17 60 30, fax 22 17 60 80). **Rainbow Hotel Terminus** is similar and closer to the station, but has a less exciting low-season deal (Friday, Saturday, or Sunday anytime or reservations within 48 hours any day during the May–August period: Sb-420 kr, small bed Db-580 kr, Db-680 kr, regular Db rate-810 kr, includes breakfast, Stenersgate 10, tel. 22 05 60 00, fax 22 17 08 98).

Sleeping in the West End
Cochs Pensjonat has 68 plain rooms (plus nine remodeled doubles) with fresh paint and stale carpets. It's right behind the palace (S-310 kr, Sb-390 kr, D-420 kr, Db-530–580 kr, all Dbs have kitchenettes, no breakfast, CC:VM, tram #11, #13, #17, or #18 to Parkveien 25, tel. 22 60 48 36, fax 22 46 54 02).

Ellingsen's Pensjonat has no lounge, no breakfasts, and dreary halls. But its rooms are great, with fluffy down comforters. It's located in a residential neighborhood 4 blocks behind the Royal Palace (a lot of S-240 kr, S with extra bed-340 kr, D-380 kr, Db-470 kr, extra bed-100 kr, call well in advance for doubles, Holtegata 25, 0355 Oslo 3, tel. 22 60 03 59, fax 22 60 99 21). Located near the Uranienborg church, it's #25 on the east side of the street (T-bane #19 from the station).

Sleeping in Rooms in Private Homes

The TI can find you a 300-kr double for a 20-kr fee (minimum two-night stay). My listings are funky, but full of memories.

Mr. Naess offers big, homey old rooms overlooking a park, and the use of a fully-equipped kitchen. This is a flat in a big ramshackle building, in a borderline-rough neighborhood with workaday shops and eateries nearby (special prices for two or more nights: S-150 kr, D-250 kr, T-375 kr, add 40 kr extra per person for one night stay, no breakfast, plenty of stairs, Toftegate 45, tel. & fax 22 37 58 94). Walk 20 minutes from the station, or take bus #30 from the tower in front of the station to Olaf Ryes Plass (five stops). Three people (or two with lots of luggage) should take a taxi.

Marius Meisfjord, a retired teacher deeply interested in imparting Norse culture, rents rooms behind the palace. Beds are 145 kr per person in a house stuffed with ancient furniture and pictures of European royalty. This eccentric place feels more like a museum than a B&B, and friendly Mr. Meisfjord looks more like Ibsen than a B&B host (breakfast extra, take tram #12 or #15 to Elisensbergveien, walk 2 blocks to Thomas Heftes Gate 46, tel. 22 55 38 46).

The **Caspari family** rents four comfortable rooms in their home (D-280 kr, breakfast-45 kr). Loosely run, it's set in a lush green yard in a peaceful suburb behind Frogner Park, a quick T-bane ride away (get off at Borgen and walk 100 yards more on the right-hand side of the tracks, Heggelbakken 1, tel. 22 14 57 70).

Sleeping in Hostels

Albertine Hostel, a huge student dorm newly opened to travelers of any age, offers the best cheap doubles in town. It feels like a bomb shelter but each room is spacious, simple, and clean. There are kitchens, free parking, and elevators (Sb-225 kr, Db-300 kr, beds in quads-125 kr, beds in six-bedded rooms-95 kr, sheets-35 kr, towel-15 kr, breakfast-45 kr; catch tram #11, #12, #15, or #17, or bus #27 or #30 from the station; Storgata 55, N-0182 Oslo, tel. 22 99 72 00, fax 22 99 72 20, Web site: www.sol.no/anker.oslo.no). In winter they use the adjacent Anker hotel reception desk.

Haraldsheim Youth Hostel (IYHF), a huge, modern hostel, is open all year, situated far from the center on a hill with a grand view, laundry, and self-service kitchen. Its 270 beds (four per room) are often completely booked. Beds in the new fancy quads with private showers and toilets are 175 kr per person, including buffet breakfast. (Beds in simple quads-155 kr, includes breakfast, sheets-35 kr, guest membership-25 kr; tram #10 or #11 from station to Sinsen, 4 km out of town, five-minute uphill hike; Haraldsheimveien 4; tel. 22 15 50 43, fax 22 22 10 25.) Eurailers can train (2/hour, to Gressen) to the hostel for free.

YMCA Sleep-In Oslo, located near the train station, offers the cheapest mattresses in town in three large rooms with 15 to 30 mattresses each, plus a left-luggage room, kitchen, and piano lounge (earplugs for sale). It's as pleasant as a sleep-in can be (100 kr, no bedding provided, you must bring a sleeping bag, reception open daily 8:00–11:00 and 17:00–24:00 July to mid-August only, Møllergata 1, entry from Grubbegata, 1 block beyond the cathedral behind Use It, tel. 22 20 83 97). They take no reservations, but call to see if there's a place.

Sleeping on the Train
Norway's trains offer 100-kr beds in triple compartments and 200-kr beds in doubles. Eurailers who sleep well to the rhythm of the rails have several very scenic overnight trips to choose from (it's light until midnight for much of the early summer at Oslo's latitude). If you have a train pass, use the station's service center (across from the ticket windows) and avoid the long lines.

Eating in Oslo
My strategy is to splurge for a hotel that includes breakfast. A 50-kr Norwegian breakfast is fit for a Viking. Have a picnic for lunch or dinner, using one of the many grocery stores. Basements of big department stores have huge first-class supermarkets with lots of picnic dinner-quality alternatives to sandwiches. The little yogurt tubs with cereal come with a collapsible spoon. The train station has a late-hours grocery.

Oslo is awash with clever little budget eateries (modern, ethnic, fast food, pizza, department store cafeterias). Here are three places for those who want to eat like my Norwegian grandparents:

Kaffistova is an alcohol-free cafeteria serving simple, hearty, and typically Norwegian (read "bland") meals for the best price around. You'll get your choice of an entrée (meatballs) and all the salad, cooked vegetables, and "flat bread" you want (or, at least, need) for around 80 kr (open Monday–Friday 12:00–20:30, until 17:00 Saturday and 18:00 Sunday in summer, closes earlier off-season, 8 Rosenkrantzgate).

Norrøna Cafeteria is another traditional budget-saver (70-kr *dagens rett*, before 14:00 you'll get the same thing for 60 kr with a cup of coffee tossed in; Monday–Friday until 18:00, later off-season; central at 19 Grensen). For a classier traditional meal with a grand view, consider the Frognerseteren restaurant (described above with the ski jump).

Vegeta Vertshus, which has been keeping Oslo vegetarians fat, happy, and low on the food chain for 60 years, serves a huge selection of hearty vegetarian food that would satisfy even a hungry Viking. Fill your plate once (small plate-73 kr, large plate-83 kr) or eternally for 114 kr. How's your balance? One plate did me fine (daily 11:00–23:00, no smoking, no meat, Munkedamsveien 3B, near top of Stortingsgata between palace and city hall, tel. 22 83 42 32).

The **Aker Brygge** (harborfront mall) development isn't cheap, but it has some cheery cafés, classy delis, open-'til-22:00 restaurants, and markets.

For a grand and traditional breakfast, consider the elegant spread at the **Bristol Hotel** (90 kr, a block off Karl Johans Gate behind the Grand Hotel).

Transportation Connections—Oslo

For train info, call 81 50 08 88 (7:00–23:00, phone tree, press 1 and wait).

By train to Bergen: Oslo and Bergen are linked by a spectacularly scenic seven-hour train ride. Reservations (20 kr) are required on all long and IC (express) trains. Departures are roughly at 7:45, 10:45, 14:45, 16:00, and 23:00 daily in both directions (500 kr, or 380 kr if you buy a day early and don't travel at peak times like Friday or Sunday).

By boat to Copenhagen: Consider the cheap quickie cruise that leaves daily from Copenhagen (departs 17:00, returns 9:15 two days later; 16 hrs sailing each way and seven hrs in Norway's capital). See Copenhagen chapter for specifics.

By plane: Oslo's new Gardermoen Airport opens in 1998. Unlike the old airport, this one is far from town (30 miles to the north) but will be connected by a slick shuttle train to the central train station.

BARCELONA

Barcelona is Spain's second city and the capital of the proud and distinct region of Catalunya (Catalonia). With Franco's fascism now history, Catalunyan flags wave once again. The local language and culture are on a roll in Spain's most cosmopolitan and European corner.

Barcelona bubbles with life in its narrow Gothic Quarter alleys, along the grand boulevards, and throughout the chic, grid-planned new town. While Barcelona had an illustrious past as a Roman colony, Visigothic capital, 14th-century maritime power, and in more modern times, a top Mediterranean trading and manufacturing center, it's most enjoyable to throw out the history books and just drift through the city. If you're in the mood to surrender to a city's charms, let it be in Barcelona.

Planning Your Time

Sandwich Barcelona between flights or overnight train rides. There's little of earth-shaking importance within eight hours by train. It's as easy to fly into Barcelona as into Madrid, Lisbon, or Paris for most travelers from the U.S.A. Those renting a car can start here, sleep on the train to Madrid, and pick up the car after seeing the city.

On the shortest visit Barcelona is worth one night, one day, and an overnight train out. The Ramblas is two different streets by day and by night. Stroll it from top to bottom at night and again the next morning, grabbing breakfast on a stool in a café in the market. Wander the Gothic Quarter, see the cathedral, and have lunch in Eixample (ay-SHAM-pla). The top two sights in town, Gaudí's Sacred Family Church and the Picasso Museum, are usually open until about 20:00. The illuminated fountains are a good finale for your day.

Barcelona

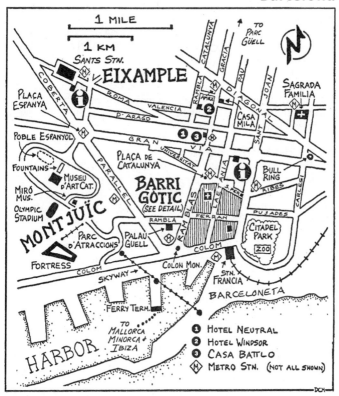

Of course, Barcelona in a day is a dash. To better appreciate the city's ample charm, spread your visit over two days.

Orientation (tel. code: 93)

Locate these orientation essentials on the map above: Barri Gòtic/Ramblas (Old Town), Eixample (fashionable modern town), Montjuïc (hill covered with sights and parks), and Sants Station (train to Madrid). The soul of Barcelona is in its compact core—the Barri Gòtic (Gothic Quarter) and the Ramblas (main boulevard). This is your strolling, shopping, and people-watching nucleus. The city's sights are widely scattered, but with a map and a willingness to figure out the sleek subway system, all is manageable.

Tourist Information

There are three useful TIs in Barcelona: at the Sants train station, the airport, and by far the best TI, on (actually, under)

Plaça de Catalunya across from Corte Inglés (Monday–Saturday, 9:00–22:00, Sunday 9:00–21:00, tel. 93/304-3135; they even have a bank with fair rates, open until 20:30 Monday–Saturday). The Sants station's TI is located at the access to platform 10 (weekdays 8:00–20:00, weekends 8:00–14:00, tel. 93/491-4431). Whichever TI you visit, get the large city map and brochures on Gaudí, Miró, Dalí, Picasso, and the Barri Gòtic. Ask for the free quarterly *Top Tips Barcelona*, a comprehensive guide listing practical information (transportation, museum hours, restaurants) and cultural information (history, festivals, and points of interest grouped by neighborhood).

Arrival in Barcelona

By Train: Although many international trains use the França Station, all domestic (and some international) trains use Sants Station. Both França and Sants have subway stations: França's is "Barceloneta" (2 blocks away), Sants' is "Sants Estacio" (under the station). Both stations have baggage lockers. Sants station has a good TI, a world of handy shops and eateries (including a juice shop with a fascinating orange-juicer behind the TI), and a classy "Club Intercity" lounge for first-class travelers (quiet, plush, TV, shower, study tables, coffee bar). There is nothing of interest within easy walking distance from the train station. Catch the subway or a taxi to your hotel.

By Plane: Barcelona's El Prat de Llobregat Airport is 12 kilometers out of town and connected cheaply and quickly by Aerobus (immediately in front of arrivals lobby, 4/hr, 20 min to Plaça de Catalunya, buy 475-pta ticket from driver) or by RENFE train (walk the tunnel overpass from airport to station, 2/hr, 20 min, 310 ptas, to Sants station and Plaça de Catalunya). A taxi to or from the airport costs about 3,000 ptas. Airport information: tel. 93/478-5000. To avoid ten-hour train trips, those continuing to Madrid or Sevilla should check the reasonable flights from Barcelona.

Getting Around Barcelona

Barcelona's subway, among Europe's best, can be faster than a taxi and connects just about every place you'll visit. It has five color-coded lines (L1 is red, L2 is lilac, L3 is green, L4 is yellow, L5 is blue). Rides cost 135 ptas each. A T-2 Card gives you ten tickets for 720 ptas; a T-1 Card is a better deal, giving you ten tickets good for the bus or Metro (subway) for the same price. Pick up the TI's guide to public transport.

The handy Tourist Bus (Bus Turistic) shuttles tourists on an 18-stop circuit covering the must-sees, funicular, and *teleférico* (mid-June–mid-October, 9:00–21:30, buy tickets on bus). The one-day ticket (for 1,400 ptas) and two-day ticket (1,800 ptas) include some serious discounts on the city's major sights. Buses run every 20 minutes and take two hours to do the entire circuit.

Taxis are plentiful and honest, and they don't charge extra for evening rides. Rides start at 285 ptas. You can go from the Ramblas to the Sants station for 600 ptas (300 ptas extra for luggage).

Helpful Hints

Theft Alert: Barcelona, after recently illuminating many of its seedier streets, is not the pickpocket paradise it was a few years back, but it's good to be alert.

American Express: The AmExCo office doesn't charge a commission for cashing any brand of traveler's check (weekdays 9:30–18:00, Saturday 10:00–12:00, Paseo de Gracia 101, tel. 93/415-2371, Metro: Diagonal).

Monday Plans: Many sights, but not all, are closed on Monday. Instead, you can stroll the Ramblas, shop at El Corte Inglés, zip up the Columbus Monument, take a *golondrina* ride, visit Parc Güell, or tour the Sagrada Familia.

Language: Although Spanish is understood here (and the basic survival words are the same), Barcelona speaks a different language—Catalan. (Most place names in this chapter are listed in Catalan.) Here are the essential Catalunyan phrases:

Hello	*Hola*	Same as Spanish
Please	*Si us plau*	(see oos plow)
Thank you	*Gracies*	Virtually the same
Goodbye	*Adeu*	(ah-DAY-oo)
Exit	*Sordida*	*Salida*
Long live Catalunya!	*Visca Catalunya!*	(BEE-skah . . .)

Sights—The Ramblas

More than a Champs-Elysées, this grand boulevard called the Ramblas takes you from rich at the top to rough at the port, a 20-minute walk. You'll find the grand opera house, ornate churches, plain prostitutes, pickpockets, con men, artists, street mimes, an outdoor bird market, elegant cafés, great shopping, and people willing to charge more for a shoeshine than you paid for the shoes. Sit on a white metal chair for 50 ptas and observe. When Hans Christian Andersen saw this street more than 100 years ago, he wrote that there could be no doubt that Barcelona was a great city.

Rambla means "stream" in Arabic. The Ramblas was a drainage ditch along the medieval wall that used to define what is now called the Gothic Quarter. It has five separately named segments, but addresses treat it as a mile-long boulevard.

Walking from Plaça de Catalunya downhill to the harbor, the Ramblas highlights are:

▲**Plaça de Catalunya**—This vast central square is the divider between old and new, and the hub for the Metro, bus, and airport shuttle. Overlooking the square, the huge El Corte Inglés department store offers everything from a travel agency and

haircuts to cheap souvenirs (10:00–21:30, closed Sunday, supermarket in basement, ninth-floor terrace cafeteria with great city
view—take elevator from west entrance, tel. 93/302-1212). Four
great boulevards start here: the Ramblas, the fashionable Passeig
de Gràcia, the cozier but still fashionable parallel Rambla
Catalunya, and the stubby, shop-filled, pedestrian-only Portal de
L'Angel.

▲▲**Mercat de Sant Josep** (a.k.a. La Boqueria)—This lively produce market (8:00–20:00, best in the morning, closed Sunday) is
an explosion of chicken legs, bags of live snails, stiff fish, delicious
oranges, sleeping dogs, and great bars for a cheap breakfast (try a
tortilla española and *café con leche*).

Gran Teatre del Liceu—Spain's only real opera house is lus-
cious but closed for a few years for renovation because of a fire
(tourable when it reopens).

Plaça Reial—This elegant, neoclassical square comes complete
with old-fashioned taverns, a Sunday coin and stamp market
(10:00–14:00), and characters who don't need the palm trees to
be shady. Escudellers, a street 1 block toward the water from the
square, is lined with bars whose counters are strewn with vampy
ladies. The area is well policed, but if you tried, you could get
into trouble.

▲**Palau Güell**—This offers the only look at a Gaudí Art Nouveau
interior, and for me, it's the most enjoyable look at Barcelona's
organic architect. The interior is a theater museum (300 ptas, usually open Monday–Saturday, 10:00–14:00, 16:00–20:00, Nou de la
Rambla 3-5, tel. 93/317-3974). Check the chimneys on the terrace—look for Gaudí's *la alcachofa* (the artichoke) and the recent
Olympic-rings chimney (with the outline of the 1992 Olympic
mascot, Cobi, at waist level on the white chimney).

Chinatown (Barri Xines)—Farther downhill, on the right-hand
side, is the world's only Chinatown with nothing even remotely
Chinese in or near it—a dingy, dangerous-after-dark nightclub
district with lots of street girls and a monument to Dr. Fuller, the
Canadian who discovered penicillin. Don't venture in.

Columbus Monument (Monument a Colóm)—At the harbor at
the end of the Ramblas, this monument offers an elevator-assisted
view from its top (225 ptas, Monday–Saturday 9:00–21:00, Sunday
10:00–19:00; off-season 10:00–13:30, 15:30–18:30, closed Monday).
It's interesting that Barcelona would so honor the man whose discoveries ultimately led to its downfall as a great trading power.

Maritime Museum (Museo Maritim)—This museum gives a
look at Barcelona's sea power before Columbus' discoveries shifted
the world's focus west. With fleets of seemingly unimportant
replicas of old boats explained in Catalan and Spanish, landlubbers
find it pretty dull (800 ptas, Tuesday–Sunday 10:00–19:00, closed
Monday).

Golondrinas—Little tourist boats make a half-hour tour of the harbor every 20 to 30 minutes from 11:00 to 18:00 at the foot of the Columbus Monument (300 ptas one-way to other side of harbor, or 440 ptas round-trip). Consider this ride or the harbor steps here for a picnic.

Maremagnum—This modern Spanish monstrosity of a mall (with a cinema, aquarium, and restaurants) offers fine city views. It's connected to the waterfront by a slick wood footbridge next to the golondrina boats.

Sights—Gothic Quarter (Barri Gòtic)

The Barri Gòtic is a bustling world of shops, bars, and nightlife packed between hard-to-be-thrilled-about 14th- and 15th-century buildings. Except for the part closest to the port, the area now feels safe, thanks to police and countless streetlights. There is a tangled grab-bag of undiscovered squares, grand squares, schoolyard plazas, art nouveau storefronts, baby flea-markets, musty antique shops, classy antique shops, and balconies with jungles behind wrought-iron bars. Go on a cultural scavenger hunt. Write a poem.

▲**Cathedral**—The colossal cathedral, a fine example of Catalan Gothic, was started in about 1300 and took 600 years to complete. Rather than stretching toward heaven, it makes a point to be simply massive (similar to the Gothic churches of Italy). The heavy choir (*coro*) in the middle confuses the dark and muddled interior. There's an admission fee to enter the *coro* from the back, but you can see everything for free from the front. Don't miss the cloister with its wispy garden and worthwhile little 50-pta museum (cathedral 8:00–13:30, 16:00–19:30; cloisters 8:45–13:15 and 16:00–18:45; museum 11:00–13:00; all closed Monday). The stirring and patriotic Sardana dances are held every weekend at the cathedral at 18:30 Saturday and noon on Sunday (and at Plaça St. Jaume at 18:30 Sunday). Drop into the courtyard of the Frederic Mares museum (down the small street running along the left side of the cathedral) for a tranquil break at its peaceful café.

Shoe Museum (Museo del Calzado)—Shoe-lovers can find this two-room shoe museum (with a we-try-harder attendant) on Plaça Sant Felip Neri, about a block beyond the outside door of the cloister (200 ptas, Tuesday–Sunday 11:00–14:00, closed Monday).

Royal Palace (Palau Reial)—The royal palace contains museums showing off Barcelona's Roman and medieval history, along with piles of medieval documents in the *Arxiu de la Corona d'Aragon* (Archives of the Kingdom of Aragon).

▲▲**Picasso Museum**—Far and away the best collection of Picasso's (1881–1973) work in Spain, this is a great chance to see his earliest sketches and paintings and better understand his genius (500 ptas, Tuesday–Saturday 10:00–20:00, Sunday 10:00–15:00, closed Monday; Montcada 15-19, Metro: Jaume; tel. 93/319-6310). He'd mastered the ability to paint realistically when just a teenager.

Barcelona's Gothic Quarter

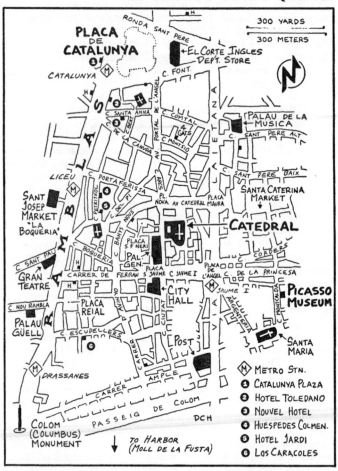

Follow his progress as his skill increased geometrically—to cubism.
Textile and Garment Museum (Museu Textil i de la Indu-mentaria)—If fabrics from the fourth to 16th century leave you
cold, have a *café con leche* on the museum's beautiful bourgeois
patio (museum, 300 ptas; patio is within walls but outside museum,
near Picasso Museum at Montcada 12-14).
▲**Catalana Concert Hall (Palau de la Música Catalana)**—
This colorful hall is an extravagant burst of modernisme, with
a floral ceramic ceiling, colored glass columns, and detailed
mosaics. To get inside, you can either take a one-hour tour
(200 ptas, Tuesday and Thursday 15:00–16:00 and Saturday

10:00–12:00, call to reserve, tel. 93/268-1000) or attend a concert (tickets as low as 600 ptas, cheapest tickets available for Sunday concerts at 11:00 or any show an hour before showtime; Calle Sant Frances de Paula 2).

Sights—Gaudí's Art and Architecture

Barcelona is an architectural scrapbook of the galloping gables and organic curves of hometown boy Antonio Gaudí. A devoted Catalan and Catholic, his toil was for his soil. Completely immersed in each project, he often lived on-site. He called Parc Güell, La Pedrera, and the Sagrada Familia all home. For more information on Gaudí, pick up a brochure at the tourist office.

▲**Sagrada Familia (Sacred Family) Church**—Gaudí's most famous and persistent work is this unfinished landmark (800 ptas, daily 9:00–20:00, off-season 9:00–18:00, Metro: Sagrada Familia, tel. 93/455-0247). From 1891 to 1925, Gaudí worked on this monumental church of eight 100-meter spires that will someday dance around a 160-meter granddaddy spire. With the cranes, rusty forests of rebar, and scaffolding requiring a powerful faith, it offers a fun look at a living, growing, bigger-than-life building. Take the lift (200 ptas) or the stairs (free) up to the dizzy lookout bridging two spires for a great city view and a gargoyle's-eye perspective of the loopy church. If there's any building on earth I'd like to see, it's the Sagrada Familia— finished. Judge for yourself how the controversial current work fits in with Gaudí's original formulation. The little on-site museum displays physical models used for the church's construction (daily 9:00–18:00).

▲**Palau Güell**—This is the best chance to enjoy a Gaudí interior (see above under Ramblas). Curvy.

▲**Casa Milà (La Pedrera)**—This house and nearby Casa Battlo have Gaudí exteriors that laugh down on the crowds that fill Passeig de Gràcia. Casa Milà, also called *La Pedrera* (The Quarry), has a much-photographed roller coaster of melting-ice-cream eaves. An elevator whisks you to the top where you can wander under brick arches; enjoy the fascinating new **Espai Gaudí**, a multimedia exhibit of models, photos, and videos of Gaudí's works (in English); and frolic on the fanciful rooftop (500 ptas, Tuesday–Saturday 10:00–20:00, Sunday 10:00–15:00, closed Monday, Passeig del Gràcia 92, Metro: Diagonal). The entrance courtyard for the Fundacio Caixa de Cataluyna, dreamily painted in pastels, is original and can be seen free of charge.

Casa Battlo—Four blocks from Casa Milà (Passeig de Gràcia 43, Metro: Passeig de Gràcia), this house's roof has a cresting wave of tiles (or is it a dragon's back?). Check out the geometric facade of the house next door (#41) by the architect Puig i Cadafalch and the modernistic house (#35) by Lluís Domènechi Muntaner, designer of the Catalana Concert Hall. This Barcelonian version of keeping up with the Joneses led to the Passeig de Gràcia's local nickname, "the street of discord." If you're tempted to frame your photo from the middle of the street, be careful—Gaudí died under a streetcar!

Parc Güell—Gaudí fans find the artist's magic in this colorful park (free, daily 10:00–20:00) and small **Gaudí Museum** (200 ptas, museum open Sunday–Friday 10:00–14:00 and 16:00–18:00, closed Saturday, Metro: Vallarca but easier by bus #24 from Plaça de Catalunya; 1,000 ptas by taxi). Gaudí didn't intend this to be a park but a planned garden city. As a high-income housing project, it flopped. As a park . . . even after reminding myself that Gaudí's work is a careful rhythm of color, shapes, and space, I was disappointed.

Modern Art Museum (Museu d'Art Modern)—East of the França train station in Parc de la Ciutadella, this manageable museum exhibits Catalan sculpture, painting, glass, and furniture by Gaudí, Casas, Llimona, and others (300 ptas, Tuesday–Sunday 10:00–19:00, closed Monday).

Sights—Barcelona's Montjuïc

The Montjuïc (Mount of the Jews), overlooking Barcelona's hazy port, has always been a show-off. Ages ago it had the impressive fortress. In 1929, it hosted an International Fair from which most of today's sights originated. And in 1992, the Summer Olympics directed the world's attention to this pincushion of sightseeing attractions. Barcelona's skyway (Transbordador Aeri) is a temptation when you see it gliding fitfully across the harbor. It's often closed for safety reasons.

There are three ways to reach Montjuïc: on the Bus Turistic (see Getting Around Barcelona, above), bus #61 from Plaza España (135 ptas, every 10 minutes), or take the subway to Metro: Parallel and catch the funicular (250 ptas one-way, 350 ptas round-trip, 10:45–20:00, later in summer). All three options leave you at the *teleférico* which you can take to the Montjuïc castle (400 ptas one-way, 600 ptas round-trip), or walk uphill 20 minutes through the pleasant park.

Amusement Park (Parc d'Atraccions de Montjuïc)—Your best chance to eat, whirl, and hurl with local families (free, open daily in summers until late, access by the skyway or by Metro: Parallel, from which you can walk or ride the Montjuïc *teleférico*, which stops here on its way up to the fortress).

Castle of Montjuïc—This offers great city views and a military museum (200 ptas, Tuesday–Sunday 9:30–13:30, 15:30–19:30, closed Monday).

▲**Fountains (Fonts Lluminoses)**—Music, colored lights, and impressive amounts of water make an artistic and coordinated splash on summer Thursday, Friday, and Saturday nights (four 30-minute shows start on the half-hour, 22:00–23:30, walk toward huge towering National Palace from the Metro: Plaça Espanya).

Spanish Village (Poble Espanyol)—This tacky 5-acre model village uses fake traditional architecture from all over Spain as a shell to contain gift shops. Craftspeople do their clichétic thing only in the morning (9:00–19:30 but dead after 13:00, not worth the time or the 950 ptas). After-hours it becomes a popular local nightspot.

Torres de Avila—The music is loud and drinks are steep (900 ptas), but this modern building is remarkable. Designed by Mariscal, it features rotating walls, a glass elevator, glass floors, and a men's room with a circular pool table. It's just outside Poble Espanyol (Thursday–Sunday, 23:00–6:00).

▲Catalonian Art Museum (Museo Nacional d'Art de Catalunya)—Often called "the Prado of Romanesque art," this is a rare and world-class collection of Romanesque frescoes, statues, and paintings, much of it from remote Catalan village churches in the Pyrenees. Also see Gothic work and paintings by the great Spanish masters (500 ptas, Tuesday–Saturday 10:00–19:00, on Thursday until 21:00, Sunday 10:00–14:30, closed Monday, tel. 93/423-7199).

▲Fundació Joan Miró—For something a bit more up-to-date, this museum showcases the modern art talents of yet another Catalonian artist (600 ptas, 10:00–20:00, Sunday 10:30–14:30, Thursday until 21:30, closed Monday).

Sights—Eixample

Uptown Barcelona is a unique variation on the grid-planned cities you find all over. Barcelona snipped off the building corners to create light and spacious eight-sided squares at every intersection (and difficulty in finding signs of crossroads). Wide sidewalks, hardy shade trees, chic shops, and plenty of art nouveau fun (by Gaudí and company) make the Eixample a refreshing break from the Old Town. For the best Eixample example, ramble Rambla Catalunya (unrelated to the more famous Ramblas) and pass through Passeig de Gràcia (Metro: Passeig de Gràcia).

The 19th century brought to Barcelona great economic and demographic growth. By the mid-1800s, the city was busting out of its medieval walls. A new modern section was planned to follow a grid-like layout and bring the city's focus uptown with the intersection of three major thoroughfares: Gran Via, Diagonal, and the Meridiana. Deemed the *Eixample*, or "Enlargement," this progressive plan would carry Barcelona well into the 20th century.

The plan envisioned a city in which everything was accessible to everyone. Each 20-block-square district would have its own hospital and large park, each 10-block-square area would have its own market and general services, each 5-block-square grid, called a *barri*, would house its own schools and day-care centers. The hollow space found inside each "block" of apartments would form a neighborhood park.

While many details were never realized, the Eixample was an urban success. Although construction was ongoing, grids were laid at the project's inception. Individuals bought plots where they built—adhering to the height, width, and depth limitations—as they pleased. The turn of the century produced the most ornate structures, many in the newly developed moderniste style. The bourgeoisie positioned themselves as close to the center as possible. For this reason, the best buildings are near the Passeig de Gràcia.

Before the age of elevators, the bourgeoisie lavishly decorated only the lower floors. Glass windows, brass handrails, and marble steps adorn the *principal* (ground floor). As you ascend, the steps get lower and narrower, and the lustrous marble is replaced by splintering wood.

Sarria and Gràcia (north of where Passeig de Gràcia turns into Gran de Gràcia) were both independent villages outside of the city. Many Barcelonans had summer homes there. Now both neighborhoods, incorporated into modern-day Barcelona, maintain their separate identities and fiestas. The charming Plaza Rovira i Trias marks the Old Town center of Gràcia.

Sleeping in Barcelona
(140 ptas = about $1, tel. code: 93)
Sleep Code: **S**=Single, **D**=Double/Twin, **T**=Triple, **Q**=Quad, **b**=bathroom, **t**=toilet only, **s**=shower only, **CC**=Credit Card (Visa, MasterCard, Amex), **SE**=Speaks English, **NSE**=No English.

Barcelona is Spain's most expensive city. Still, it has reasonable rooms. Your big decision is which neighborhood. A few places raise their rates for "high season," which, for business hotels, is outside of summer, on weekdays, and during conventions. Since dumpy, cheap hotels cater only to tourists, their high season is summer. Most prices listed do not include the 7 percent tax or the optional breakfast.

Sleeping near the Ramblas and in the Gothic Quarter
(zip code: 08002)
(These accommodations are listed in roughly geographical order downhill from Plaça de Catalunya.)

Catalunya Plaza is a business hotel with all the air-con, minibar comforts (Sb-13,000 ptas, Db-15,000 ptas, CC:VMA, on the plaza at Plaça de Catalunya 7, tel. 93/317-7171, fax 93/317-7855, SE).

Hotel Barcelona is another big American-style hotel with soft prices (Sb-13,000 ptas, Db-17,000 ptas, with a sun-roof terrace, 1 block away at Caspe 1-13, tel. 93/302-5858, fax 93/301-8674).

Hotel Toledano's elevator takes you high above the noise and into the *zona bella vista*. Request a view balcony to overlook the Ramblas. This small and folksy hotel is run by the helpful English-speaking owner Juan Sanz and his son Albert (Sb-3,900 ptas,

Db-6,900 ptas, Tb-8,600 ptas, Qb-9,600 ptas, cheaper off-season, TV with BBC in every room, CC:VMA, Rambla de Canaletas 138, tel. 93/301-0872, fax 93/412-3142, e-mail: Toledano@idgrup.iber-net.com). Juan runs **Hostal Residencia Capitol** one floor above, which is cheaper and appropriate for backpackers (S-2,900 ptas, D-4,600 ptas, Db-5,200 ptas; you can share six-bedded rooms for hostel prices).

The **Hotel Lloret** is a big, Old World, dark place right on the Ramblas. Its worn rooms have almost all been renovated with air-conditioning (S-3,500 ptas, Sb-4,800 ptas, Db-6,800 ptas, extra bed-1,000 ptas, continental buffet breakfast-450 ptas, choose between a Ramblas balcony with street noise or *tranquilo* in the back, elevator dominates the stairwell, CC:VMA, Rambla de Canaletas 125, tel. 93/317-3366, fax 93/301-9283, SE). If you want to immerse yourself in the Ramblas, do it here.

Huéspedes Santa Ana, nearby on Carrer de Santa Ana, a wonderful pedestrian street 1 block down the Ramblas, is plain, clean, and quiet (S-2,600 ptas, D-4,200 ptas, Db-5,200 ptas, T-4,800 ptas, Carrer de Santa Ana 23, tel. 93/301-2246). The friendly owner, Maria, plans lots of renovations, but the rooms will remain small and cramped.

Nouvel Hotel, an elegant Victorian-style building on the same great street, has very comfortable rooms (Sb-8,000 ptas, Db without balcony-10,800 ptas, Db with balcony-12,800 ptas, huge Db suite-19,600 ptas, air-con and royal, CC:VMA, Carrer de Santa Ana 18, tel. 93/301-8274, fax 93/301-8370, SE).

Sister hotels straddling the same street and run by one company, with shiny, modern bathrooms, all the comforts, and similar prices (Sb-5,400 ptas, Db-8,800 ptas with breakfast, CC:VMA), but in buildings that feel more concrete than Victorian, are **Hotel Cataluña** (elevator, Carrer de Santa Ana 24, tel. 93/301-9120, fax 93/302-7870) and **Hotel Cortes** (Carrer de Santa Ana 25, elevator, tel. 93/317-9112, fax 93/302-7870). **Hostal Campi**, big, musty, and ramshackle, is a few doors off the Ramblas (D-3,500 ptas, Db-4,600 ptas, no elevator, Canuda 4, tel. 93/301-3545, NSE).

Hostal Residencia Lausanne, housed in an art nouveau building, has recently been renovated. The friendly owner, Javier, promotes a worldly, harmonious setting (S-2,500 ptas, D-3,500 ptas, Ds-4,500 ptas, Db-6,000 ptas, a few great triples and quads, out-door terrace, TV room, Avenida Portal de l'Angel 24, tel. 93/302-1139, SE).

Hostal Residencia Rembrandt, on a lively pedestrian street between the Ramblas and the cathedral, has a southern-Spain garden-patio feel and bad beds (S-2,700 ptas, Sb-3,500 ptas, D-4,000 ptas, Db-5,500 ptas, breakfast-350 ptas, Portaferrisa 23, tel. & fax 93/318-1011, SE). Join the locals on their evening pil-grimage (18:00–20:00) to nearby Petritxol, a street brimming with art galleries and *churros* shops.

Huéspedes Colmenero is very clean and family-run on a great, safe but noisy alley, with seven cute rooms and tiny balconies. Rosa speaks French but no English and offers the best cheap rooms in the Old Town (S-3,000 ptas, D-4,000 ptas, Db-5,500 ptas, 1,000 ptas more if staying only one night; two streets toward the cathedral from the Ramblas at Petritxol 12, tel. 93/302-6634, fax: what's that?).

Hotel Jardi is a hard-working, clean, plain place on the happiest little square in the Gothic Quarter. Room prices vary according to newness, view, and balconies (in the old wing: D-5,000–5,500 ptas, T-5,600–6,500 ptas; in the new wing: Sb-6,000 ptas, Db-7,000 ptas, Tb-8,500 ptas, continental breakfast-650 ptas, no elevator, CC:VMA, halfway between the Ramblas and the cathedral on Plaça Sant Josep Oriol #1, tel. 93/301-5900, fax 93/318-3664, NSE). Rooms with balconies enjoy a classic plaza setting.

To sleep safely and quietly—but deeper—in the Gothic Quarter, these two new, modern neighbors keep businesspeople happy with TV, telephone, and air-con: **Hotel Adagio** (Sb-6,600 ptas, Db-8,250 ptas, Tb-9,900 ptas, includes breakfast, elevator, CC:VMA, Fernan 21, tel. 93/318-9061, fax 93/318-3724) and across the street, the **Hotel California** (Sb-5,500 ptas, Db-8,000 ptas, Tb-11,000 ptas, includes breakfast, CC:VMA, Raurich 14, tel. 93/317-7766, fax 93/317-5474). The California lacks an elevator but has bigger and brighter halls and bathrooms.

Sleeping in Eixample
(zip code: 08008)
For a more elegant and boulevardian neighborhood, sleep north of Gran Vía Cortes Catalanes in Eixample, a ten-minute walk from the Ramblas action.

There's nothing noncommittal about **Hotel Residencia Neutral**. With 35 cheery rooms, classy public rooms, mosaic floors, high ceilings, and a passion for cleanliness, it's the best Eixample value (tiny Sb-3,000 ptas, big Sb-4,400 ptas, Ds-4,500 ptas, Db-5,800 ptas, Ts-5,100 ptas, Tb-6,200 ptas, CC:VM, elegantly located 2 blocks north of Gran Vía at Rambla Catalunya 42, 08007 Barcelona, tel. 93/487-6390).

Hostal Residencia Windsor, newly refurbished, is peaceful, polished, and a decent value (S-3,200 ptas, Sb-4,000 ptas, Ds-5,600 ptas, Db-6,700 ptas, elevator, some balconies, Rambla Catalunya 84, tel. 93/215-1198, SE).

Pensión Fani is a budget cheapie. It's dark, quiet, and basic (S-2,000 ptas, D-4,500 ptas, elevator, Valencia 278, second floor, tel. 93/215-3645 and 93/215-3044).

Hostels
Hostal de Joves is clean and well-run (1,400 ptas per person with breakfast if you're under 26, 1,500 ptas otherwise, communal

kitchen, Passeig de Pujades 29, next to Parc de la Ciutadella and Metro: Arc de Triomf, tel. 93/300-3104; open 7:00–10:00 and 15:00–24:00). **Hostal Mare de Deu de Montserrat** is much cheerier than Hostal de Joves and worth the extra commute time (1,600 ptas with a hostel card, or 1,800 ptas without, for bed and breakfast if you're under 26, 2,200 ptas otherwise, dinner available, sheets-350 ptas, Passeig Mare de Deu del Coll 41, near Parc Güell, Metro: Vallcarca, follow Republica Argentina exit, tel. 93/210-5151, fax 93/210-0798). **Hostal Pere Tarres** is also good and accepts nonmembers who are willing to pay a bit more (1,450 ptas with breakfast, Calle Numancia 149, near the Sants station and Metro: Les Corts, tel. 93/410-2309).

Eating in Barcelona

Barcelona, the capital of Catalonian cuisine, offers a tremendous variety of colorful places to eat. The harbor area, especially Barceloneta, is famous for fish. The best *tapas* bars are in the Gothic Quarter and around the Picasso Museum. Many restaurants are closed in August when the owners, like you, are on vacation.

Eating in the Gothic Quarter

Los Caracoles, at Escudellers 14, a block off the Plaça Reial in red-light bar country, is a huge and trendy Spanish wine cellar dripping in atmosphere (pricey, daily 13:00–24:00, Metro: Drassanes, tel. 93/302-3185). You'll eat better on a budget at the very popular and neighboring **La Fonda** (Escudellers 10, tel. 93/301-7515). A fine place for local-style food in a local-style setting is **Restaurant Agut** (inexpensive, closed in July or August, huge servings, Calle Gignas 16, tel. 93/315-1709). **El Portalon**, in the bowels of the Gothic Quarter (between Ramblas and the cathedral), is a fair value (closed Sunday, Calle Banys Nous 20).

Taverna Basca Irati has great *tapas* in a bustling atmosphere full of locals (Calle Cardenal Casanyes 17, Metro: Liceu, tel. 93/302-3084).

Els Quatre Gats, Picasso's hangout, is popular with locals. Before it was founded in 1897, the idea of a café for artists was mocked as a place where only *quatre gats* ("four cats," meaning nobody) would come (Monday–Saturday 8:30–1:30, Sunday 17:00–01:30, CC:VMA, Montsio 3, tel. 93/302-4140).

Eating near Plaza Catalunya

Self Naturista is a bright and cheery buffet that will make vegetarians and health-food-lovers feel right at home. Others may find a few unidentifiable plates and drinks (11:30–22:00, closed Sunday, near several recommended hotels, just off the top of Ramblas at Carrer de Santa Ana 13). Another vegetarian choice is **Bio Center** (9:00–23:00, closed Sunday, Pintor Fortuny 25, Metro: Catalunya, tel. 93/301-4583).

Julivert Meu teams up regional specialties like *pan con tomate* (bread with tomato and olive oil), *jamón serrano* (cured ham), and *escalivadas* (grilled vegetables) in a rustic interior (Monday–Saturday 13:00–1:00, Sunday 13:00–16:00 and 20:00–1:00, Bonsuccés 7, Metro: Catalunya, tel. 93/318-0343).

Eating Elsewhere in Barcelona

In the Eixample, at **La Bodegueta**, have a *carajillos* (coffee with rum) and a *flauta* (sandwich on flute-thin baguette) in this authentic below-street-level bodega (Monday–Saturday 8:00–1:30, Sunday 7:00–13:00, Rambla Catalunya 100, at intersection with Provenza, Metro: Diagonal, tel. 93/215-4894) or slip into the classy **Quasi Queviures** for upscale *tapas*, sandwiches, or the whole nine yards (Passeig de Gracia 24).

El Café de Internet provides an easy way to munch a sandwich while sending e-mail messages to mom (600 ptas for a half-hour, Monday–Saturday 10:00–24:00, closed Sunday, Gran Vía 656, Metro: Passeig de Gràcia, tel. 93/302-1154, Web site: www.cafeinternet.es).

Café de L'Ópera, one of Barcelona's mainstays, serves a great *café con leche* (daily 9:00–2:30, La Rambla 74, tel. 93/317-7585).

Egipte, with its old sewing-machine tables, high ceilings, and rooms separated by tall French doors, simmers with charisma. Try the *pebrots amb bacalao*—cod-stuffed red bell peppers over rice (daily 13:00–1:00, Jerusalem 3, behind the Boqueria, Metro: Liceu, tel. 93/317-7480).

For a quick meal, pick up a healthy sandwich at **Pans & Company**. This Catalan chain puts the food back in fast-food. Its sister establishment, **Pastafiore**, dishes up salads and pasta at a fair price (500–800 ptas). Both are a lifesaver on Sunday, when many restaurants are closed (daily 8:00–24:00, opens at 9:00 on Sunday, located on Plaza Urquinaona, Provenza, La Rambla, Portal de l'Angel, and just about everywhere else).

Tapas and Tascas

A regional joke sums up eating habits in Catalunya. A person from Madrid takes a Catalan friend on a lengthy run of *tapas* bars. At each stop they sample lots of munchies. Hours later, the night ends and the Madrileño, stuffed to the gills, says to the Catalan, "Good, no?" The Catalan replies, "Not bad. But when do we eat?"

Tapas may not be standard fare in Catalunya but Barcelona boasts some of the region's finest "dive bars," called *tascas*. These colorful, historic bars are unlike anything else you'll see in Barcelona. You're most likely to enjoy local crowds from 22:00 until the wee hours. For the most fun and flavorful route through the Gothic Quarter, go to the Plaza de la Merce (Metro: Drassanes), then follow the small street that runs along the right side of the church (Carrer Merce), stopping at whichever *tascas* look fun. Consider these: **La Jarra** is known for its tender *jamón canario* (baked ham) and salty potatoes. **El Corral** makes one of the neighborhood's best *chorizo al diablo* (hell sausage), which you sauté yourself. It's great with the regional specialty *pan con tomate*. Across the street **La Plata** keeps things wonderfully simple, serving extremely cheap plates of sardines and small glasses of keg wine. You can smell **Las Campanas'** fragrant sausage a block away, whew. . . Or try *fuet*, a mini-salami from nearby **Vic**. After a stop at **El Born**, a former *pescaderia* (fish market), have a chat with the parrot at **Bar la Choza del Sopas. Miramelindo** and **Berimbao** are all well worth a stop for their ambience and specialty drinks (*mojitos* and *caiparinas*). At the end of Carrer Merce, **Bar Vendimia** serves up tasty clams and mussels. The street paralleling Carrer Merce, Carrer Ample, has ample additional bar-hopping possibilities in more refined confines.

In the Gothic Quarter, **Cavateca Vinoteca** is a great *cava* bar, bubbling with Spain's sparkling wine (Verdaguer i Callis 10, near the Palau de la Música Catalana, tel. 93/310-0938).

Transportation Connections—Barcelona
By train to: Lisbon (2/day, 20 hrs with change in Madrid), **Madrid** (6/day, 7–9 hrs, $50 with a *couchette*), **Paris** (3/day, 11–15 hrs, $70 night-train reservation required), **Sevilla** (6/day, 9 hrs), **Málaga** (3/day, 14 hrs), **Nice** (1/day, 12 hrs, change in Cerbere). Train info: tel. 93/490-0202.

By bus to: Madrid (6/day, 8 hrs, half the price of a train ticket).

MADRID

Today's Madrid is upbeat and vibrant, enjoying a kind of post-Franco renaissance. You'll feel it. Even the statue-maker beggars have a twinkle in their eyes.

Madrid is the hub of Spain. This modern capital—Europe's highest, at over 2,000 feet—has a population of more than 4 million and is young by European standards. Only 400 years ago, King Philip II decided to move the capital of his empire from Toledo to Madrid. One hundred years ago Madrid had only 400,000 people, so nine-tenths of the city is modern sprawl, surrounding an intact, easy-to-navigate historic center.

Dive headlong into the grandeur and intimate charm of Madrid. The lavish Royal Palace, with its gilded rooms and frescoed ceilings, rivals Versailles. The Prado has Europe's top collection of paintings. The city's huge Retiro Park invites you for a shady siesta and a hopscotch through a mosaic of lovers, families, skateboarders, pets walking their masters, and expert bench-sitters. Make time for Madrid's elegant shops and people-friendly pedestrian zones. Enjoy the shade in an arcade. On Sundays, cheer for the bull at a bullfight or bargain like mad at a mega-flea market. Lively Madrid has enough street singing, barhopping, and people-watching vitality to give any visitor a boost of youth.

Planning Your Time

Madrid's top two sights, the Prado and the palace, are worth a day. If you hit the city on a Sunday, allot another day for the flea market and a bullfight. Ideally, give Madrid two days (outside of Sunday events) and spend them this way:

Day 1: Breakfast of *churros*, as recommended below, before a brisk, good-morning-Madrid walk for 20 minutes from Puerta del Sol to the Prado; 9:00 to noon in the Prado; lunch at La Plaza; take an

afternoon siesta in the Retiro Park or lap up the modern art at Reina Sofia *(Guernica)* and/or the Thyssen-Bornemisza Museum; early evening *paseo*, *tapas* for dinner around Plaza Santa Ana.
Day 2: Breakfast and browse through San Miguel market, tour Royal Palace, lunch near Plaza Mayor; afternoon free for other sights, shopping, or side trip to El Escorial (open until 19:00). Note that the Prado, the T-B Museum, and El Escorial are closed on Monday.

Orientation (tel. code: 91)

The historic center can easily be covered on foot. No major sight is more than a 20-minute walk from the Puerta del Sol, Madrid's central square. Your time will be divided between the city's two major sights—the palace and the Prado—and its barhopping, car-honking, contemporary scene.

The Puerta del Sol is at the dead center of Madrid and of Spain itself; notice the "kilometer zero" marker, from which all of Spain is surveyed, at the police station (southwest corner). The Royal Palace to the west and the Prado Museum and Retiro Park to the east frame Madrid's historic center.

Southwest of Puerta del Sol is a 17th-century district with the slow-down-and-smell-the-cobbles Plaza Mayor and plenty of relics from pre-industrial Spain.

North of Puerta del Sol runs the Gran Vía, and between the two are lively pedestrian shopping streets. The Gran Vía, bubbling with business, expensive shops, and cinemas, leads down to the impressively modern Plaza de España. North of the Gran Vía is the gritty Malasana quarter, with its colorful small houses, shoemakers' shops, sleazy-looking *hombres*, milk vendors, bars, and hip night scene.

Tourist Information

Madrid has four handy Turismos: one on the Plaza Mayor at #3 (open 10:00–20:00, Saturday 10:00–14:00, closed Sunday; tel. 91/366-5477); another near the Prado Museum, across from the front door of the giant Palace Hotel (weekdays 8:00–20:00, Saturday 9:00–13:00, Duque de Medinaceli 2, tel. 91/429-4951); and smaller offices at the Chamartin train station (same hours, tel. 91/315-9976) and at the airport (weekdays 9:00–19:00, Saturday 9:00–13:00, tel. 91/305-8656). Confirm your sightseeing plans and pick up a map and *Enjoy Madrid*, the free monthly city guide. (The TI's free guide to city events, *En Madrid*, is not as good as the easy-to-decipher weekly entertainment guide, *Guía del Ocio*, on sale at streetside newsstands for 125 ptas.) If interested, ask at the TI about bullfights and *Zarzuela* (the local light opera). The free and amazingly informative *Mapa de Comunicaciones España* lists all the Turismos, *paradores*, RENFE train information telephone numbers, and highway SOS numbers, with a road map of Spain.

Madrid

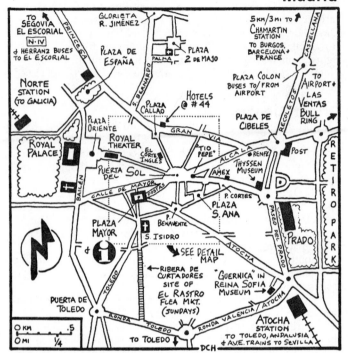

Arrival in Madrid

By Train: The two main rail stations, Atocha and Chamartin, are both on subway lines with easy access to downtown Madrid. Each station has all the services, though there is no TI at Atocha. In Spain, train rides longer than about three hours require reservations, even if you have a Eurailpass. To avoid needless running around, arrange your departure upon arrival.

Chamartin handles most international trains, and Atocha runs AVE trains to Sevilla. Both stations offer *largo recorrido* (long-distance) trains as well as *cercanias* (local trains to nearby destinations). Atocha is more clearly split into two halves (local and long-distance trains) with separate schedules; this is initially confusing if you're in the wrong side of building. Atocha also has two helpful (necessary) customer-service offices called *Atencion al Cliente* (daily 7:00–23:00), one office for each half of the building. The Chamartin station is less confusing. Its customer-service office is called *Atencion al Viajero* (behind the ticket windows, in the middle of the building) and the helpful TI is opposite track 20. Club AVE in Atocha (upstairs) is a lounge reserved solely for AVE ticketholders. Club Intercity in Chamartin is less exclusive—you can get in if you have a first-class railpass or sleeper reservation, or Intercity or Talgo ticket.

Both train stations have Metro stops named after themselves (i.e., Metro: Chamartin). Note that there are two Atocha Metro stops in Madrid. The train station's Metro station is "Atocha RENFE." If you're traveling between Chamartin and Atocha, use the Cercanias trains (free with a railpass); it's far quicker than the subway.

At the downtown RENFE office, you can get train information, reservations, and tickets (Monday–Friday 9:30–20:00, credit cards accepted, best to go in person, 2 blocks north of the Prado museum at Calle Alcala 44, tel. 91/328-9020).

By Bus: Madrid's three key bus stations are all connected by Metro: La Sepulvedana (handles Segovia and Avila, Metro: Principe Pio), the brand-new Estación sur Autobuses (covers Toledo, Metro: Menendez-Alvaro), and Estación Herranz (serves El Escorial, Metro: Moncloa).

By Plane: Madrid's Barajas Airport, 10 miles east of downtown, comes well-equipped to help new arrivals. It has a 24-hour bank with fair rates, an ATM, a TI, a telephone office where you can buy a phone card, a RENFE desk for rail information, a pharmacy, on-the-spot car-rental agencies, and easy public transportation into town. Airport info: tel. 91/305-8343.

Use your phone card to call and confirm your hotel and the price, then take the yellow bus into Madrid (to Plaza Colón, 4/hr, 30 min, 375 ptas). From Plaza Colón, take the subway to your hotel (walk up the stairs and face the blue "URBIS" sign high on a building—the subway stop, M. Serrano, is 50 yards to your right). If you take a taxi (easily available from the airport bus station at Plaza Colon), insist on the meter. For a taxi to or from the airport, allow at least 2,500 ptas. To get a rough idea of the price before you hop in, ask "*¿Cuanto cuesta a Madrid, mas o menos?*" (How much is it to Madrid, more or less?)

Getting Around Madrid

By Subway and Bus: Madrid's subway is simple, cheap (130 ptas/ ride, buy the ten-ride ticket for 660 ptas), and speedy (outside of rush hour you'll go about seven stops in ten minutes). The city's broad streets can be hot and exhausting. A subway trip of even a stop or two can save time and energy. Pick up a free map (*Plano del Metro*) at most stations. Navigate by subway stops (shown on city maps). To transfer, follow signs to the next subway line (numbered and color-coded). End stops are used to indicate directions. Insert your ticket in the turnstile; retrieve it as you pass through. Green *Salida* signs point to the exit.

City buses, while not so easy, can be useful. If interested, get a bus map at the TI or the info booth on Puerta del Sol. Tickets are 130 ptas (buy on bus) or 660 ptas for ten tickets, called a *bonobus* (buy at kiosks or tobacco shops). Bus and Metro tickets aren't interchangeable.

By Taxi: Taxis are reasonable, but you'll go faster and cheaper by subway.

Helpful Hints

The American Express office at Plaza Cortes 2 (Metro: Sevilla) is a handy place to cash any kind of traveler's checks at a decent rate with no commission (Monday–Friday 9:00–17:30, Saturday 9:00–12:00, tel. 91/577-4000). They also sell AVE train tickets, but can't help you with AVE reservations if you have a train pass. The U.S. Embassy is at Serrano 75 (tel. 91/577-4000) and the Canadian Embassy is at Nuñez de Balboa 35 (tel. 91/431-4300). The grand department store, El Corte Inglés (Monday–Saturday 10:00–21:30, just off Puerta del Sol) has a travel agency and gives free Madrid maps (at the information desk, just inside the door at northwest intersection of Preciados and Tetuan). The telephone office, centrally located at Gran Vía 30, has metered phones and accepts credit cards for charges over 500 ptas (daily 10:00–23:00).

Theft Alert: Be wary of pickpockets, anywhere, anytime, but particularly on Puerta del Sol (main square), the subway, and crowded streets. On my last trip, half the American couples I met had experienced a pickpocket attempt. Wear your money belt. In crowds, keep your daybag in front of you. Some thieves "accidentally" spill ketchup on your clothes, then pick your pocket as they help you clean up. Fortunately, violent crime against tourists is very rare.

Museum Pass: If you plan to visit the Prado, Reina Sofia, and Thyssen-Bornemisza museums, buy the Paseo del Arte pass (1,050 ptas, available at all three museums and valid for one year). Remember, the Prado and Reina Sofia are free Saturday afternoon and Sunday.

Monday Plans: If you're in Madrid on a Monday (when most museums are closed), you can see Picasso's *Guernica* (Centro Reina Sofia), rent a boat at Retiro Park, tour the nearby botanical gardens, visit the Royal Palace, shop, or café-hop.

Sights—Madrid

▲▲▲**Prado Museum**—The Prado is my favorite collection of paintings anywhere. With more than 3,000 canvases, including entire rooms of masterpieces by Velázquez, Goya, El Greco, and Bosch, it's overwhelming. Take a tour or buy a guidebook (or bring me along by ripping out and packing the Prado chapter from *Mona Winks*). Focus on the Flemish and northern (Bosch, Dürer, Rubens), the Italian (Fra Angelico, Raphael, Botticelli, Titian), and the Spanish art (El Greco, Velázquez, Goya).

Follow Goya through his cheery (*The Parasol*), political (*The Third of May*), and dark (*Saturn Devouring His Children*) stages. In each stage, Goya asserted his independence from artistic conventions. Even the standard court portraits from his "first" stage reflect his politically liberal viewpoint, subtly showing the vanity and stupidity of his subjects by the looks in their goony eyes. His political stage, with paintings like *The Third of May*, depicting a massacre of Spaniards by Napoleon's troops, makes him one of the first artists with a social conscience. Finally, in his gloomy "dark stage," Goya probed the inner world of fears and nightmares, anticipating the 20th-century preoccupation with dreams. Also don't miss Bosch's *The Garden of Earthly Delights*. Most art is grouped by painters, and any guard can point you in the right direction if you say "*¿Dónde está . . . ?*" and the painter's name as Españoled as you can (e.g., Titian is "*Ticiano*" and Bosch is "*El Bosco*"). The Prado is quietest at lunchtime from 14:00–16:00 (500 ptas, free Saturday after 14:30 and Sunday; Tuesday–Saturday 9:00–19:00, Sunday 9:00–14:00, closed Monday; Paseo de Prado, Metro: Banco de España or Atocha—each a 20-minute walk from the museum, tel. 91/420-2836).

▲▲**Centro Reina Sofia**—This exceptional modern art museum is most famous for Picasso's *Guernica*, a massive painting showing the horror of modern war. It deserves much study. Franco's death ended the work's exile in America, and now it reigns as Spain's national piece of art. The museum also houses an easy-to-enjoy collection of other modern artists whom Picasso influenced so much, from Dalí to Miró (500 ptas, free Saturday after 14:30 and Sunday; open 10:00–21:00, Sunday 10:00–14:30, closed Tuesday; Santa Isabel 52, Metro: Atocha, across from the Atocha train station, look for the exterior glass elevators, tel. 91/467-5062).

▲▲**Thyssen-Bornemisza Museum**—This stunning new museum displays the impressive collection of Baron Thyssen, a wealthy German married to a former Miss Spain. Art-lovers appreciate how the good baron's art complements the Prado's collection. For a fine walk through art history, start on the top floor and do the rooms in numerical order. While it's basically minor works by major artists and major works by minor artists (the real big guns are over at the Prado), the Thyssen is stronger in Impressionism and 20th-century art. Located across from the Prado at Paseo del Prado 8 in the Palacio de Villahermosa (600 ptas, 10:00–19:00, closed Monday, Metro: Banco de España or Atocha, tel. 91/369-0151).

▲▲**Plaza Mayor and Medieval Madrid**—The Plaza Mayor, a vast, cobbled, traffic-free chunk of 17th-century Spain, is just a short walk from the Puerta del Sol. Each side of the square is uniform, as if a grand palace were turned inside out. Throughout Spain, lesser *plazas mayores* provide peaceful pools for the river of Spanish life. A stamp-and-coin market bustles here on Sundays from 10:00 to 14:00, and on any day it's a colorful and affordable place to enjoy a cup of coffee. The TI is at #3.

Medieval Madrid is now a rather sterile tangle of narrow

Heart of Madrid

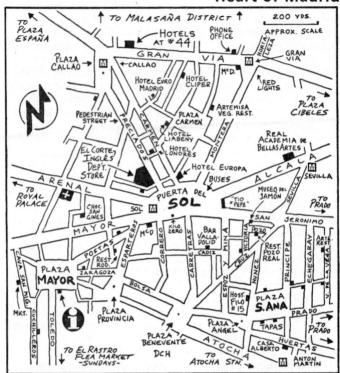

streets bounded by the Royal Palace, Plaza Mayor, Teatro Real, and Plaza Puerta de Moros. The uninviting old Plaza de la Villa was the center of Madrid before Madrid was the center of Spain. The most enjoyable action in this area is contained in a glass-and-iron cage called the Mercado de San Miguel (produce market, closed Sunday) next to the Plaza Mayor. Drop by for the morning flurry and pull up a stool for breakfast (Metro: Opera).

▲▲▲Royal Palace *(Palacio Real)*—Europe's third-greatest palace (after Versailles and Vienna) is packed with tourists and royal antiques. You can wander on your own through its clock-filled, lavish interior, or join a free English tour. Tours start whenever a group of ten to 20 gathers; if you just missed one, try to catch up with it (950 ptas admission, Monday–Saturday 9:30–18:00, Sunday 9:00–15:00, closes one hour earlier in winter, very crowded in summer, arrive early or late, Metro: Opera, tel. 91/542-0059). The Palace is free on Wednesday. Your ticket includes the impressive armory and the pharmacy, both on the courtyard. The nearby

Museo de Carruajes Reales, with its excellent collection of royal carriages, should reopen in 1998 after extensive renovation; confirm at the TI or Palace. The adjacent, newly consecrated **Catedral de la Almudena** is refreshingly clean, modern, and utilitarian (free, Monday–Saturday 10:00–13:00 and 18:00–20:00, Sunday 10:00–14:00).

▲▲**Zarzuela**—For a delightful look at Spanish light opera that even English-speakers can enjoy, try an evening of Zarzuela. Guitar-strumming Napoleons in red capes, buxom women with masks and fans, castanets and stomping feet, aficionados singing along from the cheap seats where the acoustics are best, Spanish-speaking pharaohs, melodramatic spotlights, the people's opera—that's Zarzuela. The TI's monthly guide has a special Zarzuela listing.

▲▲**El Rastro**—Europe's biggest flea market is a field day for shoppers, people-watchers, and thieves (Sundays and holidays 9:00–15:00, best before 12:00). Thousands of stalls titillate more than a million browsers. If you brake for garage sales, you'll pull a U-turn for El Rastro—you can buy or sell nearly anything here. Start at the Plaza Mayor and head south, or take the subway to Tirso de Molina. Hang on to your wallet. Munch on a *relleno* or *pepito* (meat-filled pastry). Europe's biggest stamp market thrives simultaneously on the Plaza Mayor.

Chapel San Antonio de la Florida—Goya's tomb stares up at a splendid cupola filled with his own frescoes (free, Tuesday–Friday 10:00–14:00 and 16:00–20:00, weekends 10:00–14:00, closed Monday; Paseo de la Florida 5, Metro: Principe Pio, tel. 91/547-0722).

▲▲**Retiro Park**—Siesta in this 350-acre green and breezy escape from the city. These peaceful gardens offer great picnicking and people-watching. Walk to the big lake (El Estanque) where you can rent a rowboat (450 ptas for 45 min), or wander through the Palacio de Crystal. A grand boulevard of statues leads to the Prado. The Botanical Garden (*Jardín Botánico*) nearby is a pleasant extension of Retiro Park to the southwest (250 ptas, daily 10:00–sunset, Plaza de Murillo 2, Metro: Atocha or Retiro).

▲▲▲**Bullfight**—Madrid's Plaza de Toros hosts Spain's top bullfights on most Sundays and holidays from Easter through October and nearly every day mid-May through early June. Top fights sell out in advance. Fights usually start punctually at 19:00. Tickets range from 1,000 to 6,000 ptas. There are no bad seats; paying more gets you in the shade and/or closer to the gore (*filas* 8, 9, and 10 tend to be closest to the action). Booking offices add 20 percent and don't sell the cheap seats (Calle de la Victoria 3, tel. 91/521-1213, or Plaça del Carmen 1, tel. 91/531-2732). To save money, buy your ticket at the bullring. Tickets go on sale the day of the fight at 10:00; 10 percent of the seats are kept available to be sold two hours before the fight (Calle

Alcala 231, Metro: Ventas, tel. 91/356-2200). The **bullfighting museum** (*Museo Taurino*) is next to the bullring (250 ptas, Monday–Friday 9:30–14:30, Calle Alcala 237, tel. 91/725-1857).

▲**Royal Tapestry Factory** (*Real Fabrica de Tapices*)—Have a look at the traditional making of tapestries (250 ptas, Monday–Friday 9:00–12:30, closed August, cheap tours in Spanish only, Calle Fuenterrabia 2, Metro: Menendez Pelayo, tel. 91/551-3400).

▲*Paseo*—The people of Madrid (Madrileños) take afternoon siestas because so much goes on in the evenings. The nightly *paseo* is Madrid on parade. Young and old, everyone's outside taking a stroll, "cruising" without cars, seeing and being seen. Gran Vía, Calle de Preciados, and the Paseo del Prado are particularly active scenes.

Parque de Atracciones—For a colorful amusement-park scene, complete with Venetian canals, dancing, eating, games, free shows, and top-notch people-watching, try Parque de Atracciones (open most afternoons and evenings from noon until around midnight, only Saturday and Sunday in off-season, Metro: Batan, tel. 91/ 463-2900 for exact times). This fair and Spain's best zoo (daily 10:00–20:30, dolphin shows, tel. 91/711-9950) are in the vast Casa de Campo Park just west of the Royal Palace.

Shopping—Shoppers can focus on the colorful pedestrian area between Gran Vía and Puerta del Sol. The giant Spanish department store El Corte Inglés, is a block off Puerta del Sol and a handy place to pick up just about anything you may need (Monday– Saturday 10:00–21:00, closed Sunday, free maps at info desk, supermarket in basement).

Sleeping in Madrid
(140 ptas = about $1, tel. code: 91)
Sleep Code: **S**=Single, **D**=Double/Twin, **T**=Triple, **Q**=Quad, **b**=bathroom, **t**=toilet only, **s**=shower only, **CC**=Credit Card (**V**isa, **M**asterCard, **A**mex), **SE**=Speaks English, **NSE**=No English. Breakfast is not included unless noted. In Madrid, the 7 percent IVA tax is generally, but not always, included in the price.

Madrid has plenty of centrally located budget hotels and *pensiónes*. You'll have no trouble finding a decent double for $30 to $60. The city is most crowded in July and August, but prices are the same throughout the year and it's almost always easy to find a place. The accommodations I've listed are all within a few minutes' walk of Puerta del Sol. Competition is stiff. Those on a budget can bargain. Nighttime Madrid's economy is brisk. Even decent areas are littered with shady-looking people after dark. Just don't invite them in.

Sleeping in the Pedestrian Zone between Puerta del Sol and Gran Vía
(zip code: 28013)
Predictable and away from the seediness, these are good values for

those wanting to spend a little more. Especially for these hotels, call first to see if the price is firm. Their formal prices may be inflated and some offer weekend deals. Use Metro: Sol for these five hotels.

Hotel Europa has red-carpet charm: a quiet courtyard, a royal salon, plush halls, polished wood floors, and squeaky-clean rooms with balconies overlooking the pedestrian zone or an inner courtyard. All rooms have TVs (CNN) and big, modern bathrooms (Sb-6,100 ptas, Db-8,200 ptas, Tb-11,100 ptas, elevator, easy phone reservations with no deposit, CC:VM, Calle del Carmen 4, tel. 91/521-2900, fax 91/521-4696, very helpful staff SE). They have a 1,400-ptas-a-day parking deal and plan on having air-conditioning by 1998. Have breakfast next door at Kenia cafeteria.

Hotel Londres is a business-class hotel: dark, stark, air-conditioned, and a little smoky (Db-9,000 ptas, renovated Db-10,500 ptas, CC:VM, elevator, don't trust their safes; Galdo 2, tel. 91/531-4105, fax 91/531-4101, some English spoken). **Hotel Euromadrid** is dull, with a concrete character rather than charm. It's all air-conditioned, with private bathrooms, TVs, and an elevator (Sb-6,500 ptas, Db-8,500 ptas, Tb-9,600 ptas, buffet breakfast included, CC:VMA, Mesonero Romanos 7, tel. 91/521-7200, fax 91/521-4582, SE). Nearby, the **Hotel Cliper** is faded-elegant, with a better combination of friendliness and character and comfortable rooms on a fairly quiet street (Sb-5,200 ptas, Db-8,000 ptas, includes breakfast, some rooms with air-con, CC:VMA, Chincilla 6, near Plaza Carmen, tel. 91/531-1700, fax 91/531-1707, SE).

The huge **Hotel Liabeny** feels classy and new, with spacious rooms and all the comforts (Sb-13,500 ptas, Db-19,000 ptas, plus 7 percent IVA tax, air-con, parking and buffet breakfast each 1,500 ptas/day, attached restaurant and bar, CC:VMA, off Plaza Carmen at Salud 3, tel. 91/531-9000, fax 91/532-7421, SE, Web site: www.apunte.es/liabeny, e-mail: liabeny@apunte.es).

Sleeping at Gran Vía #44
(zip code: 28013)

The pulse (and noise) of today's Madrid is best felt along the Gran Vía. This main drag in the heart of the city stays awake all night. Despite the dreary pile of prostitutes just a block north, there's a certain urban decency about it. My choices (all at Gran Vía #44, entrance between the Lladro shop and the Lotería) are across from Plaza del Callão, a colorful 4 blocks of pedestrian malls up from the Puerta del Sol. Although many rooms are high above the traffic noise, I'd request *tranquilo* for a brick-wall view on the back side. The Café & Te next door provides a classy way to breakfast. The Callão Metro stop is at your doorstep, and the handy Gran Vía stop (direct to Atocha) is 2 blocks away. The first two listings are especially popular; call well in advance to reserve.

Hostal Residencia Valencia is bright, cheery, and professional. The friendly manager, Antonio Ramirez, speaks English (Sb-4,000 ptas, big Sb-4,500 ptas, Ds-5,300 ptas, Db-5,800 ptas, CC:VM, fifth floor, tel. 91/522-1115, fax 91/522-1113). Also a good value but a bit smoky and with less character is friendly **Hostal Residencia Continental** (Sb-3,600 ptas, Db-5,000 ptas, CC:VMA, fourth floor, tel. 91/521-4640, fax 91/521-4649, SE).

Hostal Residencia Miami is clean and quiet, with lovely, well-lit rooms, padded doors, and plastic-flower decor throughout. It's like staying at your eccentric aunt's in Miami Beach. The bubbly landlady, Sra. Sanz, and her too-careful husband, who dresses up each day for work here, speak no English (S-2,500–3,000 ptas, D-3,500 ptas, Db-4,500 ptas, closed August—if they take reservations in August, they are booking you elsewhere, eighth floor, tel. 91/521-1464).

Across the hall, **Hostal Alibel**, like Miami with less sugar, rents eight big, airy, quiet rooms (D-3,500 ptas, Ds-4,200 ptas, Db-4,500 ptas, tel. 91/521-0051, NSE). Downstairs, **Hostal Josefina** has creaky vinyl floors and junkyard doors but strong beds in museum-warehouse rooms and a pleasant owner (S-2,700 ptas, Sb-3,000 ptas, Ds-4,000 ptas, Ts-6,000 ptas, seventh floor, tel. 91/521-8131 and 91/531-0466, NSE).

Sleeping on or near Plaza Santa Ana
(zip code: 28012)

The Plaza Santa Ana area has plenty of small, cheap places. While well-worn and noisy at night, it has an almost Parisian ambience, with colorful bars and very central location (three minutes from Puerta del Sol's "Tío Pepe" sign; walk down Calle San Jeronimo and turn right on Principe). At most of these hotels, fluent Spanish is spoken, toilets and showers are usually down the hall, and there's no heat during winter. Metro: Sol.

In the beautifully tiled Plaza Santa Ana 15 building, on the corner of the square closest to Puerta del Sol and all the good *tapas* bars, and up a dark wooden staircase (flick on the light) are three of my favorites: **Hostal la Rosa**, on the third floor, has pleasant rooms and shiny wood floors. If you can stay on her good side, Encarnita is a kick. She speaks no English (and is sure you speak Spanish). For 900 ptas you can use her washing machine (S-1,800 ptas, Ss-2,000 ptas, small D-2,800 ptas, D/double bed-3,000 ptas, D/twins-3,400 ptas, Ds-4,400 ptas, T-4,000 ptas, Ts-5,200 ptas, Qs-6,000 ptas, Quint/s-7,000 ptas, tel. 91/532-5805). **Hostal Filo** is squeaky clean with a nervous but helpful management and 20 rooms hiding in a confusing floor plan (S-2,000 ptas, Ss-3,000 ptas, D-3,500 ptas, Ds-4,500 ptas, T-4,500 ptas, Ts-5,000 ptas, closed in August, second floor, tel. 91/522-4056). **Hostal Delvi** is simple, clean, and friendly (S-1,800 ptas, D-2,500 ptas, Ds-3,500 ptas, Ts-4,500 ptas, third floor, tel. 91/522-5998, Marie NSE). Marie promises these discounted prices to those with this book.

The cheapest beds are across the street at **Hostal Lucense** (S-1,500 ptas, D-2,300 ptas, Ds-3,000 ptas, T-3,500 ptas, 200 ptas per shower, Nuñez de Arce 15, tel. 91/522-4888, run by Sr. and Sra. Muñoz, both interesting characters, Sr. SE) and **Casa Huéspedes Poza** (same prices and owners, Nuñez de Arce 9, tel. 91/222-4871). Hopeless romantics might enjoy playing corkscrew up the rickety cut-glass elevator to the very simple yet homey **Pensión La Valenciana**'s old and funky rooms, with springy beds. All rooms have balconies, three of them overlooking the square (S-1,500 ptas, D-3,500 ptas, Principe 27, fourth floor, right on Plaza Santa Ana next to the theater with flags, tel. 91/429-6317, NSE). Because of these three places, I list no Madrid youth hostels.

Hostal R. Veracruz II, 2 blocks north of Puerta del Sol, is a tranquil oasis with spotless, well-maintained rooms (Sb-3,500 ptas, Db-4,900 ptas, Tb-6,600 ptas, elevator, air-con, CC:VM, Victoria 1, third floor, 28012 Madrid, tel. 91/522-7635, fax 91/522-6749, NSE).

Splurges: To be on the same square and spend in a day what others spend in a week, luxuriate in **Hotel Reina Victoria** (Sb-20,500 ptas, Db-27,000 ptas, includes breakfast, CC:VM, Plaza Santa Ana 14, tel. 91/531-4500, fax 91/522-0307, SE). For a royal, air-conditioned breather and some cheap entertainment, spit out your gum, step into its lobby, grab a sofa, and watch the bellboys push the beggars back out of the revolving doors. **Suite Prado**, 2 blocks south of Plaza Santa Ana, is expensive but a better value, offering attractive, air-conditioned suites with a homier feel (Sb/suite-16,000 ptas, Db/suite-20,000 ptas, cheaper off-season, suites have fridges and comfy sitting rooms, CC:VMA, Manuel Fernandez y Gonzalez 10, at the intersection with Venture de la Vega, 28014 Madrid, tel. 91/420-2318, fax 91/420-0559, SE).

Sleeping Elsewhere in Central Madrid

Just off the Plaza Mayor, **Hostal Montalvo** is sprawling, family-run, comfortable, and just east of the elegant Plaza Mayor on a quiet, traffic-free street (S-2,700 ptas, Sb-3,700 ptas, D-4,000 ptas, Db-5,000 ptas, Tb-7,300 ptas, elevator, CC:VM, Zaragoza 6, 28012 Madrid, third floor, Metro: Opera, tel. 91/365-5910, some English spoken).

Halfway between the Prado Museum and the Plaza Santa Ana in a quiet, stately neighborhood lie two gems and one suitable hotel, all in the same building with an elevator. At #34 Cervantes (28014 Madrid, Metro: Anton Martin), you'll find the spotless, friendly and comfortable **Hotel Cervantes** (Sb-4,500 ptas, Db-6,000 ptas, CC:VM, third floor, tel. 91/429-2745, NSE), and the equally polished and friendly **Hotel Gonzalo** (Sb-3,800 ptas, Db-5,000 ptas, second floor, tel. 91/429-2714, CC:VM, NSE). The **Hotel**

Cobrero is less welcoming, but clean and perfectly sleepable (Sb-3,700, Db-4,700, first floor, tel. 91/429-4171, NSE).

Eating in Madrid
In Spain only Barcelona rivals Madrid for taste-bud thrills. You have two basic dining choices: an atmospheric sit-down meal in a well-chosen restaurant, or a meal of *tapas* (appetizers) in a bar or (more likely) in several bars. Many restaurants are closed in August.

Eating in the Pedestrian Zone between Puerta del Sol and Gran Vía
Restaurante Puerto Rico has fine food, good prices, and few tourists. Try it now before the menu has English translations (13:00–16:30 and 20:30–24:00, closed Sunday, Chinchilla 2, off Gran Vía on same street as Hotel Cliper, tel. 91/532-2040). Carnivores will devour the grilled meats at **El Gaucho** (Tetuan 34) while vegetarians will prefer the fare and rare non-smoking ambience at **Artemisa II** at Tres Cruces 4, just off Plaza Carmen (closed Sunday night, CC:VMA, tel. 91/521-8721).

Eating between the Puerta del Sol and Plaza Santa Ana
For an inexpensive, local-style dinner within 2 blocks of the Puerta del Sol, consider **Restaurante Pozo Real**. It's friendly and popular with locals, with quiet tables in the back (daily 9:00–24:30, Calle del Pozo 6, tel. 91/521-7951). Madrid's best pastry shop is next door (closed Monday). The vegetarian **Artemesia I** offers tasty meals in smoke-free comfort (daily 13:30–16:00 and 21:00–midnight, non-veggie options available, CC:VMA, Via de la Vega 4 off San Jeronimo, tel. 91/429-5092).

    Tapas: For maximum fun, people, and atmosphere, go mobile and do the *"tapa* tango"—a local tradition of going from one bar to the next, munching, drinking, and socializing. *Tapas* are toothpick appetizers, salads, and deep-fried foods served in most bars. Madrid is Spain's *tapa* capital. Grab a toothpick and stab something strange—but establish the prices first. Some items are very pricey, and most bars offer larger *raciónes* rather than smaller *tapas*. *Un pincho* is a bite-sized serving (not always available), *una tapa* is a bit more, and *una ración* is half a meal. Say *"un bocadillo"* and it comes on bread as a sandwich. *Caña* is a glass of draft beer.

    Prowl the area between Puerta del Sol and Plaza Santa Ana. There's no ideal route, but the little streets (in this book's map) between Puerta del Sol, San Jeronimo, and Plaza Santa Ana hold tasty surprises. From Puerta del Sol, head east to Carrera de San Jeronimo 6 for your first stop: the **Museo del Jamón** (Museum of Ham)—tastefully decorated, unless you're a pig. This frenetic, cheap, stand-up bar is an assembly line of fast and deliciously simple *bocadillos* and *raciónes*. Options are shown in photographs with prices. Just point and eat (daily 9:00–24:00, sit-down restaurant upstairs). Shrimp-lovers, head up the street to tiny **La Casa del Abuelo**, at Victoria 12, where sizzling, expensive little *gambas* go down great with the house wine (daily 11:00–15:30 and 18:00–23:30). Fan out from there, walking each little street within 100 yards. On outdoor restaurant row, the **La Ria** *tapas* bar (Pasaje Matheu 5), has cheap plates of ten mussels—toss the shells on the floor as you smack your lips. Follow Nuñez de Arce up to Plaza Santa Ana, where (on the far side) several upscale *cervecerías*, relaxing and comfortable spots for *tapas*, spill onto the sidewalk. The more civil **Casa Alberto**, a block south of Plaza Santa Ana at the end of Calle Principe, is a classy, tasty *tapas* bar (11:00–1:00, closed Sunday evening and all day Monday, Huertas 18); it's hard to stop at just one *canape de salmon ahumado* (smoked salmon appetizer). The popular dining room in the back has a different, pricier menu (lunch starts at 13:30, dinner at 21:00).

Plaza Santa Ana offers a great late-night scene. Just off the plaza, a tiny alley called Manuel Fernandez y Gonzalez offers plenty of distractions. Try the tiled **Los Gabrieles, Viva Madrid,** or **La Toscana.** As the night progresses, head over to Calle Huertas for more proof that this city never sleeps. Beware the potent concoctions at **La Lupe**.

Eating near the Plaza Mayor

At **Restaurante Rodriguez**, the food's not fancy but hearty (San Cristobal 15, 1 block toward Puerta del Sol from Plaza Mayor, tel. 91/231-1136). Many Americans are drawn to Hemingway's favorite, **Sobrino del Botín** (daily 13:00–16:00 and 20:00–24:00, Cuchilleros 17 near Plaza Mayor, tel. 91/366-4217). Touristy and pricey, it's the last place he'd go now. Those in need of a dirt-cheap but tasty *bocadillo* line up at the **Casa Rua** on Plaza Mayor's southwest corner. Picnic shoppers forage at the San Miguel market (below).

Fast-Food, Picnics, and Breakfast

Fast-Food: For an easy, light, cheap meal, try **Rodilla**, on the northeast corner of Puerta del Sol at #13 (daily 8:30–20:30). **Pans & Company**, a chain with shops throughout Madrid, offers healthy, tasty sandwiches. Skip the soppy salads (daily 9:00–24:00, Plaza Callão 3, Gran Vía 30, and many more).

Picnics: The department store **El Corte Inglés** has a well-stocked deli, but its produce is sold only in large quantities (10:00–21:00, closed Sunday). A perfect place to assemble a cheap picnic is downtown Madrid's neighborhood market, **Mercado de San Miguel** (9:00–14:00 and 16:00–19:00, closed Saturday afternoon and Sunday; from the Plaza Mayor, face the colorful building and exit from the upper left-hand corner). How about breakfast surrounded by early morning shoppers in the market's café? Get a couple of oranges to go.

Churros con chocolate **for breakfast:** If you like hash browns and eggs in American greasy-spoon joints, you must try the Spanish equivalent: greasy, cigar-shaped fritters dipped in pudding-like chocolate at **Bar Valladolid** (open daily from 7:00, Sunday from 8:00, 2 blocks off the Tío Pepe end of Puerta del Sol, south on Espoz y Mina, turn right on Calle de Cadiz). It's the changing of the guard, as workers of the night finish their day by downing a cognac, and workers of the day start theirs by dipping *churros* into chocolate. (One serving is often plenty for two.) With luck, the *churros* machine in the back will be cooking. Throw your napkin on the floor like you own the place. For something with less grease and more substance, ask for a *tortilla española* (potato omelet), *zumo de naranja* (orange juice), and *café con leche*.

The classier **Chocolatería San Ginés** is another Madrid magnet for *churros* and chocolate (Pasadizo de San Ginés 5, off Calle Arenal near Disco "Joy," tel. 93/365-6546).

Transportation Connections—Madrid

By train to: Toledo (9/day, 75 min, from Madrid Atocha), **Segovia** (9/day, 2 hrs, from Chamartin and 6/day from Atocha), **Ávila** (10/day, 1 hr, from Chamartin and Atocha), **Salamanca** (3/day, 3 hrs, from Chamartin), **Barcelona** (5/day, 8 hrs, from Chamartin and Atocha), **Granada** (3/day including an overnight, 6–9 hrs, from Chamartin and Atocha), **Sevilla** (12/day, 9 hrs, or 3 hrs by AVE, from Atocha), **Córdoba** (11 AVE trains/day, 2 hrs, from Chamartin and Atocha), **Lisbon** (2/day, 8–10 hrs, including an overnight, from Chamartin), **Paris** (5/day, 12–16 hrs, two direct overnights, from Chamartin). Train information: tel. 91/328-9020.

GIMMELWALD
AND THE BERNER
OBERLAND

Frolic and hike high above the stress and clouds of the real world.
Take a vacation from your busy vacation. Recharge your touristic
batteries up here in the Alps, where distant avalanches, cowbells,
the fluff of a down comforter, and the crunchy footsteps of happy
hikers are the dominant sounds. If the weather's good (and your
budget's healthy), ride a gondola from the traffic-free village of
Gimmelwald to a hearty breakfast at Schilthorn's 10,000-foot
revolving Piz Gloria restaurant. Linger among Alpine whitecaps
before riding, hiking, or hang gliding down (5,000 feet) to Mürren
and home to Gimmelwald. Your gateway to the wonderfully
mountainous Berner Oberland is the grand old resort town of
Interlaken. Near Interlaken is Switzerland's open-air folk museum,
Ballenberg, where you climb through traditional houses from
every corner of this diverse country.

Ah, but the weather's fine and the Alps beckon. Head deep
into the heart of the Alps and ride the gondola to the stop just this
side of heaven—Gimmelwald.

Planning Your Time

Rather than tackling a checklist of famous Swiss mountains and
resorts, choose one region to savor—the Berner Oberland. Interlaken is the administrative headquarters (fine transportation hub,
banking, post office, laundry, shopping). Use it for business and as
a springboard for Alpine thrills. With decent weather, explore the
two areas (south of Interlaken) which tower above either side of
the Lauterbrunnen Valley: Kleine Scheidegg/Jungfrau and
Schilthorn/Mürren. Ideally, home-base three nights in the village
of Gimmelwald and spend a day in each area. On a speedy train
trip, you can overnight into and out of Interlaken. For the fastest
look, consider a night in Gimmelwald, breakfast at the Schilthorn,
an afternoon doing the Männlichen-to-Wengen hike, and an
evening or night train out. For a nature lover not to spend the
night high in the Alps is Alpus-interruptus.

Getting Around the Berner Oberland

For more than 100 years, this has been the target of nature-worshiping pilgrims. And the Swiss have made the most exciting Alpine perches accessible by lift or train. Part of the fun (and most of the expense) of the area is riding the many lifts. Generally scenic trains and lifts are not covered on train passes (but a Eurail or Europass gets you a 25 percent discount on even the highest lifts). Ask about discounts for earlybirds, youths, seniors, groups, and those staying awhile. A Family Card gives traveling families enough of a discount to pay for itself on the first hour of trains and lifts; children under age 16 travel free with parents, age 16 to 23 pay half-price (20 SF at any Swiss train station but not gondola stations). Get a list of discounts and the free fare and time schedule at any train station or in Interlaken. Study the "Alpine Lifts in the Berner Oberland" chart in this chapter. Lifts generally go at least twice an hour, from about 7:00 to about 20:00.

INTERLAKEN

When the 19th-century Romantics redefined mountains as something more than cold and troublesome obstacles, Interlaken became the original Alpine resort. Ever since then, tourists have flocked to the Alps "because they're there." Interlaken's glory days are long gone, its elegant old hotels eclipsed by the new, more jet-setty Alpine resorts. Today its shops are filled with chocolate bars, Swiss Army knives, and sunburned backpackers.

Orientation (tel. code: 033)

Efficient Interlaken is a good administrative and shopping center. Take care of business, give the town a quick look, view the live TV coverage of the Jungfrau and Schilthorn weather in the window of the Schilthornbahn office on the main street (at Höheweg 2), and head for the hills. Stay in Interlaken only if you suffer from alptitude sickness (see Sleeping, below).

　　Tourist Information: The TI has good information for the whole region, advice on Alpine lift discounts, and a room-finding service (July–September Monday–Friday 8:00–12:00 and 13:30–18:30, Saturday 8:00–17:00, Sunday 17:00–19:00; off-season weekdays 8:00–12:00 and 14:00–18:00, Saturday 8:00–12:00, closed Sunday; tel. 033/822-2121). It's on the main street, a five-minute walk from the West station. While the Jungfrau region map costs 2 SF, a perfectly good mini-version of it is in the free Jungfrau region train timetable. Pick up a Bern map if that's your next destination.

　　Arrival in Interlaken: Interlaken has two train stations. Most major trains stop at the Interlaken-West station. The station's train information desk will also answer tourist questions and has an exchange desk with fair rates (daily 8:00–12:00 and 14:00–18:00). Ask at the station about discount passes, special

Interlaken

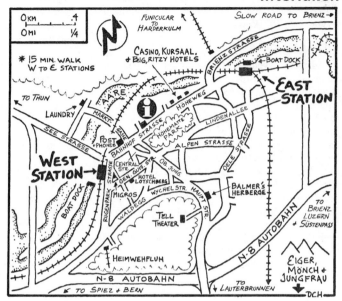

fares, Eurail discounts, and schedules for the scenic mountain trains (tel. 033/826-4750). An open-late Migros supermarket is across the street with a self-service cafeteria upstairs (Monday–Thursday 8:00–18:30, Friday 8:00–21:00, Saturday 7:30–16:00, closed Sunday).

It's a pleasant 15-minute walk between the West and East stations, or an easy, frequent train connection. From the Interlaken-East station, private trains take you deep into the mountainous Jungfrau region (see Transportation Connections, below).

Helpful Hints

Telephone: Phone booths cluster outside the post office in the center of town. Inside the office, you'll find metered phone booths (talk first, pay later; Monday–Friday 7:45–18:15, Saturday 8:30–11:00, closed Sunday).

Laundry: Helen Schmocker's Wascherei Laundry has a change machine, soap, English instructions, and a pleasant riverside place in which to hang out (daily 7:00–22:00 for self-service, 11 SF to wash and dry 10 pounds; Monday–Saturday 8:00–12:00 and 13:30–18:00 for full service: Drop off 10 pounds and 12 SF in the morning and pick up clean clothes that afternoon; from the post office, follow Marktgasse over two bridges to Beatenbergstrasse, tel. 033/822-1566).

Activities: For the adventurer with money, Alpin Raft offers high-adrenalin trips such as rafting, canyoning (rapeling down watery gorges), bungee jumping, and paragliding (Postfach 78, tel. 033/823-4100, Web site: www.alpinraft.ch).

GIMMELWALD

Saved from developers by its "avalanche zone" classification, Gimmelwald is one of the poorest places in Switzerland. Its economy is stuck in the hay, and its farmers, unable to make it in their disadvantaged trade, are subsidized by the Swiss government (and work the ski lifts in the winter). For some travelers, there's little to see in the village. Others enjoy a fascinating day sitting on a bench and learning why they say, "If heaven isn't what it's cracked up to be, send me back to Gimmelwald."

Take a walk through the town. This place is for real. Most of the 130 residents have the same last name. They are tough and proud. Raising hay in this rugged terrain is labor-intensive. One family harvests enough to feed only 15 or 20 cows. But they'd have it no other way and, unlike absentee landlord Mürren, Gimmelwald is locally owned. (When word got out that urban planners wished to develop Gimmelwald into a town of 1,000, locals pulled some strings to secure the town's bogus "avalanche zone" building code.)

Notice the traditional log-cabin architecture and blond-braided children. The numbers on the buildings are not addresses, but fire insurance numbers. The cute little hut near the station is for storing and aging cheese, not youth hostelers. In Catholic-Swiss towns, the biggest building is the church. In Protestant towns, it's the school. Protestant Gimmelwald's biggest building is the schoolhouse (one teacher, 17 students, and a room that doubles as a chapel when the pastor makes his once-a-month visit). Do not confuse obscure Gimmelwald with touristy and commercialized Grindelwald just over the Kleine Scheidegg ridge.

Evening fun in Gimmelwald is found at the youth hostel (lots of young Alp-aholics and a good chance to share information on the surrounding mountains) and up at Walter's Hotel Mittaghorn (see Sleeping, below).

Walter's bar is a local farmer's hangout. When they've made their hay, they come here to play. They look like what we'd call "hicks" (former city-slicker Walter still isn't fully accepted by the gang), but they speak some English and can be fun to get to know. For less smoke and some powerful solitude, sit outside (benches just below the rails, 100 yards down the lane from Walter's) and watch the sun tuck the mountaintops into bed as the moon rises over the Jungfrau.

Alpine Hikes

There are days of possible hikes from Gimmelwald. Many are a fun combination of trails, mountain trains, and gondola rides.

Lauterbrunnen Valley: West Side Story

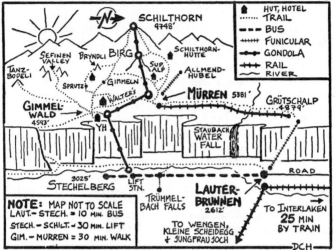

Don't mind the fences, cross at will; a hiker has the right of way in Switzerland. But as late as May, snow can curtail your hiking plans.

▲▲▲**Hike 1: The Schilthorn: Hikes, Lifts, and a 10,000-foot Breakfast**—If the weather's good, have breakfast atop the Schilthorn, in the slowly revolving, mountain-capping restaurant (of James Bond movie fame). The early-bird-special gondola tickets (rides before 9:00) take you from Gimmelwald to the Schilthorn and back at a discount. Nag the Schilthorn station in Mürren for a gondola souvenir decal (Schilthorn info: tel. 033/231-444).

Breakfast costs from 13.50 SF to 22 SF. Expect slow service and ask for more hot drinks if necessary. If you're not revolving, ask them to turn it on. Linger on top. Piz Gloria has a souvenir shop, the rocks of the region on the restaurant wall, telescopes, and a "touristorama" film room showing a multi-screen slide show and explosive highlights from the James Bond thriller that featured the Schilthorn (free and self-serve; push the button for slides or, after a long pause for the projector to rewind, push for 007).

Watch hang gliders set up, psych up, and take off, flying 30 minutes with the birds to distant Interlaken. Walk along the ridge out back. This is a great place for a photo of the "mountain-climber you." For another cheap thrill, ask the gondola attendant to crank down the window, stick your head out, and pretend you're hang gliding, ideally over the bump going down from Gimmelwald.

Lifts go twice an hour, and the ride (including two transfers) to the Schilthorn takes 30 minutes. Watch the altitude meter in the gondola. (The Gimmelwald–Schilthorn hike is free, if you don't mind a 5,000-foot altitude gain.) You can ride up to the Schilthorn and hike down, but I wouldn't (weather can change; have good shoes). For a less scary hike, go halfway down by cable car and walk down from the Birg station. Buy the round-trip excursion early-bird fare (cheaper than the Gimmelwald–Schilthorn–Birg ticket) and decide at Birg if you want to hike or ride down.

Hiking down from Birg is very steep and gravelly. Just below Birg is the Schilthorn-Hutte. Drop in for soup, cocoa, or a coffee schnapps. You can spend the night in the hut's crude loft (40 mattresses; a ridiculous 60 SF for bed, breakfast, and dinner; open July–September, tel. 033/855-1167). Youth hostelers scream down the ice fields on plastic-bag sleds from the Schilthorn. (English-speaking doctor in Mürren.)

The most interesting trail from Birg to Gimmelwald is the high one via Grauseewli Lake and Wasenegg Ridge to Brünli, down to Spielbodenalp, and the Sprutz waterfall. From the Birg lift, hike towards the Schilthorn, taking your first left down to the little, newly made Grauseewli Lake. From the lake a gravelly trail leads down the rough switchbacks until it levels out. When you see a rock painted with arrows pointing to "Mürren" and "Rotstockhütte," follow the path to "Rotstockhütte," traversing the cow-grazed mountainside. Follow Wasenegg Ridge left/down and along the barbed wire fence which dead-ends at Brünli below. (For maximum thrills, stay on the ridge and climb all the way to the knobby little summit where you'll enjoy an incredible 360-degree view and a chance to sign your name on the register stored in the little wooden box.) A steep trail winds directly down from Brünli towards Gimmelwald, soon hitting a bigger, easy trail. The trail bends right (just before the popular restaurant/mountain hut at Spielbodenalp) leading to Sprutz. Walk under the Sprutz waterfall, and a steep wooded trail deposits you in a meadow of flowers at the top side of Gimmelwald. For any hike, get local advice and believe it more than me.

For an expensive thrill, you can bungee-jump from the Stechelberg–Mürren service gondola: 129 SF for a 330-foot drop, 259 SF for 590 feet, drop head-first or feet-first, tel. 033/826-7711).

▲▲▲**Hike 2: The Männlichen–Kleine Scheidegg Hike**—This is my favorite easy Alpine hike, entertaining you all the way with glorious Jungfrau, Eiger, and Mönch views. (That's the Young Maiden being protected from the Ogre by the Monk.)

If the weather's good, descend from Gimmelwald bright and early. Catch the post bus to the Lauterbrunnen train station (or drive, parking at the large multi-storied pay lot behind the station). Buy a ticket to Männlichen and catch the train. Ride past great valley views to Wengen, where you'll walk across town (buy a picnic, but don't waste time here if it's sunny), and catch the Männlichen lift (departing every 15 minutes) to the top of the ridge high above you.

From the tip of the Männlichen lift, hike 20 minutes north to the little peak for that king- or queen-of-the-mountain feeling. It's an easy hour's walk from there to Kleine Scheidegg for a picnic or restaurant lunch. (For accommodations, see Sleeping, below.) If you've got an extra 100 SF and the weather's perfect, ride the train from Kleine Scheidegg through the Eiger to the towering Jungfraujoch and back. Check for discount trips up to Jungfraujoch (three trips a day—early or late, tel. 033/826-4750, weather info: tel. 033/855-1022). Jungfraujoch crowds can be frightening. The price has been jacked up to reduce the mobs, but sunny days are still a mess.

From Kleine Scheidegg, enjoy the ever-changing Alpine panorama of the north nace of the Eiger, Jungfrau, and Mönch, probably accompanied by the valley-filling mellow sound of Alphorns and distant avalanches, as you ride the train or hike downhill (30 gorgeous minutes to Wengeralp, 90 more steep minutes from there into the town of Wengen). If the weather turns bad, or you run out of steam, catch the train early at the little Wengeralp station along the way. After Wengeralp, the trail to Wengen is steep and, while not dangerous, requires a good set of knees. Wengen is a fine shopping town. (For accommodations, see Sleeping, below.) The boring final descent from Wengen to Lauterbrunnen is knee-killer steep, so catch the train. Trails may be snowbound into early June. Ask about conditions at the lift stations or local TI. If the Männlichen lift is closed, take the train straight from Lauterbrunnen to Kleine Scheidegg. Many take the risk of slipping and enjoy the Kleine Scheidegg-to-Wengeralp hike even with a little snow.

▲▲**Hike 3: Schynige Platte to First**—The best day I've had hiking in the Berner Oberland is the demanding six-hour ridge walk high above Lake Brienz on one side and all that Jungfrau beauty on the other. Start at Wilderswil train station (just above Interlaken), where you catch the little train up to Schynige Platte (2,000 meters). Walk through the Alpine flower display garden and into the wild Alpine yonder. The high point is Faulhorn (2,680 meters, with its famous mountaintop hotel). Hike to a chairlift called First (2,168 meters), where you descend to Grindelwald and catch a train back to your starting point, Wilderswil—or, if you have a regional train pass or no car but endless money, return to Gimmelwald via Lauterbrunnen from Grindelwald over Kleine Scheidegg.

▲▲**Hike 4: Cloudy Day Lauterbrunnen Valley Walk**—For a smell-the-cows-and-flowers lowland walk, ideal for a cloudy day, weary body, or tight budget, follow the riverside trail 5 kilometers from Lauterbrunnen's Staubach Falls (just after the town church) to the Schilthornbahn station at Stechelberg. Detour to Trümmelbach Falls en route (see below).

If you're staying in Gimmelwald: To get to Lauterbrunnen, walk up to Mürren (30 min), walk or ride the train to Grütschalp (60-min hike), ride the funicular down to Lauterbrunnen

Berner Oberland

NOTE: THIS BIRD'S EYE VIEW LOOKS SOUTH...

EIGER 13026'   MONCH 13449'   JUNGFRAU 13642'   SCHILT-HORN 9748'

JUNG-FRAU-JOCH

TUNNEL

KLEINE SCHEIDEGG 6762'

GIMMEL-WALD 4593'

BIRG 8784'

HIKE #1

HIKE #2

W. ALP

MÜRREN 5381'

GRINDEL-WALD 3393'

MÄNN-LICHEN 7317'

STECHEL-BERG 3025'

← NICE WALK

GRÜTSCHALP 4879'

← TO FIRST

GRUND

WENGEN 4180'

LAUTERBRUNNEN 2612'

ISENFLUH

HIKE #3

SCHYNIGE PLATTE 6454'

WILDERSWIL 1916'

ISELT-WALD

SPIEZ

TO LUZERN

LAKE BRIENZ

E.   W.

INTER-LAKEN 1860'

LAKE   THUN

TO BERN

BRIENZ

BALLENBERG

+—+ PRIVATE RAIL - EURAIL NOT VALID   - - - BUS
+—+ OTHER RAIL - EURAIL VALID   •••• BOAT
o—o MTN. LIFTS   ••••• TRAIL

NOT TO SCALE!

—DCH—

(10 min), walk through town, and take the riverside trail ending up at Stechelberg (75 min) where you can ride the lift back up to Gimmelwald (10 min).

▲**Other Hikes near Gimmelwald**—For a not-too-tough three-hour walk (there's a scary 20-minute stretch that comes with ropes) with great Jungfrau views and some mountain farm action, ride the funicular from Mürren to Allmendhübel (1,934 meters), and walk to Marchegg, Saustal, and Grütschalp (a drop of about 500 meters), where you can catch the panorama train back to Mürren. An easier version is the lower "Bergweg" from Allmenhü-bel to Grütschalp via Winteregg. For an easy family stroll with grand views, walk from Mürren just above the train tracks to either Winteregg (40 min, restaurant, playground, train station) or Grütschalp (60 min, train station) and catch the panorama train back to Mürren. An easy, go-as-far-as-you-like trail from Gimmelwald is up the Sefinen Valley. Or you can wind from Gimmelwald down to Stechelberg (1 hour).

You can get specifics at the Mürren TI. The TI, Guesthouse Belmont, and Hotel Mittaghorn each have a "Hiking Possibilities: Schilthorn—Panoramaland" flier that describes 12 recommended

Alpine Lifts in the Berner Oberland

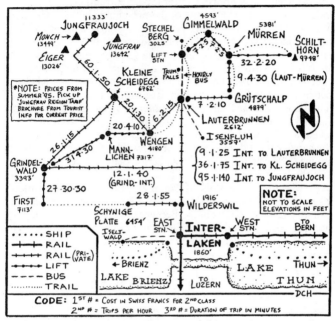

hikes. The 3-D map of the Mürren mountainside, which includes hiking trails, makes a useful, attractive souvenir (2 SF at TI and lift station. For an extensive rundown on the region, get Don Chmura's fine 5-SF Gimmelwald guidebook (includes info on hikes, flora, fauna, culture, and travel tips; available at Hotel Mittaghorn).

Rainy Day Options

If clouds roll in, don't despair. They can roll out just as quickly, and there are some good bad-weather options. There are easy trails and pleasant walks along the floor of the Lauterbrunnen Valley (see above). If all the waterfalls have you intrigued, sneak a behind-the-scenes look at the valley's most powerful one, **Trümmelbach Falls** (10 SF, daily April–October 9:00–18:00, on the Lauterbrunnen–Stechelberg road, tel. 033/855-3232). You'll ride an elevator up through the mountain and climb through several caves to see the melt from the Eiger, Mönch, and Jungfrau grinding like God's bandsaw through the mountain at the rate of up to 20,000 liters a second (nearly double the beer consumption at Oktoberfest). The upper area, "chutes 6 to 10," are the best, so if your legs ache, you can skip the lower ones and ride the lift down.

Lauterbrunnen's **Heimatmuseum** shows off the local folk culture (3 SF, mid-June–September, Tuesday, Thursday, Saturday, and Sunday 14:00–17:30, just over the bridge).

Mürren's slick **Sports Center** (Sportzentrum) offers a world of indoor activities (12 SF for use of the swimming pool and whirlpool, 7 SF for Mürren hotel guests, pool open Monday–Saturday afternoon, mid-June–October). Mürren also has plenty of shops, bakeries, banks, a TI, and accommodations (see Sleeping, below).

Boat Trips from Interlaken—From Interlaken (which means "between the lakes"), you can take daily boat trips on the lakes it's between (8/day, fewer off-season, free with Eurail). The Lake Thun boat stops at Beatushöhlen (interesting caves, 30 min from Interlaken) and two visit-worthy towns: Spiez (1 hr from Interlaken) and Thun (1.75 hrs away). The Lake Brienz boat stops at the super-cute and quiet village of Iseltwald (45 min away), and Brienz (1.25 hrs away, near Ballenberg Open-Air Folk Museum). Get the latest schedule at the TI.

▲▲**Swiss Open-Air Folk Museum at Ballenberg**—Near Interlaken, the Swiss Open-Air Museum of Vernacular Architecture, Country Life and Crafts in the Bernese Oberland is a rich collection of traditional and historic farmhouses from every region of the country. Each house is carefully furnished, and many feature traditional craftspeople at work. The sprawling 50-acre park, laid out roughly as a huge Swiss map, is a natural preserve providing a wonderful setting for this culture-on-a-lazy-Susan look at Switzerland.

The Thurgau house (#621) has an interesting wattle-and-daub (half-timbered construction) display and house #331 has a fun bread museum. Use the 2-SF map/guide. The more expensive picture book is a better souvenir than guide. (14-SF entry, half-price after 16:00, daily mid-April–October 10:00–17:00, houses close at 17:00, park stays open later, craft demonstration schedules are listed just inside the entry, tel. 039/511-123.) There's a reasonable outdoor cafeteria inside the west entrance, and fresh-baked bread, sausage, mountain cheese, and other goodies on sale in several houses. Picnic tables and grills with free firewood are scattered throughout the park. The little wooden village of Brienzwiler (near the east entrance) is a museum in itself with a lovely little church. Trains run frequently from Interlaken to Brienzwiler, an easy walk from the museum.

Sleeping in the Berner Oberland
(1.5 SF = about $1, tel. code: 033)
Sleep Code: **S**=Single, **D**=Double/Twin, **T**=Triple, **Q**=Quad, **b**=bathroom, **t**=toilet only, **s**=shower only, **CC**=Credit Card (Visa, MasterCard, Amex), **SE**=Speaks English, **NSE**=No English. Unless otherwise noted, breakfast is included.

Sleeping in Gimmelwald
(4,500 feet, tel code: 033, zip code: 3826)
To inhale the Alps and really hold it in, sleep high in Gimmelwald. Poor but pleasantly stuck in the past, the village has a happy

hostel, a comfy B&B, a decent pension, and a creaky hotel. The bad news is that the lift costs 7.20 SF each way to get there.

Hotel Mittaghorn, the treasure of Gimmelwald, is run by Walter Mittler, a perfect Swiss gentleman. The hotel is a classic, creaky, Alpine-style place with memorable beds, ancient down comforters (short and fat; wear socks and drape the blanket over your feet), and a million-dollar view of the Jungfrau Alps. The loft has a dozen real beds on either side of a divider, with several sinks, down comforters, and a fire ladder out the back window. The hotel has one shower for ten rooms (1 SF for five minutes). Walter is careful not to let his place get too hectic or big and enjoys sensitive Back Door travelers. He runs the hotel by himself, keeping it simple, but with class. This is a good place to receive mail from home (check the mail barrel in entry hall).

To some, Hotel Mittaghorn is a fire waiting to happen—with a kitchen that would never pass code, lumpy beds, teeny towels, and nowhere near enough plumbing—run by an eccentric grouch. These people enjoy Interlaken, Wengen, or Mürren, and that's where they should sleep. Be warned, you may meet more of my readers than you hoped for, but it's a fun crowd—an extended family (D-60–70 SF, T-85 SF, Q-105 SF, loft beds-25 SF, all with breakfast, CH-3826 Gimmelwald/Bern, tel. 033/855-1658, SE). Reserve by telephone only, and then you must reconfirm by telephone the day before your arrival. Walter usually serves a cheap, simple spaghetti or soup supper. Off-season only, lofters pay just 20 SF for a bed with breakfast and can eat their evening picnic in the bar with a free pot of coffee or tea, courtesy of Walter. The hotel is closed mid-November through early May.

Mountain Hostel is goat-simple, as clean as its guests, cheap, and very friendly. Its 50 dorm beds are often taken in July and August, so call ahead (easy same-day telephone reservations, call after 10:00). The hostel has low ceilings, a self-serve kitchen (pack in groceries), and new plumbing. Petra Brunner has filled the place with flowers. This relaxed hostel survives with the help of its guests. Please read the signs, respect its rules, and leave it cleaner than you found it. Guests are asked to do a small duty. The place is one of those rare spots where a family atmosphere spontaneously combusts, and spaghetti becomes communal as it softens (15 SF per bed in six- to 15-bed rooms, showers-1 SF, no breakfast, hostel membership not required, 20 yards uphill from the lift station, tel. & fax 033/855-1704, SE).

Next door, **Pension Restaurant Gimmelwald** serves meals and offers pleasant rooms (D-90 SF, Db-110 SF) and sheetless dorm beds (20 SF on top floor, 25 SF in smaller rooms), including breakfast. It's closed in November and the first half of May (a minute's walk from gondola station, non-smoking, CC:VM, tel. & fax 033/855-1730, Nicole SE).

Maria and Olle Eggimann rent out three rooms in their

Alpine-sleek chalet. These are the most comfortable rooms in town, but they're tough to get in the summer. Twelve-year town residents Maria and Olle, who job-share the village's only teaching position and raise three young children of their own, offer visitors a rare inside peek at this community (D-100 SF, Db with kitchenette-60 SF apiece for two or three people, optional breakfast 15 SF, last check-in 18:30, three-night minimum for advance reservations; from the gondola station, continue straight for 100 yards past the town's only intersection, B&B is on your left, CH-3826 Gimmelwald, tel. 033/855-3575, e-mail: oeggimann@bluewin.ch, SE fluently).

Schalf im Stroh ("Sleep in Straw") offers exactly that, in an actual barn. After the cows head for higher ground in the summer, the friendly von Allmen family hoses out their barn and fills it with straw and budget travelers. Blankets are free, but bring your own sheet, sleep sack, or sleeping bag. No beds, no bunks, no mattresses, no kidding (19 SF, 13 SF for kids under 12, breakfast included, showers-2 SF, open mid-June–mid-October, depending on grass and snow levels; from the lift, continue straight through the only intersection, barn marked "1995" is on your right, tel. 033/855-3381, fax 855-4681, NSE). The family also rents two of the town's cheapest double rooms (St-30 SF, Dt-55 SF, across from post office, shower in the barn a block away). The nicer rooms upstairs (with bath) require a four-night minimum stay.

Eating in Gimmelwald: Gimmelwald feeds its goats better than its people. The hostel has a decent members' kitchen but serves no food. There are no groceries in town. The wise and frugal pack in food from the Co-ops in Mürren or Lauterbrunnen or the Migros in Interlaken. Hostelers enjoy the communal kitchen followed by an evening of conversation, wine, and occasional local music in the hostel dining room. Walter's guests are best off eating at Walter's. Follow dinner with a Heidi Cocoa (cocoa *mit* peppermint schnapps) or Virgin Heidis. Affordable Swiss meals are also served at Pension Gimmelwald next to the hostel.

Sleeping in Mürren
(5,500 feet, tel. code: 033, zip code: 3825)

Mürren is as pleasant as an Alpine resort can be. It's traffic-free, filled with bakeries, cafés, souvenirs, old-timers with walking sticks, GE employees enjoying incentive trips, and Japanese making movies of each other with a Fujichrome backdrop. Its chalets are prefab-rustic. Sitting on a ledge 2,000 feet above the Lauterbrunnen Valley, surrounded by a fortissimo chorus of mountains, it has all the comforts of home and then some, with Alp-high prices. Mürren's TI can find you a room, give hiking advice, rent mountain bikes (20 SF/half day, 30 SF/full day), and change money. It's located in the Sportzentrum (TI open mid-July–mid-September 9:00–12:00 and 13:00–18:30, Thursday until

20:30, Saturday 13:00–18:00, Sunday 13:00–17:30, less off-season, tel. 033/856-8686, Web site: www.muerren.ch, e-mail: info@ muerren.ch).

Guesthouse Belmont offers some of Mürren's best budget rooms. This is a friendly home away from home (S-45 SF, D-90 SF, Db-130 SF, includes breakfast, 35-SF beds in four-person dorms, closed November, CC:VMA, across from the train station, tel. 033/855-3535, fax 033/855-3531, SE).

The nearby **Hotel Alpenblick** (Db-130 –140 SF, closed off-season; exit right from station, walk two minutes downhill, tel. 033/855-1327, fax 033/855-1391) and cliff-hanging **Hotel Alpina** (exit left from station, walk two minutes downhill, tel. 033/855-1361) also have affordable rooms.

Chalet Fontana, run by an Englishwoman, Denise Fussell, is worn and basic but a rare budget option in Mürren (35–45 SF per person in small doubles or triples with breakfast, 5 SF cheaper without breakfast, one three-bed room with kitchenette-45 SF per person, open mid-May–October, across the street from the Stäger-stübli restaurant in the town center, tel. 033/855-2686, e-mail: 106501.2731@compuserve.com). If no one's home, check at the Ed Abegglen shop next door (tel. 033/855-1245, SE).

Hotel Jungfrau has pricey, plush rooms (Sb-90–115 SF, Db-140 SF–190 SF) and also offers cheaper, slightly worn rooms in its neighboring lodge (Db-110–140 SF). Many rooms have views (elevator, includes free entrance to pool, CC:VMA, near TI and Sportzentrum, tel. 033/855-4545, fax 033/855-4549, Web site: www.muerren.ch/jungfrau, e-mail: jungfrau@muerren.ch).

Hotel Alpenruh is expensive and yuppie-rustic, but it's the only hotel in Mürren that's open year-round. Run by Andreas and Anne Marie Goetschi, former travelers with a great Back Door perspective, this hotel's comfortable rooms come with views and some balconies (Sb-80–100 SF, Db-160–200 SF depending on season, elevator, attached restaurant, sauna, free tickets for breakfast atop Schilthorn, CC:VMA, 10 yards from gondola station, tel. 033/855-1055, fax 033/855-4277).

Eating in Mürren: For a rare bit of ruggedness, eat at the Stägerstübli (10–30 SF lunches and dinners, closed Tuesday). For picnic fixings, shop at the Co-op (normally open 8:00–12:00 and 14:00–18:30, closed afternoons on Tuesday and Saturday and all day Sunday).

Sleeping in Wengen
(4,200 feet, tel. code: 033, zip code: 3823)
Wengen, a fancy Mürren on the other side of the valley, has more tennis courts than budget beds. This traffic-free resort is an easy train ride above Lauterbrunnen and halfway up to Kleine Schei-degg and Männlichen.

Hotel Bernerhof has double rooms and dorm beds (D-90 SF,

Db-130 SF, includes breakfast, dorm bed-20 SF, BYO sheet, tel. 033/855-2721, fax 033/855-3358). **Chalet Bergheim,** open June through mid-October, has reasonable doubles and six 20-SF dorm beds (plus 6 SF for sheets and 15 SF for breakfast, tel. 033/855-2755), and **Chalet Schweizerheim Garni** is decent (Db-120 SF, summer only, tel. 033/855-1581).

Hotel Eden has comfy rooms, an inviting breakfast room, and views (S-62 SF, D-116 SF, Db-144 SF, dorm beds-26 SF, breakfast for dormers-15 SF, tel. 033/855-1634, fax 033/855-3950, Kerstin Bucher SE). The same hotel runs **Eddy's Hostel,** a block away, with 33-SF dorm beds. Prices include 7-SF surcharge for one- to two-night stays.

Sleeping in Kleine Scheidegg
(6,762 feet, tel. code: 033, zip code: 3801)
For dorm beds with breakfast high in the mountains, sleep at Kleine Scheidegg's **Bahnhof Buffet** (38 SF per bed, tel. 033/855-1151) or at **Restaurant Grindelwaldblick** (32 SF for bed in 12-bed room, no sheets, open June–October, tel. 033/855-1374). Confirm price and availability before ascending.

Sleeping near the Stechelberg Lift
(2,800 feet, tel. code: 033, zip code: 3824)
The local **Naturfreundehaus Alpenhof,** at the far end of Lauterbrunnen Valley, is a rugged Alpine lodge for hikers (60 coed beds, four to eight per room, 17.50 SF per bed, two D-80 SF, breakfast-8 SF, dinner-14 SF, no sheets, closed November, get off bus at "Hotel Stechelberg" stop, tel. 033/855-1202). The neighboring **Hotel Stechelberg** has 20 clean and quiet rooms (S-45 SF, D-74–100 SF, Db-112–132 SF, CC:VMA, tel. 033/855-2921, SE). **Klara von Allmen** rents out three rooms in a quiet, scenic, and folksy setting (S-27 SF, D-50 SF, minimum two nights, just over the river behind the Stechelberg post office at big "Zimmer" sign, get off bus at "Stechelberg Post" stop, tel. 033/855-3930, some English spoken).

Mountain Hotel Obersteinberg, a 2.5 hour hike from Stechelberg, is primitive: no shower, hot water, or electricity. Candles light up the night (dorm beds-57 SF, S-74 SF, D-148 SF, open June–September, mules carry your bags if you're staying for a week, tel. 033/855-2033).

Sleeping in Lauterbrunnen
(2,600 feet, tel. code: 033, zip code: 3822)
Masenlager Stocki is a great value (12 SF a night with sheets in an easygoing little 30-bed coed dorm with a kitchen, closed November–mid-December, across the river, take the first left, tel. 033/855-1754). **Chalet im Rohr** offers 26-SF beds in one- to four-bed rooms (near the church, tel. 033/855-1507). Hotel

Jungfrau's fine 12-SF breakfast buffet is open to the public.

Two campgrounds just south of town work very hard to provide 15- to 25-SF beds. They each have dorms, two-, four-, and six-bed bungalows, no sheets, kitchen facilities, and big English-speaking tour groups. **Camping Jungfrau**, romantically situated just beyond the stones hurled by Staubach Falls, is huge and well-organized, with a Heidi Shop and clocks showing the time in Sydney and Vancouver (tel. 033/855-2010). It also has fancier cabins and trailers for the classier camper (18 SF per person). **Schützenbach Campground**, on the left just past Lauterbrunnen toward Stechelberg, is much simpler (tel. 033/855-1268).

Sleeping in Isenfluh
(3,560 feet, tel. code: 033, zip code: 3807)
In the tiny hamlet of Isenfluh, which is smaller than Gimmelwald and offers even better views, **Pension Waldrand** rents six reasonable rooms (tel. 033/855-1227; hourly shuttle bus from Lauterbrunnen).

Sleeping in Interlaken
(tel. code: 033, zip code: 3800)
I'd head for Gimmelwald. Interlaken is not the Alps. But if you must stay, here are some good choices.

Hotel Lotschberg, with easy parking and a sun terrace, is run by English-speaking Susi and Fritz (Sb-98 SF, Db-135–180 SF, cheaper off-season, elevator, bar, laundry service-3 SF, free to check e-mail, CC:VMA, free pick-up from station or four-minute walk from the West Station, look for the wall painting on hotel, General Guisanstrasse 31, tel. 033/822-2545, fax 033/822-2579, Web site: www.beoswiss.ch/lotschberg, e-mail: lotschberg@Interlaken-Tourism.ch). They also run **Guest House Susi's B&B** in their backyard, which has simple, cozy, cheaper rooms (Sb-85 SF, Db-105 SF, apartments with kitchenettes for two people-100 SF; for four–five people-165 SF, cheaper off-season).

Hotel Beau-Site has bright, airy rooms and a large yard with deck chairs. Well-maintained with flowers and personal touches, this is a fine splurge (S-75 SF, Sb-130–158 SF, small D-110 SF, Db-200–250 SF, extra bed-45 SF, cheaper off-season, great views, free parking, CC:VMA, four-minute walk from West train station: following "Spital" signs from station, turn left on Bahnhofstrasse, cross the tracks and bridge, and turn left on Seestrasse, tel. 033/826-7575, fax 033/826-7585, run by the Ritter family).

Backpackers enjoy **Balmer's Herberge**. This Interlaken institution is run by creative tornadoes of entrepreneurial energy, Eric and Katrin Balmer. With movies, ping-pong, a Laundromat, bar, restaurant, secondhand English book-swapping library, tiny grocery, bike rental, currency exchange, rafting excursions, shuttle-bus service into the mountains, plenty of tips on budget eating and hiking, and a friendly, hardworking, mostly American staff, this

little Nebraska is home for those who miss their fraternity (19–20
SF for dorms beds, 22–28 SF in doubles, triples, and quads, 12 SF
in overflow on-the-floor accommodations, all with breakfast,
open year-round, CC:VMA, Haupstrasse 23, in Matten, a 15-minute
walk from either Interlaken station, tel. 033/822-1961, fax
033/823-3261, SE). They recently opened up **Balmer's Tent**
about 3 blocks away; you can stay in the huge tent for dorm prices.

Transportation Connections—Interlaken

By train to: Spiez (2/hr, 15 min), **Brienz** (hrly, 20 min), **Bern**
(hrly, 1 hr). While there are a few long trains from Interlaken,
you'll generally connect from Bern.

By train from Bern to: Lausanne (hrly, 70 min) **Zurich**
(hrly, 75 min), **Salzburg** (4/day, 8 hrs, transfers include Zurich),
Munich (4/day, 5.5 hrs), **Frankfurt** (hrly, 4.5 hrs, transfers in
Basel and Mannheim), **Paris** (4/day, 4.5 hrs).

Interlaken to Gimmelwald: Take the train from the
Interlaken-East station to Lauterbrunnen, then cross the street
to catch the funicular to Mürren. You'll ride up to Grütschalp,
where a special scenic train (*Panorama Fahrt* in German) rolls you
along the cliff into Mürren. From there, either walk an easy, paved
30 minutes downhill to Gimmelwald or walk ten minutes across
Mürren to catch the gondola (7.20 SF and a five-minute steep
uphill backtrack) to Gimmelwald. A good bad-weather option (or
vice versa) is to ride the post bus from Lauterbrunnen (leaves at
five minutes past the hour) to Stechelberg and the base of the
Schilthornbahn (a big, gray gondola station, tel. 033/823-1444 or
033/555-2141).

APPENDIX

National Tourist Offices in the U.S.A.

Austrian National Tourist Office: Box 1142 Times Square, New York, NY 10108-1142, tel. 212/944-6880, fax 212/730-4568, Web site: www.anto.com. Ask for their "Vacation Kit" map. Fine hikes and Vienna material.

Belgian National Tourist Office: 780 3rd Ave., #1501, New York, NY 10017, tel. 212/758-8130, fax 212/355-7675, Web site: www.visitbelgium.com. Good country map.

British Tourist Authority: 551 5th Ave., 7th floor, New York, NY 10176, tel. 800/462-2748 or 212/986-2200, Web site: www.bta.org.uk. Free maps of London and Britain. Meaty material, responsive to individual needs.

Denmark (see Scandinavia)

French Tourist Offices: 444 Madison Ave., 16th floor, New York, NY 10022, Web site: www.francetourism.com; 676 N. Michigan Ave., Chicago, IL 60611-2819; 9454 Wilshire Blvd., #303, Beverly Hills, CA 90212-2967. Write rather than mess with their flaky 900 number (tel. 900/990-0040).

German National Tourist Offices: 122 E. 42nd St., 52nd floor, New York, NY 10168-0072, tel. 212/661-7200, fax 212/661-7174, Web site: www.germany-tourism.de; 11766 Wilshire Blvd., #750, Los Angeles, CA 90025, tel. 310/575-9799, fax 310/575-1565. Maps, Rhine schedules, events; very helpful.

Irish Tourist Board: 345 Park Ave., 17th floor, New York, NY 10154, tel. 800/223-6470 or 212/418-0800, fax 212/371-9052, Web site: www.ireland.travel.ie.

Italian Government Travel Offices: 630 Fifth Ave., #1565, New York, NY 10111, tel. 212/245-4822, fax 212/586-9249; 12400 Wilshire Blvd., #550, Los Angeles, CA 90025, tel. 310/820-0098, fax 310/820-6357.

Netherlands National Tourist Office: 225 North Michigan Ave., #1854, Chicago, IL 60601, tel. 888/GO-HOLLAND (automated) or tel. 312/819-1500 (live), fax 312/819-1740, Web site: www.nbt.nl/holland. Great country map.

Norway (see Scandinavia)

Portuguese National Tourist Office: 590 Fifth Ave., 4th floor, New York, NY 10036, tel. 212/354-4403, fax 212/764-6137, Web site: www.portugal.org.

Scandinavian Tourism: P.O. Box 4649, Grand Central Station, New York, NY 10163-4649, tel. 212/885-9700, fax 212/885-9710, Web site: www.goscandinavia.com. Good general booklets on all the Scandinavian countries, but be sure to ask for city maps and specifics.

Spanish National Tourist Offices: 666 Fifth Ave., 35th floor, New York, NY 10103, tel. 212/265-8822, fax 212/265-8864, Web site: www.okspain.org; 845 N. Michigan Ave., Chicago, IL 60611, tel. 312/642-1992, fax 312/642-9817; 1221 Breckell Ave., #1850, Miami, FL 33131, tel. 305/358-1992, fax 305/358-8223; San Vicente Plaza Bldg., 8383 Wilshire Blvd., #960, Beverly Hills, CA 90211, tel. 213/658-7188, fax 213/658-1061.

Sweden (see Scandinavia)

Swiss National Tourist Offices: 608 Fifth Ave., New York, NY 10020, tel. 212/757-5944, fax 212/262-6116, Web site: www.switzerlandtourism.com;

150 North Michigan Ave., #2930, Chicago IL 60601, tel. 312/630-5840, fax 312/630-5848; 222 North Sepulveda Blvd., #1570, El Segundo, CA 90245, tel. 310/335-5980, fax 310/335-5982. Great maps and rail and hiking material.

Let's Talk Telephones
In Europe, you can make your calls from public phone booths using a phone card or coins. At post offices, you'll often find easy-to-use "talk now-pay later" metered phones. Avoid using hotel room phones, which are major rip-offs for anything other than local calls or calling card calls (see below). For more information, see Introduction: Telephones and Mail.

Dialing Direct
Calling Between Countries: First dial the international access code, then the country code followed by the area code (if it starts with zero, drop the zero), then the local number.

  Calling Long Distance Within a Country: First dial the area code (including its zero), then the local number.

  Some of Europe's Exceptions: In Spain, area codes start with nine instead of zero (just drop or add the nine instead of a zero as in other countries). A few countries lack area codes, such as Denmark, Norway, and France. You still use the above sequence and codes to dial, just skip the area code.

International Access Codes
When dialing direct, first dial the international access code of the country you're calling from.

Austria:	00	France:	00	Norway:	00
Belgium:	00	Germany:	00	Portugal:	000
Britain:	00	Ireland:	00	Russia:	810
Czech Rep:	00	Italy:	00	Spain:	07
Denmark:	00	Latvia:	00	Sweden:	009
Estonia:	800	Lithuania:	810	Switzerland:	00
Finland:	990	Netherlands:	00	USA/Canada:	011

Country Codes
After you've dialed the international access code, dial the code of the country you're calling.

Austria:	43	France:	33	Norway:	47
Belgium:	32	Germany:	49	Portugal:	351
Britain:	44	Ireland:	353	Russia:	7
Czech Rep:	42	Italy:	39	Spain:	34
Denmark:	45	Latvia:	371	Sweden:	46
Estonia:	372	Lithuania:	370	Switzerland:	41
Finland:	358	Netherlands:	31	USA/Canada:	1

Calling Card Operators

Calling home from Europe is easy from any type of phone if you have a calling card. From a private phone, just dial the toll-free number to reach the operator. Using a public phone, first insert a small-value coin or a phone card. Then dial the operator, who will ask you for your calling card number and then place your call. You'll save money on calls of three minutes or more. When you finish, your coin should be returned (or if using a card, no money should have been deducted). Your bill awaits you at home (one more reason to prolong your vacation).

	AT&T	**MCI**	**SPRINT**
Austria	022-903-011	022-903-012	022-903-014
Belgium	0800-100-10	0800-100-12	0800-100-14
Britain	0800-89-0011	0800-89-0222	0800-89-0877
Denmark	8001-0010	8001-0022	8001-0877
France	0800-990-011	0800-990-019	0800-990-087
Germany	0130-0010	0130-0012	0130-0013
Ireland	1800-550-000	1800-551-001	1800-552-001
Italy	172-1011	172-1022	172-1877
Netherlands	0800-022-9111	0800-022-9122	0800-022-9119
Norway	800-19-011	800-19-912	800-19-877
Portugal	050-171-288	050-171-234	050-171-877
Spain	900-990-011	900-99-0014	900-99-0013
Sweden	020-795-611	020-795-922	020-799-011
Switzerland	0800-89-0011	0800-89-0222	0800-89-9777

Exchange Rates

Country	**$1 equals roughly . . .**
Austria	12 Austrian schillings (AS)
Belgium	35 Belgian francs (BF)
Denmark	7 kroner (kr)
France	5.5 francs (F)
Germany	1.7 Deutsche marks (DM)
Great Britain	.60 pound (£)
Ireland	.60 punt (£)
Italy	1,600 lire (L)
Netherlands	1.9 guilders (f)
Norway	7 kroner (kr)
Portugal	170 escudos ($)
Spain	140 pesetas (ptas)
Sweden	7 kroner (kr)
Switzerland	1.5 Swiss francs (SF)

Numbers and Stumblers

• Europeans write a few of their numbers differently than we do: 1 1 , 4 4 , 7 7 . Learn the difference or miss your train.
• In Europe, dates appear as day/month/year, so Christmas is 25/12/98.

• Commas are decimal points and decimals, commas. A dollar and a half is 1,50 and there are 5.280 feet in a mile.
• When pointing, use your whole hand, palm downward.
• When counting with fingers, start with your thumb. If you hold up your index finger to request one item, you'll probably get two.
• What we Americans call the second floor of a building is the first floor in Europe.
• Europeans keep the left "lane" open for passing on escalators and moving sidewalks. Keep to the right.

Metric Conversions
(approximate)

1 inch = 25 millimeters	32 degrees F = 0 degrees C
1 foot = 0.3 meter	82 degrees F = about 28 degrees C
1 yard = 0.9 meter	1 ounce = 28 grams
1 mile = 1.6 kilometers	1 kilogram = 2.2 pounds
1 centimeter = 0.4 inch	1 quart = 0.95 liter
1 meter = 39.4 inches	1 square yard = 0.8 square meter
1 kilometer = .62 mile	1 acre = 0.4 hectare

Weather Chart

Here is a list of average temperatures and days of no rain. This can be helpful in planning your itinerary, but I have never found European weather to be particularly predictable, and these charts ignore humidity.

(1st line, avg. daily low; 2nd line, avg. daily high; 3rd line, days of no rain)

	J	F	M	A	M	J	J	A	S	O	N	D
France	32°	34°	36°	41°	47°	52°	55°	55°	50°	44°	38°	33°
Paris	42°	45°	52°	60°	67°	73°	76°	75°	69°	59°	49°	43°
	16	15	16	16	18	19	19	19	19	17	15	14
Germany	29°	31°	35°	41°	48°	53°	56°	55°	51°	43°	36°	31°
Frankfurt	37°	42°	49°	58°	67°	72°	75°	74°	67°	56°	45°	39°
	22	19	22	21	22	21	21	21	21	22	21	20°
Great Britain	35°	35°	37°	40°	45°	51°	55°	54°	51°	44°	39°	36°
London	44°	45°	51°	56°	63°	69°	73°	72°	67°	58°	49°	45°
	14	15	20	16	18	19	18	18	17	17	14	15
Italy	39°	39°	42°	46°	55°	60°	64°	64°	61°	53°	46°	41°
Rome	54°	56°	62°	68°	74°	82°	88°	88°	83°	73°	63°	56°
	23	17	26	24	25	28	29	28	24	22	22	22
Netherlands	34°	34°	37°	43°	50°	55°	59°	59°	56°	48°	41°	35°
Amsterdam	40°	41°	46°	52°	60°	65°	69°	68°	64°	56°	47°	41°
	12	13	18	16	19	18	17	17	15	13	11	12
Switzerland	29°	30°	35°	41°	48°	55°	58°	57°	52°	44°	37°	31°
Geneva	39°	43°	51°	58°	66°	73°	77°	76°	69°	58°	47°	40°
	20	19	21	19	19	19	22	21	20	20	19	21

Road Scholar Feedback for

BEST OF EUROPE 1998

*We're all in the same travelers' school of hard knocks. Your feedback helps us improve this guidebook for future travelers. Please fill this out (attach more info or any tips/favorite discoveries if you like) and send it to us. As thanks for your help, we'll send you our quarterly travel newsletter free for one year. Thanks! **Rick***

I traveled mainly by: ___ Car ___ Train/bus tickets
___ Railpass   Other (please list _____)

Number of people traveling together:
___ Solo ___ 2 ___ 3 ___ 4 ___ Over 4 ___ Tour

Ages of traveler/s (including children):

_____

I visited _____countries in _____weeks.

I traveled in: ___ Spring ___ Summer ___ Fall ___ Winter

My daily budget per person (excluding transportation):
___ Under $40 ___ $40–$60 ___ $60–$80 ___ $80–$120
___ over $120 ___ Don't know

Average cost of hotel rooms: Single room $_____
Double room $_____   Other (type _____) $_____

Favorite tip from this book:

_____

Biggest waste of time or money caused by this book:

_____

Other Rick Steves books used for this trip:

_____

Hotel listings from this book should be geared toward places

that are:

___Cheaper   ___More expensive   ___About the same

Of the recommended accommodations/restaurants used, which was:

Best _____

    Why? _____

Worst _____

    Why? _____

I reserved rooms:

____from USA   ____in advance as I traveled

____same day by phone   ____just showed up

Getting rooms in recommended hotels was:

____easy   ____mixed   ____frustrating

Of the sights/experiences/destinations recommended by this book, which was:

Most overrated _____

    Why? _____

Most underrated _____

    Why? _____

Best ways to improve this book:

_____

I'd like a free newsletter subscription:

___ Yes   ___ No   ___ Already on list

_____

Name

_____

Address

_____

City, State, Zip

_____

E-mail Address

Please send to: ETBD, Box 2009, Edmonds, WA 98020

Faxing Your Hotel Reservation

Most hotel managers know basic "hotel English." Faxing is the preferred method for reserving a room. It's more accurate and cheaper
than telephoning and much faster than writing a letter. Use this
handy form for your fax. Photocopy and fax away.

One-Page Fax

To: _____ @ _____
                   hotel   *fax*

From: _____ @ _____
                   name   *fax*

Today's date: ____ / ____ / ___
                    day   *month* *year*

Dear Hotel _____,

Please make this reservation for me:

Name: _____

Total # of people: _____   # of rooms: _____   # of nights: _____

Arriving: ___ / ____ / ___ My time of arrival (24-hr clock): _____
              day *month* *year* (I will telephone if I will be late)

Departing: ___ / ____ / ___
               day   *month* *year*

Room(s): Single___ Double___ Twin___ Triple___ Quad___

With: Toilet___ Shower___ Bath___ Sink only___

Special needs: View___ Quiet___ Cheapest Room___

Credit card: Visa___ MasterCard___ American Express___

Card #: _____

Expiration Date:_____

Name on card: _____

You may charge me for the first night as a deposit. Please fax or mail me
 confirmation of my reservation, along with the type of room reserved,
the price, and whether the price includes breakfast. Thank you.

_____
Signature

_____
Name

_____
Address

INDEX

Rick Steves' Phrase Books

Unlike other phrase books and dictionaries on the market, my well-tested phrases and key words cover every situation a traveler is likely to encounter. With these books you'll laugh with your cabby, disarm street thieves with insults, and charm new European friends.

Each book in the series is 4" x 6", with maps.

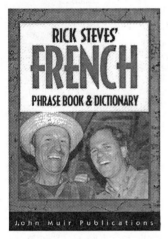
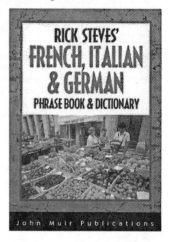

RICK STEVES' FRENCH PHRASE BOOK & DICTIONARY
U.S. $5.95/Canada $8.50

RICK STEVES' GERMAN PHRASE BOOK & DICTIONARY
U.S. $5.95/Canada $8.50

RICK STEVES' ITALIAN PHRASE BOOK & DICTIONARY
U.S. $5.95/Canada $8.50

RICK STEVES' SPANISH & PORTUGUESE PHRASE BOOK
& DICTIONARY
U.S. $7.95/Canada $11.25

RICK STEVES' FRENCH, ITALIAN & GERMAN PHRASE
BOOK & DICTIONARY
U.S. $7.95/Canada $11.25

Books from John Muir Publications

Rick Steves' Books

Asia Through the Back Door, $17.95

Europe 101: History and Art for the Traveler, $17.95

Mona Winks: Self-Guided Tours of Europe's Top Museums, $18.95

Rick Steves' Europe Through the Back Door, $19.95

Rick Steves' Best of Europe, $18.95

Rick Steves' France, Belgium & the Netherlands, $16.95

Rick Steves' Germany, Austria & Switzerland, $15.95

Rick Steves' Great Britain & Ireland, $16.95

Rick Steves' Italy, $14.95

Rick Steves' Russia & the Baltics, $9.95

Rick Steves' Scandinavia, $13.95

Rick Steves' Spain & Portugal, $14.95

Rick Steves' French Phrase Book, $5.95

Rick Steves' German Phrase Book, $5.95

Rick Steves' Italian Phrase Book, $5.95

Rick Steves' Spanish & Portuguese Phrase Book, $7.95

Rick Steves' French/Italian/German Phrase Book, $7.95

City•Smart™ Guidebooks

Albuquerque, $12.95 (avail. 4/98)

Anchorage, $12.95

Austin, $12.95

Calgary, $12.95

Cincinnati, $12.95 (avail. 5/98)

Cleveland, $14.95

Denver, $14.95

Indianapolis, $12.95

Kansas City, $12.95

Memphis, $12.95

Milwaukee, $12.95

Minneapolis/St. Paul, $14.95

Nashville, $14.95

Portland, $14.95

Richmond, $12.95

San Antonio, $12.95

St. Louis, $12.95 (avail. 5/98)

Tampa/St. Petersburg, $14.95

Travel✦Smart™ Guidebooks

Alaska, $14.95

American Southwest, $14.95

Carolinas, $14.95

Colorado, $14.95

Deep South, $17.95

Eastern Canada, $15.95

Florida Gulf Coast, $14.95

Hawaii, $14.95

Kentucky/Tennessee, $14.95

Michigan, $14.95

Minnesota/Wisconsin, $14.95

Montana, Wyoming, & Idaho, $16.95

New England, $14.95

New York State, $15.95

Northern California, $15.95

Ohio, $14.95 (avail. 5/98)

Pacific Northwest, $14.95

Southern California, $14.95

South Florida and the Keys, $14.95

Texas, $14.95

Western Canada, $16.95

Adventures in Nature Series

Alaska, $18.95

Belize, $18.95

Guatemala, $18.95

Honduras, $17.95

Kidding Around™ Travel Titles

$7.95 each

Kidding Around Atlanta

Kidding Around Austin

Kidding Around Boston

Kidding Around Chicago

Kidding Around Cleveland

Kids Go! Denver

Kidding Around Indianapolis

Kidding Around Kansas City

Kidding Around Miami

Kidding Around Milwaukee

Kidding Around Minneapolis/St. Paul

Kidding Around Nashville

Kidding Around Portland

Kidding Around San Francisco

Kids Go! Seattle

Kidding Around Washington, D.C.